TEXTILES

SARA J. KADOLPH
Iowa State University

ANNA L. LANGFORD

NORMA HOLLEN
Emeritus, Iowa State University

JANE SADDLER
Emeritus, Iowa State University, Deceased

SEVENTH EDITION

Macmillan Publishing Company
New York

Maxwell Macmillan Canada
Toronto

Maxwell Macmillan International
New York   Oxford   Singapore   Sydney

Cover photo by Joel Conison
Editor: Kevin M. Davis
Developmental Editor: Molly Kyle
Production Editor: Rex Davidson
Art Coordinator: Lorraine Woost
Text Designer: Jill E. Bonar
Cover Designer: Cathleen Norz
Production Buyer: Patricia A. Tonneman

This book was set in Garamond by V & M Graphics and was printed and bound by
Semline, Inc., a Quebecor America Book Group Company. The cover was printed by
Lehigh Press, Inc.

Macmillan Publishing Company
866 Third Avenue
New York, New York 10022

Macmillan Publishing Company is part of the
Maxwell Communication Group of Companies.

Maxwell Macmillan Canada, Inc.
1200 Eglinton Avenue East, Suite 200
Don Mills, Ontario M3C 3N1

Library of Congress Cataloging-in-Publication Data
Textiles/Sara J. Kadolph . . . [et al.].—7th ed.
    p.   cm.
   Sixth ed. written by Norma Hollen and others.
   Includes bibliographical references and index.
   ISBN 0-02-361601-6
   1. Textile industry. 2. Textile fibers. 3. Textile fabrics.
I. Kadolph, Sara J.
TS1446.T47 1993
677—dc20   92-20613
                                                                      CIP

Printing: 2   3   4   5   6   7   8   9   Year: 3   4   5   6   7

PREFACE

Textiles is intended to equip beginning professionals with a basic understanding of how the textile components of products are made and how appropriate fabric or product performance is achieved. A solid understanding of textiles (the fibers, yarns, fabrics, and finishes), the interrelationships among these components, and their impact on product performance and product satisfaction is fundamentally related to day-to-day responsibilities in many specific career choices.

In this text, serviceability of the textile is the basis of the discussion. The emphasis is on the contributions of each component as it is incorporated in or combined with other components in a textile product (fiber and yarn type, fabrication method, and finishes). The reader will also come to understand the interrelationships among the components.

MAJOR CHANGES AND ADDITIONS

For this revision, I have updated and added material where new concerns have arisen in the professional workplace, in the textile industry, or with consumers. You will find additional explanations, expanded discussions, and clarified concepts in areas where my own students and reviewers have indicated the need. Terminology has been revised to incorporate an industry perspective. Since most students will be working in one industry segment or another, they need to understand terms that both their suppliers and their customers use so they will be able to communicate effectively.

Throughout the text, you will find discussion of contemporary industry and societal concerns that have arisen or grown more important since the last

edition was published. We will also address the impact on the industry of technological advances. We cover these concerns and advances by means of a more focused discussion of product serviceability and product performance, and through greater emphasis on computer use in yarn and fabric production and finishing. The focus of the book has expanded to include a broader discussion of textile products, with equal attention to apparel and furnishings and an introduction to industrial products.

NEW MATERIAL

Information on laws and regulations regarding labeling of textiles has been combined in one place (Chapter 21) rather than scattered throughout the text, and this chapter has been expanded to include other legal aspects of being a professional, including legal responsibilities and liabilities. The chapter also includes a discussion of environmental issues and environmental laws and regulations. The discussion of environmental issues focuses on the impact this trend is having and will continue to have on the textile industry. There is no doubt that concern for the environment will continue in the 1990s and that the impact will increase.

The discussion of dyeing and printing has been expanded to provide more information on the basic processes of adding color to fabric and to include new techniques. The discussion of finishing now includes more aesthetic finishes, especially those designed to add a softer or stressed look to goods and products. The chapter on care has been expanded to include information on cleaning furnishings, especially upholstery and carpeting.

Microfibers and other fiber developments have been included in the fiber section. Discussion of furnishings as a major end use for textiles has been included throughout the text.

Finally, a new chapter (Chapter 22) on career opportunities has been added. This chapter will help students see the many possibilities open to them when they have an understanding of textiles and textile products. All too often, students tend to look at career opportunities from a narrow perspective. Although this chapter need not be used as an assigned reading in all beginning textile courses, students can use it as a means of exploring career possibilities on their own and as a starting point for considering other career options beyond those that are most readily visible to them.

ORGANIZATION

The order of several chapters has been changed, with the intention of helping the student better understand the content. In several chapters, content has been reorganized, with key concepts grouped to more closely integrate related processes, structures, or ideas. For example, the fiber chapters (Section 2) are now grouped by their basic types, rather than discussing a single fiber in each chapter. The number of chapters has been reduced. Although no one chapter was eliminated completely, related material is now located within a single chapter instead of spread throughout the book. For example, all fancy weaves and structural design woven fabrics are located in one chapter instead of several chapters. In addition, fancy weave (Chapter 13) follows the basic weaves to help students organize and learn the material.

Each section of the book focuses on a basic component or aspect of fabrics and textile products or on general issues important to use, production, or satisfaction with textile products. The sections are complete enough that they can be used in any order desired. The four center sections follow the normal sequence used in production of textiles: fiber (Section 2), yarn (Section 3), fabrication (Section 4), and finishing (Section 5). Section 1 introduces the study of textiles and the concept of serviceability by explaining the processes used in selection and evaluation of several textile products, taking textile examples from the furnishing and apparel areas. Section 2 focuses on fibers: their production, serviceability, effect on product performance, and use. Section 3 focuses on yarn produc-

tion, yarn types, and relationship of yarn type to product performance and serviceability. Section 4 examines fabrication methods. These chapters are organized by basic fabrication method, standard or classic fabric names and types, and the relationships between fabrication and product performance. Section 5 deals with finishes; finishes are grouped by type or effect. This section also includes dyeing, printing, and problems that consumers and producers experience with dyed or printed fabrics. The final section, Section 6, deals with other issues related to textiles. Chapter 20 focuses on care of textile products; Chapter 21 investigates legal and environmental issues; and the final chapter explores career opportunities that require some textiles knowledge.

STUDY AIDS

Instructors and students have always told us they liked the summary and reference tables and charts, the clear and consistent presentation of information, the emphasis on serviceability, and the numerous illustrations, graphics, and photographs. These strengths have been improved upon: the number of tables has been enlarged; tables have been revised, reorganized, or updated where necessary, or where students or colleagues have suggested improvements; and, presentation of information has been refined. Serviceability remains the focus. Many new illustrations and photographs are included to expand on the topics covered in the text.

While the basic content and flavor of *Textiles* remain intact, changes have been incorporated to help the student recognize and focus on the most important material. Objectives at the beginning of each chapter will help students identify and understand the major concepts. Lists of key words introduce terminology and important concepts. After reading and studying each chapter, students should be able to define each term and explain how the term relates to other terms and to the content of the chapter. Study questions provide students with an opportunity to demonstrate their level of understanding, focus on key concepts or applications, and integrate the information. Finally, for those who would like to investigate topics beyond the scope of the text, lists of current references direct students to additional material. For the first time for this book, an instructor's manual has been developed. The manual includes an outline of the material for each chapter, a list of suggested activities, a bank of test questions of various formats, and transparency masters for use in class.

PHILOSOPHY OF THIS BOOK

The overall philosophy regarding the knowledge of textiles required in professional careers remains unchanged. References to individual home use and home production of textiles, especially relating to how to sew with specific textiles, have been minimized so that the book focuses on the textile itself. The previous focus on apparel products as examples in the text has been shifted to widen the student's perspective. Furnishings and industrial products are equally important and the book's broader focus reflects the importance of all three areas: furnishing, industrial, and apparel products. Specific fiber performance charts have been expanded to include care of furnishing fabrics, and discussion of fiber performance, and end uses now includes furnishings and some industrial products.

This textbook takes the stance that the student will need basic information about textiles so as to perform professional responsibilities adequately and to communicate intelligently with other professionals. Hence, certain changes to this seventh edition make the book more useful both as a text and as a part of a professional's reference library. Key terms are defined in both the text and the glossary, and the glossary now contains more than basic or classic fabric names—it incorporates fiber modifications, finishes, and terminology related to performance. The expanded index will help students locate information for this class and for other classes that build on or use basic textile information, as well as when they need it later on the job. Finally, because of the quantity of textiles purchased in the international marketplace, a list of fiber names in several languages commonly encountered in international trading has been included in an appendix.

This book will benefit students in numerous ways. They will come to

- Use textile terminology correctly.
- Know laws and labeling requirements that regulate textile distribution.
- Understand the impact of production processes and selection of components on product performance, product cost, and consumer satisfaction.
- Understand past developments and recognize some of the forces that drive future developments in the textile industry.

- Identify fiber type, yarn type, or fabrication method based on visual or simple microscopic analysis.
- Predict fabric or product performance based on a knowledge of fibers, yarns, fabrication methods, and finishes in conjunction with informative labeling.
- Make appropriate selection of textile products or textile components based on specified end uses and target market expectations for performance and serviceability.
- Select appropriate care procedures for textile products.
- Develop an interest in and appreciation of textiles that will motivate further study.

A student swatch kit has been developed by Textile Fabric Consultants to use in conjunction with this edition of *Textiles*. It is available through Textile Fabric Consultants, P. O. Box 111431, Nashville, Tennessee 37222 (contact Nancy Henig or Amy White at 615/459-7510).

ACKNOWLEDGMENTS

I have used the comments and contributions of many students and colleagues in preparing this revision. I find students' comments help me the most in evaluating the approach, wording, and style of presentation. Colleagues' comments help me determine what content to include and the depth of coverage. Both perspectives are invaluable in the process of revision. I would especially like to thank Darlene Fratzke of Iowa State University and Frank Rankin of Mayfair Cleaners in Ames, Iowa, for their help with the care chapter; Carolyn Kundel, Ruth Glock, Grace Kunz, and Jean Hassebrock, all of Iowa State University, for their suggestions throughout the book; Laura Kidd, Linda Manikowske, and Criss Krabbe, all graduate teaching assistants at Iowa State University, who shared with me their perspectives and students' comments regarding the book and course material; and Teresa Heard, also a graduate assistant at Iowa State University, and Criss Krabbe for their assistance with some of the research for the book. A special thanks to Chuck Greiner of the Front Porch Photography Studio, Huxley, Iowa, for his help with the photography.

This seventh edition reflects changes in the industry and includes a great deal of new material. For their many suggestions in this regard and assistance with rewording and refocusing this edition, I thank my reviewers: Jan Petsch, Michigan State University; Chloe D. Merrill, Weber State University; Kathleen M. Delaney, Interior Designers Institute; Gajanan Bhat, University of Tennessee, Knoxville; Kay Hagan, St. Louis Community College—Meramec; Christine Ladisch, Purdue University; and Mary J. Thompson, Brigham Young University. They have helped me immeasurably.

The people at Macmillan have been great. In particular, I thank Ron Nurmi for his periodic words of encouragement, information, and assistance; Kevin Davis for his confidence in me and his people skills in organizing this revision of *Textiles*; Molly Kyle for her humor and assistance with problems and questions; Rex Davidson for his timely reminders and planning; and Sheryl Rose for her unflagging attention to detail with the manuscript copyedit.

Revising this textbook is always an exciting challenge. I have enjoyed the opportunity to dig into the textiles literature in more depth than my university responsibilities usually allow. I also enjoy the chance to share this exciting area of textiles with so many others. I hope this book intrigues some of you and hooks you on textiles—as the third edition did for me when I was a college sophomore just beginning to learn about textiles.

Sara J. Kadolph

CONTENTS

SECTION 1

INTRODUCTION TO TEXTILES

CHAPTER

1

Introduction

OBJECTIVES

- To become aware of the diversity of textile products.

- To understand the importance of studying textiles from a professional perspective.

- To recognize the importance of textiles in modern life when used as apparel, furnishings, and industrial products.

*T*HIS SECTION IS DIVIDED INTO TWO CHAPTERS. The first chapter introduces the study of textiles by briefly identifying examples of textile products, surveying the diversity of textiles currently available, and discussing the importance of the industry to the U.S. economy. The second chapter discusses selecting and evaluating textile products.

An ideal starting place to gain an understanding of textiles is by defining several basic terms.

Fiber   Any substance, natural or manufactured, with a high length-to-width ratio and with suitable characteristics for being processed into fabric.

Yarn   An assemblage of fibers, twisted or laid together so as to form a continuous strand that can be made into a textile fabric.

Fabric   A planar substance constructed from solutions, fibers, yarns, fabrics, or any combination of these.

Finish   Any process used to convert gray goods (unfinished fabric) into finished fabric.

Textile   A term generally applied to fibers, yarns, fabrics, or products made of fibers, yarns, or fabrics.

Food, shelter, and clothing are the basic needs of everyone. Most clothing is made from textiles, and shelters are made more comfortable and attractive by the use of textiles. In fact, some shelters are made from textiles. Textiles are used in the production or processing of many things used in day-to-day living, such as food and manufactured goods.

We are surrounded by textiles from birth to death. We walk on and wear textile products; we sit on fabric-covered chairs and sofas; we sleep on and under fabrics; textiles dry us or keep us dry; they keep us warm and protect us from the sun, fire, and infection. Clothing and furnishing textiles are aesthetically pleasing, and they vary in color, design, and texture. They are also available in a variety of price ranges.

The industrial and medical uses of textiles are many and varied. The automotive industry uses tex-

Fig. 1–1   *Apparel textile products.*

tiles to make tire cords, upholstery, carpeting, head liners, window runners, seat belts, shoulder harnesses, and many other parts.

Travel to the moon was done in a 20-layer, $100,000 space suit that has nylon water-cooled underwear. Life is prolonged by replacing wornout parts of the body with textile parts such as polyester arteries and velour heart valves. Disposable garments are worn by medical personnel. Bulletproof vests protect police, hunters, and soldiers, and safety belts make automobile travel less dangerous. Three-dimensional, inflatable structures keep out desert heat and Arctic cold.

This text was written to aid students in learning and understanding what to expect in fabric performance and why fabrics perform as they do. Textiles are always changing. They change as fashion changes and as the needs of people change. New developments in production processes also cause changes in textiles, as do government standards for safety, environmental quality, and energy conservation. These changes are discussed, but the bulk of the text is devoted to basic information about textile products, with an emphasis on fibers, yarns, fabric construction, and finishes. All of these elements are interdependent and contribute to the beauty, the durability, the care, and the comfort of fabrics.

Much of the terminology used in the text may be new to students and many facts must be memorized. But to understand textiles in a broad aspect one must first learn the basics. The historical development, the basic concepts, and new developments

Fig. 1–2   Furnishing textile products.

in textiles are discussed. Production processes are explained briefly. A knowledge of production should give the student a better understanding of, and appreciation for, the textile industry.

In the United States, the textile industry is a tremendous complex. It includes the natural and manufactured fiber producers, spinners, weavers, knitters, throwsters, yarn converters, tufters, fiber-web producers and finishers, machinery makers, and many others. More people are employed in the textile industry than in any other manufacturing industry, over 1.6 million. Textile products valued at over $54 billion in 1990 are produced by computer-ized systems. In Japan, for example, at the push of a button an operator can dye wool fabric in over 2,000 color combinations without flaw or error.

The textile industry has developed from an art-and-craft industry perpetuated by guilds in the early centuries, through the Industrial Revolution in the 18th and 19th centuries, when the emphasis was on mechanization and mass production, to the 20th century, with its emphasis on science and technology.

In this century, manufactured fibers were developed and modified textured yarns were created. New fabrications and increased production of knits

Fig. 1–3   Industrial textiles and industrial products incorporating textiles.

occurred, and many finishes and sophisticated textile production and marketing systems were developed. These developments have been beneficial to consumers. Manufactured fibers and durable press finishes have made many items of clothing easy care. New developments in textiles have also created some problems for consumers, particularly in the selection of apparel and furnishing textiles. Many items look alike. Knitted fabrics look like woven fabrics and vice versa, vinyl and polyurethane films look like leather, fur fabrics look like real furs, acrylic and polyester fabrics look like wool. Traditional cotton fabrics are now often polyester or polyester/cotton blends.

To make textile selection easier for consumers, textile producers and their associations have set standards and established quality-control programs for many textile products. The federal government has passed laws to protect and inform consumers.

Emphasis on energy conservation, environmental quality, noise abatement, health, and safety affect the textile industry as well as other industries. The efforts of the textile industry to meet standards set by the federal government affect the consumer by raising prices for merchandise or by limiting the choices available.

Textile fabrics can be beautiful, durable, comfortable, and easy care. They can satisfy the needs of all people at all times. Knowing how fabrics are created and used will give a better basis for their selection and an understanding of their limitations.

A knowledge of textiles and their production will result in a more informed selection of a textile product for a particular use. A knowledgeable selection will result in a more satisfied user.

KEY TERMS

Fiber

Yarn

Fabric

Finish

Textile

QUESTIONS

1. Define the key terms, explain the differences among them, and describe how these terms relate to textiles.
2. How do textiles influence contemporary lifestyles?
3. Describe textiles used in normal daily activities. Be sure to consider furnishing, industrial, and apparel products. How do these products assist in or make these activities possible?

SUGGESTED READINGS

Examine several of these trade publications to see what items are included and how detailed the discussion is: *America's Textiles International, Industrial Products Review, Textile Chemist and Colorist, Textile Horizons, Textile Month, Textile Progress, Textile Research Journal,* and *Textile World.*

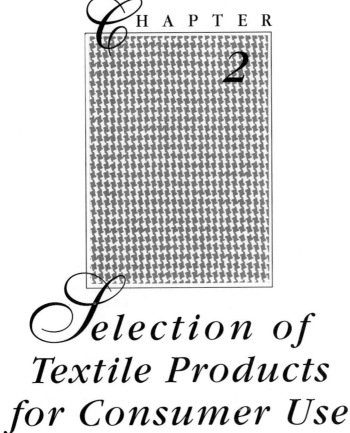

CHAPTER 2

Selection of
Textile Products
for Consumer Use

OBJECTIVES

- To understand the components of serviceability of textile products.

- To relate end-use requirements to both product selection and product evaluation.

- To apply the serviceability concepts when selecting textile products for specific target markets, situations, or consumers.

*M*ANY TEXTILES ARE USED AS A PART OF daily life. Ready-to-wear apparel, over-the-counter fabrics that will be sewn into apparel or furnishing items, and home furnishings are chosen by consumers for their use.

The selection of textile products is a personal decision based on many factors, including current fashion, lifestyle, income, sex, and age. The selection is influenced by aesthetic, psychological, sociological, and economic aspects. The decision to buy a product may be rational or it may be impulsive. This chapter provides a framework to help consumers make rational decisions about textile products.

This same framework is very useful for people whose jobs are related to textile products. People employed in merchandising, design, or production—such as retail and wholesale buyers and salespersons, and fabric, garment, and interior designers—can all benefit from a better understanding of textiles and the ways customers use these products. Persons in these jobs can be called preselectors. What they select determines what the consumer has available to purchase. Hence, the decisions made by the preselector influence, to a large degree, the consumer's choice and ultimate satisfaction.

Before the market research begins, the consumer will have decided on the item of interest. Consumers should also think through pertinent factors: Who will be using the item? How will it be used? When will it be used? How long will it need to last? Usually this thinking is in terms of what the item will be used for, or the end use.

The end use that is identified affects the subsequent selection. Is the coat to be worn by a college student or for school and play by a rambunctious nine-year-old? Will the fabric be made into a pair of slacks for a teenager or for an elderly person in a nursing home? Are the sheets and bedspread for college use, where they must serve both living and sleeping functions, or are they for the master bedroom of a carefully decorated model home? Is the suit to be worn in the summer for casual wear or will it be worn at work throughout the fall, winter, and spring? Is the upholstery for a chair to used in a formal dining room or in a shoe store by customers trying on shoes?

With the end use clearly in mind, additional factors need to be considered. What factors are important in making the item serviceable for its purpose? Factors frequently considered by consumers include price, color, fashion, style, appearance, quality of construction, durability, comfort, and care. Which factors are most important for this item and its end use? Which are least important? What are the rankings of the other factors?

With the end use and a realization of the factors that are important for serviceability of the item in mind, a possible sequence of steps in making the decision might include:

1. Determine a price range or price ceiling for the textile product.
2. Find items that are acceptable by checking available sources, such as local stores, showrooms, and catalogs.
3. Evaluate color, fashion, style, appearance, and quality of construction.
4. Evaluate the serviceability of the textile components of the item.
5. Buy a specific item or continue the search.

The satisfaction that the consumer receives from the textile material will depend on individual values as well as on the performance of the product. The performance and care of the product depend on the fibers, yarns, fabric construction, and finishes. The manufacturer has decided what combination would be appropriate for the item. The buyer has determined the selection available to the consumer. The final step in the decision-making process is for the consumer to select the item that is most appropriate for his or her own use.

This seems like an involved procedure to follow when searching for an item, but most of the steps are almost automatic. The choice of where to search limits the selection. Once the location of the search has been determined, price, color, fashion, style, appearance, and quality of construction can be quickly evaluated. When the selection is narrowed down to two or three items, the consumer can evaluate the serviceability of the textile components of each item. This is where a student of textiles will have more knowledge than a typical customer and will be better able to match end-use requirements to the realistic expected performance of the item.

The serviceability concepts that are used in organizing the material in this book are simple and straightforward. These concepts provide a framework for combining textile facts with personal needs and preferences in a way that will help consumers make wiser decisions about the textile products they purchase and use. As the concepts are combined with the consumer's past and present experiences, they can act as a simple checklist while the purchasing decision is made. The serviceability concepts also provide an excellent framework for the preselector. Combined with their experience of what sells and what works for their clients, the serviceability concepts can improve their purchasing decisions.

The five serviceability concepts will be used by following through with the examples discussed earlier in this chapter.

1. *Aesthetics.* The bedspread for the model home should be attractive in and of itself; it must also coordinate with the décor of the master bedroom and blend well with the overall effect intended for the entire house. The teenager's slacks will need to look good as judged by both the individual and the peer group. The upholstered chair for the formal dining room needs to be attractive and retain its appearance for several years.

2. *Durability.* The coat for the nine-year-old should be durable enough to withstand hard use. Is it intended to be a summer, fall, spring, or winter jacket? How different are the seasons in that specific location? How quickly is the child growing—does the child tend to wear out clothes or outgrow them? Is the jacket expected to last a season, a year, or several years? The bedspread for college use may be expected to last several years and will be subjected to hard use since dorm beds usually function as sofas. The chair upholstery for the shoe store must be durable since it will be used frequently and on a daily basis for years.

3. *Comfort.* This factor may be of great importance for a summer suit worn primarily out-of-doors in a hot and humid climate. Comfort also is very important for the person in the nursing home. The fabric must be comfortable next to delicate skin. Upholstery should be soft and flexible enough so that users are neither distracted by nor made uncomfortable by the fabric.

4. *Appearance retention.* The suit that will be worn at work needs to resist wrinkles during wear. It should maintain its shape during use. Over the period of time it is worn, it should continue to look professional. The sheets and bedspread for college use will undoubtedly last several years, but how will they look the last year?

5. *Care.* The college student's coat may not need cleaning often. If infrequent dry cleaning is required, the coat may be acceptable. On the other hand, the child's jacket and the teenager's slacks probably should be washable. Slacks used in a nursing home will need to withstand frequent high-temperature washing and will look better after care if made from a wrinkle-resistant fabric. With the daily use of the dorm bedspread and the limited budget of many college students, a machine-washable bedspread would be ideal. Dry cleaning would be more appropriate for the bedspread for the model home. Both pieces of upholstery need to be resistant to stains one might normally expect the chairs to be exposed to. Stains would require immediate treatment. Severe soiling might require steam cleaning.

When selecting among several possibly acceptable items for a specific end use, the serviceability concepts can be posed as questions. See Table 2–1.

To further emphasize the importance of defining the end use for a textile item and to better understand the impact this has on selection, the five serviceability concepts for each suit and upholstered chair discussed above have been ranked by a consumer. See Tables 2–2 and 2–3. The most important concept is ranked "1," the least important concept is ranked "5."

It is most unlikely that a single textile product would be serviceable for both end uses, for either the suit or the upholstery, because the performance requirements differ. Also, another consumer might have ranked the concepts in a different order or two concepts might be equally important.

Finally, more than one factor will need to be considered in each end use. First, consider the upholstery for the shoe store. Aesthetic factors might include the look appropriate for the type of shoe the store carries and its target customer. Compare the look of an upscale shoe store in a new shopping center with that of an off-price shoe store in a discount mall. Durability requirements would specify

Table 2–1 Serviceability Questions

Aesthetics	Is this item attractive and appropriate in appearance for its end use? How does it look and feel?
Durability	Will this item continue to be useable for as long as expected? Or will it wear out sooner than desired?
Comfort	Is this item comfortable enough for use in its purpose? Will it be too warm or too cool? Will it feel good against the skin? Will the comfort change as the fabric wears? Will the comfort be altered by required care procedures?
Appearance retention	Will this item retain its appearance during use and care? Will it resist wrinkles? Will it retain its shape? Do the aspects that make this item attractive have suitable durability, comfort, and care characteristics? Will the item look and feel good as long as it lasts?
Care	Are the treatments required to maintain the new look of this item during use, cleaning, and storage acceptable considering the money and time available? Is the care realistic considering the cost of the item?
Serviceability	What combination of these five concepts is important in making this item useable for its purpose?

the abrasion resistance for the upholstery fabric. Comfort features are probably minimal because of the use, but if it is too uncomfortable customers won't spend much time trying on shoes. Appearance-retention factors might relate to pilling and soiling. Care for upholstery is limited, but might include steam cleaning.

Next, let us look at the suit for work. Aesthetics factors might include a fashion look appropriate for that particular job and company of a color and style becoming to the wearer. Durability requirements would specify how long the suit is expected to be worn—one, two, or more years? Comfort factors include some minimum level of comfort because it is difficult to concentrate if clothes are scratchy or otherwise uncomfortable. Appearance-retention factors might relate to wrinkle resistance. The suit should

retain its shape. It should continue to look professional for a reasonable time. Care factors include the method required. Frequently, dry cleaning is required for suits. Care was ranked of lowest priority, so presumably any care method is acceptable.

Now, to return to the search—once several acceptable items have been identified, evaluate the serviceability concepts of aesthetics, durability, comfort, appearance retention, and care. Which item best satisfies the requirements of the end use? Is the cost appropriate? Are all the other selection factors acceptable? Based on this evaluation, make the decision to purchase a specific item.

In summary, end use determines performance requirements. During selection, relate end-use performance requirements to realistic expected performance in the five serviceability areas. Within this framework, textile knowledge can be critical in satisfying needs and wants. The serviceability concepts are defined and discussed in detail in Chapter 3. The concepts are referred to frequently throughout the remainder of the book.

It must be stressed that neither this book nor any course in textiles will give students the answers for any end use. This book will not answer the question: What is the best combination of fiber, yarn, fabrication, and finish for a coat or chair? Consumers make choices based on their knowledge of themselves, their needs and expectations, and the use the product will get. If they know about textiles, they can make an intelligent selection. However, with any selection, there will be some good and some not-so-good features. The more knowledge consumers have, the more serviceable the product should be.

Consumers have information available to them on labels, hang tags, and packages. Federal legislation requires that fiber content be stated. With the

Table 2–2 Suit

End Use	Casual: Summer	Work: Fall, Winter, and Spring
Aesthetics	3	1
Durability	5	4
Comfort	1	3
Appearance retention	4	2
Care	2	5

Table 2–3 **Upholstered Chair**

End Use	Formal Dining Room	Shoe Store
Aesthetics	1	2
Durability	4	1
Comfort	3	5
Appearance retention	2	3
Care	5	4

information in this book, fiber content information will provide some basis for predicting performance related to durability, comfort, and appearance retention. Aesthetics can be judged by the consumer. Care labels are required by federal legislation. Thus some information is available on which to base rational decisions. How wisely that information is used, or how meaningful that information is to any one person, depends on the person making the choices. In addition, evaluation of other aspects of the product, such as yarn and fabric type, will provide more information on which to base a decision.

KEY TERMS

Serviceability   Comfort
Aesthetics   Appearance retention
Durability   Care

QUESTIONS

1. Consider the most recent textile product you purchased. On what basis was that selection made?
2. Suggest priorities for each of the five serviceability components for the items and consumers listed below:
   carpeting in the eating area of a fast-food restaurant
   shirt/blouse for a management trainee in a retail firm
   housecoat/robe for a resident in a nursing home
   chair upholstery in the receptionist's area of a corporate office
   adhesive bandage for a child's scraped knee

SUGGESTED READINGS

Belck, Nancy, Butler, Sara M., and Wamhoff, Marlene (1990). *Textiles for the Consumer*. East Lansing, MI: Michigan State University Press.
Merkel, Robert (1991). *Textile Product Serviceability*. New York: Macmillan.

SECTION 2

FIBERS

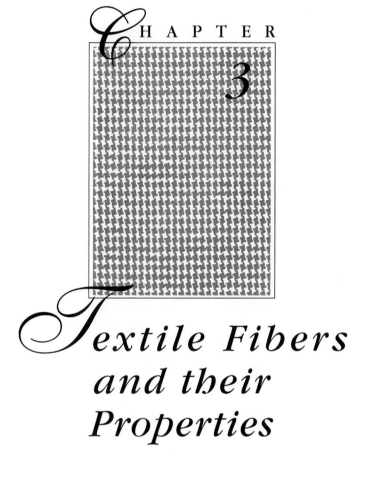

CHAPTER 3

Textile Fibers and their Properties

OBJECTIVES

- To understand terms describing textile fibers and their properties.

- To use terminology correctly.

- To understand the relationships between fiber structure and fiber properties or characteristics.

- To match fiber performance to end use requirements.

- To select and perform appropriate identification procedures for basic fibers.

*I*T IS IMPORTANT TO UNDERSTAND FIBERS AND their performance because fibers are the basic unit of most fabrics. Fibers contribute to the aesthetic appearance of fabrics; they influence durability, comfort, and appearance retention; they influence the care required for fabrics; and they influence the cost. Successful textile fibers must be readily available, constantly in supply, and cost effective. They must have sufficient strength, pliability, length, and cohesiveness to be spun into yarns.

Textile fibers have been used to make cloth for several thousand years. Until 1885, when the first *manufactured fiber* was produced commercially, fibers were produced by plants and animals. The fibers most commonly used were wool, flax, cotton, and silk. These four *natural fibers* continue to be used and valued today, although their economic importance relative to all fibers has decreased.

Textile processes—spinning, weaving, knitting, dyeing, and finishing of fabrics—were developed for the natural fibers. These traditional processes have been modified for manufactured fibers. New processes have been developed specifically for manufactured fibers.

For example, silk has always been a highly prized fiber because of its smoothness, luster, and softness; it has always been expensive and comparatively scarce. It was logical to try to duplicate silk. Rayon (called artificial silk until 1925) was the first manufactured fiber. Rayon was produced in filament length until the early 1930s when an enterprising textile worker discovered that the broken and wasted rayon filaments could be used as staple fiber. Acetate and nylon were also introduced as filaments to be used in silklike fabrics.

Many manufactured fibers were developed in the first half of the 20th century. Since then tremendous advances have been made in the manufactured fiber industry, primarily modifications of parent fibers to provide the best combination of properties for specific end uses. The manufactured fibers most commonly used in contemporary apparel and furnishing fabrics include polyester, nylon, olefin, acrylic, rayon, and acetate. Fibers for special and industrial applications include spandex, aramid, PBI, and sulfar. From time to time, new fibers or new fiber modifications are introduced.

FIBER PROPERTIES

Fiber properties contribute to the properties of a fabric. For example, strong fibers contribute to the durability of fabrics; absorbent fibers are good for skin-contact apparel and for towels and diapers; flame-retardant fibers are good for children's sleepwear and protective clothing.

To analyze a fabric in order to predict its performance, start with the fiber. Knowledge of the fiber's properties will help to anticipate the fiber's contribution to the performance of a fabric and the product made from it. Some contributions of fibers are desirable and some are not. Figure 3–1 illustrates this fact by identifying some contributions of a low-absorbency fiber. However, it is important to note that product characteristics also result from other components beyond the fiber itself. Fibers are used to produce yarns. The type of yarn and its structure influence hand and performance. For example, yarns made from short fibers tend to be comfortable, but pill. The process used to produce the

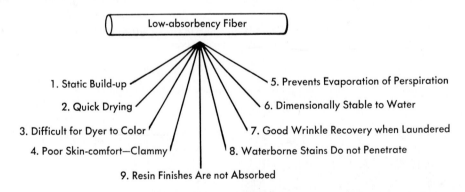

Fig. 3–1 *Properties usually related to low absorbency.*

fabric influences the product's appearance and texture, performance during use and care, and cost. Finishes are used to alter the fabric's hand, appearance, and performance. These three components (yarn, fabrication, and finishing) will be discussed in detail in the chapters in Sections 3, 4, and 5.

Fiber properties are determined by the nature of their physical structure, chemical composition, and molecular arrangement.

Physical Structure

The physical structure, or morphology, can be identified by observing the fiber using a microscope. In the text, photomicrographs at magnifications of 250-1,000× will be used to clarify details of the fiber's physical structure.

LENGTH Fibers are sold by the fiber producer as staple, filament, or filament tow. *Staple fibers* are measured in inches or centimeters and range in length from 2 to 46 cm (¾ of an inch to 18 inches), as illustrated in Figure 3-2. All the natural fibers except silk are available only in staple form. *Filaments* are long, continuous fiber strands of indefinite length, measured in yards or meters. They may be either monofilament (one fiber) or multifilament (a number of filaments). Filaments may be smooth or bulked (crimped in some way), as shown in Figure 3-3. Smooth filaments are used to produce silklike fabrics; bulked filaments are used in more cottonlike or wool-like fabrics. Filament tow is produced as a loose rope of several thousand fibers, crimped or textured, and cut to staple length.

SIZE Fiber size plays a big part in determining the performance and hand of a fabric (how it feels).

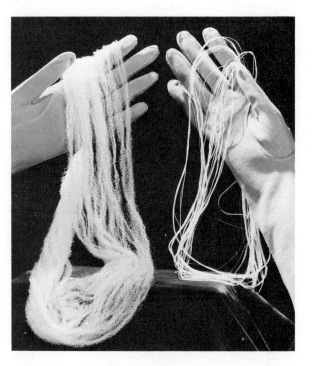

Fig. 3–3   Manufactured filaments: textured-bulk yarn (left); *smooth-filament yarn* (right).

Large fibers give crispness, roughness, body, and stiffness. Large fibers also resist crushing—a property that is important in products like carpets. Fine fibers give softness and pliability. Fabrics made with fine fibers will drape more easily.

Natural fibers are subject to growth irregularities and are not uniform in size or development. In natural fibers, fineness is a major factor in determining quality. Fine fibers are of better quality. Fineness is measured in micrometers (a micrometer is 1/1,000 millimeter or 1/25,400 inch). Table 3-1 lists the fineness of the natural fibers.

In manufactured fibers, diameter is controlled by the size of the spinneret holes, by stretching or drawing during or after spinning, or by controlling the rate of extrusion of the spinning solution through the spinneret. Manufactured fibers can be

Fig. 3–2   Manufactured staple fiber.

Table 3–1   Natural Fiber Diameter Range (micrometers)

Cotton	16–20
Flax	12–16
Wool	10–50
Silk	11–12

made uniform in diameter or can be thick-and-thin at regular intervals throughout their length. The fineness of manufactured fibers is measured in denier. *Denier* is the weight in grams of 9,000 meters of fiber or yarn. When the term denier is used to describe a fiber, the number refers to the fineness or coarseness of the fiber. Small numbers describe fine fibers; large numbers describe large or coarse fibers. *Tex* is the weight in grams of 1,000 meters of fiber or yarn. Staple fiber is sold by denier and fiber length; filament fiber is sold by the denier of the yarn or tow. Yarn denier can be divided by the number of filaments to give denier per filament or dpf. For example:

$$\frac{40 \text{ denier yarn}}{20 \text{ filaments}} = 2 \text{ denier per filament}$$

One to 3 denier corresponds to fine cotton, cashmere, or wool; 5 to 8 denier is similar to average cotton, wool, or alpaca; 15 denier corresponds to carpet wool size. Apparel fibers range from less than 1 to 7 denier. Carpet fibers may range in denier from 15 to 24.

Fibers of the same denier are not necessarily suitable for all end uses. Apparel fibers do not make serviceable carpets and carpet fibers do not make serviceable clothing. Apparel fibers are too soft and pliable, and the carpets made of apparel fibers do not have good crush resistance.

CROSS–SECTIONAL SHAPE Shape is important in luster, bulk, body, texture, and hand or feel of a fabric. Figure 3–4 shows typical cross-sectional shapes. These shapes may be round, dog-bone, triangular, lobal, bean-shaped, flat, or strawlike.

The natural fibers derive their shape from (1) the way the cellulose is built up during plant growth, (2) the shape of the hair follicle and the formation of protein substances in animals, or (3) the shape of the orifice through which the silk fiber is extruded.

The shape of manufactured fibers is controlled by the spinneret and the spinning method. The size, shape, luster, length, and other properties of manufactured fibers can be varied by changes in the production process.

SURFACE CONTOUR *Surface contour* describes the outer surface of the fiber along its length. Surface contour may be smooth, serrated, striated, or rough. It is important to the luster, hand, texture, and apparent soiling of the fabric. Figure 3–4 shows surface contours of selected fibers.

CRIMP Crimp may be found in textile materials as fiber crimp or fabric crimp. *Fiber crimp* refers to the waves, bends, twists, coils, or curls along the length of the fiber. Fiber crimp increases cohesiveness, resiliency, resistance to abrasion, stretch, bulk, and warmth. Crimp increases absorbency and skin-contact comfort but reduces luster. Inherent crimp occurs in wool. Inherent crimp also exists in an undeveloped state in bicomponent manufactured fibers where it is developed in the fabric or the completed garment (such as a sweater) by using the suitable treatment.

Fabric crimp refers to the bends caused by distortion of yarns in a fabric. When a yarn is unraveled from a fabric, fabric crimp can easily be seen in the yarn. It also may be visible in fibers removed from the yarn.

FIBER PARTS The natural fibers, except for silk, have three distinct parts: an outer covering called a *cuticle* or skin; an inner area; and a central core that may be hollow.

The manufactured fibers are not as complex as the natural fibers. They usually consist of a skin and a core.

Chemical Composition and Molecular Arrangement

Fibers are classified into groups by their chemical composition. Fibers with similar chemical compositions are placed in the same *generic group*. Fibers in one generic group have different properties from fibers in another group.

Fibers are composed of millions of molecular chains. *Polymerization* is the process of joining small molecules—monomers—together to form a long chain or a *polymer*. The length of the chains, which varies just as the length of fibers varies, depends on the number of molecules connected in a chain; it is described as *degree of polymerization*. Long chains indicate a high degree of polymerization and a high degree of fiber strength. Molecular chains are too small to be seen, even with the assistance of a microscope.

Molecular chains are sometimes described in terms of weight. The molecular weight is a factor in properties such as fiber strength and extensibility. A fiber of longer chains has a higher strength and is more difficult to pull apart than a fiber of shorter chains of equal weight.

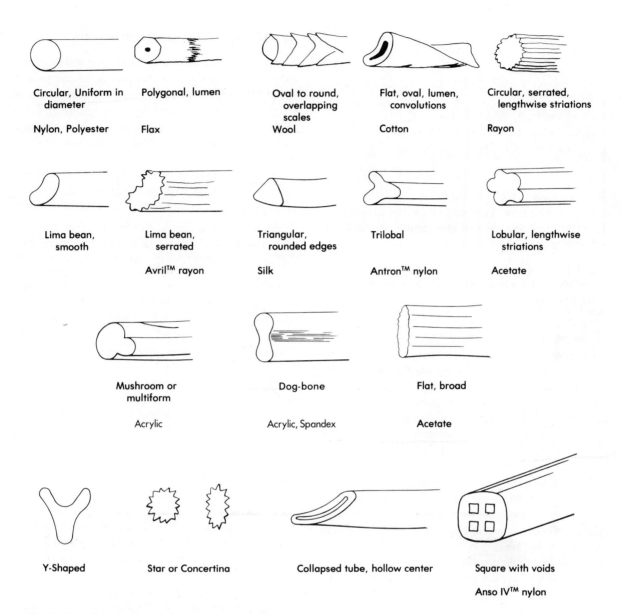

Fig. 3–4 *Cross-sectional shapes and fiber contours.*

Molecular chains have different configurations in fibers. When molecular chains are arranged in a random or disorganized way within the fiber, they are *amorphous*. When the molecular chains are parallel to each other or arranged in an organized fashion, they are *crystalline*. Molecular chains that are parallel to each other and to the lengthwise axis of the fiber are oriented. When most molecular chains are oriented, they have a high degree of *orientation* or are highly oriented. Fibers that are highly oriented must also be highly crystalline. However, highly crystalline fibers are not necessarily highly oriented (see Figure 3–5). Fibers vary in their proportion of oriented, crystalline, and amorphous regions.

The polymers in manufactured fibers are in a random, unoriented state when extruded from the spinneret. *Stretching*, or *drawing*, increases their crystallinity and orients them, reduces their diameter, and packs their molecules together (Figure 3–6). Fiber properties related to the degree of crystallinity and orientation include strength, elongation, moisture absorption, abrasion resistance, and dyeability.

Fibers that are amorphous are relatively weak and easily elongated. Amorphous fibers also have good moisture absorbency and dyeability, good flexibility, and poor elasticity. Examples of amorphous fibers include wool and rayon.

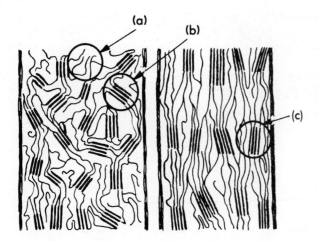

Fig. 3–5   Polymers: (a) amorphous area; (b) crystalline, but not oriented, area; (c) oriented and crystalline area.

Oriented and crystalline fibers are strong and stiff. They are difficult to elongate, but have good elasticity. They tend to be nonabsorbent and difficult to dye. Highly oriented and crystalline fibers include polyester, nylon, and aramid.

Molecular chains are held to one another by intermolecular forces called *hydrogen bonds* and *van der Waals forces*. The forces are similar to the attraction of a magnet for a piece of iron. The closer the chains are to each other, the stronger the bonds are. Hydrogen bonding is the attraction of positive hydrogen atoms of one chain for negative oxygen or nitrogen atoms of an adjacent chain. Van der Waals forces are similar but weaker bonds. It is in the crystalline area that hydrogen bonding and van der Waals forces occur. These intermolecular forces help make crystalline polymers stronger than amorphous polymers.

SERVICEABILITY

Textile serviceability includes the five concepts of aesthetics, durability, comfort, appearance retention, and care. Each concept will be discussed in terms of properties that affect it (Table 3-2). For example, the aesthetic properties of luster, drape, texture, and hand, as they relate to apparel and furnishing fabrics, will be defined and discussed.

Learning the definitions of the properties is important in gaining a more in-depth understanding of textile fiber performance. The tables in this chapter will assist you in making comparisons among fibers. Relating this to past experience with fabrics made of that fiber will contribute to a better understanding of fiber performance and serviceability.

Aesthetic Properties

A textile product should be attractive and appropriate in appearance for its end use. Aesthetic properties relate to the way the senses, such as touch and sight, assist in the perception of the textile. In evaluating the aesthetics of a textile product, the consumer usually determines whether the item is attractive and appropriate in appearance for its end use.

Luster results from the way light is reflected by a fabric's surface. Shiny or bright fabrics reflect a great amount of light and are used for certain end uses. Lustrous fabrics reflect a fair amount of light and are used in formal apparel and furnishings. Matte, or dull, fabrics reflect little light and are used most frequently for less-formal looks in apparel and furnishings. Silk fabrics are usually lustrous. Cotton and wool fabrics are usually matte. The luster of manufactured fibers can be varied during manufacturing to result in bright, semibright, or dull fibers. Yarn structure, finish, and fabric structure may enhance or decrease the luster of any fiber.

Drape is the way a fabric falls over a three-dimensional form like a body or table. Fabric may be soft and free-flowing like chiffon, or it may fall in graceful folds like percale, or it may be stiff and heavy like satin. Fibers influence drape to a degree, but yarns and fabric structure may be more important in determining drape.

Texture describes the nature of the fabric surface. It is identified by both visual and tactile senses. Fabrics may have a smooth or rough texture. Natural fibers tend to give a fabric more texture than manufactured fibers because of their inherent variations. Yarns, finishes, and fabric structure greatly affect the texture of a fabric.

Hand is the way a fabric feels to the touch. Fabrics may feel warm or cool, bulky or thin, slick or soft. Many other adjectives may be used. Hand may be evaluated by feeling a fabric between the fingers and thumb. The hand of fabric may also be evaluated by the way it feels against the skin. Subjective evaluation determines the fabric's acceptability for a particular end use; however, an objective means of assessing hand has been developed.

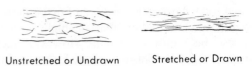

Unstretched or Undrawn   Stretched or Drawn

Fig. 3–6   Before and after drawing the fiber.

Table 3–2   Fiber Properties

Fiber Property	Is Due to	Contributes to Fabric Property
Abrasion resistance is the ability of a fiber to withstand the rubbing or abrasion it gets in everyday use.	Tough outer layer, scales, or skin Fiber toughness Flexible molecular chains	Durability Abrasion resistance Resistance to splitting
Absorbency or moisture regain is the percentage of moisture a bone-dry fiber will absorb from the air under standard conditions of temperature and moisture.	Hydroxyl groups Amorphous areas	Comfort, warmth, water repellency, absorbency, static buildup Dyeability, soiling Shrinkage Wrinkle resistance
Aging resistance	Chemical structure	Storing of fabrics
Allergenic potential is the ability to cause some physical reaction, such as skin irritation or watery eyes.	Chemical composition, additives	Comfort
Chemical reactivity is the effect of acids, alkali, oxidizing agents, solvents, or other chemicals.	Polar groups of molecules Chemical composition	Care required in cleaning—bleaching, ability to take acid or alkali finishes
Cohesiveness is the ability of fibers to cling together during spinning.	Crimp or twists, surface contour	Resistance to raveling Resistance to yarn slippage
Cover is the ability to occupy space for concealment or protection.	Crimp, curl, or twist Cross-sectional shape	Warmth in fabric Cost—less fiber needed
Creep is delayed recovery from elongation. Recovers gradually from strain.	Lack of side chains, cross links, strong bonds; poor orientation	Streak dyeing and shiners in fabric
Density—see *Specific gravity.*		
Dimensional stability is the ability to retain a given size and shape through use and care.	Physical structure, chemical structure, coatings	Shrinkage, growth, care, appearance, durability
Drape is the manner in which a fabric falls or hangs over a three-dimensional form.	Fiber size and stiffness	Appearance
Dyeability is the fiber's receptivity to coloration by dyes; dye affinity.	Amorphous areas and dye sites, chemical structure	Aesthetics and colorfastness
Elastic recovery is the degree to which fibers will recover from strain.	Chemical and molecular structure; side chains, cross linkages, strong bonds	Processability of fabrics Resiliency Delayed elasticity or creep
Elasticity is the ability of a strained material to recover its original size and shape immediately after removal of stress.	Chemical and molecular structure; side chains, cross linkages, strong bonds	Fit and appearance; resiliency
Electrical conductivity is the ability to transfer electrical charges.	Chemical structure: polar groups	Poor conductivity causes fabric to cling to the body, electric shocks
Elongation is the ability to be stretched, extended, or lengthened. Varies at different temperatures and when wet or dry.	Fiber crimp Molecular structure: molecular crimp orientation	Increases tear strength Reduces brittleness Provides "give"
Feltability refers to the ability of fibers to mat together.	Scale structure of wool	Fabrics can be made directly from fibers Special care required during washing

Table 3–2 **Fiber Properties** *(continued)*

Fiber Property	*Is Due to*	*Contributes to Fabric Property*
Flammability is the ability to ignite and burn.	Chemical composition	Fabrics burn
Flexibility is the ability to bend repeatedly without breaking.	Flexible molecular chain	Stiffness, drape, comfort
Hand is the way a fiber feels: silky, harsh, soft, crisp, dry.	Cross-sectional shape, surface properties, crimp, diameter, length	Hand of fabric
Heat conductivity is the ability to conduct heat away from the body.	Crimp, chemical composition Cross-sectional shape	Comfort: cooling effect
Heat retention is the ability to retain heat or insulate.	Crimp, chemical composition Cross-sectional shape	Comfort: warming effect, insulating
Heat sensitivity is the ability to soften, melt, or shrink when subjected to heat.	Chemical and molecular structure Fewer intermolecular forces and cross links	Determine safe washing and ironing temperatures
Hydrophilic, hygroscopic—see *Absorbency.*		
Loft, or compressional resiliency, is the ability to spring back to original thickness after being compressed.	Fiber crimp Stiffness	Springiness, good cover Resistance to flattening
Luster is the light reflected from a surface. More subdued than shine; light rays are broken up.	Smoothness Fiber length Flat or lobal shape Additives	Luster

Matte   Shiny

Fiber Property	*Is Due to*	*Contributes to Fabric Property*
Mildew resistance	Low absorption	Storage
Modulus is the resistance to stress/strain to which a fiber is exposed.	Molecular arrangement, chemical composition	Tenacity, elongation, and elasticity
Moth resistance	Molecule has no sulfur	Storage
Oleophilic describes fibers with a strong affinity or attraction for oil.	Chemical composition	Soiling; care; appearance
Pilling is the balling up of fiber ends on the surface of fabrics.	Fiber strength High molecular weight	Pilling Unsightly appearance
Resiliency is the ability to return to original shape after bending, twisting, compressing, or a combination of deformations.	Molecular structure: side chains, cross linkages, strong bonds	Wrinkle recovery, crease retention, appearance, care
Specific gravity and density are measures of the weight of a fiber. Density is the weight in grams per cubic centimeter. Specific gravity is the ratio of the mass of the fiber to an equal volume of water at 4° C.	Molecular weight and structure	Warmth without weight Loftiness—full and light Buoyancy to fabric
Stiffness or rigidity is the opposite of flexibility. It is the resistance to bending or creasing.	Chemical and molecular structure	Body of fabric Resistance to insertion of yarn twist
Strength is the ability to resist stress and is expressed as *tensile strength* (pounds per square inch) or as *tenacity* (grams per denier).	Molecular structure: orientation, crystallinity, degree of polymerization	Durability, tear strength, sagging, pilling Sheerest fabrics possible with strong fine fibers

Table 3–2 **Fiber Properties** (*continued*)

Fiber Property	Is Due to	Contributes to Fabric Property
Sunlight resistance is the ability to withstand degradation from direct sunlight.	Chemical composition Additives	Durability of curtains and draperies, outdoor furniture, outdoor carpeting
Texture is the nature of the fiber or fabric surface.	Physical structure	Luster, appearance
Translucence is the ability of a fiber, yarn, or fabric to allow light to pass through the structure.	Physical and chemical structure	Appearance
Wicking is the ability of a fiber to transfer moisture along its surface.	Chemical and physical composition of outer surface	Makes fabrics comfortable

Durability Properties

A durable textile product should last an adequate period of time for its end use. Durability properties can be tested in the laboratory, but lab results do not always accurately predict performance during actual use.

Abrasion resistance is the ability of a fabric to withstand the rubbing it gets in use (Table 3-3). Abrasion can occur when the fabric is fairly flat, as when the knees of jeans scrape along a cement sidewalk. Edge abrasion can occur when the fabric is folded, as when the bottom of a drapery fabric rubs against a carpet. Flex abrasion can occur when the fabric is moving and bending, as in shoelaces that wear out where they are laced through the shoe.

Table 3–3 **Abrasion Resistance**

Fiber	Rating
Aramid	Excellent
Nylon	
Olefin	
Polyester	
Saran	
Spandex	
Flax	
Acrylics	to
PBI	
Sulfar	
Cotton	
Silk	
Wool*	
Rayon	
Vinyon	
Acetate	
Glass	Poor

*Varies with coarseness of fiber.

Flexibility, the ability to bend repeatedly without breaking, is a very important property related to abrasion resistance.

Tenacity, or tensile strength, is the ability of a fabric to withstand a pulling force (Table 3-4). Tenacity for a fiber is the force, in grams per denier or tex, required to break the fiber. The tenacity

Table 3–4 **Fiber Strength**

Fiber*	Tenacity (grams/denier)	
	Dry	Wet
Rubber	0.34	same
Spandex	0.7–1.0	same
Vinyon	0.7–1.0	same
Fluorocarbon	0.9–4.0	same
Acetate	1.2–1.4	1.0–1.3
Saran	1.4–2.4	same
Wool	1.5	1.0
Novoloid	1.5–2.5	1.3–2.3
Modacrylic	1.7–2.6	1.5–2.4
Acrylic	2.0–3.0	1.8–2.7
Polyester	2.4–7.0	same
Rayon (HWM)	2.5–5.0	3.0
PBI	2.6–3.0	2.1–2.5
Nylon 6,6	2.9–7.2	2.5–6.1
Sulfar	3.0–3.5	same
Cotton	3.5–4.0	4.5–5.0
Olefin	3.5–4.5	same
Flax	3.5–5.0	6.5
Nylon 6	3.5–7.2	same
Vinal	3.5–6.5	2.6–4.9
Silk	4.5	2.8–4.0
Aramid (Nomex)	4.0–5.3	3.0–4.1
Glass (multifilament)	9.6	6.7

*For fibers that are available in several lengths and modifications, the values are for staple fibers with unmodified cross sections.

of a wet fiber frequently differs from the tenacity of that same fiber when it is dry. Although the fabric strength depends, to a large degree, on fiber strength, yarn and fabric structure may be varied to yield stronger or weaker fabrics made from the same fibers. Strength may also be measured by how much force it takes to rip the fabric (tearing strength) or to rupture the fabric (bursting strength).

Elongation refers to the degree to which a fiber may be stretched without breaking, measured as percent elongation at break (Table 3–5). Elongation should be considered in relation to elasticity.

Comfort Properties

A textile product should be comfortable as it is worn or used. This is primarily a matter of personal preference and individual perception of comfort under different climatic conditions and degrees of physical activity. Comfort is complex and dependent on characteristics such as absorbency, heat retention, density, and elongation.

Table 3–5   Elongation

Fiber*	% Elongation at Break Standard**	Wet
Flax	2.0	2.2
Cotton	3–7	9.5
Glass	3.1	2.2
Rayon	9–18	20
Polyester	12–55	same
Vinyon	12–125	same
Vinal	15–30	11–23
Saran	15–35	same
Nylon 6,6	16–75	18–78
Silk	20	30
Aramid (Nomex)	22–32	20–30
Wool	25	35
Acetate	25–45	35–50
PBI	25–30	26–32
Modacrylic	30–60	same
Nylon 6	30–90	42–100
Sulfar	35–45	same
Acrylic	35–45	41–50
Olefin	70–100	same
Spandex	400–700	same
Rubber	500	same

*A minimum of 10% is desirable for ease in textile processing. For fibers that are available in several lengths and modifications, the values are for staple fibers with unmodified cross sections.

**Standard conditions: 65% relative humidity; 70° F.

Table 3–6   Absorbency

Fiber	Moisture Regain*
Glass	0.0
Olefin	0.01–0.1
Saran	0.1
Vinyon	0.1
Polyester	0.4
Sulfar	0.6
Acrylic	1.0–1.5
Spandex	1.3
Modacrylic	2.5
Nylon 6	2.8–5.0
Nylon 6, 6	4.0–4.5
Vinal	5.0
Acetate	6.3–6.5
Aramid (Nomex)	6.5
Cotton	7–11
Silk	11
Rayon	11.5–12.5
Flax	12
Wool	13–18
PBI	15

*Moisture regain is expressed as a percentage of the moisture-free weight at 70°F and 65% relative humidity.

Absorbency is the ability of a fiber to take up moisture from the body or from the environment. It is measured as moisture regain where the moisture in the material is expressed as a percentage of the weight of the moisture-free material (Table 3–6). Absorbency is also related to static buildup. *Hydrophilic* fibers absorb moisture readily. *Hydrophobic* fibers have little or no absorbency. *Hygroscopic* fibers absorb moisture without feeling wet.

Heat or thermal retention is the ability of a fabric to hold heat (Table 3–7). It is important for a person to feel comfortably warm in cool weather or comfortably cool in hot weather. A low level of thermal retention is favored in hot weather. This property accounts for the fact that most people use textiles differently in summer and winter weather. Yarn and fabric structure and layering of fabrics affect this property.

Fibers differ in their reaction when exposed to heat (Table 3–8). Some fibers soften and melt; others are heat resistant. These thermal properties determine safe pressing or ironing temperatures.

Density or specific gravity is a measure of fiber weight in weight per unit volume (Table 3–9). Lighter-weight fibers can be made into thick fabrics that are more comfortable than heavier-weight fibers made into heavy, thick fabrics.

Table 3–7 Thermal Retention

Fiber	Rating
Wool	Excellent
Acrylic/Modacrylic	
Polyester	
Olefin	
Nylon	
Aramid	to
Silk	
Spandex	
Flax	
Cotton	
Rayon	
Acetate	Poor

Appearance-Retention Properties

A textile product should retain its original appearance during wear and care.

Resiliency is the ability of a fabric to return to its original shape after bending, twisting, or crushing (Table 3-10). A common test is to crunch a fabric in your hand and watch how it responds when you open your hand. A resilient fabric springs back. It is wrinkle resistant if it does not wrinkle easily. It has good wrinkle recovery if it returns to its original look after having been wrinkled.

Dimensional stability is defined as the ability of a fabric to retain a given size and shape through use and care. Dimensional stability is a desirable characteristic that includes the properties of shrinkage resistance and elastic recovery.

Shrinkage resistance is the ability of a fabric to retain a given size after care. It is related to the fabric's reaction to water or heat. A fabric that shrinks is smaller after care. The item may no longer be attractive and it may no longer be suitable for its original end use. Residual shrinkage refers to additional shrinkage that may occur after the first care cycle.

Table 3–8 Thermal Properties

Fiber	Melting Point °F	°C	Softening Sticking Point °F	°C	Safe Pressing/Ironing Temperature* °F	°C
Natural Fibers						
Cotton	Does not melt				425	218
Flax	Does not melt				450	232
Silk	Does not melt				300	149
Wool	Does not melt				300	149
Manufactured Fibers						
Acetate	500	230	350-375	184	350	177
Acrylic			430-450	204-254	300	149-176
Aramid	Does not melt; carbonizes above 700°F (Nomex) or 900°F (Kevlar)				Do not iron	
Glass	2,720		1,560	1,778	Do not iron	
Modacrylic	Does not melt				200-250	93-121
Nylon 6	419-430		340	171	300	149
Nylon 6, 6	480-500		445	229	350	177
Olefin	320-350		285-330	127	150	66
PBI	Does not melt		Decomposes at 860°F			
Polyester PET	482		440-445	238	325	163
Polyester PCDT	478-490		470	254	350	177
Rayon	Does not melt				375	191
Saran	350	177	240	115	Do not iron	
Spandex	446	230	420	175	300	149

*Lowest setting on irons: 185-225°F.

Table 3–9   Specific Gravity*

Fiber	Specific Gravity (g/cc)
Fluorocarbon	0.8–2.2
Olefin	0.90–0.91
Nylon	1.13–1.14
Acrylic	1.17
Spandex	1.2
Novoloid	1.25
Silk	1.25
Vinal	1.26
Acetate	1.32
Wool	1.32
Vinyon	1.33–1.43
Polyester	1.34–1.38
Modacrylic	1.35
Sulfar	1.37
Aramid	1.38–1.44
PBI	1.43
Cotton	1.52
Flax	1.52
Saran	1.70
Glass	2.48–2.69

*Ratio of weight of a given volume of fiber to an equal volume of water.

Elasticity or *elastic recovery* is the ability of a fabric to return to its original dimension or shape after elongation (Table 3-11). It is measured as the percentage of return to original length. Since recovery varies with the amount of elongation as well as with the length of time the fabric is stretched, the measurement identifies the percent elongation, or stretch, and the recovery. Fabrics with poor elastic

Table 3–10   Resiliency

Fiber	Rating
Nylon	Excellent
Wool	
Olefin	
Acrylic/Modacrylic	to
Polyester	
Silk	
Flax	Poor
Cotton	
Rayon	
Acetate	

Table 3–11   Elastic Recovery

Fiber	% Recovery at 3% Stretch*
Acetate	48–65 (at 4%)
Flax	65
Cotton	75
Polyester	81
Nylon 6, 6	82–89
Silk	90
Acrylic	92
Rayon	95 (at 2%)
Olefin	96 (at 5%)
Nylon 6	98–100
Spandex	99 (at 50%)
Wool	99
Modacrylic	99.5 (at 2%)

*Unless otherwise noted.

recovery tend to stretch out of shape. Fabrics with good elastic recovery maintain their shape.

Resistance to Chemicals

Fibers differ in their reaction to chemicals. Some fibers are quite resistant to most chemicals. Other fibers are resistant to some groups of chemicals but easily harmed by other groups of chemicals. Resistance to chemicals determines appropriateness of care procedures and end uses for fibers. Tables 3-12 and 3-13 summarize fiber reactions to acids and alkalis.

Resistance to Light

Exposure to light (both natural sunlight and artificial light) may damage fibers. The energy in light, especially in the ultraviolet region of the spectrum, causes irreversible damage to the chemical structure of the fiber. This damage may appear as a slight weakening of the fabric or, eventually, the complete disintegration of the fabric (Table 3-14).

Care Properties

Any treatments that are required to maintain the new look of a textile product during use, cleaning, or storage are referred to as care. Improper care procedures can result in items that are unattractive, not as durable as expected, and uncomfortable. The way fibers react to water, chemicals, and heat in pressing/ironing and drying will be discussed in each fiber chapter. Special requirements of storage will also be discussed.

Fiber Property Charts

The fibers within each generic family have individual differences. These differences are not reflected in the tables in this chapter, except in a few specific instances. The numerical values are averages, or medians, and are intended as a general characterization of each generic group. (The values were compiled from "Man-Made Fiber Chart," *Textile World*, August 1990, and "Textile Fibers and Their Properties," AATCC Council on Technology, 1977.)

FIBER IDENTIFICATION

The procedure for identification of the fiber content of a fabric depends on the nature of the sample, the experience of the analyst, and the facilities available. Because laws require the fiber content of apparel and furnishing textiles to be indicated on the label, the consumer may only need to look for identification labels. If the consumer wishes to confirm or check the information on the label, burning and some simple solubility tests may be used.

Table 3–12   Effect of Acids*

Fiber	Effect
Natural Fibers	
Cotton	Harmed
Flax	Harmed
Silk	Harmed by strong mineral acids, resistant to organic acids
Wool	Resistant
Manufactured Fibers	
Acetate	Unaffected by weak acids
Acrylic	Resistant to most acids
Aramid	Resistant to most acids
Glass	Resistant
Modacrylic	Resistant to most acids
Nylon	Harmed, especially nylon 6
Olefin	Resistant
PBI	Resistant
Polyester	Resistant
Rayon	Harmed
Spandex	Resistant
Sulfar	Resistant

*Examples of acids: organic (acetic, formic); mineral (sulfuric, hydrochloric).

Table 3–13   Effect of Alkalis/Bases*

Fiber	Effect
Natural Fibers	
Cotton	Resistant
Flax	Resistant
Silk	Harmed
Wool	Harmed
Manufactured Fibers	
Acetate	Little effect
Acrylic	Resistant to weak alkalis
Aramid	Resistant
Glass	Resistant
Modacrylic	Resistant
Nylon	Resistant
Olefin	Highly resistant
PBI	Resistant to most alkalis
Polyester	Degraded by strong alkalis
Rayon	Resistant to weak alkalis
Spandex	Resistant
Sulfar	Resistant

*Examples of alkalis: weak (ammonium hydroxide); strong (sodium hydroxide).

Visual Inspection

Visual inspection of a fabric for appearance and hand is always the first step in fiber identification. It is no longer possible to make an identification of the

Table 3–14   Light Resistance

Fiber	Rating
Glass	Excellent
Acrylic	
Modacrylic	
Polyester	
Sulfar	
Flax	
Cotton	
Rayon	to
PBI	
Triacetate	
Acetate	
Olefin	
Nylon	
Wool	
Silk	Poor

fiber content by appearance and hand alone because manufactured fibers can resemble natural fibers or other manufactured fibers. However, observation of certain characteristics is helpful. These characteristics are apparent to the unaided eye and are visual clues used to narrow the number of possibilities.

1. Length of fiber. Untwist the yarn to determine fiber length. Any fiber can be made in staple length, but not all fibers can be filament. For example, cotton and wool are always staple and never filament.

2. Luster or lack of luster. Manufactured fiber luster may range from harsh and shiny to dull and matte.

3. Body, texture, hand—soft-to-hard, rough-to-smooth, warm-to-cool, or stiff-to-flexible. These aspects relate to fiber size, surface contour, stiffness, and cross-sectional shape.

Burning Test

The burning test can be used to identify the general chemical composition of a fiber, such as cellulose, protein, mineral, or manufactured polymers, and thus identify the group to which the fiber belongs (Table 3–15). Blends cannot be identified by the burning test. If visual inspection is used along with the burning test, fiber identification can be carried

Table 3–15   Identification by Burning

Fibers	When Approaching Flame	When in Flame	After Removal from Flame	Ash	Odor
Cellulose Cotton Flax Rayon	Does not fuse or shrink from flame	Burns	Continues to burn, afterglow	Gray, feathery, smooth edge	Burning paper
Protein Silk Wool	Curls away from flame	Burns slowly	Usually self-extinguishing	Crushable black ash	Burning Hair
Acetate	Fuses away from flame	Burns with melting	Continues to burn and melt	Brittle black, hard bead	Acrid
Acrylic	Fuses away from flame	Burns with melting	Continues to burn and melt	Brittle black, hard bead	Chemical odor
Glass	No reaction	Does not burn	No reaction	Fiber remains	None
Modacrylic	Fuses away from flame	Burns very slowly with melting	Self-extinguishing, white smoke	Brittle black, hard bead	Chemical odor
Nylon	Fuses and shrinks away from flame	Burns slowly with melting white smoke	Usually self-extinguishing	Hard gray or tan bead	Celerylike
Olefin	Fuses and shrinks away from flame	Burns with melting	Usually self-extinguishing	Hard tan bead	Chemical odor
Polyester	Fuses and shrinks away from flame	Burns slowly with melting; black smoke	Usually self-extinguishing	Hard black bead	Sweetish odor
Saran	Fuses and shrinks away from flame	Burns very slowly with melting	Self-extinguishing	Hard black bead	Chemical odor
Spandex	Fuses but does not shrink from flame	Burns with melting	Continues to burn with melting	Soft black ash	Chemical odor

Fig. 3–7 *Fiber identification by the burning test.*

further. For example, if the sample is cellulose and also filament, it is probably rayon; but if it is staple, a positive identification for a specific cellulosic fiber cannot be made.

The following are general directions for the burning test:

1. Ravel out and test several yarns from each direction of the fabric to see if they have the same fiber content. Differences in luster, twist, and color indicate that there might be two or more generic fibers in the fabric.

2. Hold the yarn horizontally, as shown in Figure 3-7. Use tweezers to protect your fingers. Feed the yarns slowly into the edge of the flame and observe what happens. Repeat this step several times to check your results.

Microscopy

A knowledge of fiber structure, obtained by seeing the fibers through the microscope and observing some of the differences among fibers in each group, is of help in understanding fibers and fabric behavior.

Positive identification of most of the natural fibers can be made by using this procedure. The manufactured fibers are more difficult to identify because some of them look alike and their appearance may be changed by variations in the manufacturing process. Positive identification of the manufactured fibers by microscopy is rather limited. A cross section of the fiber is helpful if more careful examination is desired.

Longitudinal and cross-sectional photomicrographs of individual fibers are included in the fiber chapters. These may be used for reference when identifying unknown fibers.

The following are directions for using the microscope:

1. Clean the lens, slide, and cover glass.

2. Place a drop of distilled water or glycerine on the slide.

3. Untwist a yarn and place the loosened fibers on the slide. Cover with the cover glass and tap to eliminate air bubbles.

4. Place the slide on the stage of the microscope. Focus with low power first. If the fibers have not been well separated, it will be difficult to focus on a single fiber. Center the fiber or fibers in the viewing field. Then move to a lens with greater magnification. As magnification increases, the size of the viewing field decreases. Thus, if fibers are not in the center of the field when a higher magnification is selected, they may disappear from the viewing field.

5. If a fabric contains two or more fiber types, examine each fiber and both warp and filling yarns.

Table 3–16   Solubility Tests

Solvent	Fiber Solubility
1. Acetic acid, 100%, 20°C	Acetate
2. Acetone, 100%, 20°C	Acetate, modacrylic, vinyon
3. Hydrochloric acid, 20% concentration, 1.096 density, 20°C	Nylon 6, nylon 6, 6, vinal
4. Sodium hypochlorite solution, 5%, 20°C	Silk and wool (silk dissolves in 70% sulfuric acid at 38°C), azlon
5. Xylene (meta), 100%, 139°C	Olefin and saran (saran in 1.4 dioxane at 101°C; olefin is not soluble), vinyon
6. Dimethyl formamide, 100%, 90°C	Spandex, modacrylic, acrylic, acetate, vinyon
7. Sulfuric acid, 70% concentration, 38°C	Cotton, flax, rayon, nylon, acetate, silk
8. Cresol (meta), 100%, 139°C	Polyester, nylon, acetate

Solubility Tests

Solubility tests are used to identify the manufactured fibers by generic class and to confirm identification of natural fibers. Two simple tests, the alkali test for wool and the acetone test for acetate, are described in Chapters 5 and 7, respectively.

Table 3-16 lists solvents from weakest to strongest. Place the specimen in the liquid in the order listed. While many solvents will dissolve some fibers, following this order will help in identifying the specific fiber in question. Stir the specimen for 5 minutes and note the effect. Fiber, yarns, or small pieces of fabric may be used. Remember that the liquids are hazardous—handle them with care! Use chemical laboratory exhaust hoods, gloves, aprons, and goggles.

KEY TERMS

Manufactured fiber
Natural fiber
Filament fiber
Staple fiber
Filament tow
Denier
Tex
Fiber crimp
Fabric crimp
Generic group
Polymerization
Polymer
Degree of polymerization
Orientation
Stretching
Drawing
Cross links
Hyodrogen bonds
Van der Waals forces

Luster
Drape
Texture
Hand
Abrasion resistance
Flexibility
Tenacity
Elongation
Absorbency
Hydrophilic
Hydrophobic
Hygroscopic
Heat retention
Density
Resiliency
Dimensional stability
Shrinkage resistance
Elasticity
Elastic recovery

QUESTIONS

1. Define each of the key terms as well as the terms listed in Table 3-2.
2. Differentiate between the following pairs of related terms:
     elongation and elasticity
     absorbency and dyeability
     loft and resiliency
     heat conductivity and heat sensitivity
3. How would performance change when a fiber's shape is changed from round to trilobal?
4. What differences in performance might you expect from fibers designed for apparel, furnishings, and industrial products?
5. Describe polymerization and the possible arrangements of molecules within fibers.
6. What performance characteristics might be preferred in the following products?
     T-shirt for sightseeing
     upholstery for recliner chair in a den
     soft-sided luggage
     blanket for baby's bed
7. What would be an efficient procedure to identify the fiber content of an unknown fabric?

SUGGESTED READINGS

AATCC Council on Technology (1977). *Textile Fibers and Their Properties.* Research Triangle Park, NC: American Association of Textile Chemists and Colorists.

American Fiber Manufacturers Association (1988). *Manufactured Fiber Fact Book.* Washington, DC: American Fiber Manufacturers Association.

American Society for Testing and Materials (1990). *Annual Book of ASTM Standards, Vol. 7.* Philadelphia, PA: ASTM.

"Man-Made Fiber Chart" (August, 1990). *Textile World.*

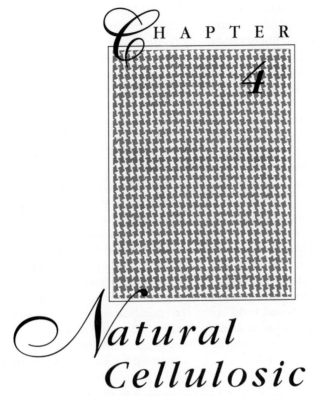

CHAPTER 4

Natural Cellulosic Fibers

OBJECTIVES

- To recognize those fibers that are classified as cellulosic fibers.

- To understand characteristics common to all cellulosic fibers and the differences among those most commonly used.

- To know the basic steps in processing the basic cellulosic fibers.

- To recognize the importance of natural cellulosic fibers to the consumer market.

$\mathcal{A}$LL PLANTS ARE FIBROUS. THE FIBER BUNdles of plants give strength and pliability to their stems, leaves, and roots. Natural cellulosic textile fibers are obtained from plants whose fibers can be readily and economically separated from the rest of the plant. These fibers can be classified according to the portion of the plant from which they are removed (see Table 4-1).

Cotton is an example of a *seed fiber*, a fiber that grows within a pod or boll from developing seeds. Flax is an example of a *bast fiber*, a fiber that is obtained from the stem of the plant. Sisal is an example of a *leaf fiber*, a fiber removed from the veins or ribs of a leaf.

These fibers are cellulosic but differ in percentage of cellulose present and in physical structure. The arrangement of the molecular chains in fibers, although similar, varies in orientation and length, so that performance characteristics related to polymer orientation and length differ. Fabrics made from these fibers thus have different appearances and hand but react to chemicals in essentially the same way and require essentially the same care. Properties common to all cellulosic fibers are summarized in Table 4-2.

Table 4–1 Natural Cellulosic Fibers

Seed Fibers	Bast Fibers	Leaf Fibers
Cotton	Flax	Piña
Kapok	Ramie	Abaca
Coir	Hemp	Sisal
	Jute	Henequen
	Kenaf	

This chapter discusses natural cellulosic fibers. Several of these fibers have limited use in the United States; nevertheless, a discussion of these fibers has a place in an introductory textiles course because some of these fibers are imported into the United States and others may be encountered during travel or in certain careers. Although these fibers are not of great importance to the U.S. economy, they may be significant to the economy of the countries where they are produced. There are, of course, many other natural cellulosic fibers that will not be discussed because of their extremely limited use.

Table 4–2 Properties Common to All Cellulosic Fibers

Properties	Importance to Consumer
Good absorbency	Comfortable for summer wear and furnishings
	Good for towels, diapers, handkerchiefs, and active sports wear, if sufficiently pliable
Good conductor of heat	Sheer fabrics cool for summer wear
Ability to withstand high temperature	Fabrics can be boiled or autoclaved to make them relatively germ free; no special precautions in pressing/ironing
Low resiliency	Fabrics wrinkle badly unless finished for recovery
Lacks loft; packs well into compact yarns	Tight, high-count fabrics can be made
	Makes wind-resistant fabrics
Good conductor of electricity	Does not build up static
Heavy fibers (density of ± 1.5)	Fabrics are heavier than comparable fabrics of other fiber content
Harmed by mineral acids, but little affected by organic acids	Fruit stains should be removed immediately to prevent setting
Attacked by mildew	Store clean items under dry conditions
Resistant to moths, but may be damaged by crickets and silverfish	Store clean items under dry conditions
Flammable	Cellulose fibers ignite quickly, burn freely, and have an afterglow and gray, feathery ash; filmy or loosely constructed garments should not be worn near an open flame; furnishings should meet required codes
Moderate resistance to sunlight	Draperies should be lined

SEED FIBERS

Seed fibers are those from the seed pod of the plant. By far the most important seed fiber is cotton. This section discusses cotton and some minor seed fibers.

The first step in the production of seed fibers is to separate the fiber from the seed. (The seed of some seed fibers also is used in producing oil and feed for animals.) After the seed and fiber have been separated, the fibers may be carded into a parallel arrangement for production of yarns or used as bundles of fibers for fiberfill.

Cotton

Cotton is the most important apparel fiber. In 1990, cotton met 48.6 percent of total world fiber demand and 54 percent of the worldwide demand for apparel fiber. Cotton has a combination of properties—pleasing appearance, comfort, easy care, moderate cost, and durability—that make it ideal for warm-weather clothing, active sportswear, work clothes, upholstery, draperies, area rugs, towels, and bedding. Even though other fibers have encroached on the markets that cotton once dominated, the cotton look is maintained. Cotton is an important part of many blended fabrics.

Cotton cloth was used by the people of ancient China, Egypt, India, Mexico, and Peru. The cotton spinning and weaving industry began in India.

Cotton was grown in the southern U.S. colonies as soon as they were established. Throughout the 1600s and 1700s, cotton fibers were separated from the cotton seeds by hand. This was a very time-consuming and tedious job; a worker could separate the seeds from the fibers of only one pound of cotton in a day.

With the invention of the saw-tooth cotton gin by Eli Whitney in 1793, things changed. The gin could process 50 pounds of cotton in a day; thus more cotton could be prepared for spinning. Within the next 20 years, a series of spinning and weaving inventions in England mechanized fabric production. The Southern states were able to meet Britain's greatly increased demand for raw cotton. By 1859, U.S. production was 4.5 million bales of cotton—two-thirds of world production. Cotton was the leading U.S. export.

The picture again changed dramatically during the Civil War. U.S. cotton production decreased to 200,000 bales in 1864, and Britain looked to other countries to fill its needs. After the war, Western states began producing cotton.

During the time of rapidly expanding cotton production in the Southern states, the New England states were building factories to manufacture yarn and fabric. Most spinning and weaving of U.S. fabrics took place in the New England states.

After the Civil War, the Southern states began building spinning and weaving mills. Between World War I and World War II, most of the New England mills moved south. Factors important in this move included proximity to the supply of cotton, cheaper power, less expensive nonunion labor, and special relocation incentives from state and local governments. By 1950, 80 percent of the mills were in the South. Yet in the 1980s, many mills closed because of increased costs and competition from imports.

Production of Cotton

Cotton grows in any part of the world where the growing season is long and the climate is temperate to hot with adequate rainfall or irrigation. Cellulose will not form if the temperature is below 70°F. In the United States, cotton is grown from southern South Carolina west to central California and south of that line. Figure 4-1 shows cotton production areas in the United States.

Major producers of cotton are China (23.3 percent), U.S. (17.0 percent), the Commonwealth of Independent States (13.8 percent), India (11.6 percent), Pakistan (7.9 percent), Brazil (3.9 percent), Turkey (3.3 percent), and Egypt (1.8 percent). Worldwide production of cotton was over 87 million bales in 1990. Mechanization and weed control have reduced the number of hours required to produce a bale of cotton and increased productivity.

Factors affecting the U.S. production of cotton include the value of the dollar compared with other currencies, imports of cotton apparel and fabrics, changes in government incentives for growing cotton, and comparable changes in other countries.

Cotton grows on bushes 3-6 feet high. The blossom appears, falls off, and the *boll* or seed pod begins its growth. Inside the boll are 7-8 seeds from which the fibers grow. When the boll is ripe, it splits open and the fluffy white fibers spread out (Figure 4-2). Each cotton seed may have as many as 20,000 fibers growing from its surface.

Cotton is picked by machine or by hand (Figure 4-3). Machine-picked cotton contains many immature fibers—an inescapable result of stripping a cotton plant. After picking, the cotton is taken to a *gin* to remove the fibers from the seed. Figure 4-4

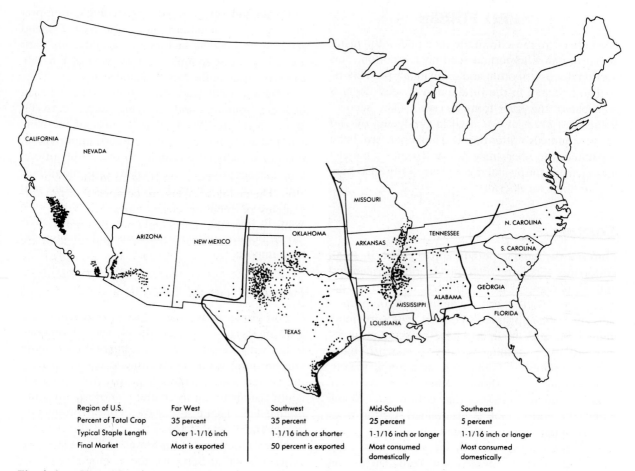

Region of U.S.	Far West	Southwest	Mid-South	Southeast
Percent of Total Crop	35 percent	35 percent	25 percent	5 percent
Typical Staple Length	Over 1-1/16 inch	1-1/16 inch or shorter	1-1/16 inch or longer	1-1/16 inch or longer
Final Market	Most is exported	50 percent is exported	Most consumed domestically	Most consumed domestically

Fig. 4–1 *United States cotton production, 1990-91. (Courtesy of National Cotton Council of America.)*

shows a saw gin, in which the whirling saws pick up the fiber and carry it to a knifelike comb, which blocks the seeds and permits the fiber to be carried through. The fibers, called *lint*, are pressed into bales weighing 480 pounds, ready for sale to a spinning mill.

After ginning, the seeds are covered with very short fibers—⅛ inch in length—called *linters*. The linters are removed from the seeds and are used to a limited extent as raw material in producing rayon and acetate. The seeds are crushed to obtain cottonseed oil and meal.

With advances in plant breeding and biotechnology, new cottons are now being developed. A transgenic cotton has been produced that is genetically engineered to be insect resistant. These fibers are in the experimental stage, but they have the potential of significantly lowering the cost of fiber production while decreasing use of insecticides by 30-40 percent, a factor of increasing importance in terms of environmental impact. These transgenic

fibers are being field tested to determine productivity. Additional testing for fiber and product performance is also a consideration. Other possibilities in genetic engineering of cotton include improving the quality of cotton before it reaches the consumer by breeding specific performance aspects into the fiber.

FIBER PROPERTIES OF COTTON

Physical Structure

Raw cotton is usually creamy white in color. The fiber is a single cell, which grows out of the seed as a hollow cylindrical tube over one thousand times as long as it is thick.

LENGTH Staple length is very important because it affects how the fiber is handled during spinning and

Fig. 4–2   Opened cotton boll. (Courtesy of National Cotton Council of America.)

relates to fiber fineness and fiber tensile strength. Longer cotton fibers are finer and make stronger yarns.

Cotton fibers range in length from ½ inch to 2 inches, depending on the variety. Three groups of cotton are commercially important:

1. Upland cottons, which are ⅞–1¼ inches in length, were developed from cottons native to Mexico and Central America.

2. Long-staple cottons, which are 1⅜₆–1½ inches in length, were developed from Egyptian and South American cottons. Varieties include American Pima, Egyptian, American Egyptian, and Sea Island cottons.

3. Short-staple cottons, which are less than ¾ inch in length, are produced primarily in India and eastern Asia.

Long-staple fibers are considered to be of finer quality because they can be made into softer, smoother, stronger, and more lustrous fabrics. Because they command a higher price and less is produced than the medium- and short-staple lengths, they are sometimes identified on a label or tag as Pima or Supima. Or they may be referred to as long-staple or extra-long-staple cotton.

DISTINCTIVE PARTS The cotton fiber is made up of a cuticle, primary wall, secondary wall, and lumen (Figure 4-5). The fiber grows to almost full length as a hollow tube before the secondary wall begins to form.

The *cuticle* is a waxlike film covering the primary, or outer, wall. The *secondary wall* is made up of layers of cellulose (Figure 4-6).

The layers deposited at night differ in density from those deposited during the day; this causes *growth rings*, which can be seen in the cross section. The cellulose layers are composed of *fibrils*—bundles of cellulose chains—arranged spirally. At some points the fibrils reverse direction. These *reverse spirals* (Figure 4-7) are important in the development of convolutions that contribute to elastic recovery and elongation of the fiber. They are also the weak spots, being 15-30 percent weaker than the rest.

Cellulose is deposited daily for 20-30 days until, in the mature fiber, the fiber tube is almost filled.

The *lumen* is the central canal, through which the nourishment travels during growth. When the fiber matures, the dried nutrients in the lumen may result in dark areas visible under the microscope.

CONVOLUTIONS *Convolutions*, or ribbonlike twists, characterize the cotton fibers (Figure 4-6).

Fig. 4–3   Cotton field with harvester. (Courtesy of National Cotton Council of America.)

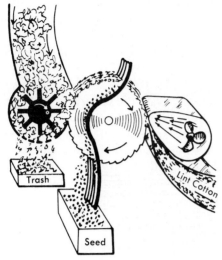

Fig. 4–4   *Cotton Gin.*

When the fibers mature, the boll opens, the fibers dry out, and the central canal collapses. Reverse spirals in the secondary wall cause the fibers to twist. The twist forms a natural crimp that enables the fibers to cohere to one another, so that despite its short length, cotton is one of the most spinnable fibers. The convolutions can be a disadvantage, since dirt collects in the twists requiring vigorous washing to remove. Long-staple cotton has about 300 convolutions per inch; short-staple cotton has less than 200.

FINENESS Cotton fibers vary from 16 to 20 micrometers in diameter. The cross-sectional shape varies with the maturity of the fiber. Immature fibers tend to be U-shaped and the cell wall is thinner; mature fibers are more nearly circular, with a very small central canal. Every cotton boll contains some immature fibers. The proportion of immature to mature fibers can cause problems in spinning and dyeing processes. Notice in Figure 4–8 the difference in size and shape of the fibers.

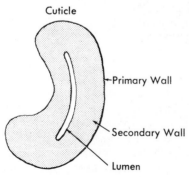

Fig. 4–5   *Cross section of mature cotton fiber.*

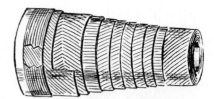

Fig. 4–6   *Layers of cellulose (schematic).*

COLOR Cotton is naturally creamy white. As it ages, it becomes more beige. If it rained on just before harvest, the fiber is grayer. White fiber is preferred.

Picking and ginning affect the appearance of cotton fibers. Carefully picked cotton is cleaner. Well-ginned cotton tends to be more uniform in appearance and whiter in color. Poorly ginned cotton has brown flecks in it called *trash*, such as bits of leaf, stem, or dirt. These brown flecks decrease the quality of the fiber. Fabrics made from such fibers include utility cloth and occasionally are fashionable when a "natural" look is popular.

Natural-colored cottons are also available. Small quantities of cotton in shades of brown, rust, and green are produced in California, Arizona, and Texas. The developer is working on growing naturally colored blue, yellow, and lavender cotton.

Cotton Classification

Grading and classing of cotton is done by hand and by machine. Inspection of staple length and color compare the cotton from the bale with standards prepared by the United States Department of Agriculture.

Cotton classification describes the quality of cotton in terms of grade and staple length. The quality of cotton is determined by several factors: fiber length, grade, and character. Fiber length classifications for cotton include very short-staple cotton (less than .25 inch), short-staple cotton (.25 to .94 inch); medium-staple cotton (.94 to 1.13 inches); ordinary long-staple cotton (1.13 to 1.38 inches); and extra-long-staple cotton (greater than 1.38 inches). *Staple length* is based on the length of a representative bundle of fibers from a bale of cotton. There are 19 staple lengths ranging from less than $^{13}\!/_{16}$ inch to $1\frac{3}{8}$ inches and beyond. A good cotton classer must be consistently able to tell differences in length of $\frac{1}{32}$ of an inch. Actually, a sample classified as $1\frac{1}{32}$ inch will have fibers ranging in length from $\frac{1}{8}$ inch to $1\frac{3}{8}$ inches as shown in Figure 4–9.

Grade refers to the color of the fiber and the absence of dirt, leaf matter, seed particles, and tangles of fiber. The best quality grade is lustrous, silky,

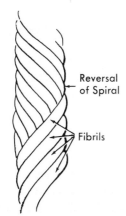

Fig. 4–7   *Reverse spirals in cotton fiber.*

white, and clean. There are 39 grades of cotton. The predominant grade of cotton produced in the United States is strict low-middling cotton. *Strict* in this case means "better than."

Color of cotton is described in terms that range from white to yellow: white, light-spotted, spotted, tinged, and yellow. Color is also described in terms of lightness to darkness: plus, light gray, and gray. This factor of appearance is a combination of grayness and the amount of leaf present in white cotton grades.

Character refers to other fiber aspects including maturity, smoothness and uniformity of fibers within the bale, fiber fineness, strength, and convolutions. Character refers to the amount of processing necessary to produce a good white fabric for commercial use. Because of yearly variations in growing conditions and variations in geographic locations, yarn and fabric producers take care in selecting and blending cotton so that cotton fabrics and products are as uniform as possible.

Cotton is a commodity crop. It is sold by grade and staple length. Strict low-middling cotton is used

in mass-produced cotton goods and in cotton/synthetic blends. Better grades of cotton and longer-staple cotton are used in quality shirtings and sheets. Extra-long-staple American Egyptian cotton is frequently identified by the terms Pima and Supima because of its higher quality and price. Pima is used in sweaters, blouses and shirts, underwear, and towels.

Fig. 4–9   *Cotton classed as 1 5/32 inch contains fibers that range in length from less than 1/8 inch up to 1 5/8 inch. (Courtesy of United States Department of Agriculture.)*

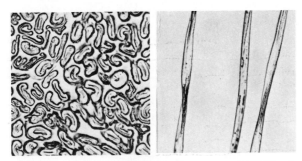

Fig. 4–8   *Photomicrographs of cotton: cross-sectional view at 500 × (left); longitudinal view 250 × (right). (Courtesy of E. I. du Pont de Nemours & Company.)*

Chemical Composition and Molecular Arrangement of Cotton

Cotton, when picked, is about 94 percent cellulose; in finished fabrics it is 99 percent cellulose. Like all cellulose fibers, cotton contains carbon, hydrogen, and oxygen with reactive hydroxyl (OH) groups. The basic unit of the cellulose molecule is the *glucose unit*, which consists of the chemical elements carbon, hydrogen, and oxygen. Cotton may have as many as 10,000 glucose units per molecule. The molecular chains are arranged in spiral form.

Chemical Nature of Cellulose

The chemical reactivity of cellulose is related to the hydroxyl groups (OH groups) of the glucose unit. These groups react readily with moisture, dyes, and many finishes. Chemicals such as chlorine bleaches break the molecular chain of the cellulose by attacking the oxygen atom and causing a rupture there.

The cellulose molecule is a long, linear chain of glucose units. The length of the chain is a factor in fiber strength.

Cotton can be altered by using chemical treatments or finishes. Mercerization (treating yarns or fabrics with sodium hydroxide, NaOH) causes a physical change in the fiber. Mercerization is done primarily to increase absorbency and to improve the dyeability of cotton yarns and fabrics. Liquid ammonia is used as an alternative to several preparation finishes, especially mercerization. Fabrics that have had the ammonia treatment have good luster and dyeability. These fabrics are not as stiff and harsh when treated to be wrinkle resistant compared to mercerized wrinkle-resistant fabrics.

Properties of Cotton

Cotton is a comfortable fiber. Appropriate for year-round use, it is the fiber most preferred for warm-weather clothing, especially where the climate is hot and humid. Cotton is also preferred for many furnishing applications.

AESTHETIC Cotton fabrics certainly have consumer acceptance. Cotton fabrics have a matte appearance. Their low luster is the standard that has been retained with cotton/polyester blends, which are increasingly important in apparel and furnishing fabrics.

Long-staple cotton fibers contribute luster to fabrics. Mercerized and ammonia-treated cotton fabrics have a soft, pleasant luster as a result of the chemical finishes; cotton sateen's luster is due to weave structure and finishes.

Drape, luster, texture, and hand are affected by choice of yarn size and type, fabric structure, and finish; cotton fabrics range from soft, sheer batiste, to crisp, sheer voile, to fine chintz, and to sturdy denim and corduroy.

DURABILITY Cotton is a medium-strength fiber having a dry breaking tenacity of 3.5–4.0 g/d (grams per denier). It is stronger when wet: wet breaking tenacity is 4.5–5.0 g/d. Long-staple cotton produces stronger yarns because there are more contact points between the fibers when they are twisted together. Because of its higher wet strength, cotton can stand rough handling during laundering and in use.

Abrasion resistance is moderate. Obviously, heavy fabrics will take longer to wear through than thinner fabrics. The elongation of cotton is low, 3 percent, and it has low elasticity.

COMFORT Cotton makes very comfortable skin-contact fabrics because of its high absorbency, soft hand, and good heat and electrical conductivity (static buildup is not a problem). It is lacking in any surface characteristics that might be irritating to the skin, an important factor to those with tender skin. Cotton has a moisture regain of 7 percent. When cotton becomes wet, the fibers swell and become somewhat plastic. This property makes it possible to give a smooth, flat finish to cotton fabrics in pressing or finishing and makes high-count woven

Table 4–3 Summary of the Performance of Cotton in Apparel and Furnishing Fabrics

Aesthetic	*Attractive*
Luster	Matte, pleasant
Drape	Soft to stiff
Texture	Pleasant
Hand	Smooth to rough
Durability	**Moderate**
Abrasion resistance	Moderate
Tenacity	Moderate
Elongation	Low
Comfort	**Excellent**
Absorbency	Excellent
Thermal retention	Low
Appearance retention	**Moderate**
Resiliency	Low
Dimensional stability	Moderate
Elastic recovery	Moderate
Recommended care	Machine wash and dry (apparel) Steam or dry clean with caution (furnishings)

fabrics water repellent. However, as cotton fabrics absorb more moisture in damp conditions, they feel wet or clammy and may be too absorbent to be comfortable.

Still, cotton is a good fiber to use in hot and humid weather. The fibers absorb moisture and feel good against the skin in high humidity. The fiber ends in the spun yarn hold the fabric slightly off the skin for greater comfort. Moisture passes freely through the fabric, thus aiding evaporation and cooling. Cotton is comfortable for use all year.

APPEARANCE RETENTION Overall appearance retention is moderate. Cotton has very low resiliency. The hydrogen bonds holding the molecular chains together are weak, and when fabrics are bent or crushed, particularly in the presence of moisture, the chains move freely to new positions. When pressure is removed, there are no forces within the fibers to pull the chains back to their original positions so the fabrics stay wrinkled. Creases can be pressed in and wrinkles can be removed, but wrinkling during use remains a problem.

Unless cotton fibers are given a durable-press finish or blended with polyester and given a durable-press finish, they wrinkle easily during both use and care.

All-cotton fabrics shrink unless they have been given a durable-press finish or a shrinkage-resistant finish. Untreated cottons shrink less when washed in cool water and drip dried; they shrink more when washed in hot water and dried in a hot dryer. When they are used again, they tend to recover some of their original dimensions—think of cotton-denim jeans or fitted cotton sheets.

All-cotton fabrics that have been given a wrinkle-resistant or durable-press finish or that have been treated for shrinkage generally should not shrink noticeably. However, a little more care may be needed with handwoven cotton fabrics or those of lower quality, short-staple fibers, unless specific information about shrinkage is available on the label.

Elastic recovery is moderate. Cotton recovers 75 percent from 2–5 percent stretch. In other words, cotton tends to stay stretched out in areas of stress, such as in the elbow or knee areas of garments.

CARE Cotton can be washed with strong detergents and requires no special care during washing and drying. White cottons can be washed in hot water. Colored cottons retain their color better if washed in warm water. If items are not heavily soiled, cold water cleans them adequately. Cotton releases all types of soil readily, but for some furnishing and apparel uses soil-resistant finishes are desirable. Chlorine bleach may be used on cottons if the directions are followed; bleaching should be considered a spot-removal method and not used routinely with every load of wash, because excessive bleaching weakens cellulosic fibers.

Less wrinkling occurs in the dryer if the cotton items are removed when they are dry and not left in the dryer longer than necessary. Cotton fabrics respond best to steam pressing or ironing while damp. Fabrics made of cotton and a heat-sensitive fiber need to be ironed at a lower temperature to avoid melting the heat-sensitive fiber. Cotton is not thermoplastic; it can be ironed safely at high temperatures. However, cotton burns readily.

Cotton draperies should be dry cleaned. Cotton upholstery may be steam cleaned with caution. If shrinkage occurs, the fabric may split or rupture where it is attached to the frame.

Cottons should be stored clean and dry. If they are damp, mildew can form. Mildew first appears as little black dots, but it can actually eat through the fabric, causing holes if enough time elapses. If the clothing merely smells of mildew, it can be laundered or bleached and it will be fine. But if the mildew has progressed to visible spots, they may not be removable. More extensive damage cannot be corrected.

Cotton is harmed by acids. Fruit and fruit juice stains should be treated promptly with cold water before they set and become even more difficult to remove. Cotton is not greatly harmed by alkalis. Cotton is resistant to organic solvents so that it can be safely dry cleaned.

Cotton oxidizes in sunlight, which causes white and pastel cottons to yellow and all cotton to degrade. Some dyes are especially sensitive to sunlight and when used in window treatment fabrics the dyed areas disintegrate.

Table 4-3 summarizes cotton's performance in apparel and furnishing fabrics.

Identification of Cotton

Microscope identification of cotton is relatively easy. Convolutions are generally clearly visible along the fiber. Burn tests will verify cellulose, but a more precise identification is not possible with this procedure. Fiber length may be of assistance in determining content, but remember that long fibers can be broken or cut to resemble shorter fibers in length. Cotton is soluble in strong mineral acids.

Uses of Cotton

Cotton is the most important apparel fiber in the United States. As a part of the total fiber market, cotton accounted for the following percentages of fiber used in these categories in 1990:

57 percent of apparel

57 percent of home furnishings

11 percent of industrial uses

Focusing on cotton alone, of the 4.7 billion pounds of cotton consumed in the United States in 1990,

64 percent was used in apparel

26 percent was used for home furnishings

10 percent was used for industrial uses or was exported

The greatest amount of cotton is used for apparel. All-cotton fabrics are used where comfort is of primary importance and appearance retention is not as important, or where a more casual fabric is acceptable. Cotton blended with polyester in durable-press fabrics is easy to find on the market, both in ready-to-wear apparel and in over-the-counter fabrics. Blends of 60 percent or 70 percent cotton mixed with other fibers are available. Most blends retain the pleasant appearance of cotton, have the same or increased durability, are less comfortable in conditions of extreme heat and humidity or high physical activity, and have better appearance retention during wear in comparison with 100 percent cotton fabrics. However, removal of oily soil is a greater problem with blends.

Cotton is a very important furnishing fabric because of its versatility, natural comfort, and ease of finishing and dyeing. Towels are mostly cotton— softness, absorbency, wide range of colors, and washability are important in this end use. Durability is increased in the base fabric, as well as in the selvages and hems by blending polyester with the cotton. However, the loops of terry towels are cotton so that maximum absorbency is retained.

Sheets and pillowcases are all cotton or blends of cotton with polyester. Blend levels and counts vary a great deal. Muslin and percale sheets are common, and flannelette sheets are available in the fall and winter. Spring- and fall-weight blankets made of cotton are also on the market. Cotton bedspreads are available in a variety of weights.

Drapes, curtains, upholstery fabrics, slipcovers, and wall coverings are made of cotton. Cotton upholstery fabrics are attractive and durable, comfortable, and easy to spot clean. They retain their appearance well. Resiliency is not a problem with heavyweight fabrics that are stretched over the furniture frame. Cotton is susceptible to abrasion, waterborne stains, and shrinkage if cleaning is too vigorous or incorrect.

Medical, surgical, and sanitary supplies are frequently made of cotton. Since cotton can be autoclaved (heated to a high temperature to sanitize it), it is very important in hospitals. Absorbency, washability, and low static buildup are also important properties in these uses.

Industrial uses include abrasives, book bindings, luggage and handbags, shoes and slippers, tobacco cloth, and woven wiping cloths.

Cotton Incorporated is the organization that promotes the use of cotton by consumers. It also promotes the use of Natural Blend® fabrics and apparel—items that contain at least 60 percent cotton (see Figure 4-10).

Fig. 4–10 Cotton® seal (top) for fabrics and apparel made of 100 percent cotton and Natural Blend® seal (bottom) for fabrics and apparel made of at least 60 percent cotton.

Kapok

Kapok is obtained from the seed of the Java kapok or silk cotton tree. The fiber is lightweight and soft. Kapok is hollow and very buoyant. With use, kapok has a tendency to break down into a powder. The fiber is difficult to spin into yarns so it is used primarily as fiberfill for personal flotation devices and for pillow and upholstery padding.

Coir

Coir is the fiber obtained from the fibrous mass between the outer shell and the husk of the coconut. The fibers are removed by soaking the husk in saline water for several months. Sri Lanka is the major producer of coir fiber. Coir is a very stiff, cinnamon-brown fiber. It has good abrasion, water, and weather resistance. Coir has become an important fiber in interiors for rugs and floor tiles. With its stiff, wiry texture and coarse size, coir provides strong visual interest and produces fabrics whose weave, pattern, or design is clearly visible. These floor textiles are extremely durable and blend with furnishings of many styles.

BAST FIBERS

Bast fibers come from the stem of the plant. Hand labor is often required to process bast fibers, so that production has flourished in countries where labor is cheap. Complete mechanization in the production of bast fibers has yet to be achieved. Since the fiber extends into the root, harvesting is done by pulling up the plant or cutting it close to the ground to keep fiber length as long as possible. After harvesting, the seeds are removed by pulling the plant through a machine in a process called rippling.

Bast fibers lie in bundles in the stem of plant just under the outer covering or bark. They are sealed together by a substance composed of pectins, waxes, and gums. To loosen the fibers so that they can be removed from the stalk, the pectin must be decomposed by a process called retting (bacterial rotting). There are some individual fiber differences in the process, but the major steps are the same. Retting can be done in the fields (dew retting); in ponds or pools (pool retting); in tanks (tank retting), where the temperature and bacterial count can be carefully controlled; or with chemicals such as sodium hydroxide. Chemical retting is a much faster process than any other method. However, extra care must be taken or irreversible damage can occur to the fiber.

After the plants have been rinsed and dried, the woody portion is removed by breaking the outer covering, a process called scutching, in which the stalks are passed between fluted metal rollers. Most of the fibers are separated from one another and the short and irregular fibers are removed by hackling, or combing. This final step removes any remaining woody portion and arranges the fibers in a parallel fashion. As an example, Figure 4–11 shows flax at different stages of processing.

The processes of spinning, weaving, and finishing cause further separation of the fibers. With most bast fibers, length and fineness dimensions are not clearly definable. The primary fibers are bound together in fiber bundles and never completely separate into individual fibers. These fiber bundles, as they are commonly used, are made up of many primary fibers. It is this characteristic of fiber bundles that give bast fiber fabrics their characteristic thick-and-thin yarns.

Flax

Flax is one of the oldest textile fibers. The term linen refers to fabric made from flax. Fragments of linen fabric were found in prehistoric lake dwellings in Switzerland; linen mummy cloths more than 3,000 years old were found in Egyptian tombs. The linen industry flourished in Europe until the 18th century. With the invention of power spinning, cotton replaced flax as the most important and widely used fiber.

Fig. 4–11 *Flax fiber at different stages of processing.*

Today flax is a prestige fiber as a result of its limited production and relatively high cost. The term linen, however, is often misused today in referring to fabrics that look like linen—fabrics that have thick-and-thin yarns and are fairly heavy or crisp. The term *Irish linen* always refers to fabrics made from flax. (The former use of flax in sheets, tablecloths, and towels has given us the term *linens* to describe textile items—for example, bed linens and table linens.)

The unique and desirable characteristics of flax are its body, strength, and thick-and-thin fiber bundles, which give texture to fabrics. The main limitations of flax are low resiliency and lack of elasticity. Many linens are given wrinkle-resistant finishes.

Most flax is produced in western Europe in Belgium, France, Italy, the United Kingdom, Austria, Germany, the Netherlands, and Switzerland. Flax is also produced in the Commonwealth of Independent States and New Zealand.

Structure of Flax

The primary fiber of flax averages 5.0–21.5 inches in length and 12–16 micrometers in diameter. Remember, these primary fibers are bound together in fiber bundles.

Flax fibers can be identified under the microscope by crosswise marking called *nodes* or *joints* (Figure 4–12). The markings on flax have been attributed to cracks or breaks during harvesting or to irregularity in growth. The fibers may appear slightly swollen at the nodes and resemble somewhat the joints in a stalk of corn or bamboo. The fibers have a small, central canal similar to the lumen in cotton. The cross section (Figure 4–12) is several-sided or polygonal with rounded edges.

Flax fibers are grayish in color when dew retted and yellowish in color when water retted. Flax has a more highly oriented molecular structure than cotton and is, therefore, stronger than the cotton fiber.

Flax is similar to cotton in its chemical composition. The major differences between the two fibers are that flax has a higher degree of polymerization (the cellulose polymer is longer) and a greater degree of orientation and crystallinity.

Short flax fibers are called *tow*; the long, combed, better quality fibers are called *line*. Line fibers are ready for spinning into yarn. The short tow fibers must be carded to prepare them for spinning into yarns that are used in less expensive fabrics.

Properties of Flax

AESTHETIC Flax has a high, natural luster that is broken up by the fiber bundles, which give an irregular appearance to yarns made from flax. This irregular appearance is part of the charm of linen fabrics. The luster of flax can be increased by flattening yarns with pressure in finishing.

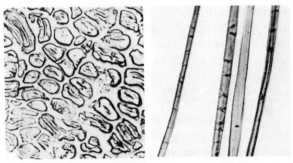

Fig. 4–12 *Photomicrographs of flax cross-sectional view (left); longitudinal view (right). (Courtesy of E. I. du Pont de Nemours & Company.)*

Because flax has a higher degree of orientation and crystallinity and the fiber diameter is larger than in cotton, the resulting fabrics are stiffer in drape and harsher in hand.

DURABILITY Flax is strong for a natural fiber. It has a breaking tenacity of 3.5–5.0 g/d when dry and 6.5 g/d when wet. Before synthetic fibers were invented, linen thread was used to sew shoes. Flax has very low elongation of approximately 7 percent. Elasticity is poor, with a 65 percent recovery at an elongation of only 2 percent. Flax also is a stiff fiber. With poor elongation, elasticity, and stiffness, fabrics made of flax should not be folded repeatedly in the same place, as repeated folding causes the fabric to break. Also, avoid pressing folds when ironing linen to minimize the stress on the fibers at the fold line. Flax has good abrasion resistance for a natural fiber. The good abrasion resistance is related to the fiber's high orientation and crystallinity.

COMFORT Flax has a high moisture regain of 12 percent and it is a good conductor of electricity. Hence, static is no problem. Flax is also a good conductor of heat, so it makes an excellent fabric for warm-weather wear. Flax has a high specific gravity of 1.52, which is the same as cotton.

CARE Flax is resistant to alkalis, organic solvents, and high temperatures. Linen fabrics can be dry cleaned or washed without special care and bleached with chlorine bleaches. For upholstery and wall coverings, steam cleaning with caution to avoid shrinkage is often recommended. Linen fabrics have very low resiliency and require frequent pressing. They are more resistant to sunlight than cotton.

Crease-resistant finishes can be used on linen, but the resins usually decrease strength and abrasion resistance. The wrinkling characteristics of flax are responsible for the strong high-fashion image of linen fabrics. Linen fabrics must be stored dry; otherwise mildew will become a problem.

Table 4-4 summarizes flax's performance when used in apparel or furnishing fabrics.

IDENTIFICATION TESTS Flax burns readily in a manner very similar to cotton. An easy way to differentiate between these two cellulosic fibers is to study their fiber length. Cotton is seldom over 2.5 inches in length; flax is almost always longer than that. Flax is also soluble in strong acids. Figure 4–12 shows the microscopic appearance of flax.

Table 4–4 Summary of the Performance of Flax in Apparel and Furnishing Fabrics

Aesthetics	*Excellent*
Luster	High
Texture	Thick and thin
Hand	Stiff
Durability	*Good*
Abrasion resistance	Good
Tenacity	Good
Elongation	Low
Comfort	*High*
Absorbency	High
Thermal retention	Good
Appearance retention	*Poor*
Resiliency	Poor
Dimensional stability	Adequate
Elastic recovery	Low
Recommended care	Dry clean or machine wash (apparel) Steam or dry clean (furnishings)

USES The International Linen Promotion Commission (ILPC), which promotes the use of linen, has developed a trademark to identify linen (see Figure 4–13). Of the fiber produced, 22 percent is used in household linens (bed, table, and bath items), 16 percent in other furnishing items for both home and commercial use, 50 percent in apparel, and 12 percent in industrial products. Furnishing items include wallpaper and wall coverings, some as wide as 120 inches. Linen fabrics are ideal for this end use because the irregular texture adds interest, hides nail holes or wall damage, and muffles noise. The wider fabrics minimize seams in the wall coverings. Linen fabrics are also used in upholstery and window treatment fabrics because of their durability, interesting and soil-hiding textures, and versatility in fabrication and design.

Apparel items of linen are usually designed for warm-weather use, high fashion aspects, or professional wear. Industrial products include luggage, bags, purses, and sewing thread.

Ramie

Ramie is also known as rhea or grasscloth. It has been used for several thousand years in China. The

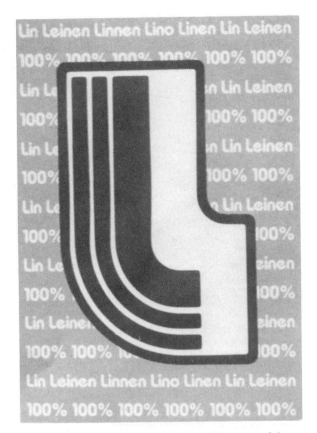

Fig. 4–13 *Linen symbol of quality. (Courtesy of the International Linen Promotion Commision.)*

ramie plant is a tall perennial shrub from the nettle family that requires a hot, humid climate. Ramie is fast-growing and can be harvested as frequently as every 60 days. Thus, several crops can be harvested each year. Because it is a perennial, it is cut, not pulled. It has been grown in the Everglades and Gulf Coast regions of the United States, but it is not currently produced in those areas.

Ramie fibers must be separated from the plant stalk by *decortication*. In this process, the bark and woody portion of the plant stem are separated from the ramie fiber. Because this process requires a lot of hand labor, ramie was not commercially important until less labor-intensive ways of decorticating were developed. Now that relatively inexpensive ways of decorticating ramie are available, ramie is a commercially important fiber. Ramie found a place in the U.S. market because it was a nonquotaed fiber in the Multi-Fiber Agreement regulating the amount of specific fibers that can be imported. For this reason and the fact that ramie blends well with many other fibers, many items of ramie or ramie blends have appeared in the United States. Ramie is produced in China, the Philippines, and Brazil.

Properties of Ramie

Ramie is long, lustrous, and fine. It has an absorbency similar to that of flax. Ramie has a density of 1.56, which is just slightly greater than that of flax.

When seen through the microscope, ramie is very similar to flax fiber (see Figure 4-14). It is pure white. It is one of the strongest natural fibers known and its strength increases when it is wet. It has silk-like luster. Ramie also has a very high resistance to rotting and mildew.

Ramie has some disadvantages. It is stiff and brittle, owing to the high crystallinity of its molecular structure. Consequently it lacks resiliency and is low in elasticity.

Ramie is resistant to shrinkage. It has a low elongation potential and will break if folded repeatedly in the same spot. Ramie has good absorbency, but does not dye as well as cotton. It has poor resiliency and should have a durable-press finish. Ramie is resistant to insects and microorganisms.

USES Ramie is used in a wide variety of imported apparel items including sweaters, shirts, blouses, and suitings (see Figure 4-15). It is often in blends, particularly with cotton or wool. It is also used in ropes, twines, nets, and industrial uses including auto upholstery, banknotes, cigarette paper, and geotextiles, such as erosion control ground-cover fabrics.

Ramie is important in furnishings, often in blends with linen or other fibers, for windows treatments, pillows, and table linens. A geotextile of ramie and polypropylene is used to reinforce steep slopes and provide a base for vegetation to minimize slumping of the ground during heavy rains. The ramie rots over time, but the polypropylene remains to add reinforcement around the plants' roots.

Table 4-5 summarizes ramie's performance in apparel and furnishing fabrics.

Fig. 4–14 *Photomicrographs of ramie cross-sectional view* (left); *longitudinal view* (right). *(Courtesy of E. I. du Pont de Nemours & Company.)*

Table 4–5   Summary of the Performance of Ramie in Apparel and Furnishing Fabrics

Aesthetics	Good
Luster	Matte
Texture	Thick and thin
Hand	Stiff
Durability	Good
Abrasion resistance	Average
Tenacity	Good
Elongation	Average
Comfort	Good
Absorbency	High
Thermal retention	Average
Appearance retention	Poor
Resiliency	Poor
Dimensional stability	Poor
Elastic recovery	Poor
Recommended care	Dry-clean or machine wash

Fig. 4–15   Imported ramie/cotton blend sweater.

Hemp

The history of *hemp* is as old as that of flax. Hemp resembles flax; however, because hemp lacks the fineness of better quality flax, it has never been able to compete with flax when used in clothing. Some varieties of hemp, though, are very difficult to distinguish from flax.

The high strength of hemp makes it particularly suitable for twine, cordage, and thread. Hemp is not very pliable or elastic. It does not rot readily when exposed to water. Hemp was commercially important up to end of World War II. After World War II, the demand for hemp declined because it was replaced in most end uses by manufactured or other natural fibers.

Jute

Jute was used as a fiber in Biblical times and probably was the fiber used in sackcloth. Jute is one the cheapest textile fibers. It is grown throughout Asia, chiefly in India and Bangladesh. The primary fibers in the fiber bundle are short and brittle, making jute one of weakest of the cellulosic fibers.

Jute is creamy white to brown in color. It is soft, lustrous, and pliable when first removed from the stalk. But it quickly turns brown, weak, and brittle. Jute has poor elasticity and elongation.

The greatest part of jute production goes into sugar and coffee bagging; it is also used for carpet backing, rope, cordage, and twine. Olefin is a strong competitor in these end uses. Because jute is losing its market, other uses for it are being investigated by jute-producing countries. For example, Bangladesh is investigating jute as a reinforcing fiber in resins to create preformed low-cost housing.

Burlap, a fabric usually made from jute, is used for decorative furnishings, for window treatments and wall coverings. Chemical finishes can be used to overcome the natural odor and stiffness of the fiber. Jute has low sunlight resistance and poor colorfastness. It is brittle and subject to splitting and snagging. It also deteriorates quickly when exposed to water.

Kenaf

Kenaf is a soft bast fiber from the kenaf plant. The fiber is light yellow to gray, long in length, and harder and more lustrous than jute. Like jute, it is used for twine, cordage, and other industrial purposes. Kenaf is produced in Central Asia, India, Africa, and some Central American countries. Kenaf is being investigated as a source of paper fiber.

LEAF FIBERS

Leaf fibers are those fibers obtained from the leaf of the plant. Most leaf fibers are long and fairly stiff. In processing, the leaf is cut from the plant and fiber is split or pulled from the leaf. Most leaf fibers have poor dye affinity and are used in their natural color.

Piña

Piña is obtained from the leaves of the pineapple plant. The fiber is soft, lustrous, and white or ivory. Piña is highly susceptible to acids and enzymes, so any acid stains should be rinsed out immediately and enzymatic presoaks should be avoided. Hand washing is recommended for piña. The fiber is used to produce lightweight sheer fabrics that are fairly stiff. These fabrics are often embroidered and used for formal wear in the Philippines. Piña is also used to make mats, bags, table linens, and other clothing (see Figure 4-16.)

Piña is the focus of current research efforts to modify processing techniques and equipment used in the linen industry. The aim of the research is to produce a commercially competitive fiber and to blend piña with other fibers.

Abaca

Abaca is obtained from a member of the banana tree family. Abaca fibers are coarse and very long; some may reach a length of 15 feet. Abaca is off-white to brown in color. The fiber is strong, durable, and flexible. It is used for ropes, cordage, floor mats, table linens, and clothing. It is produced in Central America and the Philippines. Abaca is sometimes referred to as Manila hemp even though it is not a true hemp (see Figure 4-17).

Sisal and Henequen

Sisal and *henequen* are closely related plants. They are grown in Africa, Central America, and the West Indies. Both fibers are smooth, straight, and yellow.

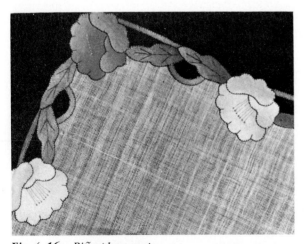

Fig. 4–16   *Piña place mat.*

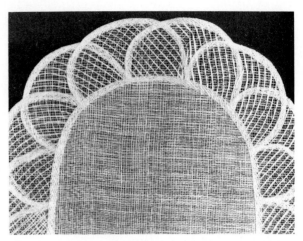

Fig. 4–17   *Abaca place mat..*

They are used for better grades of rope, twine, and brush bristles. However, since both fibers are degraded by salt water, they are not used in maritime ropes. In addition to these end uses, sisal may be substituted for horsehair in upholstery.

Sisal is also important in furnishings for carpet and custom rugs. These rugs can be hand painted to give an individual look. Sisal provides a complementary texture and background for many furnishing styles. Sisal may be used by itself or in blends with wool and acrylic for a softer hand. The dry extraction cleaning method (see Chapter 20) is recommended. Sisal is used in wall coverings, especially in heavy-duty commercial applications, because of its durability and ease of application to a variety of surfaces.

OTHER CELLULOSIC MATERIALS

Other cellulosic materials are important in furnishings. Rush (stems of a marsh plant), seagrass, and maize or cornhusks are used in area rugs because of their resistance to dry heat. Yarns made from paper (wood pulp) add interest and texture in wall coverings for interiors. Wooden slats and grasses are found in window treatments. Grasses are especially appealing; the variable thicknesses and textures add a natural look to interiors.

KEY TERMS

Seed fiber

Bast fiber

Leaf fiber

Cotton

Gin

Lint

Linters

Cuticle

Lumen

Convolutions

Kapok

Coir

Rippling

Retting

Scutching

Hackling

Primary fiber bundle

Flax

Linen

Nodes

Tow

Line

Ramie

Decortication

Hemp

Jute

Kenaf

Piña

Abaca

Sisal

Henequen

QUESTIONS

1. Explain the properties that are common to all cellulosics.
2. To what fiber aspects are differences among cellulosic fibers attributed?
3. Compare the performance characteristics of ramie and cotton. Why are blends of these two fibers currently available?
4. Identify a cellulosic fiber that would be an appropriate choice for each of the end uses listed below and explain why that fiber was selected.

   sheets for double bed for master bedroom

   tablecloth for an expensive French restaurant

   area rug for a designer's showroom

   woman's sweater for summer wear

   socks for active four-year-old child

   corduroy slacks for high school student

SUGGESTED READINGS

Grayon, Martin, ed. (1984). *Encyclopedia of Textiles, Fibers, and Nonwoven Fabrics.* New York: John Wiley & Sons.

LaBarthe, Jules (1975). *Elements of Textiles.* New York: Macmillan.

Stout, Evelyn E. (1970). *Introduction to Textiles.* New York: John Wiley & Sons.

Trotman, E.R. (1984). *Dyeing and Chemical Technology of Textile Fibres*, 6th ed. New York: John Wiley & Sons.

5

Natural Protein Fibers

OBJECTIVES

- To know the characteristics common to protein fibers and the differences among the basic protein fibers.

- To understand the processing required to produce goods from natural protein fibers.

- To recognize the importance of natural protein fibers in the consumer market.

- To recognize those fibers that are classified as natural protein fibers.

*N*ATURAL PROTEIN FIBERS ARE OF ANIMAL origin: wool and specialty wools are the hair and fur of animals and silk is the secretion of the silkworm. The natural protein fibers are prestige fibers today. Silk, vicuña, cashmere, and camel's hair have always been in this category. Wool is still the most widely used protein fiber, but it is no longer as readily nor as inexpensively available as it was.

Protein fibers are composed of various amino acids that have been formed in nature into polypeptide chains with high molecular weight, containing carbon, hydrogen, oxygen, and nitrogen. Wool also contains sulfur. Protein fibers are amphoteric, having both acidic and basic reactive groups. The protein of wool is keratin, whereas that of silk is fibroin.

The following is a simple formula for an amino acid:

amino group   carboxyl group
(basic)   (acidic)

Protein fibers have some properties in common because of their chemical composition. These properties are important because they indicate the care required for the fabrics. All animal fibers are superior to other fibers in that they absorb moisture without surface wetting; they are *hygroscopic*. This phenomenon has long been recognized as a major factor in understanding why items made from protein fibers are so comfortable to use. Hygroscopic fibers minimize sudden temperature changes at the skin. This is illustrated by the difference in warmth between an all–polyester suit and an all-wool suit. In the winter, when people go from a dry indoor atmosphere into the damp outdoor air, the wool fibers absorb moisture and generate heat, protecting the wearers from the cold. Silk and wool have some different properties because their physical and molecular structures are different. Table 5-1 lists the properties common to protein fibers.

Table 5–1 **Properties Common to All Protein Fibers**

Properties	Importance to Consumer
Resiliency	Resist wrinkling. Wrinkles hang out between uses. Fabrics tend to hold their shape during use.
Hygroscopic	Comfortable in cool, damp climate. Moisture prevents brittleness in carpets.
Weaker when wet	Handle carefully during washing. Wool loses about 40 percent of its strength and silk loses about 15 percent.
Specific gravity	Fabrics feel lighter than cellulosics of the same thickness.
Harmed by alkali	Use neutral or slightly alkaline soap or detergent. Perspiration weakens the fiber.
Harmed by oxidizing agents	Chlorine bleaches damage fiber so should not be used. Sunlight causes white fabrics to turn yellowish.
Harmed by dry heat	Wool becomes harsh and brittle and scorches easily with dry heat. Use steam! White silk and wool turn yellow.
Flame resistance	Do not burn readily; are self-extinguishing; have odor of burning hair, and form a black, crushable ash.

WOOL

Wool was one of the first fibers to be spun into yarns and woven into cloth. Wool was one of the most widely used textile fibers before the Industrial Revolution. Now, wool is a luxury fiber, used extensively in designers' collections.

The consumer is most likely to have a wool sweater, suit or coat. The high initial cost of wool products and the cost of their care have led many customers to classify wool garments as investment clothing. These factors have encouraged the substitution of acrylic, polyester, or wool/synthetic blends in many end-use products. However, wool has a combination of properties that are unequaled by any manufactured fiber: ability to be shaped by heat and moisture, good moisture absorption without feeling wet, excellent heat retention, water repellency, feltability, and flame retardance.

Sheep were probably among the first animals domesticated. The covering of primitive sheep consisted of a long, hairy outercoat (kemp) and a light, downy undercoat. The fleece of present-day domesticated sheep is primarily the soft undercoat. The Spanish developed the *Merino* sheep, whose fleece contains no hair or kemp fiber. Kemp is still found in wools of all breeds of sheep except the Merino.

Sheep raising on the Atlantic seaboard began in the Jamestown, Virginia, colony in 1609 and in the Massachusetts settlements in 1630. From these centers, the sheep-raising industry spread rapidly. In 1643, English wool combers and carders settled in the Massachusetts Bay colony, where they produced and finished wool fabric. This was the beginning of the New England textile industry. Following the U. S. Civil War, the opening of free grazing lands west of the Mississippi prepared the way for the expansion of sheep production. By 1884, the peak year, 50 million sheep were found in the U.S. The U.S. sheep population has declined steadily since then.

Production of Wool

In 1990, major producers of wool were Australia (32.0 percent), Eastern Europe and China (25.7 percent), New Zealand (9.5 percent), and Argentina (4.6 percent). The United States ranked ninth with only 1.3 percent of world production. Total amount produced was almost 7.5 billion pounds of greasy wool.

Merino sheep produce the most valuable wool (Figure 5-1). About 43 percent of Merino wool comes from Australia. Good quality ewes produce 15 pounds of wool per fleece, while rams produce 20 pounds. Australian Merino wool is 3-5 inches long and very fine.

Fine wool is produced in the United States by four breeds of sheep: Delaine-Merino, Rambouillet, Debouillet, and Targhee. More than half of this fine wool is produced in Texas and California. It is 2½ inches long.

The greatest share of U.S. wool production is of medium-grade wools removed from animals raised more for meat than fiber. These fibers have a larger diameter than the fine wools and a greater variation in length, from 1½-6 inches. Fifteen breeds of sheep

Fig. 5–1 *Merino sheep. (Courtesy of Australian Wool Corporation.)*

are commonly found in the United States. The breeds vary tremendously in appearance and type of wool produced. Sheep are raised in every state of the United States, with the exception of Hawaii, but most sheep are raised in the western U.S.

Sheep are generally sheared once a year in the spring. The fleece is removed with power shears that look like large barber's shears. A good shearer can handle 100-225 sheep per day. An expert can shear a sheep in less than 5 minutes. The fleece is removed with long, smooth strokes, beginning at the legs and belly. A good shearer leaves the fleece in one piece. After shearing, the fleece is folded together and put in bags to be shipped to market.

As an alternative to shearing, a chemical additive to the sheep's diet has been tried. When the chemical is digested it causes the wool to become brittle. Several weeks later, the fleece can be pulled off the sheep.

The sheared (or pulled) wool is *raw wool* or *grease wool.* It contains impurities such as sand, dirt, grease, and dried sweat *(suint),* which account for 30-70 percent of the weight of the fleece. Once these impurities are removed, the wool is *clean,* or *scoured, wool.* The grease is a valuable byproduct; in its purified state, it is *lanolin* used in manufacturing creams, cosmetics, soaps, and ointments.

Grading and sorting are two marketing operations that group wools of like character together. In *grading,* the whole fleece is judged for fineness and length. Each fleece contains more than one quality of wool. In *sorting,* the individual fleece is pulled apart into sections of different-quality fibers. The best-quality wool comes from the sides, shoulders, and back; the poorest wool comes from the lower legs.

Different qualities of wool are used differently. For example, fine wool may be used in a lightweight worsted fabric while a coarse wool could be used in carpets.

The quality of wool is based on fineness and length and does not necessarily imply durability because fine fibers are not as durable as coarse fibers. Fineness, color, crimp, strength, length, and elasticity are characteristics that vary with the breed of the sheep.

Types and Kinds of Wool

Many different qualities of wool are available for the production of yarns and fabrics. Although breeds of sheep produce wools with different characteristics, labels on wool products almost never give that information; the fiber is simply identified as wool. The term *wool* legally includes fiber from various animals, such as sheep, Angora goat, Cashmere goat, camel, alpaca, llama, and vicuña. In addition, wool may be identified as:

• Sheared wool—from live sheep

• Pulled wool—from the pelts of meat-type sheep

• Recycled wool—from worn clothing and cutters' scraps

Wool is often blended with less expensive fibers to reduce the cost of the fabric or to extend its use. The terms that appear on the label of a garment made of wool fiber are defined by the Federal Trade Commission as follows:

1. Virgin wool—wool that has never been processed. If only the term "wool" is used, it implies a virgin wool. The phrase virgin wool on a label is a helpful marketing tool.

2. Wool—new wool or wool fibers reclaimed from knit scraps, broken thread, and noils. (Noils are the short fibers that are combed out in the making of worsted yarns.)

3. Recycled wool—scraps of new woven or felted fabrics that are *garnetted* (shredded) back to the fibrous state and used again in the manufacture of woolens. Shoddy wool from old clothing and rags is cleaned, sorted, and shredded into fibers. Recycled wool is often blended with new wool before being respun. It is usually used in thick, boardy fabrics.

Recycled wool is important in the textile industry. However, these fibers lose some of the desirable properties of new wool during garnetting. Some fibers are broken by the mechanical action and/or wear. The fibers are not as resilient, strong, or durable as new wool, yet the fabrics made from them perform well. The terms *recycled wool* or *virgin wool* on a label do not refer to the quality of the fiber, but to the past use of the fiber.

Lamb's wool comes from young animals technically defined as less than 7 months old. This wool is finer and softer because it is the first shearing and the fiber has only one cut end: the other end is the natural tip (Figure 5–2). Lamb's wool is usually identified on a label.

Physical Structure of Wool

LENGTH The length of Merino wool fibers ranges from 1½ to 5 inches, depending on the animal and the length of time between shearings. Long, fine wool fibers, used for worsted yarns and fabrics, have an average length of 2½ inches. Worsted refers to a yarn type and implies long fibers, greater uniformity of fiber length, and more compact yarns. The shorter fibers, which average 1½ inches in length, are used in woolen fabrics. Woolen also refers to yarns and implies shorter, less parallel, softer, and looser yarns with greater variety of fiber length. Certain breeds of sheep produce coarse, long wools

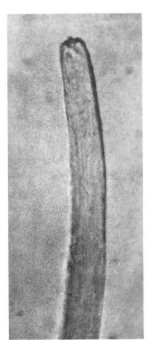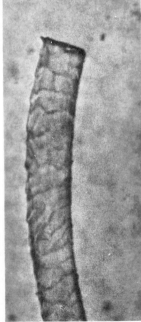

Fig. 5–2. Lamb's wool fiber: natural tip (left); cut tip (right).

that measure from 5 to 15 inches in length. These long wools are used in specialty fabrics and hand weaving.

The diameter of wool fiber varies from 10 to 50 micrometers. Merino lamb's wool may average 15 micrometers in diameter. The wool fiber is made up of a cuticle, cortex, and medulla (Figure 5-3).

MEDULLA When present, the *medulla* is a honeycomblike core containing air spaces that increase the insulating power of the fiber. It appears as a dark area when seen through the microscope, but is usually absent in fine wools.

CORTEX The *cortex* is the main part of the fiber. It is made up of long, flattened, cigar-shaped cells with a nucleus near the center. In natural-colored wools, the cortical cells contain *melanin,* a colored pigment.

The cortical cells on the two sides of the wool fiber react differently to moisture and temperature. These cells are responsible for the three-dimensional *crimp,* which is unique to the wool fiber. This irregular lengthwise waviness gives wool fabrics three very important properties: cohesiveness, elasticity, and loft. Figure 5-4 shows the crimp in wool fiber. Fine Merino wool may have as many as 30 crimps per inch. Lower-quality wools may have only 1-5 crimps per inch. Crimp helps individual fibers cling together in a yarn, which increases the strength of the yarn. Elasticity is increased because crimp helps the fiber act like a spring. As force is exerted on the fiber, the fiber first straightens out from its naturally wavy state to a flat state, without any damage to the fiber. Once the force is released, the wool fiber gradually returns to its crimped posi-

Fig. 5–4 *Natural crimp in wool fiber.*

tion. Crimp also is an important factor in the loft that wool fabrics exhibit. Because of the crimp of the fibers, yarns and fabrics made from wool are lofty or bulky and retain this loftiness throughout use.

The crimp in wool is three-dimensional. As the fiber bends back and forth, it twists around its axis. This is drawn in Figure 5-5. Remember that the cortical cells on the two different sides of the fiber react differently to heat and moisture. Because wool has these two different parts, it is called a *natural bicomponent fiber.* To illustrate this bicomponent nature, consider how a wool fiber reacts to water. One side of the fiber swells more than the other side; this causes a decrease in the natural crimp of the fiber. When the fiber dries, the crimp returns.

Wool has been described as a giant molecular coil spring with outstanding resiliency. This resiliency is excellent when the fiber is dry and poor when it is wet. If dry wool fabric is crushed in the hand, it tends to spring back to its original shape when the hand is opened. The wool fiber can be stretched to as much as 30 percent of its original length. When stress is applied, the waves and bends of the fiber straighten out; when stress is removed, the fiber recovers its original length. Recovery takes place more slowly when the fabric is dry. Steam, humidity, and water hasten recovery. This is why wool items lose wrinkles more rapidly when exposed to a steamy or humid environment.

CUTICLE The cuticle consists of an epicuticle and a horny, nonfibrous layer of scales. The *epicuticle* is a thin, nonprotein membrane that covers the scales. This layer gives water repellency to the fiber, but is easily damaged by mechanical treatment. In fine

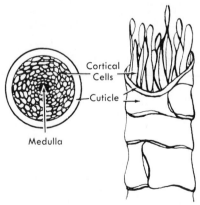

Fig. 5–3 *Physical structure of wool fibers. (Courtesy of Werner von Bergen from* Industrial and Engineering Chemistry, *September 1952; reprinted by permission.)*

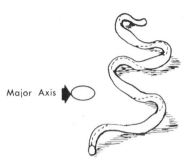

Fig. 5-5 *Three-dimensional crimp of wool fiber. (From G. E. Hopkins,* Wool As an Apparel Fiber. *Copyright 1953 by Holt, Rinehart and Winston, Inc.)*

wools, the *scales* completely encircle the shaft and each scale overlaps the bottom of the preceding scale like parts of a telescope. In medium and coarse wools, the scale arrangement resembles shingles on a roof or scales on a fish (Figure 5-6). The free edges of the scales project outward and point toward the tip of the fiber. The scale covering gives wool its abrasion resistance and felting property, but it can cause skin irritation for some people.

Felting, a unique and important property of wool, is based on the structure of the fiber. Under mechanical action combining agitation, friction, and pressure with heat and moisture, the wool fiber tends to move rootward and the edges of the scales interlock, thus preventing the fiber from returning to its original position and resulting in shrinkage, or felting, of the fabric.

The movement of the fibers is speeded up and felting occurs more rapidly under extreme or severe conditions. Wool items can be shrunk to half their original size. Lamb's wool felts more readily than other wool. In soft, fluffy fabrics the fibers are not firmly held in position and are free to move, so these fabrics are more susceptible to felting than are the firmly woven worsteds. The felting property is an advantage in making felt fabric directly from fibers without spinning or weaving, yet it can be a disadvantage because it makes the laundering of wool more difficult. Treatments to prevent felting shrinkage (see Chapter 18) are available.

Chemical Composition and Molecular Arrangement of Wool

Wool fiber is a protein called *keratin.* It is the same protein that is found in human hair, fingernails, horns, and hooves. Keratin consists of carbon, hydrogen, oxygen, nitrogen, and sulfur. These combine to form over 17 different amino acids. Five amino acids are shown in Figure 5-7. The wool mol-

ecule consists of flexible molecular chains held together by natural cross-links—cystine (or sulfur) linkages and salt bridges—that connect adjacent molecules.

Figure 5-7 resembles a ladder, with the cross-links analogous to the crossbars of the ladder. This simple structure can be useful in understanding some of the properties of wool. Imagine a ladder made of plastic that is pulled askew. When wool is pulled, its inherent tendency is to recover its original shape; the cross-links are very important in this recovery. However, if the cross-links are damaged, the structure is destroyed and recovery cannot occur.

A more realistic model of the structure of wool molecules would show this ladderlike structure alternating with a helical structure. About 40 percent of the chains are in a spiral formation, with hydrogen bonding occurring between the closer parts. The ladderlike formation occurs at the cystine cross-links or where other bulky amino acids meet and the chains cannot pack closely together. The spiral formation works like a spring and is also important in the resilience, elongation, and elastic

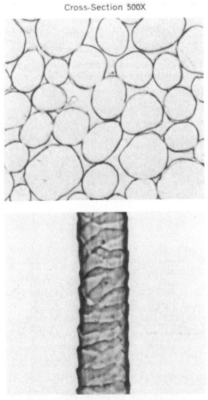

Fig. 5-6 *Photomicrographs of wool. (Courtesy of American Association of Textile Chemists and Colorists.)*

recovery of wool fibers. Figure 5-8 shows the helical structure of wool.

The cystine linkage is the most important part of the molecule. Any chemical, such as alkali, that damages this linkage can destroy the entire structure. In controlled reactions, the linkage can be broken and

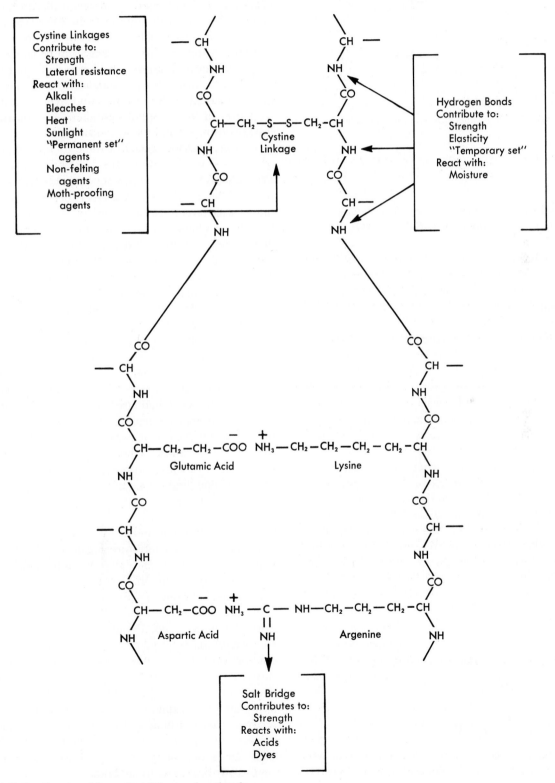

Fig. 5-7   *Structural formula of the wool molecule.*

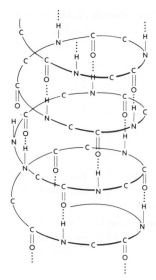

Fig. 5–8 *Helical arrangement of the wool molecule. (Courtesy of International Wool Secretariat.)*

then reformed. Minor modifications of the cystine linkage that result from pressing and steaming have a beneficial effect; those from careless washing and exposure to light have a detrimental effect.

SHAPING OF WOOL FABRICS Wool fabrics can be shaped by heat and moisture—a definite aid in producing wool products. Puckers can be pressed out; excess fabric can be eased and then pressed flat or rounded as desired. Pleats can be pressed into wool cloth with heat, steam, and pressure, but they will not last through washing. This excerpt from *Textile Industries* explains the process:

Hydrogen bonds are broken by moisture and heat so the wool structure can be re-shaped by the mechanical action of the iron or press. Simultaneously, the heat dries the wool and new hydrogen bonds are formed in the wool structure as the water escapes as steam. The new hydrogen bonds maintain the wool in the new shape so long as the humidity is low. In high humidity or if the wool is dampened with water, the new hydrogen bonds are broken and the molecular structure reverts to its former shape. This is why garments shaped by ironing lose their creases or flatness and show relaxation shrinkage on wetting.—From "What Happens When Setting Wool," *Textile Industries,* 130 (October 1966): 344.

Properties of Wool

AESTHETIC Because of its physical structure, wool contributes loft and body to fabrics. Wool sweaters,

suits, carpets, and upholstery are the standard "looks" by which manufactured fiber fabrics are measured.

Wool has a matte appearance. Fibers are sometimes blended with wool from sheep that produce longer fibers or with specialty hair fibers such as mohair to modify the fabric's luster or texture.

Drape, luster, texture, and hand can be varied by choice of yarn structure, fabric structure, and finish. Sheer-wool voile, medium-weight printed-wool challis, medium-weight flannels and tweeds, heavy-weight coating and upholstery fabrics demonstrate the spectrum of possibilities. No wonder designers love to work with wool!

DURABILITY Wool fabrics are very durable. They have moderate abrasion resistance because of the fiber's scale structure and flexibility, which is excellent. Wool fibers can be bent back on themselves 20,000 times without breaking, as compared to 3,000 times for cotton and 75 times for rayon. Atmospheric moisture helps wool retain its flexibility. Wool carpets, for example, become brittle if the air is too dry. The crimp and scale structure of wool fibers make them very cohesive so they cling together to make strong yarns.

Wool fibers have a low tenacity, 1.5 g/d dry and 1.0 g/d wet. The durability of wool relates to their excellent elongation (25 percent) and elastic recovery (99 percent). When stress is put on the fabric, the crimped fibers elongate as the molecular chains unfold. When stress is removed, the cross-links pull the fibers back almost to their original positions. The combination of these properties, excellent flexibility, elongation, and elastic recovery, results in wool fabrics that can be used and enjoyed for many years.

COMFORT Wool is more hygroscopic than any other fiber. It has a moisture regain of 13–18 percent under standard conditions. Wool fibers are initially water repellent. In a light rain or snow, the water runs off or remains on the fabric surface.

Wool is a poor conductor of heat so that warmth from the body is not dissipated readily. Outdoor sports enthusiasts have long recognized the superior comfort provided by wool. Drying of wool occurs slowly enough that the wearer is more comfortable than in any other fiber. Wool's excellent resiliency is important in providing warmth. The wool fibers can recover from crushing and the fabrics will remain porous and capable of incorporating much air. This "still" air is one of the best insulators because it keeps body heat close to the body.

Some people are allergic to the chemical components of wool and itch, break out in a rash, or sneeze when they touch wool. Fabrics that irritate may be coarse, low-quality wools.

Wool has a medium density (1.32 g/cc). People often associate heavy fabrics with wool since it is used in fall and winter wear when the additional warmth of heavy fabrics is desirable. Lightweight wools are very comfortable in the changeable temperatures of spring and early fall.

One way to compare fiber densities is to think of blankets. A winter blanket of wool is heavy and warm. An equally thick blanket of cotton would be even heavier (cotton has a higher density), but not as warm. A winter blanket of acrylic would be lighter in weight (acrylic has a lower density than either). Personal preferences need to be considered before deciding which fiber would be more comfortable.

APPEARANCE RETENTION Wool is a very resilient fiber. It resists wrinkling and recovers well from wrinkles. It wrinkles more readily when wet. Wool maintains its shape fairly well during normal use. Often wool apparel is lined to maintain its shape.

When wool fabrics are dry cleaned, they retain their size and shape well. When wool items are hand washed, they need to be cared for properly to avoid shrinking. Follow care instructions for washable woolens.

Wool has an excellent elastic recovery—99 percent at 2 percent elongation. Even at 20 percent elongation, recovery is 63 percent. Recovery is excellent from the stresses of normal usage. Wool carpet maintains an attractive appearance for years.

CARE Wool does not soil readily, and the removal of soil from wool is relatively simple. Grease and oils do not spot wool fabrics as readily as they do fabrics made of other fibers. Wool items do not need to be washed or dry cleaned after every use. They do not wrinkle very much. They can be spot treated. Layer wool garments with washable ones to decrease odor pickup.

A firm, soft brush not only removes dust but also gently lifts matted fibers back to their natural springiness. Damp fabrics should be allowed to dry before brushing. Garments should have a period of rest between wearings to recover from deformations. Hanging the item in a humid environment or spraying a fine mist of water on the cloth speeds up recovery.

Wool is very susceptible to damage when it is wet. Its wet tenacity is a third lower than its relatively low dry strength. Wet elongation increases to 35 percent before breaking. Resiliency and elastic recovery decrease. The redeeming properties of dry wool that make it durable in spite of its low tenacity do not operate when it is wet. Handle wet wool very gently.

Dry cleaning is the recommended method of caring for most wool items. Dry cleaning minimizes potential problems that may occur during hand or machine washing. Incorrect care procedures can be disastrous and costly; the item can be ruined.

Some items can be hand washed if correct procedures are followed. Use warm water that is comfortable to the hand. Avoid agitation; squeeze gently. Support the item, especially if it is knit, so it does not stretch unnecessarily. Air dry flat. Do not machine or tumble dry or felting will occur. Woven or knit items that are labeled machine washable are usually blends or have been given a special finish so they can be laundered safely. Follow any special instructions given. These special instructions usually require using warm or lukewarm water and a gentle cycle for a short period of time, with line or flat drying recommended.

Chlorine bleach, an oxidizing agent, damages wool. Verify this by putting a small piece of wool in fresh chlorine bleach. What happens? The wool dissolves! Wool is also very sensitive to the action of alkali, such as strong detergents. The wool reacts to the alkali by turning yellow, then becoming slick and jellylike, and finally dissolving. If the fabric is a blend, the wool in the blend disintegrates, leaving only the other fibers.

Wool is attacked by moth larvae and other insects. Regular, liberal use of mothballs or crystals is discouraged due to the toxic nature of these pesticides. However, they should be used when evidence of insects is apparent, such as when moths or traces of larvae are seen. Moth larvae also eat, but do not digest, any fiber that is blended with wool.

Unless mothproofed, wool fabrics should be stored so that they will not be accessible to moths. Wool fabrics should be cleaned before storage.

Wool burns very slowly and is self-extinguishing. It is normally regarded as flame-resistant. This is one of the reasons why wool is so popular with interior designers. However, when wool is used in public buildings, a flame-retardant finish may be applied to meet building code requirements.

Table 5-2 summarizes wool's performance in apparel and furnishing fabrics.

Table 5–2 Summary of the Performance of Wool in Apparel and Furnishing Fabrics

Aesthetic	Variable
Luster	Matte
Durability	**High**
Abrasion resistance	Moderate
Tenacity	Low
Elongation	High
Comfort	**High**
Absorbency	High
Thermal retention	High
Appearance retention	**High**
Resiliency	High
Dimensional stability	Low
Elastic recovery	Excellent
Recommended care	Dry clean (apparel)
	Steam clean (furnishings)

Uses of Wool

Only a small amount of wool is used in the United States. In 1990 domestic consumption of wool was 185 million pounds, or approximately 2 percent of all fiber used in the United States. The most important use of wool is for adult apparel (see Table 5-3).

Wool suits perform well and look great. They fit well because they can be shaped through tailoring. The fabrics drape well and are durable. They are comfortable under a variety of conditions and retain their good looks during wear and care. Suits are usually dry cleaned to retain their best looks and because of the shaping components. Blends of synthetic fibers with wool for suiting materials are also important.

The Wool Bureau has adopted two symbols to assist in the promotion of wool: the Woolmark® used on all 100 percent wool merchandise that meets the Wool Bureau's specifications for quality and the Woolblend® mark for blends with at least 60 percent wool. Both symbols are shown in Figure 5-9.

Wool is extremely important for furnishings, even though the actual percentage of furnishing products that are wool is small. Wool is the standard by which carpet appearance is judged. Obviously, a major use of wool is in carpets and custom rugs, often special-order or one-of-a-kind rugs. Many woven Axminster and Wilton rugs with Persian-type designs are made from wool. More contemporary

PURE WOOL   WOOLBLEND MARK

Fig. 5–9 *Woolmark® and Woolblend® symbols of quality. (Courtesy of the Wool Bureau, Inc.)*

looks are also available. Most rugs are imported, although some are made in the United States. Wool rugs are more expensive than nylon carpets, but people who prefer them like the patterns and appreciate the color, texture, and appearance of wool. Wool rugs account for a very small share of the rug market.

Wool is also found in upholstery fabrics. Both wool and wool blend fabrics are used in upholstery because of their aesthetic characteristics, good appearance retention, durable nature, and natural flame resistance. For residential use no additional flame retardant treatment may be necessary, but for many commercial and contract uses the wool or wool blend upholstery fabric may require flame retardant treatment.

Table 5–3 Uses of Wool

Percent	End Use	Million Pounds
72.7	Apparel	
	Top weight	3.3
	Bottom weight	108.1
	Underwear and nightwear	2.6
	Sweaters	14.6
	Retail piece goods	1.0
	Socks	3.3
	Hand-knitting yarns	2.2
23.0	Home Furnishing	
	Carpets	24.5
	Upholstery	13.7
	Blankets	5.3
4.2	Industrial	
	Felts	8.0

Source: *Fiber Organon 61* (9), Sept. 1990.

Handcrafted wall hangings and true woven tapestries are often made of wool because textile artists prefer the way the fiber handles and designers, artists, and consumers appreciate the way the finished item looks and wears.

Many school laboratories have fire blankets of wool for safety. Stadium blankets and throws are often made of wool for warmth and an attractive appearance.

In industrial uses, wool is important in felts, which are used under heavy machinery to help decrease noise, or for a variety of other uses. Wool is also used to clean up oil spills. Tiny balls of wool absorb up to 40 times their weight in oil.

SPECIALTY WOOLS

Most specialty wools are obtained from the goat, rabbit, and camel families (see Table 5-4).

Specialty wools are available in smaller quantities than sheep's wool so they are usually more expensive. Like all natural fibers, specialty wools vary in quality.

Specialty wool fibers are of two kinds: the coarse long outerhair and the soft, fine undercoat. Coarse fibers are used for interlinings, upholstery, and some coatings; the very fine fibers are used in luxury coatings, sweaters, shawls, suits, and dress fabrics.

Mohair

Mohair is the hair fiber of the Angora goat. In 1989, 50 million pounds of mohair were produced worldwide. Major producers are South Africa, the U.S., and Turkey. Texas is the major producer in the United States. Most U.S. mohair is exported. The goats (see Figure 5-10) are usually sheared twice a year, in the early fall and early spring. The fiber length is 4 to 6 inches if sheared twice or 8 to 12 inches if sheared once.

Fig. 5–10 *Angora goats produce mohair fibers. (Courtesy of the Mohair Council of America.)*

Mohair fibers have a circular cross section. Scales on the surface are scarcely visible and the cortical cells show through as lengthwise striations. There are some air ducts between the cells that give mohair its lightness and fluffiness. Few of the fibers have a medulla.

Mohair is one of the most resilient fibers and has none of the crimp found in sheep's wool, giving it a silk-like luster and a smoother surface that is more resistant to dust than wool. Mohair has fewer scales than wool, so mohair fibers are smoother than wool fibers (see Figure 5-11). Mohair is very strong and has good affinity for dye. The washed fleece is a lustrous white.

Mohair's chemical properties are the same as those of wool. Mohair makes a better novelty loop yarn than wool or the other specialty hair fibers.

Mohair is used for:

- Upholstery and draperies
- Suitings and coatings
- Pile fabrics (embossed and curled like fur)
- Laces
- Wigs and hairpieces
- Hand-produced rugs and wall hangings

Figure 5-12 shows the quality symbol used on all mohair products that meet performance standards established by the Mohair Council of America.

Qiviut

Qiviut, a rare and luxurious fiber, is the underwool of the domesticated musk ox (see Fig. 5-13). Successful musk ox domestication projects have

Table 5–4   **Groupings of Specialty Wools**

Goat Family	Camel Family	Others
Angora goat—mohair	Camel's hair	Angora rabbit—angora
Cashmere goat—cashmere	Llama	Fur fibers
	Alpaca	Musk ox—qiviut
	Vicuña	
	Guanaco	

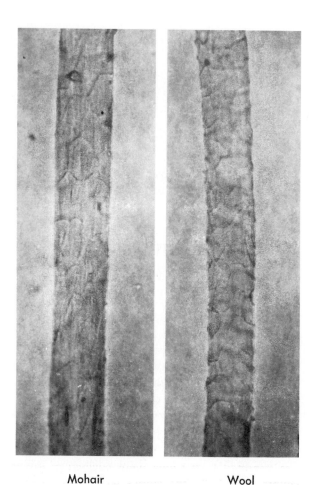

| Mohair | Wool |

Fig. 5–11 *Microscopic view of mohair and wool. (Courtesy of U.S.D.A., Livestock Division , Wool and Mohair Lab.)*

been conducted in Alaska. A large musk ox provides 6 pounds of wool each year. The fiber can be used just as it comes from the animal, for it is protected from debris by the long guard hairs and has a low lanolin content. The fleece is not shorn but is shed naturally and is removed from the guard hairs as soon as it becomes visible. Qiviut is an expensive fiber, over $150 an ounce.

Eskimo women hand knit with qiviut. Their first products were lacy scarves with designs taken from Eskimo artifacts. Each pattern is identified with a particular village.

Angora

Angora is hair of the Angora rabbit. These rabbits are raised in France and the U.S. (see Figure 5-14). Each rabbit produces only a few ounces of fiber, which is very fine, fluffy, soft, slippery, and fairly long. It is pure white or a natural color.

Fig. 5–12 *Mohair symbol of quality. (Courtesy of the Mohair Council of America.)*

Angora does not take dye well and usually has a lighter color than other fibers with which it is blended. It is usually blended with wool to facilitate spinning because the slick fiber has poor cohesiveness. Angora is most often used in apparel such as sweaters.

Camel's Hair

Camel's hair is obtained from the two-hump Bactrian camel. These camels are found from Turkey east to China and north to Siberia. Camel's hair is said to have the best insulation of any of the wool fibers. The hair is collected by a "trailer" who follows the camel caravan, picks up the hair as it is shed, and places it in a basket carried by the last camel. The trailer also gathers the hair in the morning at the spot where the camels lay down for the night. A camel produces about 5 pounds of hair a year.

Fig. 5–13 *The musk ox of Alaska produces qiviut fiber. (Courtesy of Fairbanks Convention and Visitor Bureau.)*

Fig.5–14 *The Angora rabbit produces a soft, white or natural color fiber. This is a photo of an English Angora rabbit. (Courtesy of Mary Goodwin.)*

Because camel's hair gives warmth without weight, the finer fibers are much prized for clothing fabrics. They are often used in blends with sheep's wool, which is dyed the tan color of camel's hair. Camel's hair is most often used in coats or jackets, scarves, and sweaters.

Cashmere

Cashmere comes from a small goat raised in Kashmir, China, Tibet, and Mongolia. The fibers vary in color from white to gray to brownish gray. The goat has an outercoat of long, coarse hair and an innercoat of down. The hair is combed by hand from the animal during the two molting seasons. Care is taken to separate the coarse hair from the fine fibers, which make up only a small part of the fleece, probably not more than one-half pound per goat. The fiber is solid with no medulla. Cashmere is used in high-quality apparel, especially women's sweaters and coats. Fabrics are warm, buttery in hand, and have beautiful draping characteristics. Cashmere is more sensitive to chemicals than wool.

Llama and Alpaca

Llama and alpaca are domesticated animals of the South American branch of the camel family. The fiber is 8-12 inches in length and is noted for its softness, fineness, and luster. The natural colors are white, light fawn, light brown, dark brown, gray, black, and piebald.

Vicuña and Guanaco

Vicuña and guanaco are wild animals of the South American camel family. They are very rare, and the animals must be killed to obtain the fiber. The governments of countries where vicuña and guanaco are found have limited the number of animals that can be harvested each year in order to protect the herds from extinction. Vicuña is the softest, finest, rarest, and most expensive of all textile fibers. The fiber is short, very lustrous, and light cinnamon in color.

SILK

Silk is a natural protein fiber. It is similar to wool in that it is composed of amino acids arranged in a polypeptide chain. Silk is produced by the larvae of a moth.

According to Chinese legend, silk culture began in 2640 B.C. when Empress Hsi Ling Shi became interested in silkworms and learned how to reel the silk and make it into fabric. Through her efforts China developed a silk industry that the country monopolized for 3,000 years. Silk culture later spread to Korea and Japan, westward to India and Persia, and then to Spain, France, and Italy. Silk fabrics imported from China were coveted in other countries; in India, the fabrics were often picked apart and rewoven into looser fabrics or combined with other fibers to provide more yardage from the same amount of silk filament. Today, major producers of silk are China (54 percent), India (14 percent), and Japan (11 percent).

Silk is universally accepted as a luxury fiber. The International Silk Association of the United States emphasizes the uniqueness of silk by its slogan "Only silk is silk." Silk has a unique combination of properties not possessed by any other fiber:

- "Dry" tactile hand
- Natural luster
- Good moisture absorption
- Lively suppleness and draping qualities
- High strength

The beauty and hand of silk and its high cost are probably responsible for the manufactured fiber industry. Silk is a solid fiber with a simple physical structure. It is this physical nature of silk that some modifications of manufactured fibers attempt to duplicate. Manufactured fibers with a triangular cross section and fine size are the most successful.

Production of Silk

Sericulture is the production of cultivated silk, which begins when the silk moth lays eggs on specially prepared paper. The cultivated silkworm is usually *Bombyx mori.* When the eggs hatch, the caterpillars, or larvae, are fed fresh, young mulberry leaves. After about 35 days and 4 moltings, the silkworms are approximately 10,000 times heavier than when hatched and ready to begin spinning a cocoon, or chrysalis case. A straw frame is placed on the tray and the silkworm starts to spin the cocoon by moving its head in a figure–eight (see Figure 5-15). The silkworm produces silk in two glands and forces the liquid silk through openings, *spinnerets,* in its head. The two strands of silk are coated with a water-soluble protective gum, *sericin.* When the silk comes in contact with the air, it solidifies. In 2 or 3 days, the silkworm has spun approximately 1 mile of filament and has completely surrounded itself in a cocoon. The silkworm then begins to change into a chrysalis and then into a moth. Usually the silkworm is killed (stifled) with heat before it reaches the moth stage. If the silkworm is allowed to reach the moth stage, it is used for breeding additional silkworms. The moth secretes a fluid that dissolves the silk at one end of the cocoon so that it can crawl out. Cocoons from which the moths have emerged cannot be used for filament silk yarns and the staple silk from these cocoons is not as valuable as filament silk.

To obtain filament silk from the cocoon after the silkworm has been stifled, the cocoons are first sorted for fiber size, fiber quality and defects, then brushed to find the outside ends of the filaments. Several filaments are gathered together and wound onto a reel. This process, referred to as *reeling,* is performed in a manufacturing plant called a *filature.* Each cocoon yields approximately 1,000 yards of silk filament. This is *raw silk,* or *silk-in-the-gum.* Several filaments are combined to form a yarn. The operators in the filature must be careful to join the fibers so that the diameter of the reeled silk remains uniform in size. Uniformly reeled filament silk is the most valuable (see Figure 5-16).

As the fibers are combined and wrapped onto the reel, twist can be added to hold the filaments together. Adding twist is referred to as *throwing* and the resulting yarn is called a *thrown yarn.* There are several types of thrown yarns. The type of yarn and amount of twist relate to the type of fabric desired. The simplest type of thrown yarn is a singles. In a *singles,* three to eight filaments are twisted

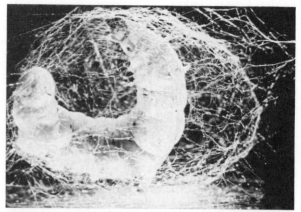

Fig. 5–15 *Silk caterpillar spinning silk fibers to form cocoon. (Courtesy of Stock, Boston. © Cary Wolinsky, 1984.)*

together to form a yarn. Commonly used for filling yarns in many silk fabrics, singles may have two or three twists per inch.

Much usable silk is not reeled because long filaments cannot be taken from a damaged cocoon. Cocoons in which the filament broke or the moth was allowed to mature and silk from the inner portions of the cocoon yield staple silk, often referred to as *silk noils,* or *silk waste.* This silk is degummed (the sericin is removed) and spun like any other staple fiber or blended with another staple fiber and spun into a yarn. Spun silk is less expensive and of lower quality than filament silk.

Wild silk production is not controlled as is production of cultivated silk. Although many species of wild silkworms produce wild silk, the two most common are *Antheraea mylitta* and *Antheraea pernyi.* The silkworms feed on oak and cherry leaves and produce fibers that are much less uni-

Fig. 5–16 *Reeling of silk. (Courtesy of The Textile Institute.)*

form in texture and color. The fiber may be brown, yellow, orange, or green, with brown the most common color. Since the cocoons are harvested after the moth has matured, the silk cannot be reeled and must be used as spun silk. *Tussah silk* is the most common type of wild silk. It is coarser, darker, and cannot be bleached. Hence, white and light colors are not available in tussah silk. *Tasar* is a type of wild silk from India. *Duppioni silk* results when two silkworms spin their cocoons together. The yarn is irregular in diameter with a thick–thin appearance. It is used in linenlike silk fabrics.

Physical Structure of Silk

Silk is the only natural filament fiber. It is a solid fiber, smooth but irregular in diameter along its shaft. The filaments are triangular in cross section with rounded corners (Figure 5-17). Silk fibers are very fine—1.25 denier/filament. Wild silks may have slight striations along the longitudinal length of the fiber.

Chemical Composition and Molecular Structure of Silk

The protein in silk is *fibroin,* which contains 15 amino acids in polypeptide chains. Silk has reactive amino (NH_2) and carboxyl (COOH) groups. Silk has no cross-linkages and no bulky side chains. The molecular chains are not folded as in wool, but are almost fully extended and packed closely together. Thus silk is highly oriented, which gives the fiber its strength. As with all fibers, there are some amorphous areas between the crystalline areas, giving silk its elasticity.

Properties of Silk

AESTHETIC Silk can be dyed and printed in brilliant colors. It is adaptable to a variety of fabrication methods, thus it is available in a wide variety of fabric types for furnishing and apparel uses. Because of cultivated silk's smooth but slightly irregular surface and triangular cross section, the luster of this fiber is soft with an occasional sparkle. It is this luster that has been the model for many manufactured fibers. Fabrics made of cultivated silk usually have a smooth appearance and a luxurious hand.

Wild silks have a duller luster because of their coarser size, less regular surface, and presence of sericin. Fabrics made of wild silk have a more pronounced texture.

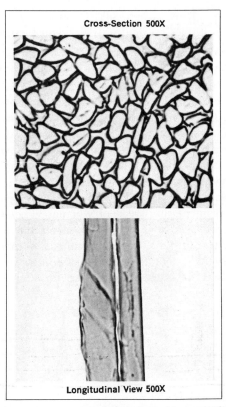

Cross-Section 500X

Longitudinal View 500X

Fig. 5–17 *Photomicrographs of silk fiber: cross-sectional view* (top); *longitudinal view* (bottom). *(Courtesy of American Association of Textile Chemists and Colorists.)*

In filament form, silk does not have good covering power. Before the development of strong synthetic fibers, silk was the only strong filament and silk fabrics were often treated with metallic salts such as tin, a process called *weighting,* to give the fabric better drape, covering power, and dye absorption. Unfortunately, these weighted silks age quickly. Silk has *scroop,* a natural rustle, which can be increased by treatment with an organic acid such as acetic or tartaric acid.

DURABILITY Silk has moderate abrasion resistance. Because of its end uses and cost, silk seldom receives harsh abrasion.

Silk is one of the strongest natural fibers, with a tenacity of 4.5 g/d dry. It may lose up to 20 percent of its strength when wet. Its strength is excellent in relation to its fineness.

Silk has a breaking elongation of 20 percent. It is not as elastic as wool because there are no cross-linkages to retract the molecular chains. When silk is elongated by 2 percent, its elasticity is only 90 percent. Thus, when silk is stretched a small amount it does not return to its original length, but remains slightly stretched.

COMFORT Silk has good absorbency with a moisture regain of 11 percent. Silk may develop static cling. This is primarily a result of the smoothness of the fibers and yarns and the fabric weight. Silk fabrics are comfortable in summer. Like wool, silk is a poor conductor of heat so that it is comfortably warm in the winter. The weight of a fabric is important in heat conductivity—sheer fabrics, possible with filament silk, are cool whereas heavy fabrics are warm. Silk is smooth and soft and thus not irritating to the skin. The density of silk is 1.25 g/cc, which gives strength and light weight to silk products. Weighted silk is not as durable as regular silk and wrinkles more readily.

APPEARANCE RETENTION Silk has moderate resistance to wrinkling. This is related to silk's elastic recovery. Because the fiber does not recover well from elongation, it does not resist wrinkling as well as some other fibers.

Silk fibers do not shrink. Because the molecular chains are not easily distorted, silk swells a small amount when wet. Fabrics made from true crepe yarns shrink if laundered, but this is caused by the yarn structure, not the fiber content.

CARE Dry cleaning solvents do not damage silk. In fact, dry cleaning often is recommended for silk items because of yarn structures, dyes that have poor fastness to water or laundering, or product or fabric-construction methods. Some washable silk items can be laundered in a mild detergent solution with gentle agitation. Since silk may lose up to 20 percent of its strength when wet, care should be taken with wet silks to avoid adding any unnecessary stress. Silk items should be pressed after laundering. Pure dye silks should be ironed damp with a press cloth. Wild silks should be dry cleaned and ironed dry to avoid losing sericin, which gives the fabric its body. Silk furnishings are generally cleaned by the dry extraction method.

Silk may water-spot easily so care should be taken to avoid this problem. Before hand or machine washing, test in an obscure place of the item to make sure the dye or finish does not water-spot.

Silk can be damaged and yellowed by strong soaps or detergent and high temperatures. Chlorine bleaches should be avoided. However, bleaches of hydrogen peroxide and sodium perborate are safe to use if the directions are followed carefully.

Silk is resistant to dilute mineral acids and organic acids, but it is damaged by strong alkaline solutions such as strong detergent solutions. A crepe-like surface effect may be created by the shrinking action of some acids.

Silk is weakened and yellowed by exposure to sunlight and perspiration. Many dyes used to color silk are damaged by sunlight and perspiration. Furnishing fabrics of silk should be protected from direct exposure to sunlight.

Silks may be attacked by insects, especially carpet beetles. Items should be stored clean because soil may attract insects that do not normally attack silk.

Weighted silks deteriorate even under good storage conditions and are especially likely to break at the folds. Historic items often exhibit a condition known as *shattered silk*, in which the weighted silk is disintegrating. The process cannot be reversed.

Table 5-5 summarizes silk's performance in apparel and furnishing fabrics.

Uses of Silk

Silk has a drape, luster, and texture that may be imitated by synthetic fibers, but cannot be duplicated exactly. Because of its unique properties

Table 5–5 Summary of the Performance of Silk in Apparel and Furnishing Fabrics

Aesthetic	*Variable*
Luster	Beautiful and soft
Durability	*High*
Abrasion resistance	Moderate
Tenacity	High for natural fibers
Elongation	Moderate
Comfort	*High*
Absorbency	High
Thermal retention	Good
Appearance Retention	*Moderate*
Resiliency	Moderate
Dimensional stability	High
Elastic recovery	Moderate
Recommended Care	Dry Clean (apparel) or dry extraction clean (furnishings)

and high cost, silk is used primarily in apparel and furnishing items. Other factors that contribute to the continued popularity of silk are its appearance, comfort, and strength. Silk is extremely versatile and can be used to create a variety of fabrics from sheer, gossamer chiffons to heavy, beautiful brocades and velvets. Because of silk's absorbency, it is appropriate for warm weather wear and active sportswear. Because of its low heat conductivity, it is also appropriate for cold weather wear. Silk underwear, socks, and leggings have become popular due to silk's soft hand, good absorbency, and wicking characteristics. Of course, silk remains an important fiber in apparel designers' collections.

Silk and silk blends are equally important in furnishings. Silk blends are often used in window treatment and upholstery fabrics because of the soft luster and drape silk contributes. Silk is also frequently used by itself in upholstery, wall covering fabrics, and wall hangings. Some designers are so enamored with silk that they drape entire rooms in silk. Wild and duppioni silks are used to cover ceilings and walls because of their texture and drape. Occasionally, beautiful and expensive hand-made rugs are made of silk. Liners for sleeping bags and bed sheets of silk help keep the user warm and feel soft and luxurious next to the skin.

Silk has limited application beyond apparel and furnishings. However, silk is used in the medical field for sutures and prosthetic arteries.

IDENTIFICATION OF NATURAL PROTEIN FIBERS

Natural protein fibers can be identified with a microscope fairly easily. The wool fibers have scales that are visible along the edge and if the fiber is white or pastel, may be seen throughout the length of the fiber. It is difficult to distinguish among the wool fibers because of their similar appearance. For example, it is easy to distinguish wool from cotton, but it is difficult to distinguish sheep's wool from camel hair. Silk can be identified with the microscope, but with greater difficulty. Since silk is a natural fiber, its surface is not as regular as that of most manufactured fibers. The trilobal cross section may not be apparent, but the fiber has slight bumps or other irregularities. Natural protein fibers are soluble in sodium hypochlorite. In the burn test, these fibers smell like burning hair. However, the odor is so strong that a very small percentage of protein fiber produces a noticeable hair odor. Hence, the burning test is not reliable for blends, nor will it distinguish among the protein fibers.

KEY TERMS

Hygroscopic
Wool
Merino
Raw or grease wool
Scoured or clean wool
Grading wool
Sorting wool
Garnetted
Recycled wool
Virgin wool
Lamb's wool
Medulla
Cortex
Crimp
Natural bicomponent fiber
Scales
Felting
Keratin
Mohair
Qiviut
Angora

Camel's hair
Cashmere
Llama
Alpaca
Vicuña
Guanaco
Silk
Sericulture
Sericin
Reeling
Filature
Raw silk
Silk-in-the-gum
Silk noils
Wild silk
Tussah silk
Duppioni silk
Fibroin
Weighting
Scroop

QUESTIONS

1. Describe the similarities in the properties common to all protein fibers.
2. For the products listed below, describe the properties of wool and silk that some manufactured fibers attempt to duplicate.
   carpeting
   blanket
   blouse
   interview suit (wool)
   interview suit (silk)
3. How is the processing of wool and silk different?
4. Identify a natural protein fiber that would be appropriate for each of the end uses listed below and identify the properties that help make it appropriate for that end use:
   area rug in front of a fireplace
   upholstery for corporate boardroom
   suit for business travel
   tie with small print pattern
5. To what fiber aspects are the differences in properties among the natural protein fibers attributed?

SUGGESTED READINGS

Grayson, Martin, ed. (1984). *Encyclopedia of Textiles, Fibers, and Nonwoven Fabrics.* New York: John Wiley & Sons.

LaBarthe, Jules (1975). *Elements of Textiles.* New York: Macmillan.

Rheinberg, L. (1991). "The Romance of Silk," *Textile Progress*, 21 (4), pp. 1–43.

Trotman, E.R. (1984). *Dyeing and Chemical Technology of Textile Fibers*, 6th ed. New York: John Wiley & Sons.

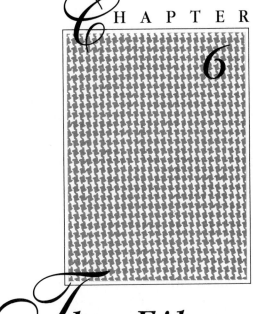

C H A P T E R

6

The Fiber Manufacturing Process

OBJECTIVES

- To understand the concepts involved in producing manufactured fibers.

- To relate production processes to fiber modifications.

- To understand the relationship between fiber engineering for end use and fiber modifications.

- To understand common fiber modifications, how they are achieved, and the functions they serve.

- To understand the differences and similarities among natural and manufactured fibers.

*M*ANUFACTURED FIBERS ARE PRODUCED TO satisfy a market or supply a special need. The first manufactured fibers made it possible for consumers to have silklike fabrics at low cost. Synthetic fibers give consumers fabrics with improved properties unlike natural fiber fabrics.

In 1664, Robert Hooke suggested that if the proper liquid were squeezed through a small aperture and allowed to congeal, a fiber like silk might be produced. In 1889, the first successful manufactured fiber (made in 1884 from a solution of cellulose by a Frenchman, Count de Chardonnet), was shown at the Paris Exhibition. In 1910, rayon fibers were commercially produced in the United States. Acetate was produced in 1924. By 1939, the first noncellulosic, or synthetic, fiber—nylon—was made. Since that time, many more generic fibers and modifications or variants of these generic fibers have appeared on the market.

Fiber manufacturers use generic names to identify particular fibers, whereas trade names are companies' names for their fibers, used to promote and market a company's fibers over competitors' fibers. The increasing number of new fiber names appearing on labels can create a great deal of confusion for the consumer. See Table 6-1 for a list of generic fibers.

The impact of manufactured fibers on the consumer and the industrial market has been far beyond original predictions. The first manufactured fibers were aimed at people who could not afford the expensive natural fibers, like silk. Yet manufactured fibers have caused tremendous changes in the way people live and the things they can do. End uses that simply were not possible or practical are now commonplace due to the use of manufactured fibers. For example, many current fashions are directly related to manufactured fibers. The current combination of fit and performance found in spandex and nylon biking shorts, swimwear, and leotards cannot be made with any natural fiber or any combination of natural fibers. The common use of carpeting in homes, businesses, and other facilities is related to the low cost and good performance characteristics of nylon, olefin, and other manufactured fibers. Carpets of wool are too expensive and do not possess the characteristics appropriate for many current uses of carpet. The use of manufactured fibers in roadbed underlays, communication cables, and replacement body parts are examples of end uses that are not possible with natural fibers. These manufactured fibers have literally revolutionized daily life!

Manufactured fibers possess the unique ability to be engineered for specific end uses. For that reason, many of these fibers are highly versatile and found in an amazing array of products. Our understanding of polymer chemistry and fiber production has expanded to the point that many inherent problems in the original fiber can be overcome through changes in the polymer, production, or finishing steps.

With current lifestyles, it is simply not possible to return to the use of natural fibers only. Table 6-2 summarizes the use of manufactured fibers in the U.S. in 1989. Worldwide, manufactured fibers comprise 46 percent of the market. In the U.S., that number is over 64 percent; 41 percent for apparel, 76 percent for furnishings, and 96 percent for industrial products. Those numbers are especially amazing when one realizes that the manufactured fiber industry uses only 1 percent of the nation's oil and natural gas supplies. The industry is highly efficient. One 300-acre polyester facility can produce as much fiber as 600,000 acres of cotton.

Table 6–1 **Manufactured Fibers: Generic Names**

Cellulosic	Noncellulosic or Synthetic		Mineral
Acetate	Acrylic	Nytril*	Glass
(Triacetate*)	Anidex*	Olefin	Metallic
Rayon	Aramid	PBI	
	Azlon*	Polyester	
	(Lastrile*)	Rubber	
	Modacrylic	Saran	
	Novoloid	Spandex	
	Nylon	Sulfar	
		Vinal*	
		Vinyon*	

*Not produced in the United States

FIBER SPINNING

It took many years to develop the first *fiber spinning* solutions and devise spinnerets to convert the

Table 6–2 Use of Manufactured Fibers

Use category	Percentage
Sheer hosiery	96
Socks/anklets	48
Sweaters	61
Craft yarn	89
Underwear	22
Lingerie	55
Robes, etc.	66
Pile fabrics	100
Linings	74
Lace apparel	66
Narrow fabrics, apparel	62
Top weight apparel	39
Bottom weight apparel	32
Other apparel	63
Bedspreads, etc.	45
Blankets	45
Sheets	43
Towels	5
Window treatments	54
Upholstery	56
Carpet	99
Other furnishings	84
Tires	99
Hose	95
Belting	79
Medical, surgical uses	85
Nonwovens	100
Fiberfill	100
Felts	65
Filtration	92
Rope, etc.	90
Sewing thread	69
Reinforcement, paper	65
Reinforcement, plastic	41
Coated fabrics	78
Transportation fabrics	92
Narrow fabrics, industrial	86
Bags, bagging	92
Miscellaneous	87

solutions into filaments. The first solutions were made by treating cellulose so it would dissolve in certain substances. It was not until the 1920s and 1930s that we first learned how to build long–chain molecules from simple substances.

All manufactured fiber spinning processes are based on these three general steps.

1. Preparing a viscous or syrupy dope.

2. Extruding the dope through a spinneret to form a fiber.

3. Solidifying the fiber by coagulation, evaporation, or cooling.

The *raw material* may be a natural product such as cellulose or protein, or it may be chemicals that are synthesized into resins. These raw materials are made into solutions by dissolving them with chemicals or by melting. The solution is referred to as the *spinning solution* or *dope*.

Extrusion is a very important part of the spinning process. It consists of forcing or pumping the spinning solution through the tiny holes of a spinneret.

A *spinneret* is a small thimblelike nozzle (Figure 6-1). Rayon is spun through a spinneret made of platinum—one of the few metals that will withstand the action of acids and alkalis. Acetate and other fibers are extruded through stainless–steel spinnerets. Spinnerets are costly—as much as $1,000 each—and new developments are closely guarded secrets. The making of the tiny holes is the critical part of the process. Fine hairlike instruments or laser beams are used. Ordinarily the holes are round, but many other shapes are used for special fiber types (see Figure 3-4).

Each hole in the spinneret forms one fiber. *Filament fibers* are spun from spinnerets with 350 holes or less. Together these fibers make a filament yarn. *Filament tow* is an untwisted rope of thousands of fibers. This rope is made by putting together the fibers from 100 or more spinnerets, each of which may have as many as three thousand holes (Figure 6-2). The tow is crimped and is then ready to be converted into staple by cutting or breaking to the desired length. (See Chapter 10 for methods of breaking filament tow into staple.)

Spinning Methods

Spinning is done by five different methods, which are compared briefly in Figure 6-3. Details of the methods are given in later chapters.

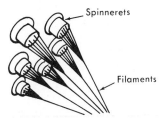

Fig. 6–1 *Spinnerets. (Courtesy of AVTEX Fibers, Inc.)*

Fig. 6–2 *Collecting fibers from several spinnerets to make a rope, called filament tow, which will be cut into staple fiber.*

The production program for a new fiber is long and expensive, and millions of dollars must be invested before any profit can be realized. First, a research program is planned to develop the new fiber. Then a pilot plant is built to translate laboratory procedures to commercial production. This pilot plant may produce as much as 5 million pounds of fiber, which are tested to determine and evaluate end uses. When the fiber is ready, a commercial plant is built.

A patent on the process gives the producer 17 years of exclusive right to the use of the process—time to recover the initial cost and make a profit. The price per pound during this time is high, but it drops later. The patent owner can license other producers to use the process. Continuing research and development programs correct any problems that arise and produce new fiber types modified for special end uses.

COMMON FIBER MODIFICATIONS

One advantage of the manufactured fibers is that each step of the production process can be pre-cisely controlled to "tailor" or modify the parent fiber. These modifications are the result of a producer's continuing research program to correct any limitations, explore the potential of its fibers, and develop properties that will give greater versatility in the end uses of the fibers.

The *parent fiber* is the fiber in its simplest form. It is often sold as a "commodity fiber" by generic name only, without benefit of a trade name. The parent fiber has been called by the following names: regular, basic, standard, conventional, or first–generation fiber.

Modifications of the parent fiber are usually sold under a brand or trade name. Modifications may also be referred to as types, variants, or *x* generation fibers where the *x* could be any number. Some fiber producers are identifying ninth and tenth generation modifications.

The following are *fiber modifications* of the second generation:

1. Modification of fiber size and shape: cross section, thick and thin, hollow
2. Modification of molecular structure and crystallinity: high tenacity, low pilling, low elongation
3. Additives to polymer or fiber solution: cross dye, antistatic, sunlight resistance, fire retardant
4. Modifications of spinning procedures: crimp, fiberfill

Complex modifications have been engineered to combine two polymers as separate entities within a single fiber or yarn. These have been referred to as third–generation fibers:

1. Bicomponent fibers
2. Blended filament yarns

Fiber Size

Fiber size is generally easy to control. The simplest way is by changing the size of the opening in the spinneret. Fiber size often dictates end use. Finer fibers, those with a denier of less than 7, are most often used for apparel. Deniers ranging from 5 to 25 are used in furnishings. Industrial applications have the widest range of denier, ranging from deniers of 1 for transportation upholstery and sewing thread to several thousand for ropes and fishline.

A relatively new denier size to come on the market is the *microdenier*. Fibers identified as microdenier are those with deniers of less than 1.0. These

Wet Spinning: Acrylic, Rayon, Spandex

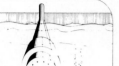

1. Raw material is dissolved by chemicals.
2. Fiber is spun into chemical bath.
3. Fiber solidifies when coagulated by bath.

Oldest process
Most complex
Weak fibers until dry
Washing, bleaching, etc., required before use

Dry Spinning:
Acetate, Acrylic, Modacrylic, Spandex, Triacetate, Vinyon

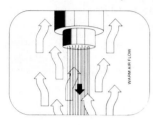

1. Resin solids are dissolved by solvent.
2. Fiber is spun into warm air.
3. Fiber solidifies by evaporation of the solvent.

Direct process
Solvent required
Solvent recovery required
No washing, etc., required

Melt Spinning: Nylon, Olefin, Polyester, Saran

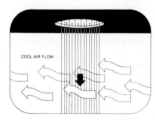

1. Resin solids are melted in autoclave.
2. Fiber is spun out into the air.
3. Fiber solidifies on cooling.

Least expensive
Direct process
High spinning speeds
No solvent, washing, etc., required
Fibers shaped like spinneret hole

Dispersion or Emulsion Spinning: Polytetrafluoroethylene

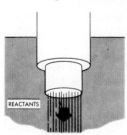

1. Polymer is dispersed as fine particles in a carrier.
2. Dispersed polymer is extruded through a spinneret and coalesced by heating.
3. Carrier is removed by heating or dissolving.

Expensive
Used only for those fibers that are insoluble
Carrier required

Reaction Spinning: Spandex

1. Monomers are placed in solution.
2. Polymerization occurs during extrusion through spinneret system of reactants.
3. Solvents may be used to control fiber size.

Simple recovery of solvents
Less expensive than dry spinning for spandex
Difficult to get uniform, light fibers

Fig. 6–3 *Methods of spinning manufactured fibers. (First three drawings courtesy of American Fiber Manufacturers Association, Inc.)*

fibers tend to range from 0.5 to 0.8 denier per filament (*dpf*). A yarn of microdenier fibers or microfibers may have as many as four times more fibers than a regular fiber yarn of the same size. Microdenier fibers currently on the market include polyester, nylon, acrylic, and rayon. These fibers are used in apparel and furnishings. Claims made for products of these fibers include softer hand and drape, more silklike characteristics, greater comfort, and water repellency.

Microfibers may be present by themselves in fabrics or in blends with natural or other manufactured fibers. In blends, at least 40 percent microfiber is needed to retain the microfiber's characteristics. These fibers are used in coats, blouses, suits, sleepwear, upholstery, window treatments, and wall coverings. The introduction of these fibers created problems in production. Yarn spinning frames, looms and sewing machines required modifications in order to handle the very small fibers. Modifications in dyeing and finishing techniques were also required. These fibers have met with great enthusiasm from both designers and consumers, in spite of their higher price.

Larger sized fibers are frequently used where greater strength, abrasion resistance, and resiliency are required. For example, carpet fiber may have deniers in the range of 15 to 24 to improve the resiliency of the generic fiber. Higher denier fibers resist crushing better than lower denier fibers.

Fiber Shape

SOLID FIBERS Changing the cross-sectional shape is the easiest way to alter the mechanical and aesthetic properties of a fiber. This is usually done by changing the shape of the spinneret hole to produce the fiber shape desired. All kinds of shapes are possible: flat, trilobal, quadralobal, pentalobal, triskelion, cruciform, cloverleaf, and alphabet shapes such as Y and T (see Figure 3-4).

The *flat shape* was one of the first variations produced. "Crystal" acetate and "sparkling" nylon were ribbonlike fibers that were extruded through a long, narrow spinneret hole. Flat fibers tend to catch and reflect light much as a mirror does, so fabrics have a glint or sparkle.

The *trilobal shape* has been widely used in both nylon and polyester fibers (Figure 6-4). It is spun through a spinneret with three triangularly arranged slits. The trilobal shape produces a fabric with a beautiful silklike hand (depending on end-use requirements), subtle opacity, soil-hiding capacity,

Fig. 6–4 Stereoscan photograph of trilobal nylon. (Courtesy of E. I. du Pont de Nemours & Company.)

built-in bulk without weight, heightened wicking action, silklike sheen and color, crush resistance in heavy deniers, and good textured crimp.

Other fiber shapes that produce similar characteristics are *triskelion* (a three-sided configuration similar to a boat propeller), *pentalobal* (see Figure 6-5), *octolobal*, and *Y-shaped.*

Thick-and-thin fiber types have variations in diameter along their length as a result of uneven drawing or stretching after spinning. When woven into cloth, these yarns give a duppioni silklike or linenlike texture. The thick areas, or nubs, dye a deeper color to create interesting tone-on-tone color effects. Many surface textures are possible by changing the size and length of the nubs or slubs.

HOLLOW OR MULTICELLULAR FIBER TYPES The hair or fur of many animals contains air cells that provide insulation in cold weather. The feathers of birds are hollow to give them buoyancy. Similar air cells and hollow filaments are possible in manufactured fibers by the use of gas-forming compounds added to the spinning solution, by air injection at the jet face as the fiber is forming, or by the shape of the spinneret holes.

Hollow melt-spun fibers can be formed by pyrolizing a portion of the polymer flowing to the spinneret to form gas and then extruding the bubble containing polymer as hollow filaments. The spinneret hole can be shaped to produce hollow fibers. When extruded through a C-shaped hole, the fiber closes immediately. Other spinneret holes spin the fiber as two halves that immediately close to make

Fig. 6–5 *Trevira® polyester pentalobal cross section 312×. (Courtesy of Hoechst Calanese.)*

the hollow fiber (see Figure 6-6). Examples of trade names of hollow fibers include Hollofil and Quallofil by Du Pont.

Molecular Structure and Crystallinity

High tenacity fibers are produced by stretching fibers. Fiber strength is increased by (1) drawing or stretching the fiber to align or orient the molecules, thus strengthening the intermolecular forces, and/or by (2) chemical modification of the fiber polymer to increase the degree of polymerization. These procedures will be discussed in more detail in Chapters 7 and 8.

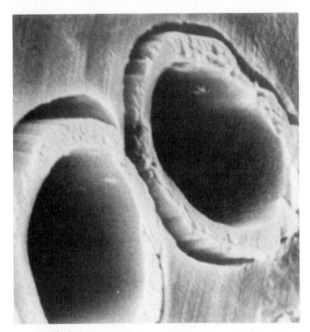

Fig. 6–6 *Cross section of Hollofil polyester. (Courtesy of E. I. du Pont de Nemours & Company.)*

Low-pilling fibers are engineered to reduce the flex life by reducing the molecular weight as measured in terms of intrinsic viscosity. When flex-abrasion resistance is reduced, the fiber pills break off almost as soon as they are formed and the fabric retains its smooth appearance. These low-pilling fibers are not as strong as other types but are durable enough for apparel uses and are particularly suited to soft knitting yarns. (Review the discussion of molecular weight in Chapter 3.)

Binder staple is a semidull, crimped polyester with a very low melting point. (Melting point relates to molecular structure.) Binder staple develops a thermoplastic bond with other fibers under heat and pressure. It sticks at 165°F and shrinks 55-75 percent at 200°F. Type 450 Fortrel is a fiber of this type.

Low-elongation fiber types are designed as reinforcing fibers to increase the strength and abrasion resistance of weak fibers blended with stronger fibers as in cotton/polyester blends. Low elongation results from changing the balance of tenacity and extension. High-tenacity fibers have lower elongation properties. End uses are mainly for work clothing and other items that get hard wear.

Additives to the Polymer or Spinning Solution

DELUSTERING The basic fiber usually reflects light from its surface. It is referred to as a *bright fiber*. (Note that here bright refers to high luster, not intense color.) To *deluster* a fiber, titanium dioxide—a white pigment—is added to the spinning solution before the fiber is extruded. In some cases, the titanium dioxide can be mixed in at an earlier stage, while the resin polymer is being formed. The degree of luster can be controlled by varying the amount of delusterant, producing dull or semidull fibers. Figure 6-7 shows three cones of yarn of different lusters.

Delustered fibers can be identified microscopically by what appear to be black spots (Figure 6-7). The particles of pigment absorb light or prevent reflection of light. Absorbed light causes degradation, or tendering, of the fiber. For this reason, bright fibers that reflect light suffer less light damage and are better for use in window treatment fabrics. The initial strength of a delustered fiber is less than that of a bright fiber. Rayon, for example, is 3-5 percent weaker when it is delustered.

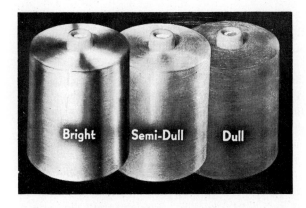

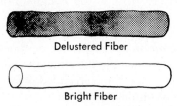

Delustered Fiber

Bright Fiber

Fig. 6–7 (Top) *Rayon yarns. (Courtesy of AVTEX Fibers, Inc.)* (Bottom) *Fibers as they would look under a microscope.*

SOLUTION DYEING OR MASS PIGMENTATION

Solution dyeing, or *mass pigmentation,* was developed in response to the gas-fading of many dyes used to dye acetate. *Solution dyeing* is the addition of colored pigments or dyes to the spinning solution. Thus, the fiber is colored when it emerges from the spinneret. These fibers are also referred to as *solution dyed, mass pigmented, dope dyed, spun dyed,* or *producer colored.* If the color is added before the fiber hardens, the term *gel dying* may be used. Solution dyeing offers the potential of providing color permanence that is not obtainable in any other way. The lightfastness and washfastness are unchanged for the life of the item. Because the color is uniformly distributed throughout the fiber, crocking and other color changes with use are not problems.

Because of the difficulty in obtaining a truly black dye that has reasonable colorfastness properties, black pigments are usually the first ones to be used. Other colors are produced as suitable colorfast pigments are developed.

Solution-dyed fibers cost more per pound than uncolored fibers. This difference is offset later by the cost of yarn or piece (fabric) dyeing. The solution-dyed fibers are used in all kinds of end uses, such as upholstery, window treatments, and apparel. One disadvantage of the solution-dyed fibers is that the manufacturer must carry a large inventory to be able to fill orders quickly. The manufacturer is also less able to adjust to fashion changes in color, because it is not possible to strip color from these fibers and redye them.

WHITENERS AND BRIGHTENERS *Whiteners* and *brighteners* are added to the spinning solution to make whiter fibers or fibers that resist yellowing. The additive used is an optical bleach or fluorescent dye that causes a whiter light to be reflected from the cloth. These whiteners are permanent in washing and dry cleaning. They are an advantage in many items because they eliminate the necessity for bleaching.

DYE AFFINITY Dye affinity or *cross-dyeable* fibers are very different from solution-dyed fibers. Solution-dyed fibers have colored pigment added to the spinning solution, so they are colored as they emerge from the spinneret. Dye affinity fibers are not colored when they emerge from the spinneret.

Cross-dyeable fibers are made by incorporating dye-accepting chemicals into the molecular structure. Some of the parent fibers are nondyeable; others have poor acceptance of certain classes of dyes. The cross-dyeable types were developed to correct this limitation. The dye affinity fibers are far easier to dye than their parent fibers.

ANTISTATIC FIBER TYPES Static is a result of the flow of electrons. Fibers conduct electricity according to how readily electrons move in them. If static builds up in a fiber so that it has an excess of electrons, it is negatively charged and it is attracted to something that is positively charged—something that has a deficiency of electrons. This attraction is illustrated by the way clothing clings to the body. Water dissipates static. Because the heat-sensitive fibers, especially the synthetics, have such low water absorbency, static charges build up rapidly during cold, dry weather, and they are slow to dissipate. If the fibers can be made wettable, the static charges will dissipate quickly and there will be no annoying static buildup.

The *antistatic fiber types* give durable protection because the fiber is made wettable by incorporating an antistatic compound—a chemical conductor—in the fiber as an integral part of it. The compound is added to the fiber-polymer raw material so that it is evenly distributed throughout the fiber dope or spinning solution. It changes the fiber's hydrophobic nature to a hydrophilic one and raises the moisture regain so that static is dissipated more quickly. The moisture content of the air should be kept high enough to provide moisture for absorption—even cotton will build up static if the air is dry enough. Static control is also achieved by incorporating a conductive filament into the filament (Figure 6–8). Table 6–3 lists trade names and end uses of some antistatic fiber variants.

The soil-resistant benefits of the antistatic fiber types are outstanding. The antistatic fibers retard soiling by minimizing the attraction and retention of dirt particles, and the opacity and luster in the yarn have soil-hiding properties. Soil redisposition in laundry is dramatically reduced. Oily stains, even motor oils, are released easily.

SUNLIGHT-RESISTANT FIBERS Ultraviolet light causes fiber degeneration as well as color fading. When ultraviolet light is absorbed, the damage results from an oxidation–reduction reaction between the radiant energy and the fiber or fiber dye. Stabilizers such as nitrogenous compounds may be added to the dope to increase light resistance. These stabilizers must be carefully selected for the fiber-dye combination. Estron SLR is a *sunlight-resistant* acetate fiber. These SLR fibers are especially important for window treatments and other furnishings in glass office buildings. SLR fibers are also important for car interiors. Delustered fibers are more sensitive to sunlight than bright fibers.

FLAME-RESISTANT FIBERS *Flame-resistant fibers* give better protection to consumers than do topical flame-retardant finishes (see Chapter 18). Some manufactured fibers are inherently flame retardant because of their chemical composition. These include aramid, novolid, modacrylic, glass, PBI, saran, sulfar, and vinyon. Other manufactured fibers can be modified by changing their polymer struc-

Fig. 6–8   Antistatic polyester. (Courtesy of E. I. du Pont de Nemours & Company.)

ture or by adding water-insoluble compounds to the spinning solution. These fiber modifications make the fibers inherently flame resistant. The fibers vary in their resistance to flame.

Fiber Spinning Procedure

When producers started to make staple fiber, mechanical crimping was done to broken filaments and later to filament tow to make the fibers more cohesive and thus easier to spin into yarns. Other techniques were developed to give permanent crimp to rayon and acetate and to provide bulk or stretch to all fibers—filaments as well as staple.

Table 6–3   Antistatic Fiber Variants

Parent Fiber	Trademark	Fiber Modification	End Use	Producer
Nylon	Antron III	Three filaments of carbon-black core surrounded by sheath of nylon	Apparel	Du Pont
Nylon	Ultron	Conjugate spun 95 percent nylon 6,6 and 5 percent nylon/carbon-black polymer stripe	Carpets	Monsanto
Nylon	Hydrofil		Apparel	Allied-Signal
Polyester	Dacron III (Figure 6–8)	Polymeric conductive core	Carpets	Du Pont

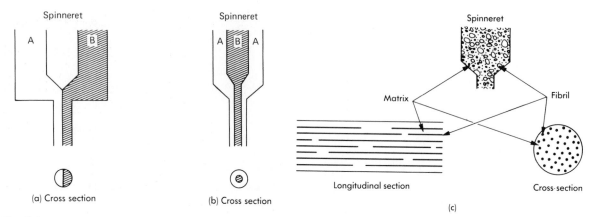

Fig. 6–9 *Bicomponent fiber structure: (a) bilateral; (b) core-sheath; (c) matrix-fibril.*

Crimping of fibers is important in many end uses for cover and loft in bulky knits, blankets, carpets, battings for quilted items, pillows, and the like, and for stretch and economy in hosiery and sportswear.

For wet spun fibers, crimp can be produced by coagulating the fiber in a bath of lower acid and higher salt concentration. A skin forms around the fiber and then bursts. A thinner skin forms over the rupture. The crimp develops when the fiber is immersed in water. Melt-spun, helically (spiral) crimped fibers are produced by cooling one side of the fiber faster than the other side as the fiber is extruded. This uneven cooling causes a curl to form in the fiber. The same effect can be achieved by heating one side of the fiber during the stretching or drawing process. This helical crimp has more springiness than the conventional mechanical sawtooth crimp. These fibers are used where high levels of compressional resistance and recovery are needed.

Third–Generation Fiber Types

BICOMPONENT FIBERS A *bicomponent fiber* is a fiber consisting of two polymers that are chemically different, physically different, or both. If the two components would fall into two different generic classes, the term *bicomponent-bigeneric* may be used. Bicomponent fibers may be of several types. Bilateral fibers are spun with the two polymers side–by–side. In core-sheath fibers, one polymer is surrounded or encircled by another polymer. In matrix-fibril fibers, short fibrils of one polymer are embedded in another polymer (see Figure 6-9).

The original discovery that the two sides of a fiber can react differently when wet was made during studies of wool in 1886. In 1953, it was discovered that the difference in reaction was the result of the bicomponent nature of wool, which results from a difference in growth rate and in chemical composition. This differential behavior is used to advantage in producing bilateral bicomponent fibers with latent or inherent crimp.

For example, acrylic fibers can be spun straight and made into a garment such as a sweater, which is then exposed to heat; one side of the fiber shrinks and the fiber takes on a helical crimp. The reaction of the fibers to water occurs during laundering. As the fiber gets wet, one side swells and the fiber uncrimps. As the crimp relaxes, the sweater increases in size. The crimp returns as the sweater dries and it will regain its original size if properly handled. Sweaters of this type should not be drip-dried or placed on a towel to dry because the weight of the water and the resistance of the towel prevent the sweater from regaining its original size. The correct way to dry the sweater is either to machine dry it at a low temperature or to place it on a smooth, flat surface and bunch it in to help the crimp recover.

Cordelan is a vinal/vinyon bicomponent-bigeneric flame-resistant fiber. It is made of three polymers: polyvinyl chloride, polyvinyl alcohol, and a copolymer of PVC/PVA. It is a matrix fibril-type fiber used in flame-retardant furnishings and apparel.

Table 6–4 U.S. Manufactured Fiber Capacity in Millions of Pounds in 1990*

Acetate and rayon	806
Acrylic	779
Nylon	2,358
Olefin	748
Polyester	3,989

*Source: *Chemical and Engineering News,* June 24, 1991, page 34.

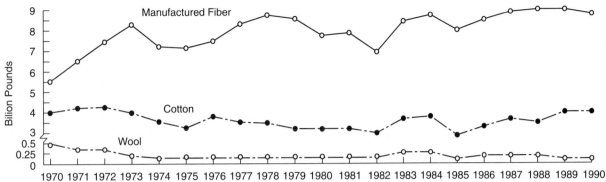

Fig. 6–10 *Domestic consumption: Manufctured fiber, cotton, and wool. (Courtesy of Textile Organon.)*

MANUFACTURED FIBER CAPACITY

In 1928, manufactured fibers accounted for 5 percent of fiber consumption in the United States; by 1990, manufactured fibers comprised over 70 percent of U.S. textile consumption. See Figure 6-10, which compares domestic consumption of manufactured fiber, cotton, and wool, and Table 6-4 which lists U.S. manufactured fiber capacity in millions of pounds.

MANUFACTURED VERSUS NATURAL FIBERS

A comparison of natural and manufactured fibers is made in Table 6-5.

Table 6–5 Comparison of Natural and Manufactured Fibers

Category	Natural	Manufactured
Production	Seasonal; stored until used	Continuous
Quality	Varies due to weather, nutrients, insects, or disease	Uniform
Uniformity	Lacking	Can be uniform or nonuniform depending on end use
Physical structure	Dependent on natural growth of plant or animal	Dependent on fiber-spinning processes and after treatments
Chemical composition and molecular strucure	Dependent on natural growth	Dependent on starting materials
Properties	Inherent; but can be changed by yarn, fabrication, and finishes	Inherent; but can be changed by varying spinning solutions and spinning conditions, fabrication, or finishes
Length	Mostly staple; only silk is avilable in filament	Any length
Versatility	Not as versatile	Versatile; changes can be made quickly
Absorbency	Highly absorbent	Most have low absorbency*
Heat sensitivity	Not heat sensitive	Most are heat sensitive**
Heat settability	Require fabric finish	Most can be heat-set*
Research, development, and promotion	By trade organizations	By individual companies as well as by trade organizations
Size	Dependent on type and variety	Any size can be produced

*Rayon and acetate are exceptions.

**Rayon is an exception.

KEY TERMS

Manufactured fiber
Fiber spinning
Dope or spinning solution
Extrusion
Spinneret
Filament fiber
Filament tow
Parent fiber
Fiber modification
Microdenier
Trilobal shape
Round cross section
Thick–and–thin fibers
Hollow fibers
High-tenacity fibers

Low-pilling fibers
Binder staple
Low-elongation fibers
Bright fibers
Delustering
Mass pigmentation
Solution dyeing
Whiteners or brighteners
Cross–dyeable fibers
Antistatic fibers
Sunlight-resistant fibers
Flame-resistant fibers
Bicomponent fibers
Bicomponent–bigeneric fibers

QUESTIONS

1. Explain, in general terms, how a manufactured fiber is produced.
2. What are the three most common spinning methods used to produce manufactured fibers? Explain briefly how they differ and give an example of a fiber produced by each of these methods.
3. What characteristics of manufactured fibers can be modified? Give an example of an end use that would benefit from each modification. How are these modifications achieved?
4. Do fiber modifications cause any negative effects? If so, what are they?
5. What modifications would be appropriate for each end use listed below?
    carpeting for restaurant floor
    window treatment for office building
    woman's slip
    child's pajamas
    fiberfill for quilt batting
    tow rope

SUGGESTED READINGS

American Fiber Manufacturers Association (1988). *Manufactured Fiber Fact Book*, Washington, D.C.: American Fiber Manufacturers Association.

Dockery, Alfred and Plott, Monte (January, 1990). "Fiber Producers in the '90s: In Style," *America's Textiles International*, pp. 50–59.

Grayson, Martin, ed. (1984). *Encyclopedia of Textiles, Fibers, and Nonwoven Fabrics*. New York: John Wiley & Sons.

CHAPTER 7

Manufactured Fibers

OBJECTIVES

- To be aware of the complex procedures necessary to produce manufactured fibers.

- To understand the properties of rayon, acetate, and azlon.

- To relate fiber properties and end use for the manufactured fibers: rayon, acetate, and azlon.

*M*ANUFACTURED FIBERS ARE PRODUCED from naturally occurring polymers. These polymers do not naturally occur as fibers; thus, processing is needed to convert them into fiber form. These fibers may also be referred to as regenerated fibers. There are two groups of manufactured or regenerated fibers: cellulosic and protein. The manufactured cellulosic fibers are more important to the textile industry and the majority of this chapter will be devoted to them. The manufactured cellulosic fibers—rayon and acetate—are used in apparel, furnishings, and industrial products. These fibers met 7.4 percent of the worldwide fiber demand in 1990. In 1990, 505 million pounds of rayon and acetate were produced in the U.S., a decline for the third straight year. In the U.S., 48 percent of the manufactured cellulosic fibers are used in apparel, 31 percent in industrial products, and 21 percent in furnishings (see Table 7-1).

A short discussion of the manufactured protein fibers will be presented at the end of this chapter.

Table 7–1 Uses of Manufactured Cellulosic Fibers (1989)

Category*	% of total fiber use
Apparel	6
Robes	11
Lingerie	3
Lining	53
Narrow fabrics/trim	4
Top weight	5
Bottom weight	3
Other	58
Furnishings	5
Sheets	1
Window treatments	19
Upholstery	7
Other	7
Industrial	6
Tires	1
Hose	7
Medical/surgical/sanitary	14
Nonwovens	21
Filtration	13
Transportation	6
Misc./consumer goods	5

*Categories where fiber usage is less than 1% are not listed.

IDENTIFICATION OF MANUFACTURED FIBERS

The manufactured cellulosic fibers appear similar microscopically. Both have striations and irregular cross sections. Rayon burns like cotton or flax. Acetate burns freely, melts, and decomposes to a black char. The solubility test is easy to use to differentiate between the two.

The *acetone test* is a specific identification test for acetate, since none of the other fibers dissolves in acetone. Figure 7-1 shows a procedure for testing the acetate content of a fabric. Use a dropper bottle, glass rod, watch glass, and tissue. Test individual yarns first to determine the presence of other fibers. Work quickly: acetone evaporates easily. The structure does not disintegrate if only a small amount of acetate is present, but as the solvent evaporates it feels sticky and stiffens permanently. If the fabric dissolves completely, it was 100 percent acetate.

RAYON

Rayon was the first manufactured cellulosic fiber. It was developed before scientists knew how molecular chains were developed in nature or how they could be produced in the laboratory. The developers of rayon were trying to make artificial silk. Frederick Schoenbein discovered in 1846 that *cellulose* pretreated with nitric acid would dissolve in a

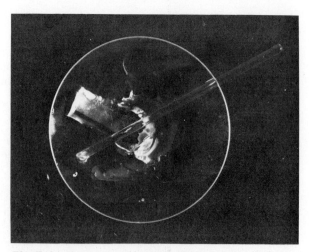

Fig. 7–1 *Acetone test for identification of acetate fiber.*

mixture of ether and alcohol, but the resulting fiber was highly explosive. In 1884 in France, Counte Hilaire de Chardonnet made the first successful rayon by changing the nitrocellulosic fiber back to cellulose. This process was dangerous and difficult; it was discontinued in 1949.

In 1890, Louis Despeissis discovered that cellulose would dissolve in a cuprammonium solution, and in 1919 J. P. Bemberg made a commercially successful cuprammonium rayon. In 1892, in England, Cross, Bevan, and Beadle developed the viscose method, which is the only process currently used in the United States.

Commercial production of viscose rayon in the United States began in 1911. The fiber was sold as artificial silk until the name "rayon" was adopted in 1924. Viscose filament fiber, the first form of the fiber to be made, was a very bright, lustrous fiber. In 1932, machinery was designed especially for making staple fiber. Large spinnerets with ten times as many holes were used; the fibers from several spinnerets were collected into tow, to be crimped and cut into staple. Rayon was originally used in crepe and linenlike apparel fabrics. The high twist that was required to make the crepe yarn reduced the bright luster of the fibers. Transparent velvet, sharkskin, tweed, challis, and chiffon were also made from these first rayons.

The physical properties of rayon remained unchanged until 1940, when high-tenacity rayon for tires was developed. It proved to be superior to cotton for that use, and by 1957 had replaced cotton in that market. After high-tenacity tire cord and heavy-denier carpet fiber were developed, 65 percent of the rayon produced went into industrial and home furnishings uses and less went into apparel.

Continued research and development led to what has been considered the greatest technological breakthrough in rayon—*high-wet-modulus rayon.* Production in the United States started in 1955. This modification expanded the use of rayon into sheets and towels. Used in blends with cotton, it stimulated a resurgence in the use of rayon in apparel.

High-wet-modulus rayon is frequently referred to as HWM rayon to distinguish it from regular or viscose rayon. In fact, HWM rayon is a viscose rayon, but in common usage viscose rayon refers to the weaker fiber. HWM rayon is also called high-performance (HP) rayon, or polynosic rayon. Polysonic is used as a generic name for HWM rayon in Europe.

Currently, there are three producers, only one of which produces filament rayon. These include BASF Corporation, Courtaulds Fibers, Inc., and North American Rayon Corporation. It is estimated that the output of rayon will not be increased because of the high cost of replacement machinery and the cost of the wet-spinning process. Rayon is no longer the inexpensive fiber it once was—now it is generally comparable in price to cotton.

Production of Rayon

In the most common method of producing rayon, purified cellulose is chemically converted to a viscous solution, forced through spinnerets into a bath, and returned to solid 100 percent cellulose filaments. This is done by the *wet-spinning* process (see Figure 6-3). Table 7-2 describes processes for making regular and high-wet-modulus rayon. The differences in the spinning process produce fibers with different properties. The high-wet-modulus process maintains maximum chain length and fibril structure as much as possible.

A *solvent-spun* rayon is being produced in Europe by Courtaulds under the name Tencel Lyocell. Courtaulds has requested a new generic classification for this rayon from the Federal Trade Commission. Courtaulds has proposed the generic name of lyocell, which is the generic term used in Europe. The cellulose polymer is dissolved in an amine oxide solvent and is spun into a weak bath of the solvent, a process referred to as solvent spinning to differentiate it from wet spinning or dry spinning. Then the fiber is washed and dried; the solvent is recovered and used again. This environmentally friendly process results in a rayon fiber that is more cottonlike than any other, including the HWM modifications. The properties of this fiber will be discussed with the other rayons later in this chapter.

Physical Structure of Rayon

Regular viscose is characterized by lengthwise lines called *striations.* The cross section is a *serrated* or indented circular shape (Figure 7-2). The shape of the fiber results from loss of the solvent during coagulation. This serrated shape is an advantage in dye absorption because of an increase in surface area. High-wet-modulus rayon has a rounder cross section (Figure 7-3). Figure 7-4 shows the round, smooth shape of Tencel rayon. Note the differences among the three.

Filament rayon yarns have from 80 to 980 filaments per yarn and vary in size from 40 to 5,000

Table 7–2   Spinning Process for Viscose Rayon

Regular or Standard		High-Wet-Modulus
1. Blotterlike sheets of purified cellulose.		1. Blotterlike sheets of purified cellulose
2. Steeped in caustic soda		2. Steeped in weaker caustic soda
3. Liquid squeezed out by rollers		3. Liquid squeezed out by rollers
4. Shredder crumbles sheets to alkali crumbs		4. Shredder crumbles sheets to alkali crumbs
5. Crumbs aged 50 hours		5. No aging
6. Crumbs treated with carbon disulfide to form cellulose xanthate, 32 percent CS_2		6. Crumbs treated with carbon disulfide to form cellulose xanthate, 39–50 percent CS_2
7. Crumbs mixed with caustic soda to form viscose solution		7. Crumbs mixed with 2.8 percent sodium hydroxide to form viscose solution
8. Solution aged 4–5 days		8. No aging
9. Solution filtered		9. Solution filtered
10. Pumped to spinneret and extruded into sulfuric acid bath		10. Pumped to spinneret and extruded into acid bath

Regular or Standard		High-Wet-Modulus
10 percent H_2SO_4	Spinning bath	1 percent H_2SO_4
16–24 percent Na_2SO_4		4–6 percent Na_2SO_4
1–2 percent $ZnSO_4$		
120 meters/minute	Spinning speed	20–30 meters/minute
45–50°C	Spinning bath temperature	25–35°C
25 percent	Filaments stretched	150–600 percent

denier. Staple fibers and tow have a range of 1.5 to 15 denier. Staple fibers are crimped mechanically or chemically (Figure 7–5).

Rayon fibers are naturally very bright, which lim-its use to more formal apparel and furnishing items. The addition of delustering pigments (see Chapter 6) remedied this problem. Solution-dyed fibers are also available.

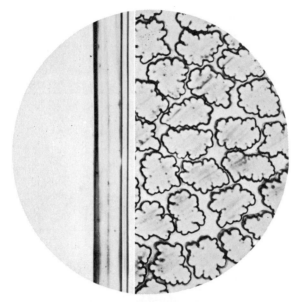

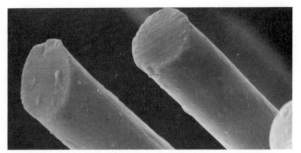

Fig. 7–4 Photomicrograph of Tencel fiber. (Courtesy of Courtaulds Fibers, Inc.)

Fig. 7–2 Photomicrographs of viscose rayon: longitudinal (left); cross-sectional (right). (Courtesy of American Association of Textile Chemists and Colorists.)

Chemical Composition and Molecular Structure of Rayon

Rayon—a manufactured fiber composed of regenerated cellulose, as well as manufactured fibers composed of regenerated cellulose in which substituents have replaced not more than 15 percent of the hydrogens of the hydroxyl groups.—Federal Trade Commission.

Rayon is 100 percent cellulose and has the same chemical composition and molecular structure as the natural cellulose found in cotton or flax, except that the rayon chains are shorter and are not as crystalline. The cellulose breaks down when the alkali cellulose and the viscose solutions are aged. When

the solution is spun into the acid bath, regeneration and coagulation take place rapidly. Stretching aligns the molecules to give strength to the filaments.

In high-wet-modulus rayon, the aging is eliminated and the molecular chains are not shortened as much. Because the acid bath is less concentrated, there is slower regeneration and coagulation so that more stretch and greater orientation of the molecules can be achieved. HWM rayon retains its microfibrilar structure. This means its performance is more similar to that of cotton than to that of regular rayon. Table 7-3 shows the similarity between cotton and the rayons.

Properties of Rayon

Rayon fibers are highly absorbent, soft, comfortable, easy to dye, and versatile. Fabrics made of rayon have a unique soft drape that designers love. Rayon is used in apparel, furnishings, and industrial products. Table 7-4 summarizes rayon's performance in apparel and furnishings.

Fig. 7–3 Stereoscan photograph of Fibro, regular rayon (left) and Vincel, high-wet-modulus rayon (right). (Courtesy of Modern Textiles magazine.)

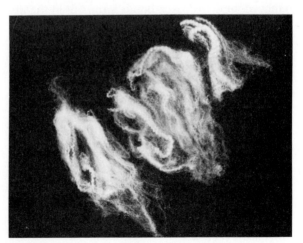

Fig. 7–5 Crimp in viscose rayon staple.

Table 7–3   **Comparison of Cotton and Rayon Types**

Properties	Cotton	Regular Rayon	High-Wet-Modulus Rayon	Tencel Rayon
Fibrils	Yes	No	Yes	Yes
Molecular chain length	10,000	300–450	450–750	—
Swelling in water, percent	6	26	18	—
Average stiffness	57–60	6–50	28–75	30
Tenacity, grams/denier				
Dry	4.0	2.0	2.5–5.0	4.3–4.7
Wet	5.0	1.0	3.0	3.8–4.2
Breaking elongation, percent	3–7	8–14	9–18	14–16

AESTHETIC Since the luster, fiber length, and diameter of the fiber can be controlled, rayon can be made into cottonlike, linenlike, wool-like, and silklike fabrics. When engineered to be used in blends, rayon can be given much the same physical characteristics as the other fiber in the blend. If it is chosen instead of cotton or to blend with cotton, rayon can give the look of mercerized long-staple cotton to a fabric. Rayon has an attractive, soft, fluid drape. Sizing may be added to increase the body and hand.

DURABILITY Regular rayon is a weak fiber that loses about 50 percent of its strength when wet. The breaking tenacity is 2.0 g/d. Rayon has a breaking elongation of 8–14 percent dry and 20 percent wet. It has the lowest elastic recovery of any fiber. All of these factors result from the amorphous regions in the fiber. Water readily enters the amorphous areas, causing the molecular chains to separate as the fiber swells, breaking the hydrogen bonds and distorting the chains. When water is removed, new hydrogen bonds form, but in the distorted state.

HWM rayon has a more crystalline and oriented structure so that the dry fiber is relatively strong. It has a breaking tenacity of 2.5–5.0 g/d, a breaking elongation of 9–18 percent dry and 20 percent wet, and an elastic recovery greater than that of cotton.

Tencel rayon performs more like cotton. Its breaking tenacity is 4.3–4.7 g/d dry and 3.8–4.2 g/d wet, only a 12 percent loss. Its breaking elongation is 14–16 percent.

COMFORT Both regular and HWM rayon make very comfortable, smooth, soft fabrics. They are absorbent, having a moisture regain of 11.5–12.5 percent. This eliminates any static. Tencel has a regain of 11.5 percent.

APPEARANCE RETENTION The resiliency of both rayons is low. This can be improved in HWM rayon fabrics by adding a durable press finish. However, the finish may decrease strength and abrasion resistance. The dimensional stability of regular rayon is low. Fabrics may shrink or stretch. The fiber is very weak when wet and has low elastic recovery. The performance of HWM rayon is better. It exhibits moderate dimensional stability that can be improved by shrinkage-control finishes. The fiber is not likely to stretch out of shape and elastic recov-

Table 7–4   **Summary of the Performance of Rayon in Apparel and Furnishing Fabrics**

	Regular Rayon	HWM Rayon
Aesthetic	*Variable*	*Variable*
Durability	*Low*	*Moderate*
Abrasion resistance	Low	Moderate
Tenacity	Low	Moderate
Elongation	Moderate	Low
Comfort	*Excellent*	*Excellent*
Absorbency	High	Excellent
Thermal retention	Low	Low
Appearance Retention	*Low*	*Moderate*
Resiliency	Low	Low
Dimensional stability	Low	Moderate
Elastic recovery	Low	Moderate
Recommended care	Dry clean	Machine wash Dry clean

ery is moderate. Tencel rayon has better appearance retention than regular rayon.

CARE Regular rayon fabrics have limited washability because of the low strength of the fibers when wet. Unless resin–treated, rayon fabrics have a tendency to shrink progressively. This shrinkage cannot be controlled by finishes. Regular rayon fabrics generally should be dry cleaned. Sizings added to increase the body and hand may water-spot or streak.

HWM and Tencel rayon fabrics have greater washability. They have stability equal to cotton and strength equal to or better than cotton; they can be mercerized and finished to minimize shrinkage; and they wrinkle less than regular rayon in washing and drying.

The chemical properties of rayon are similar to those of the other cellulosic fibers. They are harmed by acids, are resistant to dilute alkalis, and are not affected by organic solvents. They can be safely dry cleaned. Rayon is attacked by silverfish and mildew.

Rayon is not greatly harmed by sunlight. It is not thermoplastic and thus can withstand a fairly high temperature for pressing. Rayon burns readily, like cotton.

Uses of Rayon

Rayon is mostly used in woven fabrics, especially in apparel and furnishing products. Antique–satin drapery fabrics in a blend of rayon and acetate continue to be a classic fabric for interior decoration.

The second most important use of rayon is in nonwoven fabrics, where absorbency is important. Items include industrial wipes; medical supplies, including bandages; diapers; sanitary napkins and tampons. These disposable products are biodegradable.

Types and Kinds of Rayon

Table 7–5 summarizes varieties of rayon on the market. The only way to determine an HWM or solvent spun rayon is by the trade name. Unfortunately, rayon producers have not used these trade names as a marketing tool with consumers.

Table 7–5   Types and Kinds of Rayon

Rayon	Trademark	Producer	Uses
Staple fiber	Fibro	Courtaulds	Apparel and furnishings
	Zantrel	BASF	
Filament, staple, tow	Narco	North American Rayon	Apparel and furnishings
Solution dyed	Fibro	Courtaulds	Furnishings and industrial
	Jetspun	BASF	
	Kolorbon	BASF	
	Skybloom	BASF	
Acid dyeable	Enkrome	BASF	Apparel and furnshings
	Fibro DD	Courtaulds	
Varied cross-section	Enkaire	BASF	Apparel
	Viloft	Courtaulds	
Intermediate or high tenacity	Hi-Narco	North American Rayon	Industrial
	Super-Narco	North American Rayon	
	I.T.	BASF	
	Fibro HT	Courtaulds	
High-wet-modulus	Polynosic	BASF	Apparel and furnishings
	Vincel	Courtaulds	
	Zantrel	BASF	
Optically brightened	Super White	BASF	All
High absorbency	Absorbit	BASF	Sanitary supplies
Adhesive-treated yarns	Beau-grip	North American Rayon	Industrial
Hollow filament	Viloft		
Solvent-spun rayon	Tencel	Courtaulds	Apparel and furnishings
Microfibers	Zantrel	BASF	Apparel and furnishings
	2001	Courtaulds	Apparel and furnishings

ACETATE

Acetate originated in Europe. Using a technique that produced a spinning solution for a silklike fiber, the Dreyfus brothers experimented with acetate in Switzerland. They went to England during World War I and perfected the acetate dope as a varnish for airplane wings. After the war, they perfected the process of making acetate fibers. Acetate was the second manufactured fiber produced in the United States; production began here in 1924.

More problems had to be solved with the acetate process than with the rayon processes. Acetate is a different chemical compound. Primary acetate (*triacetate*), contains no hydroxyl groups; modified or secondary acetate (acetate fiber) has only a few hydroxyl groups. Because of the unique chemical nature of the fibers, they could not be dyed with any existing dyes. Disperse dyes were developed especially for acetate and triacetate.

Acetate was the first *thermoplastic* or *heat-sensitive* fiber. Consumers were confronted with fabrics that melted under a hot iron. This was at a time when consumers were accustomed to ironing all apparel. The problem was further compounded when manufacturers introduced acetate as a kind of rayon.

Still another problem with acetate was fume fading—a condition in which certain disperse dyes changed color (blue to pink, green to brown, gray to pink) as a result of atmospheric fumes, now referred to as atmospheric pollutants. Solution dyeing was developed to correct this problem and can now be used for all manufactured fibers. In 1955, an inhibitor was developed that gave greatly improved protection to the dyes under all conditions that cause fading. However, *fume and pollution fading* continues to be a problem.

Production of Acetate

In 1990, two companies were producing acetate: Eastman Chemical Products, Inc. and Hoechst Celanese. The basic steps in the manufacturing process are listed in Table 7-6.

Triacetate was produced until the end of 1986, when the last triacetate plant was closed because the Environmental Protection Agency (EPA) banned use of the solvent methylene chloride. Some triacetate is imported into the United States, so it is important for consumers to be aware that triacetate is a thermoplastic fiber. It can be heat set for resiliency and dimensional stability and is machine washable.

Physical Structure of Acetate

Acetate is available as staple or filament. Much more filament is produced because of its silklike appearance. Staple fibers are crimped and usually blended with other fibers. The cross section of acetate is lobular or flower petal-shaped. (A lobular shape is characteristic of silklike fibers.) The shape results from the evaporation of the solvent as the fiber solidifies in spinning. Notice in Figure 7-7 that the lobes may appear as a false lumen.

The cross-sectional shape can be varied. Y-shaped fibers have been produced for fiberfill for pillows and battings; flat filaments have been produced to give glitter to fabrics.

Chemical Composition and Molecular Arrangement of Acetate

Acetate—a manufactured fiber in which the fiber-forming substance is cellulose acetate. Where not less than 92 percent of the hydroxyl groups are acetylated, the term triacetate may be used as a generic description of the fiber.
—Federal Trade Commission.

Acetate is an ester of cellulose and therefore has a different chemical structure than rayon or cotton. In acetate, two of the hydroxyl groups have been replaced by acetyl groups (see Fig. 7-8). The bulky acetyl groups keep the molecules apart so they do not pack into crystalline areas. There is less attraction between the molecular chains as a result of a lack of hydrogen bonding. Water molecules do not penetrate as readily, which accounts for the lower

Table 7-6 Acetate Manufacturing Process

1. Purified cellulose from wood pulp or cotton linters
2. Mixed with glacial acetic acid, acetic anhydride, and a catalyst
3. Aged 20 hours—partial hydrolysis occurs
4. Precipitated as acid-resin flakes
5. Flakes dissolved in acetone
6. Solution is filtered
7. Spinning solution extruded in column of warm air. Solvent recovered (see Fig. 7-6)
8. Filaments are stretched a bit and wound onto beams, cones, or bobbins ready for use

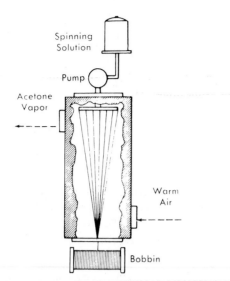

Fig. 7–6 *Acetate spinning chamber. (Courtesy of Tennessee Eastman Co.)*

absorbency of acetate. The changed chemical structure also explains the different dye affinity of acetate. Acetate is thermoplastic.

Properties of Acetate

Acetate has a combination of properties that make it a valuable textile fiber. It is low in cost and has good draping qualities. Table 7-7 summarizes acetate's performance in apparel and furnishing fabrics.

Fig. 7–7 *Photomicrographs of acetate fiber: longitudinal view* (left) *cross-sectional view* (right). *(Courtesy of American Association of Textile Chemists and Colorists.)*

***Table* 7–7 Summary of the Performance of Acetate in Apparel and Furnishing Fabrics**

Aesthetic	*Excellent*
Luster	High
Drape	High
Texture	Smooth
Hand	Smooth
Durability	*Low*
Abrasion resistance	Low
Tenacity	Low
Elongation	Moderate
Comfort	*Moderate*
Absorbency	Moderate
Thermal retention	Moderate
Appearance retention	*Low*
Resiliency	Low
Dimensional stability	Moderate
Elastic recovery	Low
Recommended care	Dry Clean

AESTHETICS Acetate has been promoted as the beauty fiber. It is widely used in satins, brocades, and taffetas in which luster, body, and beauty of fabric are more important than durability or ease of care. Acetate has, and keeps, a good white color. This is one of its advantages over silk, which yellows readily.

DURABILITY Acetate is a weak fiber having a breaking tenacity of 1.2–1.4 g/d. It loses some strength when wet. Other weak fibers have some compensating factor, such as good elastic recovery in wool or spandex, but acetate does not. Acetate has a breaking elongation of 25 percent. Acetate also has poor resistance to abrasion. A small percentage of nylon may be combined with acetate to produce a stronger fabric.

COMFORT Acetate has a moisture regain of 6.3–6.5 percent and is subject to static buildup. The fiber is soft and has no allergenic potential.

APPEARANCE RETENTION Acetate fabrics are not very resilient and wrinkle during use. When the fabrics are washed, they may develop wrinkles that are difficult to remove. Acetate has moderate dimensional stability. The fibers are weaker when wet and

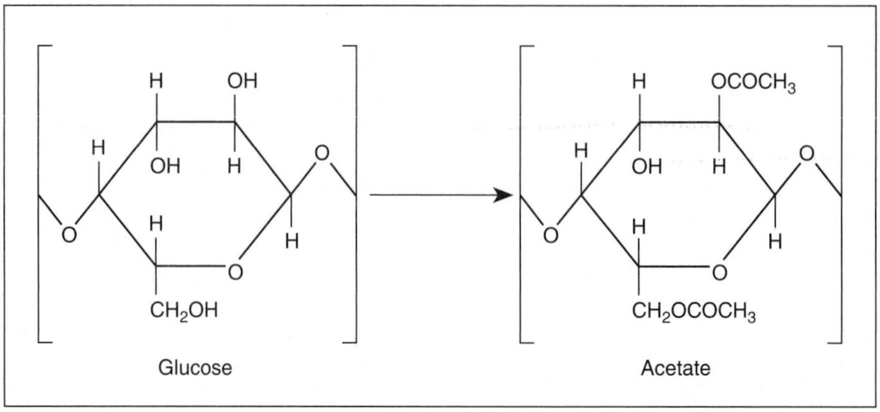

Fig. 7–8   Chemical structure of acetate.

can be shrunk by excess heat. Elastic recovery is low, 58 percent.

CARE Acetate should be dry cleaned unless other care procedures are identified on the care label. Acetate is resistant to weak acids and to alkalis. It can be bleached with hypochlorite or peroxide bleaches. Acetate is soluble in acetone. Acetate cannot be heat-set at a temperature high enough to give permanent shape to fabrics or to ensure that embossing is durable.

Acetate is thermoplastic and heat sensitive; it becomes sticky at low temperatures (177-191°C, 350-375°F) and melts at 230°C (446°F). Triacetate has a higher melting point than acetate.

Acetate has better sunlight resistance than silk or nylon but less than the cellulose fibers. It is resistant to moths, mildew, and bacteria.

COMPARISON WITH RAYON Rayon and acetate are the two oldest manufactured fibers and have been produced in large quantities, filling an important need for less expensive fibers in the textile industry. They lack the easy care, resilience, and strength of the synthetics and have had difficulty competing in uses where these characteristics are important. Rayon and acetate have some similarities because they are made from the same raw material, cellulose. The manufacturing processes differ, so the fibers have many individual characteristics and uses. Some of these are listed in Table 7-8.

Uses of Acetate

Acetate is a minor fiber in terms of usage. Acetate is used in apparel, furnishings, and industrial products.

An important use of acetate is in lining fabrics. The aesthetics of acetate—its luster, hand, and body—its relatively low cost, and its ease in handling contribute to its wide use here. However, since acetate is not a durable fiber, the fabric must be carefully selected for the end use or the consumer will be dissatisfied with the product.

A second important use of acetate is in robes and loungewear. It is frequently seen in brushed-tricot and fleece fabrics. In knits, the fiber is washable and performs well. Acetate is very important in drapery

Table 7–8   Comparison of Rayon and Acetate

Rayon	Acetate
Differences	
Wet spun	Dry spun
Regenerated cellulose	Chemical derivative of cellulose
Serrated cross section	Lobular cross section
More staple produced	More filament produced
Scorches	Melts
High absorbency	Fair absorbency
No static	Static
Not soluble in acetone	Soluble in acetone
Industrial uses—tires	Very few industrial uses
Not used for fiberfill	Used for fiberfill
Color may crock or bleed	Color may fume or pollution fade
Mildews	Resists mildew
Moderate cost	Low cost
Similarities	
Low strength	Low strength
Low abrasion resistance	Low abrasion resistance
Chlorine bleaches can be used	Chlorine bleaches can be used
Flammable, but can be made flame retardant	Flammable, but can be made flame retardant

fabrics. Sunlight-resistant modifications contribute to the fiber's popularity here as do its luster and soft drape. Antique-satin fabrics made of blends of acetate and rayon are very common. Fabrics of 50 percent acetate and 50 percent cotton are used where draperies need to match bedspreads or lightly used upholstery. Acetate and acetate-blend fabrics come in an amazingly wide assortment of colors—nearly any décor can be matched.

A third important use of acetate is in fabrics for formal wear, such as dresses and blouses. Taffeta, moiré taffeta, satin, and brocade are very common and popular fabrics.

Other important uses of acetate fabrics include bedspreads and quilts, satin sheets, fabrics sold for home sewing, ribbons, and cigarette filters.

Types and Kinds of Acetate

Types of acetate are solution dyed, flame retardant, sunlight resistant, fiberfill, textured filament, modified cross section, and thick-and-thin slublike filament. See Table 7-9.

AZLON

Manufactured protein fibers, *azlon*, are made by dissolving and resolidifying protein substances from animal or grain sources. They are not currently made in the United States although some research involving these fibers is being conducted. In the 1940s and 1950s, Aralac, made from milk casein,

Table 7–9 Types and Kinds of Acetate

Acetate	Trademarks	Producer
Regular	Celebrate	Hoechst Celanese
	Estron	Eastman
Solution dyed	Celaperm	Hoechst Celanese
	Chromspun	Eastman
Modified cross section	Celafil	Hoechst Celanese
	Celacloud (fiberfill)	Hoechst Celanese
Textured or crimpable	Celco	Hoechst Celanese
	Loftura	Eastman
Sunlight and weathering resistant	SLR	Eastman

and Vicara, made from the zein of corn, were produced, but these fibers were not successful because they were too weak to be used alone and too expensive to compete with other blending fibers, particularly rayon and acetate.

An azlon fiber is manufactured in Japan, imported to the United States, and sold under the Japanese generic name of promix and the trade name of Chinon. It is made from milk casein copolymerized with acrylic. Its characteristics are silklike; it is used in scarves, ties, blouses, and sweaters. It is also used in the pharmaceutical industry to purify medications.

KEY TERMS

Manufactured fiber
Acetone test
Rayon
Cellulose
High wet modulus rayon
Wet spinning
Solvent-spun rayon
Striations

Acetate
Triacetate
Dry spinning
Heat sensitive
Thermoplastic
Fume or pollution fading
Azlon

QUESTIONS

1. How do the properties of rayon and acetate differ from those of the natural cellulosic fibers?
2. How do the properties of azlon differ from those of the natural protein fibers?
3. Why do the properties of rayon, acetate, and azlon differ from those of the natural fibers?

4. How can the manufactured fibers be changed to enhance their performance for specific end uses?
5. For each end use listed below, identify a fiber discussed in this chapter that would be appropriate. Indicate why that fiber was selected as well as any fiber modifications that might enhance the fiber's performance for that end use.

    inexpensive kitchen wipes
    draperies for formal dining room
    lining for suit jacket
    summer-weight linen-look suit

SUGGESTED READINGS

Davies, Stan (February, 1989). "All You Need to Know About Tencel." *Textile Horizons,* pp. 62–63.

Grayson, Martin, ed. (1984). *Encyclopedia of Textiles, Fibers, and Nonwoven Fabrics.* New York: John Wiley & Sons.

Trotman, E. R. (1984). *Dyeing and Chemical Technology of Textile Fibers,* 6th ed. New York: John Wiley & Sons.

Ward, Derek (August, 1988). "World's Largest Viscose Producers." *Textile Month,* pp. 23–24.

CHAPTER 8

Synthetic Fibers

OBJECTIVES

- To know the properties common to most synthetic fibers.

- To understand the processes used in producing synthetic fibers.

- To know the performance characteristics of the common synthetic fibers.

- To relate performance characteristics of synthetic fibers to end uses.

- To recognize the importance of synthetic fibers to the industrial products industry.

- To recognize the widespread use of synthetics in apparel and furnishing products in both 100 percent synthetic fibers and blends with natural fibers.

OVERVIEW OF THE SYNTHETIC FIBERS

$\mathcal{S}$YNTHETIC FIBERS ARE ALSO CONSIDERED manufactured fibers. Before the synthetic fiber can be produced, the polymer must be synthesized or made. Once the polymer is available, the fiber is made; hence, the name synthetic fiber. Although other names like chemical fibers and non-cellulosic manufactured fibers are used, these fibers are most often referred to as synthetic fibers.

In producing synthetic fibers, the fiber-forming compounds must be made from basic raw materials. The procedures involved in creating the fiber-forming raw materials from the starting materials are complex and beyond the scope of this text. Many synthetic fibers are made from petrochemicals (petroleum-based chemicals). Even though the synthetic fiber industry is a huge one (see Table 8-1), the consumption of petrochemicals is less than 1 percent of the total petroleum consumed in the U.S. in one year.

Once the raw materials are available, they are polymerized or connected into one extremely large linear compound called a polymer. The polymerization process is either addition or condensation polymerization. In many cases, the basic unit of the polymer, the monomer, is fairly simple; in other cases, the monomer is more complex. In addition polymerization, a double bond between 2 carbon atoms is broken and many monomers are connected together. In condensation polymerization, 1 or 2 compounds are connected to form a monomer and a small molecule, often water, is a by-product of the reaction. Many monomers are then connected to form the polymer (see Figure 8-1).

(a) $3(A = B) \longrightarrow A - B - A - B - A - B$
Addition polymerization

(b) $3D - H + 3E - OH \longrightarrow D - E - D - E - D - E + 3H_2O$
Condensation polymerization

Fig. 8–1 *Polymerization: (a) addition and (b) condensation.*

Different chemical compounds are used as the raw materials to make the polymer for nylon, polyester, olefin, acrylic, and modacrylic. These fibers are found in a wide variety of apparel, furnishing, and industrial applications and will be discussed in this chapter. The next chapter will focus on many other synthetic fibers as well as other fibers that have special uses or applications in the textile industry. The synthetic fibers have many properties and processes in common (see Table 8-2).

Synthetic fibers have acquired a negative image related to previous end uses and the fashion characteristics of those end uses. Synthetic fiber producers are developing new marketing strategies to strengthen the industry and change the public's perception of these fibers through advertising and touch tests. The industry is working hard to help the public understand the high-tech versatility, easy care, durability, and high-fashion appeal of these fibers.

Common Properties of Synthetic Fibers

HEAT SENSITIVITY Most manufactured fibers, except rayon, are heat sensitive. *Heat sensitivity* refers to fibers that soften or melt with heat; those that scorch or decompose are described as being heat resistant. Heat sensitivity is important in manufacturing processes because of the heat in dyeing, scouring, singeing, and other finishing and production processing. Heat sensitivity is equally important in use and care because of heat encountered in washing, ironing, and dry cleaning.

Fibers differ in their level of heat sensitivity. This difference is reflected in Table 3-8. Because of the speed of the iron in normal ironing, the fabric never gets as hot as the sole plate of the iron. If the iron speed slows or the iron stands in one spot, the heat builds up. When heat-sensitive fabrics get too hot,

Table 8–1 Million Pounds of Fiber Used

Fiber	(1990)	Percent
Cotton	3,352	27.8
Polyester	3,195	26.5
Nylon	2,662	22.0
Olefin and vinyon	1,822	15.1
Acrylic	506	4.2
Rayon and acetate	505	4.2
Total	12,042	99.8

Table 8–2   Properties Common to Synthetic Fibers

Properties	Importance to Consumers
Heat sensitive	Fabrics will shrink and melt if exposed to excess heat. Holes may appear. Pleats, creases, and other three-dimensional effects can be heat-set in fabrics. Fabric can be stabilized by heat setting. Yarns can be textured for bulk. Fur-like fabrics can be produced.
Resistant to most chemicals	Used in industrial applications where chemical resistance is required.
Resistant to moths and fungi	Storage is no problem. Used in geotextiles, sandbags, fishlines, tenting and other industrial applications
Low moisture absorbency	Products dry quickly, resist waterborne stains. Lack of comfort in humid weather. Increases possibility of static. Water does not cause shrinkage. Difficult to dye.
Oleophilic	Oil and grease absorbed into the fiber must be removed by dry cleaning agents.
Electrostatic	Clothes cling to wearer. May cause sparks that can cause explosions or fires. Shocks in cold, dry weather are unpleasant.
Abrasion resistance good to excellent (acrylics lowest)	Good appearance retained longer because holes and worn places do not appear as soon. Used in many industrial applications.
Strength good to excellent	Strongest fibers make good ropes, belts, and women's hosiery. Resist breaking under stress.
Resilience excellent	Easy-care apparel, packable for travel. Less wrinkling during wear. Resilient carpeting.
Sunlight resistence good to excellent (nylon modified to improve resistence)	Webbing for outdoor furniture. Indoor/outdoor carpet. Curtains and draperies. Flags, banners, and awnings.
Flame resistance	Varies from poor to excellent. Check individual fibers.
Density of specific gravity	Varies as a group but tend to the lightweight. More product per unit mass.
Pilling	May occur in staple-length fiber products.

the yarns soften and pressure from the iron flattens them permanently (Figure 8-2). This effect is referred to as *glazing*. Glazing can be used to achieve embossed and shiny surfaces on fabrics.

Alterations are difficult to make in heat–sensitive fabrics because creases, seams, and hems are hard to press in or out. Fullness cannot be shrunk out for shaping, so patterns have to be adjusted to remove some of the fullness in areas where fullness is usually controlled by shrinkage.

PILLING Fiber tenacity is a basic factor in *pilling*, the formation of tiny balls of entangled fiber ends on

Before

After

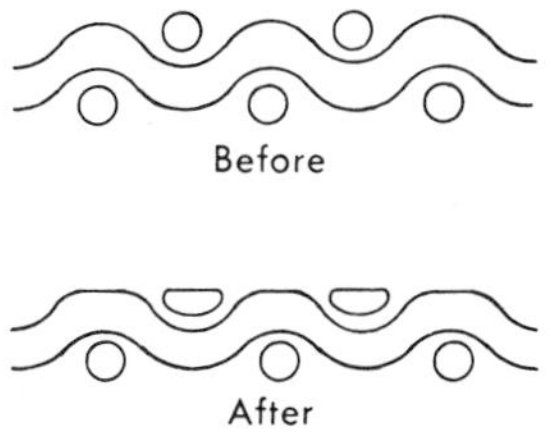

Fig. 8–2 *Heat and pressure cause permanent flattening of the yarn (glazing).*

the surface of the fabric. Pilling occurs on staple fiber fabrics where fiber ends get tangled by rubbing. The pills may break off before the item becomes unsightly, but with most synthetics the fibers are so strong that pills accumulate on the fabric's surface. Pills are of two kinds: lint and fabric. *Lint pills* are more unsightly, because they contain not only fibers from the item but also fibers picked up during care, in use, through contact with other fabrics, and even through static attraction. Pilling can be minimized by fiber modification or finishes.

Fabric construction is an important factor in minimizing pilling. Close weaves, high-yarn twist or plied yarns, and longer-staple fibers are recommended. Resin finishes of cotton and fulling of wool also help prevent pilling.

STATIC ELECTRICITY Static electricity is generated by the friction of a fabric when it is rubbed against itself or other objects. If the electrical charge is not removed, it builds up on the surface. When the fabric comes in contact with a good conductor, a shock, or electron transfer, occurs. This transfer may produce sparks that, in a gaseous atmosphere, can cause explosions. Static tends to build up more rapidly in dry, cold regions. Problems involving static include the following:

1. Soil and lint cling to the surface of the fabric and dark colors become very unsightly. Brushing simply increases the problem.

2. Dust and dirt are attracted during storage and to furnishings.

3. Fabrics cling to equipment in production facilities and make cutting and handling very difficult. Static is responsible for increased defects contributing to a higher percentage of seconds.

4. Clothes cling to the wearer and cause discomfort and an unsightly appearance. Static can be minimized by the use of fabric softeners, when used as directed.

Antistatic finishes are applied to many fabrics at the factory, but they may not be permanent.

OLEOPHILIC Fibers that have low moisture absorption usually have a high affinity for oils and greases. They are *oleophilic.* Exposure to oily substances may cause these fibers to swell. Oily stains are very difficult to remove and may require prespotting with a concentrated liquid soap or a dry cleaning solvent.

Common Manufacturing Processes

MELT SPINNING Many synthetic fibers are melt spun. The basic steps in the melt-spinning process for filament and staple fiber made from filaments are shown in Figure 8-3. *Melt spinning* is essentially a simple process. It can be demonstrated by a laboratory experiment that is fun to do. A flame, a pair of tweezers, and a piece of nylon are needed. Heat the fabric until quite a little melt has formed, then quickly draw out the melt with tweezers as shown in Figure 8-4.

Commercial melt spinning consists of forcing the melt through the holes of the stainless–steel plate of a heated spinneret. The fiber cools in contact with the air, solidifies, and is wound on a bobbin. Figure 8-5 shows commercial spinning of nylon as it is extruded through the spinneret into cool air.

DRAWING After extrusion of the fiber, its chain-like molecules are in an amorphous or disordered arrangement. The filament fiber must be *drawn* to develop the desirable strength, pliability, toughness,

and elasticity properties of the fiber. Some fibers are cold drawn; others must be hot drawn. Drawing aligns the molecules, placing them parallel to one another and bringing them closer together so they are more crystalline and oriented. The fiber is also reduced in size. The amount of draw varies with intended use. The draw ratio determines the decrease in fiber size and the increase in strength.

HEAT SETTING *Heat setting* is a process that uses heat to stabilize yarns or fabrics made of heat-sensitive fibers. The yarn or fabric is heated to bring it almost to the melting point specific for the fiber being heat set or the glass transition temperature (Tg). At this temperature the fiber molecules move freely, dissipating stresses within the fiber. The fabric is kept under tension until it cools, to lock this shape into the molecular structure of the fiber. After cooling, the fabric or yarn will be stable to any heat lower than that at which it was set, but changes can be made by higher temperatures. Heat setting may be done at any stage of finishing, depending on the level of heat resistance of the fiber and other qualities (see Table 8-3).

Identification of Synthetic Fibers

Burn tests identify the presence of several synthetic fibers if the product is all synthetic because of the melting and dripping that occurs with several fibers in this group. However, the burn test is not good for blends or for fibers that are flame retardant. The burn test also cannot identify a specific generic fiber since the differences may be masked by fiber additives or finishes. See Table 3-15 for the slight differences in the burn tests for each synthetic fiber.

Microscopic appearance is not a reliable method of identification for these fibers. Since these are synthetic fibers, fiber appearance can be easily modi-

Table 8–3 **Heating Settting**

Advantages	Disadvantages
Embossed designs are permanent.	"Set" creases and wrinkles are hard to remove in ironing or in garment alteration.
Pleats and shape are permanent.	
Size is stabilized.	Care must be taken in washing or ironing to prevent the formation of set wrinkles.
Pile is crush resistant.	
Knits do not need to be blocked.	
Clothing resists wrinkling during wear.	

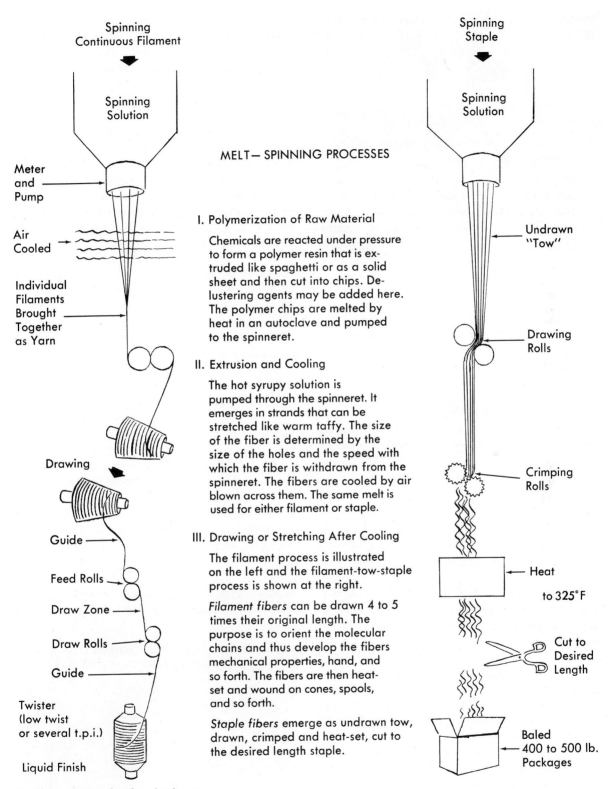

Fig. 8–3 *Chart of melt–spinning processes.*

fied. Fibers in this group have no unique visible characteristics at either the microscopic or macroscopic level. Photomicrographs included in this chapter clearly illustrate this.

Solubility tests are the only procedures that differentiate among the synthetic fibers. Table · 3–16

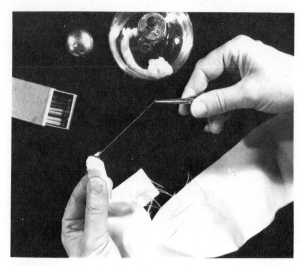

Fig. 8–4 *Spinning a melt–spun fiber by hand.*

lists solvents commonly used to identify synthetic fibers. Several solvents used in identification of fibers are toxic and hazardous. Appropriate care should be taken when using any solvent.

Common Fiber Modifications

FIBER SHAPE AND SIZE Since many synthetic fibers are melt spun, changing the fiber's cross-sectional shape is relatively easy. Fiber shape can be changed by altering the shape of the spinneret hole. Many modifications are possible. Hollow fibers for fiberfill are common because of better thermal properties and lighter weight aspects. Trilobal, pentalobal, and multilobal fibers are used for apparel and furnishings, especially carpeting. Voided fibers help hide soil on carpeting. Flat ribbon fibers are used in formal and special occasion apparel. Channel fibers like Du Pont's CoolMax are used in active sportswear to wick moisture away from the skin's surface.

Microfibers are fibers with a denier per filament (dpf) of less than 1.0. Many synthetic microfibers are available; the most common are nylon and polyester varieties. These fibers are produced by conventional melt spinning, splitting bicomponent fibers, or dissolving one of the components of bicomponent fibers. All three techniques provide commercially important microfibers for apparel, furnishing, and industrial applications. Apparel and furnishing markets have had the strongest industry focus to date. End uses include fashion apparel, intimate apparel, upholstery, wall coverings, and wiping cloths for the precision and glass industries.

LOW PILLING FIBERS Low-pilling fibers are engineered to minimize pill formation. This is accomplished by decreasing the fiber's flex life by reducing the molecular weight slightly. When the flex abrasion resistance is reduced, the fiber pills break off almost as soon as they are formed, thus maintaining the fabric's original appearance. The low–pilling fibers are not as strong as other fiber types, but are durable enough for most apparel and many furnishing uses. They are also especially applicable for soft knitting yarns. Some low-pilling fiber modifications are especially designed for blending with natural fibers. For example, there are polyester low-pilling types available for blending with cotton or rayon.

HIGH-TENACITY FIBERS Stretching a fiber changes its stress/strain curve, which is the basis of tenacity. Fiber strength is increased in several ways. Drawing or stretching the fiber to align or orient the molecules strengthens the intermolecular forces. Chemical modifications of the fiber polymer increase the degree of polymerization, the length of the polymer chain. Some high-tenacity fibers are produced by combining drawing with chemical modification.

In synthetic fibers, the molecular chain length can be varied by chemical modification by changes in time, temperature, pressure, and chemicals. Long molecules are harder to pull apart than short molecules. Drawing of synthetic fibers also increases tenacity.

LOW-ELONGATION FIBERS Low-elongation fibers are designed as reinforcing fibers to increase the strength and abrasion resistance of cellulosic-blend

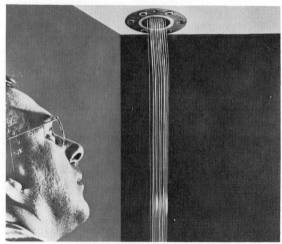

Fig. 8–5 *Spinning nylon fiber. (Courtesy of E. I. du Pont de Nemours & Company.)*

fabrics. The low elongation is a result of changing the balance of tenacity and extension. High-tenacity fibers have lower elongation properties. Primary end uses are apparel and furnishing items that get hard use like work clothing and heavy-duty upholstery fabrics.

NYLON

Nylon was the first synthetic fiber and the first fiber conceived in the United States. In 1928, the Du Pont Company decided to establish a fundamental research program as a means of diversification. Du Pont hired Dr. Wallace H. Carothers, who had done research on high polymers, to direct a team of scientists. The team created many kinds of polymers, starting with single molecules and building them up into long molecular chains. One team member discovered that one of the solutions could be stretched out into a stable solid filament. This stimulated the group to concentrate on textile fibers. By 1939, Du Pont was making a polyamide fiber in a pilot plant. This fiber, nylon 6,6, was introduced to the public in women's hosiery where it was an instant success. The name *nylon* was chosen for the fiber. It has no special meaning but sounds like cotton and rayon. At the time there were no laws specifying generic names for fibers.

Nylon had a combination of properties unlike any other fiber in use in the 1940s. It was stronger and more resistant to abrasion; it had excellent elasticity and could be heat set. Permanent pleats became a reality. For the first time, gossamer-sheer fabrics were durable and machine washable. Nylon's high strength, light weight, and resistance to chemicals made it suitable for ropes, cords, sails, parachutes, and other industrial products.

As nylon entered more end-use markets, its disadvantages became apparent—static buildup, poor hand, lack of comfort in skin-contact fabrics, and low resistance to sunlight. But fortunately, as each problem appeared, ways were developed to overcome the disadvantages.

Production of Nylon

Nylon or polyamides are made from various substances. The numbers after the word nylon indicate the number of carbon atoms in the starting materials. Nylon 6,6 is made from hexamethylene diamine, which has six carbon atoms, and adipic acid, which also has six carbon atoms.

While nylon 6,6 was being developed in the United States, scientists in Germany were working on nylon 6. It is made from a single substance, caprolactam, which has six carbon atoms.

Physical Structure of Nylon

Nylon is available in multifilament, monofilament, staple, and tow in a wide range of deniers and shapes. Many staple lengths are also available. They are produced in bright, semidull, and dull lusters. They vary in degree of polymerization and thus in strength. They are available as partially drawn or completely finished filaments.

Regular nylon has a round cross section and is perfectly uniform throughout the filament (Figure 8-6). Microscopically, the fibers look like fine glass rods. They are transparent unless they have been delustered or solution dyed.

At first, the uniformity of nylon filaments was a distinct advantage over the natural fibers, especially silk. However, the perfect uniformity of nylon produced woven fabrics with a dead feel. They lacked the liveliness of silk. This condition is reduced by changing the shape of the spinneret holes. Melt-spun fibers, like nylon, tend to retain the shape of the spinneret hole. In nylon carpets, trilobal fibers and square fibers with voids give good soil-hiding characteristics (see Figures 8-7 and 8-8).

Fig. 8–6 *Photomicrographs of nylon fiber: longitudinal and cross-sectional* (inset) *views. (Courtesy of E. I. du Pont de Nemours & Company.)*

Fig. 8–7 *Photomicrograph of trilobal nylon. (Courtesy of E. I. du Pont de Nemours & Company.)*

Chemical Composition and Molecular Arrangement of Nylon

Nylon—a manufactured fiber in which the fiber-forming substance is any long-chain, synthetic polyamide in which less than 85 percent of the amide linkages

$$\left[\begin{array}{c} -C-NH- \\ \parallel \\ O \end{array} \right]$$

are attached directly to two aromatic rings.—Federal Trade Commision.

Nylons are polyamides with recurring amide groups that contain the elements carbon, oxygen, nitrogen, and hydrogen. They differ in their chemical arrangement and this accounts for slight differences in properties.

The molecular chains of nylon vary in length. They are long, straight chains with no side chains or cross-linkages. Cold drawing aligns the chains so that they are oriented with the lengthwise direction and are highly crystalline. High-tenacity filaments have a longer chain length than regular nylon. Staple fibers are not cold drawn after spinning, have lower degrees of crystallinity, and have lower tenacity than filament fibers.

Nylon is related chemically to the protein fibers silk and wool. Both have amino dye sites that are important in dyeing, but nylon possesses far fewer dye sites than wool.

Properties of Nylon

Nylon's performance in apparel and furnishing fabrics is summarized in Table 8-4.

AESTHETIC Nylon has been very successful in hosiery and in knitted–filament fabrics such as tricot and jersey because of its smoothness, light weight, and high strength. The luster of nylon can be selected for the end use—it can be lustrous, semilustrous, or dull. Trilobal nylons have a pleasant luster.

The drape of fabrics made from nylon can be varied, depending largely on the yarn size and fabric

Fig. 8–8 *Nylon fiber with voids. (Courtesy of E. I. du Pont de Nemours & Company.)*

Table 8–4 Summary of the Performance of Nylon in Apparel and Furnishing Fabrics

Aesthetic	**Variable**
Durability	**Excellent**
Abrasion resistance	Excellent
Tenacity	Excellent
Elongation	High
Comfort	**Low**
Absorbency	Low
Thermal retention	Moderate
Appearance Retention	**High**
Resiliency	High
Dimensional stability	High
Elastic recovery	Excellent
Recommended Care	**Machine wash** (apparel) Dry extraction method (furnishings)

structure selected. High-drape fabrics are found in draperies and in sheer overlays for nightgowns and in formals. Stiff fabrics are found in taffetas for formal wear, parkas, furnishings, or industrial uses. Very stiff fabrics include webbing for luggage handles and seat belts. These also vary in filament size.

Smooth textures are frequently found. These too can be varied by using spun yarns or by changing the knit or woven structure. The hand frequently associated with nylon fabrics is smooth because of the filament yarn and flat tricot-knit construction. Textured-yarn fabrics are bulkier.

Nonround fibers are generally used in carpets. Trilobal, pentalobal, and voided fibers are used for several reasons. Round fibers tend to magnify soil and look dirty very quickly. The nonround fibers hide the soil. Even though the carpets may be quite dirty, they may not look soiled at all. In addition, voids and flat sides of the fibers scatter light, which assists in hiding the soil and more closely duplicates the matte luster of wool (see Figures 8-7 and 8-8).

DURABILITY Nylon has outstanding durability. High-tenacity fibers are used for seat belts, tire cords, ballistic cloth, and other industrial uses. Regular-tenacity fibers are used in apparel (see Table 8-5).

High-tenacity fibers are stronger, but have lower elongation than regular-tenacity fibers. During production the high-tenacity fibers are drawn to a

Table 8–5
Comparison of Nylon 6,6 and Nylon 6

Nylon 6,6	Nylon 6
Made of hexamethylene diamine and adipic acid	Made of captolactam
$$\left[\begin{matrix} O & O \\ \parallel & \parallel \\ C\,(CH_2)_4\,C\,NH(CH_2)_6\,NH \end{matrix} \right]_n$$	

Advantages	Advantages
Heat setting 205°C (401°F)	Heat setting 150° (302°F)
Pleats and creases, can be heat set at higher temperatures	Softening point 220°C (428°F)
Softening point 250°C (482°F)	Better dye affinity than nylon 6,6; takes deeper shades
Difficult to dye	Softer hand
	Greater elasticity, elastic recovery, and fatigue resistance
	Better weathering properties, including better sunlight resistance

Performance				Performance		
Tenacity dry/wet	Breaking Elongation, %	Elastic Recovery, %	Fiber Type	Tenacity dry/wet	Breaking Elongation, %	Elastic Recovery, %
5.9–9.8/ 5.1–8.0	15–28/ 18–32	89	High-Tenacity Filament	6.5–9.0 5.8–8.2	16–20/ 19–33	99–100
2.3–6.0/ 2.0–5.5	25–65/ 30–70	88	Regular Tenacity Filament	4.0–7.2 3.7–6.2	17–45/ 20–47	98–100
2.9–7.2 2.5–6.1	16–75/ 18–78	82	Staple	3.5–7.2/ —	30–90/ 42–100	100
—	—	—	Bulked Continuous Filament	2.0–4.0/ 1.7–3.6	30–50/ 30–60	—

greater degree than the regular-tenacity fibers. Thus, the HT fibers are more crystalline and oriented.

In addition to excellent strength and high elongation, nylon has excellent abrasion resistance. For example, nylon carpet fibers outwear all other fibers including wool (see Table 8-6).

A major end use for nylon is carpet. The ideal carpet is durable, resilient, and resistant to pilling, shedding, fading, traffic, abrasion, soil, and stains. Nylon meets or exceeds many of these demands. In terms of durability, nylon is unexcelled in abrasion resistance.

This combination of properties makes nylon the fiber for women's hosiery. No other fiber has been able to compete with nylon in pantyhose. The sheer, almost transparent fiber is flattering to the wearer. The fiber is more durable in wear than any other fiber for its sheerness. Filament hosiery develops runs because the fine yarns break and the knit loop is no longer secure. Very sheer hosiery is less durable.

The high elongation and excellent elastic recovery of nylon account for its outstanding performance in hosiery. Hosiery is subjected to relatively high degrees of elongation; nylon recovers better after high elongation than other fibers do. Another factor that helps it retain its shape during wear is that the shape of hosiery can be heat or steam set.

Nylon is used for lining fabrics in coats and jackets. These linings are more durable; however, the cost is greater because of the greater difficulty in sewing nylon fabrics and because nylon fabrics are more expensive than acetate fabrics.

Nylon is not very durable as a curtain or drapery fabric because it is weakened by the sun. Sunlight- or ultraviolet-resistant modifications are available. These modified fibers are used in sheer glass curtains, draperies, car interiors, seat belts, and other industrial applications.

COMFORT Nylon has low absorbency. Even though its moisture regain is the highest of the synthetic fibers (4.0-4.5 percent for nylon 6,6 and 2.8-5.0 for nylon 6), nylon is not as comfortable a fiber to wear as the natural fibers.

Compact yarns of filament nylon originally were used in men's woven sports shirts. The shirts became transparent when wet from perspiration. The yarn and fabric structure resulted in a shirt that felt like a plastic sheet wrapped around the body. As the man perspired, the fiber did not absorb the moisture nor did the dense fabric let any moisture escape. The shirts were especially uncomfortable in warm, humid weather. Later, open-structure woven fabrics and crimped yarns were used to improve comfort.

Because of this early and inappropriate use, fiber producers began to develop fabric quality-control programs through which they could exercise control over the final product and thus protect the

Table 8–6   Comparison of Wool and Manufactured Carpet Fibers

Fiber Characteristic	Wool	Manufactured
Fiber diameter	Coarse-blends of various wools	15–18 denier or blend of various deniers
Fiber length	Staple	Staple or filament blend of various lengths
Crimp	3D Crimp	Sawtooth crimp, 3D crimp, bicomponent, textured filament
Cross-section	Oval	Round, trilobal, multilobal, square with voids, 5 pointed star
Resiliency and resistance to crushing	Good	Medium to excellent depending on fiber
Resistance to abrasion	Good	Good to excellent
Resistance to water-borne stains	Poor	Good to excellent
Resistance to oily stains	Good	Poor
Fire retardancy	Good	Modified fiber or topical finish
Static resistance	Good	Poor to good depending on fiber

image of their fibers. Today, textured and spun yarns used in knit fabrics result in more comfortable shirts. Knit fabrics of nylon are more comfortable than woven-nylon fabrics because the additional air spaces within the fabric structure allow heat and moisture to escape more readily.

The very factors that make nylon uncomfortable under one set of conditions make it very comfortable under a different set. Nylon is widely used for wind-resistant jackets and parkas. The smooth, straight fibers pack closely together into yarns that can be woven into a compact fabric with very little space for wind to penetrate.

With a density of 1.14, nylon is one of the lightest fibers on the market. Compared to polyester, nylon yields 21 percent more yardage per pound of fabric. This lighter weight corresponds to lighter products and lower costs of moving fabrics and finishing fabrics.

Another disadvantage of low absorbency is the development of static electricity by friction at times of low humidity. This disadvantage can be overcome by using antistatic-type nylon fibers, or antistatic finishes, and by blending with high-absorbency, low-static fibers.

Antistatic fiber modifications and finishes are common with carpets. Metallic and carbon fibers are also used to minimize static in carpets. Static creates problems with comfort, soiling, and function.

APPEARANCE RETENTION Nylon fabrics are highly resilient because they have been heat set. The same process can be used to make permanent pleats, creases, and embossed designs that last for the life of the product.

Most nylon carpet yarns are heat set before they are incorporated in the carpet. This heat set improves the compressional resiliency of the fibers in the pile yarns. Compressional resiliency refers to the tendency of the carpet fibers to spring back to their original height after being bent or otherwise deformed. Nylon has excellent compressional resiliency. Thus, traffic paths do not develop quickly. In addition, depressions from heavy furniture are less likely to be permanent. Marks of heavy furniture can be minimized by steaming these areas. In addition, most carpet fibers are made in a large denier, often 15 or greater. Larger denier fibers have improved compressional resiliency and appearance retention.

Shrinkage resistance is also high because the heat setting and the low-absorbency fiber are not affected by water. Elastic recovery is excellent. Nylon recovers fully from 8 percent stretch; no other fiber does as well. At 16 percent elongation, it recovers 91 percent

immediately. This property makes nylon an excellent fiber for hosiery, tights, ski pants, swimsuits, and other active sportswear (see Table 8-5).

Solution-dyed carpet fibers are available where fading, especially from exposure to sunlight, may be a problem. These carpets are specifically aimed at the low-priced contract/commercial markets. Nylon does not wrinkle much in use, it is stable, and it has excellent elastic recovery, so it retains its appearance very well during use.

CARE Nylon introduced the concept of easy-care garments. In addition to retaining their appearance and shape during use, nylon fabrics retain their appearance and shape during care.

The wet strength of nylon is 80-90 percent of its dry strength. Wet elongation increases slightly. Little swelling occurs in wet fabric made of nylon. This is in marked contrast to cellulosic fibers: nylon, up to 14 percent; cotton, 40-45 percent; and viscose rayon, 80-110 percent.

To minimize wrinkling, warm wash water, gentle agitation, and spin cycles are recommended. Hot water may cause wrinkling in some fabric constructions. Wrinkles set by hot wash water can be permanent. Hot water will remove greasy and oily stains when necessary. Usually the additional wrinkling that occurs in the wash can be pressed out without any problem.

Nylon is a *color scavenger*. White and light-colored nylon fabrics pick up color from other fabrics or dirt that is in the wash water. A red sock that loses color into the wash water of a load of whites will turn the white nylon fabrics a dingy pink-gray. This extra color may be extremely difficult to remove. Prolonged use of chlorine bleach may also cause yellowing of white nylon. Discolored nylon and grayed or yellowed nylon can be avoided by following correct laundry procedures.

Since nylon has low absorbency, it dries quickly. Hence, fabrics need to be dried only for a short time. Do not overdry the fabrics. Dryer temperatures should be warm or low. Avoid using the hot setting on commercial gas dryers. Figure 8-9 shows the melted and fused result of a nylon garment dried in an overheated gas dryer with socks of a different fiber content.

Nylon does have problems with static, particularly when the air is dry, so a fabric softener may be used in the washer or dryer. Nylon should be pressed or ironed at a low temperature setting, 270-300°F, to avoid glazing. Home-ironing temperatures are not high enough to press seams, creases,

Fig. 8–9 *The melted and fused remains of nylon garments dried in an overheated gas dryer.*

and pleats permanently in items or to press out wrinkles acquired in washing.

The chemical resistance of nylon is generally good. Nylon has excellent resistance to alkali and chlorine bleaches but is damaged by strong acids. Pollutants in the atmosphere can damage nylon or create problems with dyes used on nylon. Certain acids, when printed on the fabric, create a puckered effect. Nylon dissolves in formic acid and phenol.

Nylon is resistant to the attacks of moths and fungi.

Nylon has low resistance to sunlight. Better resistance is achieved in end uses where sunlight exposure is a concern by using bright rather than delustered fibers, which absorb rather than reflect light. In addition, sunlight-resistant modifications of nylon are available.

Carpet soiling can be a real problem. Soiling in carpets is related to fiber cross section, carpet color, and fiber opacity/translucence. Round cross sections tend to magnify soil. Nonround cross sections, such as trilobal, pentalobal, and voided, hide soil (see Figures 8-7 and 8-8). Soil resistant fiber modifications are frequently used in carpeting to minimize soil adherence and permanent staining. In addition, many carpets now combine soil-resistant fiber modifications with soil-resistant finishes. See Chapter 18 for information on soil-resistant finishes for carpets.

Uses of Nylon

In 1990, there were twenty-four firms in the United States producing nylon: five produced only nylon 6,6; ten produced only nylon 6; and eight produced both nylon 6 and nylon 6,6. Three companies in the last group produced one or two additional nylons as well, including nylon 6,12; nylon 6,10; or nylon 12.

Nylon is the third most widely used fiber in the United States. It follows cotton and polyester in pounds used and is far ahead of all other fibers.

The single most important use of nylon is for carpets. Tufted carpets are an excellent end use for nylon because of its aesthetic appearance, durability, appearance retention, and ability to be cleaned in place. The combination of nylon fiber and the tufting process results in relatively low-cost and highly serviceable carpeting, contributing to the widespread use of carpeting in both residential and commercial buildings.

A second important use of nylon is for apparel. Lingerie fabrics are an end use for which nylon is an important fiber. The fabrics are attractive and durable; they retain their appearance well and are easy-care. Panties, bras, nightgowns, pajamas, and lightweight robes are frequently made from nylon. A copolymer absorbent nylon by Allied-Signal Fibers, Hydrofil, is used in sports bras and panties for greater comfort.

Women's sheer hosiery is an important end use of nylon. How frequently they are simply called "nylons"! No other fiber has the combination of properties that make it so ideal for that use. The very sheer hosiery is often 12–15 denier instead of the once standard 30 denier yarn or monofilament. Sheers give the look that is wanted, but they are less durable. Hosiery yarns may be monofilament or multifilament-stretch nylon. They may be plain or textured.

Short socks or knee-high socks are sometimes made from nylon. More frequently they are nylon blends with cotton or acrylic, with the nylon adding strength and stretch.

Active sportswear in which comfort stretch is important—leotards, tights, swimsuits, and ski wear—is another end use for nylon. Nylon-taffeta windbreakers and parkas are commonly seen in cooler weather. Lining fabrics, especially for jackets and coats, are sometimes made of nylon.

Industrial uses for nylon are varied. Within this group, an important use of nylon is for tire cord. The nylon or polyester fibers that are used in the cord of radial tires go rim to rim over the curve of the tire. Nylon is facing stiff competition in this specialized market, and may lose the market to polyester, aramid, and/or steel.

Although nylon is strong and abrasion resistant, with high elongation and high elasticity, it has a tendency to "flat spot." Flat spotting occurs when a car has been stationary for some time and a flattened place forms on the tire. The car will have a bumpy ride for the first mile or so until the tire recovers from flattening. With the advent of belted-radial

Table 8–7 Nylon Microfibers

Producer	Fiber Trade Name	Fiber Size	End Use
BASF	Silky Touch	0.8 dpf	Lingerie, swimwear
Du Pont	Supplex	1.0 dpf	Woven fabrics in sportswear for skiing, golfing, and bicycling
	MicroSupplex	0.7 dpf	

tires and the availability of heat-resistant aramid and steel, the market is changing.

Car interiors are another example of the varied uses for nylon. The average car uses 25 pounds of fiber, most of which may be nylon. Upholstery fabric (called body cloth), carpet for the interior, trunk lining, door and visor trims, head liners on the interior of the car roof, and seat belt webbing are all nylon fabrics of one kind or another. Some may be modified to be sunlight resistant, heat resistant, or high tenacity. In addition, clutch pads, brake linings, and yarns to reinforce radiator hoses and other hoses are needed. This is also a very competitive market. Polyester is gaining importance. Allied-Signal Fibers' nylon, StayGard, is used in airbags.

Additional industrial uses include parachute fabric, cords and harnesses, glider tow ropes, ropes and cordage, conveyor belts, fishing nets, mail bags, and webbings.

The category of industrial uses also includes consumer uses, sporting goods, and leisure fabrics. Consumer uses include umbrellas, clotheslines, toothbrush bristles, hairbrush bristles, paint brushes, and luggage. Leisure goods include soft luggage, backpacks, book bags, camera bags, golf bags, hunting gear, and horse blankets. Cordura nylon by Du Pont is used in many leisure goods. Blends of Cordura with other fibers are used in protective apparel, work wear, and career apparel.

Nylon is important in sporting goods. It is used for tents, sleeping bags, spinnaker sails, fishing lines and nets, racket strings, backpacks, and duffle bags.

Nylon microfibers are used in apparel and furnishings. These fibers are 26–36 percent softer than regular nylon fibers and range in size from 0.7 to 1.0 dpf, compared to a denier of 2.0 for regular nylon. The micro nylons are available from several manufacturers and are used in a variety of applications. These fibers are water repellent, wind and wear resistant, and vapor permeable and comfortable. They are used in 100 percent nylon formations and in blends with natural fibers like wool and cotton (see Table 8-7).

Types and Kinds of Nylon

It has been said that as soon as a new need arose, a new type of nylon was produced to fill the need. This has led to a large number of types of nylon that are identified by trademarks.

The list in Table 8-8 illustrates many modifications of nylon. Table 8-9 lists trade names for several producers of nylon.

Table 8–8 Types and Kinds of Nylon

Cross-section	Dyeability	Crimp or Textured	Others
Round	Acid dyeable	Mechanical crimp	Antistatic
Heart-shaped	Cationic dyeable	Crimp-set	Soil hiding
Y-shaped	Disperse dyeable	Producer textured	Bicomponent
8-shaped	Deep dye	Undrawn	Faciated
Delta	Solution dye	Partially drawn	Thick and thin
Trilobal	Heather	Steam crimped	Antimicrobial
Triskelion	Optically	Bulked continuous	Sunlight resistant
Trinode	whitened	filament	Flame resistant
Pentagonal		Latent crimp	Delustered
Hollow			High tenacity
Voided			Cross-linked

Table 8–9   Some Trademarks and Producers

Nylon 6,6 Trade Names	Producer	Nylon 6 Trade Names	Producer
Antron, Cantrece, Cordura	Du Pont	Anso-Tex, Caprolan, Captiva, Hydrofil, SeaGard, StayGard	Allied-Signal
Ultron, Wear-Dated	Monsanto	Natural Touch Zefran Zefsport Zeftron	BASF Fibers
		Shareen	Courtaulds

POLYESTER

The first polyester fiber, Terylene, was produced in England. It was first introduced in the U.S. in 1951 by Du Pont under the trade name Dacron (pronounced day'kron). The outstanding resiliency of polyester, whether dry or wet, coupled with its excellent dimensional stability after heat setting made it an instant favorite.

Sometimes referred to as the workhorse fiber of the industry, polyester is the most widely used synthetic fiber. The filament form of the fiber is extremely versatile and the staple form can be blended with many other fibers, contributing its good properties to the blend without destroying the desirable properties of the other fiber. Its versatility in blending is one of the unique advantages of polyester.

The polyesters have undergone significant research and developmental work. The polymer is endlessly engineerable, with many physical and chemical variations possible. These modified fibers improve the performance of the original polyester. One important physical difference has been changing from the standard round shape to other shapes to give different properties. A chemical modification, high-tenacity staple, was developed for use in durable-press fabrics. The strength of the polyester reinforces the cotton fibers, which are weakened by the finishing process. Other developments focus on more natural polyesters—with a hand and absorbency more like the natural fibers.

The properties of polyester are listed in Table 8-10.

Production of Polyester

Polyester is produced by reacting dicarboxylic acid with dihydric alcohol. The fibers are melt spun by a process that is very similar to the one used to make nylon. The polyester fibers are hot drawn to orient the molecules and improve strength, elongation, and the stress/strain properties. Since polyester is melt spun, it has the ability to retain the shape of the spinneret hole. Modifications in cross-sectional shape are possible.

Physical Structure of Polyester

Polyester fibers are produced in many types. Filaments are high tenacity or regular, bright or delustered, white or solution dyed. Staple fibers are available in deniers from 1.5 to 10 and are delustered. They may be regular, low pilling, or high tenacity. Regular polyester fibers are smooth rodlike fibers that have a circular cross section (Figure 8-10). The fibers are not as transparent as the nylon fibers. They are white, so they normally do not need to be bleached. However, whiter types of polyester fibers have been produced by the addition of optical whiteners to the fiber-spinning solution. The pitted appearance of the fiber is caused by delusterant.

A variety of cross-sectional shapes are produced: round, trilobal, octolobal, oval, hollow, voided, hexalobal, and pentalobal (star-shaped).

Chemical Composition and Molecular Arrangement of Polyester

Polyester fibers—manufactured fibers in which the fiber-forming substance is any long-chain synthetic polymer composed of at least 85 percent by weight of an ester of a substituted aromatic carboxylic acid, including but not restricted to substituted terephthalate units,

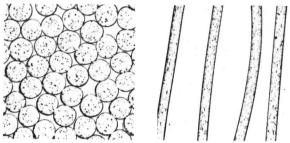

Fig. 8–10 *Photomicrographs of Dacron polyester: cross section of regular-delustered Dacron 500 times* (left); *longitudinal view 250 times* (right). *(Courtesy of E. I. du Pont de Nemours & Company.)*

$$p(-R-O-\underset{\underset{O}{\|}}{C}-C_6H_4-\underset{\underset{O}{\|}}{C}-O-), \text{ and para}$$

substituted hydroxybenzoate units,

$$p(-R-O-C_6H_4-\underset{\underset{O}{\|}}{C}-O-).$$

—Federal Trade Commission.

Polyester fibers are made from two kinds of terephthalate polymers: polyethylene terephthalate (PET) and 1,4 cyclohexylene-dimethylene terephthalate (PCDT). The differences are listed in Table 8-11. Both PET and PCDT polymers may be homopolymers or copolymers. The copolymers are pill-resistant, lower-strength staple fibers used primarily in knits, blends, and carpets.

Polyester fibers have straight molecular chains that are packed closely together and are well oriented with very strong hydrogen bonds.

Properties of Polyester

Polyester's performance in apparel and furnishing fabrics is summarized in Table 8-12.

AESTHETIC Polyester fibers blend well so that a natural fiber look and texture are maintained with the advantage of easy care for apparel and furnishings. The fabrics look like the natural fiber in the blend; their appearance retention during use and care clearly illustrates the influence of polyester.

Thick-and-thin yarns of polyester and rayon give a linen look to summer-weight blouse and suit fabrics. Wool-like fabrics are found in both summer-weight and winter-weight men's suiting fabrics.

Silklike polyesters have been very satisfactory in appearance and hand. The trilobal polyester fibers resulted from a study by Du Pont to find a manufactured filament that would have the aesthetic properties of silk. The study, made in cooperation with a silk-finishing company, began by investigating the effect of silk-finishing processes on the aesthetic properties of silk fabrics, since silk seemed to acquire added richness in the fabric form.

The silk fabric study found that the unique properties of silk—liveliness, suppleness, and drape of the fabric; dry "tactile" hand; and good covering power of the yarns—resulted from (1) the triangular shape of the silk fiber; (2) the fine denier per filament; (3) the loose, bulky yarn and fabric structure; and (4) the highly crimped fabric structure. These results were applied to polyester. The fibers are spun with a trilobal shape and made into fabrics processed by a silk-finishing treatment. They are unique because they can be treated with a caustic soda to dissolve away the surface, leaving a thinner, less uniform fiber, yarn, or fabric without basically changing the fiber.

Polyester microfibers are particularly suited to high fashion apparel and furnishing items because of the versatility and durability of the fibers. Designers find the microfibers' drape and hand

Table 8–10 Properties of Polyester

Properties	Importance to Consumers
Resilient—wet and dry	Easy-care apparel, furnishings, packable garments
Dimensional stability	Machine washable
Resistant to sunlight degradation	Good for glass curtains and draperies
Durable, abrasion resistant	Industrial uses, sewing thread, good for work clothes
Aesthetics superior to nylon	Blends well with other fibers, good silklike filaments

Table 8–11   Comparison of PET and PCDT Fibers

PET	PCDT

PET polyester	PCDT polyester
Dacron, Fortrel, Trevira	Kodel
Filaments are hot drawn	Drawn at higher temperatures
Filament or staple	Filament or staple
Textured yarns	Textured yarns
Stronger, more resistant to abrasion	More elastic
	Greater bulking properties
	Greater resiliency
Higher density, 1.38	Lower density, 1.22
Lower melting point, 480°F	Higher melting point, 540°F

exciting and challenging. Consumers have been willing to pay the additional cost of products incorporating microfibers. Microfibers yield softer and more drapeable fabrics than conventional fibers do. Figure 8-11 illustrates the differences between fiber sizes in yarn aspects. Items of polyester microfibers, both 100 percent polyesters and blends with other fibers, include coats, suits, blouses, dresses, wall coverings, upholstery, sleeping bags, tents, filters, and toweling (see Figure 8-12). See Table 8-13 for U.S. producers, trade names, and current products. The European market is more advanced in microfiber applications than the U.S. market.

DURABILITY   The abrasion resistance and strength of polyesters are excellent. Wet strength is comparable to dry strength. The high strength is produced by hot drawing to develop crystallinity and by increasing the molecular weight. As Table 8-14 shows, the breaking tenacity of polyester varies depending on the end use. The stronger fibers have been stretched more; their elongation is lower than the weaker fibers. This is particularly dramatic in the case of partially oriented filament fibers, which are sold to manufacturers who will stretch them more during the production of textured yarns. Their tenacity is 2.0-2.5 g/d. These filament fibers are

lower in strength than the staple fibers, yet their elongation far exceeds that of the other fibers, 120-150 percent! They can be thought of as being partially manufactured fibers until the texturing is completed.

COMFORT   Absorbency is quite low for the polyesters, 0.4-0.8 percent. Poor absorbency lowers the comfort factor of skin-contact apparel and upholstery.

Woven fabrics made from round polyester fibers can be very uncomfortable to use in warm, humid weather. Moisture does not escape easily from between the skin and the fabric, and the fabric feels slick and clammy.

To increase comfort, select blends with absorbent fibers or comfort-modified fibers, a thin and somewhat open fabric design, spun rather than filament yarns, trilobal rather than round fibers, and finishes that absorb, or wick, moisture. The soil-release finishes have improved the wicking characteristics of the polyesters, thus improving the breatheability and comfort of the fabrics. Finishes and fiber modifications also increase the comfort of polyester.

Blends of polyester and cotton are more comfortable in humid weather than are 100 percent poly-

Table 8–12   Summary of the Performance of Polyester in Furnishings and Apparel Fabrics

Aesthetic	Variable
Durability	**Excellent**
Abrasion resistance	Excellent
Tenacity	Excellent
Elongation	High
Comfort	**Low**
Absorbency	Low
Thermal retention	Moderate
Appearance Retention	**High**
Resiliency	Excellent
Dimensional stability	High
Elastic recovery	High
Recommended care	Machine wash (apparel) Dry extraction (furnishings)

Fig. 8–12   *Velvet gown by Nicole Miller made of Micromattique™ microdenier polyester. (Courtesy of E. I. du Pont de Nemours & Company)*

ester fabrics. Moisture is wicked along the outer surface of the polyester fibers to the fabric surface, where it evaporates. Polyester is resilient when it is wet, so the fabric does not mat down. Polyester is light in weight and dries quickly.

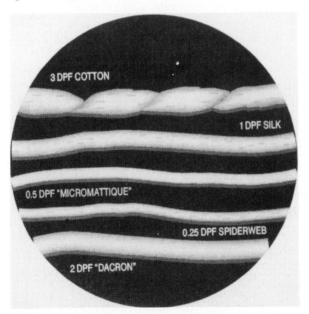

Fig. 8–11   *Comparison of fiber size: cotton, silk, Micromattique™ polyester, spiderweb, and Dacron® polyester. (Courtesy of E.I. du Pont de Nemours & Company)*

Polyester exhibits moderate thermal retention. It is generally not as comfortable as wool or acrylic for cold-weather wear. Blends with wool are very successful in increasing its comfort. Polyesters have been specifically engineered for a variety of fiberfill applications. Fiber modifications—including hollow fibers, binder staple, and crimped fibers—are performing very well.

Because of their low absorbency, polyesters are more *electrostatic* than the other fibers in the heat-sensitive group. The static potential of polyester can be lowered by modifying the fiber's cross section, incorporating special water-absorbing compounds in the spinning solution prior to extrusion, or adding topical finishes such as soil-release and antistat finishes. Cross-sectional modifications include incorporating compounds that make the fiber surface porous, which traps moisture. Other cross-sectional modifications expand the surface area per unit mass ratio, thus slightly increasing the absorbency. The density of polyester fibers ranges from 1.22 to 1.38. Hollow variants for fiberfill are lower in density.

APPEARANCE RETENTION *Resiliency* relates to tensile-work recovery and refers to the extent and manner of recovery from deformation. Polyester has a high recovery when the elongation is low, an important factor in the apparel and furnishings markets. When only small deformations are involved in wrinkling, polyester recovers better than nylon. This recovery is similar to that of wool at higher

Table 8–13 Polyester Microfibers

Producer	Fiber Trade Name	Fiber Size	End Use
Fiber Industries	Fortrel Microspun	.5–1.0	Outerwear, ski and sports wear, furnishings
Du Pont	Micromattique	.6–.7	Skiwear, outerwear, intimate apparel, furnishings
Hoechst Celanese	Trevira Finesse or Micronesse	.55–.9	Apparel, furnishings, industrial uses

elongations, which helps explain the suitability of polyester and wool blends. Nylon exhibits better recovery at the higher elongations, so it performs better in products that are subject to greater elongation—hosiery, for example (see Table 8-15).

Polyester has an advantage over wool in many uses, since wool has poor wrinkle recovery when wet. Under conditions of high humidity, polyester fabrics do not shrink and are very resistant to wrinkling. However, when polyester products wrinkle and where body heat and moisture set wrinkles, they may be difficult to remove, even with pressing.

Resiliency makes the polyesters especially good for fiberfill in quilted fabrics such as quilts, bedspreads, parkas, and robes, and in padding for furniture, futons, and mattresses.

The heat properties of the polyesters are used to advantage in fiberfill for pillows, quilts, and linings. If the fiber is flattened on one side or made asymmetrical, it takes on a tight spiral curl of outstanding springiness. Fiberfill of a blend of fiber deniers gives different levels of support. Lumpiness in pillows can be prevented by running hot needles through the bat to spot-weld the fibers to each other. Fiberfills with one, four, or seven hollow channels are available. See Figure 8-13.

To summarize, the resiliency of polyester is excellent; it resists wrinkles and, when wrinkled, it recovers well whether wet or dry. Elastic recovery is high for most apparel items. The dimensional stability of polyester is high. When properly heat set, it retains its size. It can be permanently creased or pleated satisfactorily.

Pilling was a severe problem with fabrics made from the unmodified polyesters. Low-pilling fiber types have been developed to minimize the problem and to make them more suitable to use in blends. The finishing process of singeing also helps control pilling.

CARE Polyester has revolutionized consumer laundering. This revolution occurred because of heat setting and the advent of durable-press finishes. Care instructions for polyester/cotton durable-press fabrics can be relatively simple: Wash in warm water; dry with medium heat in a dryer; remove promptly when the cycle is over; hang; and touch-up with a steam iron if necessary.

The excellent abrasion resistance and tenacity, and the high elongation of polyester are unaffected by water; there is no difference in wet or dry performance. The low absorbency of polyester (0.4 percent) means that it resists water-borne stains and is quick

Table 8–14 Performance Aspects of Modified Polyester Fibers

Fiber Modification	Tenacity g/d	Breaking Elongation, %	End use
High-tenacity filament	6.8–9.5	9–27	Tire cord, industrial uses
Regular-tenacity filament	2.8–5.6	18–42	Apparel and furnishings
High-tenacity staple	5.8–7.0	24–28	Durable-press items
Regular-tenacity staple	2.4–5.5	40–45	Apparel and furnishings

Table 8–15 Tensile Recovery from Elongation

Fiber	1%	3%	5%	15%
Polyester 56 (regular)	91	76	63	40
Nylon 200 (regular)	81	88	86	77

Source: E.I. du Pont de Nemours & Company, *Technical Bulletin X-142* (September 1961).

to dry. The excellent resiliency of polyester keeps it looking good during use and minimizes wrinkling during care so only light pressing may be required. Because of heat setting, dimensional stability is excellent.

Warm water is generally recommended to minimize wrinkling. Hot water may cause fabrics to wrinkle more and may cause color loss. However, hot water (120–140°F) may be needed to remove greasy or oily stains or built-up body soil because polyester is oleophilic; it has a tendency to retain oily soil. A familiar example of this is "ring around the collar." With polyester shirts or polyester/cotton blends, the soil usually responds to pretreatment, then laundering.

The oleophilic nature of polyester may also result in redisposition of oily soil on fabrics, making them look dingy. However, polyester is not the color scavenger that nylon is. Soil-release finishes applied to fabrics can improve soil removal.

Another problem with polyester, especially noticeable with apparel, is a tendency to exhibit bacterial odor. This problem occurs when soil has built up on the fabric; bacteria grow there and an odor results. Use of hot water wash, laundry agents such as borax, which minimizes odor, or bleach to remove the soil buildup and kill the bacteria may minimize the odor. Several detergents are available that focus on this problem.

Polyester fibers are resistant to both acids and alkalis and can be bleached with either chlorine or oxygen bleaches. Polyester fibers are resistant to biological attack and to sunlight damage, especially important for sheer drapery casement fabrics.

Uses of Polyester

In 1991, there were 25 producers of polyester fibers, including Allied-Signal, Du Pont, BASF Fibers, Hoechst Celanese, and Fiber Industries. Polyester is the most widely used manufactured

fiber in the United States. Peak mill consumption of polyester was 4,176 million pounds in 1981.

Polyester is very important in woven fabrics for apparel and furnishings. Frequently, spun yarns blended with cotton or rayon are seen. Polyester filament yarns may be used in one or both directions of the fabric. Many of the woven fabrics are blends made into durable-press fabrics. These blended fabrics are attractive, durable, comfortable (except in very hot and humid conditions), retain their appearance well, and are easy care. Their excellent performance has resulted in their widespread use and continued popularity. Woven fabrics are used in top weight and bottom weight apparel, sheets, blankets, bedspreads, curtains that match bedspreads, mattress ticking, table linens, and upholstery fabrics. The filaments are used in glass curtains, where the excellent light resistance of the fibers and the fineness of denier makes them particularly suitable for ninon and marquisette.

A second important use of polyester is in knitted fabrics. Slightly more filament yarns than spun yarns are used. Polyester as well as polyester/cotton blend yarns are used. Knit fabrics of polyester wear well, are comfortable, retain their appearance well, and are easy care.

The first use of polyester filaments was in knit shirts for men and blouses for women. The use of fil-

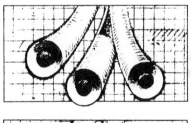

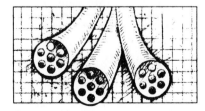

Fig. 8–13 *Hollow polyester fibers: 1-Hollofil, 4-Qallofil, and 7-Hollofil. (Courtesy of E. I. du Pont de Nemours & Company)*

ament polyester increased tremendously when textured yarns were developed. Both smooth and textured filaments are used in career apparel such as uniforms and in furnishings such as tricot sheets, warp knit upholstery, and warp knit window treatment fabrics.

A third important use of polyester is in fiberfill. Used in pillows, comforters, bedspreads, other quilted household and apparel fabrics, and winter jackets, polyester dominates the market. Other fiberfill materials include down, feathers, or acetate. The polyester used for fiberfill is engineered for resiliency and loft. The durability, comfort, and easy care of polyester also make it appropriate for this end use. Fiberfill is not visible during use—but poor performance shows up in lumpy products. A new fiberfill from Japan creates the soft, feathery feel of down.

Nonwoven or fiberweb fabrics are a fourth important use of polyester. Interfacings or interlinings, pillow covers, and mattress interlinings are examples of uses for nonwoven fabrics. They are used where the durability of rayon is inadequate and where absorbency is not needed. Olefin is a strong competitor in many industrial uses.

Tire cord is a fifth important use of polyester. Polyester tires do not "flat spot" as nylon tires do.

Polyester accounts for a small percentage of carpets that are produced. Polyester carpets have a softer hand than most nylon carpets. The performance of polyester carpets has not been quite as high as that of nylon carpets under most conditions of use. However, polyester carpets perform well in low-use areas like bedrooms. The first polyester carpets suffered from a "walked down" look after a period of wear in heavy-traffic areas. This problem has been minimized by autoclave heat setting the fibers. Hoechst Celanese has a polyester carpet fiber, Trevira XPS, with enhanced resistance to matting and crushing.

Polyester is chosen for many other consumer and industrial uses: pile fabrics, tents, ropes, cording, fishing line, cover stock for disposable diapers, garden hoses, sails, seat belts, filters, fabrics used in road building, seed and fertilizer bags, sewing threads, and artificial arteries, veins, and hearts. Research continues to increase industrial applications.

Types and Kinds of Polyester

Some of the more commonly seen trade names for polyester fibers, and the companies that produce

Table 8–16   Variants of Polyester

Cross Section	Dyeability	Crimp or Textured	Tenacity
Round	Disperse dyeable	Producer textured	Regular tenacity
Trilobal	Cationic dyeable	Partially oriented	Intermediate tenacity
Triangular	Solution dyed	Undrawn filament	High tenacity
Trilateral	Optically whitened		High elongation
Pentalobal	Deep dye		Mid-modulus
Scalloped oval	Extra bright		High-modulus
Octolobal	Bright heather		
Heptalobol	Dark heather		
Hollow (7, 4, or 1 channels)			

Shrinkage	Other
High shrinkage	Pill resistant
Normal shrinkage	Homopolymer
Low shrinkage	Copolymer
Heat stabilized	Bicomponent
Chemically stabilized, adhesive activated	Bigeneric
	Polished high luster
	Binder fiber
	Soft luster

Table 8–17 Polyester for Specialized Uses

Producer	Trade Name	Use
Allied-Signal	A.C.E.	Tire cord, furniture webbing
Du Pont	Hollofil, Quallofil	Fiberfill and insulating fibers
	Sontara	Spunlaced nonwoven fabrics
Hoechst-Celanese	ESP	
	Ceylon	
	Comfort Fiber	Staple fiber for apparel uses
	Loftguard	Staple fiber for industrial uses
	Polar Guard	
	Lambda	Filament yarns with spun-yarn characteristics
	Serene	
	Superba	
	Trevira HT	Marine & military uses; ropes, cordage.
	Trevira XPS	Carpeting
	BTU	Cold-weather apparel

them, include: Fortrel by Fiber Industries, Dacron by Du Pont, Kodel by Eastman, and Trevira by Hoechst Celanese. Tables 8-16 and 8-17 describe fiber modifications and fibers engineered for special end uses. Each company has a large variety of specific fibers or yarns that combine one or more modifications.

OLEFIN

Many attempts were made to polymerize ethylene in the 1920s. Ethylene was polymerized and used as an important plastic during World War II, but filaments made from it did not have sufficient properties for use in textile fibers. In 1954, Karl Ziegler in Germany developed a process in which the melting point of polymerized ethylene filaments was raised but it still was too low for many uses. In Italy, Giulio Natta worked with polypropylene and was successful in making linear polymers of high molecular weight that proved to be suitable for most textile applications. By 1957, Italy was producing olefin fibers; U.S. production of olefin fibers started in 1960.

Olefin fibers have a combination of properties that make them good for furnishings, apparel that does not need ironing, and industrial uses. Olefin fibers are strong and resistant to abrasion, inexpensive, chemically inert, and thermoplastic but static resistant.

Production of Olefin

There were 76 producers of polypropylene in the United States in 1990.

Two processes are used to produce olefin. The high-pressure system, at a pressure of 10 tons per square inch, is used to produce polyethylene film. The low-pressure system, at a lower temperature and in the presence of a catalyst and hydrocarbon solvent, is less expensive and produces a polymer (polyethylene) more suitable for textile uses. The extrusion process is similar to that of nylon and polyester. Olefin is melt spun into water or cool air and cold drawn to six times its spun length. Olefins differ from polyester and nylon in that the solution crystallizes very rapidly (undrawn fibers are crystalline), so that the spinning conditions and after treatments greatly affect the fiber properties. Olefin is an inexpensive fiber with extremely good performance characteristics for many end uses. The low price of olefin, coupled with its properties, explains its widespread use in industrial uses, furnishings, and apparel. Olefin is one synthetic fiber with a growing production (see Table 8-18).

Physical Structure of Olefin

Olefins are produced as monofilament, multifilament, staple fiber, and tow with variable tenacities. The fibers are colorless, usually round in cross section, and have a somewhat waxy feel (Figure 8-14).

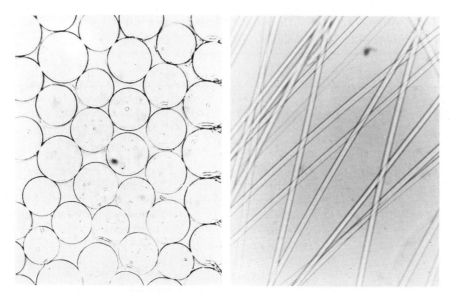

Fig. 8–14 *Photomicrographs showing cross-sectional* (left) *and longitudinal* (right) *views of olefin. (Courtesy of Hercules, Inc.)*

The cross section can be modified depending on end use.

Chemical Composition and Molecular Arrangement of Olefin

Olefin fibers—manufactured fibers in which the fiber-forming substance is any long-chain synthetic polymer composed of at least 85 percent by weight of ethylene, propylene, or other olefin units except amorphous (noncrystalline) polyolefins qualifying . . . as rubber. —Federal Trade Commission.

Olefin is often referred to as polypropylene. Polypropylene has a three-dimensional structure with a backbone of carbon atoms and methyl groups ($-CH_3$) protruding from the chain. Giulio

Table 8–18   Production of Synthetic Fibers (millions of pounds)

Fibers	1990	1985	1980	1975	(peak year)
Acrylic	506	631	779	525	1981
Nylon	2,662	2,343	2,358	1,857	1989
Olefin	1,822	1,249	748	497	still growing
Polyester	3,195	3,341	3,989	2,995	1980

Source: Chemical and Engineering News, June 9, 1986, p. 38 and June 24, 1991, p. 34.

Natta observed that three configurations could be developed when propylene was polymerized and that when all the methyl groups were on one side of the chain, the molecular chains could pack together and crystallize. Natta developed the process in which polymerization would take place in this manner and, together with Karl Ziegler, received the Nobel Prize in 1963 for their work.

Karl Ziegler's work on catalysts to polymerize ethylene and Giulio Natta's discovery of steriospecific polymerization made it possible to obtain high-molecular-weight crystalline polypropylene polymers. *Steriospecific polymerization* means that the molecules are specifically arranged in space so that all the methyl groups have the same spatial arrangement. Natta called this phenomenon *isotactic*. In the atactic form, the methyl groups are randomly arranged, resulting in an amorphous polymer that would qualify as rubber.

Methyl groups

Olefin fibers have no polar groups. The chains are held together by crystallinity alone; the fiber is highly crystalline. The absence of polar groups makes dyeing a problem. Solution dyeing is expensive and less versatile than other methods of adding color to fibers or fabrics. An acid-dyeable olefin has been developed.

Properties of Olefin

Olefin's performance in apparel and furnishing fabrics is summarized in Table 8-19.

AESTHETICS Olefins are usually produced with a medium luster and smooth texture, but the luster and texture can be modified depending on the end use. Olefin has a waxy hand; crimped fibers with modified cross sections have a much more attractive hand. Fibers modified in this manner are most often used for apparel and furnishing products. Drape can be varied relative to end use by selection of fiber modification, fabric-construction method, and finish. Finer denier fibers produce a softer, natural drape.

Current olefins do not look artificial as the early olefins did. These contemporary olefins can be modified easily by changing their cross section, fiber size, crimp, and luster. Olefin fibers are most often solution dyed; many producers provide a wide variety of color choices for olefins designed for furnishing or apparel uses. Some interior designers prefer

Table 8–19 Summary of the Performance of Olefin in Apparel and Furnishing Fabrics

Aesthetic	Variable
Luster	Medium
Durability	**High**
Abrasion resistance	Very good
Tenacity	High
Elongation	Variable
Comfort	**Moderate**
Absorbency	Low
Thermal retention	Good
Appearance Retention	**Excellent**
Resiliency	Excellent
Dimensional stability	Excellent
Elastic recovery	Excellent
Recommended care	Machine wash, dry at low temperature (apparel) Dry extraction method (furnishings)

olefin to most other fibers because of its attractive appearance and other positive performance aspects coupled with its relatively low price compared to similar products of different fibers.

DURABILITY Olefins may be produced with different strengths suited to the end use. The tenacity of polypropylenes ranges from 3.5 to 8.0 g/d; that of polyethylenes ranges from 1.5-7.0 g/d. Wet strength is equal to dry strength for both types. An ultra-high-strength olefin, Spectra by Allied-Signal, has a tenacity of up to 30 g/d and is used in industrial end uses. Fibers produced for less demanding end uses have tenacities of 4.5 to 6.0 g/d. Olefin fibers have very good abrasion resistance. Elongation varies with the type of olefin. For olefins normally used in apparel and furnishings, the elongation is 10-45 percent with excellent recovery.

Olefin products are extremely durable. Olefin has excellent strength characteristics. With its low density, it is possible to produce highly durable, lightweight products. Resistance to abrasion and chemicals is excellent. This combination of characteristics and low cost means that olefin is very competitive with other fibers with equal or superior durability characteristics. In end uses where durability, low cost, and low density are critical, such as ropes and cables of great size or length, olefin is often selected.

COMFORT Olefins have a low moisture regain, less than 0.1 percent, hence they are not absorbent. Color is normally added during fiber production; most olefin fibers are solution dyed.

Because olefins are nonpolar in nature, they are not prone to static electricity problems. Olefins do have excellent wicking abilities, so the fibers are able to wick moisture away from the surface of the skin. For this reason, olefin is becoming more important in some apparel end uses, such as active sportswear. Olefin is also suited for its use in disposable diapers. As a cover stock, it does not absorb moisture, thus minimizing problems with leakage.

Olefin has good heat retention. However, it is olefin's ability to wick moisture that dictates its use in active sportswear, socks, and underwear. It is used in active sportswear to wick perspiration away from the body and to aid in heat loss. In cold-weather wear and active sportswear, olefin is used to keep the skin dry by wicking moisture away from the skin's surface.

Olefin fibers are the lightest of the textile fibers. Polypropylene has a specific gravity of .90 to .91;

polyethylene, .92 to .96. This low specific gravity provides more fiber per pound for better cover. Producers are working to minimize problems with low softening and melting temperatures, difficulty in dyeing, and unpleasant hand. When these problems are solved, olefins would be good for warmth-without-weight fabrics for sweaters and blankets. It takes 1.27 pounds of nylon or 1.71 pounds of cotton to cover the same volume as 1 pound of olefin.

With modifications of cross section, crimp, and fiber size, it is possible to produce olefin upholstery fabrics that are extremely comfortable. Olefins with deniers of 1.7 are used in upholstery fabrics to minimize problems with the hand and texture of the fabric. Compare that low denier with the normal denier of 2 or greater for most other upholstery fibers. Olefin fibers with a similar small denier are also used in apparel fabrics. Soft and lightweight olefin fibers with good wicking characteristics are prized by both amateur and professional athletes for the edge they contribute to their performance.

APPEARANCE RETENTION Olefin has excellent resiliency and recovers quickly from wrinkling. Olefin has outstanding shrinkage resistance as long as it is not heated. It also has excellent elastic recovery. Olefin is able to retain its attractive appearance for years. Since the fiber can be heat set, wrinkles will be minimal and crimp and other three-dimensional effects will be permanent. The fiber does not react with most chemicals so it does not soil or stain readily. Designers often find olefin carpeting and upholstery fabrics ideal for a wide variety of end uses.

CARE Olefins have easy-care characteristics that make them suited to a number of end uses. Because they are hydrophobic, they are not affected by water-borne stains. They dry quickly after washing. Dry cleaning is seldom recommended because olefins are swollen by common dry cleaning solvents such as perchloroethylene. Petroleum dry cleaning solvents are acceptable for cleaning olefins, but if perchloroethylene is used, the damage cannot be reversed.

Since olefin is not absorbent, water-borne stains are not a problem. The fiber does not pick up color from stains or items that bleed in the wash. The major problems with olefin relate to its oleophilic and heat-sensitive nature. Oily stains are extremely difficult to remove. Exposure to oil may cause the fiber to swell. Exposure to excess heat causes the fiber to shrink and melt. Furnishing items of olefin should never be treated with soil removal agents that contain perchloroethylene since this solvent causes the fiber to swell and, thus, alters the appearance of the treated area.

Olefins have excellent resistance to acids, alkalis, insects, and microorganisms. They are affected by sunlight, but stabilizers can be added to correct this disadvantage. Indoor/outdoor carpeting made of olefin fibers can be hosed off.

Olefins have a low melting point (325-335°F), which limits their use in apparel. Warm or cold water should be used for spot cleaning or washing. Olefin fabrics should be air dried. Olefins should be dried and ironed at low temperatures.

Uses of Olefin

Olefin is found in an ever-widening array of end uses. In apparel, it is used for underwear, socks, sweaters, and active sportswear (Figure 8-15). Thinsulate is a low-bulk, ultra-fine-microdenier fiberfill of olefin and polyester produced by 3M and used in ski jackets and other outerwear where a less bulky silhouette is desired. In furnishings, olefin is used in carpeting as face yarns and in tufted carpets as backing; as nonwoven, needle-punched carpets and carpet tiles; and as upholstery, draperies, and slipcovers.

Olefin is used in furnishings, by itself and in blends with other fibers. Olefin has almost completely replaced jute in carpet backing because of its low cost, ease of processing, excellent durability characteristics, and suitability to a wide variety of

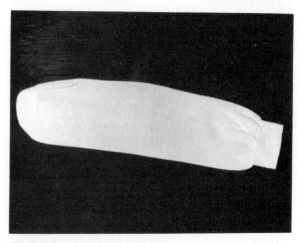

Fig. 8–15 Sock knit of olefin.

face yarns, end uses, and finishing procedures. Duon olefin by Phillips Fiber Corp. is used for non-woven fabrics for furniture webbing because it is versatile, efficient, easy to handle, and economic.

It is in industrial applications that olefin really proves itself. Olefin's continued growth, at a time when the market for most other fibers is stable or receding, is due to its versatility, serviceability, and low cost in a wide array of applications. Olefin makes an ideal geotextile, those textiles that are used in contact with the soil. It is used to produce roadbed support fabrics, like Petromat and Petrotak, that provide a water and particle barrier between road surfaces and the underlying soil foundation. Roadbed support fabrics are used on highways and streets, rail lines, and parking lots to extend their life. Geotextiles of olefin are extremely important in minimizing damage to the environment. For example, olefin is used in drainage systems to keep soil in place and minimize erosion. Supergro is an erosion control blanket used in landscaping to protect newly seeded areas and prevent soil erosion. Fabrisoil is a reusable cover for landfills that minimizes the cost of daily covering the site with soil and scraping the soil off for the next day's additions.

Alpha olefin, a moldable fiber by Phillips Fiber Corp., is used in many places in car interiors: floor coverings, upholstery, headliners, sun visors, instrument panels, arm rests, package shelf fabric, door and side panels, and carpeting in trunks and cargo areas. It is also a popular fiber in boats for furnishings and finishing fabrics and as surface coverings on docks and decks.

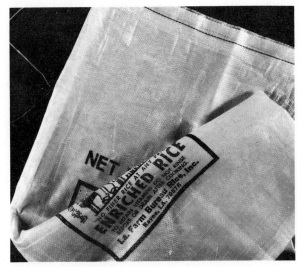

Fig. 8–16 *Bag woven with slit-olefin yarns.*

Table 8–20 Types and Kinds of Olefin Fibers

Heat stabilized	Acid dyeable
Light stabilized	Solution dyed
Modified cross section	Bicomponent
Pigmented	Fibrillated

In industrial end uses, olefin is found in carpet backing such as Typar, dye nets, cover stock for diapers, filter fabrics, laundry and sand bags, wall–panel fabrics such as Tyvek, envelopes (also Tyvek), banners, geotextiles, ground-control fabrics such as Mirafi and Supac, protective clothing such as Tyvek, substrate for coated fabrics, ropes and twines, and roadbed stabilizer fabrics such as Petromat. Figure 8-16 shows a rice bag of olefin.

Tables 8-20 and 8-21 list modifications, trade names, and producers of olefin. Table 8-22 compares the characteristics of nylon, polyester, and olefin, the three melt-spun fibers discussed in this chapter.

ACRYLIC

Acrylonitrile, the substance from which *acrylic fibers* are made and from which the generic name is derived, was first made in Germany in 1893. It was another chemical used by Carothers and his team in their fundamental research on high polymers for the Du Pont Company.

Table 8–21 Some Trade Names and Producers of Olefins

Patlon, Marquessa Lana, Propex III	Amoco Fabrics & Fibers Co.
Tyvek	Du Pont
Fibrilawn, Fibrilon	Fibron Corp.
Herculon	Hercules, Inc.
Duraguard, Evolution, Evolution III	Kimberly-Clark
Marvess, Duon, Petromat	Phillips Fibers
Polyloom	Polyloom Corp.
Typar, Biobarrier	Reemay, Inc.
Spectra 900, Spectra 1000	Allied-Signal, Inc.

Table 8–22   Comparison of Melt-Spun Fibers

	Nylon	*Polyester*	*Olefin*
Breaking tenacity g/d	2.3–9.8 filament	2.8–9.5 filament	3.5–8.0 filament
	2.9–7.2 staple	2.4–7.0 staple	
Specific gravity	1.14	1.22 or 1.38	0.91
Moisture regain %	4.0–4.5	0.4–0.8	Less than 1
Melting point	482° or 414°F	540° or 482°F	325°–335°F
Safe ironing temperature	270°–300°F	325°–350°F	250°F–lowest setting
Effect of light	Poor resistance	Good resistance	Poor resistance

Du Pont developed an acrylic fiber in 1944 and started commercial production of this fiber in 1950. Du Pont ceased acrylic production in 1991.

The marketing of acrylic fibers frequently takes advantage of its wool-like characteristics. Terms like "virgin acrylic", "mothproof", and "moth–resistant" apparently appeal to consumers. These terms do not convey anything significant since acrylics are inherently moth resistant and are not recycled in the same way that wool is recycled.

Production of Acrylic

Three companies produced acrylic in 1991. Some acrylic fibers are dry or solvent spun and others are wet spun. In *solvent spinning*, or *dry spinning*, the polymers are dissolved in a suitable solvent, such as dimethyl formamide, extruded into warm air, and solidified by evaporation of the solvent. After spinning, the fibers are stretched hot, three to ten times their original length, and then crimped, and marketed as cut staple or tow. In *wet spinning*, the polymer is dissolved in solvent, extruded into a coagulating bath, dried, crimped, and collected as tow for use in the high–bulk process or cut into staple and baled.

Physical Structure of Acrylic

The cross-sectional shape of acrylic fibers varies as a result of the spinning method used to produce them (Figure 8-17). Dry spinning produces a dog-bone shape. Wet spinning imparts a round or lima–bean shape to Acrilan, Creslan, and Zefran. Differences in cross-sectional shape affect physical and aesthetic properties and thus can be a factor in determining appropriate end use. Round and lima–bean shapes have a higher bending stiffness, which contributes to resiliency, and are appropriate for bulky sweaters

and blankets. Dog-bone shape gives the softness and luster desirable for other uses.

All the production of acrylic fibers in the United States is staple fiber and tow. Staple fiber is available in deniers and lengths suitable for all spinning systems. Acrylic fibers also vary in shrinkage potential. Bicomponent fibers were first produced as acrylics. Some filament yarn acrylic fabrics are imported, mostly in window treatments.

Chemical Composition and Molecular Arrangement of Acrylic

Acrylic fibers—manufactured fibers in which the fiber-forming substance is any long-chain synthetic polymer composed of at least 85 percent by weight of acrylonitrile units ($-CH_2-CH-$).
$$\underset{CN}{|}$$

—*Federal Trade Commission.*

Fibers of 100 percent polyacrylonitrile have a compact, highly oriented internal structure that

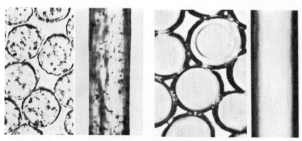

Fig. 8–17 *Photomicrographs of acrylic fibers: cross-sectional and longitudinal views. (From left to right) Acrilan and Creslan. (Acrilan courtesy of Fibers Division of Monsanto Chemical Co., a unit of Monsanto Co., Creslan courtesy of the Cyanamid Company.)*

makes them virtually undyeable. They are an example of a *homopolymer*, a fiber composed of a single substance. Schematically, a homopolymer could be diagrammed:

x x x x x x x x x x x x x x   **Homopolymer**

Since this structure in acrylic fibers makes dyeing so difficult, most acrylics are made as *copolymers* with up to 15 percent additives, which give a more open structure and permit dye to be absorbed into the fiber. The additives furnish dye sites that can be modified for specific dye classes, which makes cross dyeing possible. Copolymer fibers are composed of two or more compounds and could be diagrammed:

O x O x O x O x O x O x O x   **Copolymer**

or:

x x x x x O x x x x O   **Copolymer**

depending on the percentage of substances and their arrangement in relations to each other.

In graft polymerization, the additive does not become a part of the main molecular chain but is a side chain. The side branches are attached to the backbone chain of the molecule, which gives the molecular chains a more open structure and less crystallinity; dye receptivity is increased.

Some fibers have molecules with chemically reactive groups; others are chemically inert. A chemically inert molecule can be made reactive by grafting it with reactive groups. It could be diagrammed:

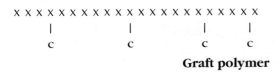

Graft polymer

The copolymer acrylics are not as strong as the homopolymers or *graft polymer* acrylics. Since the end uses for acrylics are mostly apparel and furnishings, the reduced strength is not a major concern.

Properties of Acrylic

Acrylic fibers are soft, warm, lightweight, and resilient. They make easy-care fabrics. Because of their low specific gravity and high-bulk properties, the acrylics have been called the "warmth without weight" fibers. Acrylics have been very successful in end uses such as sweaters and blankets that were previously dominated by wool. They are superior to wool in their easy-care properties and are nonallergenic. Bulky acrylic yarns are also popular in socks, fleece fabrics, fake-fur fabrics, and craft yarns. Table 8-23 summarizes the performance characteristics of acrylics.

AESTHETIC Acrylic fibers possess favorable aesthetic properties. They are attractive and have a soft, pleasant hand. The fibers are usually textured. The resulting bulky spun yarns are wool-like in texture. Indeed, acrylic fabrics imitate wool fabrics more successfully than any of the other manufactured fibers.

Apparel and furnishing items of all acrylic or acrylic blends are attractive. Their luster is matte due to delustering, the irregular cross-sectional fiber shape, and the crimp. Since these products are almost always staple, that wool-like appearance is maintained. Bulky yarns and bicomponent fibers contribute to the wool-like appearance, too.

Table 8–23 **Summary of the Performance of Acrylic in Apparel and Furnishing Fabrics**

Aesthetic	*Wool-like*
Durability	*Moderate*
Abrasion resistance	Moderate
Tenacity	Moderate
Elongation	Moderate-high
Comfort	*Moderate*
Absorbency	Low
Thermal retention	Moderate
Appearance	
Retention	*Moderate*
Resiliency	Moderate
Dimensional stability	Moderate
Elastic recovery	Moderate
Recommended care	Machine wash; follow care label (apparel) Dry clean or dry extraction method (furnishings)

American Cyanamid has introduced an acrylic microfiber, MicroSupreme. It has a denier per filament of 0.8 and is used in fine-gauge knitted and woven apparel, hosiery, and furnishings.

DURABILITY Acrylics are not as durable as nylon, polyester, or olefin fibers, but, in apparel and furnishings, the strength of acrylics is satisfactory. Dry tenacity ranges from 2.0 to 3.0 g/d, which is moderate. Abrasion resistance is moderate. The elongation at break is 35 percent. Elongation increases when the fiber is wet. The overall durability of acrylic fibers is moderate, similar to that of wool and cotton.

Furnishings of acrylic or acrylic blends are highly durable. They provide reasonable resistance to abrasion for upholstery fabrics. They are sufficiently strong to withstand laundering (table linens), dry cleaning (draperies), and dry extraction cleaning (carpet). Pilling can be a noticeable problem with these staple fiber fabrics, however. Some low-pilling fiber modifications are available. In addition, fabric finishes can be used to reduce pilling.

Monsanto has introduced a Wear Dated Traffic Control Carpet of 88 percent nylon/12 percent acrylic. The carpet has high bulk and is more durable than nylon alone. Both fibers are blended together in the carpet yarn, twisted, and heat set. Since the acrylic is a high shrinkage modification, it shrinks and tightens the yarn tuft, giving it its good durability characteristics.

Because of its exceptional resistance to weathering, acrylic is widely used in awnings and tarpaulins. Table 8–24 shows that acrylic fibers are comparable to wool in their durability properties.

COMFORT The fiber surface of acrylic fibers is much less regular than that of other synthetic fibers. Photomicrographs show irregularities and indentations on the surface (see Figure 8-18). In spite of

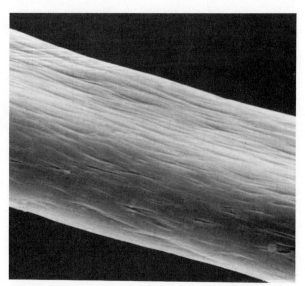

Fig. 8–18 *Acrylic that is magnified 3,000 times shows a pitted and irregular surface.*

the relatively low moisture regain of 1.0–2.5 percent, acrylics are moderately comfortable because of the irregular fiber surface. Instead of absorbing moisture and becoming wet to the touch, acrylic fibers tend to wick moisture to the outside of the fabric where it evaporates more readily. The evaporation aids in cooling the body.

Another factor that makes acrylics comfortable is that the fibers and yarns can be made with high bulk. Acrylic fibers can be produced with a *latent shrinkage potential* and retain the bulk indefinitely at room temperature. The resulting bulky fabrics retain body heat well so they are warm in cold temperatures. Bulky knit sweaters are a familiar example of this.

The structure of the yarn and fabric can be varied to make a warmer or cooler product, depending on how it is used. In general, acrylics are more comfortable than nylon and polyester, but not as comfortable as cotton in hot, humid weather, or as wool in very cold or cold, humid weather.

The density of acrylic is similar to that of nylon. Thus, the fabrics are lightweight with good durability. In apparel, this means bulky sweaters of acrylic are not as heavy as wool sweaters. Acrylic blankets are lighter than similar wool blankets.

APPEARANCE RETENTION Acrylic fibers exhibit moderate resiliency and recovery from bending, thus they resist wrinkling during use and care. They have moderate dimensional stability. When proper yarn and fabric structures are utilized, the dimen-

Table 8–24 Comparison of Acrylic Fibers With Wool—Durability

Fiber Property	Acrylic	Wool
Abrasion resistance	Good	Fair
Breaking tenacity	2.0–3.0 g/d dry	1.5 g/d dry
	1.8–2.7 g/d wet	1.0 g/d wet
Elongation at break	35 percent	25 percent
Elastic recovery	92 percent	99 percent

sional stability of acrylic fabrics is good. Acrylics shrink when exposed to boiling water, so high temperatures and steam should be avoided. The fibers have poor hot–wet properties.

Acrylic fibers cannot be heat set like nylon and polyester because acrylic does not melt, but decomposes and discolors when heated. However, some acrylics can have pleats or creases set in that are not affected by normal use or care. With the application of heat and/or steam, the crease or pleats can be removed.

Another way that acrylics differ from nylon and polyester is that dimensional stability is not as good. Fabrics may shrink or stretch.

Pills form on some acrylic fabrics. Acrylics tend to fibrillate, or crack, with abrasion, which may contribute to pilling.

Acrylics and blends with acrylic maintain their appearance well. The bulk characteristics are permanent if the product receives the appropriate care. These fibers are less likely to mat than some fibers. With solution dyeing of some upholstery, drapery, and awning fabrics, colors are permanent. Awning fabrics of solution-dyed acrylic have become quite popular in finishing window exteriors, entries, and outdoor entertainment areas.

CARE In caring for items made of acrylic, it is especially important to follow the instructions found on care labels. There are several basic acrylic fibers with slightly differing properties due to the polymer composition and manufacturing methods. With the additional variations available through shrinkage potentials of acrylic fibers, as well as of bicomponent fibers, there are many factors that can affect appropriate care.

The acrylics have good resistance to most chemicals except strong alkalis and chlorine bleaches. This is not surprising; fibers containing nitrogen are usually susceptible to damage from alkali and chlorine. Except for the furlike fabrics, acrylic fabrics have good wash-and-wear characteristics. They do not wrinkle if handled properly and if directions on the label are followed.

Some items made from high-bulk yarns of bicomponent fibers need to be machine dried to regain their shape after washing. If they are blocked, dried flat, or drip dried, they may be too large or misshapen. Rewash and then tumble dry the knit, and it should recover its original shape.

Acrylics can be dry cleaned. However, with some fabrics the finish is removed, resulting in a harsh feel. Thus, care labeling should be followed.

Acrylics are resistant to moth damage and mildew, and have excellent resistance to sunlight.

Following the recommended care procedures for acrylic or acrylic blend products is especially true for electric blankets. They are usually made of acrylic and should never be dry cleaned. Dry cleaning solvents dissolve the protective coating on the wiring of the blanket, resulting in a high risk of electric shock or fire. Steam cleaning of draperies, upholstery, and carpeting is generally not recommended because acrylics may shrink.

Mann Industries has developed a new antimicrobial fiber, Biokryl, to be used in apparel, furnishing, and industrial applications. Products include nursing uniforms, socks, shoe liners, sportswear, contract carpet and upholstery, and surgical barrier fabrics and industrial filters.

Uses of Acrylic

Acrylic accounted for approximately 5 percent of the fiber produced in the United States in 1990, approximately 506 million pounds. Although more acrylic is used in apparel, it is also important in furnishings and industrial products. Knitted apparel items of acrylic include fleece fabrics, sweaters, and socks (Figure 8-19). Fleece fabrics are a frequently used item in jogging outfits and active sportswear and are available in many colors and prints.

Craft yarns are another important end use of acrylic fibers. Craft yarns are often made of a heavier denier (5-6 denier). Many sweaters, vests, and afghans are knit or crocheted with these yarns. Acrylic yarns are also used for embroidery, weaving, and other crafts.

Another important use for acrylic is for pile fabrics; thick, snuggly fun furs that are used for coats, jackets, linings, or soft, cuddly stuffed animals.

Acrylic is used in furnishings. Upholstery fabrics may be flat-woven fabrics or velvets. Usually they have a wool-like appearance. Drapery fabrics of acrylic are available in this country and are imported from Europe. This is an appropriate and growing end use for acrylics because of their good sunlight resistance and weathering properties.

Acrylics are used in blankets. A variety of fabrics and fabric construction methods are used. Both lightweight and winter-weight blankets are available. Blankets are an appropriate use for acrylics because the cost is lower, the bulky fabrics are lighter weight, and the care is easier than for wool blankets.

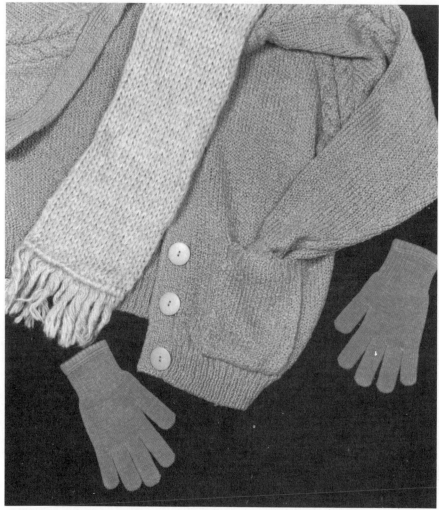

Fig. 8–19   *Acrylic is used in fleece, socks, sweaters, and other knits.*

Carpets and rugs of acrylic or blends look more wool-like than several other synthetic fibers, and have easier care requirements and lower cost than wool carpets.

Acrylics are found in a number of industrial uses for which their chemical resistance and good weathering properties make them suitable: awnings and tarpaulins, luggage, boat and other vehicle covers, outdoor furniture, tents, carbon fiber precursors, office room dividers, and sandbags.

Types and Kinds of Acrylic

Each company that produces acrylic in the United States identifies its fiber by a trade name:

Trade Name	Company	Type
Acrilan, Acrilan II, Bi-Loft, Du-Rel, Fi-Lana, Pa-Qel, So-Lara	Monsanto Chemical Co.	Staple and tow
Creslan	American Cyanamid	Staple and tow
Zefran, Biokryl, Mann Aeryl, Acry Pulp	Mann Industries, Inc.	Staple

Fiber variants that are tailored for a specific end use or differ in performance are also produced. See Table 8-26 for a list of fiber and yarn types available. Trade names and modifications for one producer, Monsanto Chemical Co., are:

Acrilan	
Bi-Loft	high bulk
So-Lara	producer colored
Fi-Lana	ultra–soft
Pa-Qel	bicomponent, high bulk
So-Qel	producer colored, bicomponent
Du-Rel	fade resistant pigmented fiber (upholstery)
Pil-Trol	pill resistant for specialty uniforms

Table 8–25 Comparison of Acrylics and Wool—Care

Fiber Property	Acrylic	Wool
Effect of alkalis	Resistant to weak alkalis	Harmed
Effect of acids	Resistant to most acids	Resistant to weak acids
Effect of solvents	Can be dry cleaned	Dry cleaning recommended
Effect of sunlight	Excellent resistance	Low resistance
Stability	Can be heat set for shape retention	Subject to felting, shrinkage
Permanence of creases	Creases can be set and removed by heat	Creases set by heat and moisture—not permanent
Effect of heat	Thermoplastic—sticks at 450–490°F	Scorches easily, becomes brittle at high temperature
Resistance to moths and fungi	Resistant	Harmed by moths; mildew forms on soiled, stored wool
Effect of water	None	May felt or mat, noticeable odor when wet

MODACRYLIC FIBERS

Modacrylic fibers are modified acrylics. They are made from acrylonitrile but a larger proportion of other polymers are added to make the copolymers. Production of modacrylic fibers started in the United States in 1949.

Modacrylics were the first inherently flame-retardant synthetic fibers; they do not support combustion, are very difficult to ignite, are self–extinguishing, and do not drip. This inherent flame retardancy makes them good for end uses such as protective clothing, children's sleepwear, contract draperies, fake furs, and wigs.

Production of Modacrylic Fibers

The modacrylic fibers are produced by polymerizing the components, dissolving the copolymer in acetone (dry spun), pumping the solution into a column of warm air, and stretching while hot. Currently Monsanto Chemical Co. is the only producer in the U.S. The trade name S.E.F. (self-extinguishing flame) is used.

Physical Structure of Modacrylic Fibers

The modacrylics are creamy white and are produced as staple or tow. They have a dog-bone or

Fig. 8–20 *Acrylics are used for luggage and outoor furniture because of their abrasion resistance and good weathering properties. (Courtesy of BASF Corp. Fibers Division.)*

Table 8–26 Types and Kinds of Acrylic Fibers and Yarns

Homopolymer
Copolymer
Graft polymer
Bicomponent
Blends of various deniers
Blends of homopolymer and copolymer
Helical, nonreversible crimp
Reversible crimp
Surface modified
Variable cross section—round, acorn, dog-bone
Variable dyeability—cationic, disperse, acidic, basic
Solution dyed

irregular cross section (Figure 8-21). Various deniers, lengths, crimp levels, and shrinkage potentials are available to fabric producers.

Chemical Composition and Molecular Arrangement of Modacrylic Fibers

Modacrylic fibers—manufactured fibers in which the fiber-forming substance is any long-chain synthetic polymer composed of less than 85 percent but at least 35 percent by weight acrylonitrile units except when the polymer qualifies as rubber. —Federal Trade Commission.

The chemicals used as copolymers include vinyl chloride (CH_2CHC1), vinylidene chloride (CH_2CC1_2), or vinylidene dicyanide (CH_2CCN_2).

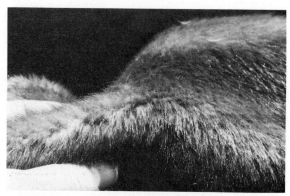

Fig. 8–22 *Furlike fabric of modacrylic. Notice the sleek guard hairs and the soft, fine undercoat.*

Properties of Modacrylic Fibers

Modacrylics are similar to the acrylics in their properties, the major differences being flame retardancy and improved heat resistance of modacrylics.

AESTHETIC Furlike fabrics, wigs, hairpieces, and fleece-type pile fabrics are important end uses for modacrylic fibers. Some are produced with different amounts of crimp and shrinkage potential. By mixing different fiber types it is possible to obtain fibers of different pile heights, long, polished fibers (guard hairs), and soft, highly crimped undercoat fibers much like real fur (Figure 8-22). Fabrics can be sheared, embossed, and printed to resemble fur.

Modacrylic has an attractive appearance similar to that of acrylic. It can be made to resemble wool with a soft, matte luster, or it can be made with a more intense luster to resemble the shiny guard hairs of fur.

Cross-Section 500X   Cross-Section 500X

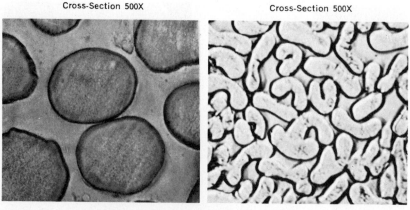

Fig. 8–21 *Photomicrographs of modacrylic fibers. (Courtesy of American Association of Textile Chemists and Colorists.)*

Table 8–27 Comparison of Modacrylic and Acrylic Fibers—Durability

Factor	Modacrylic	Acrylic
Strength	1.7–2.6 g/d	2.0–3.0 g/d
Elongation	30–60 percent	35 percent
Elastic recovery	99.5 percent	92 percent
Sunlight resistance	Excellent	Excellent

DURABILITY Modacrylics are less durable than acrylics but they have adequate durability for their end uses. A comparison of durability factors of modacrylics and acrylics is listed in Table 8–27.

The strength of modacrylics is similar to that of wool. Abrasion resistance is similar to acrylic. Elastic recovery is superior to that of acrylic. Modacrylic is generally used in products where safety is the number one concern and durability must be adequate, but does not need to be great.

COMFORT Modacrylics are poor conductors of heat. Fabrics are soft, warm, and resilient, but have a tendency to pill. Their absorbency is low, varying from 2 to 4 percent moisture regain.

Modacrylics combine flame retardancy with a relatively low density (1.35). This means that protective apparel need not be uncomfortably heavy. Flame-retardant furnishings, especially draperies, can be produced without great weight.

APPEARANCE RETENTION Modacrylic fibers exhibit moderate resiliency. In typical end uses, they do not wrinkle. They have moderate dimensional stability and high elastic recovery.

Modacrylics do pill more quickly than acrylics and are more sensitive to heat. They also mat more readily and are not as resilient as acrylics. Modacrylics tend to retain color well.

CARE Modacrylics are resistant to acids, weak alkalis, and most organic solvents. Most modacrylics dissolve in boiling acetone. They are resistant to mildew and moths. They have very good resistance to sunlight and very good flame resistance.

Modacrylics can be washed or dry cleaned, but special care must be taken. Excessive rubbing may cause fabrics to pill. Fibers are heat sensitive; they shrink at 250°F and stiffen at temperatures over 300°F. If fabrics are machine washed, use warm water and tumble dry at a low setting. Most fabrics need little ironing; the lowest setting should be used. Some of the furlike fabrics are dry cleanable; some require special care in dry cleaning (no steam, no tumble, tumble cold); some should be cleaned by a furrier method. Look for instructions on labels (Figure 8–23).

Modacrylics are more sensitive to loss of appearance from improper care than the acrylics. Note the precautions in the paragraph above. The precautions regarding steam cleaning discussed with acrylics also apply to modacrylics.

USES OF MODACRYLIC FIBERS Modacrylics are used primarily in those applications where flame retardancy is necessary or required by law or building codes (See Chapter 21). End uses include protective clothing such as pajamas and robes for children and the elderly and shirts and trousers for electric line personnel; furnishings including upholstery, window treatment fabrics, and blankets; and industrial applications including filters, blankets and upholstery in airplanes. Modacrylics are also used in applications where its heat sensitivity plays an important role including realistic fake furs and wigs or hair pieces that can be curled with a curling iron.

Fig. 8–23 *Label giving directions for cleaning furlike fabric.*

KEY TERMS

Synthetic fibers
Heat sensitivity
Glazing
Pilling
Oleophilic
Melt spinning
Heat setting
Nylon
Polyamides
Polyester
Polypropylene

Olefin
Polyethylene
Isotactic
Acrylic fibers
Solvent or dry spinning
Wet spinning
Copolymer
Homopolymer
Graft polymer
Modacrylic fibers

QUESTIONS

1. Explain the differences in chemical composition between these groups of fibers:
   polyethylene and polypropylene
   acrylic and modacrylic

2. Identify the differences in properties between the pairs of fibers listed in question 1.

3. What are the major performance characteristics of each of these fibers: nylon, polyester, olefin, acrylic, and modacrylic?

4. What spinning process is used to produce each of these fibers: nylon, polyester, olefin, acrylic, modacrylic? How does the spinning process relate to the fiber's cross-sectional shape?

5. How do the characteristics of these fibers differ from those of the natural fibers and those produced from naturally occurring polymers?

6. Identify a synthetic fiber that would be an appropriate choice for each end use listed below and explain, using performance characteristics, why that fiber was selected:
   carpet for department store boutique area
   pantyhose
   man's sweater vest
   geotextile for use as roadbed underlay
   lead rope for horses or ponies
   upholstery fabric for theater seats

SUGGESTED READINGS

Jerg, Gunter, and Baumann, Josef (1990). "Polyester Microfibers: A New Generation of Fabrics." *Textile Chemist and Colorist*, 22 (12), pp. 12–14.

Mansfield, Richard G. (August, 1990). "Polypropylene: Strong Backing in Carpets." *America's Textiles International*, pp. 46–48.

Moore, Ronald A. F. (1989). "Nylon 6 and Nylon 6,6: How Different Are They?" *Textile Chemist and Colorist*, 21 (2), pp. 19–22.

Trotman, E. R. (1984). *Dyeing and Chemical Technology of Textile Fibers.* New York: John Wiley & Sons.

Zeronian, S. Haig, and Collins, Martha J. (1988). "Improving the Comfort of Polyester Fabrics." *Textile Chemist and Colorist*, 20 (4), pp. 25–28.

CHAPTER 9

Special Use Fibers

OBJECTIVES

- To understand the properties of the special use fibers.

- To relate the properties of these fibers to their end uses.

- To recognize the importance of these fibers in apparel, furnishings, and industrial products.

*T*HIS CHAPTER FOCUSES ON FIBERS WITH UNIQUE characteristics. Although some of these fibers are in common consumer products, consumers may not be aware of them. Many of these fibers are used in applications so specialized that the average consumer would have little contact with them. However, these textiles contribute significantly to the technological advances we accept as commonplace and necessary for the lives we lead. The fibers are grouped by the purposes they serve: elastomeric or protective.

ELASTOMERIC FIBERS

According to the American Society of Testing and Materials (ASTM), an *elastomer* is a natural or synthetic polymer that, at room temperature, can be stretched repeatedly to at least twice its original length and that, after removal of the tensile load, will immediately and forcibly return to approximately its original length. Elastomeric fibers include spandex, rubber, and anidex. Anidex is no longer produced in the United States.

Many textile products need some stretch or elasticity. There are two kinds of stretch: power stretch and comfort stretch. *Power stretch* is important in end uses where holding power and elasticity are needed. Elastic fibers that have a high retractive force must be used to attain this kind of stretch. Some end uses are foundation garments, surgical-support garments, swimsuits, garters, belts, and suspenders.

Comfort stretch is important in products where only elasticity is desired. Comfort-stretch fabrics look no different than nonstretch fabrics and are usually lighter in weight than power-stretch fabrics.

Rubber

Rubber—manufactured fiber in which the fiber-forming substance is comprised of natural or synthetic rubber, including:

1. A manufactured fiber in which the fiber-forming substance is a hydrocarbon such as natural rubber, polyisoprene, polybutadiene, copolymers of dienes and hydrocarbons, or amorphous (noncrystalline) polyolefins.

2. A manufactured fiber in which the fiber-forming substance is a copolymer of acrylonitrile

and a diene (such as butadiene) composed of not more than 50 percent but at least 10 percent by weight of acrylonitrile units $(-CH_2-CH-)$.
$$\underset{CN}{|}$$

The term lastrile *may be used as a generic description for fibers falling in this category.*

3. A manufactured fiber in which the fiber-forming substance is a polychloroprene or a copolymer of chloroprene in which at least 35 percent by weight of the fiber-forming substance is composed of chloroprene units $(-CH_2-C=CH-CH_2-)$.
$$\underset{Cl}{|}$$

—Federal Trade Commission.

Natural *rubber* is the oldest elastomer and the least expensive. It is obtained by coagulation of the latex from the rubber tree *Hevea brasiliensis*. In 1905, sheets of rubber were cut into strips that made the yarns used in foundation garments and the like. During and shortly after World War II, synthetic rubbers were developed. These synthetic rubbers are cross-linked diene polymers, copolymers containing dienes, or amorphous polyolefins. Both synthetic and natural rubbers must be vulcanized or cross-linked with sulfur in order to develop elastomeric properties. Natural and synthetic rubbers are large in cross section. The shape of the cross section is round if extruded or rectangular if cut.

Rubber has excellent elongation characteristics of 700–900 percent with excellent recovery, but it has low tenacity ranging from .5 to 1.0 g/d, limiting its use in lightweight garments. The finest rubber yarns must be three times as large as spandex yarns to be comparable in strength. Because of rubber's low dye acceptance, hand, and appearance, it is almost always covered by a yarn of another fiber content or by other yarns used to produce the fabric.

Rubber has been replaced in many uses by spandex, but it continues to be used in narrow elastic fabrics. It is more common to find synthetic rubber in these elastic fabrics than it is to find natural rubber.

Although antioxidants are incorporated in the spinning solution, rubber still does not have good resistance to oxidizing agents and is damaged by aging, sunlight, oil, and perspiration. Rubber's resistance to alkali is generally good, but it is damaged by heat, chlorine, and solvents, so it should be washed with care and should not be dry cleaned.

Neoprene, a type of synthetic rubber made from polychloroprene, is used as an elastomeric fiber or a supported elastic film. It is resistant to acids, alkalis, alcohols, oils, caustics, and solvents. It is found in a variety of products including protective gloves and clothing, wetsuits, framing for window glass, industrial hoses and belts, anticorrosive seals and membranes, and coatings for wiring.

Spandex

After many years of research, Du Pont introduced the first manufactured elastic fiber, a spandex fiber called Lycra, in 1958.

There was much interest in spandex fibers; they were superior to rubber in strength and durability. At present, spandex is produced by Du Pont under the trade name of Lycra and by Globe Manufacturing Company under the trade names of Glospan and Cleerspan.

PRODUCTION Spandex fibers are made by reacting preformed polyester or polyether molecules with di-isocyanate and then polymerizing into long molecular chains. Filaments are obtained by wet or solvent spinning. Like that for all manufactured fibers, the spinning solution may contain delustering agents, dye receptors, whiteners, and lubricants.

PHYSICAL STRUCTURE Spandex is produced as monofilament or multifilament yarns in a variety of deniers. Monofilaments are round in cross section whereas multifilaments are coalesced or partly fused together at intervals (Figures 9-1 and 9-2). When sewing multifilament yarns, the needle goes between the fine filaments rather than breaking them. When sewing monofilament yarns with a ballpoint needle, the needle pushes the monofilament aside rather than rupturing it. Spandex is delustered and usually white or gray.

Deniers range from 20 to 4,300. Twenty-denier spandex is used in lightweight support hosiery where a large amount of stretch is desirable. Much coarser yarns, 1,500 to 2,240 denier, stretch less and are used for support in hosiery tops, swimwear, and foundation garments.

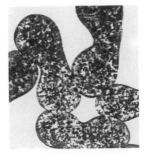

Fig. 9–1 *Lycra spandex fiber: cross section* (left); *lengthwise* (right). *(Courtesy of E. I. du Pont de Nemours & Company.)*

CHEMICAL COMPOSITION AND MOLECULAR ARRANGEMENT

Spandex—a manufactured fiber in which the fiber-forming substance is a long-chain synthetic polymer consisting of at least 85 percent of a segmented polyurethane. —Federal Trade Commission.

Spandex is a generic name, but it is not derived from the chemical nature of the fiber as are most of the manufactured fibers. The name was coined by shifting the syllables of the word expand.

Spandex is made up of rigid and flexible segments in the polymer chain; the soft segments provide the stretch and the rigid segments hold the chain together. When force is applied, the folded, or coiled, segments straighten out; when force is removed, they return to their original positions (Figure 9-3). Varying proportions of hard and soft segments control the amount of stretch.

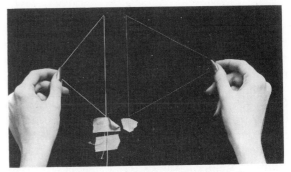

Fig. 9–2 *Comparison of heavy 1,500 denier Lycra spandex fibers* (left) *and fine 20 denier yarn* (right). *(Courtesy of E. I. du Pont de Nemours & Company.)*

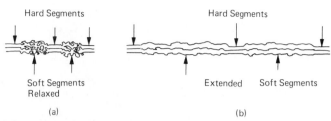

Fig. 9–3 *Spandex molecular chains: (a) relaxed; (b) extended.*

PROPERTIES Table 9-1 compares the performance of spandex and rubber in apparel and furnishing fabrics.

Aesthetics Spandex is seldom used alone in fabrics. Other yarns or fibers are added to achieve the desired hand and appearance. Even in power-stretch fabrics for foundation garments and surgical hose, where beauty is not of major importance, nylon or other yarns are used. The characteristics of spandex that contribute to beauty in fabrics are dyeability of the fiber and good strength, making it possible to have fashionable colors and prints in sheer garments. Rubber does not take dye, which limited the use of color in foundation garments.

Spandex needs no cover yarns since it takes dye. Eliminating the cover yarn reduces the cost and results in lighter weight garments. This is important not only for beauty but also for comfort.

Durability As Table 9-2 shows, spandex is more durable than rubber because it does not deteriorate with age. (Nylon is included in the table because it has more stretch than other manufactured filaments and illustrates the difference between a hard fiber and an elastomeric fiber.)

Spandex is resistant to body oils, perspiration, and cosmetics, which cause degradation of rubber. It also has good shelf life; that is, it does not deteriorate with age. Its flex life is ten times greater than that of rubber.

Comfort Spandex fibers have a moisture regain of 0.75-1.3 percent, making them uncomfortable for skin contact. Lighter-weight foundation garments of spandex have the same holding power as heavy garments of rubber. Spandex has a specific gravity of 1.2-1.25, which is greater than that of rubber. However, because of the greater tenacity of spandex, smaller denier yarns are used and lightweight products are available.

Care Spandex is resistant to dilute acids and to alkalis. It has good resistance to cosmetic oils and lotions.

Most spandex fibers are resistant to bleaches. They have good resistance to dry cleaning solvents. Spandex is thermoplastic, with a melting point of 446-518°F.

Spandex has superior aging resistance compared to rubber, resists soiling, and has superior elasticity and elongation properties. Spandex items retain an attractive appearance. However, over time the coarser spandex fibers may rupture and work through the fabric so that short, thick gray-white fibers show. In these areas, the fabric loses its elasticity and elongation properties because the fiber has ruptured. This problem is sometimes referred to as grin-through because the broken ends of spandex appear on the surface. Once the problem has developed, it cannot be remedied. It occurs most often in products that have aged or have been stressed to extremes (see Figure 9-4).

USES Spandex is used in foundation garments, active sportswear, hosiery, furnishings, and narrow

Table 9–1 Summary of the Perfomance of Spandex and Rubber in Apparel and Furnishing Fabrics

	Spandex	Rubber
Aesthetic	*Adequate*	*Poor*
Durability	*Adequate*	*Poor*
Abrasion resistance	Low	Low
Tenacity	Low	Low
Elongation	Excellent	Excellent
Comfort	*Adequate*	*Poor*
Appearance Retention	*Good*	*Good*
Resiliency	Good	Good
Dimensional stability	Good	Good
Elastic recovery	Excellent	Excellent
Recommended care	*Machine wash or Dry clean*	*Wash with care*

Table 9–2 Durability Factors of Spandex, Rubber, and Nylon

Fiber Property	Spandex	Rubber	Nylon
Breaking tenacity g/d	0.6–0.9	0.34	3.0–9.5
Breaking elongation	400–700 percent	500–600 percent	23 percent
Flex life	Excellent	Fair	Excellent
Recovery from stretch	99 percent	97 percent	100 percent

fabrics. It is used in swimwear, skiwear, leotards and other dancewear, leggings, biking shorts, and other body-fitting apparel. It also has medical uses, such as surgical and support hose, bandages, and surgical wraps. It is used in fitted sheets and slipcovers.

See Tables 9–3 and 9–4 for fiber modifications and a summary of end uses related to stretch properties.

OTHER ELASTOMERS

Anidex—a manufactured fiber in which the fiber-forming substance is any long-chain synthetic polymer composed of at least 50 percent by weight of one or more esters of a monohydric alcohol and acrylic acid.
($CH_2=CH-COOH$) . —Federal Trade Commission

Fig. 9–4 *Grin-through in a spandex garment.*

Anidex was produced by Rohm and Haas Company between 1970 and 1975. *Lastrile* and *anidex* are generic names established by the Federal Trade Commission for elastomeric fibers. Rohm and Haas experimented with lastrile but did not produce it commercially.

Lastrile fibers are made from copolymers of acrylonitrile or polychloroprene. The properties of lastrile fibers are similar to those of the other rubber fibers. At present, no lastrile or anidex fibers are produced in the United States.

A new elastomer based on polyether-ester has been introduced by the Japanese textile firm Teijin, Ltd. under the trade name Rexe. The fiber has an elongation potential of 600 percent, a tenacity of 1.0 gpd, and elasticity of 80 percent at elongations over 200 percent. Those properties are slightly less than the properties of spandex. However, Rexe has superior strength retention in wet heat and after treatment with alkalis. It is also superior in its resistance to chlorine bleach. It may be treated to

Table 9–3 Stretch Properties of Spandex

Major End Uses	Important Properties
Athletic apparel	Power stretch, washability
Foundation garments (Power net, tricot)	Power stretch, washability, lightweight
Bathing suits	Power stretch, resistance to salt and chlorine-treated water, dyeability
Golf jackets	Comfort stretch
Ski pants	Comfort stretch
Support and surgical hose	Power stretch, lightweight
Elastic webbing	Power stretch
Slipcovers, bottom sheets	Comfort stretch, washability

***Table 9–4* Types and Kinds of Spandex**

White—delustered
Transparent—clear luster
20–210 denier—support hosiery
140–560 denier (core spun)—men's hosiery
70–2240 denier—laces, foundation garments, swimwear, narrow fabrics, hosiery tops, fitted sheets
Bicomponent

increase dyeability and print clarity, which also give a more silklike hand to the fiber. Its potential for use in fashion outerwear and fitted furnishings is strong.

FIBERS WITH CHEMICAL, HEAT, OR FIRE RESISTANCE

The protective fibers are produced for specialized applications. In almost all cases, their costs are prohibitive for normal apparel and furnishing products. Some of these fibers cost over $40 per pound. Compare that to prices of less than $1 per pound for the fibers generally found in apparel and furnishings like cotton and polyester. Clearly, these fibers provide sufficient performance for their cost or they would not be used. With their unique properties of resistance to chemicals, heat, and flame, these fibers have generated products not possible before they were available. The field of industrial textiles is very much related to these specialty fibers.

Aramid

Aramid—a manufactured fiber in which the fiber-forming substance is a long-chain synthetic polyamide in which at least 85 percent of the amide linkages $\left(\begin{array}{c} -C-NH- \\ \parallel \\ O \end{array} \right)$ *are attached directly to two aromatic rings . —Federal Trade Commission.*

Nylon is a polyamide fiber; *aramid* is an aromatic polyamide fiber. Du Pont introduced a nylon variant with exceptional heat and flame resistance in 1963 under the trade name Nomex nylon. Another variant of nylon was introduced by Du Pont in 1973 as Kevlar. This fiber had exceptional strength in addition to fire resistance. The Federal Trade Commission

established the generic classification of aramid in 1974 for these fibers.

Aramid can be wet or dry spun and is usually round or dog-bone shaped (Figure 9-5). Aramid fibers have high tenacity and high resistance to stretch, to most chemicals, and to high temperatures. The fiber can be produced as a high-tenacity fiber. Table 9-5 compares normal-tenacity aramids with high-tenacity aramids. These fibers maintain their shape and form at high temperatures. Aramid fibers have excellent impact and abrasion resistance.

Hollow aramid fibers are used to produce fresh water from sea water through reverse osmosis. The thin, dense skin of the fiber allows only water to pass through. Aramids are difficult to dye and have poor resistance to acids. Trade names for aramid fibers are Nomex, Kevlar, Conex, Fenilon, Arenka, and Kermel. Nomex and Kevlar, trade names owned by Du Pont, are the most common trade names found in the United States. Solution-dyed forms of Nomex and Kevlar are used extensively in the military.

Kevlar is lightweight and fatigue and damage resistant. It is five times stronger than steel on an equal weight basis and 43 percent lower in density

Cross-Section 600X

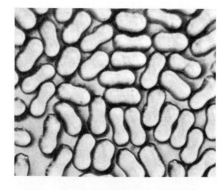

Longitudinal View 600X

Fig. 9–5 *Photomicrographs of aramid. (Courtesy of American Association of Textile Chemists and Colorists.)*

Table 9–5   Properties of Aramid

Property	Normal Tenacity	High Tenacity
Breaking tenacity	4.3–5.1 g/d—filament	21.5 g/d
	3.7–5.3 g/d—staple	
Specific gravity	1.38	1.44
Moisture regain	4.5 percent	3.5–7.0 percent
Effect of heat	Carbonizes above 800°F	
	Very resistant to flame	
	Does not melt	
Resistance to acids	Better than nylon	
Resistance to alkalis	Good	
Resistance to organic solvents	Good	
Resistance to sunlight	Poor	
Oleophilic	Yes, unless special finishes are used	
Static buildup	Yes, unless special finishes are used	

than fiberglass. Kevlar is used primarily in reinforcements of radial tires and other mechanical rubber goods. Kevlar 29 is found in protective apparel, cables, and cordage, and as a replacement for asbestos, such as in brake linings and gaskets. A 7-layer body-armor undervest of Kevlar 29 weighing 2.5 pounds can deflect a knife slash and stop a .38-caliber bullet fired from 10 feet (Figure 9–6). Kevlar 49 has the highest tenacity of the aramids and is found as a plastic-reinforcement fiber for boat hulls, aircraft, aerospace uses, and other composite uses.

Nomex is used where resistance to heat and combustion with low-smoke generation are required. Protective clothing, such as firefighters' apparel and race-car drivers' suits, and flame-retardant furnishings for aircraft are made of Nomex. Hot-gas filtration systems and electrical insulation are constructed of Nomex. This heat-resistant fiber is also found in covers for laundry presses and ironing boards.

Glass

Glass—a manufactured fiber in which the fiber-forming substance is glass. —Federal Trade Commission.

Glass is an incombustible textile fiber; it does not burn. This makes it especially suitable for end uses where the danger of fire is a problem—such as in draperies for motels, nursing homes, public buildings, and homes. The problems of severe skin irritation from tiny broken fibers has limited the use of glass fibers in apparel.

The process of drawing out glass into hairlike strands dates back to ancient times. It is thought that Phoenician fishermen noticed small pools of molten material among the coals of the fires they built on the sands of the Aegean beaches and while poking at the strange substances, they drew out a long strand—the first glass fiber.

The raw materials for glass are sand, silica, and limestone, combined with additives of feldspar and boric acid. These materials are melted in large elec-

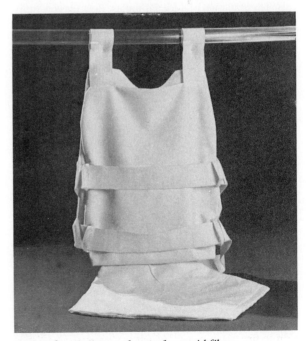

Fig. 9–6   Bulletproof vest of aramid fibers.

tric furnaces (2,400°F). For filament yarns, each furnace has holes in the base of the melting chamber. Fine streams of glass flow through the holes and are carried through a hole in the floor to a winder in the room below. The winder revolves faster than the glass comes from the furnace, thus stretching the fibers and reducing them in size before they harden. The round rodlike filaments are shown in Figure 9-7. When staple yarn is spun, the glass flows out in thin streams from holes in the base of the furnace, and jets of high-pressure air or steam break the strands into fibers 8-10 inches long. These fibers are collected on a revolving drum and made into a thin web, which is then formed into a sliver, or soft, untwisted yarn.

Beta Fiberglas, by the Owens-Corning Fiberglas Corporation, has one-sixth the denier of common glass fibers. The extremely fine filaments are resistant to breaking and thus more resistant to abrasion. Beta Fiberglas has about half the strength of regular glass fiber, but its tenacity of 8.2 is still greater than that of most fibers. It is used in products like window treatment fabrics, where greater fiber flexibility is needed.

Glass has a tenacity of 6-10 g/d dry and 5-8 g/d wet. Glass has a low elongation of only 3-4 percent but excellent elasticity in this narrow range. Glass fibers are brittle and break when bent; they exhibit poor flex resistance to abrasion. These fibers are very heavy, with a specific gravity of 2.5. The fibers have no absorbency and are resistant to most chemicals. Trade names include Fiberglas, Beta glass, Chemglass, J-M fiberglass, PPG fiberglass, and Vitron.

Hand washing is preferred to machine washing, which causes excessive breaking of the fibers.

Figure 9-8 shows the remnants of a fiberglass laundry bag that was machine washed. A residue of tiny glass fibers in the washing machine will contaminate the next load and cause severe skin irritation for people who use those textiles. Even with hand washing, severe skin irritation can occur. Care labels should disclose this possibility.

Glass textiles should not require frequent washing, however, because glass fibers resist soil, and spots and stains can be wiped off with a damp cloth. No ironing is necessary. Items can be smoothed and hung to dry. Oils used in finishing have caused graying in white fabrics. Oil holds the dirt persistently and also oxidizes with age. Washing has not proved to be a very satisfactory way to whiten the material, and dry cleaning is not recommended.

Glass fiber is used in furnishings such as flame-retardant draperies. Here the fiber performs best if bending and abrasion can be limited. Thus, movement from drafts, opening/closing the fabric, and people and pets should be kept to a minimum. The weight of the fabrics may mean that special rods are necessary (see Table 9-6).

Glass fiber has wide industrial use where noise abatement, fire protection, temperature control (insulation), and air purification are needed. Glass is common as a reinforcement fiber in molded plastics

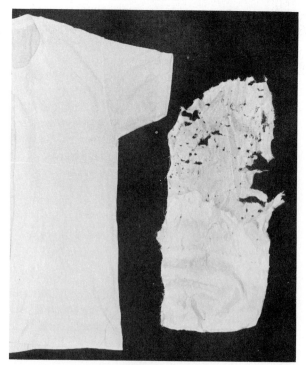

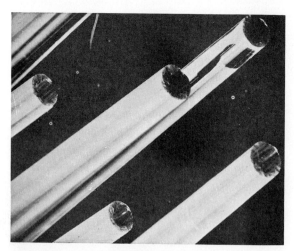

Fig. 9-7 *Photomicrograph of fiberglass. (Courtesy of the Owens-Corning Fiberglas Corporation.)*

Fig. 9-8 *Glass fiber laundry bag after being washed with regular family wash.*

Table 9–6 Glass Fiber Properties Important in Draperies

Flexibility	Breaks easily
Specific gravity	Heavy
Absorbency, percent of moisture regain	None
Effect of sunlight	None
Effect of acid and alkali	None
Effect of heat	Flameproof

in boat and airplane parts. Insulation in buildings and transportation vehicles, such as boats and railway cars, are made of glass. In addition, glass is found in ironing-board covers and space suits. Flame-resistant-glass mattress covers are produced for hotels, dormitories, and hospitals. A silica-glass quilt called AFRSI (Advanced Flexible Reuseable Surface Insulation) was used on several space shuttles. Glass is used in geotextiles. Filters, fire blankets, and heat and electrical-resistant tapes and braids are other industrial products made of glass. A lightweight, durable, water-resistant cast material is available from 3M for supporting broken bones as they heal. Owens-Corning is researching glass yarns suitable for apparel.

Additional end uses are the optical fibers, very fine fibers of pure glass. Laser beams, rather than electricity, activate the fibers. Glass optical fibers are free of electrical interference. Optical fibers are found in communication and medical equipment.

Metal and Metallic Fibers

Metallic—a manufactured fiber composed of metal, plastic-coated metal, metal-coated plastic, or a core completely covered by metal.
—Federal Trade Commission.

Gold and silver have been used since ancient times as yarns for fabric decoration. More recently, aluminum yarns, aluminized plastic yarns, and aluminized nylon yarns have replaced gold and silver. Metallic filaments can be coated with transparent films to minimize tarnishing. A common film is polyester with the trade name of Lurex. These fibers are often found as a decorative touch in apparel and home furnishings.

Two processes are used to make these decorative fibers. The *laminating process* seals a layer of aluminum between two layers of acetate or polyester (mylar) film, which is then cut into strips for yarn

(see Figure 9-9). The film may be colorless so the aluminum foil shows through, or the film and/or the adhesive may be colored before the laminating process. The *metalizing process* vaporizes the aluminum under high pressure and deposits it on the polyester film. The metalizing process produces thinner, more flexible, more durable, and more comfortable fibers. Monsanto has introduced a new line of metallized fiber, fabrics and film called Flectron. The fine layers of metal are bonded to almost any fiber or film surface for fabrics in computer rooms and specialized composites.

Fabric containing a large amount of metal can be embossed. Ironing is a problem when metallic film yarns are used because a high temperature melts the plastic. The best way to remove wrinkles is to set the iron on its end and draw the edge of the fabric across the sole of the iron.

Stainless-steel fibers were developed in 1960, and other metal fibers have also been made into fibers and yarns. Stainless steel has had the most extensive development.

The use of stainless steel as a textile fiber was an outgrowth of research for fibers to meet aerospace requirements. Superfine-stainless-steel filaments (3–15 micrometers) are a bundle of fine wires (0.002 inch) pickled in nitric acid and drawn to their final diameter. Several problems had to be solved, one of which involved twist. Each filament tended to act like a tiny coil spring, so the yarns required special treatment to deaden the twist.

Stainless-steel fibers are produced as both filament and staple. They can be woven or knitted and can be used in complex yarns. The staple fiber can be blended with other textile fibers to reduce static permanently. Only 1–3 percent of the stainless-steel fiber is needed. The limitation on the use of stainless steel in clothing is its inability to be dyed, although some producers claim that such a small amount will not affect the color of white fabrics. Stainless steel is used in carpets to reduce static.

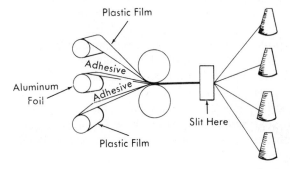

Fig. 9–9 *Laminating layers to produce a metal yarn.*

Static is one of the annoying problems associated with carpets in terms of comfort (static shock) and soiling. Brunsmet, a stainless-steel fiber from 2 to 3 inches long, can be mixed throughout any kind of spun yarn to make the yarn a good conductor. Only one or two fibers per tuft will carry the static from the face fiber to the backing. This kind of carpet yarn is used where static is a special problem, such as in rooms where sensitive computer equipment is kept. It is also suitable for this purpose in upholstery, blankets, and work clothing, but until the cost of stainless-steel fibers is reduced, its use in such articles will not be practical. Stainless-steel fibers are used for industrial purposes, such as tire cord, wiring, and missile nose cones, and in corrective heart surgery.

Metal fibers are blended with other fibers to produce static-free clothing worn in clean rooms in computer-production facilities. Metals do not have many of the properties usually attributed to textile fibers. They are much heavier than the organic materials that compose most fibers—the specific gravity of metal fibers is 7.88 g/cc as compared to 1.14 for nylon. They cannot bend without leaving permanent crease lines, have very little or no drape characteristics, and do not have the hand associated with textiles. Reduction in the denier of the fiber improves its properties, but the finer fibers are more expensive. Metal fibers are used in industrial products like wiring and cables. Figure 9-10 shows a copper braid used in wiring.

Novoloid

Novoloid—a manufactured fiber in which the fiber-forming substance contains at least 35 percent by weight of cross-linked novolac (a cross-linked phenolformaldehyde polymer). —Federal Trade Commission.

Kynol, a type of novoloid fiber, was introduced in 1969 with commercial production beginning in 1972.

Novoloid shows outstanding flame resistance to a blaze of 2500°C from an oxyacetylene torch, and it can meet any flammability requirements that might be legislated. The yarns do not melt, burn, or fuse but carbonize while maintaining their construction.

Novoloid has an elasticity of 35 percent. It has good resistance to sunlight and is inert to acids and organic solvents but susceptible to highly alkaline substances. Table 9-7 presents the properties of novoloid.

Novoloid fiber is gold in color, so its dyeing possibilities are somewhat limited—darker shades pre-

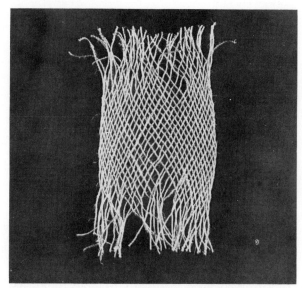

Fig. 9–10   *Copper braid used in wiring.*

sent no problem. It is produced as staple and filament (see Figures 9–11 and 9–12).

PBI

PBI is a manufactured fiber in which the fiber-forming substance is a long-chain aromatic polymer having reoccurring imidazole groups as an integral part of the polymer chain. PBI is produced by Hoechst Celanese Corporation. The trade name Arazole may be used. PBI is a condensation polymer that is dry spun. Its specific gravity is 1.39; if the fiber has been stabilized, the specific gravity is 1.43. PBI has a tenacity of 3.1–1.42 g/d and a breaking elongation of 30 percent. PBI has a high moisture regain of 15 percent, but it is difficult to dye, hence the most common coloration method currently used is mass pigmentation. PBI does not burn or melt and has

Table 9–7   Properties of Novoloid

Cross section	Elliptical
Tenacity (grams/denier)	1.5–2.5
Specific gravity (grams/cc)	1.27
Moisture regain (percent)	6.0
Chemical resistance	Excellent

Uses
Fireproof clothing and fabrics
Chemical filters
Friction materials
Gaskets, packings

Cross-Section 500X

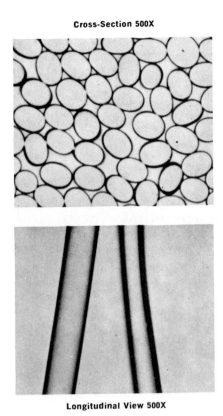

Longitudinal View 500X

Fig. 9–11   Photomicrographs of novoloid. (Courtesy of American Association of Textile Chemists and Colorists.)

Fig. 9–12   Heat- and flame-resistant apparel of Kynol™ novoloid. (Courtesy of American Kynol, Inc.)

very low shrinkage when exposed to flame. Even when charred, PBI fabrics remain supple and intact. Because of its heat resistance, it is ideal for use in heat–resistant apparel for firefighters, astronauts, fuel handlers, race-car drivers, welders, foundry workers, and hospital workers (Figure 9–13). The fiber is found in upholstery, window-treatment fabrics, and carpets for aircraft, hospitals, and submarines. PBI is also used as a flue-gas filter in coal-fired boilers and in reverse-osmosis membranes.

Sulfar

Sulfar is a manufactured fiber in which the fiber-forming substance is a long-chain synthetic polysulfide in which at least 85 percent of the sulfide (—S—) linkages are attached directly to two (2) aromatic rings. Sulfar is produced by Phillips Fibers Corporation by melt spinning. The fiber is gold in color. The trade name Ryton PPS may be used. Sulfar has a tenacity of 3.0–3.5 g/d and a breaking elongation of 25–35 percent. It has excellent elasticity. Moisture regain is low (0.6 percent), and specific gravity is 1.37. Sulfar is highly resistant to acids

and alkalis and not soluble in any known solvent below 200°C (392°F). Sulfar is used in filtration fabrics, paper-making felts, electrolysis membranes, high-performance membranes, rubber reinforcement, electrical insulation, fire fighting suits, and other protective clothing (Figure 9–14). Sulfar helps maintain a clean environment because of its use in filters in plants that generate electricity by burning garbage.

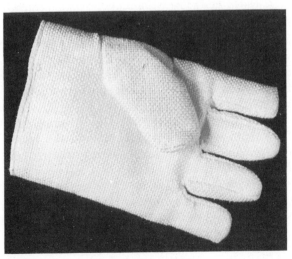

Fig. 9–13 Heat–resistant glove of PBI.

Fig. 9–14 *Firefighting outfits made from sulfar fiber. (Courtesy of Thomas D. Lowes, Buffalo, N. Y.)*

Saran

Saran—a manufactured fiber in which the fiber-forming substance is any long-chain synthetic polymer composed of at least 80 percent by weight of vinylidene chloride units. (CH_2CCl_2). —Federal Trade Commission.

Saran is a vinylidene-chloride/vinyl-chloride co-polymer developed in 1940. The raw material is melt spun and stretched to orient the molecules. Both filament and staple forms are produced. Much of the filament fiber is produced as a monofilament for seat covers, furniture webbing, and screenings. Monofilaments may also be used in doll's hair and wigs. The staple form is made straight, curled, or crimped. The curled form is unique in that the curl is inherent and closely resembles the curl of natural wool.

Saran production is low because of competition from olefin, which has similar properties at a lower cost. Saran is used as an agricultural protective fabric to shade delicate plants such as tobacco and ginseng. It is also used in rugs, draperies, and upholstery (see Figure 9–15). In addition to its use as a fiber, saran has wide use in the plastics field.

Saran has good weathering properties, chemical resistance, and stretch resistance. It is an unusually tough, durable fiber. Saran has a tenacity of 1.4–2.4 g/d with no change when wet, an elongation of 15–30 percent with excellent recovery, and good resiliency. It is an off-white fiber with a slight yellowish tint.

Like the other melt-spun fibers, Saran is perfectly round and smooth. It has a moisture regain of less than 0.1 percent. Saran absorbs little or no moisture, so it dries rapidly. It is difficult to dye; for this reason, solution dyeing is used. Saran also has no static charge. It is heavy, with a specific gravity of 1.7. Saran does not support combustion. When exposed to flame it softens, chars, and decomposes. It softens at 115°C (240°F). It has excellent size and shape retention and is resistant to acids, alkalis, and organic solvents. Exposure to sunlight causes light-colored objects to darken, but no strength loss occurs. Saran is immune to biological attack.

Vinyon

Vinyon—a manufactured fiber in which the fiber-forming substance is any long-chain synthetic polymer composed of at least 85 percent by weight of vinyl chloride units ($-CH_2CHCl-$) —Federal Trade Commission.

Commercial production of vinyon was begun in 1939. It is a copolymer of vinyl chloride (86 percent) and vinyl acetate (14 percent). The raw material is dissolved in acetone and dry spun.

Vinyon has an irregular-, round-, dog-bone-, or dumbbell-shaped cross section. The fiber is white and somewhat translucent. Vinyon is very sensitive to heat. The fibers soften at 150–170°F, shrink at 175°F, and do not withstand the elevated tempera-

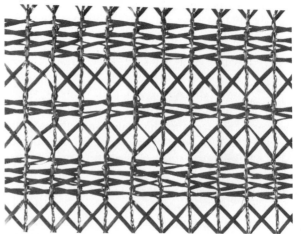

Fig. 9–15 *Saran casement cloth designed by Jack Lenor Larsen.*

tures experienced in home ironing. They are unaffected by moisture, chemically stable, resistant to moths and biological attack, poor conductors of electricity, and flame retardant. These properties make vinyon especially good as a bonding agent for rugs, papers, and nonwoven fabrics. The amorphous undrawn fibers have a tenacity of 0.7–1.0 g/d. These fibers have a warm, pleasant hand. Elongation ranges from 12 to 125 percent. Specific gravity ranges from 1.33 to 1.43. Moisture regain is 0.1 percent.

Vinyon is also used for wigs, flame-retardant Christmas trees, filter pads, fishing lines and nets, and protective clothing. Some trade names of vinyon are Leavil, Teviron, and Viclon.

One modification of vinyon is a bicomponent-bigeneric fiber called Cordelan. It is a matrix-fibril fiber of 50 percent vinyl/50 percent vinyon. It is produced in Japan and used for flame-retardant apparel, airplane blankets, and furnishings.

Vinal

Vinal—a manufactured fiber in which the fiber-forming substance is any long-chain synthetic polymer composed of at least 50 percent by weight of vinyl alcohol units ($-CH_2CHOH-$) and in which the total of the vinyl alcohol units and any one or more of the various acetal units is at least 85 percent by weight of the fiber. —Federal Trade Commission.

No vinal fibers are produced in the United States. Modified vinal fibers are imported for use in some protective clothing because of their inherent flame-retardant properties. Vinal is made in Japan and Germany under the trade names of Kuralon, Mewlon, Solvron, Vilon, Vinol, and Vinylal.

When the fibers are extruded, they are water soluble. The fibers must be treated with formaldehyde in order to form cross-links, which make the fiber nonwater soluble. The fiber has a smooth, slightly grainy appearance with a U-shaped cross section. Vinal has a tenacity of 3.5–6.5 g/d, an elongation of 15–30 percent, and is 25 percent weaker when wet. The specific gravity of vinal is 1.26. It has a moisture regain of 5.0 percent. It does not support combustion, but softens at 200°C (390°F) and melts at 220°C (425°F). It has good chemical resistance and is unaffected by alkalis and common solvents. Concentrated acids harm the fiber. Vinal has excellent resistance to biological attack. Mass pigmentation is used to color the fiber.

In other countries, vinal is used in protective apparel. Major uses in the United States are industrial: fishing nets, filter fabrics, tarpaulins, and brush bristles. In water-soluble forms, the fiber is used as a ground fabric to create laces and other sheer fabrics. Once the fabric has been produced, the vinal ground is dissolved and the sheer fabric remains.

Cordelan is a matrix-fibril fiber of 50 percent vinal/50 percent vinyon. See the preceding discussion of vinyon for end uses. Vinal is also used in film form, often labeled vinyl. It is used for rainwear, umbrellas, clear table coverings and upholstery protectors in showrooms.

Nytril

Nytril—a manufactured fiber containing at least 85 percent of a long-chain polymer of vinylidene dinitrile ($-CH_2C(CN)_2-$) where the vinylidene dinitrile content is no less than every other unit in the polymer chain. —Federal Trade Commission.

Nytril is no longer produced anywhere in the world. Other fibers with similar properties and lower costs have replaced nytril in all end uses.

Polytetrafluoroethylene

Polytetrafluoroethylene (PTFE) is not defined by the Textile Fiber Products Identification Act. Polytetrafluoroethylene is common as a coating for cookware under the trade name Teflon. It is also used as a coating in plastic forms.

PTFE is polymerized under pressure and heat in the presence of a catalyst. Emulsion spinning can be used. In *emulsion spinning,* polymerization and extrusion occur simultaneously. PTFE has the following repeat unit ($-CF_2-CF_2-$). It has a tenacity of 1.6 g/d, with low elongation and good pliability. The fiber is heavy, with a specific gravity of 2.3, and it can withstand temperatures up to 260°C (500°F) without damage. It is resistant to chemicals, sunlight, weathering, and aging. The fibers are chemically inert. PTFE does produce electrical charges. It is tan in color, but can be bleached white with sulfuric acid. Gore-Tex is a trade name for fabrics that have a thin microporous film of PTFE applied to a fabric for use in outerwear. Gore-Tex can be dry cleaned but needs to be rinsed well to prevent impairment of the film's functions. PTFE is used industrially in filter fabrics (to reduce smokestack emissions), packing fabrics, gaskets, industrial felts, covers for presses in commercial laundries, electrical tape, and as a layer of some protective fabrics.

Carbon

Carbon is a heat-stabilized cyclic and cross-linked polyacrylonitrile. The fiber has exceptional heat resistance and does not ignite or melt. It maintains its full strength of 1.5 g/d after prolonged exposure to temperatures of more than 200°C. Carbon has a density of 1.4, a moisture regain of 10 percent, and an elongation of 10 percent. Carbon fibers have very low coefficients of thermal expansion, are chemically inert, and biocompatible. They also dissipate static quickly. Because of these properties and its comfortable hand, carbon is used in protective clothing, to reinforce lightweight metal components in golf clubs and bicycle bodies, in aerospace uses, in bone grafts, and as a substitute for asbestos in industrial products. It is produced by BASF under the trade name Celiox. Under the tradename Resista it is used as a coating of nylon for carpeting, upholstery, apparel, and industrial brushes and belts.

Table 9-8 compares some properties of aramid, glass, PBI, sulfar, PTFE, and carbon.

Table 9–8   Comparison of Selected Chemical, Heat, and Fire Resistant Fibers: Aramid, Glass, PBI, Sulfar, PTFE, and Carbon

Fiber	Tenacity g/d	Elongation % dry	Elasticity %	Regain %	Specific Gravity	Heat/Chemical Resistance
Aramid	23	4.0	100	4.3	1.44	Difficult to ignite, does not melt, decomposes at 900°F, resistant to dilute acids and bases, degraded by strong mineral acids, excellent solvent resistance
Glass	15.3	4.8	100	0	2.48	Does not burn, softens at + 1350°F, resists most acids and alkalis, unaffected by solvents
PBI	2.6-3.0	25–30	—	15	1.43	Does not ignite or melt, chars at 860°F, unaffected by most acids, alkalis, and solvents
Sulfar	3.0-3.5	35–45	100	0.6	1.37	Outstanding heat resistance, melts at 545°F, outstanding resistance to most acids, alkalis, and solvents
PTFE	0.9-2.0	19–140	—	0	2.1	Extremely heat resistant, melts at + 550°F, most chemically resistant fiber known
Carbon	15.9	0.7	100	—	1.77	Does not melt, excellent resistance to hot, concentrated acids and alkalis, unaffected by solvents, degraded by strong oxidizers (chlorine bleach)

KEY TERMS

Elastomer
Comfort stretch
Power stretch
Rubber
Lastrile
Spandex
Anidex
Aramid
Glass
Metallic fibers

Stainless steel
Novoloid
PBI
Sulfar
Saran
Vinyon
Vinal
Polytetrafluoroethylene (PTFE)
Carbon

QUESTIONS

1. Compare the performance characteristics of rubber and spandex.
2. What are the differences and similarities between power and comfort stretch?
3. Explain why glass and metal are included as textiles.
4. Identify a fiber from this chapter that would be an appropriate choice for each end use listed below and explain, using performance characteristics, why that fiber was selected. (Some of these fibers may actually be used in blend form in the product.)

    insulation for electrical wiring
    support hosiery
    theater costume for a performance of *King Lear*
    apron for welder
    firefighting suit

SUGGESTED READINGS

Coffee, D. R., Serad, G. A., Hicks, H. L., and Montgomery, R. T. (1982). "Properties and Applications of Celanese PBI-Polybenzimidazole Fiber." *Textile Research Journal, 52,* pp. 466–472.

Grayson, Martin, ed. (1984). *Encyclopedia of Textiles, Fibers, and Nonwoven Fabrics.* New York: John Wiley & Sons.

Pfister, Fred V. (January, 1991). "Technology Trends." *Textile Month,* pp. 8–10.

Reisch, Marc S. (February 2, 1987). "High Performance Fibers Find Expanding Military, Industrial Uses." *Chemical and Engineering News,* pp. 9–14.

Trotman, E. R. (1984). *Dyeing and Chemical Technology of Textile Fibers,* 6th ed. New York: John Wiley & Sons.

SECTION 3

YARNS

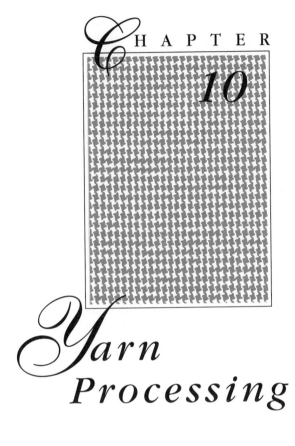

C H A P T E R

10

Yarn Processing

OBJECTIVES

- To understand the processes used in producing yarns from filament and staple fibers.

- To recognize the different types and qualities of yarns produced from filament and staple fibers.

- To relate yarn selection to end use performance.

- To integrate fiber properties with yarn properties.

- To understand the reasons for blending fibers and their effects on product performance.

A YARN IS A CONTINUOUS STRAND OF TEXTILE fibers, filaments, or materials in a form suitable for knitting, weaving, or otherwise intertwining to form a textile fabric (ASTM, p. 54). In this chapter, the process of making a yarn from fibers or other starting materials will be explored. For filament yarns, this is a relatively quick and easy process. For spun yarns, a series of operations is needed to make the fibers parallel and bond them in some manner.

Yarn processing attracts a great deal of industry attention, but not much consumer interest. However, yarn type and quality has a great deal to do with product cost and performance. Thus, a general understanding of the making of yarn will help in understanding products made from yarns.

Many changes have occurred in the ways yarns are made. This evolutionary process continues. Current efforts relate to ways of improving productivity, decreasing costs, increasing uniformity and quality, solving problems with current systems, and developing new systems or approaches to deal with changes in other segments of the industry. For example, yarn processing systems had to be modified to work with microfibers and yarn characteristics were modified to cope with the faster and faster production speeds of fabrication equipment. In fact, yarns are often the limiting factor in fabric production rates. Computer systems monitor yarn production and quality of yarns. Computerization of yarn processing continues with computers becoming more function specific and more user friendly.

FILAMENT YARNS

Filament yarns are primarily manufactured fibers because silk, the only natural filament, accounts for less than 1 percent of fiber and yarn production. Manufactured filament yarns are made by chemical spinning. In this process a polymer solution is extruded through a spinneret, solidified in fiber form, and then the individual filaments are immediately brought together with or without a slight twist (see Figure 8–3). The bringing together of the filaments and/or the addition of twist creates the filament yarn. The spinning machine winds the yarn on a bobbin. The yarn is then rewound on spools or cones and is a finished product unless some addi-

tional treatment is required, such as crimping, twisting, texturing, or finishing.

Throwing, originally a process for twisting silk filaments, evolved into the twisting of manufactured fibers and then into texturing. Throwing provides the fabricator with the kind of yarn needed for a particular product. The throwster performs a service for the industry; some throwsters now place trade names on products made from their yarns. Some fiber producers texture yarns as a final step in the fiber–spinning process.

Smooth-Filament Yarn

Filament yarns are more expensive in price per pound; however, the cost of making tow into staple and then spinning it into yarn by the mechanical spinning process usually makes the final cost about the same. The number of holes in the spinneret determines the number of filaments in the yarn.

Regular-filament, or conventional-filament, yarns are *smooth* and silklike as they come from the spinneret. Their smooth nature gives them more luster than spun yarns, but the luster varies with the amount of delustering agent used in the fiber-spinning solution and the amount of twist in the yarn. Maximum luster is obtained by the use of bright filaments with little or no twist. Crepe yarns, yarns with very high twist, were developed to reduce the luster of the filaments. With thermoplastic fibers, the crepe twist can be heat set. Filament yarns generally have either high twist or low twist.

Filament yarns have no protruding ends, so they do not shed lint; they resist pilling; and fabrics made from them tend to shed soil. Filaments of round cross section pack well into compact yarns that give little bulk, loft, or cover to fabric. Compactness is a disadvantage in some end uses, where bulk and absorbency are necessary for comfort. Nonround or lobal filaments create more open space for air and moisture permeability and give greater cover.

The strength of a filament yarn depends on the strength of the individual fibers and on the number of filaments in the yarn. Filament fiber strength is usually greater than that of staple fibers. Using polyester as an example, staple strength is 3–5.5 gpd (grams per denier); filament strength is 5–8 gpd.

The strength of each filament is fully utilized. In order to break the yarn, all the filaments must be broken. It is possible to make very sheer fabrics of fine filaments that have good strength. Filament yarns reach their maximum strength at about 3–6 turns per inch; then strength remains constant or decreases.

Fine-filament yarns are soft and supple. However, they are not as resistant to abrasion as coarse filaments, so for durability it may be desirable to have fewer but coarser filaments in the yarn.

Monofilament Yarns

Monofilament yarns are used primarily in industrial uses. These yarns usually are coarse-filament fibers. End uses include sewing thread, fishline, fruit and vegetable bags, nets, and other woven or knitted fabrics where low cost and high durability are the most important characteristics desired.

Tape Yarns

Tape yarns are produced from extruded polymer films. *Extrusion*—forcing a liquid through a spinneret to form fine strands—is the standard method of spinning fibers and some films. The *split-fiber method* is less expensive than the traditional extrusion process and can be done with a minimum investment in equipment. Some fiber polymers cannot be processed by the split-fiber method; polypropylene is used extensively because of its ease of processing and economic factors.

Pellets of polypropylene with appropriate additives are melted, then extruded as a film 0.005 to 0.020 inch thick onto a chill roll or cooled quickly by quenching in water. The film is slit into tapes 0.1 inch wide. The slit tapes are then heat-stretched to orient the molecular chains. The stretching is carried to a point where the film develops a tendency to fibrillate (split into fibers), or the film is passed over needles to produce the slits. Twisting or other mechanical action completes the fibrillation. Split-fiber yarns have high strength.

Yarns as low as 250 denier have been made from split fibers. Tape yarns are coarse and usually used in carpet backing, rope, cord, fishnets, bagging, and furnishings where ribbonlike yarn is needed.

Olefin films are slit into yarns that are used for the same textile products as split-fiber olefin. Slit-film-tape yarns are much more regular than fibrillated film-tape yarns. However, fibrillated yarns are less expensive and quicker to produce. These tape yarns are found most often in industrial textiles such as carpet backing and bagging.

Bulk Yarns

A *bulk yarn* is a yarn that has been prepared to have greater covering power or apparent volume than that of a conventional yarn of equal linear density and of the same basic material with normal twist (ASTM). Often these bulk yarns are referred to as *bulk-continuous-filament yarns*. A common shorthand notation used when referring to these yarns is *BCF*. BCF yarns include any continuous-filament yarn whose smooth, straight fibers have been displaced from their closely packed, parallel position by the introduction of some form of crimp, curl, loop, or coil (Figure 10–1).

The characteristics of bulk yarns are quite different from those of smooth-filament yarns. Bulking gives filaments the aesthetic properties of spun yarns by altering the surface characteristics and creating space between the fibers. Fabrics have better bulk, cover, and elasticity, are more breathable and permeable by moisture, absorbent, and comfortable. Static buildup is lower. Bulk yarns can have spun yarn qualities without pilling and shedding.

There are three classes of bulk yarns: bulky yarns, stretch yarns, and textured yarns. These three classes will be discussed after texturing processes are discussed.

TEXTURING FILAMENT YARNS The texturing processes discussed here are mechanical texturing methods based on the use of thermoplastic fibers and heat and chemical methods of achieving texture by means of bicomponent fibers.

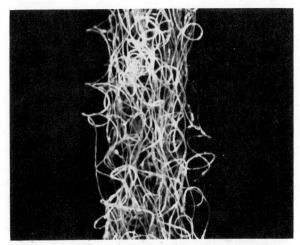

Fig. 10–1 *Typical bulk yarn. (Courtesy of the Fibers Division of Monsanto Chemical Co., a unit of Monsanto Co.)*

Gear Crimp The filament yarn passes between the teeth of two heated gears that mesh and thus give the yarn the shape of the gear teeth—a sawtooth crimp (Figure 10-2). The bends are angular in contrast to the rounded waves and bends of natural crimp. When thermoplastic fibers are gear crimped, the crimp is permanent.

Stuffer Box The stuffer box produces a sawtooth crimp of considerable bulk. Straight-filament yarns are literally stuffed into one end of a heated box (see Figure 10-3) and then withdrawn at the other end in crimped form. The apparent volume increase is 200-300 percent, with some elasticity. The stuffer box is a fast method, one of the least costly, and one of the most widely used processes.

Air Jet Conventional filament is fed over an air jet (Figure 10-4) at a faster rate than it is drawn off. The blast of air forces some of the filaments into very tiny loops; the velocity of the air affects the size of the loops. This is not a high-speed process and is relatively costly, but it is commonly used because of its versatility.

Volume increases in the yarn are between 50 and 150 percent with more texture and a change in lus-

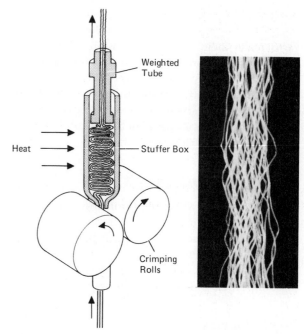

Fig. 10–3 *"Stuffing box" process* (left); *bulky yarn used in apparel* (right). *(Courtesy of the Fibers Division of Monsanto Chemical Co., a unit of Monsanto Co.)*

ter. The process is very versatile. Any kind of fiber can be used and styling possibilities are diverse.

Air-jet yarns maintain their size and bulk under tension because the straight areas bear the strain and the loops remain relatively unaffected. The yarns have little or no stretch. Heat setting is not necessary, so the process can be used for non-heat-settable yarns. Under magnification the yarn resembles a novelty yarn.

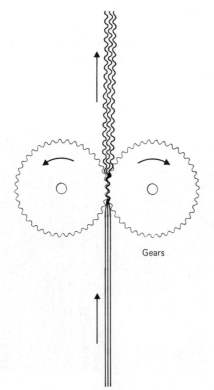

Fig. 10–2 *Filament yarn passes through heated gears to receive crimped shape.*

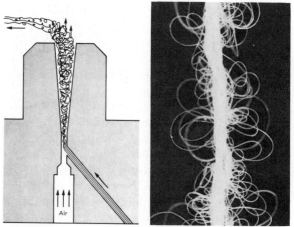

Fig. 10–4 *Air-jet process* (left); *bulky yarn* (right). *(Courtesy of the Fibers Division of Monsanto Chemical Co., a unit of Monsanto Co.)*

Draw-Texturing In draw-texturing unoriented filaments or partially oriented filaments are fed directly through the double-heater false-twist spinner, eliminating a separate stretching process. Another type of draw-textured yarn is made by a machine similar to that shown in Figure 10–5 with a second heating zone. The false-twisted yarn is stretched slightly and stabilized at a temperature higher than that used for texturing. This yarn may be referred to as a flat-drawn textured yarn. Draw texturing is a much faster and cheaper way of making textured bulk yarns and the finished yarns are as good as or better than those made by conventional means.

False-Twist The false-twist spindle whirls at 600,000 revolutions per minute and generates such an intense sound that its effect on health and hearing is an industry concern. The process is continuous; the yarn is twisted, heat set, and untwisted as it travels through the spindle (Figure 10–5). As the false-twist spindle turns, it creates an S-twist in the yarn on one side and a Z-twist in the yarn on the other side (Figure 10–6). When the yarn untwists, the filaments are essentially in the form of a helical coil distorted by the untwisting (Figure 10–5). If the yarn is pulled at each end, the coils straighten out—thus the stretch.

Fig. 10–6 *False-twist spindle.*

False-twist is a widely used method of texturing yarns. These yarns have easy-care properties and excellent performance characteristics. They are often used in crepelike fabrics.

Friction texturing is another type of false-twist texturing. POY yarns (partially oriented yarns) are fed into machines that put twist into the yarns by using friction surfaces rather than false-twisters or spindles.

Edge-Crimp Curl-type stretch yarns are made by drawing heated filaments over a knifelike edge (Figure 10–7), which flattens the filaments on one side and causes the yarn to curl. A similar effect is obtained by pulling a ribbon over a scissors blade to curl it. The filament cross section changes from round to flattened on one side (Figure 10–8). The flattened side is shortened, so differential shrinkage of the sides causes an effect similar to that of bicomponent stretch. The process is low cost and speedy.

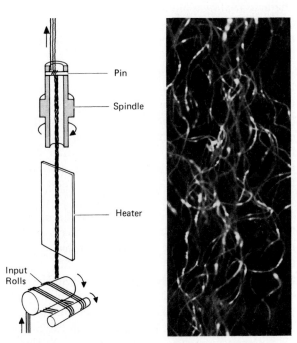

Fig. 10–5 *"False-twist" process* (left); *yarn* (right). *(Courtesy of the Fibers Division of Monsanto Chemical Co., a unit of Monsanto Co.)*

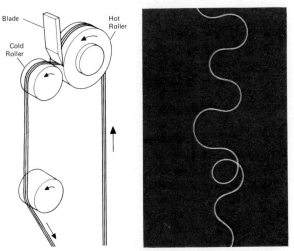

Fig. 10–7 *Edge-crimp yarn process* (left); *fiber* (right). *(Photograph courtesy of Milliken Research Corporation.)*

Round Filament   Flattened

Fig. 10–8   *Edge-crimping flattens one side of the filament.*

It can be used on monofilaments as well as multi-filaments.

Knit-de-Knit   A small-diameter tube is knit at a rapid speed (Figure 10-9, 10-10). It is then heat set, unraveled, and wound on cones. Crimp size and frequency can be varied by difference in stitch size and tension. The knitting stitch used to make the fabric must be of different gauge than that of the knit-de-knit tube or pinholes will form where the crimp gauge and knit gauge match.

BULK YARN TYPES

Bulky Yarns   *Bulky yarns* are yarns formed from inherently bulky fibers, such as manufactured fibers that are hollow along part or all of their length, or yarns formed from fibers that cannot be closely packed because of their cross-sectional shape, fiber alignment, stiffness, resilience, or natural crimp (ASTM).

Bulky texturing processes can be used with any kind of filament fiber or spun yarn. The yarns have

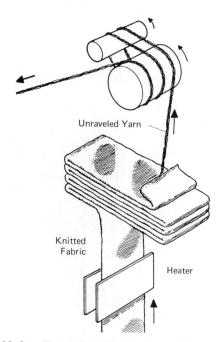

Unraveled Yarn

Knitted
Fabric

Heater

Fig. 10–9   *Knit-de-knit fabric is heat set, then unraveled.*

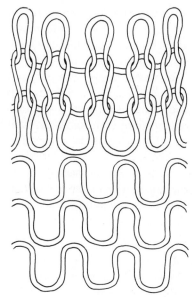

Fig. 10–10   *Knit-de-knit crimp.*

less stretch than either stretch or textured yarns. Bulky yarns are used in a wide array of products from carpeting to lingerie and sweaters to shoelaces.

Stretch Yarns   Stretch yarns are thermoplastic filament or spun yarns having a high degree of potential elastic stretch and rapid recovery, and characterized by a high degree of yarn curl (ASTM). Stretch yarns are characterized by high elongation (300–500 percent), rapid recovery, and moderate bulk per unit of weight.

Stretch yarns are made primarily of nylon fiber, have been used extensively in men's and women's hosiery, pantyhose, leotards, swimwear, ski pants, football pants and jerseys. Stretch yarns make it possible to manufacture fewer sizes, as one-size items fit wearers of different sizes. Stretch yarns should not be confused with yarns made with elastomeric fibers.

Textured Yarns   *Textured or bulked yarns* are filament or spun yarns that have been given notably greater apparent volume than a conventional yarn of similar fiber (filament) count and linear density (ASTM). These yarns have much lower elastic stretch than stretch yarns, but greater stretch than bulky yarns. They are stable enough to present no unusual problems in subsequent processing or in use by the ultimate consumer. The apparent increase in volume may be achieved through physical, chemical, or heat treatments or a combination of these.

Textured yarns are stabilized stretch yarns—they have bulk and some comfort stretch. Fabrics made from these yarns maintain their original size and shape during wear and care.

Table 10-1 summarizes the three major types of bulk-filament yarns.

SPUN YARNS

Spun yarns are continuous strands of staple fibers held together by some mechanism. Often the mechanism is a mechanical twist that takes advantage of the fiber's irregularities and natural cohesiveness to bind the fibers together into one yarn. The process of producing yarns from staple fibers by twisting is an old one. The initial discovery of twisting fibers together has been lost in history. Ways of producing spun yarns without twist have been developed.

Spun yarns have protruding fiber ends that hold the yarn away from close contact with the skin; thus a fabric made of spun yarn is more comfortable on a hot, humid day than a fabric of smooth-filament yarns that does not allow perspiration to evaporate.

Many of the insulating characteristics of a fabric are due to the structure of the yarns used to produce that fabric. There is more space between fibers in a spun yarn than in a filament yarn. A spun yarn with low twist has more space than a spun yarn with a high twist. Hence a spun yarn with low twist is better at insulating than a highly twisted yarn. For that reason, most fabrics designed for warmth have lower twist yarns. If wind resistance is desired, fabrics with high-twist yarns and a high count are more desirable because air permeability is reduced.

Carded yarns, made of short-staple fibers, have more protruding fiber ends than *combed yarns,* which are made of long-staple fibers. Protruding ends contribute to greater comfort and warmth but also to a dull, fuzzy appearance; the shedding of lint; and to the formation of pills on the surface of the fabric. Fuzzy fiber ends can be removed from the surface of the fabric by singeing (Chapter 16).

The strength of the individual staple fiber is a less important factor in spun yarn strength than it is in filament yarns. Spun yarn strength is dependent on the cohesiveness or clinging power of the fibers and on the points of contact resulting from twist or other binding mechanisms used to produce the spun yarn. The greater the number of points of contact, the greater the resistance to fiber slippage within the yarn. Fibers with crimp or convolutions have a greater number of points of contact. The friction of one fiber against another also gives resistance to lengthwise fiber slippage. A fiber with a rough or irregular surface—wool scales, for example—creates more friction than a smooth fiber.

The mechanical spinning of staple fibers into yarns is one of the oldest manufacturing arts and has been described as an invention as significant as that of the wheel. The basic principles of spinning are the same now as they were when yarns were first made.

Primitive spinning consisted of drawing out the fibers, which were held on a stick called a distaff, twisting them by the rotation of a spindle, which could be spun like a top, and then winding up the spun yarn (Figure 10-11). The spinning wheel was invented by the spinners of India and was introduced into Europe in the 14th century. The factory system began in the 18th century when James

Table 10–1 Bulk Yarns

	Bulky Yarns	Stretch Yarns	Textured Yarns
Nature	Inherently bulky	High degree of yarn curl	High degree of bulk
Fiber Type	May be hollow or crimped fibers	Any thermoplastic fiber	Any fiber that can be treated with moisture, heat, or chemical to develop crimp
Stretch characteristics	Least stretch Sawtooth, loops in individual fibers	300–500 percent stretch Torque and nontorque	Moderate amount of stretch Loopy, high bulk, crimped
Processes	Gear crimping, stuffer box, air jet, draw-texturing, friction texturing	False-twist, edge-crimp, knit-de-knit, draw-texturing, friction texturing	Air jet, flat-drawn textured, draw-texturing, friction texturing

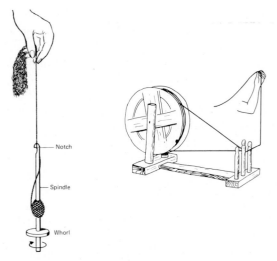

Fig. 10–11 *Hand spinning* (left); *early spinning wheel* (right).

Hargreaves invented the first spinning jenny—a machine that could turn more than one spinning wheel at a time. Other inventions for improving the spinning process followed and led to the Industrial Revolution, when power machines took over hand processes and made mass production possible. Machines were developed for each separate step in the spinning process.

Spinning continues to evolve. Progress has been made in reducing the number of steps involved, in automating the process, and in making it faster, simpler, and more economical with higher production speeds and more user-friendly computerization. Spun-yarn processes are shown in Table 10-2.

Processing Staple Fibers

CONVENTIONAL OR RING SPINNING *Conventional or ring spinning* consists of a series of operations designed to (1) clean and parallel-align staple

Table 10–2 Spun Yarn Processes

From Staple Fiber	From Filament Tow
Conventional ring	Tow-to-top
Direct	Tow-to-yarn
Open-end	High-bulk yarns
Friction	
Twistless	
Self-twist	

fibers, (2) draw them out into a fine strand, and (3) twist them to keep them together and give them strength. Conventional spinning remains the standard by which spun yarns are judged. Many mills are returning to ring spinning. Although continuous spinning, higher speeds, and automation have come into use, spinning is still a long and expensive process. Conventional spun yarns are finer, have better quality, are more uniform, and create fewer problems in fabrication. Conventional spinning is more automated than alternate spinning systems. Approximately 56 percent of the spun yarns are processed by this system.

Spinning may be done by any one of five conventional systems (cotton, woolen, French, Bradford, and American) that are adapted to the characteristics of the fiber—length, cohesiveness, diameter, elasticity, and surface contour. Because the cotton system is representative of the rest, it is discussed here in detail. Table 10-3 summarizes the steps in producing a spun yarn.

Opening Machine-picked cotton contains a high percentage of trash and dirt. The fibers have been compressed very tightly in a bale and may have been stored in this state for a year or more. *Opening* loosens, cleans, and blends the fibers. Cotton varies from bale to bale, so the fibers from several bales are blended together to achieve more uniform quality in the finished yarn. Two types of opening units are used: a chute-feed system and a rotating carousel (Figure 10-12). In both systems bale pluckers (Figure 10-13) pull small tufts of fiber from the bales and drop the tufts on a screen or lattice. High-velocity air removes dirt and trash. The loosened, cleaned fibers are fed to the carding machine in sheet form.

There are several possibilities for blending different generic fiber types in the opening operation. In one method, several bales of fiber are laid around the picker and fibers from each bale are fed alternately into the machine. Another method is called *sandwich blending.* The desired amounts of each fiber are weighed out and a layer of each is spread over the preceding layer to build up a sandwich composed of many layers. Vertical sections are then taken through the sandwich and fed into the picker. *Feeder blending* is an automatic process in which each type of fiber is fed to a mixing apron from individual hoppers (Figure 10-14).

Carding *Carding* partially straightens the fibers and forms them into a thin web, which is brought

Table 10–3   The Cotton System

Operation	Purpose
Opening	Loosens, blends, cleans, forms lap.
Carding	Cleans, straightens, forms carded sliver.
Drawing	Parallels, blends, forms drawn sliver.
Combing	Parallels, removes short fibers, forms combed sliver (used for long-staple cotton only).
Roving	Reduces size, inserts slight twist, forms roving.
Spinning	Reduces size, twists, winds the finished yarn on a bobbin.
Winding	Rewinds yarn from bobbins to spools or cones.

together as a soft, very weak rope of fibers called a *carded sliver* (Figure 10-15). The carding machine consists of cylinders covered with heavy fabric embedded with specially bent wires or with granular cards that are covered with a rough surface similar to rough sandpaper.

Drawing *Drawing* increases the parallelism of the fibers and combines several carded slivers into one *drawn sliver*. This is a blending operation that contributes to greater yarn uniformity. Drawing is done by sets of rollers, each set running successively faster than the preceding set (Figure 10-16).

As slivers are combined, their size is reduced and a small amount of twist is added.

The drawing process may be repeated more than once. It is at this stage that fibers of different generic types often are blended because of the differences in their physical properties. Blending during the drawing process also eliminates mixed wastes.

Combing If long-staple fibers are to be spun, another step is added to the process. *Combing* is done to achieve a yarn that is superior to a carded yarn in smoothness, fineness, evenness, and

Fig. 10–12 *Karousel opener-picker machine. (Courtesy of the Reiter Company, Inc.)*

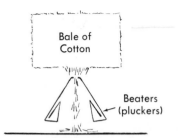

Fig. 10–13   *Beaters (pluckers) pull fibers from the bale.*

Fig. 10–15   *Carding. (Courtesy of Coats & Clark, Inc.)*

strength. Combing parallel-aligns fibers and removes any short fibers from the long staple so that the combed fibers will be more uniform in length. Fibers emerge from the combing machines as *combed sliver*. The combing operation and the long-staple fiber are costly and as much as one-fourth of the fiber is combed out as waste. When working with cotton or cotton blends, the term *combed yarn* is used. When working with wool or wool blends, the term *worsted yarn* is used. Yarns that have not received this process are called carded (cotton and cotton blends) or woolen (wool or wool blends).

Roving   The *roving* process reduces the drawn sliver, increases the parallelism of the fibers, and inserts a small amount of twist in the strand, now called the roving. The roving is a softly twisted strand of fibers about the size of a pencil (see Figure 10–17). Successive roving operations that gradually reduce the size of the strand may be used.

Spinning   *Spinning* adds the twist that makes the single-spun yarn. Ring spinning draws, twists, and winds in one continuous operation. The traveler (Figure 10–18) carries the yarn as it slides around the ring, thus inserting the twist. Ring spinning is a slow textile process in terms of productivity, with rates of 25,000 to 30,000 rpm compared to rates of 110,000 to 120,000 rpm for open-end spinning. Figure 10–19 shows a ring-spinning frame—a multi-

ple-spinning machine that holds a number of individual units.

Blending can also take place during roving or spinning because several fiber strands are combined in these processes. Blending is usually done during roving or spinning to achieve a blending of color.

Ring-frame spinning is most commonly used for woolen yarns. It is similar to ring spinning of cotton yarns.

COMPARISON OF CARDED-COMBED AND WOOLEN-WORSTED YARNS   The length and parallelism of fibers in spun yarns is a major factor in the kind of fabric produced, the cost of the yarns and fabrics, and the terminology used to designate these characteristics.

Yarns made from carded sliver are called *carded* yarns. Carded sliver of short wool fibers is made into *woolen* yarns and the fabrics are called *woolen* fabrics. (The term *woolen* refers to yarn type and is not a synonym for wool.)

Yarns made from combed sliver are called *combed* yarns. With wool, the combed sliver is referred to as *top* and the yarns made from top are called *worsted* yarns. The short fibers that are combed out are called *noils* and are a source of fiber supply for

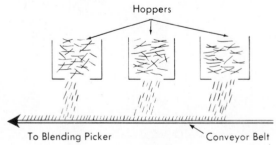

Fig. 10–14   *Fibers from various hoppers are blended on a conveyor belt.*

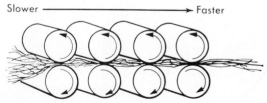

Fig. 10–16   *Drawing rolls.*

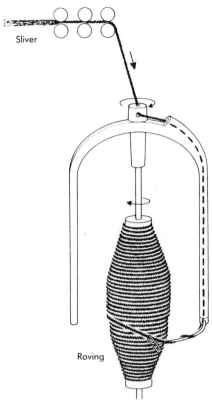

Fig. 10–17 *Roving.*

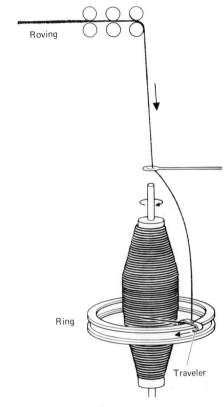

Fig. 10–18 *Ring spinning.*

woolen yarns (see Figure 10–20). Fine-combed cotton yarns are made from the fibers that measure more than 1⅛ inches.

Carded and combed yarns are compared in Table 10–4.

Alternate Spun Yarn Processes

These procedures focus on shortening or simplifying yarn spinning by eliminating or bypassing some of the steps in the conventional ring-spinning system. Most processes focus on eliminating one or more of these steps: drawing, roving, ring spinning, and rewinding.

DIRECT SPINNING *Direct spinning* eliminates the roving but still uses the ring-spinning device for inserting the twist (see Figure 10–21). The sliver is fed directly to the spinning frame. This machine is used to make heavier yarn for pile fabrics and carpets.

OPEN-END SPINNING *Open-end spinning* eliminates the roving and twisting by the ring. Knots are eliminated, and larger packages of yarn are formed,

less operator supervision is needed, and production speeds are about four times that of ring spinning, but the yarns produced are slightly coarser. There are two types of open-end spinning: rotor spinning and air-vortex spinning.

Fig. 10–19 *A spinning frame holds multiple ring spinners.*

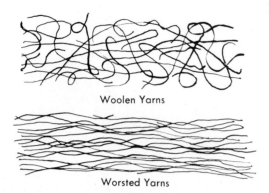

Woolen Yarns

Worsted Yarns

Fig. 10–20 *Woolen and worsted yarns: short-staple wool fibers in carded or woolen yarns (top); long-parallel wool fibers in combed or worsted yarn (bottom).*

In the rotor-spinning process, sliver is broken up so that individual fibers are fed by an air stream and deposited on the inner surface of a rotating device driven at high speed. As the fibers are drawn off, twist is inserted by the rotation of the rotor, making a yarn (Figure 10-22). Approximately 42 percent of all spun yarns are processed by this system.

The air-vortex spinning process is similar to the rotor process except that an even, regular yarn is formed by moving air rather than a rotor. Yarns made in this way are stronger than rotor yarns, but tend to pill more readily.

FRICTION SPINNING *Friction spinning* uses a modification of open-end spinning that combines the rotor and air techniques. The sliver is separated into fibers that are spread onto carding or combing rolls and delivered by air to two cylinders that rotate in the same direction. These two cylinders pull the fibers into a yarn. The feed angle into the cylinder controls fiber alignment. Friction-spun yarns are more even, freer of lint and other debris, and loftier, but they are weaker when compared to conventional yarns.

TWISTLESS SPINNING *Twistless spinning* eliminates the twisting process. A roving is wetted, drawn out, sprayed with sizing or adhesive, wound on a package, and steamed to bond the fibers together (Figure 10-23). The yarns are flat and ribbonlike in shape and are quite stiff because of the sizing. They lack strength as individual yarns but gain strength in the fabric from the pressure between the warp and filling. The absence of twist gives the yarns a soft hand, good luster, and opacity after the sizing is removed. The yarns are easy to dye and have good durability but are not suitable to very open weaves.

SELF-TWISTING SPINNING In *self-twist spinning*, two strands of roving are carried between two rollers that draw out the roving and put in twist. The yarns have areas of S-twist and areas of Z-twist. When the two twisted yarns are brought together, they intermesh and entangle, and, when pressure is released, the yarns ply over each other (Figure 10-24). This process can be used to combine staple plies, filament plies, or staple and filament plies.

Spinning Filament Tow into Spun Yarns

Filament tow of any manufactured fiber can be made into spun yarns by direct spinning without

Table 10–4 Carded and Combed Yarn Comparison

	Carded	Combed
Fibers used	Short staple	Long staple
Yarns	Medium to low twist	Medium to high twist
	More protruding ends	Fewer protruding ends
	Bulkier, softer, fuzzier	Parallel fibers, finer count
		Longer wearing, stronger
Fabrics	May become baggy in areas of stress	Smoother surface, lighter weight
	Fabrics may be soft to firm	Do not sag
	Blankets always carded	Take and hold press
	Wide range of uses	Fabrics range from sheers to suitings

Fig. 10–21 *Mackie direct spinner turns sliver into finished yarn—eliminates roving. (Courtesy of Lumus Mackie Ltd.)*

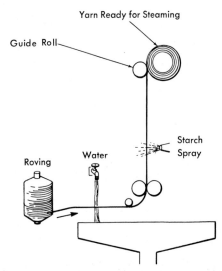

Fig. 10–23 *Twistless spinning.*

disrupting the continuity of the strand. The two systems are tow-to-top or tow-to-yarn.

TOW-TO-TOP (SLIVER) SYSTEM The *tow-to-top system* bypasses the opening, picking, and carding steps of conventional spinning. In this system the filament tow is reduced to staple and formed into sliver (or top) by either diagonal cutting or break stretching. The sliver is made into regular-spun yarn by conventional spinning.

The diagonal cutting stapler changes tow into staple of equal or variable lengths and forms it into a crimped sliver (Figure 10–25). The break-stretch stapler operates on the principle that, when tow is stretched, the fibers break at their weakest points (random breakage) without disrupting the continuity of the strand. The resultant staple is of various lengths.

TOW-TO-YARN SYSTEM *Tow-to-yarn spinning* is done by a machine called a direct spinner. Light tow (4,400 denier) is fed into the machine through leveling rolls, passes between two nip rolls, and then to a second pair of nip rolls, which travel at a faster rate of speed and create tension that causes the fibers to break at their weakest points. The resulting strand is drawn out to yarn size, twisted, and wound on a bobbin (Figure 10–26).

HIGH-BULK YARNS

High-bulk yarns are yarns essentially free from stretch. A fraction of the fibers (in any cross section) has been forced to assume a relatively high random crimp by shrinkage of the remaining fibers that, in general, have very low crimp (ASTM).

Some fibers can be produced with a *latent shrinkage potential* and retain the bulk indefinitely at room temperature. Latent shrinkage in a fiber is achieved by heating, stretching, and then cooling while in the stretched condition. These heat-stretched fibers are called *high-shrinkage fibers* and are combined with nonshrinkage fibers

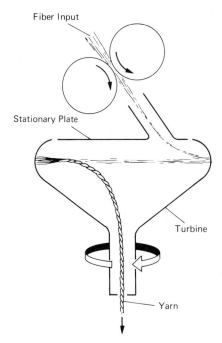

Fig. 10–22 *Open-end, or break, spinning.*

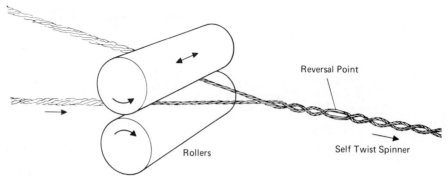

Fig. 10–24 *Self-twist spinning.*

in the same yarn, which is then made into a product. Heat treatment of the product causes the high-shrinkage fibers to relax or shrink, forcing the nonshrinkage fibers to bulk (see Figure 10–27). This makes high-bulk sweaters, knitting yarns, and other products. High-shrinkage fibers tend to migrate to the center of the yarn. Thus, if fine-denier nonshrinkage fibers are combined with coarse-denier high-shrinkage fibers, the fine-denier fibers end up on the outer surface of the yarn. The amount of bulk can be controlled by regulating the amount of heat stretching.

The high-bulk principle can be used to achieve interesting effects, such as "guard hairs" in synthetic furs and sculptured high-low effects in carpets. Carpet pile or furlike fabrics can be made more dense by using a high-shrinkage-type fiber for the ground yarns. When the yarns shrink, the fibers are brought much closer together.

FIBER BLENDS

A *blend* is an intimate mixture of fibers of different composition, length, diameter, or color spun together into a yarn. A *mixture* is a fabric that has yarn of one fiber content in the warp and yarn of a different fiber content in the filling. A *combination* yarn has two unlike fiber strands twisted together as a ply. Blends, mixtures, and combinations give properties to fabrics that are different from those obtained with one fiber only. The following discussion relates to blends because they are most common, but comments apply to mixtures and combinations as well.

Blending is done for several reasons:

1. To produce fabrics with a better combination of performance characteristics in the product. In end uses where durability is important, nylon or polyester blended with cotton or wool provide

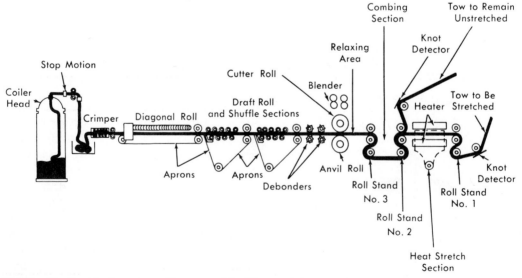

Fig. 10–25 *The Pacific Converter. (Courtesy of the Warner & Swasey Co.)*

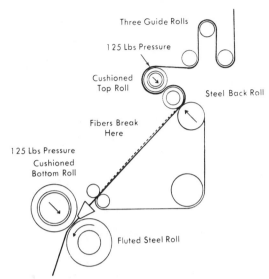

Fig. 10–26 *Direct spinning of yarn from filament tow.*

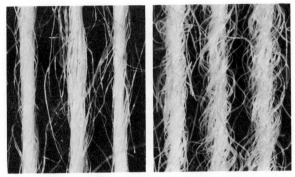

Fig. 10–27 *High-bulk yarn before* (left) *and after* (right) *steaming.*

strength and resistance to abrasion, while the wool or cotton look is maintained. A classic example is durable-press fabrics, where 100 percent cotton fabrics are not as durable as polyester/cotton blends.

2. To improve spinning, weaving, and finishing efficiency and to improve uniformity.

3. To obtain better texture, hand, or fabric appearance. A small amount of a specialty wool may be used to give a buttery or slick hand to wool fabrics, or a small amount of rayon may give luster and softness to a cotton fabric. Fibers with different shrinkage properties are blended to produce bulky, lofty fabrics or fur like fabrics with guard hairs.

4. To minimize fiber cost. Expensive fibers can be extended by blending them with more plentiful fibers. Labeling requirements minimize the use of improper labels when an expensive fiber is used in small amounts but advertised in large print; for example, CASHMERE and wool.

5. To obtain cross-dyed effects or create new color effects such as heather. Fibers with unlike dye affinity are blended together and then piece dyed.

Blending is a complicated and expensive process, but the combination of properties it provides are permanent. Blends offer better serviceability of fabrics as well as improved appearance and hand.

In Table 10-5 some fiber properties are rated. Notice that each fiber is deficient in one or more important properties. Try different fiber combinations to see how a blend of two fibers might give different performance than either fiber used alone.

Table 10–5 Fiber Properties

Properties	Cotton	Rayon	Wool	Acetate	Nylon	Polyester	Acrylic	Modacrylic	Olefin
Bulk and loft	−	−	+++		−	−	+++	+++	
Wrinkle recovery	−	−	+++	++	++	+++	++	++	++
Press (wet) retention	−	−	−	+	++	+++			
Absorbency	+++	+++	+++	+	−	−	−	−	−
Static resistance	+++	+++	++	+	+	−	+	+	++
Resistance to pilling	+++	+++	+	+++	+			+	++
Strength	++	+	+	+	+++	+++	+	+	+++
Abrasion resistance	+	−	++	−	+++	+++	+	+	+++
Stability	++	−	−	+++	+++	+++	+++	+++	+++
Resistance to heat	+++	+++	++	+	+	+	++	−	−

+++, excellent;   ++, good;   +, fair;   −, deficient

Blend Levels

A blend of fibers that complement each other may give more satisfactory all-round performance than a 100 percent fiber fabric. For example, compare two fabrics, one of Fiber A and the other of Fiber B, across 5 properties. A fabric made of 50 percent A and 50 percent B will have values for each property that are neither as high as possible nor as low as possible (Caplan) (see Table 10–6). By blending the fibers, a fabric with intermediate values is obtained. Unfortunately, in a blend the real values do not come out in the same proportion as their respective percentage.

Much research has been done by fiber manufacturers to determine the percentage of each fiber necessary in various products. It is very difficult to generalize about percentages, because the percentage varies with the kind of fiber, the fabric construction, and the expected performance. For example, a small amount of nylon (15 percent) improves the strength of wool, but 60 percent nylon is needed to improve the strength of rayon. For stability, 50 percent acrylic blended with wool in a woven fabric is satisfactory, but 75 percent acrylic is necessary in knitted fabrics.

Fiber producers have controlled blend levels fairly well by setting standards for fabrics identified with their trademarks. For example, the Du Pont Company recommends a blend level of 65 percent Dacron polyester/35 percent cotton in light- or medium-weight fabrics, whereas 50/50 Dacron/cotton is satisfactory for suiting-weight fabrics. This assures satisfactory performance of the fabric and maintains a positive fiber image for Dacron. The fabric manufacturer profits from the large-scale promotion by the fiber producer.

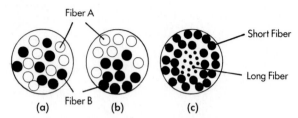

Fig. 10–28   *Cross section of yarn showing the location of the fiber in the blend: (a) blended at the opening stage; (b) blended at the roving stage; (c) blend of short and long fibers.*

By using specially designed fiber variants, it is possible to obtain desired performance and appearance in fabrics. For example, fading, shrinkage, and softening over time are desirable characteristics for denim jeans, but are undesirable in most other apparel. For this market Du Pont has developed a Dacron polyester variant that, when blended with cotton, fades, shrinks uniformly, and becomes softer.

Blending Methods

Blending of staple can be done at any stage prior to the spinning operation including opening-picking, drawing, or roving. One of the disadvantages of direct spinning is that blending cannot be done before the sliver is formed.

The earlier the fibers are blended in processing, the better the blend. Figure 10–28 shows a cross section of yarns in which the fibers were blended in opening and in which the fibers were blended at the roving stage.

Long, fine fibers tend to move to the center of a yarn, whereas coarse, short fibers migrate to the periphery of a yarn (see Figure 10–28c).

Table 10–6   Effect of Blending on Performance

Property	Known Values		Predicted Values 50/50 A and B
	A	*B*	
1	12	4	8
2	9	12	10.5
3	15	2	8.5
4	7	9	8
5	12	8	10

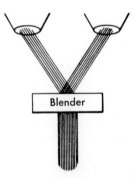

Fig. 10–29   *Blended filament yarn. Different fibers are spun, then blended to form a yarn.*

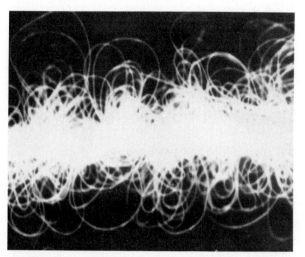

Fig. 10–30 *Lanese yarn. (Courtesy of Hoechst Celanese.)*

Fabrics are also produced that are mixtures of bulk-filament yarns and spun yarns. These fabrics may have filament yarns in only one direction and spun yarns in the other or they may have different yarns in bands in the warp or filling to create a design in the fabric.

Blended Filament Yarns

A *blended filament yarn* is one in which unlike filaments of different deniers or generic types are blended together. This is usually done to improve the performance and appearance of fabrics (see Figures 10–29 and 10–30). The yarns are used in apparel and furnishings.

ROTOFIL OR FACIATED YARNS These yarns give better texture and hand to fabrics. The yarns are combinations of coarse filaments for strength and fine broken filaments for softness. They are made by a combination of crimping and twisting.

KEY TERMS

Yarn	Sliver
Filament yarn	Combing
Throwing	Worsted yarn
Smooth-filament yarn	Roving
Tape yarn	Spinning
Bulk yarn	Woolen yarn
Bulk-continuous-filament yarn	Top
BCF	Direct spinning
Texturing	Open-end spinning
Stretch yarn	Friction spinning
Bulky yarn	Twistless spinning
Textured or bulked yarn	Self-twist spinning
Spun yarn	Tow-to-top system
Carded yarn	Tow-to-yarn system
Combed yarn	High-bulk yarn
Conventional or ring spinning	Blend
Opening	Mixture
Carding	Combination
Drawing	

QUESTIONS

1. Explain the processes used to produce each of these yarns: smooth filament, BCF, carded spun yarn, worsted spun yarn.
2. Using the serviceability concepts, explain why cotton and polyester are often blended for furnishing and apparel items.
3. Compare and contrast the appearance, processing, and performance of the yarn pairs listed:
     carded and combed yarns

  smooth and bulk filament yarns

  woolen and worsted yarns

4. How would the performance of two similar products differ if one were made of filament yarns of polyester and the other of spun yarns of polyester?

5. What are the differences between these two products: a blend of nylon and wool and a mixture of nylon and wool?

SUGGESTED READINGS

American Society for Testing and Materials (1990). *Annual Book of ASTM Standards, Vol 7.01.* Philadelphia, PA: American Society for Testing and Materials.

Caplan, M. J. (1959). "Fiber Translation in Blends." *Modern Textile Magazine, 40,* p. 39.

Krause, H. W., and Soliman, H. A. (July, 1990). "Do Higher Speeds Demand Better Yarns?" *Textile Month,* pp. 19–22.

"Slit Film Extrusion of Polypropylene Yarns." (May, 1990). *Textile Month,* pp. 53–54.

Wilson, D. K., and Kollu, T. (1991). "The Production of Textured Yarns by the False-Twist Technique." *Textile Progress, 21* (3), pp 1–42.

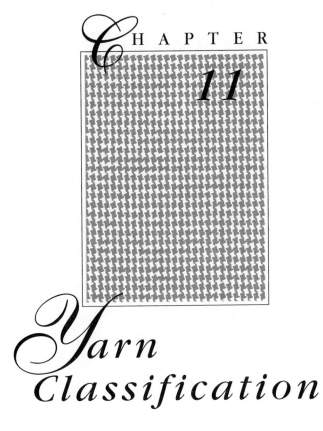

CHAPTER 11

Yarn Classification

OBJECTIVES

- To understand the classification of yarns based on appearance and structure.

- To classify and name yarns when seen in fabrics.

- To explain performance of yarns in textile products.

- To understand relationships between yarn characteristics and fiber performance.

- To relate yarn selection to end uses and expected performance.

*A*YARN IS CLASSIFIED AND IDENTIFIED BY several aspects: fiber length (staple/filament), yarn twist, yarn size, and yarn regularity/irregularity along its length. These factors contribute to the performance of the fabric made from the yarn.

Fabric producers select from a wide variety of yarns based on end use. Yarns play an important part in determining the hand and performance of the fabric. For example, yarns with high twist create the texture in true crepe fabrics, and yarns with low twist are napped in flannel fabrics and blankets. Yarn may enhance good fiber performance or compensate for poor fiber performance. The effectiveness of a finish may depend on the proper choice of yarn. Most yarns can be easily identified.

FIBER LENGTH

The names of the most common yarns are based on the length of the fibers within them, and the appearance and parallelism of those fibers. When a typical yarn is unraveled from a fabric and examined, it appears uniformly smooth, or uniformly bulky, or fuzzy with protruding fiber ends. It can be untwisted until it separates into individual fibers. These fibers are either short, typically ½–2½ inches, or as long as the piece of fabric from which the yarn was pulled.

A *spun yarn* is composed of short-staple fibers that are twisted or otherwise bonded together, resulting in a fuzzy yarn with protruding fiber ends. Spun yarns of felted wool are available in some specialty sweaters.

A *filament yarn* is composed of long fibers that are grouped together or slightly twisted together. Filament yarns may be smooth—with straight, almost parallel fibers—or uniformly bulky, in which case they are called *textured-bulk-filament yarns* or just *textured-bulk yarns*. Table 11–1 summarizes the properties that result from the use of these yarns in fabrics. Processing of spun yarns, smooth filament yarns, and textured bulk yarns was discussed in Chapter 10.

YARN TWIST

Twist, the spiral arrangement of the fibers around the axis of the yarn, is produced by rotating one end of a fiber strand while the other end is held stationary. Twist binds the fibers together and contributes strength to the spun yarn. The use of a twist helps to vary the appearance of fabrics.

The number of twists has a direct bearing on the cost of the yarn. Higher twist yarns are more expensive because yarn yield is lower. Twist is identified by the number of turns per unit length: *turns per inch (tpi)* or turns per meter (tpm).

Direction of Twist

The direction of twist is described as S-twist or Z-twist. A yarn has *S-twist* if, when held in a vertical position, the spirals conform to the direction of slope of the central portion of the letter "S." It is called *Z-twist* if the direction of spirals conforms to the slope of the central portion of the letter "Z." Z-twist is the standard twist used for weaving yarns (Figure 11–1).

Amount of Twist

The amount of twist varies with (1) the length of the fibers, (2) the size of the yarn, and (3) its intended use. Increasing the amount of twist to the point of perfect fiber-to-fiber cohesion increases the strength of the yarn. However, excess twist places the fibers at right angles to the axis of the yarn causing a shearing action between fibers; the yarn loses strength (Figure 11–2).

Combed yarns with long fibers do not require as much twist as carded yarns with short fibers because long, parallel fibers have more points of contact per fiber giving a stronger yarn for the same amount of twist. Fine yarns require more twist than coarse yarns. Knitting yarns have less twist than filling yarns used in weaving. Table 11–2 and the following discussion give examples of uses for yarns with different amounts of twist.

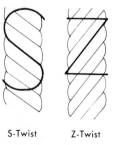

S-Twist   Z-Twist

Fig. 11–1 *S- and Z-twist yarns.*

Table 11–1   Comparison of Spun, Smooth-Filament, and Textured-Bulk Yarns

Spun Yarns	Smooth-Filament Yarns	Textured-Bulk Yarns (BCF)
I. Fabrics are cottonlike or wool-like.	I. Fabrics are silklike.	I. Fabrics have the strength of filament yarns and the appearance of spun yarns.
II. Strength of fibers is not completely utilized.	II. Strength of fiber is completely utilized.	II. Strength may or may not be completely utilized.
III. Short fibers twisted into continuous strand, has protruding ends. 1. Dull, fuzzy look. 2. Lint. 3. Subject to pilling. 4. Soil readily. 5. Warm (not slippery). 6. Loft and bulk depend on size and twist. 7. Do not snag readily. 8. Stretch depends on amount of twist. 9. More cover (more opaque).	III. Long continuous, smooth, closely packed strand. 1. Smooth, lustrous. 2. Do not lint. 3. Do not pill readily. 4. Shed soil. 5. Cool, slick. 6. Little loft or bulk. 7. Snagging depends on fabric contruction. 8. Stretch depends on amount of twist. 9. Less cover (less opaque).	III. Long continuous, irregular, porous, flexible strand. 1. Bulky, dull. 2. Do not lint. 3. Pilling depends on fabric construction. 4. Soil more easily than plain filament. 5. Warmer than plain filament. 6. Loft, bulk, and/or stretch. 7. Snag easily. 8. Stretch depends on method of processing. 9. More cover (more opaque).
IV. Absorbency depends on fiber content. Most absorbent type. 1. Good for skin contact (most absorbent). 2. Less static buildup.	IV. Absorbency depends on fiber content. 1. Thermoplastics are low in absorbency. 2. Static buildup high in thermoplastics.	IV. More absorbent than plain-filament yarns of same fiber content. 1. Most manufacturing processes require thermoplastic fibers. 2. Static buildup.
V. Size often expressed in yarn number.	V. Size in denier.	V. Size in denier.
VI. Various amounts of twist used.	VI. Usually very low or very high twist.	VI. Usually low twist.
VII. Most complex manufacturing process.	VII. Least complicated manufacturing process.	VII. Manufacturing process is more complex than for plain filament.

Low twist in spun yarns results in lofty yarns. They are used in filling yarns of fabrics that are to be napped. Napping teases out the ends of the staple fibers and creates the soft, fuzzy surface. (See "Napped," Chapter 17.) See Figures 11-3b and 11-3c.

Average twist is frequently used for yarns made of staple fibers and is very seldom used for filament yarns. Yarns with average twist are the most common and durable type of spun yarns. These yarns can be of long-staple fibers with a parallel arrangement as in combed and worsted yarns or they can be of short-staple fibers with a less parallel arrangement (carded and woolen yarns). See Figure 11-3d.

Hard twist or *voile twist* yarns have a harsher hand and 30-40 turns per inch. The hardness of the yarn results when twist brings the fibers closer together and makes the yarn more compact. This effect is more pronounced when a twist-on-twist ply yarn is used. *Twist-on-twist* means that the direction of twist in the singles is the same as that of plying twist (Figure 11-4). This results in a buildup of the total amount of twist in the yarn. (See discussion of voile under "Lightweight Sheer Fabrics," Chapter 12.) See Figure 11-3e.

Crepe yarns are made of either staple or filament fiber with the highest number of turns per inch (40-80) inserted in the yarn. These yarns are also

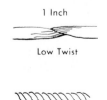

1 Inch

Low Twist

High Twist

Fig. 11–2 *Low and high turns per inch.*

Table 11–2   Amount of Twist

Amount	Example	Characteristics
Low twist	Filament yarns: 2–3 tpi*	Smooth and slick or bulky; may be difficult to recognize any twist.
Napping twist	Blanket warps: 12 tpi Filling: 6–8 tpi	Bulky, soft, fuzzy, may be weak.
Average twist	Percale warps: 25 tpi Filling: 20 tpi Nylon hosiery: 25–30 tpi	Most common, smooth, regular, durable, comfortable. Produces smooth, regular fabrics.
Voile twist	Hard-twist singles: 35–40 tpi are plied with 16–18 tpi	Strong, fine yarns. Fabrics have harsher hand due to yarn twist.
Crepe twist	Singles: 40–80 or more tpi are plied with 2–5 tpi	Lively yarns tend to kink and twist in fabric. Creates good drape and texture in fabrics.

*Turns per inch.

referred to as unbalanced yarns since they tend to twist and kink when removed from the fabric. This makes the yarn so lively and kinky that it must be twist-set before it can be woven or knitted. *Twist-setting* is a yarn finishing process.

Increasing the amount of crepe yarn twist and alternating the direction of twist increases the amount of crinkle in a crepe fabric. For example, 6S filling yarns in a band followed by 6Z filling yarns in a band gives a more prominent crinkle than 2S filling yarns in a band followed by 2Z filling yarns in a band.

To identify crepe yarns, ravel adjacent sides to obtain a fringe on each of the two edges. Test the yarns that are removed by pulling on the yarn and then letting one end go. The yarn will twist as shown in Figure 11–5. Also see Figure 11–3f.

Do not confuse kink with yarn crimp. Examine the fringe of the fabric. If yarns other than crepe

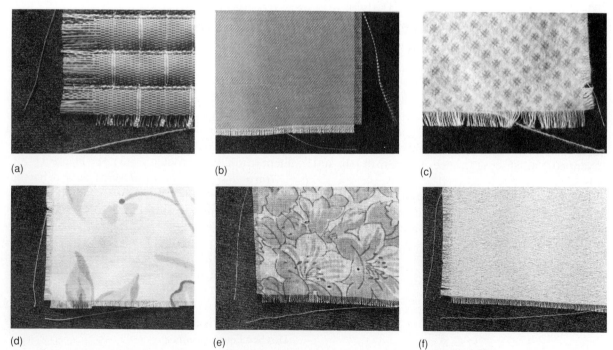

(a)　　　　　　　(b)　　　　　　　(c)

(d)　　　　　　　(e)　　　　　　　(f)

Fig. 11–3   *Examples of yarn twist and fabrics of these yarns: (a) monofilament, (b) low twist, (c) napping twist, (d) average twist, (e) voile twist, and (f) crepe twist.*

Fig. 11–4   Twist-on-twist two-ply yarn.

yarns are used in the fabric, they will probably be of very low twist. The majority of crepe fabrics have crepe yarns in the crosswise direction, although some are in the lengthwise direction, and some have crepe yarns in both directions. Crepe fabrics are discussed in Chapters 12 and 13.

YARN SIZE

Yarn Number

Spun-yarn size is referred to as *yarn number* and is expressed in terms of length per unit of weight. The precise weights and lengths differ according to the fiber in the yarn. The cotton system is discussed here since many yarns are numbered by the cotton system. It is an indirect or fixed-weight system: the finer the yarn, the larger the number. The yarn number or cotton count is based on the number of hanks (1 hank is 840 yards) in 1 pound of yarn (see Table 11-3). Some examples that show how the size of the weaving yarn affects the weight of the fabric are given in the second half of the table.

The woolen and worsted systems are similar to the cotton system, except that hanks are of different lengths.

Denier

Denier refers to yarns made from filament fibers. The term refers to both smooth and bulky-textured yarns.

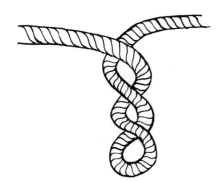

Fig. 11–5   Kink in crepe yarn.

Table 11–3   Cotton System

Number or Count of Spun Yarn	Hanks	Weight (pounds)
No. 1	1 (840 yards)	1
No. 2	2 (1,680 yards)	1
No. 3	3 (2,520 yards)	1

Examples of Fabric Weight	Yarn Size	
	Warp	Filling
Sheer lawn (2.0 oz/yd^2)	70s*	100s
Medium-weight print cloth (4.5 oz/yd^2)	30s	40s
Heavyweight sailcloth (7.5 oz/yd^2)	13s	20s

*The "s" after the number means that the yarn is single.

The size of filament yarns is based on the size of the individual fibers in the yarn and the number of those fibers grouped into the yarn. The size of both filament fibers and filament yarns is expressed in terms of weight per unit of length—denier. In this system, the unit of length remains constant. The numbering system is direct, also referred to as a fixed-length system, because the finer the yarn, the smaller the number. See Table 11-4 for examples of filament yarns made in a specific denier for certain end uses.

Tex System

The International Organization for Standardization has adopted the *tex* system, which determines yarn count or number in the same way for all fiber yarns and uses metric units (weight in grams of 1 thousand meters of yarn). One tex is equal to 0.11 denier (tex = denier/9). Because the size can be small, the

Table 11–4   Filament Yarn Size

Yarn Denier	Use	Yarn Tex
20	Sheer hosiery	2.2
40–70	Tricot lingerie, blouses , shirts, support hosiery, glass curtains	4.4–7.8
140–520	Outerwear, draperies	15.6–57.8
520–840	Upholstery	57.8–93.3
1,040	Carpets, some knitting yarns	115.6

term decitex (dtex) may be used. One dtex is 10 times larger than one tex. This system is not widely used in the United States.

YARN REGULARITY

Yarn regularity describes the uniformity of the yarn throughout its length in terms of its appearance and structure. Regular yarns have a similar appearance and structure throughout. There may be some slight variation due to uniformity of fiber distribution and fiber length, degree of parallelism of fibers within the yarn, and regularity of fiber size or diameter. For example, yarns with a wide variety of fiber length, unparalleled fibers, or fibers from bast sources like flax or ramie may be slightly less regular than other yarns.

Fancy or novelty yarns have deliberately introduced appearance and structural variations. These irregularities tend to appear at a regular interval due to processing. Composite yarns have components that differ from each other. All three general yarn types will be discussed in more detail in this section.

Simple Yarns

A *simple yarn* is alike in all its parts. It can be described as a spun or filament yarn based on the length of the fibers. A simple yarn also can be described by the number of parts it has, by the direction and amount of twist in the yarn, and by the size of the yarn. Figure 11–6 outlines the relationship of yarns in this category to each other.

Simple yarns are classified as single, ply, or cord yarns. A *single yarn* is the simplest type of the three. It is the product of the first twisting operation that is performed by the spinning machine (Figure 11–7a). These simple single yarns require no additional processing once the yarns have been formed.

Spun, filament, and textured yarns are each examples of simple single yarns. Since these three yarns are most commonly found in apparel and furnishing fabrics, they usually are referred to as spun, filament, or textured-bulk yarns. They are simple yarns, alike in all parts. They are single yarns, consisting of one strand of fibers.

A *ply yarn* is made by a second twisting operation, which combines two or more singles (Figure 11–7b). Each part of the yarn is called a ply. The twist is inserted by a machine called a twister. Most ply yarns are twisted in the opposite direction to the twist of the singles from which they are made; thus the first few revolutions tend to untwist the singles and straighten the fibers somewhat from their spiral position and the yarn becomes softer.

Plying tends to increase the diameter, strength, uniformity, and quality of the yarn. Ply yarns are commonly used in the warp direction of woven fabrics to increase the strength of the fabric. Two-ply yarns are found in the best-quality men's broadcloth shirts. Ply yarns are frequently seen in knits and furnishings. Two-ply and three-ply yarns are found in sewing thread and string used to tie packages. If simple ply yarns are used only in the filling direction, they are used for some fabric effect other than strength.

A *cord* is made by a third twisting operation, which twists ply yarns together (Figure 11–7c). Some types of sewing thread and some ropes belong to this group. Cord yarns are seldom used in apparel and furnishing fabrics, but are used in industrial-weight fabrics such as duck and canvas.

Fancy Yarns

Fancy yarns may be defined as yarns that deliberately have unlike parts and that are irregular at regu-

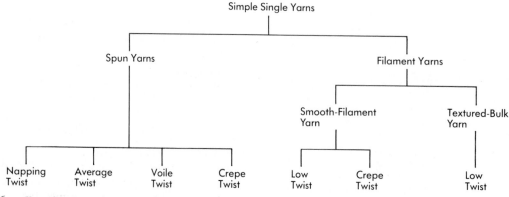

Fig. 11–6 *Classification of simple single yarns.*

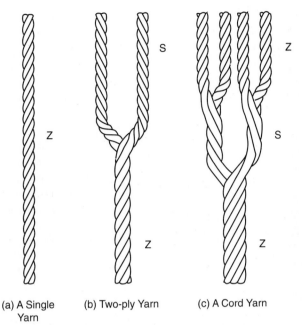

(a) A Single   (b) Two-ply Yarn   (c) A Cord Yarn
Yarn

Fig. 11–7   *Parts of a yarn: (a) single yarn; (b) two-ply yarn; (c) cord yarn.*

lar intervals. The regular intervals may or may not be obvious at first to the observer.

Fancy yarns may be single, plied, or cord yarns. They may be spun, filament, or textured yarns—or any combination of yarn types. They are called fancy yarns or novelty yarns because of their appearance: They lend an interesting or novel effect to fabrics made with them. Their structure may be complex and consist of several yarn plies.

Fancy yarns can be classified according to the number of parts and named for the effect that dominates the fabric. Usually more common in furnishing fabrics than in apparel fabrics, fancy yarns are used by artists and craft people to create interest in otherwise plain fabrics. They are seen in wool fabrics, especially suitings and coatings.

Fancy yarns are made on twisters with special attachments for giving different tensions and rates of delivery to the different plies (parts), thus allowing loose, curled, twisted, or looped areas in the yarn. Slubs and flakes of color are introduced into the yarn by special attachments. Knots or slubs are made at regular cycles of the machine operation (Figure 11–8).

The following are some facts about *novelty yarns*:

1. Novelty yarns are usually plied yarns, but they are not used to add strength to the fabric.

2. If novelty yarns are used in one direction only, they are usually in the filling direction. They are more economical in that direction (there is less waste), are subject to less strain, and are easier to vary for design purposes.

3. Novelty yarns add permanent interest to plain-weave fabrics at lower cost than if effects were obtained from variations in weave.

4. Novelty yarns that are loose and bulky give crease resistance to a fabric, but they make the fabric spongy and hard to handle.

5. The durability of novelty yarn fabrics is dependent on the size of the novelty effect, how well the novelty effect is held in the yarn, and on the firmness of the weave of the fabric. Generally speaking, the smaller the novelty effect, the more durable the fabric, since the yarns are less affected by abrasion and do not tend to catch and snag so readily.

Figure 11-9 classifies the most common fancy yarns according to whether they are typically single or ply yarns.

Tweed yarn is an example of a single, spun, fancy yarn. Flecks of color from short fibers are twisted into the yarn to add interest. The cohesiveness of wool fibers explains why tweeds are often made of wool. Tweed yarns are found in apparel, upholstery, and draperies.

A *slub yarn* is another single, spun, novelty yarn. This thick-and-thin yarn is made by varying the amount of twist in the yarn at regular intervals. The

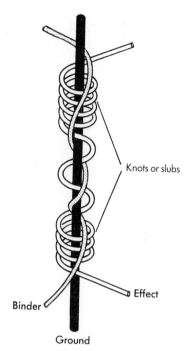

Fig. 11–8 *Fancy yarn, showing the three basic parts.*

thicker part of the yarn is twisted less; the thinner part of the yarn is twisted more. Slub yarns can be found in shantung, drapery, and upholstery fabrics as well as in hand-knitting yarns and sweaters.

Other fancy yarns have two plies. One ply may be of one color, the other of a different color. The plies may be of differing thicknesses. A two-ply fancy yarn may have one spun ply combined with a filament ply.

Frequently fancy yarns have three basic parts:

1. The ground, or foundation, or core
2. The effect, or fancy
3. The binder

As a fancy yarn is examined, the *binder* is the first ply that can be unwound from the yarn. Its purpose is to hold the effect ply in place. The *effect ply* is mainly responsible for the appearance of the yarn, as well as the name given to the yarn. The *ground ply*

forms the foundation of the yarn. Figure 11–8 shows a three-ply novelty yarn. For clarity in the illustration, each ply appears to be a simple, single, monofilament (single-fiber) yarn. In actuality, each ply could be spun, filament, BCF, or complex. Metallic components may also be used. For example, the ground may be a simple, single, filament yarn; the effect could be two-ply, with one ply a monofilament metallic yarn and the other ply a spun yarn; and the binder could be a simple, single, spun yarn. Each ply in two or more ply fancy yarns may have a different fiber content. Endless variations are possible!

The following are typical novelty yarns:

1. In *ratiné yarns,* the effect ply is twisted in a somewhat spiral arrangement around the ground ply. At intervals, a longer loop is thrown out, kinks back on itself, and is held in place by the binder (Figure 11–10a).

2. The *spiral* or *corkscrew yarn* is made by twisting together two plies that differ in size, type, or twist. These two parts may be delivered to the twister at different rates of speed (Figure 11–10b).

3. The *knot, spot, nub,* or *knop yarn* is made by twisting the effect ply many times in the same place (Figure 11–10c). Two effect plies of different colors may be used and the knots arranged so the colored spots are alternated along the length of the yarn. A binder is added during the twisting operation.

4. In the *spike* or *snarl,* the effect ply forms alternating unclosed loops along both sides of the yarn (Figure 11–10d).

5. The *loop, curl,* or *bouclé yarn* has closed loops at regular intervals along the yarn (Figure 11–10e). These yarns are used in fabrics to create a looped pile that resembles caracul lambskin and is called *astrakhan cloth.* They are also used to give textured effects to other fabrics. Mohair, rayon, and acetate are often used for the effect ply.

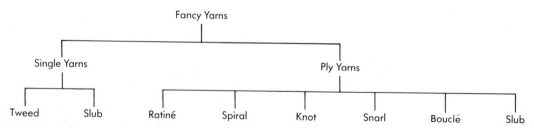

Fig. 11–9 *Classification of fancy yarns.*

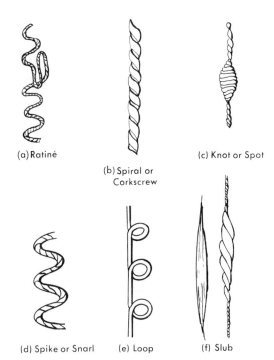

(a) Ratiné

(b) Spiral or Corkscrew

(c) Knot or Spot

(d) Spike or Snarl   (e) Loop   (f) Slub

Fig. 11–10   *Effect ply of several kinds of fancy yarns.*

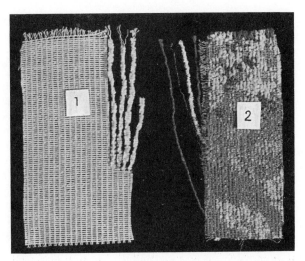

Fig. 11–12   *(1) Chenille yarn is made by cutting a specially woven fabric into strips. (2) Fabric made from chenille yarn.*

6. *Slub effects* are achieved in two ways (Figure 11–10f). True slubs are made by varying the amount of the twist at regular intervals. Intermittently spun flake or slub effects are made by incorporating soft, thick, elongated tufts of fiber into the yarn at regular intervals. A core or binder is needed in the latter situation.

7. *Metallic yarns* have been used for thousands of years. See Chapter 9 for processing and use information. Metallic yarns may be monofilament fibers or combined in ply yarns.

8. *Chenille yarn* is made by cutting a specially woven ladderlike fabric into warpwise strips (Figures 11–11 and 11–12). The cut ends of the softly twisted yarns loosen and form a fringe. This fringed yarn may be woven to produce pile on one side or on both sides of the fabric. If the pile is on one side only, the yarn must be

folded before it is woven. This yarn is sometimes referred to as a "caterpillar" yarn. Chenille-type yarns can also be made by flocking or gluing short fibers on the surface of the yarn. Other chenille-type yarns are made by twisting the effect yarn around the core yarn, securing it in place with the binder, and cutting the effect so it forms a fringe or pile. Chenille yarns are mainly used in furnishings and apparel.

Table 11–5 summarizes information about yarns relative to aesthetics, durability, comfort, and care. Use it to review the major yarns and compare their performance.

Composite Yarns

Composite yarns, regular in appearance along their length, have several unlike components; they have both staple-fiber and filament-fiber components. Composite yarns include covered yarns, core-spun yarns, filament-wrapped yarns, and molten-polymer yarns. The relationship of the basic composite yarns is shown in Figure 11–13.

Covered yarns have a central yarn that is completely covered by fiber or another yarn. These yarns were developed to make rubber more comfortable in foundation garments and surgical hose. These stretch-covered yarns consist of a central core of rubber or spandex covered with yarns. There are two kinds: single covered and double covered. Single-covered yarns have a single yarn wrapped around them. They are lighter, more resilient, and

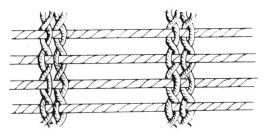

Fig. 11–11   *Fabric from which chenille yarn is cut.*

Table 11–5   Performance of Yarns in Fabrics

Yarn Type	Aesthetics	Durability	Comfort	Care
Spun yarns	Fabrics are cottonlike or wool-like in appearance Fabrics lint and pill	Weaker than filament yarns of same fiber Ply yarns stronger than simple yarns Yarns are more cohesive so fabrics tend to resist raveling and running	Warmer More absorbent because of larger surface area	Yarns do not snag readily Soil readily
Smooth-filament yarns	Fabrics are smooth and lustrous Fabrics do not lint or pill readily	Stronger than spun yarns of same fiber Fabrics ravel and run readily	Cooler Least absorbent but more likely to wick moisture	Yarns may snag Resist soiling
Bulk yarns	Fabrics are less lustrous; more similar to those made of spun yarns Fabrics do not lint, but may pill	Stronger than spun yarns of same fiber Yarns are more cohesive so fabrics ravel and run less than those made with filament yarns, but more than those made with spun yarns	Bulkier and warmer than smooth-filament yarns More absorbent than fialment yarns Stretch more than other yarns	Yarns likely to snag Soil more readily than filament yarns
Fancy yarns	Interesting texture Greater novelty effects show wear sooner than smaller novelty effects Fabrics lint and pill	Weaker than filament yarns Most resist raveling Less abrasion-resistant	Warmer More absorbent if part is spun	Yarns likely to snag Soil readily
Composite	Varies, yarns may be large, may have spun or filament appearance	Related to process	May have stretch, larger than many other yarns	Large yarns may snag

more economical than double-covered yarns and can be used in satin, batiste, broadcloth, and suiting as well as for lightweight foundation garments. Most ordinary elastic yarns are double-covered to give them balance and better coverage. Fabrics made with these yarns are heavier. A double-covered yarn

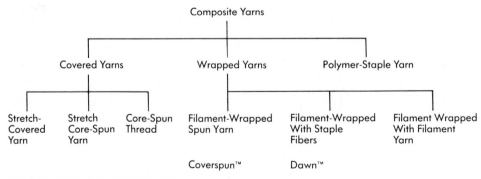

Fig. 11–13 *Classification of composite yarns.*

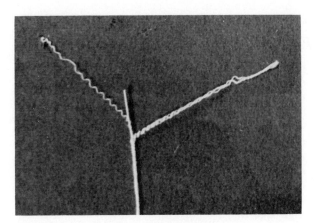

Fig. 11–14 *Double-wrapped elastic yarn.*

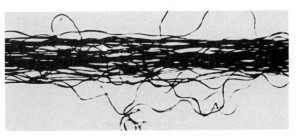

Fig. 11–16 *Filament-wrapped filament yarn. (Courtesy of Hercules, Inc.)*

is shown in Figure 11-14. Covered yarns are subject to "grin-through" (see Figure 9-4).

An alternate way of making a stretch yarn is to make a stretch *core-spun yarn,* spinning a sheath of staple fibers (roving) around a core. When working with elastomeric cores, the core is stretched while the sheath is spun around it. The core is completely hidden and does not change the fabric surface. The sheath gives aesthetic properties to the yarn, and the core gives just enough stretch for comfort. Core-spun yarns can be used to given woven fabrics an elasticity more like that of the knits.

Polyester/cotton core-spun thread has a high-strength filament polyester core around which is spun a sheath of high-quality cotton. The cotton outer cover gives the thread excellent sewability, and the polyester core provides high strength and resistance to abrasion. Polyester/cotton thread also provides the slight stretch that is necessary in knits.

In *wrap-spun yarns,* a core of staple fibers (often

a twistless yarn) is wrapped in a helix with filament fibers that serve as a binder. These yarns can be produced economically to have good evenness, strength, appearance, and finishing properties.

Filament yarn wrapped with staple fibers, or fasciated yarns are a bundle of filaments wrapped with staple fibers. The yarns are combinations of coarse filaments for strength and fine broken filaments for softness (Figure 11-15). They are produced by running the filaments and stretch-broken tow through a device that spins the staple around the bundle of filaments. Production of these yarns is very fast. These yarns give better texture and hand to fabrics. Another variation is a *filament-wrapped filament yarn* (Figure 11-16).

Yarns can be produced by pressing staple fibers of any length or generic class into a molten polymer stream. As the polymer solidifies, the fibers that are partially embedded become firmly attached and form a sheath of staple fiber. The resultant yarn is about two-thirds staple fiber and one-third coagulated polymer. The polymer, which is extruded as manufactured fibers are, is a less expensive product than other melt-spun filaments.

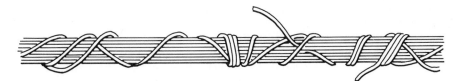

Fig. 11–15 *Fasciated yarn.*

KEY TERMS

Yarn	Ply yarn
Spun yarn	Cord
Filament yarn	Fancy yarn
Textured-bulk-filament yarn	Novelty yarn
Textured-bulk yarn	Slub yarn
Twist	Binder
Turns per inch (tpi)	Effect ply
S-twist	Ground ply
Z-twist	Ratiné yarn
Low twist	Spiral or corkscrew yarn
Soft twist	Knot, spot, nub, or knop yarn
Napping twist	Spike or snarl
Average twist	Loop, curl, or bouclé yarn
Hard twist	Astrakhan cloth
Voile twist	Slub effects
Twist-on-twist	Metallic yarn
Crepe yarn	Chenille yarn
Twist setting	Composite yarn
Yarn number	Covered yarn
Denier	Core spun yarn
Tex	Wrap-spun yarn
Simple yarn	Filament yarn wrapped with staple fibers
Single yarn	Filament-wrapped filament yarn

QUESTIONS

1. What type of yarn (in terms of fiber length, yarn twist, yarn complexity, regularity, and size) would likely be found in each of the following products? Explain the performance of each yarn selected.

   percale sheeting in luxury hotel suite

   muslin sheeting in budget motel room

   tweed for woman's blazer

   carpet for family room

   upholstery for antique formal settee

   casual T-shirt

   denim jeans

   elastic wrap for sprained ankle

   casement cloth for draperies in medical center waiting room

2. What differences in fiber length and turns per inch would you expect between a low twist yarn and an average twist yarn?

3. Why are fancy or novelty yarns used? In what kinds of fabrics and for what uses are they most common?

4. What are the differences and similarities between the denier and tex systems?

SUGGESTED READINGS

American Society for Testing and Materials (1990). *Annual Book of ASTM Standards, Vol 7.01*. Philadelphia, PA: American Society for Testing and Materials.

Merkel, Robert S. (1991). *Textile Product Serviceability*. New York: Macmillan Publishing Co.

Wiberley, James S. (1984) "The Analysis of Textile Structure." In William J. Weaver, ed., *Analytical Methods for a Textile Laboratory*. Research Triangle Park, SC: American Association of Textile Chemists and Colorists.

SECTION 4

FABRICATION

CHAPTER

12

Basic Weaves and Fabrics

OBJECTIVES

- To understand the loom, the process of weaving, and the three basic weaves.
- To identify fabrics made using any of the three basic weaves.
- To name basic fabrics.
- To predict performance of fabrics based on fabrication, yarn structure, and fiber.

A FABRIC IS A PLIABLE, PLANELIKE STRUC-
ture that can be made into two- or three-dimensional
products where some shaping and flexibility is
needed. Fabrics are used in apparel, furnishings, and
many industrial products. The four chapters in this
section focus on methods used to produce fabrics
and introduce many fabrics by name for each
method. Not all fabrics will be discussed for each
process. Many fabrics have very specialized applications; others are no longer fashionable due to
changes in tastes or lifestyles. Some fabrics are no
longer commercially available due to changes in
expectations by consumers, different lifestyles, or
cost of production. Some remain important, but
their names have changed. Current names, especially names used in the industry, will be identified.

The fabric-forming process (fabrication) contributes to the fabric's appearance and texture, performance, and cost. The process may determine the
name of the fabric, like felt, lace, double knit, and
tricot. The cost in relation to fabrication process
depends on the number of steps involved and the
speed. The fewer the steps and the faster the
process, the cheaper the fabric.

Fabrics can be made from a wide variety of starting materials: solutions (films and foams), fibers
(felts and fiberwebs or nonwovens), yarns (braids,
knits, laces, and wovens), and fabrics (multiplex fabrics combining solutions, fibers, yarns, or fabrics to
produce a fabric). The first three chapters of this
section focus on fabrics made from yarns: woven
and knitted fabrics. The final chapter focuses on all
the other processes.

With the exception of triaxial fabrics, all woven
fabrics are made with two or more sets of yarns
interlaced at right angles to each other. The yarns
running in the lengthwise direction are called *warp
yarns* or *ends,* and the yarns running crosswise are
called *filling, weft,* or *picks.* The right-angle position
of the yarns gives the cloth more firmness and rigidity than yarn arrangements in knits, braids, or laces.
Because of this structure, yarns can be raveled from
adjacent sides. Woven fabrics vary in the ways the
yarns interlace, pattern, number of yarns per inch,
and ratio of warp to filling yarns.

Woven fabrics are widely used, and weaving is
one of the oldest methods of making cloth. Fabric
names are based on the end use (hopsacking used in
bags for collecting hops; tobacco cloth as shade for
tobacco plants; cheesecloth to wrap cheeses; and
ticking in mattress covers, which were called
"ticks"); the town in which the fabric was woven
(bedford cord from New Bedford, Massachusetts;
calico from Calcutta, India; chambray from Cambrai,
France; and shantung from Shantung, China); or the
person who originated or was noted for that fabric
(batiste for Jean Baptiste, a linen weaver; and
jacquard for Joseph Jacquard).

Weaving is the most widely used construction
technique. (In 1989, 70 percent of all two-dimen-
sional fabric was woven.)

Woven fabrics generally have these characteristics:

- Two or more sets of yarns are interlaced at right
  angles to each other.
- Many different interlacing patterns give interest to
  the fabric.
- Fabrics can be raveled from adjacent sides.
- Fabrics have grain.
- Fabrics are relatively rigid—they do not have
  much stretch in warp or filling.
- Fabrics are used in apparel, furnishings, and
  industrial products.

WEAVING AND THE LOOM

Weaving is done on a machine called a *loom.* All the
weaves that are known today have been made for
thousands of years. The loom has undergone significant modifications, but the basic principles and
operations remain the same. Warp yarns are held
taut, and filling yarns are inserted and pushed in
place to make the cloth.

In primitive looms, the warp yarns were kept
upright or horizontal (Figure 12–1). Backstrap
looms, used for hand weaving in many countries,
keep the warp yarns taut by attaching one beam to a
tree or post and the other beam to a strap that fits
around the weaver's hips as the weaver squats or
sits (Figure 12–1). Filling yarns are inserted by a
shuttle batted through raised warp yarns. To separate the warp yarns and weave faster, alternate warp
yarns were attached to bars that could be raised,
bringing the alternate warp yarns up. A toothed
device very much like a comb pushed the filling
yarns in place. The bar developed into heddles and

(a)

(b)

Fig. 12–1 *Hand looms: backstrap* (left) *and horizontal* (right). *(Courtesy of Mary Littrell.)*

harnesses attached to foot pedals so the weaver could separate the warp yarns by stepping on the pedals, leaving the hands free for inserting the filling yarns.

During the Industrial Revolution, mass production high-speed looms were developed. The modern loom consists of two beams, a warp beam and a cloth beam, holding the warp yarns between them (Figure 12–2). The warp is raised and lowered by a harness-heddle arrangement. A *harness* is a frame to hold the heddles. The harness position determines the weave pattern or interlacing. A *heddle* (heicle) is a wire with a hole in its center through which the warp yarn is threaded. There are as many heddles as there are warp yarns in the cloth, and the heddles are held in two or more harnesses. As can be seen in the diagram of a simple two-harness loom, as one harness is raised, the yarns form a *shed* through which the filling can be inserted. Filling yarns are carried through the shed by carriers of several types. The name of the loom often refers to the carrier used to insert the filling yarn. Originally, these carriers were fairly large, somewhat oval wooden shuttles with a bobbin of yarn in the center. In the shuttle loom, a *shuttle* is flung through the shed by picker sticks at both sides of the loom. These sticks bat the shuttle first from one side and then, after the shed has changed, back to the other side so quickly the shuttle is a blur. Shuttle looms are limited to about 200 picks or filling insertions per minute. The noise of the picker sticks striking the shuttle is deafening. Looms with quieter and more efficient carriers, called shuttleless looms, will be discussed later in this chapter.

A *reed,* or *batten,* beats or pushes the filling yarn into place to make the fabric firm. A reed is a set of wires in a frame; the spaces between the wires are called *dents.* Warp yarns are threaded through the dents in the reed. The spacing in the reed is related to the desired number of warp yarns per inch in the woven fabric. Reeds are available with a wide variety of spacings related to the density of the yarns in the finished fabric and the size of the yarns. For example, 20-dent reeds are used for low-density fabrics where the yarns are often large; 80-dent reeds are used for higher density fabrics where the yarns are finer.

Weaving consists of the following steps:

1. *Shedding*: raising one or more harnesses to separate the warp yarns and form a shed.

2. *Picking*: passing the shuttle through the shed to insert the filling.

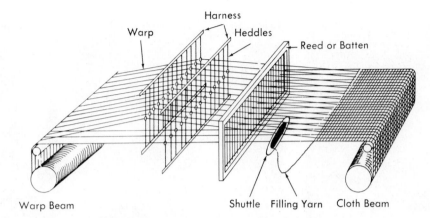

Fig. 12–2 *Simplified drawing of a two-harness shuttle loom.*

3. *Beating up*: pushing the filling yarn into place in the cloth with the reed.

4. *Take-up*: winding finished cloth on the cloth beam.

The most frequent type of commercial loom is a four-harness loom. This loom is extremely versatile for its cost and can be used to produce most simple woven fabrics. These fabrics comprise the greatest percentage of woven fabrics currently on the market and explain the popularity of the four-harness loom. Additional harnesses or other devices that control the position of the warp yarns are used to make more intricate designs. However, generally six harnesses is the limit in terms of efficiency. Patterns that require more than six harnesses are usually made on looms that utilize other devices to control the warp yarns. These other devices will be discussed later in this chapter.

Preparing for Weaving

WINDING Yarns are repackaged so that they can be used on the particular equipment to be used in making the fabric. This step is called *winding*. In this process, spun yarns can be given more twist or combined with other singles to make ply yarns.

CREELING Yarn packages are placed on a large frame called a *creel* (Figure 12–3). The purpose of the creel is to hold the yarn as it is wound onto a warp beam. To protect warp yarns from damage during weaving, they are treated with a sizing agent. After weaving, the cloth is removed from the cloth beam, washed to remove the sizing, finished to specification, and wound on bolts or tubes for sale to cutters or consumers. (See Chapters 16–19.)

Loom Developments

Loom developments over the years have centered on (1) devices to weave intricate designs; (2) computers and electronic monitoring systems to increase speed, patterning capabilities, and quality; and (3) quicker and more efficient means of inserting filling yarns.

PATTERNING CAPABILITIES Devices that control the position (up or down) of the warp yarns have included dobby, doup, lappet, and leno attachments, and the jacquard loom. These have become so sophisticated that pictures can be woven in cloth (see Chapter 13). In some new looms now available the pattern is controlled by microcomputers.

COMPUTER SYSTEMS *Computer* and *electronic devices* play an important part in developing design tables for setting up "maximum weavability" properties, such as tightness and compactness in wind-repellent fabrics or tickings. The computer plays a part in textile designing. Designs can be controlled by microcomputers that control the operation of individual warp yarns.

Computerization of weaving has made tremendous advances in the past few years. Some mills now perform weaverless weaving. This refers to the use of automatic looms with microcomputers that function in many ways. The computer can alter loom operation so that high speeds of filling insertion are maintained while adjusting for minor changes in tension of both warp and filling yarns and winding up woven cloth. These computers also detect incorrect filling insertions, remove the incorrect insertion, correct the problem, and begin the weaving operation. All these steps occur without the assistance of a human operator. Weaving quality

Fig. 12–3   *Creeling. Spools of yarns are placed on a large creel and wound onto a warp beam.*

and efficiency are improved. These weaverless looms are not yet common, but they are commercially available.

LOOM EFFICIENCY Because of their noise and slower speeds, many companies are replacing shuttle looms with faster, quieter, more versatile shuttleless looms.

Four types of shuttleless looms have been developed—water-jet, air-jet, rapier, and projectile looms with higher weaving speeds and reduced noise levels—a factor of great importance to the worker. In these looms, the filling yarns are measured, inserted, and cut, leaving a fringe along the side. These ends may make a fused selvage if the yarns are thermoplastic, or the ends may be tucked into the cloth.

At the end of 1988, there were 129,640 looms in the United States. Of these, 49.5 percent were shuttleless. Most shuttleless looms are air-jet or rapier types. Water-jet and projectile looms are less common.

Water-Jet Loom   The water-jet loom uses a high-pressure jet of water to carry the filling yarn across the warp (Figure 12–4). It can weave fabrics without yarn streaks or barré (a type of yarn streak).

The water is removed from the loom by suction. Since water from the jet dissolves regular warp sizings, water-resistant sizings are used. The fabric is wet when it comes from the loom, so drying is an added expense. This loom is more compact, less noisy, and takes up less space than the conventional

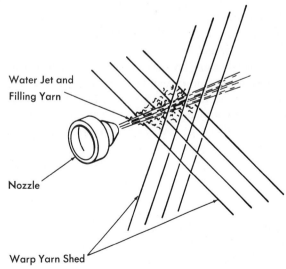

Fig. 12–4   *Water jet carries filling yarn through warp shed.*

loom. It can operate at 400–600 picks per minute—two or three times faster than the conventional loom.

Air-Jet Loom In the air-jet loom the filling is premeasured and guided through a nozzle, where a blast of air sends it across. The loom can operate at speeds up to 1000 picks per minute and is suitable for spun yarns. Good warp preparation is required. There are limitations in the types of filling yarns this loom can handle. Air-jet looms can now weave fabrics up to 400 centimeters (157 inches) in width.

Rapier Loom The rapier loom weaves primarily spun yarns at up to 650 picks per minute. The double-rapier loom has two metal arms about the size of a small penknife, called carriers or "dummy shuttles," one on the right side and the other on the left side of the loom. A measuring mechanism on the right side of the loom measures and cuts the correct length of filling yarn to be drawn into the shed by the carriers. The two carriers enter the warp shed at the same time and meet in the center. The left-side carrier takes the yarn from the right-side carrier and pulls it across to the left side of the loom. Figure 12-5 shows the carrier arms. This loom has found wide acceptance for use with basic cotton and woolen/worsted fabrics. It is more flexible than the air-jet loom.

Projectile Loom In the projectile loom, one projectile with grippers carries the yarn across the full width of the shed. The yarn may be inserted from one or both sides. This loom is also called the missile or gripper loom.

Multiple-Shed Loom In each of the looms discussed so far one shed forms at a time. In *multiple-shed weaving* more than one shed is formed at a time. In some looms, as a yarn carrier enters one portion of the warp, a shed is formed; as the carrier leaves that area, the shed changes. This action may occur simultaneously across the width of the warp several times. In other multiple-shed looms, several sheds form along the length of the warp yarns and open at the same time, one filling yarn is inserted into each shed, and then the sheds change.

As many as 16 to 20 filling carriers insert the precut filling in a continuous process instead of the intermittent process of single-shed weaving. Beating up and shedding arrangements are different. In this continuous-weaving process, the number of picks per minute (ppm) is doubled.

Circular Loom Most looms weave flat widths of fabric. Circular looms weave tubular fabric. The *circular loom* in Figure 12-6 weaves sacks of split-film polypropylene. Pillowcases are also tubular woven.

Triaxial Loom This system weaves three sets of yarns at 60° angles to each other (see Figure 12-7). These *triaxial* fabrics are stable in all directions—horizontally, vertically, and on the bias. Biaxial-woven fabrics, in which the two sets of yarns are woven at right angles to each other, are not stable on the bias.

In triaxial weaving, all the yarns are usually alike in size and twist. Two yarn sets are warp and the other set is filling. Fabrics can be produced more quickly than other weaves because there are fewer picks per inch and speed of weaving is based on the number of picks per minute.

The end uses of triaxial fabrics include balloons, air structures, sailcloth, diaphragms, truck covers, and outerwear apparel.

CHARACTERISTICS OF WOVEN FABRICS

All yarns in woven fabrics interlace at right angles to one another (Figure 12-8). An *interlacing* is the point at which a yarn changes its position from one side of the fabric to the other. When a yarn crosses over more than one yarn at a time, *floats* are formed and the fabric has fewer interlacings.

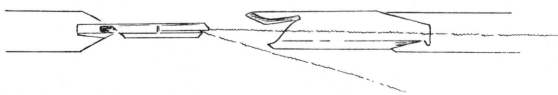

Fig. 12–5 *Carrier arms of a rapier shuttleless loom.*

Fig. 12–6 *Circular loom used to weave bagging. (Courtesy of Amoco Fabrics & Fibers Co.)*

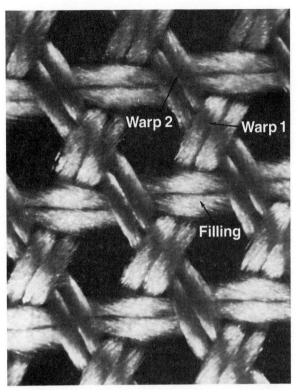

Fig. 12–7 *Triaxial-weave pattern. (Courtesy of Reed-Chatwood, Inc.)*

Warp And Filling

Warp and *filling yarns* have different characteristics, resulting in different performance characteristics. The warp must withstand the high tensions of the loom and the abrasion of weaving, so the warp yarns are stronger and more uniform with higher twist. Filling yarns are more apt to be fancy or special-function yarns, such as high-twist crepe yarns, low-twist napping yarns, or bouclé yarns.

It is possible to differentiate between warp and filling:

1. The selvage always runs in the lengthwise (warp) direction of all fabrics.

2. Most fabrics have lower elongation in the warp direction.

3. The warp yarns lie straighter and are more parallel in the fabric because of loom tension.

4. Fancy or special-function yarns are usually in the filling direction.

5. Specific fabric characteristics may indicate the warp and filling directions. For example, poplin has a filling rib and satin has warp floats.

6. Warp yarns tend to be smaller, with higher twist.

7. Fabric crimp is usually greater for filling yarns since they must bend or flex over or under warp yarns due to the way the loom operates.

Grain

Grain refers to the geometry or position of warp yarns relative to filling yarns in the fabric. A fabric

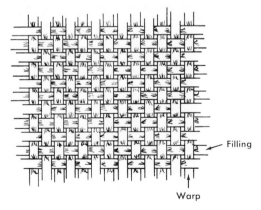

Fig. 12–8 *Yarn arrangement in weaving.*

that is on-grain has warp yarns parallel to each other and perpendicular to the filling yarns, which move straight across the fabric. Lengthwise grain is parallel to the warp yarns. Crosswise grain is parallel to the filling yarns. Fabrics are almost always woven on-grain. Handling, finishing, or stress due to yarn twist, weave, or other fabric aspects may cause fabrics to distort and lose their on-grain characteristic. These fabrics are off-grain.

Off-grain fabrics create problems in production and for consumers. At the factory, off-grain causes reruns or repeating finishing steps and lowers fabric quality. Products do not drape properly or hang evenly and printed designs are not straight. Figure 12-9 shows a design that has been printed slightly off-grain—the print does not follow the yarns or a torn edge.

There are two kinds of off-grain. *Skew* occurs when the filling yarn is at an angle other than 90° to the warp. It usually results in finishing when one side of the fabric travels ahead of the other (see Figure 12-9).

Bow occurs when the filling yarns dip in the center of the fabric and usually develops when the center of the fabric lags behind the two sides as the fabric is finished (see Figure 12-10). Fabrics should always be examined for grain. On-grain fabrics usually indicate high quality standards.

Fabric Count

Fabric count, or *count,* is the number of warp and filling yarns per square inch of gray goods (fabric as it comes from the loom). Count may increase due to shrinkage during dyeing and finishing. Count is written with the warp number first, for example, 80 × 76; or it may be written as the total of the two, or 156. Count is not synonymous with yarn number.

Count is an indication of the quality of the fabric—the higher the count, the better the quality for any one fabric. Higher count also may mean less potential shrinkage and less raveling of seam edges. Catalogs sometimes give count because the customer must judge the quality from printed information rather than from the fabric itself.

Count can be determined with a fabric counter (Figure 12-11) or by hand where the number of yarns in each direction are counted for an inch.

Count may vary depending on the end use or quality of fabric. Often it is listed as a total and may be described on labels as thread count. For example, two-plain weave fabrics often used in bed sheets are percale and muslin. Percale is a better quality fabric made of combed yarns in counts of 160, 180, or 200. The 200-count fabric is the best quality of the three. Muslin is a harder wearing fabric designed for lower price points. It is usually made of carded yarns in counts of 112, 128, or 140. It is frequently used in bed linens for budget motels

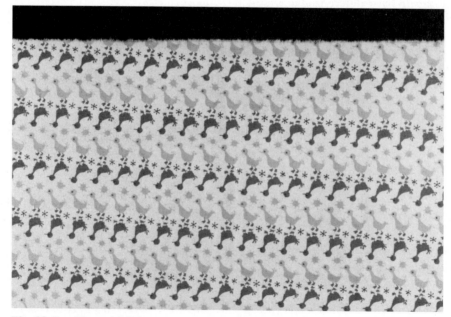

Fig. 12–9 *Skewed fabric.*

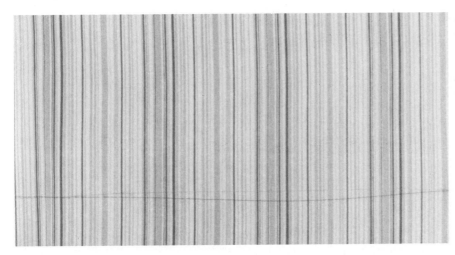

Fig. 12–10   Bowed fabric. Note the horizontal lines traced on the fabric. The darker line traces an actual yarn; the lighter line traces the straight crosswise grain of the fabric.

and hospitals. The 140-count fabric is best quality of the three.

Balance

Balance is the ratio of warp yarns to filling yarns in a fabric. A balanced fabric has approximately one warp yarn for every filling yarn, or a ratio of 1:1. An example of a balanced fabric is 78 × 78 print cloth. An unbalanced fabric has significantly more of one set of yarns than the other. A typical unbalanced fabric is broadcloth, with a count of 144 × 76 and a ratio of about 2:1.

Balance is helpful in recognizing and naming fabrics and in distinguishing the warp direction of a fabric. Balance plus count is helpful in predicting slippage. If the count is low, there will be more slippage in unbalanced fabrics than in balanced fabrics.

Selvages

A *selvage* is the self-edge of a fabric formed by the filling yarn when it turns to go back across the fabric. The conventional loom makes the same kind of selvage on both sides of the fabric, but shuttleless looms have different selvages because the filling yarn is cut and the selvage looks like a fringe (see Figure 12-12). In some fabrics, different yarns or interlacing patterns are used to weave the selvage.

Plain selvages are similar to the rest of the fabric. They do not shrink and can be used for seam edges. *Tape selvages* of larger and/or plied yarns for strength are wider than the plain selvage and may be a different weave to maintain a flat selvage, such as in bed sheets. *Split selvages* are used when narrower items such as towels are woven two or more side by side and cut apart after weaving. These edges require finishing. *Fused selvages* are found in narrow fabrics cut from wide fabric.

Fig. 12–11   Fabric yarn counter. (Courtesy of Alfred Suter Co.)

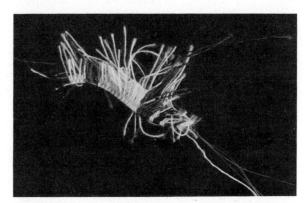

Fig. 12–12   Fringe selvage woven on a shuttleless loom.

Fabric Width

The loom determines the width of the fabric. Handwoven fabrics are narrow, often 27–36 inches wide. Fabric widths have been increasing because wide fabrics are more economical to weave and allow for more efficient use of fabric in products. Looms weave cotton fabrics 45 or 60 inches wide. Wool fabrics are 54–60 inches wide and silk-type fabrics are 40–45 inches wide.

Properties of Woven Fabrics

Fabric properties resulting from weaving variables are summarized in Table 12-1.

The weave or interlacing pattern influences fabric properties as well as fabric appearance. Table 12-2 summarizes the various weaves. This chapter and Chapter 13 deal with woven fabrics.

PLAIN WEAVE

The *plain weave* is the simplest of the three basic weaves that can be made on a loom without any modification. It is formed by yarns at right angles passing alternately over and under each other. Each warp yarn interlaces with each filling yarn to form the maximum number of interlacings (Figure 12-13). Plain weave requires only a two-harness loom and is the least expensive weave to produce. It is described as a $\frac{1}{1}$ weave, read as one harness up and one harness down, which describes the position of the harness when forming the shed.

Figure 12-13 shows several ways of diagramming a plain weave. The top drawing is a cross-sectional view of a fabric cut parallel to a filling yarn. The cut

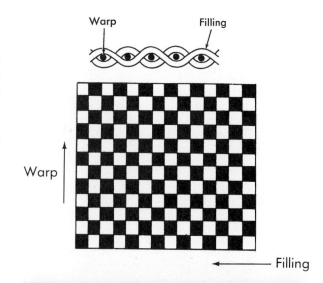

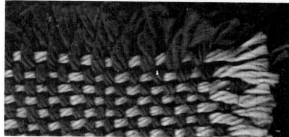

Fig. 12–13   *Three ways to show the yarn-interlacing pattern of plain weave: cross section* (top); *checkerboard* (center); *photograph* (bottom).

ends of the warp yarns appear as black circles. The filling yarn goes over the first warp yarn and under the second warp yarn. In a plain-weave fabric, this same pattern is repeated until the filling yarn has interlaced with all the warp yarns across the width of the loom. The second filling yarn goes under the

Table 12–1   Properties of Woven Fabrics

Fabric Type	Properties
High count	Firm, strong, good cover and body, compact, stable, wind and water repellent, fire retardant, reduced raveling of edges.
Low count	Flexible, permeable, pliable, better drape, higher shrinkage potential, more edge raveling.
Balanced	Less seam slippage, warp and filling wear more evenly.
Unbalanced (usually more warp)	Seam slippage in low count; surface yarns wear out first, leaving slits (common in upholstery fabrics). Add visual and tactile interest.
Floats	Lustrous, smooth, flexible, resilient, may ravel and snag, seam slippage in low count.

first warp yarn and over the second. This pattern also is repeated across the width of the loom. Notice how these two filling yarns interlace with the warp yarns to achieve the maximum number of interlacings. In a plain weave, all odd-numbered filling yarns have the same interlacing pattern as the first filling yarn, and all even-numbered filling yarns have the same interlacing pattern as the second filling yarn.

The photograph of the fabric at the bottom of Figure 12–13 shows the same interlacing pattern as in the cross section. In the photograph, the yarns are opaque and only yarns on the surface are visible. Hence, a pattern of dark warp yarns and light filling yarns develops.

The checkerboard pattern in the center of Figure 12–13 is a simple representation of the photograph of the plain-weave fabric. In the checkerboard pattern, each square represents one yarn on the surface of the fabric; dark squares represent warp yarns on the surface and light squares represent filling yarns on the surface. Starting at the upper left-hand corner of the checkerboard and moving across the row, a filling yarn is on the surface, then a warp yarn is on the surface, and so on. The second row is just the opposite and represents the interlacing pattern of the second filling yarn. All woven fabrics can be diagrammed using this technique. These diagrams are an easy way to represent the interlacing patterns and help identify the weave in a fabric.

Plain-weave fabrics have no technical face or back due to the weave. Printing and some surface finishes may create a technical face. Plain weave's uninteresting surface serves as a good ground for printed designs and many finishes. Because there are many interlacings per square inch, plain-weave fabrics tend to wrinkle more, ravel less, and be less absorbent than other weaves. Interesting effects can be achieved by the use of different fibers, novelty or textured yarns, yarns of different sizes, high- or low-twist yarns, filament or staple yarns, and finishes.

Balanced Plain Weave

The simplest plain weave is one in which warp and filling yarns are the same size and the same distance apart so they show equally on the surface—*balanced plain weave* (see Figure 12–14). Balanced plain-weave fabrics have a wider range of end uses than fabrics of any other weave and are the largest group of woven fabrics. They can be made in any weight, from very sheer to very heavy (see Table 12–3).

One convenient way of grouping fabrics is by fabric weight. Balanced plain-weave fabrics will be discussed in five groups: lightweight sheer, lightweight opaque, low-count sheer, medium weight, and heavyweight.

LIGHTWEIGHT SHEER FABRICS Lightweight sheer fabrics are very thin, light, and transparent or semitransparent. High-count sheers are transparent as a result of the fineness of yarns.

Filament-yarn sheers may be designated by the fiber content; for example, polyester sheer or nylon sheer. *Ninon* is a filament sheer that is widely used for glass curtains. It is usually 100 percent polyester because of that fiber's good resistance to sunlight, excellent resiliency, and easy washability. Although ninon is a plain weave, warp yarn spacing is not uniform across the fabric. Two yarns are a little closer to each other and spaced a little farther away from the yarns on either side. Ninon has medium body and hangs well.

Georgette and *chiffon* are made with filament-crepe yarns, the latter being smoother and more lustrous. Both are very lightweight, drape well, and are used in apparel. Both fabrics were originally made of silk but now often are made from manufactured filament yarns. The crepe twist yarns can be found in either warp or filling or in both directions.

Voile is a sheer made with special high-twist spun yarns. Voile was originally a cotton or wool fabric, but it is now found on the market in many fiber contents.

Organdy is the sheerest cotton cloth made. Its sheerness and crispness are the result of an acid finish on lawn gray goods (see Chapter 17). Because of its stiffness and fiber content, it wrinkles badly. *Organza* is the filament-yarn counterpart to organdy. It has a lot of body. These sheer fabrics are used for glass curtains and for summer-weight apparel.

LIGHTWEIGHT OPAQUE FABRICS Lightweight opaque fabrics are very thin and light, but are not as transparent as sheer fabrics. The distinction between the two groups of fabrics is not always pronounced.

Organdy (a sheer fabric), lawn, and batiste are finished from the same gray goods, lawn gray goods. They differ from one another in the way they are finished. The better qualities are made of combed yarns. *Lawn* is a fabric that is often printed. Lawn is usually all cotton or cotton/polyester.

Batiste is the softest of the lightweight opaque fabrics. Batiste fabrics are made of cotton, wool,

Table 12–2 Basic Weaves

Name	Interlacing Patterns	General Characteristics	Typical Fabrics	Chapter Reference
Plain $\frac{1}{1}$	Each warp interlaces with each filling.	Most interlacings per square inch. Balanced or unbalanced. Wrinkles most. Ravels. Less absorbent.	Batiste Voile Percale Gingham Broadcloth Crash Cretonne Printcloth Glazed chintz	12
Basket $\frac{2}{1}$ $\frac{2}{2}$ $\frac{4}{4}$	Two or more yarns in warp, filling, or both directions woven as one in a plain weave.	Looks balanced. Fewer interlacings than plain weave. Flat looking. Wrinkles less. Ravels more.	Oxford Monk's cloth Duck Sailcloth	12
Twill $\frac{2}{1}$ $\frac{2}{2}$ $\frac{5}{1}$	Warp and filling yarns float over two or more yarns from the opposite direction in a regular progression of one to the right or left.	Diagonal lines or wales. Fewer interlacings than plain weave. Wrinkles less. Ravels more. More pliable than plain weave. Higher counts possible.	Serge Surah Denim Gabardine Herringbone Flannel	12
Satin $\frac{4}{1}$ $\frac{1}{4}$	Warp and filling yarns float over four or more yarns from the opposite direction in a progression of two to the right or left.	Flat surface. Most are lustrous. High counts possible. Fewer interlacings. Long floats subject to slippage and snagging. Ravels.	Satin Sateen Antique satin Peau de soie	12
Momie or crepe	An irregular interlacing of yarns. Floats of unequal lengths in no discernable pattern.	Rough-looking surface. Crepe-like.	Granite cloth Moss crepe Sand crepe Bark cloth	13
Dobby	Many different interlacings. Possible to create geometric patterns.	Cord-type fabrics. Simple patterns.	Shirting madras Huck toweling Waffle cloth Piqué	13
Jacquard	Each warp yarn controlled individually. An infinite number of interlacings is possible.	Intricate patterns	Damask Brocade Tapestry	13
Doublecloth	Several possible patterns use three, four, or five sets of yarns.	Thick, stiff, warm fabrics	Doublecloth Suitings Coatings	13

Table 12–2   **Basic Weaves** (continued)

Name	Interlacing Patterns	General Characteristics	Typical Fabrics	Chapter Reference
Pile	Extra warp or filling yarns are woven in to give a cut or an uncut three-dimensional fabric.	Plush or looped surface. Warm. Wrinkles less. Pile may flatten.	Velvet Velveteen Corduroy Furlike fabrics Wilton rugs Terrycloth	13
Slack-tension	A type of pile weave. Some warp yarns can be released from tension to form raised areas in the cloth or a pile surface.	Crinkle stripes or pile surface. Absorbent. Nonwrinkling.	Seersucker Terrycloth Friezé	13
Leno	A doup attachment on the loom causes one of two warp yarns to be carried over the other on alternate passings of the filling yarns.	Meshlike fabric. Lower count fabrics that are resistant to slippage.	Marquisette Curtain fabrics	13
Swivel	An attachment to the loom. Small shuttles carrying extra filling yarns weave in small dots.	Dots on both sides of fabric as filling floats.	Dotted swiss	13

polyester, and blends. *Tissue ginghams* and *chambray* are similar in weight but are yarn-dyed.

China silk is also similar to batiste, except that it is made from fine-filament yarns. It is a soft fabric that was originally made of silk and used for women's suit linings and matching blouses. *Habutai* is slightly heavier than China silk.

Crepe de Chine, traditionally a filling crepe-silk fabric, drapes beautifully. It has a dry and very pleasant hand and medium luster. The fabric is more commonly found now as a filament polyester for blouses and fine linings.

Challis tends to be heavier than the fabrics discussed so far and, depending on fiber content and fashion, it may be a medium-weight fabric. A classic challis fabric is wool in a paisley print. It is soft and drapes well. Challis usually is printed and slightly napped and frequently is made from rayon.

LOW-COUNT SHEER FABRICS Low-count sheer fabrics are characterized by open spaces between the yarns, making them transparent. They are made of carded yarns of size 28s and 30s in the warp and 39s and 42s in the filling. Count ranges from 10×12 to 48×44. These fabrics are neither strong nor durable, are seldom printed, and differ in the way they are finished. They are functional fabrics that may be used for decorative and industrial purposes, or as shaping fabrics in apparel. Included in this group are cheesecloth, crinoline, buckram, and bunting. (See the Glossary at the end of the book.)

MEDIUM-WEIGHT FABRICS Medium-weight fabrics comprise the largest group of woven fabrics because they have many more uses than either lightweight or heavyweight fabrics. These fabrics have medium-sized yarns and a medium count with carded or combed yarns. They may be finished in different ways or woven from dyed yarns. They are also called top-weight fabrics because they are frequently used for blouses and shirts. Medium-weight fabrics are also used to produce many furnishing items, such as window-treatment fabrics, bed and table linens, and some upholstery fabrics.

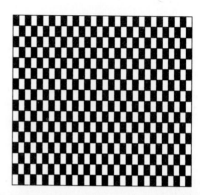

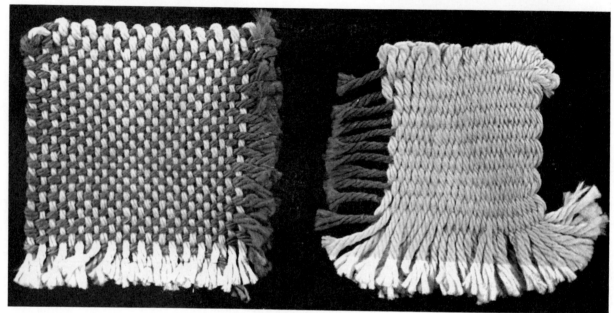

Fig. 12–14 *Comparison of balanced plain-weave fabric* (left) *and unbalanced plain-weave fabric* (right).

The carded-yarn fabrics in this group are converted from a gray goods cloth called *print cloth*. Figure 17–1 shows the variety of ways it can be finished. Chapter 17 can be used as a supplement in understanding some of the differences in fabrics due to finishing. For example, two fabrics converted from print cloth are plissé and embossed.

Most print cloth is made into *percale*, a smooth, slightly crisp, printed or plain-colored fabric. In percale bed sheets, counts of 160, 180, and 200 are available. Percale is called *calico* if it has a small, quaint, printed design; *chintz* if it has a printed design; and *cretonne* if it has a large-scale floral design. When a solid-color fabric is given a glazed calendar finish, it is called *polished cotton*. When chintz is glazed, it is called *glazed chintz*. Glazed chintz is made in solid colors as well as prints. These fabrics are often made with blends of cotton

and polyester or high-wet-modulus rayon. They are used for shirts, dresses, blouses, pajamas, matching curtains and bedspreads, upholstery, slipcovers, draperies, and wall coverings.

Any plain-woven, balanced fabric ranging in weight from lawn to heavy bed sheeting may be called *muslin*. Muslin is usually available in counts of 112, 128, or 140. This is also a specific name for medium-weight fabric that is unbleached or white.

Napped fabrics may be either medium- or heavy-weight. Flannel and outing flannel may be either plain weave or twill weave. *Flannelette* is a plain-weave fabric that is lightly napped on one side. *Outing flannel* is heavier and stiffer than flannelette; it may be napped on one or both sides. It is used for shirts, dresses, lightweight jackets, and jacket linings. Some outing flannels are made with a twill weave.

Ginghams are yarn-dyed fabrics in checks, plaids, or solids (Figure 12–15). *Chambrays* are yarn dyed. They may look solid color but have white filling and colored-warp yarns, or they may have darker yarns in the filling (*iridescent chambray*), or they may have stripes. Some chambray is unbalanced with high warp count and a filling rib similar to that of broadcloth and poplin.

Ginghams and chambrays are usually made of cotton or cotton blends. When they are made of another fiber, the fiber content is included in the name; for example, silk gingham. When filament yarns are used, these fabrics are given a crisp finish and called *taffetas*. In wool, similar fabrics are called wool checks, plaids, and shepherd's checks, *Madras*, or *Indian madras,* is frequently all cotton, often of a lower count than gingham. Madras is a yarn-dyed plaid fabric.

Stripes, plaids, and checks present problems that do not occur in solid-colored fabrics. Ginghams may have a design with an up and down, a right and left, or both. More time is needed to cut out an item in plaid than in plain material, more attention must be given to the choice of design, and more care must be taken during production to match seams.

Imitations of yarn-dyed fabrics are made by printing. There is, however, a technical face and a techni- cal back to the print, whereas true yarn-dyed fabrics are the same on both sides. Lengthwise printed stripes are usually on-grain, but the crosswise stripes may be off-grain. These printed fabrics may be per- cale if the fabric was converted from a print cloth.

Pongee is a filament-yarn, medium-weight fabric. It has a fine warp of regular yarns with filling yarns that are irregular in size. It was originally silk with slub-filling yarns, but is now made of a variety of fibers. *Honan* is similar to pongee, but it is charac- terized by slub yarns in both the warp and the filling.

Plain-weave fabrics with crepe yarns in either warp or filling or in both warp and filling are often referred to as *true crepe*. These fabrics can be any weight, but are most often found in medium weight or heavyweight fabrics. Because of their interesting texture and lively drape, these fabrics are frequently used by designers for apparel and furnishings. In apparel, true crepes are found in both weights and are most commonly used in suits, coats, and dresses. In furnishings, true crepes are common in uphol- stery, draperies, and wall coverings. True crepes are also found in table linens, but are not as common in that use.

HEAVY-WEIGHT FABRICS Heavy weight fabrics are also known as *suiting-weight* or *bottom-weight*

Table 12–3 Balanced Plain-Weave Fabrics

Fabric	Range in Count	Yarn Size		Category
		Warp	Filling	
Lawn	88 × 80	70s*	100s*	High count sheer
Organdy	Similar to lawn	Similar to lawn		High count sheer
Batiste	Similar to lawn	Similar to lawn		High count sheer
Percale, carded (muslin, plissé, calico, chintz, and so forth)	80 × 80 to 44 × 48	30s	42s	Medium weight
Combed cotton	96 × 80	40s	50s	Medium weight
Gingham, cotton	64 × 76	Same as percale		Medium weight
Carded	to 48 × 44			
Combed	88 × 84 to 84 × 76			
Cotton suiting	48 × 48 to 66 × 76	13s to 20s		Heavyweight

*The "s" after the number means that the yarn is a single yarn.

Fig. 12–15 *Gingham fabrics: yarn-dyed checks or plaids.*

fabrics. These fabrics are heavy enough to tailor and drape well. Their filling yarns are usually larger than the warp yarns and have slightly lower twist. Because of their weight, these fabrics are more durable and more resistant to wrinkling than sheer or medium-weight fabrics, but they tend to ravel more because of their low count.

Weaver's cloth is a more general name for cotton suiting, which is converted from a gray goods called *coarse sheeting*. Cotton suiting is plain in color or printed.

Homespun is a name used for furnishing fabrics with slightly irregular yarns, a lower count, and a handwoven look.

Crash is made with yarns that have thick-and-thin areas, giving it an uneven nubby look. It is often linen or a manufactured fiber or fiber blend that looks like linen. The irregular surface shows wrinkles less than a plain surface does.

Butcher rayon is a crashlike fabric of 100 percent rayon or rayon/polyester. In heavier weights it looks like linen suiting.

Burlap has a much lower count than crash, and is used in furnishings rather than apparel. It has characteristic coarse thick-and-thin yarns and is usually made of jute.

Osnaburg is a variable-weight fabric most often found in suiting weight. Like muslin, it may be unbleached or bleached. In general it is a lower-quality fabric than muslin, with a lower count and bits of leaf and bark from the cotton plant giving it a characteristic spotted appearance. It is a utility fabric that occasionally becomes fashionable. It is seen as a drapery-lining fabric. When printed

or dyed, it may be used in upholstery and drapery fabrics.

Flannel is a plain-weave suiting fabric that is napped. Made in woolen yarns, it is used for women's suits, slacks, skirts, and jackets. It may have a plain or twill weave.

Tweed is made of any fiber or mixture of fibers and is always characterized by novelty yarns with nubs of different colors. Harris tweed is handwoven in the Outer Hebrides Islands, and Donegal tweed is handwoven in Donegal County, Ireland.

Tropical worsted suitings are made from long-fiber worsted yarns in the lightest weight. They are wool-like fabrics made for men's suits, intended for use in tropical countries or for summer use in temperate climates. They are frequently made of fiber blends.

Heavyweight balanced plain-weave fabrics are often used in furnishings. They are used in wall coverings, upholstery, and draperies. Often producers give these fabrics a company name.

Unbalanced Plain Weave

Increasing the number of warp yarns in a plain-woven fabric until the count is about twice that of the filling yarns creates a crosswise ridge called a filling *rib*. It also creates a fabric in which the warp yarns completely cover the filling yarns. Ribs in fabric can be produced by increasing the reed pressure (pushing more yarns into the same area) or by changing yarn size. Small ridges are formed when the warp and filling yarns are the same size; larger ridges are formed where the filling yarns are larger than the warp. Yarn sizes are given in Table 12–4.

When the yarns are of different colors, the color showing on the surface will be that of the warp yarns. Figure 12–14 shows the high warp count, the warp surface, and a difference in color in a ribbed fabric.

Identification of an unbalanced fabric may not be easy. To assist in identification, ravel adjacent sides until a yarn fringe can be seen. Observe the difference in density of warp and filling yarns. Broadcloth has a very thick fringe of warp yarns (144 × 76). Percale (78 × 78) has a fringe of equal density for both warp and filling (see Figure 12–16).

Slippage is a problem in ribbed fabrics made with filament yarns, especially those of lower quality and lower count (see Figure 12–17). Slippage occurs when one set of yarns is pushed to one side, exposing the yarns that are normally covered. It usually happens at points of wear and tension, such as at seams.

Table 12–4 Unbalanced Plain-Weave Fabrics

Fabric	Count*	Yarn Size		Category
		Warp	Filling	
Staple fiber				
Combed broadcloth	144 × 76	100/2	100/2	Medium weight
Carded broadcloth	100 × 60	40s	40s	Medium weight
Filament fiber				
Rayon taffeta	60 × 15	10/2	3s	Medium weight
Acetate taffeta	140 × 64	75 denier	150 denier	Medium weight
Faille	200 × 64	75 denier	200 denier	Medium weight
Rep	88 × 31	30/2	5s	Heavyweight
Bengaline	92 × 40	150 denier	15s spun	Heavyweight
Shantung	140 × 44	150 denier	30/2	Heavyweight

*Counts may be high for polyester/cotton and durable-press fabrics.

Wear occurs on the surface of the ribs. The warp yarns wear out first and splits occur in the fabric. The filling yarns, which are covered by the warp, are protected from wear.

Ribbed fabrics with fine ribs are softer and more drapeable than comparable balanced fabrics—broadcloth is softer than percale. Fabrics with large ribs have more body and are stiffer. A few sheer rib fabrics are used in glass curtains.

MEDIUM-WEIGHT RIBBED FABRICS Medium weight is the largest group of ribbed fabrics. *Broadcloth* has the finest rib of any of the staple-fiber fabrics because the warp and filling yarns are the same in size. The better quality fabrics are made of long-staple combed cotton, plied yarns and are usually mercerized for luster. Slub broadcloth is made with a yarn that contains slubs at regular intervals. Silk broadcloth has filament warp and staple filling.

Taffeta is a fine-rib, filament-yarn fabric with crispness and body. *Moiré taffeta* has a water-marked, embossed design (Figure 12–18).

Shantung has an irregular rib surface produced by long, irregular areas in the yarn. It may be made in medium or suiting weight and of various kinds of fiber.

 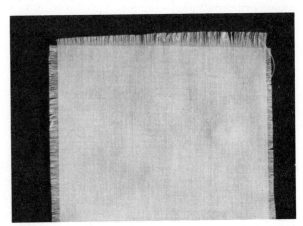

Fig. 12–16 *Compare the count and balance of the print cloth (percale)* (left) *and broadcloth* (right).

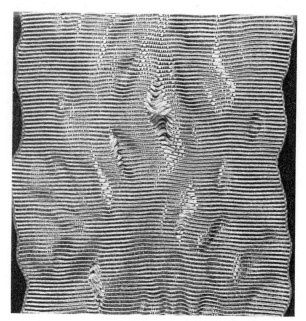

Fig. 12–17 *Slippage of yarns in a ribbed fabric.*

HEAVYWEIGHT RIBBED FABRICS *Poplin* is similar to broadcloth, but the ribs are heavier because of larger filling yarns, and it is usually suiting weight. Polyester/cotton blends are widely used.

Faille (pronounced file) is made of filament-warp and spun filling yarns. *Rep* is a heavy, coarse fabric with a pronounced rib effect. *Bengaline* is similar to faille and often made with rayon warp and cotton filling. It is sometimes woven with two warps at a time to emphasize the rib. *Ottoman* has alternating large-and-small ribs that are adjacent to each other, created by using filling yarns of different sizes or using different numbers of filling yarns in adjacent ribs. *Grosgrain* (pronounced grow'-grane) has a rounder rib than faille.

Bedford cord is seen occasionally in apparel fabrics, but more commonly in furnishing fabrics like bedspreads. It has spun warp yarns that are larger than the filling yarns. There are other ways of producing bedford cord (see Chapter 13).

Basket Weave

Basket weaves are made with two or more adjacent warps controlled by the same harnesses, and with two or more fillings placed in the same shed. A full basket would have the basket feature used in both warp and filling: both warp and filling are grouped. A half basket would have the basket feature in only warp or filling; only one yarn set would

be grouped. The most common basket weaves are 2 × 2 and 4 × 4, but variations of the basket weave include 2 × 1 and 2 × 3. These fabrics have greater flexibility and more wrinkle resistance because there are few interlacings per square inch. The fabrics have a flatter appearance than a comparable regular plain-weave fabric would have. Long floats snag easily. Figure 12–19 shows a 2 × 2 basket weave. Although most basket weaves are balanced, some are unbalanced.

Dimity is a sheer unbalanced fabric used for apparel and for window treatments. It has heavy-warp cords at intervals across the fabric. The cords may be formed by yarns significantly larger than those used elsewhere in the fabric, or by grouping yarns together in that area. Either technique produces the unique narrow band or stripe indicative of dimity. Dimity is often white or printed.

Oxford is usually a 2 × 1 or 3 × 2 basket weave. It is most common as a 2 × 1 half basket weave. It may have a yarn-dyed warp and white filling and be called an *oxford chambray*. Oxford looks like a bal-

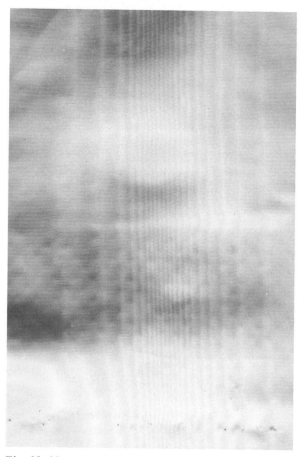

Fig. 12–18 *Moiré taffeta.*

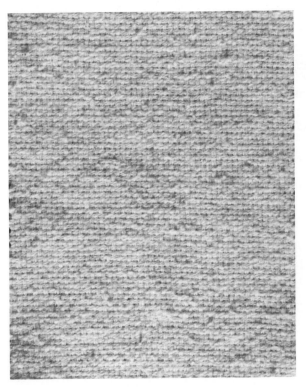

Fig. 12–19   A 2 × 2 basket weave.

anced fabric because the warp yarns are finer and have higher twist than the filling. Because of soft yarns and loose weave, yarn slippage is likely to occur at the seams and within the fabric itself. Oxford fabrics are soft, porous, and lustrous. Oxford is a medium-weight fabric.

Most basket weaves are heavyweight fabrics. Common ones include sailcloth, duck, or canvas. Sailcloth is lighter weight than duck or canvas. Duck is usually 100 percent cotton. Sailcloth is used in slacks, skirts, summer-weight suits, and furnishings. Furnishings and industrial variations of these fabrics come in many different weights and range from soft to stiff in drape. They are usually 2 × 1 or 3 × 2 basket weaves that are used for slipcovers, boat covers, shoe fabrics, and house and store awnings.

Hopsacking is an open basket-weave fabric made of cotton, linen, or wool. It is primarily used for coats, suits, upholstery, and wallcoverings. It gets its name from the sacks used to gather hops.

Monk's cloth, friar's cloth, druid's cloth, and mission cloth are some of the oldest full-basket-weave fabrics. They are usually brownish white or oatmeal color. These fabrics are usually 2 × 2, 3 × 3, 4 × 4, or 6 × 6. They are used primarily in furnishings.

TWILL WEAVE

In a *twill weave,* each warp or filling yarn floats across two or more filling or warp yarns with a progression of interlacings by one to the right or left, forming a distinct diagonal line, or *wale.* A *float* is the portion of a yarn that crosses over two or more yarns from the opposite direction. Twill weaves require three or more harnesses depending on the complexity of the weave. Twill weave is the second basic weave that can be made on the simple loom. Although it is possible to create elaborate patterns using a twill weave, this chapter will focus only on basic fabrics and patterns.

Twill weave is often designated by a fraction—such as $\frac{2}{1}$—in which the numerator indicates the number of harnesses that are raised and the denominator indicates the number of harnesses that are lowered when a filling yarn is inserted. The fraction $\frac{2}{1}$ would be read as "two up, one down."

In order to weave any twill, the loom must be properly warped. To weave a $\frac{2}{1}$ twill, the threading and shedding processes described here must be followed. Any change in this process will produce something other than a $\frac{2}{1}$ twill. The first warp yarn is threaded through a heddle in the first harness, the second warp yarn through a heddle in the second harness and the third warp yarn through a heddle in the third harness. This process repeats until the entire set of warp yarns are threaded through the three harnesses. In weaving the first filling yarn, the first two harnesses are raised and the third harness is lowered. For the second filling yarn, the shed changes so that harnesses 2 and 3 are raised, harness 1 is lowered, and the yarn is inserted. The third filling yarn is inserted into a shed created by raising harnesses 1 and 3 and lowering harness 2. This pattern is repeated until the entire fabric has been woven. Thus, by following the steps of threading and shedding, the $\frac{2}{1}$ twill has been made. The number of harnesses needed to produce a simple twill can be determined by adding the numerator and the denominator. A $\frac{2}{1}$ twill is shown in Figure 12–20. The distance between the arrows demonstrates the length of the float. The floats on the surface are warp yarns, making it a warp surface; it is classified as a warp-faced twill.

Characteristics of Twill Weave

Twill fabrics have a technical face and a technical back. The technical face is the side of the fabric with the most pronounced wale. It is usually more

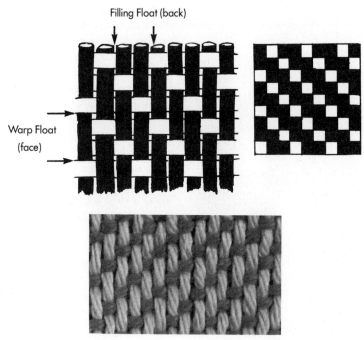

Filling Float (back)

Warp Float
(face)

Fig. 12–20 *A $\frac{2}{1}$ twill weave.*

durable, more attractive, and most often used as the fashion side of the fabric. The face usually is the side visible on the loom during weaving. If there are warp floats on the technical face, there will be filling floats on the technical back. If the twill wale goes up to the right on one side, it will go up to the left on the other side. Twill fabrics have no up and down as they are woven. Check this fact by turning the fabric end to end and then examining the direction of the twill wale.

Sheer fabrics are seldom made with a twill weave. Because a twill surface has interesting texture and design, printed twills are much less common than printed plain weaves. Printed twills are more likely to be light weight fabrics. Soil shows less on the uneven surface of twills than it does on smooth surfaces such as plain weaves.

Fewer interlacings permit the yarns to move more freely and give the fabric more softness, pliability, and wrinkle recovery than a comparable plain-weave fabric. When there are fewer interlacings, yarns can be packed closer together to produce a higher-count fabric (Figure 12–21). If a plain-weave fabric and a twill-weave fabric have the same kind and number of yarns, the plain-weave fabric would be stronger because it has more interlacings. In twills with higher counts, the fabric is more durable and air or water resistant.

The prominence of a twill wale may be increased by the use of long floats, combed yarns, plied yarns, hard-twist yarns, twist yarns opposite to the direction of the twill line, and high counts. Fabrics with prominent wales, such as gabardine, may become shiny because of flattening caused by pressure and wear.

The direction of the twill wale usually goes from lower left to upper right in wool and wool-like fabrics—right-hand twills—and from lower right to upper left in cotton or cottonlike fabrics—left-hand twills. This fact is important only in deciding which is the face and back side of a twill fabric. In some fabrics that have a very prominent wale or are made with white and colored yarns, design implications relative to the wale should be considered.

The degree of angle of the wale depends on the balance of the cloth. The twill line may be *steep*, *regular*, or reclining. The greater the difference between the number of warp and filling yarns, the steeper the twill line. Steep-twill fabrics have a high warp count and therefore are stronger in the warp direction. The importance of the angle is that it serves as a guide in determining the strength and name of a fabric. Figure 12–21 shows how the twill line changes in steepness when the warp yarn density increases and the filling yarn density remains the same. Note that all three diagrams are for a $\frac{2}{1}$ left-handed twill. The only change is in the number of warp yarns, yet the wale angle changes drastically.

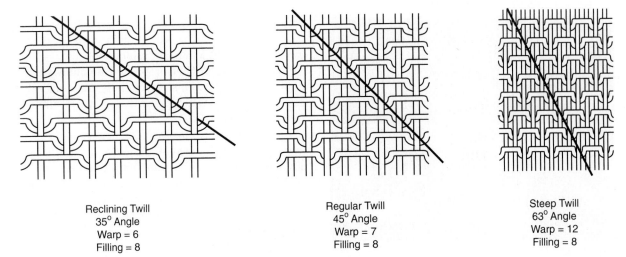

Reclining Twill	Regular Twill	Steep Twill
35° Angle	45° Angle	63° Angle
Warp = 6	Warp = 7	Warp = 12
Filling = 8	Filling = 8	Filling = 8

Fig. 12–21 *Twill angle depends on ratio of warp to filling. These diagrams show left-handed twills.*

Filling-faced twills are not discussed in this text because they are seldom used. They are usually reclining twills and are less durable than the others.

Even-Sided Twills

Even-sided twills have an equal percentage of warp and filling yarn exposed on both sides of the fabric. They are sometimes called *reversible twills* because they look alike on both sides, although the direction of the twill line differs. Better-quality filling yarns must be used in these fabrics than in the warp-faced twills because both sets of yarn are exposed to wear. They are $\frac{2}{2}$ twills and have the best balance of all the twill weaves (see Table 12–5).

Foulard or *surah* is a printed filament-twill fabric of $\frac{2}{2}$ construction that is used in silklike dresses, linings, ties, and scarves. It is soft, smooth, and lightweight. Sometimes it is piece dyed instead of printed.

Serge is a $\frac{2}{2}$ twill with a rather subdued wale and a clear finish. Cotton serge of fine yarn and high count is often given a water-repellent finish and used for jackets, snowsuits, and raincoats. Heavy-yarn cotton serge is used for work pants. Wool serge is also used in apparel.

Twill flannel is a $\frac{2}{2}$ or $\frac{2}{1}$ twill. The filling yarns are low-twist larger yarns, specially made for napping. They may be either woolen or worsted. Worsted flannels have less nap, take and hold a sharp crease better, and are less apt to show wear or get baggy, as compared with woolen flannels. These are found in both apparel and furnishings, most often in upholstery.

Sharkskin is a $\frac{2}{2}$ twill with a sleek appearance. It has a small-step pattern because yarns in both the warp and the filling alternate one white yarn with one colored yarn. Sharkskin is used primarily for slacks and suits.

Herringbone fabrics have the twill line reversed at regular intervals to give a design that resembles the backbone of a fish (Figure 12–22). Two different color yarns may be used to accentuate the pattern. Herringbone patterns can be very subtle or very apparent. Herringbone is used in both apparel and furnishings.

Another woven-in pattern is called *houndstooth*. This $\frac{2}{2}$ twill fabric is basically a check, but is unique in appearance because it is pointed—rather like an eight-point star (see Figure 17–15). Houndstooth fabrics are also used in apparel and furnishings.

Table 12–5   Even-Sided Twills

Fabric	Count	Range in Yarn Size	
		Warp	**Filling**
Serge	48 × 34 to 62 × 58	Varies with fiber content	
Flannel	56 × 30 to 86 × 52	Varies with fiber content	

Fig. 12–22   Herringbone.

Warp-Faced Twills

Warp-faced twills have a predominance of warp yarns on the face of the fabric. Since warp yarns are made with higher twist, these fabrics are stronger and more resistant to abrasion. Table 12–6 summarizes warp-faced twills.

Lining twill is a medium-weight $\frac{2}{1}$ fabric made from filament yarns and usually piece dyed or printed in a small pattern. It is similar to foulard in appearance and use.

Denim is a yarn-dyed cotton twill made in two weights: for sportswear and for overalls. Its use in casual wear has been popular for decades, and the

nature of denim has also changed. It is often napped, printed, made with stretch yarns, or otherwise modified for a current fashion look.

Jean is a piece-dyed or printed medium-weight twill used for children's playclothes, draperies, slipcovers, and work shirts. Jean is not heavy enough for work pants.

Drill is a strong, medium- to heavyweight twill fabric. It is a $\frac{2}{1}$ or $\frac{3}{1}$ twill that is piece dyed. It is usually seen in work clothing and industrial fabrics.

Covert is a twill fabric with a mottled appearance resulting from two colors of fibers being used in the yarns or from two colors of plies twisted together to form the yarns. It is usually a $\frac{2}{1}$ heavyweight twill.

Chino is a hard-wearing steep-twill fabric. It has a slight sheen and is frequently made from combed yarns. Usually two-ply yarns are used in both the warp and the filling directions. Chino is typically a summer-weight military uniform fabric.

Gabardine is a warp-faced steep twill with a very prominent, distinct wale. It has a 63° angle or greater and always has many more warp than filling. Cotton gabardine is made with 11, 13, or 15 harnesses. Rayon and wool gabardine are sometimes made with a three-harness arrangement in which the warp yarns are crowded close together, giving a steep twill.

Cavalry twill also has a pronounced steep-twill line. Its unique characteristic is that it has a double-twill line; that is, two diagonal lines that are very close together separated by a little space from the next pair of diagonal lines.

Fancy twill interlacings are used to create more interesting textures and patterns in the fabric for uses in upholstery, window treatment fabrics, wall coverings, and apparel. These twills may be altered so that the wale is not continuous, such as broken twills, or so that fairly elaborate patterns are created within the fabric (see Figure 12–23).

Table 12–6   **Warp-Faced Twills**

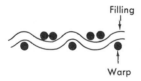

		Range in Yarn Size	
Fabric	*Count*	*Warp*	*Filling*
Jean	84 × 56 to 100 × 64	21s to 24s	24s to 30s
Denim	60 × 36 to 72 × 44	7s to 16s	8s to 23s
Gabardine	110 × 76 to 130 × 80	15s to 39/2	15s to 26s

Fig. 12–23   Examples of broken twill fabrics.

SATIN WEAVE

In a *satin weave*, each warp yarn floats over four filling yarns ($\frac{4}{1}$) and interlaces with the fifth filling yarn, with a progression of interlacings by two to the right or the left (Figure 12-24); or each filling yarn floats over four warps and interlaces with the fifth warp ($\frac{1}{4}$) with a progression of interlacings by two to the right or left (Figure 12-25). In certain fabrics each yarn floats across seven yarns and interlaces with the eighth yarn. Satin weave is the third basic weave that can be made on the simple loom; however, this weave requires at least five harnesses to achieve the inter-lacing pattern. Thus, basic four-harness looms cannot be used to produce a satin weave. Basic fabrics made with this weave are *satin* and *sateen*.

Satin-weave fabrics are characterized by luster due to the long floats that cover the surface. Note in Figure 12-25 the checkerboard designs show few interlacings; the yarns can be packed close together

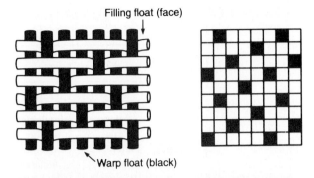

Filling float (face)

Warp float (black)

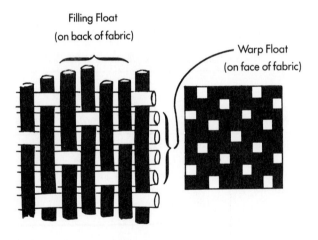

Filling Float
(on back of fabric)

Warp Float
(on face of fabric)

Fig. 12–24 *Warp-faced satin weave: $\frac{4}{1}$ yarn arrangement.*

Fig. 12–25 *Filling-faced satin weave: $\frac{1}{4}$ yarn arrangement.*

to produce a very high-count fabric. Also note that no two interlacings are adjacent to one another. However, unless examined carefully, some satin weaves may resemble twill weaves on the back. This is especially common when the count is high.

When warp yarns cover the surface, the fabric is a warp-faced fabric—satin—and the warp count is high. When filling floats cover the surface, the fabric is a filling-faced fabric—sateen—and the filling count is high. These fabrics are unbalanced, but the high count compensates for the lack of balance.

All these fabrics have a face and back side. A high count gives them strength, durability, body, firmness, and wind repellency. Fewer interlacings give pliability and resistance to wrinkling but may permit yarn slippage and raveling.

Satin Fabrics

Satin fabrics are usually made of bright filament yarns with very low twist. Warp floats almost completely cover the surface. Because of the bright fibers, low twist, and long floats, satin is one of the most lustrous fabrics made. It is made in many weights (see Table 12-7) for use in dresses, linings,

Table 12–7   Typical Satin Fabrics

		Kind of Yarn	
Fabric	Count	Warp	Filling
Satin	200 × 65	100-denier acetate	100-denier acetate
Slipper satin	300 × 74	75-denier acetate	300-denier acetate
Crepe-backed satin	128 × 68	100-denier acetate	100-denier rayon crepe

lingerie, draperies, drapery linings, and upholstery. It seldom has printed designs. It is especially good for linings because the high count makes it very durable and smooth. Satin makes a more pliable lining than taffeta and thus does not split as readily at hems. Quality is particularly important in linings. Low-count satins pull at the seams and rough up in use. Floats may shift in position and bubble or wrinkle.

In *crepe-back satin*, crepe yarns are used in the filling and the low-twist warp floats give the smooth, satiny surface to the fabric. The crepe yarns give softness and drapeability. In antique satin, novelty filling yarns are used to add visual interest to the fabric. Antique satin is often used with the technical back as the fashion side in furnishings, especially upholstery and window treatments.

Sateen

Sateen is a lustrous fabric made of spun yarns. In order to achieve luster with staple fibers, medium-twist yarns form the float surface. The filling yarn count is greater (see Table 12–8). Finishes are used to enhance the luster and durability. (See Chapter 17.)

Filling sateen is a smooth, lustrous cotton fabric used for draperies, drapery linings, and dress fabrics. It is often made with carded yarns with a high filling count. Yarns are similar in size to those used in print cloth, but the filling yarns are larger in size than the warp yarns. Combed sateens are usually finished for added luster. (See Chapter 17.)

Warp sateens are cotton fabrics made with warp floats in a $\frac{4}{1}$ interlacing pattern. They have a rounded wale effect that makes them resemble a twill fabric. They are stronger and heavier than filling sateens because of the high warp count. They are less lustrous than filling sateen and used where durability is more important than luster. Warp sateens are used in slacks, skirts, pillow and bed tickings, draperies, and upholstery fabrics. Warp sateens are the most likely type of satin fabrics to be printed.

Table 12–8   Typical Sateen Fabrics

		Kind of Yarn	
Fabric	Count	Warp	Filling
Filling sateen	60 × 104 carded	32s	38s
	84 × 136 carded	40s	50s
	96 × 108 combed	40s	60s
Warp sateen	84 × 64 carded	12s	11s
	160 × 96 carded	52s	44s

KEY TERMS

Fabric
Warp
Filling
Loom
Harness
Heddle
Shed
Shuttle
Reed
Dents
Shedding

Picking
Beating up
Take-up
Water-jet loom
Air-jet loom
Rapier loom
Projectile loom
Multiple-shed weaving
Circular loom
Triaxial
Interlacing

Floats
Grain
Off-grain
Skew
Bow
Count
Balance
Selvage
Plain weave
Balanced plain weave
Ninon
Georgette
Chiffon
Voile
Organdy
Organza
Lawn
Batiste
Tissue ginghams
Chambray
China silk
Habutai
Crepe de chine
Challis
Percale
Print cloth
Calico
Chintz
Cretonne
Polished cotton
Glazed chintz
Muslin
Flannelette
Outing flannel
Gingham
Taffeta
Madras
Pongee
Honan
True crepe
Suiting-weight fabrics
Bottom-weight fabrics
Weaver's cloth
Crash
Burlap

Osnaburg
Flannel
Tweed
Unbalanced plain weave
Rib
Broadcloth
Shantung
Poplin
Faille
Rep
Bengaline
Ottoman
Grosgrain
Bedford cord
Basket weave
Dimity
Oxford cloth
Hopsacking
Monk's cloth
Twill weave
Wale
Float
Warp-faced twill
Steep twill
Regular twill
Filling-faced twill
Even-sided twill
Foulard
Surah
Serge
Twill Flannel
Herringbone
Houndstooth
Lining twill
Denim
Drill
Chino
Gabardine
Satin weave
Satin
Sateen
Filling sateen
Warp sateen
Crepe-back satin

QUESTIONS

1. Describe the way a loom produces a woven fabric.
2. Diagram the interlacing patterns for the three basic weaves. Try both the cross section diagram and the checkerboard.
3. What are the criteria to use in determining the name of a fabric?
4. Identify the similarities and differences between these paired groups of fabrics:
   gingham and plissé
   flannelette and challis
   organdy and georgette
   oxford cloth and monk's cloth

satin and sateen
herringbone and gabardine
denim and chambray
5. Compare and contrast the characteristics of fabrics made from the three basic weaves.
6. Predict the performance of the following textile products:
   100 percent olefin tweed upholstery with flake filling yarns and fine filament warp yarns.
   50 percent cotton/50 percent polyester broadcloth shirt/blouse with combed yarns in both warp and filling
   100 percent acetate antique satin drapery
   100 percent nylon taffeta backpack with BCF yarns in the warp and filling
   100 percent rayon challis skirt and blouse

SUGGESTED READINGS

Emery, Irene (1980). *The Primary Structures of Fabrics.* Washington, D.C.: The Textile Museum.

Krause, H. W., and Soliman, H. A. (July, 1990). "Do Higher Speeds Demand Better Yarns?" *Textile Month,* pp. 19-22.

Schwartz, Peter, Rhodes, Trevor, and Mohamed, Mansour (1982). *Fabric Forming Systems.* Park Ridge, NJ: Noyes Publications.

Suzuki, Hajime (February, 1990). "Automated Weaving: A Japanese Perspective." *Textile Month,* pp. 26-28.

"Textile Machinery Technology," (April, 1991). *Textile World,* pp. 61-68.

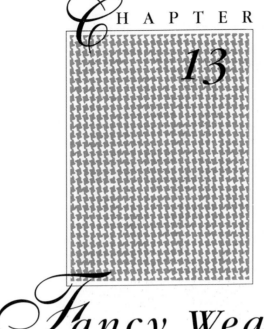

C H A P T E R

13

Fancy Weaves and Fabrics

OBJECTIVES

- To understand the production of fancy woven fabrics.

- To identify the technique or process used to produce fancy woven fabrics.

- To integrate fabrication, yarn type, and fiber in predicting performance of products.

- To relate technological advances in producing fabrics to market availability and cost.

*F*ANCY FABRICS HAVE AN APPEARANCE UNIQUELY different from basic fabrics. This difference in appearance is produced while the fabric is made. It is an inherent part of the fabric and cannot be removed without dismantling the fabric. The appearance of the fabric is permanent. Some fabrics may require additional treatment in order for these differences to be fully developed, as in the pile fabrics that require shearing or napping.

The characteristics that all these *fancy weaves* have in common are that the production process is more involved than for the basic weaves, fabric costs are higher, and the fabric tends to have a more specialized application. For all these fabrics, the unique appearance aspect is inherent in the fabric and results from the weave used. The techniques used to obtain these fabrics vary in complexity and influence the cost and serviceability of the fabric. Recognition of the technique used in manufacturing the fabric assists in selecting a serviceable fabric for the intended end use.

Woven figures are made by changing the interlacing pattern in the design from that of the background. The interlacing pattern is controlled by the warp yarns' position during weaving. In a three-harness loom there are three possible arrangements of the warp yarns; in a four-harness loom there are as many as 12 different arrangements. As the number of harnesses increases, the number of possible different interlacings also increases. But there is a limit to the number of harnesses that can be used efficiently. Consider the number of interlacings needed to make a figure: If the figure is ¼ inch in length, in an 80 × 80 fabric, it may require 20 different interlacings; if the figure is ½ inch long on a nylon-satin background (320 × 140), it may require 70 different interlacings. Special looms, attachments, or controls are necessary to make these fabrics competitive in price with imitations.

DOBBY WEAVES

Small-figured designs, which require fewer than 25 different yarn arrangements to complete one repeat of the design, are made on a loom with a dobby attachment—usually referred to as a *dobby loom* (Figure 13-1). Two methods are used to control the pattern.

In the older method, the weave pattern is controlled by a plastic tape with punched holes (Figure 13-2). These tapes somewhat resemble the rolls for a player piano. The holes control the raising and lowering of the warp yarns. The newer method of creating a simple geometric pattern in the fabric uses a computer. The computer's floppy disks control the position of the warp yarns. This system is faster, compatible with several computer-aided design systems (CADs), and allows for easy and quick pattern changes in the fabric.

Many designs made on either type of dobby loom are small geometric figures. There are many dobby fabrics (see Figure 13-3); a few readily available and identifiable ones are discussed here. Figure 13-4 illustrates several generic patterned fabrics found in apparel and furnishings.

Bird's-eye has a small diamond-shaped filling-float design with a dot in the center that resembles the eye of a bird. This design was originally used in costly white silk fabric for ecclesiastical vestments. At one time, it was widely used for kitchen and hand towels and diapers. *Huck* or *huck-a-back* has a pebbly surface made by filling floats. It is used primarily in roller, face, and medical-office towels.

Shirting madras has small, satin-float designs on a ribbed or plain ground. *Waffle cloth* is made with a dobby attachment and has a three-dimensional honeycomb appearance.

Extra-Yarn Weaves

When yarns of various colors or types different from the background are wanted for a figure, *extra yarns* are woven into the fabric. The figure portion has warp or filling floats. When not used in the figure, the extra yarns float across the back of the fabric and are usually cut away during finishing. In hand-woven fabrics the warp yarns are manipulated by hand and the extra yarns can be laid in where wanted by using small shuttles. But in power looms an automatic attachment must be used.

Extra-warp yarns are wound on a separate beam and threaded into separate heddles. The extra yarns interlace with the regular filling yarns to form a design and float about the fabric until needed for the repeat. The floats are then clipped close to the design or clipped long enough to give an eyelash effect. Figure 13-5 shows a fabric before and after clipping.

Fig. 13–1   *Loom with a dobby attachment* (upper left).

Extra-filling yarns are inserted in several ways. *Clipped-dot designs* are made with low-twist filling yarns inserted by separate shuttles. The shedding is done so that the extra yarns interlace with some warp yarns and float across the back of other warp yarns. Clipped spots are woven on a box loom that has a wire along the edge to hold the extra yarns so that they need not be woven in the selvage. Figure 13–6 shows a clipped fabric, dotted swiss, before and after clipping.

Many of the fabrics that have small-dot designs are called dotted swiss. The dots may be structural designs: clipped-dot designs, as described above, or swivel-dot designs. *Swivel-dot designs* are made on a loom that has an attachment holding tiny shuttles. The fabric is woven so the shuttles and extra yarns are above the ground fabric. Each shuttle carrying the extra yarn goes four times around the warp yarns in the ground fabric and then the yarn is carried along the surface to the next spot. The yarn is sheared off between the spots (Figure 13–7). Swivel-dot fabrics are rarely seen in the

United States, except as imported designer fabrics. Either side of swivel-dot fabrics, clipped-dot fabrics, and the larger clipped-spot fabrics may be the fashion side.

Fig. 13–2   *Pattern roll that controls warp shedding on a dobby loom. (Courtesy of Crompton & Knowles Corp.)*

Fig. 13–3 *Dobby fabrics: bird's eye fabric* (left) *and buck* (right).

Dotted swiss may also be an applied design. (See Chapter 17 for more details.) A comparison of several different types of dotted swiss is an interesting exercise in determining the serviceability of fabrics.

Piqué Weaves

The word *piqué* comes from the French word meaning quilted; the raised effect in these fabrics is similar to that in quilts.

Piqué weave produces a fabric with ridges, called wales or cords, that are held up by floats on the back. The wales vary in width. *Widewale piqué* (0.25 inch) is woven with 20 or more warp yarns in the face of the wale and then two warps in between. *Pinwale piqué* (0.05 inch) is a six-warp wale with two consecutive filling yarns floating across the back of the odd-numbered wales and then woven in the face of the even-numbered wales. The next two consecutive picks alternate with the first two by floating across the back of the even-numbered wales. Figure 13–8 shows a six-warp pinwale piqué.

Stuffer yarns are laid under the ridges in better-quality piqué fabrics to emphasize the roundness,

Fig. 13–4 *Generic dobby fabrics for use in apparel and furnishings.*

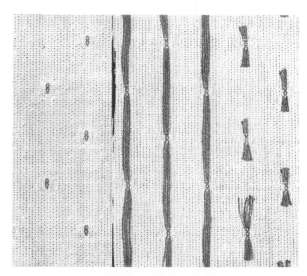

Fig. 13–5 *Fabric made with extra warp yarns: face of fabric* (left); *back, before and after clipping* (right).

and their presence or absence is one way of determining quality. The stuffer yarns are not interlaced with the surface yarns of the fabric and may be easily removed when analyzing a swatch of fabric. Piqué fabrics are woven on either a dobby or jacquard loom depending on the complexity of the design.

Cords or wales usually run in the lengthwise direction. In bird's-eye and bull's-eye piqués the cords run crosswise. Cord fabrics have a definite technical face and technical back. In wear, the floats on the wrong side usually wear out first. Figure 13-9 shows the right and wrong side of a piqué fab-

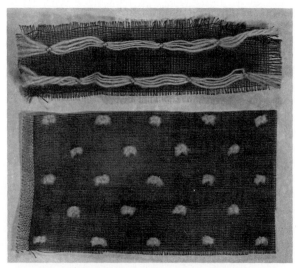

Fig. 13–6 *Dotted swiss made with extra filling yarns: before* (above) *and after clipping* (below).

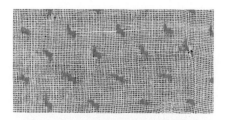

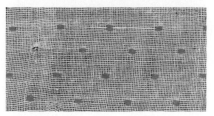

Fig. 13–7 *Dotted swiss showing both sides of a swivel-dot fabric.*

ric. Piqué fabrics are more resistant to wrinkling and have more body than flat fabrics.

Fabrics in this group are called piqué, with the exception of bedford cord. *Bedford cord* is a heavy fabric with warp cords used for bedspreads, upholstery, window treatments, slacks, trousers, and uniforms. It is made of a variety of fibers. Its spun warp yarns are larger than the filling yarns. Cords located at intervals across the fabric are formed by extra filling yarn floating across the back, giving a raised effect. Stuffer yarns are sometimes used to give a more pronounced cord. The lengthwise cords may be the same size, or alternately larger and smaller. The wales are wide and stuffer yarns are usually present.

Piqué is lighter in weight than bedford cord and has a narrower wale. Better-quality piqué fabrics are made with long-staple, combed, mercerized yarns and have one stuffer yarn. Carded yarn piqués are made without the stuffer and are sometimes printed.

Bird's-eye piqué has the tiny design formed by the wavy arrangements of the cords and by the use of stuffer yarns. *Bull's-eye piqué* is made like bird's-eye but has a much larger design. Both these fabrics have crosswise rather than lengthwise cords. They are used for apparel and furnishings.

JACQUARD WEAVES

Large-figured designs, which require more than 25 different arrangements of the warp yarns to complete one repeat design, are woven on the *jacquard loom* (Figure 13-10). Two types of looms are used to produce jacquard weaves. In the older type of loom, each warp is controlled independently by punched cards that are laced together in a continuous strip. As the cards move over the loom, all the warp yarns are raised by rods attached to them. When the rods hit the cards, some go through the holes and thus raise the warp yarns; others remain down. In this manner the shed is formed for the passage of the filling yarn. Figure 13-11 shows a picture woven with fine silk yarns on a jacquard loom. Notice that there is no repeat of this pattern from top to bottom or from side to side. The repeat would be another picture.

The newer method for producing these large patterns in the fabric uses a computer, often designed to be used with an air-jet loom. The computer's floppy disks control the position of the warp yarns and the insertion of different colored filling yarns. This system is fast with weaving speeds of 600 picks per minute, compatible with several computer-aided design systems (CADs), and allows for easy and quick pattern changes in the fabric. Fabrics produced on the electronic jacquard looms include fancy mattress ticking, upholstery, and apparel.

Fabrics made on a jacquard loom include damask, brocade, tapestry, and a variety of other patterns (see Figure 13-12). *Damask* has satin floats on a satin background, with the floats in the design opposite those in the background. It can be made from any fiber and in many different weights for apparel and furnishings. Damask is the flattest-looking of the jacquard fabrics and is often finished to maintain that flat look. Quality and durability are dependent on high count. Low-count damask is not durable because the long floats rough up, snag, and shift during use.

Brocade has satin or twill floats on a plain, ribbed, twill, or satin background (Figure 13-13). Brocade differs from damask in that the floats in the

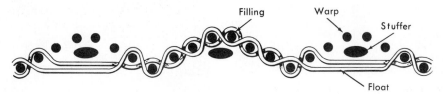

Fig. 13–8 *Six-warp pinwale piqué.*

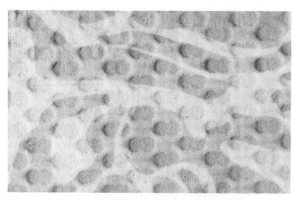

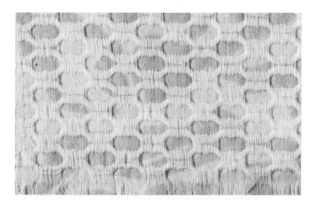

Fig. 13–9   *Piqué: right side of fabric* (left); *reverse side of fabric* (right). *Note stuffer yarns running vertically.*

design are more varied in length and are often of several colors.

Brocatelle fabrics are similar to brocade fabrics, except that they have a raised pattern. This jacquard-woven fabric frequently is made with filament yarns, using a warp-faced pattern and filling-faced ground. Coarse cotton stuffer filling yarns may be used to help maintain the three-dimensional appearance of the fabric when intended for upholstery.

Originally, *tapestry* was an intricate picture that was handwoven with discontinuous filling yarns. It was usually a wall hanging and took years to weave. Today's jacquard tapestry is mass produced for upholstery, handbags, and the like. It is a complicated structure consisting of two or more sets of warp and two or more sets of filling interlaced so that the face warp is never woven into the back and the back filling does not show on the face. Upholstery tapestry is durable if warp and filling yarns are comparable. Very often, however, fine yarns are combined with coarse yarns, and when the fine yarns are abraded away, the coarse yarns are left loose and are unsightly.

Wilton rugs are figured pile fabrics made on a jacquard loom. These rugs, once considered imitations of Oriental rugs, are so expensive to weave that the tufting industry has found a way to create similar figures through printing techniques.

MOMIE WEAVES

Momie is a class of weaves that present no twilled or other distinct weave effect but give the cloth the appearance of being sprinkled with small spots or seeds. The appearance resembles crepe made from

Fig. 13–10   *Jacquard loom for weaving large-figured fabrics. (Courtesy of Crompton & Knowles Corp.)*

Fig. 13-11   *Jacquard-woven picture.*

Fig. 13–12 *Jacquard patterned fabrics.*

yarns of high twist. Fabrics are made on a loom with a dobby attachment or computer control. Some are variations of satin weave, with filling yarns forming the irregular floats. Some are even-sided and some have a decided warp effect. Momie weave is also called *granite* or *crepe weave*. Fibers such as wool, cotton, and rayon, which do not lend themselves to high-twist-yarn crepe fabrics, are often used in making crepe-weave fabrics. An irregular interlacing pattern of crepe weave is shown in Figure 13–14.

Sand crepe is a common momie-weave fabric. It has a repeat pattern of 16 warp yarns and 16 filling yarns and requires 16 harnesses. No float is greater than two yarns in length. It is woven of either spun or filament yarns.

Granite cloth is made with the momie weave, based on the satin weave. It is an even-sided fabric with no long floats and no twilled effect. It is used for furnishings and apparel.

Moss crepe is a combination of high-twist crepe yarns and crepe weave. The yarns are plied yarns with one ply made of a crepe-twist single yarn. Regular yarns may be alternated with the plied yarns or they may be used in one direction while the plied yarns are used in the other direction. This fabric

Fig. 13–13 *Brocade.*

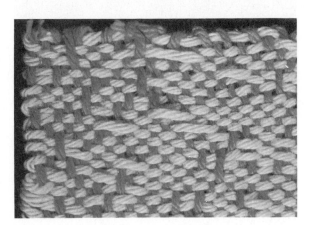

Fig. 13–14 *Crepe weave with irregular interlacings.*

should be treated as a high-twist crepe fabric. Moss crepe is used in dresses and blouses.

Bark cloth is a momie weave fabric used primarily in furnishings. The interlacing pattern is usually executed with spun yarns and creates a fabric with a rough texture somewhat like that of tree bark, hence the fabric's name. The fabric may be printed or solid. The rough texture adds visual interest to the fabric and minimizes the appearance of soiling.

LENO WEAVES

Leno is a weave in which the warp yarns do not lie parallel to each other. Warp yarns work in groups, usually pairs of two; one yarn of each pair is *crossed* over the other before the filling yarn is inserted, as shown in Figure 13–15.

Leno is made with a *doup attachment*, which may be used with a plain or a dobby loom. The attachment consists of a thin hairpinlike needle supported by two heddles. One yarn of each pair is threaded through an eye at the upper end of the needle, and the other yarn is drawn between the two heddles. Both yarns are drawn through the same dent in the reed. During weaving, when one of the two heddles is raised, the doup-warp yarn that is threaded through the doup needle is drawn across to the left. When the other heddle is raised, the same doup-warp yarn is drawn across to the right.

By glancing at a leno fabric, one might think that the yarns were twisted fully around each other, but this is not true. Careful examination shows that they are *crossed* and that one yarn of the pair is always above the other. The fabrics made with leno weave are lacelike in character.

Fabrics made by leno weave include *marquisette* (Figure 13–16); mosquito netting; and some bags for laundry, fruit, and vegetables. Polyester marquisettes are widely used for glass curtains. Casement draperies are frequently made with leno weave and novelty yarns. Thermal blankets are sometimes made of leno weave. All these fabrics are characterized by sheerness or open spaces between the yarns. The crossed-yarn arrangement gives greater firmness and strength than plain-weave fabrics of the same low count and also gives resistance to slippage of yarns. Snagging may be a problem in use and care, however.

DOUBLE CLOTH

Double-cloth fabrics have a different appearance on the two sides due to the method of producing the fabric. Double-cloth fabrics tend to be heavier and have more body than single cloths. A single cloth, such as percale, is made from one set of warp yarns and one set of filling yarns—two sets of yarns. Double cloth is a woven fabric made from three or more sets of yarns.

The following are three types of woven double cloth:

1. Double cloth—coat fabrics: melton and kersey.
2. Double weave—apparel and upholstery fabrics: matelassé.

Fig. 13–15   *Leno weave.*

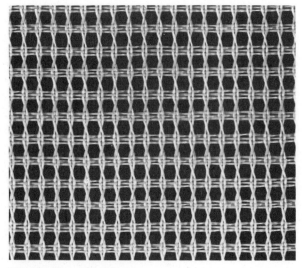

Fig. 13–16   *Marquisette.*

3. Double-faced—blanket cloth, double-satin ribbon, lining fabric, and silence cloth.

Double cloth is made with five sets of yarns: two fabrics woven one above the other on the same loom with the fifth yarn (warp) interlacing with both cloths (Figure 13-17). This technique is used to produce velvet. (See Pile Weaves, this chapter.) True double cloth can be separated by pulling out the yarns holding the two cloths together. It can be used in reversible garments such as capes and skirts.

Double cloth is expensive to make because it requires special looms and the production rate is slower than for single fabrics. Double cloth is more pliable than the same weight single fabric because finer yarns can be used. The two specific fabrics that may be either true double cloth or single cloth are melton and kersey. Both of these heavyweight-wool coating fabrics are twill-weave fabrics that have been heavily finished so that it is difficult to identify the weave.

Melton tends to have a smoother surface than kersey. *Kersey* is usually heavier than melton and has a shorter, more lustrous nap. Both fabrics are used in winter coats, overcoats, riding habits, and military uniforms.

Double Weaves

Double weave is made with four sets of yarns, creating two separate layers of fabric that periodically reverse position from top to bottom, thus interlocking the two layers of fabric. Between the interlocking points the two layers are completely separate, creating pockets in the fabric (Figure 13-18).

Double-weave fabrics can also be called *pocket fabrics*, *pocket cloth*, or *pocket weave*. They are

Fig. 13-18   *Double weave: face of fabric* (bottom); *back of fabric* (top).

most commonly seen in high-quality upholstery fabrics. The main advantage of the fabrics is the designs that can be achieved. An additional advantage is their heavier weight. They are usually closely woven, durable fabrics.

Matelassé crepe is a double-cloth construction with either three or four sets of yarns woven on a jacquard or dobby loom. Two of the sets are always the regular warp and filling yarns and the others are crepe or coarse cotton yarns. They are woven together so that the two sets crisscross, as shown in Figure 13-19. When the fabrics are finished, the crepe or cotton yarns shrink, giving the fabric a puckered appearance. Heavy cotton yarns are used as stuffer yarns beneath the fabric face to emphasize the three-dimensional appearance of the fabric. Matelassé is used in apparel and upholstery (see Figure 13-20).

Double-Faced Fabrics

Double-faced fabrics are made with three sets of yarns: two warp and one filling, or two sets of filling and one set of warp. Blankets, satin ribbons, interlinings, and silence cloth can be made by this process (Figure 13-21).

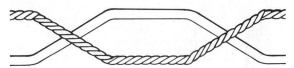

Fig. 13-19   *Interlacing of yarns between fabric surfaces of matelassé.*

Fig. 13-17   *Double cloth made with five sets of yarns.*

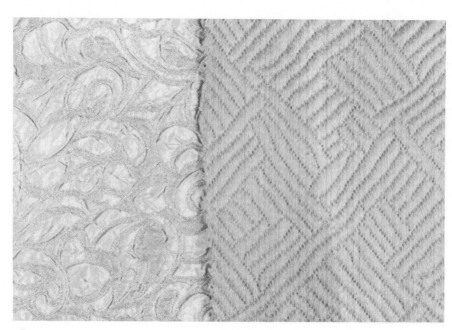

Fig. 13–20 Two examples of matelassé.

Blankets with one color on one side and another color on the other side are usually double-faced blankets. One set of warp yarns is used, with two sets of different-colored filling yarns. Sometimes designs are made by interchanging the colors from one side to the other. Double-faced blankets are usually expensive woven-wool blankets.

Satin ribbons, which have a lustrous satin face on both sides of the ribbon, are used in designer lingerie and evening wear. These ribbons have two sets of warp yarns that form the surface on both sides of the ribbon. They are interlaced with one set of filling yarns.

A double-faced interlining fabric is used to add warmth to winter jackets and coats. The face of the fabric is a filament-yarn satin weave that takes the place of a lining fabric and slides easily over other clothing. The back of the fabric uses a third set of low-twist yarns that are heavily napped for warmth. Thus the fabric functions as a combination lining and interlining fabric.

Silence cloth is a heavy cotton fabric that has been napped on both sides. Available in white, it is used under fine tablecloths to silence the noise of china and silverware while dining.

PILE WEAVES

Woven-pile fabrics are three-dimensional structures made by weaving an extra set of warp or filling yarns into the ground yarns to make loops or cut ends on the surface (Figure 13–22). The pile is usually 1/2 inch or less in height. Woven-pile fabric is less pliable than other pile fabrics. Sometimes when the fabric is folded, the rows of tufts permit the back to show, or "grin through." Pile fabrics can be both functional and beautiful. A high pile is used to give warmth as either the shell or the lining of coats, jackets, gloves, and boots. High-count fabrics give durability and beauty in carpets, upholstery, and bedspreads. Low-twist yarns give absorbency in towels and washcloths. Other uses for pile fabrics are stuffed toys, wigs, paint rollers, buffing and polishing cloths, and decubicare pads for bedridden

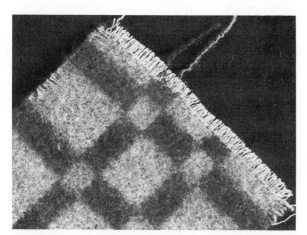

Fig. 13-21 Double-faced blanket. One set of warp yarns and two sets of filling yarns.

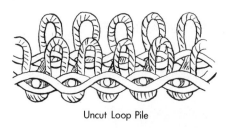

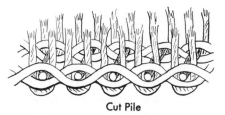

Fig. 13–22   Cut pile and loop pile: woven fabric.

Fig. 13–23   Filling pile. Cross section of weave in corduroy.

patients. Interesting effects can be achieved by combinations of cut and uncut pile (Figure 13–22), pile of various heights, high- and low-twist yarns, areas of pile on a flat surface, and curling and crushing or forcing pile into a position other than upright.

In pile fabrics, the pile receives the surface abrasion and the base weave receives the stress. A durable base structure contributes significantly to a satisfactory pile fabric. A compact ground or base weave increases the resistance of a looped or uncut pile to snagging and of a cut pile to shedding and pulling out. A dense pile stands erect, resists crushing, and gives better cover. Care must be taken in cleaning and pressing to keep the pile erect. Cut pile usually looks better if dry cleaned, but some pile fabrics—such as pinwale corduroy—can be washed, depending on the fiber content. Incorrect pressing may flatten the pile and cause the fabric to appear lighter in color. Special pressing aids or techniques are used with pile fabrics, like steaming or using needleboards.

Many pile fabrics are pressed during finishing so that the pile slants in one direction, giving an up and down. It is more important that the pile be directed in the same way in all pieces of a product. Otherwise, light will be reflected differently and the product will appear to be made of two colors.

Filling-Pile Fabrics

The pile in *filling-pile fabrics* is made by long filling floats on the surface that are cut after weaving (Figure 13–23). Two sets of filling yarns and one set of warp are used. The ground fabric is made with one set of filling yarns and the warp yarn set. During weaving, the extra filling yarns float across the ground yarns, interlacing occasionally. In *corduroy*, the floats are arranged in lengthwise rows; in *velveteen*, they are scattered over the base fabric.

Cutting is done by a special machine consisting of guides that lift the individual floating yarns from the ground fabric and revolving knives that cut the floats (Figure 13–24). A gray-goods corduroy with some of the floats cut is shown in Figure 13–25. When widewale corduroy is cut, the guides and knives can be set to cut all the floats in one operation. For narrow corduroy and velveteen, the rows are so close together that alternate rows are cut with each pass and the fabric must be run through the machine twice.

After cutting, the surface is brushed crosswise and lengthwise to bloom open the yarn tuft, raise the pile, and merge the separate pile tufts. Finishing gives the fabric its final appearance.

Both velveteen and corduroy are made with long-staple, combed, mercerized cotton for the pile. In good-quality fabrics, long-staple cotton is used for the ground as well. Polyester/cotton blends are available with polyester in the ground yarns for strength. The ground may be made with plain- or twill-weave interlacing patterns. With the twill pattern, it is possible to have a higher count and therefore a denser pile. Corduroy can be recognized by lengthwise wales. Velveteen has more body and less drapeability than velvet. The pile is not over 1/8 inch high. Both corduroy and velveteen are commonly seen as solid-color and printed fabrics. Table 13–1 gives characteristics of different kinds of corduroy.

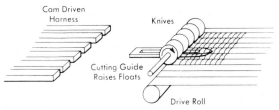

Fig. 13–24   Process for cutting floats to make corduroy.

Fig. 13–25 *Corduroy gray goods showing some of the floats cut and brushed open.*

Warp-Pile Fabrics

Warp-pile fabrics are made with two sets of warp yarns and one set of filling. One set of warp yarns and the filling yarn set form the ground fabric. The extra set of warp makes the pile. Several methods are used.

DOUBLE-CLOTH METHOD Two fabrics are woven, one above the other, with the extra set of warp yarns interlacing with both fabrics. There are two sheds, one above the other, and one filling yarn is inserted in each shed. The fabrics are cut apart while still on the loom by a traveling knife that passes back and forth across the loom. With the

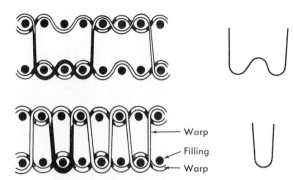

Fig. 13–26 *Warp pile: double-cloth method. W-interlacing* (above); *V-interlacing* (below).

double-cloth method of weaving, the depth of the pile is determined by the space between the two fabrics (Figure 13-26).

Velvet is made of filaments with a pile 1/16 inch high or shorter. Velvet is not wound on bolts, as are other fabrics, but is hung on a special bolt so that there are no folds or creases in the fabric.

Velvet and velveteen can often be distinguished by fiber length, since velvet is usually made with filaments and velveteen with staple. To tell warp directions in these fabrics, ravel adjacent sides. In velvet, the tufts are interlaced with a filling yarn (Figure 13-27). Another way to tell warp direction is to bend the fabric. In velveteen, the pile "breaks" into lengthwise rows because the filling tufts are interlaced with the warp yarns. In velvet, the pile breaks in crosswise rows because the warp tufts are interlaced with the ground-filling yarns. This technique works best with medium- to poor-quality fabrics.

Crushed velvet is made by mechanically twisting the wet cloth. The surface yarns are randomly flattened in different directions.

Panné velvet is an elegant fabric that has had the pile pressed flat by heavy pressure in one direction to give high luster. If the pile is disturbed or

Table 13–1 Kinds of Corduroy

	Wales per inch	Ounces per yard	Characteristics
Featherwale	18–19	5 ±	Shallow pile, flexible
Pinwale	14–16	7 ±	Shallow pile, flexible
Midwale	11	10 ±	Men's and women's outerwear
Widewale	3–9	12 ±	Coats, most durable corduroy made

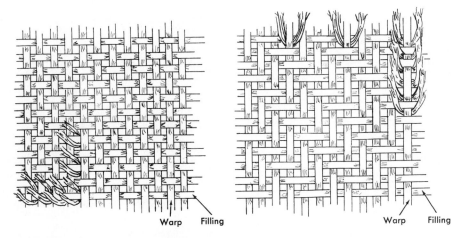

Fig. 13–27 *Comparison of filling pile and warp pile. Velvet: warp-pile yarn is interlaced with ground filling (left). Velveteen: filling-pile yarn is interlaced with ground warp (right).*

brushed in the other direction, the smooth, lustrous look is destroyed.

Velour is a warp-pile cotton fabric used primarily for upholstery and draperies. It has a deeper pile than velveteen and is heavier in weight. *Plush* has a deeper pile than velour or velvet and is usually longer than 1/4 inch.

Furlike fabrics may be finished by curling, shearing, sculpturing, or printing to resemble different kinds of real fur (see Figure 13–28). (Most furlike fabrics are made by other processes; see Chapters 14 and 15.)

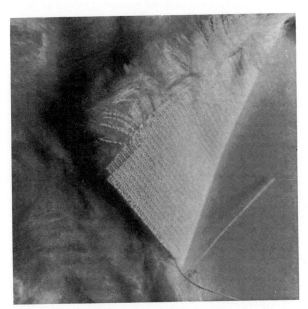

Fig. 13–28 *Woven furlike fabric.*

OVER-WIRE METHOD In the *over-wire method* a single cloth is woven with wires placed across the width of the loom over the ground warp and under the pile warp. For cut pile fabrics, each wire has a knife edge that cuts all the yarns looped over it as it is withdrawn. Uncut pile can be made over wires without knives or over waste picks of filling yarns. The wires are removed before the cloth is off the loom, and the waste picks are removed after the fabric is off the loom. Friezé and mohair-pile plush are made in this way. Most woven carpets are made over wires.

Friezé, an uncut or combination cut/uncut pile fabric, is an upholstery fabric that usually has a lower pile density than most other pile fabrics. There are fewer tufts per square inch than found in velvet. The durability of friezé depends on the closeness of the weave (Figure 13–29).

Velvet can also be made by the over-wire method. Complex patterns using different-color yarns and loops combined with cut pile result in a wide variety of fabrics.

SLACK-TENSION PILE METHOD The pile in *terrycloth* is formed by a special weaving arrangement in which three picks are put through and beaten up with one motion of the reed. After the

Fig. 13–29 *Friezé is woven over wires.*

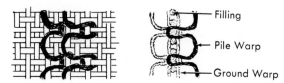

Fig. 13–30 *Warp pile: slack-tension method for terrycloth.*

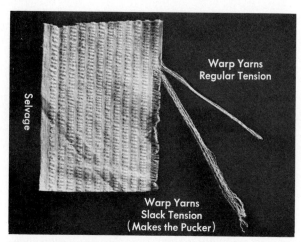

Fig. 13–31 *Seersucker, showing the difference in length of slack- and regular-tension yarns.*

second pick in a set is inserted, there is a let-off motion that causes the yarns on the warp-pile beam to slacken, while the yarns on the ground-pile beam are held at tension. The third pick is inserted, the reed moves forward all the way, and all three picks are beaten up firmly into the fell of the fabric (Figure 13–30). These picks move along the ground warp and push the pile-warp yarns into loops. The loops can be on one side only or on both sides. The height of the loops is determined by the distance the first two picks are left back from the fell of the fabric.

Terrycloth is used for bath towels, beach robes, and sportswear. Each loop acts as a tiny sponge. When the loops are sheared and the surface is brushed to loosen and intermesh the fibers of adjacent yarns, the surface becomes more compact, less porous, and therefore less absorbent than the loop-pile terry. Cotton/polyester terry towels have blended ground yarns and cotton pile, the pile yarns for absorbency and the polyester ground yarns for strength and durability, especially in selvages.

There is no up and down in terrycloth unless the cloth is printed. Some friezés are made by the terrycloth method. *Shagbark*, which has spaced rows of loops, is also made this way.

SLACK-TENSION WEAVES

In *slack-tension weaving* two warp beams are used. The yarns on one beam are held at regular tension and those on the other beam are held at slack tension. As the reed beats the filling yarn into place, the slack yarns crinkle or buckle to form the puckered stripe and the regular-tensioned yarns form the flat stripe. Loop-pile fabrics, such as terrycloth, are made by a similar weave; see the previous section. *Seersucker* is the fabric made by slack-tension weave (Figure 13–31).

The yarns are wound onto the two warp beams in groups of 10 to 16 for a narrow stripe. The crinkle stripe may have slightly larger yarns to enhance the crinkle, and this stripe may also have a 2 × 1

basket weave. The stripes are always in the warp direction. Seersucker is produced by a limited number of manufacturers. It is a low-profit, high-cost item to produce because of slow weaving speed. Seersuckers are made in 45- or 60-inch widths in plain colors, stripes, plaids, checks and prints. Seersucker is used in summer suiting, dresses, and sportswear.

NARROW FABRICS

Narrow fabrics encompass a diverse range of products that are up to 12 inches wide and made by a variety of techniques. Woven narrow fabrics will be discussed here. Narrow fabrics include ribbons of all sorts, elastics, zipper tapes, Venetian-blind tapes, couturier's labels, hook and loop tapes such as

Fig. 13–32 *Narrow fabric* (left to right): *woven fancy, grosgrain ribbon, woven satin ribbon, bias tape, zipper tape, and rickrack.*

Velcro, pipings, carpet-edge tapes, trims, safety belts, and harnesses (Figure 13-32). Webbings are an important group of narrow fabrics used in packaging, cargo handling, furniture, and for animal control, like leashes or lead ropes for dogs, horses, and show cattle. Narrow fabrics are only a minor end use for fibers—2.1 percent of fibers are used in their production. Industrial uses of narrow fabrics are more important than apparel and furnishing uses. In 1990, 133.5 million pounds of fiber were used in narrow-fabric industrial uses, compared with 80.2 million pounds in apparel uses and only 4.0 million pounds in furnishing uses.

Narrow-fabric looms weave many fabrics side by side. Each fabric has its own shuttle but shares all other loom mechanisms. Plain, twill, satin, jacquard, and pile are the kinds of weaves made.

Woven elastics are available in a variety of weaves. They are used in apparel where tight fit and holding power are needed, such as women's undergarments. They have better stability and rigidity than knit elastics and are less prone to riding up, but are more expensive.

Table 13-2 compares the characteristics of the fancy weaves discussed in this chapter.

Table 13–2   Comparison of Fancy Weaves

Weave	Fabrication Details	Appearance	Uses/Fabrics
Dobby	Warp controlled in groups	Small geometric patterns	Apparel, furnishings, bird's-eye diaper, waffle cloth
Extra yarn	Additional yarn sets in warp or filling, excess removed or on back, yarn ends may add interest	Small geometric patterns, yarn fringe	Apparel, furnishings, dotted swiss, eyelash
Piqué	Dobby or jacquard technique, raised pattern areas	Floats on back or stuffer yarns create raised areas	Apparel, furnishings, bedford cord, pinwale piqué, bull's-eye piqué
Jacquard	Warp controlled individually	Elaborate, intricate designs	Apparel, furnishings, brocade, damask, tapestry
Momie	Irregular interlacing	Pebbly, uneven surface	Apparel, furnishings, crepe, bark cloth, moss crepe
Leno	Warp yarns cross over each other	Stable, open fabric	Apparel, furnishings, leno, casement cloth, marquisette
Double cloth	Three, four, or five sets of yarns used	Double-faced, pockets in fabric, or thick, stiff, heavy fabrics	Apparel, furnishings, matelassé melton, blankets
Pile	Extra yarns in warp or filling create surface pile	Thick, bulky, warm, durable fabrics	Apparel, furnishings, corduroy, velveteen, velvet, friezé, terrycloth, wilton carpets
Slack tension	Warp bands under different tensions during weaving	Puckered stripes in warp direction	Apparel, furnishings, seersucker

KEY TERMS

Fancy weaves
Dobby weave
Dobby loom
Bird's-eye
Huck or huck-a-back
Shirting madras
Waffle cloth
Extra yarns
Extra-warp yarns
Extra-filling yarns
Clipped-dot fabric
Swivel-dot fabric
Piqué
Jacquard loom
Damask
Brocade
Brocatelle
Tapestry
Momie weave
Crepe or granite weave
Sand crepe
Granite cloth
Moss crepe
Leno
Doup attachment
Marquisette

Double cloth
Melton
Kersey
Double weave
Pocket weave
Matelassé
Double-faced fabric
Silence cloth
Pile weave
Woven-pile fabrics
Filling pile fabrics
Corduroy
Velveteen
Warp-pile fabrics
Velvet
Crushed velvet
Panné velvet
Velour
Plush
Over-wire method
Friezé
Terrycloth
Shagbark
Slack-tension weave
Seersucker
Narrow fabrics

QUESTIONS

1. Why are the fabrics in this chapter referred to as fancy?
2. Summarize the structural characteristics of these weaves: dobby, jacquard, momie, leno, double cloth, pile, slack tension.
3. What performance differences would be expected among the fabrics in question 2?
4. Name a fabric for each of these weaves and discuss the appearance characteristics that are useful in recognizing that fabric.

SUGGESTED READINGS

Emery, Irene (1980). *The Primary Structures of Fabrics.* Washington, D.C.: The Textile Museum.

Schwartz, Peter, Rhodes, Trevor, and Mohamed, Mansour (1982). *Fabric Forming Systems.* Park Ridge, NJ: Noyes Publications.

Suzuki, Hajime (February, 1990). "Automated Weaving: A Japanese Perspective." *Textile Month*, pp. 26–28.

"Textile Machinery Technology." (April, 1991). *Textile World*, pp. 61–68.

14

Knitting and Knit Fabrics

OBJECTIVES

- To know the differences between woven and knit fabrics.

- To differentiate between warp- and filling-knit fabrics.

- To understand the characteristics of warp- and filling-knit fabrics.

- To integrate fabrication, yarn type, and fiber to end use.

- To understand the versatility of knit fabrics for apparel, furnishing, and industrial products.

*K*NITTING IS THE FORMATION OF A FABRIC by the interlooping of one or more sets of yarns. Knitting has been the traditional method of producing some items, such as sweaters, underwear, hosiery, and baby blankets. Knits are very popular in active sportswear. Stabilized knits have increased the use of knit fabrics in furnishing and industrial products.

The technique of knitting is probably not as old as that of weaving. Remnants of knit fabrics dating back to A.D. 250 were found near the borders of ancient Palestine. Knitting was a hand process until 1589, when the Reverend William Lee of England invented a flat-bed machine for knitting cloth for hosiery. This machine could produce cloth at 10 times the rate of hand knitting. The circular-knitting machine and the warp-knitting machine were developed about 200 years later. Other devices invented about that time include the ribbing device and the latch needle.

A unique advantage of knitting is that a completed garment can be produced or fashioned directly on the knitting machine. Sweaters and hosiery are good examples. The knitting of a completed garment has been possible since 1863 when William Cotton invented a machine that could shape garment parts by adding or dropping stitches.

The rate of production of knitting machines is relatively high—about four times as many square yards or meters per hour as for looms since machine width is not related to operating speeds. This speed should be an economic factor in favor of knitting as a method of fabrication, but the increased cost of the yarn more than offsets any savings in the cost of manufacture. There are several reasons for this. First, because the looped position of the yarn imparts bulk, more yarn is required to produce a knit fabric than to produce a comparable woven fabric. Second, the looped structure is porous—has holes or spaces—and provides less cover than a woven fabric in which yarns lie side by side. So, in order to achieve an equal amount of cover, small stitches (finer gauge) and finer and more expensive yarns are used. Knitting yarns are more expensive because they must be much more uniform to prevent the formation of thick-and-thin places in the fabric.

Knitting is a very efficient and versatile method of making fabric. This versatility has resulted from the use of computer-aided design systems wherein electronic-patterning mechanisms permit rapid adjustment to fashion changes. In addition, microcomputers are being used in a manner similar to their use in pattern weaves. Electronic controls identify the type of stitch for each needle, the yarn to be used in the stitch, and the tension on the yarn. Electronic controls for knitting machines make knitting faster, more efficient, and more practical. These machines are more versatile than other machines and changing patterns is much simpler and quicker. There is now a knitted counterpart for almost every woven fabric—knitted seersucker, piqué, denim, crepe, satin, terrycloth, and velour.

Other knitting machine technological developments helped broaden the range of end uses. Attachments to the knitting machine produce fabrics whose stability is more like that of wovens. The weft-insertion knitting machine introduced filling yarn for more crosswise stability and the warp-insertion knitting machine added warp yarns for greater lengthwise stability.

The major advantages of knits are comfort and appearance retention. Comfort is based on the ability to adapt to body movement. The loop structure provides the fabric with outstanding elasticity (stretch/recovery) that is distinct from any elastic properties of the fibers and yarns that are used. The loop can change shape by lengthening or widening to give stretch in either direction of the cloth (Figure 14-1). However, knits may sag, bag, or snag.

Knitted fabrics have higher potential shrinkage than woven fabrics. The accepted standard is 5 percent for knits, whereas 2 percent is standard for wovens. However, the performance specifications developed by the American Society for Testing and Materials list a recommended maximum shrinkage for both woven and knit products of 3 percent in both vertical and horizontal directions.

The bulky structure of a knit provides many dead-air cells for good insulation in still air but a wind-

Loop Lengthened   Loop Widened   Loop Normal

Fig. 14–1 *The loop can change its shape to give stretch.*

repellent outer layer is needed to prevent chill winds from penetrating. On a warm, humid day, knits may be too warm because they tend to fit snugly and insulate too well.

Appearance retention means lack of wrinkles during use, care, and packing or storage. Wrinkle recovery is based somewhat on the loop structure, but it is also strongly influenced by fiber content and kind of yarn. Snagging is probably the single most serious problem encountered in the use of knit fabric. When a yarn is snagged so it pulls out and stands away from the surface of the fabric, "shiners" or tight yarns are formed on either side of the snag. If snags are cut off (rather than being worked back into their original position), a run may start in some knits, particularly in filling knits.

A run occurs when the stitches in a wale collapse or pull out. A run occurs in a stepwise fashion when one stitch in a wale after another collapses due to stress on the loop and when a yarn is severed.

The *mace test* is a particularly tough test for snagging. It consists of running a round, spiked iron ball a specified number of times along the surface of the cloth to test its resistance to snags (Figure 14–2). Finer yarns, smaller stitches, and higher twist all contribute to snag resistance. This test has been found to give good results in terms of correlation with actual wear.

Table 14–1 summarizes some of the major differences between the processes of knitting and weaving and the fabrics made by these processes. Performance and appearance characteristics of knits include:

- One or more yarns are formed into a series of interlocking loops.
- Knitting is a faster technique than weaving, requiring more yarn per unit of cover. Knits may be bowed or skewed.
- Knits are stretchy, elastic fabrics.
- Knits are porous and resilient; they may be bulky.
- Knits are used for apparel, furnishing, and industrial purposes.

KNITTING

Knitting is a fabrication process in which needles are used to form a series of interlocking loops from one or more yarns or from a set of yarns. *Filling*, or *weft*, *knitting* is a process in which one yarn or yarn set is carried back and forth (or around) and under needles to form a fabric. Yarns run horizontally in the fabric. *Warp knitting* is a process in which a warp beam is set into a machine and yarn sets are interlooped to form a fabric. Yarns run vertically in the fabric. These names were borrowed from weaving and refer to the direction the yarns move in the fabric. Note that in knitted fabrics, yarns do not move in both directions as they do in weaving.

Needles

Knitting is done by needles: *spring-beard, latch*, or *compound*, which are shown in Figure 14–3. Most filling knits are formed with the latch needle. The spring-beard, or bearded, needle may be used to produce fully fashioned garments and knit-fleece fabrics. Spring-beard needles are usually used with fine yarns, whereas latch needles may be used in making coarse fabrics. A double-latch needle is used to make purl loops. The compound needle is used primarily in warp knitting.

Stitches

Stitches or loops are made by needles. The stitches are named based on the way they are made. Stitches may be open or closed, depending

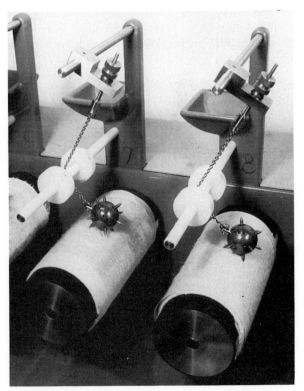

Fig. 14–2   Mace test. (Courtesy of Crosrol, Inc.)

Table 14–1   Comparison of Knit and Woven Fabrics

Knitting	Weaving
Comfort and Appearance Retention	
Mobile, elastic fabric. Adapts easily to body movement. Good recovery from wrinkles.	Rigid to stress (unless made with stretch yarns). Varies with the weave.
Cover	
Porous, less opaque. More open spaces between yarns let winds penetrate.	Provides maximum hiding power. Maximum cover per weight of yarn. Less air permeable, especially if count is high.
Fabric Stability	
Less stable in use and care. Many shrink more than 5 percent unless synthetic fibers have been heat set.	More stable in use and care. Many shrink less than 2 percent.
Versatility	
Sheer to heavyweight fabrics. Plain and fancy knits. Can be made to look like many other fabrics.	Sheer to heavyweight fabrics. Many different textures and designs.
Economics	
Design patterns can be changed quickly to meet fashion needs.	Machinery less adaptable to rapid changes in fashion.
Process is less expensive but is offset by expensive raw material costs. Speedier regardless of fabric width.	Most economical method of producing a unit of cover. Wider looms weave slower.

on how the stitch is formed. Open stitches are most common in filling knitting. In warp knitting either kind may be found, depending on the design of the knit. Open or closed stitches are useful primarily in identifying the way the fabric was made and have little relationship to performance characteristics.

Fabric Characteristics

Wales are vertical columns of stitches in the knit fabric. *Courses* are horizontal rows of stitches. In machine knitting, each wale is formed by a single needle. Wales and courses show clearly on filling-knit jersey (see Figures 14-4 and 14-5).

Gauge, or *cut*, indicates the fineness of the stitch; it is measured as the number of needles in a specific space on the needle bar and often expressed as needles per inch (npi).

The higher the gauge, or cut, the finer the fabric. The finished fabric may not have the same gauge as the machine on which it was made because of shrinkage or stretching during finishing. A fine-gauge, filling-knitting machine may have 28 npi or more.

It may be difficult to identify the technical face of the fabric. The following list identifies some charac-

teristics for which to look in determining the technical face of a knitted fabric (see Figures 14-4 and 14-5). *Technical face* refers to the outer side of fabric as knitted. This may not be the side used as the fashion side in a product.

1. The technical face side has a better finish.
2. If two kinds of yarn or fiber are used, the more expensive one is used on the face side.
3. If floats are present, the least snaggable ones are on the face.
4. Finer yarns are on the face.
5. If the two sides differ, the design is on the face side.
6. If the fabric curls, it curls to the *technical back*, parallel to the wales.

FILLING (OR WEFT) KNITTING

Filling knitting can be either a hand or a machine process. In *hand knitting*, a yarn is cast (looped) onto one needle, another needle is inserted into the first stitch, the yarn is thrown around the needle, and by manipulating the needle the new stitch is taken off onto the second needle. The process is

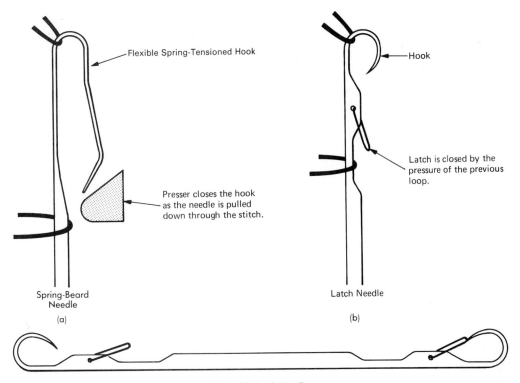

(c) Double Latch Needle

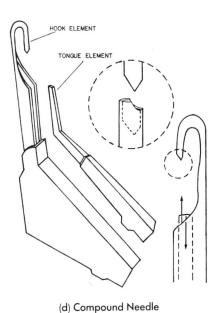

(d) Compound Needle

Fig. 14–3   *Knitting needles: (a) spring-beard needle; (b) latch needle; (c) double-latch needle; (d) compound needle.*

repeated with all the stitches being taken off from one needle to the other.

In *machine knitting*, many needles (one for each wale) are set into a machine and the stitch is made in a series of steps. In the *running position*, the stitch begins to move down the needle. In *clearing*, the old stitch is moved down to the stem of the needle. During the *yarn-feed step*, the new yarn is positioned in front of the needle. In the *knockover step*, the old stitch is removed from the needle. The final

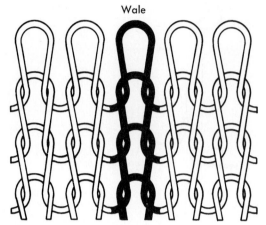

Fig. 14–4 *Wale from the technical face of filling-knit jersey fabric.*

step is the *pulling step*, when the new stitch is formed at the hook of the needle. These five steps are repeated in one continuous motion to form a knit (see Figure 14-6).

Knitting can be flat, in which the yarn is carried back and forth on a flat-bed machine (see Figure 14-7), or circular, in which the yarn is carried in a spiral like the threads in a screw on a circular machine (see Figure 14-8). In hand knitting, many kinds of stitches can be made by varying the way the yarn is placed around the needle (in front or behind) and by knitting stitches together, dropping stitches, or transferring stitches. Special mechanisms have to be used to obtain these variations in machine knitting.

Fabrics may be categorized by the machine used to produce them or by the number of yarn sets in the fabric. Knits are classified by several factors: the machine on which the knit is made, the number of yarn sets in the knit, and the type of stitch or stitches used in the knit. Categorizing filling knits by the number of yarn sets is a carryover from hand knitting. Some fabrics, such as ribknits, are made with one set of yarns on a machine with two needle beds. Thus, ribknits could be categorized as single

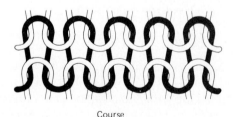

Fig. 14–5 *Course from the technical back of jersey.*

or double knits. In this book, knits are categorized by the machine used to produce them.

Machines Used In Filling Knitting

Machine knitting is done on single- and double-knit circular and flat-bed machines. The *circular machines* are faster in production. They make yardage primarily, but are also used to make sweater bodies, panty hose, and socks. The *flat-bed machines* knit full-fashioned parts and have much slower operating speeds.

Filling-Knit Structures—Stitches

Filling-knit fabrics are classified according to the stitch type used. There are four possible stitch types. Each is controlled by the selection of *cams*, or guides, that control the motion of the needle. The first stitch is the *knit stitch*. This is the basic stitch used to produce the majority of filling-knit fabrics (see Figure 14-9). These fabrics have greater elongation crosswise and less elongation lengthwise. The sides of the stitches appear on the face of jersey; the back is comprised of the tops and bottoms of the stitches. Figure 14-10 illustrates the appearance of both sides of the fabric. When jerseys are printed, they are printed on the face since that is the smoothest and most regular surface. However, many jerseys, especially the pile types, are used with the technical back as the fashion side because of the loop formation.

The *tuck stitch* is used to create a pattern in the fabric. In the tuck stitch, the old stitch is not cleared from the needle. Thus there are two stitches on the needle. Figures 14-11 and 14-12 show how the tuck stitch looks in a fabric. In a knit fabric with tuck stitches, the fabric is thicker and slightly less likely to stretch crosswise than a basic-knit fabric with the same number of stitches. With the tuck stitch, the fabric has bubbles, blisters, or puckers for visual interest, which may be incorporated in a pattern or added randomly to create texture. These are usually referred to as jacquard jerseys.

The *float* or *miss stitch* is also used to create a pattern in the fabric. In the float stitch, no new stitch is formed at the needle while adjacent needles form new stitches. The float stitch can be used when yarns of different colors are used to create patterns. Figure 14-13 shows how the float stitch

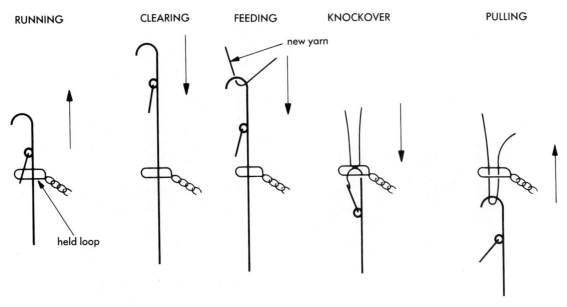

RUNNING   CLEARING   FEEDING   KNOCKOVER   PULLING

new yarn

held loop

Fig. 14–6   *Latch-needle knitting action.*

looks in a fabric. A knit fabric with float stitches is thinner and much less likely to stretch crosswise than a basic-knit fabric with the same number of stitches. In jacquard jerseys, float stitches are very common because of the combination of colors in the fabric. For example, if a fabric incorporates two or more colors in a pattern, float stitches are necessary as one color comes to the face and the other floats in this area. Figure 14–14 shows the face and back of a jacquard jersey with float stitches.

The *purl*, or *reverse*, *stitch* forms a fabric that looks like the technical back of a basic-knit fabric on both sides. The fabric is reversible (see Figure 14–15).

Filling-Knit Fabrics

SINGLE-FILLING KNITS *Single-filling knits* are made using a machine with one set of needles. This machine is usually a circular one, but it may also be a flat-bed one.

Single knits can be any pattern or weight. They are less stable than double knits, tend to curl at the edges, and run readily, especially if made of filament yarns.

Single or Plain Jersey Single jersey fabric is the simplest of the filling-knit structures. The face side has prominent wales—columns of stitches running lengthwise. The back has prominent courses—rows

Fig. 14–7   *Flat-bed knitting machine. (Courtesy of H. Stoll GmbH & Co.)*

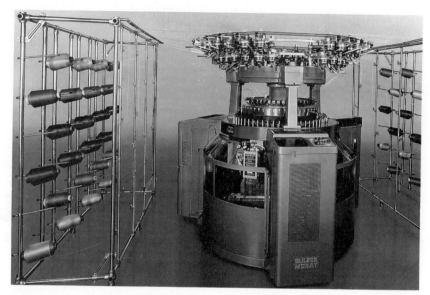

Fig. 14–8   *Circular knitting machine. (Courtesy of Sulzer Morat GmbH.)*

of stitches running crosswise (see Figure 14-9). Stretch a swatch of jersey crosswise and it will curl to the back at the lengthwise edges. The ends will curl toward the face. Yarns ravel crosswise because the yarns run horizontally in the fabric. Cut edges or broken yarns may create problems with runs. Single jerseys made of staple-fiber yarns resist running because of fiber cohesiveness.

The single-jersey structure, or plain knit, is widely used because it is the fastest method of filling knitting and is made on the least complicated knitting machine.

Jersey is a light- to heavyweight fabric usually knitted on a circular-jersey machine and sold in tubular form or cut and sold as flat goods. When tubular fabrics are pressed in finishing, the creases are seldom parallel to the wales of the fabric—they are off-grain. The tubular cloth does not need to be cut and opened out when cutting out product parts, unless there is a specific reason for doing so.

Figure 14-16 shows a T-shirt that was cut from tubular cotton jersey with crosswise stripes. When

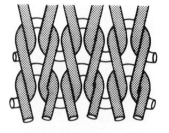

(a) Technical Face

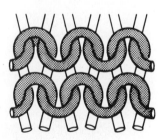

(b) Technical Back

Fig. 14–9   *Close-up of a plain-jersey stitch: technical face* (left); *technical back* (right).

Fig. 14–10   *Single jersey: (a) technical face; (b) technical back.*

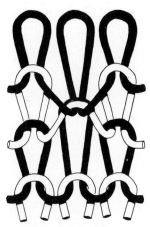

Single needle, single course
tuck stitch

Fig. 14–11 *Tuck stitch. (Courtesy of* Knitting Times, *the official publication of National Knitwear and Sportswear Association.)*

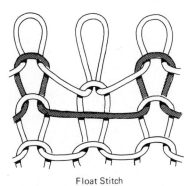

Float Stitch

Fig. 14–13 *Float, or miss, stitch. (Courtesy of* Knitting Times, *the official publication of National Knitwear and Sportswear Association.)*

purchased, the stripes were parallel and the side seam was perpendicular to the lower edge. After washing, the fabric assumed its normal position, causing the side seams to twist and the stripes to spiral.

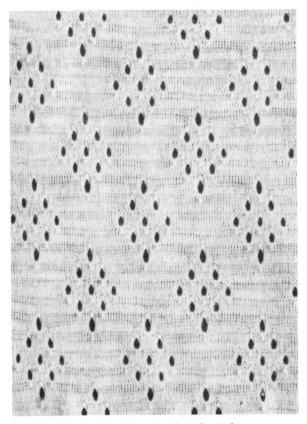

Fig. 14–12 *Fabric knitted with tuck stitch.*

End uses for plain-knit structures include hosiery, underwear, shirts, T-shirts, dresses, and sweaters.

Variations in plain knit are made by programming the machines to knit stitches together, to drop stitches, and to use colored yarns to form patterns or vertical stripes. Extra yarns or slivers are used to make pile fabrics like terrycloth, velour, and fake-fur fabrics.

Two stitches commonly used to make jersey variations are the tuck stitch and the float stitch. *Tuck stitches* are used to create blisters, puckers, or other special effects and to secure laid-in yarns or long floats of yarns on the back of the fabric. Figure 14-12 shows tuck stitches in fabric. *Float stitches* are used to carry yarns of different colors on the back of fabric for knitted-in designs. *Stockinette* is another name for jersey. This term usually implies a coarser spun yarn and a heavier or bulkier fabric.

Jacquard Jerseys *Single-figured jerseys* are made by a jacquard mechanism on circular-jersey machines. An alternative is the use of electronic controls to knit patterns in as the fabric is being produced. These patterns can consist of combinations of stitches such as knit, tuck, and float, combinations of yarns that vary by color or texture, or incorporation of yarns in specific areas within the fabric, much like a true tapestry weave for woven fabrics. Jacquard jerseys are the simplest of these patterned fabrics. In a jacquard jersey, the pattern develops because of different stitch types, yarn colors, or a combination of stitch type and yarn color. Figure 14-14 shows the face and back of a simple jacquard jersey where the color knit on the face changes to create the pattern.

In a more complicated patterned single knit fabric, the yarn used to create a pattern in the fabric is knit into the fabric in that area only. This is the knit

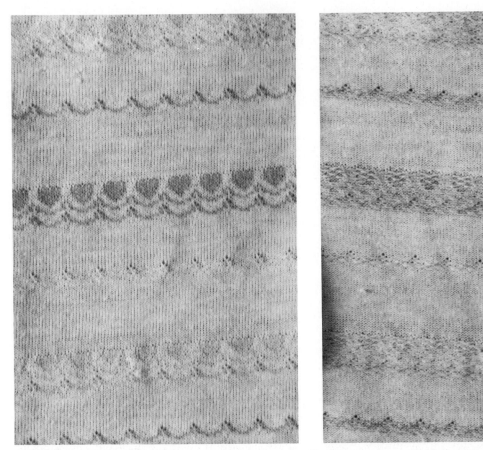

Fig. 14–14 *Jacquard jersey: face* (left) *and back* (right). *Note the pattern on the face and the floats on the back.*

counterpart to a true tapestry weave. This fabric is referred to as an intarsia.

Intarsia designs in jersey are made by laying in colored yarns. True intarsia designs have a clear pattern on both the right and wrong side of the cloth with no bird's eye backing that is characteristic of jacquard designs. Fabrics have no extra weight, and the stretch is not impaired. Mock intarsia designs are made by knitting and float-knitting (float or miss stitch), which results in a heavier-weight fabric with

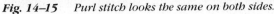

Fig. 14–15 *Purl stitch looks the same on both sides.*

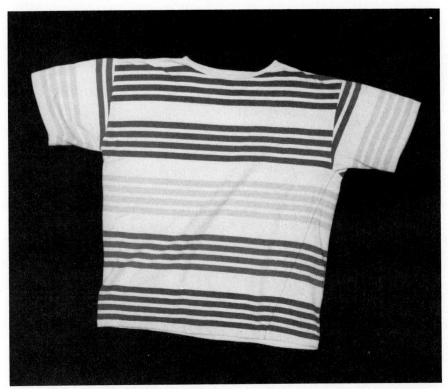

Fig. 14–16 *T-shirt showing skew of the circular knit jersey fabric. Note how the side seam twists toward the front of the shirt.*

floating yarns on the reverse side. These floating yarns reduce the elasticity of the fabric and may snag readily. Compare both fabrics in Figure 14-17.

Pile Jerseys *Pile jerseys* are made on a modified circular jersey machine. The fabrics look like woven pile but are more pliable and stretchy. The pile surface may consist of (1) cut or uncut loops of yarn or (2) fibers (see the following discussion of sliver knits). In velour and knit terrycloth, the fabric is made with two sets of yarns. One yarn set is spun yarns and will eventually form the pile surface of the finished fabric. The other set is a BCF yarn that has been processed in such a way as to shrink when heated. Both yarn sets are knit together to form the fabric. At this point, the fabric looks like a very loose, poor-quality jersey. The fabric is heat set and the BCF yarn shrinks. The spun yarns form the pile and the fabric is finished to produce the appropriate look.

Knitted terrycloth is a loop pile used for beachwear, robes, and babies' towels and washcloths. It is softer and more absorbent than woven terry but does not hold its shape as well. *Velour* is a cut-pile fashion fabric used in men's wear, in women's pantsuits, and in robes. Velour is knit with loops that are cut evenly. Then the yarn twist is uncurled to give better coverage and the fabric is dyed, tentered, and steamed.

Sliver-pile knits are made on a special weft-knit, circular, sliver-knitting machine and are called furlike, high-pile, or deep-pile fabrics. Examine Figure 14-19 and notice that yarns are used for the ground; the *sliver* furnishes the fibers for the pile. Sliver is an untwisted rope of fiber and is the product of either carding, drawing, or combing (Chapter 10).

Fibers from the sliver are picked up by the knitting needles—along with the ground yarns—and are knit into place as the stitch is formed. A denser pile can be obtained with sliver than with yarn because the amount of face fiber is not limited by yarn size or by the distance between yarns (Figure 14-20).

The surface pile can be made with heat-sensitive manufactured fibers to resemble guard hairs for a more realistic look, printed to resemble more exotic furs like pony, jaguar, or leopard, or used in other designs for fun furs. Fibers are usually solution dyed because piece dyeing distorts the pile. Furlike fabrics are used for the shells (the outer layer) and for linings (the inner layer) of coats and jackets. Some *fake furs* are also used for casual upholstery fabrics.

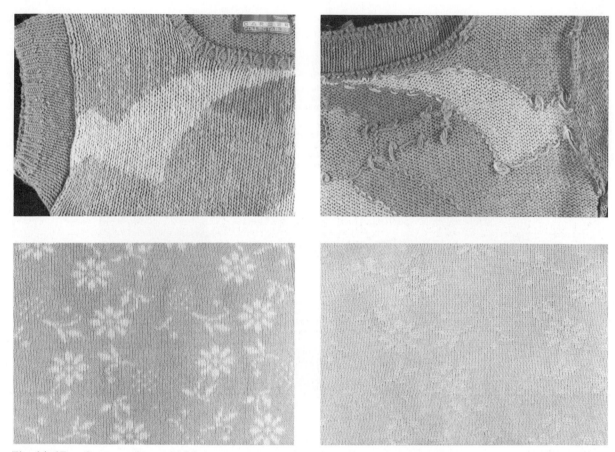

Fig. 14–17 *Compare these two fabrics: true intarsia, face* (top left) *and back* (top right); *mock intarsia, face* (bottom left) *and back* (bottom right).

Furlike fabrics are much lighter in weight, are much more pliable, and have better comfort characteristics than real fur. They require no special storage. A dry cleaner can successfully clean furlike fabrics by using a cold tumble dryer and combing the pile rather than steam pressing it.

Weft-Insertion Jersey In *weft insertion*, a yarn of any type is laid in a course as that course is being knit. The yarn is not knit into stitches, but is laid in the loops of the stitches as they are being formed. The yarn may be novelty, large, irregular, or very low twist, and thus not suitable for normal knitting. The laid-in yarn increases the crosswise stability of the fabric. This yarn may be used for decorative, strength, stability, or comfort reasons; it may be designed to produce a nap during finishing. In-laid yarns for pile-effect fabrics such as napped jerseys may have so little twist that they are too weak to withstand the stress of knitting (see Figure 14-21).

DOUBLE-FILLING KNITS *Double-filling knits* are made using a machine with two sets of needles, with the second bed or set of needles located at a right angle to the first bed of needles. Most double-knitting machines have the two needle beds arranged in an inverted V and are called *vee-bed machines*. The double-knit fabric may be made with one or more sets of yarns. Double knits are categorized based on the arrangement of the needles in the double-knitting machine, or the gait of the machine. In a *rib-gait machine*, the two beds of needles are positioned so that both needles can be knitting at the same time. The needles of one bed are located in the spaces between the needles of the other bed. In *interlock gaiting*, the needles are positioned so that only one needle bed can be knitting at a time. The needles of one bed are located directly across from the needles of the other bed (see Figure 14–22 for rib and interlock gaiting).

Double-knit fabrics can be made with any combination of the four stitches. In the flat-bed machine,

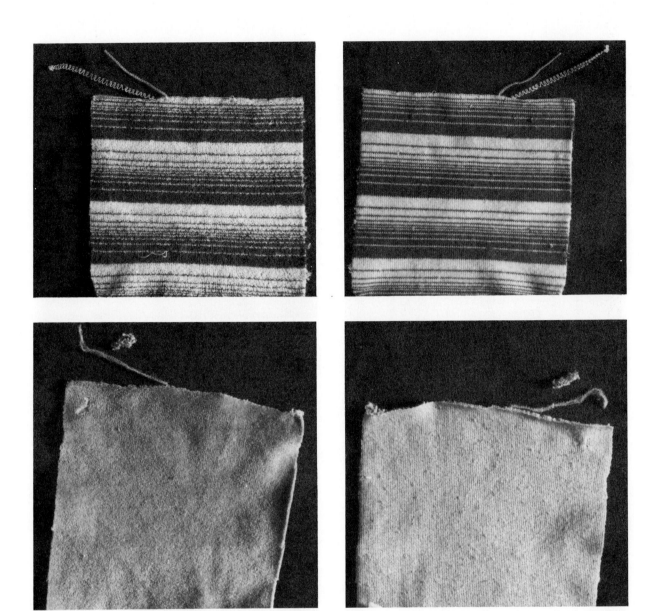

Fig. 14–18 *Pile filling knit fabrics: knit terry, face* (top left) *and back* (top right); *velour, face* (bottom left) *and back* (bottom right). *Note the yarns ravelled from each fabric and the side that forms the fashion side of the fabrics.*

the needles from one bed pull the loops to the back and those in the other bed pull the loops to the front (Figure 14-23). In the circular machine, the loops are pulled to the face and back by setting one set of needles vertically in a cylinder and the other set of needles horizontally in a dial or cam (Figure 14-24).

Double-knit fabrics have two-way stretch and relatively high dimensional stability. They do not curl at the edges and are less apt to stretch out than single knits. They do not run. Double knits can resemble any woven structure and are often given the

woven fabric name—denim, seersucker, double piqué, and the like.

A technique used to illustrate the production of double knits is a diagram based on the two needle beds and the type of gaiting. A center horizontal line represents the space between the beds. A short vertical line represents a needle. In *interlock gaiting*, the short vertical lines are directly opposite each other (Figure 14-25). In *rib gaiting*, the needle lines stop at the horizontal line and needle lines on one side of the line are staggered with needle lines on the opposite side (Figure 14-26). In the diagram, a

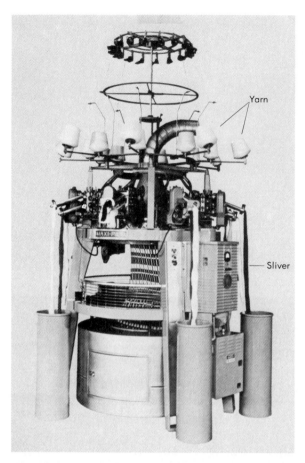

Fig. 14–19 *Sliver-knitting machine. (Courtesy of Rockwell International Corp.)*

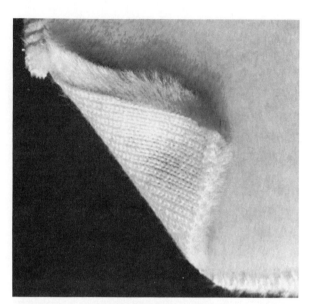

Fig. 14–20 *Sliver-knit furlike fabric.*

Double-knit jersey, like *interlock jersey*, looks the same on both sides. It differs in that it is made on rib gaiting and needles from the cam and cylinder are not opposite each other but are positioned so that the needles from one bed work between the needles from the other bed. They knit a 1 × 1 rib. To distinguish between an interlock and a rib-gaiting fabric, cut along a course and stretch the edge widthwise. Examine the edge. If it is interlock, there

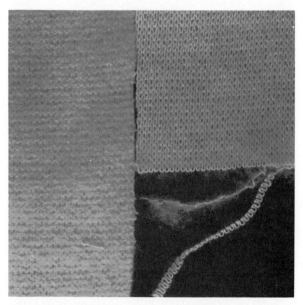

Fig. 14–21 *Weft-insertion weft or filling knit: napped side* (left) *and technical face with knitting and inlaid yarns* (right).

loop represents a knit stitch, an inverted V represents a tuck stitch, and a — represents a float or miss stitch. Thus a 1 × 1 rib would be diagrammed on rib gaiting, as shown in Figure 14-27. Each course required to produce the pattern is diagrammed separately and is referred to as a step. A simple interlock would be diagrammed in two steps on interlock gaiting because two steps are required to create the interlock fabric (see Figure 14-28). A double knit on interlock gaiting might be a ponte de roma, which requires four steps to create the fabric (see Figure 14-29). A double knit on rib gaiting might be a la coste, which requires eight steps in knitting (see Figure 14-30). An easy way to identify a double knit is to look at the edge of the fabric parallel to a course. If all loops point in one direction it is a single knit. If some of the loops point toward the front and some toward the back, it is a double knit. If the loops are directly opposite each other, it is made with interlock gaiting. If the loops are not directly opposite each other, it is made with rib gaiting.

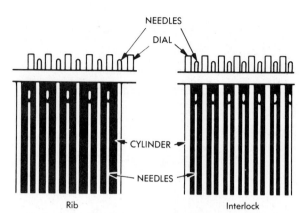

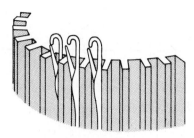

Fig. 14–22   *Gaiting: rib* (left); *interlock* (right).

(a) Section of Cylinder

(b) Cylinder

Fig. 14–24   *(a) Needle beds and (b) knitting action in circular-knitting machine, rib gait. (Courtesy of* Knitting Times, *the official publication of National Knitwear and Sportswear Association.)*

will be a back stitch opposite each front stitch; if it is rib double knit, the back stitches will alternate between the front stitches.

Rib Structure   A *rib structure* is made of face wales and back wales. The lengthwise ridges are formed on both sides of the fabric by pulling stitches first to the face and next to the back of the

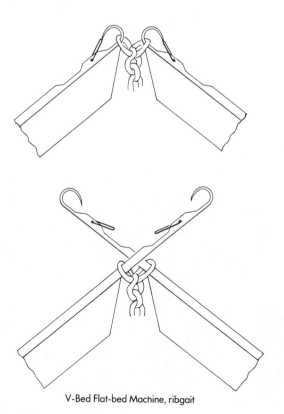

V-Bed Flat-bed Machine, ribgait

Fig. 14–23   *Needle action in flat-bed machine. (Courtesy of* Knitting Times, *the official publication of National Knitwear and Sportswear Association.)*

fabric in adjacent stitches or groups of stitches. These may be in various combinations, 1×1, 2×2, 2×3, and so on (Figure 14–31). Figure 14–32 shows a T-shirt fabric in a combination plain and rib knit. The 1×1 rib is the simplest double-knit fabric produced using rib gaiting. It usually consists of one set of yarns.

Rib knits have the same appearance on the face and back. They generally have twice the extensibility crosswise as that of single jersey. Rib knits do not curl at the edges, but they run. They unravel from the end knit last. They are usually twice as thick as single jersey.

Jacquard double knits have almost limitless design possibilities. The intermeshing of the two yarns is the same as for the double-knit jersey but with added needle-selecting mechanisms (Figure 14–33). Although the names of woven fabrics are often used for double knits that resemble them, more often the term double knit is the only name used to identify this type of fabric.

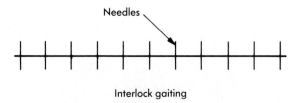

Fig. 14–25   Interlock gaiting.

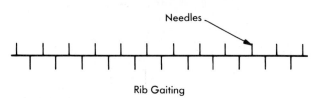

Fig. 14–26   Rib gaiting.

Fig. 14–27   1 × 1 rib (rib gaiting).

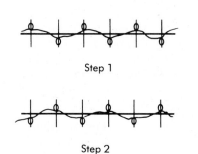

Fig. 14–28   Interlock diagram.

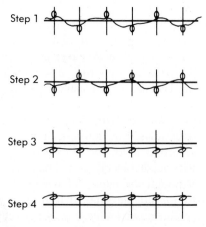

Fig. 14–29   Ponte de roma (interlock gaiting).

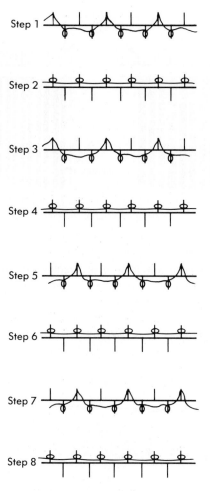

Fig. 14–30   La coste (rib gaiting).

Purl Structure   *Purl knits* usually are made on machines with two needle beds and double-hooked needles with either type of gaiting. Purl is generally the slowest form of knitting, but it is also the most versatile. The purl is the only filling-knitting machine that can produce all three types of filling-knit fabrics—plain, rib, and purl—although as a rule not as economically. Thus a purl machine can make a fabric that is part plain, part rib, and part purl.

Fabrics produced by the purl stitch are thick, wide, and short as compared to single jersey with the same number of plain stitches. Fabrics do not curl, but they do run and may be made to unravel from both ends (see Figure 14–34).

The two major end uses for purl structures are children's and infants' wear and sweaters. Purl stitches may be used at the shoulder seams of sweaters to stabilize the garment due to low crosswise stretch compared to plain knits.

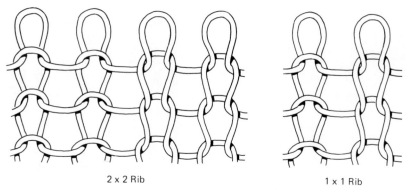

Fig. 14–31 *Rib stitches: 2 × 2 rib (left); 1 × 1 rib (right).*

A less expensive alternative to a purl knit is the use of the technical back of a jersey or stockinette as the fashion side of the fabric. The appearance is the same, but the performance of the fabric is slightly different. Most consumers would not be aware of the difference and would get the look desired without the additional cost due to the more specialized nature of the knitting machine and the slower knitting speeds.

Interlock Structure The *interlock* is the simplest double-knit fabric produced using interlock gaiting (see Figure 14–28). Interlock fabrics are composed of two 1 × 1 rib stitches intermeshed. (Figure 14–35 is offset for clarity.)

Both sides of the fabric look alike and resemble the face side of single jersey. Interlock stretches like plain jersey, but the fabric is firmer. Interlocks do not curl and fabrics run and unravel from one end only.

Most interlock fabrics are plain or printed. Colored yarns can be knitted to give spot effects or horizontal or vertical stripes.

SHAPING ON THE KNITTING MACHINE Garment parts—sweater bodies, fronts, backs, sleeves, skirts, socks, seamed hosiery, and collars—can be knitted to shape on flat-bed machines. The stitch used for shaping is called *loop transfer.* A knit stitch is transferred from one needle to another, usually near the end of a course, so that the width of the fabric is decreased. The process, called *fashioning,* is used to shape parts like armholes, neckline curves, collar points, and finish edges.

A *looping machine* is used to join the shoulders and sleeves of the shaped parts with the effect of continuous knitting rather than of seams. This machine is also used to join collars to cut-and-sewn knit garments.

Fig. 14–32 *Rib-knit fabric: fabric relaxed, left side 2 × 2 rib, technical face (top); fabric stretched to show difference in stitches (bottom).*

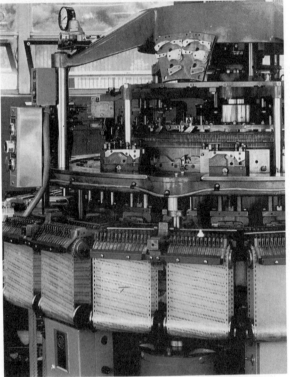

Fig. 14–33 *Jacquard knitting machine. (Courtesy of Rockwell International).*

To identify fashioned garments, look for "fashion marks" accompanied by an increase or decrease in the number of wales (Figure 14–36). Mock fashion marks are sometimes put in the garment but they are not accompanied by an increase or decrease in the number of wales, so no shaping is done by the mock fashion marks (Figure 14–37). Full-fashioned sweaters are almost always made with a jersey stitch. Circular jersey sweaters are cut and sewn.

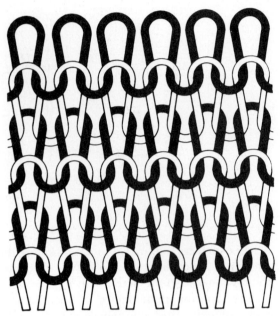

Fig. 14–34 *Purl fabric. (Courtesy of* Knitting Times, *the official publication of National Knitwear and Sportswear Association.)*

Full-fashioned garments do not necessarily fit better than cut-and-sewn garments because fit depends on the size and shape of the pieces. But full-fashioned garments are always on-grain, look better to the discerning eye, and should not become misshapen during washing due to twisted seams.

See Table 14–2 for a summary of the differences and similarities between flat-bed and circular machines from a single- and double-knit perspective.

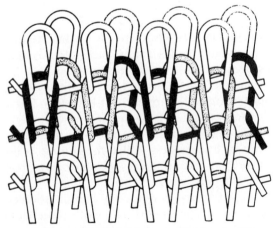

Fig. 14–35 *Interlock (diagram offset for clarity). (Courtesy of* Knitting Times, *the official publication of National Knitwear and Sportswear Association.)*

Fig. 14–36 *Raglan sleeve portion of full-fashioned sweater. Note that stitches are dropped.*

Fig. 14–37 *Raglan sleeve portion of cut-and-sewn sweater. Note the mock fashion marks.*

HOSIERY Fashion and manufactured fibers have been responsible for many of the developments in hosiery. Spun yarns are used for socks, of any fiber content. Two-ply mercerized cotton, called *lisle,* is stronger and more durable than regular cotton. Spandex is used in the tops of socks. Nylon is commonly used as reinforcement in the heels and toes of socks. Filament nylon yarns, which may be monofilament or multifilament, are used in women's hosiery and lighter weight socks (see Figure 14–38).

All hosiery is a filling knit. The types include plain (or jersey), rib, mesh, and micromesh. The plain knit has stretch in both directions, and hose can be very sheer if made of fine denier fibers. Plain knit has the disadvantage of running readily when a loop is broken. Mesh hose are lacelike knits that do not run, but they snag and holes will develop. Micromesh has loops knitted so that a run goes up only. Mesh and micromesh stockings are not as elastic or as smooth as plain jersey. Rib stitches and jersey are used in socks. Fancy knits such as cables and argyles are often used in socks.

Seamless hose have the same number of stitches from top to toe and are knit on circular machines. Shaping may be done by decreasing the size of the loop gradually from top to toe. If shaping is done at toe and heel, a circular fashioning mechanism that drops stitches is used. Heavier yarn can be knit into toe and heel to give greater comfort and durability. Seamless hosiery is knit in one piece as a continuous operation. When knitting is finished, the toe is closed and the stocking is turned right side out.

Hosiery with shaped heels are *preboarded,* a process in which stockings are placed on metal leg forms of the correct size and shape and then steamed to press. Tube socks and stockings do not have shaped heels. They are seamed across the toe end.

Panty hose are usually made from textured stretch nylon. The panty portion is heavier than the stocking portion. Panty hose are knitted in tube shape with a guide for slitting. After the panty section is slit, two tubes are stitched together in a U-shaped crotch seam with a firm, serged stitch. A separate crotch section is often inserted for better fit.

WARP KNITTING

Warp knitting is unique in that it developed as a machine technique without ever having been a hand technique. Warp knitting started about 1775 with the invention of the *tricot* (pronounced tree-*ko*) *machine* by Crane of England. The tricot machine is sometimes called a warp loom because it uses one or more sets of yarns that are wound on warp beams and mounted on the knitting machine.

Warp knitting provides the fastest means of making fabric from yarns. It has been said that warp knits combine the best qualities of both double

Table 14–2   Filling-Knitting Machines and Fabrics

| | Single Knit | | Double Knit | |
	Jersey—Flat	Jersey—Circular	Flat (Rib/Interlock)	Circular (Rib/Interlock)
Description	Straight bar holding one set of latch needles	See Figure 14–10. One set of latch needles	Two flat needle beds formed in Λ position, see Figure 14–23	See Figure 14–24. One set of needles mounted on dial, one set on cylinder
	Yarn carried back and forth	Yarn carried around	Yarns carried back and forth	Multiple-feed yarn carried around needle selection mechanism
	Purpose is to shape items	Electronic control patterns make range of designs	Stitch-transfer carriage can switch from one bed to another to make variety of stitches	
Kinds of knits and end uses	Basic knit stitch	Workhorse of knitting industry		Double knits—plain and jacquard double knits
	Fabric has different appearance on face and back	Fabric has different appearance face and back	Same appearance face and back	
	Full-fashioned garments	High-volume production Seamless hose Jersey, velour, terry	Used when fabric must have finished edge Collars, trims	
Advantages	Economical use of yarn Garments always on grain Design variations possible	Fastest method	Less waste than circular rib	High-speed production Excellent design flexibility Versatile in yarn usage
Limitations	Quite slow in production Higher priced end product Single-feed system	Variety of pattern possibilities available	Slow speed	Complex machine Downtime can be a problem

knits and wovens. Warp-knit fabrics tend to be less resilient and lighter weight than filling knits. They can have stability in both directions of the fabric or exhibit a degree of stretch, as determined by the control of the knitting stitch.

Warp knitting produces a vertical-loop construction (see Figure 14–39). It is a machine process of making fabric in flat or sheet form using one or more *sets* of warp yarns that are fed from warp beams to a row of knitting needles extending across the width of the machine. Each set of yarns is controlled by yarn guides mounted in a guide bar that also extends across the width of the machine. Warp-knitting machines are wider than most looms. If there is one set of yarns, the machine will have one warp beam and one guide bar; if there are two sets of yarns, there will be two warp beams and two guide bars, and so on: hence the terms *one-bar tricot* and *two-bar tricot*. All guide bars feed yarn to the same set of needles. Each yarn guide on the bar guides one yarn represent the movement of the guide bar that controls yarn movement. Since all the needles knit at one time, each row of points represents the needles used to produce one course. The guide bar diagram shows yarn movement for each course. Thus the diagram for each row of points represents the movement of the guide bar to create the yarn loops for that course. The next row of points would represent the next course, and so on until one complete repeat has been represented. The diagram starts at the bottom row of points and moves up the paper from course to course as time progresses. Figure 14–39 is a diagram for a warp knit. In Figure 14–40, steps (a) through (g) show the movement of the guide bar as it directs the yarn's movement to create that warp-knit stitch. In (a) of Figure 14–41, the seven steps are combined in one diagram; in (b), the resulting yarn loop is shown; in (c), the two repeats of the pattern are shown. In Figure 14–42, the knitting action of a tricot machine is diagrammed.

Yarn from the front bar usually predominates on the surface, whereas yarn from the back bars provides run resistance, elasticity, and weight.

Apparel end uses for warp knits include lingerie, underwear, sportswear, and outerwear. Industrial end uses are the most rapidly expanding area and include fabrics for sun and light protection, for controlling rock falls, for grass collection, for snow barriers, and for dam reinforcement. Warp-knit fabrics are also used as medical implants such as artificial veins and tissue-support fabrics.

Even though warp knitting is fast, warp knits are not inexpensive because the process requires very regular yarns. The cost of the yarns offsets the fast speed of the process.

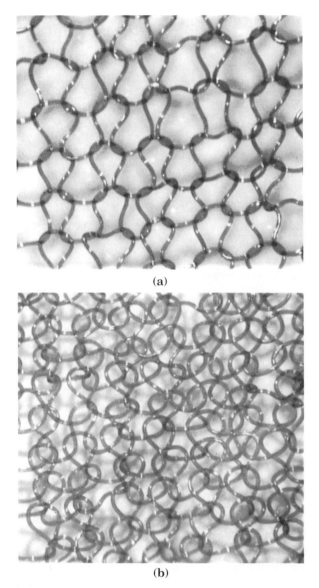

(a)

(b)

Fig. 14–38 *Nylon Cantrece: (a) stretched; (b) relaxed. (Courtesy of E. I. du Pont de Nemours & Company.)*

to the hook of one knitting needle. Chains with links of various heights control the movement of the guide bars. More guide bars give greater design flexibility. The loops of one course are all made simultaneously when the guide bar rises and moves sideways, laying the yarns around the needles to form the loops, which are then pulled down through the loops of the preceding course.

Warp knits are usually diagrammed using a *point-paper notation*. In this notation, each point in a horizontal row represents a needle. Arrows

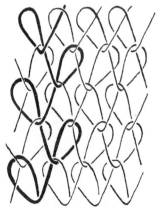

Fig. 14–39 *Warp-knitting stitch.*

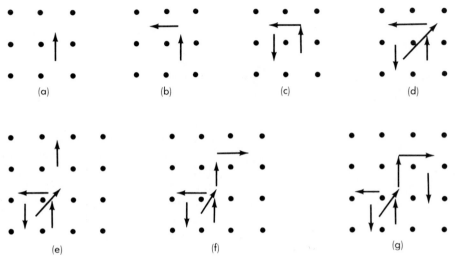

Fig. 14–40   *Guide-bar movements, step by step, for warp-knit stitch.*

Machines Used in Warp Knitting

Warp knits are classified by the equipment type used to produce the fabric and the characteristics of the resulting fabric. Tricot machines use a single set of spring-beard or compound needles. Tricot-knitting machines with computer-controlled guide bars, electronic beam control, and computerized take-up are able to knit 2,000 courses per minute. Raschel machines use one or two sets of vertically mounted latch needles. Jacquard raschel knitting machines with computer-controlled guide bars are available. The differences between the fabrics produced by these machines have become less distinct. Several types of warp knitting machine are listed in Table 14-3. Tricot and raschel machines, however, account for the manufacture of more than 95 percent of all warp-knit goods.

Warp Knits Versus Filling Knits

Warp and filling knits differ because of the different knitting techniques and the machines used in their manufacture. The major differences are summarized in Table 14-4.

Warp-Knit Fabrics

TRICOT WARP KNITS   The name *tricot* has been used as a generic name for all warp-knit fabric. Tricot comes from the French word *tricoter*, meaning *to knit*. It is the fabric produced on the tricot machine using the *plain stitch.*

The plain stitch is shown in Figure 14–43. The face of the fabric is formed of the vertical portion of loops and the back has the horizontal portion of loops. The face has a much finer appearance than

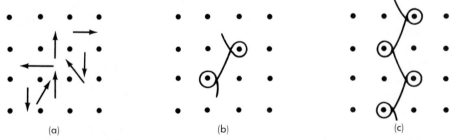

Fig. 14–41   *Guide-bar movements: (a) all steps of the guide-bar movement; (b) yarn movement following the guide-bar movement; (c) series of yarn loops creating warp-knit fabric.*

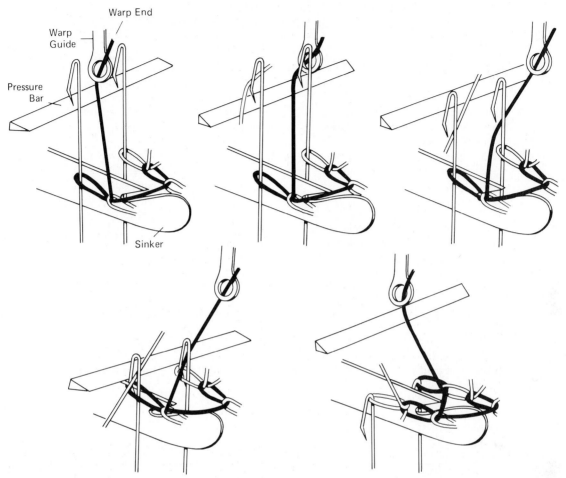

Fig. 14-42 *Knitting action of tricot machine. (Courtesy of* Knitting Times, *the official publication of National Knitwear and Sportswear Association.)*

the back. Tricot is runproof and nonraveling. The fabric will curl just as filling-knit jersey does. Tricot has greater elasticity in the crosswise direction. Some important end uses of tricot fabrics include lingerie, sleepwear, shirts, blouses, uniforms, dresses, and automotive upholstery.

The tricot machine is the mainstay of the warp-knitting industry (Figure 14-44). It is a high-speed machine that can knit flat fabric up to 170 inches wide. The machine makes a plain-jersey stitch or can be modified to make many designs. Another modification is the attachment for laying in yarn in a tricot structure.

Plain tricot is made on a machine employing one set of needles and two guide bars. Filament yarns are used in either smooth or textured form. In the standard ranges of 15-40 denier, nylon tricot is lightweight (17.5-6.5 yards/pound), has excep-

tional strength and durability, and can be heat set for dimensional stability. One of the unique features of nylon tricot is that the same piece of gray goods can be finished under different tensions to different widths and different appearances; for example, 168-inch gray goods can be finished at 98, 108, 120, 180, or 200 inches wide.

Brushed tricots have a velvetlike surface of loops raised from the surface. Heat-set nylon must be used, so it is possible to raise the loops without breaking them. The fabric is versatile and is used in evening gowns, shoes, slacks, upholstery, and draperies.

The knit stitches have long underlaps. One set of yarns is carried over 3-5 wales to form floats; the second set of yarns interloops with adjacent yarns. Nylon is used for the adjacent looping to provide strength and durability. The long floats are broken

Table 14–3   Warp-Knitting Machines

Tricot	Raschel	Simplex	Milanese
Single bed	One or two needle beds	Two sets of needles	Flat—spring-beard needles
Spring-beard needles or compound needles	Latch needles Coarse guage	Spring-beard needles	Circular—latch needles
2-3-4 bars indicate number of sets of warp yarns	May have as many as 65 guide bars		Yarn travels diagonally from one side of material to the other
Simple fabric	Complex fabric		
High-speed, high-volume	Great design possibilities	Seldom used	Seldom used
Usually filament yarns	Usually spun or spun and filament yarns		
Wide fabric, 170 inches	Narrow fabric, 100 inches		
End Uses			
Plain, patterned, striped, brushed fabric Underwear Outerwear Upholstery	Sheer laces and nets Draperies Power net Thermal cloth Outerwear	Warp double knits Gloves	Underwear Outerwear

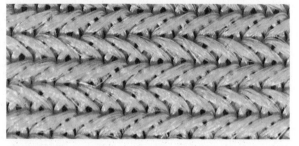

Fig. 14–43   *Two-bar tricot: technical face* (top); *technical back* (bottom).

when the fabric is finished. The napped side is used as the fashion side of the fabric even though it is the technical back (Figure 14–45).

Satinlike tricots are made in the same way as napped tricots except that the finishing processes differ. These fabrics are usually 100 percent nylon or polyester and the floats are longer.

Tricot-net fabric can be made by skipping every other needle so only half as much yarn is used and open spaces are created in the fabric.

Tuck effects use the same yarns as in the striped fabrics, but a change in the yarn arrangement forms a tuck. The tucks may be straight, wavy, irregular, intermittent, wide, or narrow.

Automotive tricot upholstery—a double-knit velvet—has been introduced (see Figure 14–46). The fabric is made in a manner similar to that of velvet. Two layers of fabric are knit face to face with a pile yarn connecting the two layers. The layers are separated when the pile yarn is cut. Pile

Fig. 14–44   *Mayer warp-knitting machine. (Courtesy of Mayer Textile Machine Corp.)*

height is related to the distance between the two layers.

RASCHEL-WARP KNITS   The raschel-warp knitting machine has one or two needle beds with latch needles set in a vertical position and as many as 78 guide bars. The fabric comes from the knitting frame almost vertically instead of horizontally as in the tricot machine. The various raschel machines knit a wide variety of fabrics from gossamer-sheer nets and veilings to very heavy carpets.

Raschel knits are used industrially for a variety of products including laundry bags, fish nets, dye nets, safety nets, and covers for swimming pools.

Raschel fabrics have rows of chainlike loops called *pillars*, with laid-in yarns in various lapping configurations (Figures 14–47 and 14–48). These fabrics can be identified by raveling the laid-in yarn and noticing that the fabric splits or comes apart length-

wise. Window treatment fabrics and outerwear fabrics are knitted on this standard-type machine.

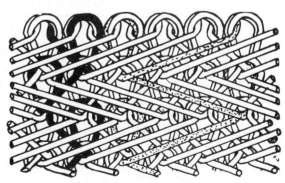

Fig. 14–45   *Warp knit velour before napping. Black yarn is nylon; white and gray yarns will be broken during napping. (Courtesy of* Knitting Times, *the official publication of National Knitwear and Sportswear Association.)*

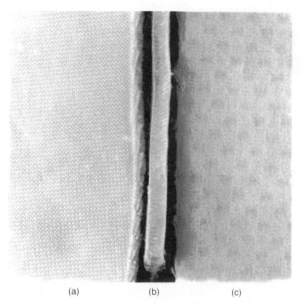

Fig. 14-46   *Knit-velour car upholstery: (a) as knit; (b) cross-sectional view; (c) after separation.*

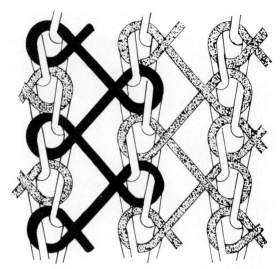

Fig. 14-47   *Raschel knit. (Courtesy of* Knitting Times, *the official publication of National Knitwear and Sportswear Association.)*

Carpets have been knitted since the early 1950s. Since their production is faster, knitted carpets are cheaper to make than woven carpets. Tufted carpets, being much cheaper to produce, have captured a major share of the carpet market. Knitted carpets have two- or three-ply warps for lengthwise stability, laid-in crosswise yarns for body and crosswise stability, and pile yarns. Knitted carpets can be identified by looking for chains of stitches on the underside. They seldom have a secondary backing. These carpets are usually commercial or contract carpets.

Lace and curtain nets of the kind made on Leavers lace machines (see Chapter 15) can be made at much higher speeds on a Raschel machine. Window-treatment nets, which can have square, dia-

Table 14-4   Comparison of Filling and Warp Knits

Filling Knits	*Warp Knits*
Yarns run horizontally	Yarns run vertically
Loops joined one to another in the same course	Loops joined one to another in adjoining course
Connections are horizontal	Connections are diagonal
More design possibilities	Higher productivity
More compact fabric	More compact fabric
Two-way stretch	Crosswise stretch, little lengthwise stretch
Run, most ravel	Do not run or ravel
Hand or machine process	Machine process
Flat or circular	Flat
Can have finished edges	
Can knit shaped garments, garment pieces, or yardage	Produced as yardage

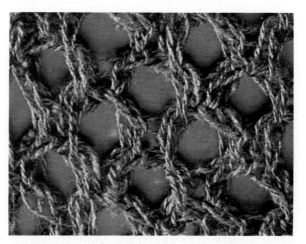

Fig. 14–49   *Raschel fabric.*

Fig. 14–48   *Raschel knit with extra yarn: technical face of fabric* (left); *technical back of fabric* (right).

mond, or hexagonal meshes, are made on tricot machines. Laces are usually made of nylon or polyester (Figure 14–49).

Thermal cloth has pockets knitted in to trap heat from the body; it looks like woven waffle cloth and is used mainly for winter underwear. This knit is also used for some thermal blankets.

Power net is an elasticized fabric used for foundation garments and bathing suits. Nylon is used for the two-bar ground construction and spandex is laid in by two other guide bars (Figure 14–50).

INSERTION WARP KNITS Insertion of yarns in the warp knit structure is a relatively simple concept. Yarns are laid in the stitches during the knitting process but do not form any stitches. These yarns provide directional stability and can be laid in in any direction or at an angle. Fabric characteristics can be engineered for desired properties. Yarns that are not appropriate for knitting can be used, such as extremely coarse, fine, or irregular yarns and yarns of fibers that have low flexibility, such as carbon or glass. These fabrics are used in aircraft and aerospace components, automotive parts, boat hulls, ballistic protective clothing, structural building elements, interlinings for apparel, and window treatment and wall covering fabrics.

Weft insertion is done by a warp knitting machine with a weft-laying attachment. Several types are available. The simplest attachment carries a single filling yarn to and fro across the warp knitter, and this yarn is then fed steadily into the needle

zone of the machine. A firm selvage is formed on each side.

More complex attachments supply a sheet of filling yarns to a conveyor that travels to and fro across the machine. The yarns are then fed into the stitching area of the machine. A cutting device trims filling yarn "tails" from the selvages and a vacuum removes the tailings.

Weft-insertion fabrics offer the best combination of properties of both woven and knitted cloth: namely, strength, comfort, cover without bulk, and

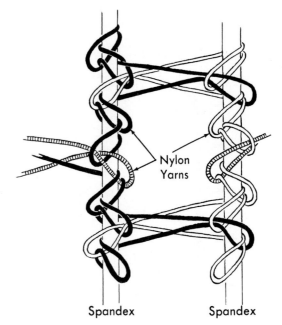

Fig. 14–50   *Raschel power-net stitch.*

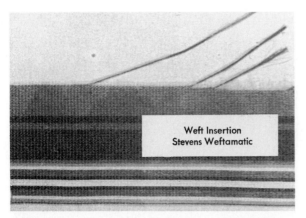

Fig. 14–51 *Weft insertion fabric. The raveled yarns are the polyester filling yarns that are inserted in the warp-knit stitches.*

Fig. 14–53 *Warp and weft insertion. Warp-knit casement fabric for windows.*

weight. They are lighter weight than double knits but have more covering power. They have increased crosswise stability of weaves but retain the comfort of knits (see Figure 14-51).

In weft-insertion warp knits, the inserted yarn is caught in a vertical chain of stitching. These fabrics are used for hospital curtains and table linens, as well as for other furnishing and industrial uses.

The insertion of *warp* yarn into a knit structure gives the fabric the vertical stability of woven cloth while retaining the horizontal stretch of knit fabric (Figure 14-52). The cloth is basically a single tricot.

Warp- and weft-insertion fabrics have characteristics very similar to woven fabrics. These fabrics can be much less expensive than woven fabrics and are available in wide widths. They are frequently used as window treatment fabrics (see Figure 14-53).

Minor Warp Knits

SIMPLEX The *simplex machine*, which is similar to the tricot machine, uses spring-beard needles, two needle bars, and two guide bars. It produces a two-faced fabric somewhat like circular double knits. End uses are fashion gloves, swimwear, and dresses.

MILANESE The *Milanese machine* is especially constructed to produce superior warp-knit fabrics. The machine can use both kinds of needles. The fabric it produces, equivalent to a two-bar tricot fabric, is made from two sets of warp yarns with one needle bar and one guide bar. But the lapping movements are arranged so each warp yarn moves across the full width of the fabric, one set knitting from right to left and the other from left to right. This results in a diagonal formation (Figure 14-54), which shows up on the back of the cloth. The face has a very fine rib. The fabric is runproof and is used for gloves and lingerie.

Narrow Knitted Fabrics

Narrow knitted fabrics are made on a few needles on a multiknit machine, either filling or warp-knitting machines. One of the more important types of narrow knitted fabrics are knit elastics. Knit elastics

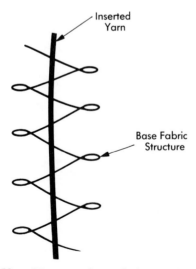

Fig. 14–52 *Diagram of warp-knit warp insertion.*

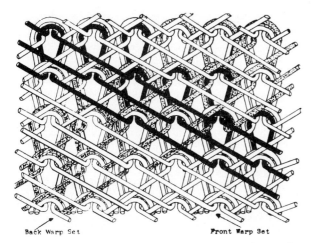

Fig. 14–54   *Milanese. (Courtesy of* Knitting Times, *the official publication of National Knitwear and Sportswear Association.)*

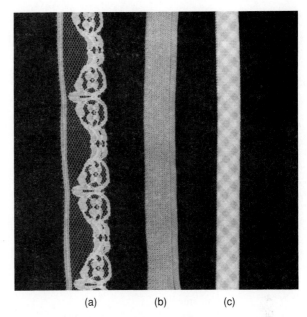

(a)   (b)   (c)

Fig. 14–56   *Narrow fabrics: (a) raschel knit; (b) flat filling knit; (c) circular knit.*

account for 35–40 percent of the narrow elastic market and are used in underwear, running shorts, slacks, fleece products, and hosiery. Hook and loop tape fasteners are warp-knit narrow fabrics (see Figure 14–55). Other trim and knit elastics are shown in Figure 14–56.

Narrow knitted fabrics of thermoplastic fiber are made on regular machines in wide widths and slit with hot knives to seal the edges. These are much cheaper to produce and are satisfactory if the heat sealing is properly done.

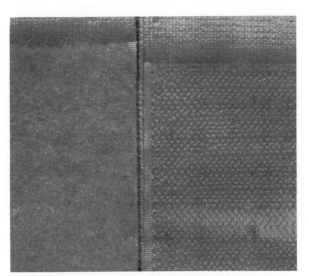

Fig. 14–55   *Velcro closure: looped fabric* (left); *hooked fabric* (right).

XXX

KEY TERMS

Mace test
Knitting
Filling or weft knitting
Warp knitting
Spring-beard needle
Latch needle
Compound needle
Stitch
Wale
Course
Gauge
Cut
Technical face
Technical back
Circular machines
Flat-bed machines
Knit stitch
Tuck stitch
Float or miss stitch
Purl or reverse stitch
Single-filling knit
Jersey
Stockinette
Jacquard jersey
Single-figured jersey
Intarsia
Pile jersey
Knitted terrycloth

Velour
Sliver-pile knit
Fake fur
Weft insertion
Double-filling knit
Vee-bed knitting machine
Rib gaiting
Interlock gaiting
Double-knit jersey
Rib
Jacquard double knit
Purl knits
Fashioning
Looping machine
Lisle
Tricot machine
Warp knitting
Point-paper notation
Tricot
Brushed tricot
Raschel
Lace
Power net
Weft insertion warp knit
Warp insertion warp knit
Simplex machine
Milanese machine

QUESTIONS

1. Compare the characteristics of woven and knit fabrics.
2. Compare the characteristics of filling and warp-knit fabrics.
3. Describe the differences in appearance and performance between the following pairs of knit fabrics:
   jersey and tricot
   ribknit and interlock
   jacquard jersey and raschel
   fleece and velour
4. Describe the performance that might be expected in the following products:
   100 percent combed cotton filling-knit jersey T-shirt
   100 percent modacrylic warp-insertion raschel casement drapery (smooth filament yarns and inserted thick-thin novelty yarns) for a public library
   100 percent olefin raschel warp-knit contract carpet of BCF yarns for hallway of office building
   80 percent nylon/20 percent spandex raschel-knit swimsuit

SUGGESTED READINGS

Raz, Sam (September, 1989). "New Concepts in Technical Fabric Engineering." *Knitting Times*, pp. 65–68.

Reisfeld, A. (April, 1989). "Multi-Axial Machine for Weft-Insertion Knits." *Knitting Times*, pp. 21–22.

Spencer, David J. (1983). *Knitting Technology.* New York: Pergamon Press.

Schwartz, Peter, Rhodes, Trevor, and Mohamed, Mansour (1982). *Fabric Forming Systems.* Park Ridge, NJ: Noyes Publications.

CHAPTER 15

Other Fabrication Methods

OBJECTIVES

- To understand fabrication processes beyond woven and knit fabrics.

- To understand the performance characteristics of film, foam, fiberweb and netlike structures, lace, braid, multiplex fabrics, leather, and fur.

- To recognize fabrics made using these techniques.

- To integrate the fabrication techniques with end uses.

*I*NCLUDED IN THIS CHAPTER ARE ITEMS MADE FROM solutions, fibers, yarns, and fabrics. This chapter discusses all fabrication methods except weaving and knitting. Many of the fabrication methods and fabrics produced by the methods discussed in this chapter do not fit the classic definition of a textile. These methods and fabrics are included in this text because they are used to produce textile products, they are used as substitutes for textiles, they are made of the same chemicals as textiles, or they are made of textile components like fibers, yarns, and fabrics. Many of these items are used for apparel and furnishings. They are equally, if not more, important to the industrial textile markets. This discussion begins with the simplest process and components and moves to the most complex.

FABRICS FROM SOLUTIONS

Films

Films are made directly from solution by melt-extrusion or by casting the solution onto a hot drum. The solutions are similar to the spinning solutions for fibers.

Apparel and furnishing textile films are made from vinyl or polyurethane solutions. They are similar in appearance but vary in the care required. Vinyl films are washable but become stiff in dry cleaning solvents. Urethane films are both washable and dry cleanable. Urethane films remain soft in cold weather, whereas vinyl films stiffen.

There are several kinds of films. *Plain films* are firm, dense, and uniform; they may also be referred to as *nonreinforced films.* These films are usually impermeable to air and water. They have excellent soil and stain resistance and recover well from deformation.

Expanded films are spongier, softer, and plumper as a result of a blowing agent that incorporates tiny air cells into the compound. They are neither as strong nor as abrasion resistant as plain films. Expanded films also may not be as impermeable to air and water. To increase the comfort characteristics of plain and expanded films, thousands of tiny pinholes called micropores may be punched in the fabric to permit air and water vapor, but not liquid water, to pass through the fabric.

Because plain films and expanded films are seldom durable enough to withstand normal use, these products are usually attached to a woven, knit, or fiberweb support fabric or substrate. The final product is a *supported, coated,* or *reinforced film.* Supported films are multiplex fabrics, but will be discussed later in this chapter. Supported films are more durable, easier to sew, and less likely to crack and split than nonreinforced films.

Plastic films and coated fabrics are better than any other material for waterproof items. The finishing process can make them look like almost any other textile (see Figure 15-1.) They can vary in thickness from very thin transparent film used to make a sandwich bag to heavy leatherette used to cover a dentist's chair. They have the advantage of being uniform in appearance and quality, they can be obtained by the yard or meter in wide widths, and they are much cheaper and easier to make into products compared to leather.

This list briefly summarizes films:

• Solution is extruded through narrow slits into warm air or cast onto a revolving drum. Molding powders may be pressed between hot rolls.

Fig. 15–1   Films.

- Films are waterproof, low cost, resistant to soil, nonfibrous.
- Films may lack permeability.
- Films may lack strength unless supported by a fabric back.
- Films have low drapeability.
- Films can be finished to look like any other fabric or to have their own characteristic appearance.
- Films are used for shoes, shower curtains, upholstery fabrics, and plastic bags.

Table 15–1 lists some polymers that are used as both films and fibers.

Fig. 15–2 *Foam carpet pad: surface view* (top) *and cross-sectional view* (bottom).

Foams

Foams are made by incorporating air into an elastic like substance. Rubber and polyurethane are the most commonly used foams. The outstanding characteristics of foams are their bulk and sponginess. They are used as carpet backings and underlays, furniture padding, and pillow forms, and are laminated to fabric for apparel and furnishing textiles (Figure 15–2). Shredded foam is used to stuff accent pillows and toys.

Polyurethane foam can be obtained in a wide range of physical properties from very stiff to rubbery. The size of the cells can be controlled.

Foams will yellow on exposure to sunlight, but this neither causes a chemical change in the urethane foam nor affects its usefulness and durability. (Exposure to sunlight does, however, cause rubber to disintegrate.) Polyurethane is prepared by the reaction of diisocyanate with a compound containing two or more hydroxyl groups in the presence of a suitable catalyst. Chemicals and foaming agents are mixed thoroughly. After the foam is formed, it is cut into blocks 200–300 yards long, and strips of the desired thickness are cut from these blocks.

Table 15–1 Films Are Made From Solutions

Solution	Fiber	Film	End Uses for Film
Acetate	Acetate	Acetate	Photographic film; projection film
Polyamide	Nylon	Nylon	Cooking bags
Polyester	Polyester	Mylar*	Packaging; metallic yarns; computer disks
Polypropylene	Olefin		
Polyethylene		Polyethylene	Packaging, garment and shopping bags, squeeze bottles
Polyurethane	Spandex	Polyurethane	Leatherlike fabrics
Polyvinyl chloride	Vinal	Vinyl	Packaging, garment bags, leatherlike fabrics for apparel and upholstery, seed tapes, water-soluble bags
Vinylidene chloride	Saran	Saran Wrap*	Packaging
Viscose (regenerated cellulose)	Rayon	Cellophane	Glitter weaving yarns—mostly in handwoven textiles

*Trade names.

This list briefly summarizes foams:

- Foams are made by incorporating air into an elastic-like substance. Rubber and polyurethane are the most commonly used foams.
- Foams are lofty, springy, bulky material, too weak to be used without backing or covering.
- Foams are used in pillows, chair cushions, mattresses, carpet padding, and apparel.

FABRICS FROM FIBERS

Some fabrics are made directly from fibers or fiber-forming solutions; thus there usually is no processing of fibers into a yarn. These operations include very old and very new processes. The origins of felt and tapa cloth are lost in antiquity; netlike structures used to bag fruits and vegetables use new technologies; multiplex fabrics are made by combining fabrics.

The first fiberweb, tapa cloth, is made from the fibrous inner bark of the fig tree. It was used chiefly for clothing by people in many areas where the fig tree grows, the Pacific Islands, Central America, and elsewhere. The cloth is made by soaking the inner bark to loosen the fibers, beating them with a mallet, smoothing them out into a paperlike sheet, and decorating them with block prints (Figure 15-3).

Today, fabrics made from fibers are the fastest growing area of the textile industry. These fabrics have industrial uses, but some are also used in apparel and furnishing items. Much research and development work is being focused on industrial fabrics; new products made from existing fibers provide expanded markets for fiber companies.

These fabrics are often referred to as *nonwovens*, meaning that they are not made from yarn. However, the term nonwoven creates confusion because knits are nonwovens as well. Nonwoven refers to a wide variety of fabric structures. Because the term is so indefinite, another classification system eliminates the problems of the nonwoven system. This system includes three categories: fiberweb structures, netlike structures, and multiplex structures (Batra, et al., 1985).

Increased usage of these fabrics is related to the increased cost of reconditioning traditional textiles—especially the labor cost; scarcity and fluctuating cost of natural fibers; production and promotion of some manufactured fibers; easier cutting and

Fig. 15–3   Tapa cloth from Samoa.

sewing, especially by unskilled labor; and new technologies that result in made-to-order inexpensive products.

Fiberweb Structures

Fiberweb structures include all textile-sheet structures made from fibrous webs, bonded by mechanical entanglement of the fibers or by the use of added resins, thermal fusion, or formation of chemical complexes. Fibers are the fundamental units of structure, arranged into a web and bonded so that the distances between fibers are several times greater than the fiber diameter. These fiberweb structures are not like paper. Fiberweb structures are more flexible than paper structures of similar construction.

The properties of fiberweb structures are controlled by selection of the geometrical arrangements of fibers in the web, the properties of the fibers used in the web, and the properties of any binders that may be used.

PRODUCTION Fiberwebs are quick to produce. The basic steps include selecting the fibers, laying the fibers to make a web, and bonding the web together to make a fabric. Any fiber can be used to make fiberwebs. The inherent characteristics of the fibers are reflected in the fabric. Filaments and strong staple fibers are used where strength and durability are important; rayon and cotton are used for absorbency; thermoplastics are used for spun-bonded webs.

Web formation can be a more involved process. The five techniques are dry laid, wet laid, spun bonded, spun laced, and melt blown.

Dry-laid fiberwebs are made by carding or air laying the fibers in either a random or oriented fashion. Webs delivered from the carding machine have the majority of fibers oriented lengthwise or parallel to the lengthwise (machine) direction. Webs can be cross-laid by stacking the carded web so that one layer is oriented lengthwise and the next layer crosswise to give added strength and pliability. *Cross-laid webs* do not have a grain and can be cut more economically than woven or knitted fabrics. *Air-laid,* or *random, webs* are made by machines that disperse the fibers by air. This web is much like the cross-laid web but has more random distribution. Oriented webs have good strength in the direction of orientation, but poor cross-orientation strength. Since random webs have the fibers oriented in different directions in a random fashion, strength is uniform in all directions. Typical end uses for dry-laid fiberwebs include wipes, wicks, battery separators, backing for quilted fabrics, interlining, insulation, abrasive bases, filters, and base fabric for laminating and coating.

Wet-laid fiberwebs are made from a slurry of short, paper-process–length and textile-length fibers and water. The water is extracted, leaving a fiber web. The advantage of these webs is their excep-tional uniformity. Typical end uses for wet-laid fiberwebs include laminating and coating bases, filters, interlining, insulation, roofing substrates, adhesive carriers, wipes, and battery separators.

Spun-bonded webs are made immediately after fibers are produced from spinnerets. The continuous filaments are laid down in a random fashion on a fast-moving belt and, in their semimelted state, fuse together at their cross points. They may be further bonded by heat and pressure. Spun-bonded fiberwebs have high tensile and tear strength and low bulk (Figure 15-4). Typical end uses for spun-bonded fiberwebs include carpet backings like Typar by Du Pont, geotextiles, adhesive carriers, envelopes like Tyvek by Du Pont, tents and tarps, wall coverings, house-wrap vapor barriers, tags and labels, bags, protective apparel, filters, insulation, and roofing substrate.

Spun-laced webs are similar to spun-bonded webs except that jets of water are forced through the web, separating the filaments into a wovenlike structure to produce a looser-bonded fabric (Figure 15-5). They have more elasticity and flexibility than spun-bonded fabrics.

These fabrics are also known as hydroentangled or water-needled fabrics. This technique makes products that are not possible with any other process. Water from high-pressure jets on both sides of the fabric entangle the fibers. The degree of entanglement is controlled by the number and force of jets and the fiber type. Computer controls main-

Fig. 15–4 *Spun-bonded filament: Reemay.*

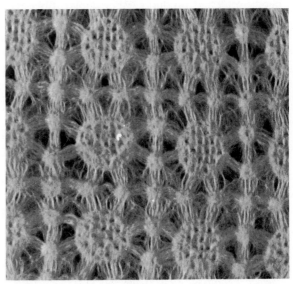

Fig. 15–5 *Spun-lace fabric.*

tain a uniform quality in the fabric. This technique is one of the fastest growing of the fiberweb process. Spun-laced textiles are used in medical gowns and drapes, battery separators, interlinings, roofing substrates, floppy disk liners, mattress pads, table linens, household wipes, wall coverings, window treatment components, protective clothing, and filters. Sontara is a spun-laced polyester produced by Du Pont.

Melt-blown fiberwebs are made by extruding the polymer through a single-extrusion orifice into a high-velocity, heated-air stream that breaks the fiber into short pieces. The fibers are collected in a web form on a moving conveyor belt and are held together by a combination of fiber interlacing and thermal bonding. Because the fibers are not drawn, the strength of the resulting fiberweb is low. Olefin and polyester are the fibers used commercially with this process to produce hospital/medical products and battery separators.

Webs become fabrics through the use of a mechanical needling process, the application of chemical substances or adhesives, or heat.

Needle punching or needling consists of passing a properly prepared dry-laid web over a needle loom as many times as is necessary to produce the desired strength and texture. A *needle loom* has barbed needles protruding 2 or 3 inches from the base (Figure 15–6). As the needles push up and down through the web, the barbs catch a few fibers, causing them to interlock mechanically. The construction process is relatively inexpensive.

Attractive blankets and carpeting are examples of needle-punched products. Fiber denier, fiber type, and product loft may be varied.

Indoor/outdoor needle-punched carpeting made of olefin fibers is used extensively for patios, porches, pools, and putting greens. The fiber is impervious to moisture. Needled nonwoven carpet backings are designed especially for use with tufted carpets.

Needled fabrics can be made of a web consisting of two layers, each with a different color. By pulling colored fibers from the lower layer to the top surface, geometric designs can be made. If the fibers are pulled above the surface, a pile fabric results. The army has developed a ballistics-protective vest for combat use from needle-punched fabrics. Needle-punched fabrics are finished by pressing, steaming, calendering, dyeing, and embossing. Solution-dyed fibers are often used.

FIBERWOVEN PROCESS

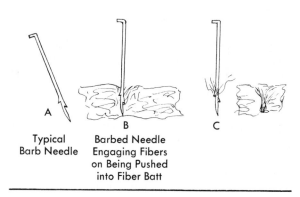

FIBERWOVEN PROCESS
Action of Cooperating Pair of Barbed Needles

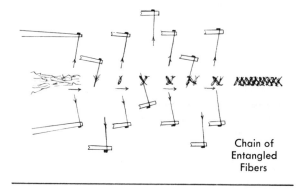

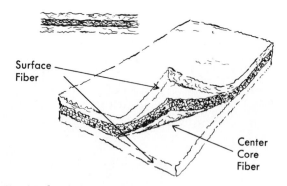

Fig. 15–6 *Needle-punch process.*

Other techniques include the use of a closed needle that penetrates the web, opens, grabs some fibers, and draws them back as a yarnlike structure that is then chain-stitched through the web. These fabrics are related to the stitch-through fabrics discussed later in this chapter.

Chemicals or *adhesives* are used with dry-laid or wet-laid webs. Acrylic emulsions are usually used.

Heat and pressure are used to bond thermoplastic-fiber webs. Figure 15–7 shows Mirafi 140 fabric, which is composed of a random mixture of polypropylene (olefin) homopolymer and bicomponent-polypropylene core-nylon sheath filaments that is heat bonded. Mirafi 140 is an industrial fabric used for roadbed and area stabilization.

FIBERFILL Batting, wadding, and fiberfill are not fabrics, but they are important components in apparel for snowsuits, ski jackets, quilted robes, and jackets, and in furnishing textiles for quilts, comforters, furniture paddings, mattresses, and mattress pads.

Batting is made from new fiber, *wadding* is made from waste fiber, and *fiberfill* is a manufactured fiber staple made especially for these end uses. Carded fibers are laid down to form the desired thickness and may be covered with a sheet of fiberweb fabric.

Fiber density relates to the weight or mass per unit volume. Fiber density is important for batting, wadding, and fiberfill in order to produce lightweight, resilient products.

Resiliency is important because fabrics that maintain their loft incorporate more air space. When fibers stay crushed, the fabric becomes thinner and more compact. *Resistance to shifting* is important in maintaining uniformity of thickness in the fabric. For instance, down comforters need to be shaken often because the filling tends to shift to the outer edges. The thermoplastic-fiber batts can be run through a needle-punch machine in which hot needles melt the parts of the fibers that they touch, fusing them and forming a more stable batt, often referred to as a bonded web. The thicker the batt, the warmer the fabric, regardless of fiber content. In

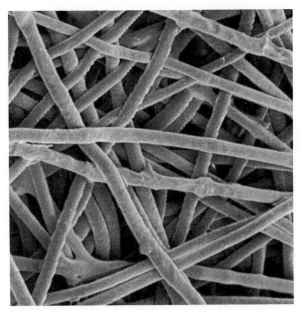

Fig. 15–7 *Photomicrograph of Mirafi 140 fabric. (Courtesy of Dominion Textiles of Canada.)*

apparel there is a limit to the thickness, however, because too much bulk restricts movement and limits styling. (See Table 15–2.)

Two types of polyester fiberfill by Du Pont are Thermoloft, a high-loft insulation, and Thermolite, a thin insulation made with microfibers.

Although not fibers, down and feathers are often used as fiberfill. These fills are defined by the Federal Trade Commission in the Code of Federal Regulations. Down refers to the undercoating of waterfowl and relates to the fine, bulky underfeathers. Items labeled 100 percent down must meet specified requirements relating to the condition of the down. Down-filled items must be 80 percent down or down fiber and may include up to 20 percent other feathers. Down is rated by its loft capacity, the volume one cubic ounce of down will fill.

Table 15–2 **Comparsion of Properties of Commonly Used Battings**

Fiber	Density	Resiliency	Resistance to Shifting	Care
Down (costly)	Lightweight	Excellent	Poor	Dry cleanable
Acetate (low cost)	1.30	Fair	Poor	Washable, dries more quickly than cotton
Polyester (medium cost)	1.30–1.38	Good	Good—can be spot welded	Washable, quick drying
Cotton (low cost)	1.52	Poor	Poor	Washable, but slow drying

Higher loft capacity downs are more expensive. Down is lightweight and warm. However, it has a tendency to shift, and when wet, it mats and loses its warmth. Down may be difficult to clean and still maintain the original loft. People who are allergic to feathers may experience difficulty with down products. Down is used in apparel, bedding, and padding for pillows and soft furniture.

FUSIBLE FIBERWEBS *Fusible fiberwebs* give body and shape to garments as interfacing or interlinings in shirts, blouses, dresses, and outerwear.

A fusible is a fabric that has been coated with a heat-sealable, thermoplastic adhesive. It also may be a thin, spiderweblike fabric of thermoplastic filaments (Figure 15-8). The fusible fabric is applied to a face fabric and bonded to it by heat and pressure.

The adhesives used are polyethylene, hydrolyzed ethylene vinyl acetate, plasticized polyvinyl chloride, and polyamides. The adhesive is usually printed on the substrate in a precisely positioned manner to give the desired hand to the end product.

Fusibles eliminate certain areas of stitching, such as zigzag stitches used in coat and suit lapels. They require less skilled labor in garment production, and when the proper technique and correct selection are combined, increase productivity. They improve the appearance of products. However, fusibles may generate problems for producers and consumers. They may separate during care. Adhesives may bleed through to the face

Fig. 15–8 *Fusible interlining. Tape under web to show sheerness of web.*

fabric. The layers may shrink differently during care. The change in hand and drape are difficult to predict.

END USES OF FIBERWEBS Fiberwebs are used for disposable goods, such as diapers and wipes, durable goods that are incorporated into other products, or alone for draperies, mattress pads, and some apparel (see Table 15–3).

To summarize, fiberwebs are:

• Produced by bonding and/or interlocking fibers by mechanical, chemical , thermal, or solvent means, or combinations of these processes.

Table 15–3 Uses of Fiberwebs

Durable	Type	Disposable	Type
Bedding and coated fabrics, mattress ticking, backing for quilting, dust cloth for box springs	Spun bonded	Diapers, underpads, sanitary napkins/tampons	Dry laid
		Surgical packs and accessories	Dry laid, melt blown
		Wipes and towels	Dry laid, or wet
Carpet backing, coated fabrics	Needled, spun bonded, dry laid	Packaging, floppy disk liners	Spun bonded
Filters			
Interfacings	Dry or wet laid		
Interlinings	Needled, dry laid		
Draperies, upholstered furniture, backings, facings, dust covers, automotive, shoe parts, geotextiles, labels, backings for wall coverings, leatherlike fabrics	Dry and wet laid, spun bonded, spun lace, melt blown		

- Cheaper than woven or knitted fabrics. Widely used for disposable or durable items. May have grain but usually do not.

- Used for apparel, furnishing, and industrial purposes.

Felt

True felt is a mat or web of wool or part-wool fibers held together by the interlocking of the scales of the wool fibers. Felting is one of the oldest methods of making fabrics. Primitive peoples made felt by washing wool fleece, spreading it out while still wet, and beating it until it had matted and shrunk together in fabriclike form. Figure 15-9 shows a Numdah felt rug made in India. In modern factories, layers of fiber webs are built up until the desired thickness is attained and then heat, soap, and vibration are used to mat the fibers together and to shrink or full the cloth. Finishing processes for felt resemble those for woven fabrics.

Felts do not have grain; they are stiff and less pliable than other structures; they do not ravel. Felts are not as strong as other fabrics and vary in quality depending on the quality of the wool fiber used.

Felt has many industrial and some clothing uses. It is used industrially for padding, soundproofing, insulation, filtering, polishing, and wicking. In the past, felt was used under practically all machinery to absorb sound. Foams, being much cheaper, have replaced felt in this end use. Felt is not used for fitted clothing because it lacks the flexibility and elasticity of fabrics made from yarns. Felt has wide use in such products as hats, house slippers, clothing decorations, and pennants. Because felt does not fray, it needs no seam finish. Colored felt letters or

Fig. 15–10   Felt (magnified).

decorations on apparel often fade in washing and should be removed or the garments should be sent to a professional dry cleaner.

The following characteristics summarize felt:

- Wool fibers are carded (and combed), laid down in a thick batt, sprayed with water, and run through hot agitating plates, which cause the fibers to become entangled and matted together (see Figure 15-10).

- Felt has no grain; it does not fray or ravel.

- Felt absorbs sound. It lacks pliability, strength, and stretch recovery.

- Felt is used in crafts and industrial matting.

Netlike Structures

Netlike structures include all textile structures formed by extruding one or more fiber-forming polymers in the form of a film or a network of ligaments or strands. In the integral-fibrillated-net process, the extruded film is embossed while molten by being passed through a pair of heated rollers that are engraved to form a pattern on the fabric. When the film is stretched biaxially, slits occur in the fabric, creating a netlike structure. In the integral-extruded-net process, the spinneret consists of two rotating dies. When the polymer is extruded, the fibers form as single strands that interconnect when the holes of the two rotating dies coincide. The process produces tubular nets that are used for packaging fruit and vegetables, agricultural nets, bird nets, and plastic fencing (Figure 15-11).

Fig. 15–9   Numdah felt rug.

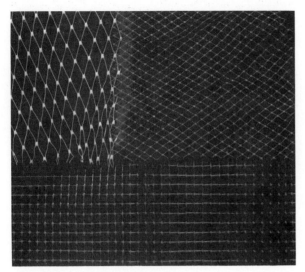

Fig. 15–11 *Netlike structures.*

FABRICS FROM YARNS

Braids

Braids are narrow fabrics in which yarns are interlaced lengthwise and diagonally (see Figure 15-12). They have good elongation characteristics. They are very pliable, curve around edges nicely, and are used primarily for trims, shoelaces, and coverings on components in industrial products like wiring and hoses for liquids like gasoline and water. Three-dimensional braids are made with two or more sets of yarns.

The characteristics of braid include the following:

• Yarns are interlaced both diagonally and lengthwise. Fabrics are narrow.

• Braid is stretchy and easily shaped.

• Braid can be made circular for shoelaces.

• Braid is used for trim and industrial purposes.

Lace

Lace is another basic fabric made from yarns. Weaving has interlaced yarns, knitting has interlooped yarns, braids have yarns interlaced diagonally, and lace has intermeshed yarns—yarns twisted around each other. Lace is an openwork fabric with complex patterns or figures, handmade or machine-made on special lace machines or on Raschel knitting machines.

It can be difficult to determine the machine used to make a fine-lace fabric without the aid of a micro-scope. However, it is a fairly simple matter to determine the origin of many laces. Some imitation lace-like fabrics are made by printing or flocking (Figure 15-13).

Lace was very important in men's and women's fashion between the 16th and 19th centuries, and all countries in Europe developed lace industries. Lace remains important today as a trim or accessory in apparel and furnishings. The names given to lace often originated from the town in which the laces were made. For example, the best quality needlepoint lace was made in Venice in the 16th century—hence the name Venetian lace. Alençon and Valenciennes are laces made in French towns.

HANDMADE LACE *Handmade lace* has always been, as it is today, a prestige textile. Some people use old lace on garments or as decorative wall hangings. With the contemporary interest in crafts, many of the old lace-making techniques are being used to make less delicate lace. For example, macramé, crochet, tatting, and hairpin laces are made as wall hangings, belts, bags, shawls, afghans, bedspreads, and tablecloths.

Lace is classified according to the way it is made and the way it appears. Handmade laces are needlepoint, bobbin, crochet, and darned.

Needlepoint Lace *Needlepoint lace* is made by drawing a pattern on paper, laying down yarns over the pattern, and making buttonhole or blanket stitches over the yarns with a needle and thread. The network of fine threads making the ground is called *reseau* or *brides*. The solid part of the

Fig. 15–12 *Braid.*

(a) Machine-made cordonnet lace. Alençon.

(b) Raschel lace.

(c) Filling knitted lace-like fabric.

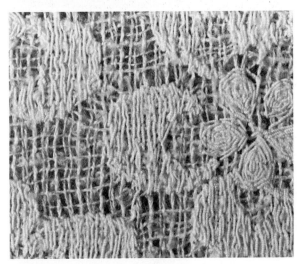

(d) Woven lace-like fabric.

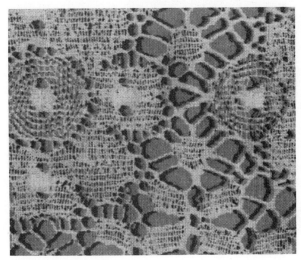

(e) Imitation lace.

Fig. 15–13 *Lace and lacelike fabrics: (a) Cordonnet or reembroidered lace made on Leavers lace machine; (b) lace fabric made on raschel-warp knitting machine; (c) lace fabric made on purl knitting machine; (d) woven lace; (e) imitation lace—cotton percale printed with a lace-like design.*

Fig. 15–14   *Needlepoint lace: machine-made* (left); *handmade* (right).

pattern, which may be made with buttonhole stitches or interlaced as a woven area, is called *toile*. Needlepoint laces are Alençon, which has a hexagonal mesh, rosepoint, and Venetian point, which have an irregular mesh. Needlepoint laces have birds, flowers, and vases as the design (Figure 15-14).

Bobbin Lace   *Bobbin lace* is made on a pillow. The pattern is drawn on paper and pins are inserted at various points. The yarns, which are on many bobbins, are twisted and plaited around the pins to form the mesh and the design (Figure 15-15). Cluny is a coarse, strong lace; Duchesse has a fine net ground with raised patterns; Maltese has the Maltese

Fig. 15–15   *Bobbin lace: machine-made lace* (left); *handmade lace* (right).

Fig. 15–16 *Close-up view of Battenburg lace tablecloth.*

cross in the pattern; Mechlin has a small hexagonal mesh and very fine yarns; Torchon is a rugged lace with very simple patterns; Valenciennes has a diamond-shaped mesh; Chantilly has a double ground with filling of flowers, baskets, or vases.

Crocheted Lace *Crocheted lace* is a combinations of stitches, but it differs from knitting in that the stitches are thrown off and finished, whereas in knitting the entire series of stitches is held on needles while new stitches are made. Crocheted laces are Irish lace and Syrian lace. Crocheting is done with a crochet hook.

Darned Lace *Darned lace* has a chain stitch outlining the design on a mesh background. The needle carries another yarn around the yarns in the mesh. The mesh is square in filet lace and rectangular in antique lace.

Battenburg Lace This handmade lace is made with loops of tape caught together by yarn brides in patterns. Figure 15-16 shows a piece of Battenburg lace. Making Battenburg lace was a common hobby in the U.S. in the early part of the 20th century. Contemporary pieces are imported from the Far East, especially China, for apparel and furnishing accessories.

MACHINE-MADE LACE In 1802 in England, Robert Brown perfected a machine that made nets on which lace motifs could be worked by hand. In 1808 John Heathcoat made the first true lace machine by developing brass bobbins to make bobbinet. In 1813, John Leavers developed a machine that made patterns and background simultaneously. A card system, similar to the technique used on card jacquard looms, made it possible to produce intricate designs with the Leavers machine (Figure 15-17).

Leavers Machine The *Leavers machine*, a machine of tremendous size and weight, consists of warp yarns placed in the machine and oscillating bobbins that are set in frames called *carriages*. The carriages move back and forth with the bobbins swinging around the warp to form a pattern. These little brass bobbins, holding 60 to 300 yards of yarn, are thin enough to swing between adjacent warp yarns and twist themselves around one warp before moving to another yarn (Figures 15-18 and 15-19). The Leavers machine has approximately 20 brass bobbins for each inch width of the machine. A machine 200 inches wide would have 4,000 brass bobbins side by side.

Laces made on the Leavers machines are fairly expensive, depending on the quality of yarns used and the intricacy of the design. On some fabrics, a yarn or cord outlines the design. These are called *Cordonnet*, or *reembroidered, lace* (Figure 15-13a).

Raschel Machines *Raschel knitting machines* (see Chapter 14) are used to make patterned laces

Fig. 15–17 *Leavers lace machine.*

that look like those made on a Leavers machine. They can be made at much higher speeds and thus are less expensive to produce. Needles are set in these machines horizontally instead of vertically. Filament yarns are commonly used to make coarser laces that are suitable for tablecloths, draperies, and casement fabrics. Raschel machines are also used to make crocheted fabric (Figure 15–20).

QUALITY OF LACE Quality in laces is determined by the following: (1) fineness of yarns, (2) number of yarns per square inch or closeness of background net, and (3) intricacy of the design.

CARE OF LACE Because lace has open spaces, it can easily snag and tear. Fragile laces should be washed by hand-squeezing suds through the fabric rather than rubbing. Some laces can be put into a protective bag and machine washed.

MULTIPLEX FABRICS

Multiplex fabrics are fabrics that combine several primary and/or secondary structures, at least one of which is a recognized textile structure, into a single structure. This broad category includes such diverse fabrics as stitch-bonded structures, laminates, tufted and flocked structures, and coated fabrics.

Coated Fabrics

A *coated fabric* combines the best characteristics of a textile fabric with a polymer film. The woven, knit, or fiberweb fabric provides such characteristics as strength and elongation control. The coating or film provides protection from environmental factors such as water, chemicals, oil, abrasion, and so forth. Common films include rubber and synthetic elastomers such as polyvinyl chloride (PVC), neoprene, and polyurethane. PVC-coated fabrics are the most common; they are used in window shades, book covers, upholstery, wall coverings, apparel, shoe liners, and shoe uppers. Neoprene is used for protective clothing like chemical gloves and wetsuits. Most polyurethane-coated fabrics are used in shoe uppers and apparel. Heavier-weight polyurethane-coated fabrics are used in industrial tarpaulins.

The coating is added to the fabric by several methods. The most common method is *lamination*, in which a prepared film is adhered to fabric with adhesive or heated to slightly melt the film. In the second method, calendering, the polymer is mixed with a filler, stabilizing agent, pigment, and plasti-

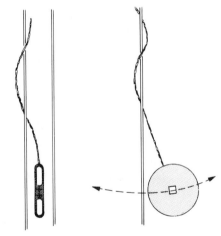

Fig. 15–18 *Brass bobbins. (Reproduced from Textiles, 1973, Vol. 2, No. 1, a periodical of the Shirley Institute, Didsbury, United Kingdom.)*

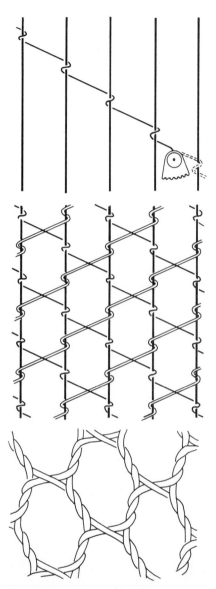

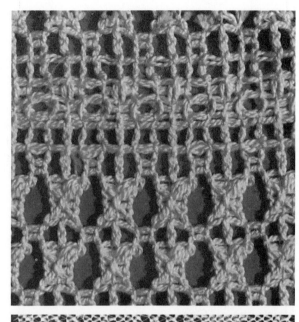

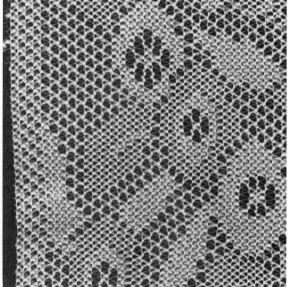

Fig. 15–19 *Brass bobbins, carrying thread, twist around warp yarns. (Reproduced from* Textiles, *1973, Vol. 2, No. 1, a periodical of the Shirley Institute, Didsbury, United Kingdom.)*

Fig. 15–20 *Raschel crochet* (top); *raschel lace* (bottom).

cizer. The mixture is calendered directly onto a preheated fabric by passing the fabric and the mixture between two large metal cylinders spaced close together. The final method is *coating*, in which a more fluid compound is required. The fluid mixture is applied by knife or roll. The degree of penetration of the mixture is controlled by allowing the mixture to solidify or gel slightly before it comes in contact with the fabric.

Coated fabrics can be printed or embossed. They are used for apparel, shoe uppers and liners, upholstery, vinyl car tops, floor and wall coverings, window shades, bandages, acoustical barriers, filters, soft-sided luggage, awnings, pond and ditch liners, and air-supported structures.

Bion II by Biotex Industries is a monolithic, or solid, polyurethane coating that is waterproof, breathable, and flame retardant. It is used in active sportswear such as running suits, outerwear such as parkas, diaper covers, mattress covers, and incontinence products. It can be applied to most fibers in woven or knit forms.

In order for these protective fabrics to be comfortable, they work in one of two ways. Coated fabrics incorporate a nonporous hydrophilic membrane or film. Sympatex by Akzo incorporates a hydrophilic polyester film. (The second method uses a microporous film, which will be discussed in the next section.) Sympatex can be laminated to an outer shell, a lining fabric, or a lightweight insert fabric such as tricot or fiberweb for use in skiwear. Sympatex is washable or dry cleanable.

A summary of coated fabrics includes these aspects:

- Coated fabrics are produced by applying semi-liquid materials to a fabric substrate. Neoprene, polyvinyl chloride, and polyurethane are usual coating materials (see Figure 15-21).

- Coated fabrics are stronger and more stable than unsupported films.

- Coated fabrics are used for upholstery, luggage and bags, and apparel (see Table 15-4).

Poromeric Fabrics

Poromeric, or *microporous, fabrics* are coated fabrics, but they are classified in a separate category because the coating is very fine and microporous. These two major distinctions determine many characteristics of the resulting fabric. The poromeric or membrane layer is processed to generate the micropores of the fabric, which are so small that they allow the passage of water vapor, but not liquid water; hence, they are water vapor–permeable. This factor greatly enhances comfort in apparel items. These fab-

Table 15–4 End Uses for Films and Coated Fabrics

Air-supported roofings	Tablecloths
Draperies	Umbrellas
Hospital-bed coverings	Upholstery
Hose container for fuel and water	Waterproof apparel such as raincoats, boots, and
Inflatable flood gates for water control	mittens
	Wetsuits
Leather-like coats, jackets	Chemical protective
Shower curtains	clothing and gloves

rics are effective due to the enormous size difference between a droplet of liquid water and the size of water vapor—the water vapor droplet is 250,000 times smaller!

Poromeric films can be made from polytetrafluorocthylene (Gore-Tex) or polyurethane (Figure 15-22). These products are waterproof, windproof, and breathable. They can be applied to a wide variety of fabrics and fibers but are used primarily in apparel because of the requirements for comfort and protection. They are used for active sportswear, rugged outdoor wear such as hunting clothes, tents, sleeping bags, medical products, filters, coatings for wires and cables, and protective apparel. Besides Gore-Tex, other poromeric fabrics include Dartexx, a warp knit with a polyurethane

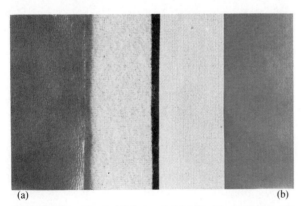

Fig. 15–21 *Coated fabrics: (a) knitted base fabric; (b) woven base fabric. The outer portions show the technical face of the fabric. The inner portions show the technical back or base of the fabric.*

Fig. 15–22 *Gore-Tex fabric: face fabric, polytetrafluoroethylene film, backing* (left); *face and back of fabric* (right).

membrane, and Entrant, which has a polyurethane membrane.

The performance of the poromeric fabrics relates directly to their price. Fabrics that are both comfortable and waterproof are expensive to make and their components are also expensive.

Suedelike Fabrics

Because of the beautiful texture and hand of suede and the problems encountered in its care, *suedelike fabrics* have been produced. These fabrics are needle-punched fabrics made from microdenier fibers combined with a resin coating and nonfibrous polyurethane. The microdenier fibers are arranged in a manner that reproduces the microscopic structure of natural suedes. The fabric is dyed and finished. The process was developed by Toray Industries of Japan. Ultrasuede® and Ultraleather® are registered trade names of Springs Industries. Both are used in apparel. Ultrasuede® is made of 60 percent microfine polyester and 40 percent polyurethane foam. Ultraleather® is 100 percent polyurethane with a knit back of 70 percent rayon and 30 percent nylon. The embossed fabric is lightweight, soft, water repellent, and has comfort stretch. Ultrasuede® may be backed with a cotton-woven fabric when used for upholstery. Belleseime® is a similar fabric of 65 percent polyester/20 percent nylon matrix fiber on a 15 percent polyurethane-foam substrate produced by Kanebo Company of Japan.

Suede- and leatherlike fabrics are used in apparel, upholstery, wall coverings, and accessories. These fabrics are made in various ways (see Table 15-5). This process can be summarized as follows:

- Fibers and polyurethane solution are mixed together, cast on a drum, or forced through a slit to make fabric, which is napped on both sides.
- The fabric looks and feels like suede.
- The fabric is machine washable and dry cleanable.
- The fabric is uniform in thickness and quality and sold by the yard or meter.

Table 15–5   Leather, Suede, and Imitations

Construction Technique	Characteristics	Trade Name
Composite fabric—polyester fibers and polyurethane mixed, cast on drum, napped or embossed	Washable, dry cleanable Looks like leather or suede	Ultrasuede® Ultraleather®
Composite fabric	Easy care Looks like natural suede	Belleseime®
Woven cotton/polyester substrate with surface coating of polyurethane	Dry cleanable Washable	
Substrate with polyurethane on both sides		
100 percent polyester-pile fabric with suedelike finish	Dry cleanable Washable	
Flocked cotton	Least expensive. Flock may wear off at edges of garment	
100 percent polyester-warp knit-napped	Washable, dry cleanable	Super-suede
Leather (cow, pig, or lamb)	Natural product, irregular in nature, available in wide variety of finishes, cleanability may not be good	None
Suede (cow, pig, or lamb)	Natural product, irregular in nature, cleanability may not be good	None

Flocked-Pile Fabrics

Flock fibers are very short fibers attached to the surface of a fabric by an adhesive to make a pile-like design or fabric. Flocking was used as a technique for wall decoration as early as the 14th century when short silk fibers were applied to freshly painted walls by a bellows. Flock can be applied to many base materials—cloth, foam, wood, metal, and concrete—or it can be applied to an adhesive film that can then be laminated to a base fabric.

Interest in flocking intensified in the 1960s with the development of new, improved adhesives that withstand repeated washings or dry cleanings. The new emulsions are not as stiff and thick as the early adhesives; they have good flexibility, durability, drape, and hand and are colorless and free of undesirable odor. Over half of the adhesives used are aqueous-based acrylic resins.

Rayon fibers are inexpensive and easy to cut, and are thus used in large quantities. Rayon can be made fire retardant. Nylon has excellent abrasion resistance and durability. Acrylics, polyesters, and olefins can also be used. Fibers for flocking must be straight, not crimped. As the fiber length is increased, the denier also must be increased so that the fiber will remain erect in the fabric. Fibers that are cut square at the ends anchor more firmly in the adhesive (Figure 15-23).

An interesting flocked product is the blanket made of soft nylon fibers electronically bonded to two layers of polyurethane foam that are permanently sealed to nylon scrim (Figure 15-24). The blanket is light in weight and very warm. It can withstand over 50 washings and dryings with no ill effect if a gentle-agitation cycle is used. The price is competitive with other types of blankets.

Some of the major end uses of flocking include velvet upholstery fabrics, draperies, bedspreads, blankets, designs on apparel fabrics, carpets, wall coverings for aesthetics and noise reduction, auto-

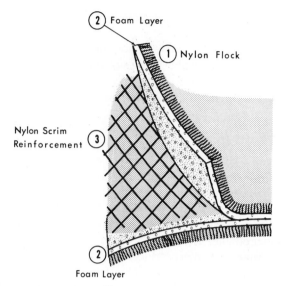

Fig. 15-24 *Foam-flocked construction. Pile surface made of fibers.*

motive fabrics, toys, books, shoes, hats, and industrial uses such as conveyor belts and air filters.

The two basic methods of applying the flock fibers are mechanical and electrostatic. In both processes the flock is placed in an erect position and, after flocking, is sent to an oven to dry the adhesive. A comparison of the two methods is given in Table 15-6. Overall flocking, or area flocking, can be done by either method. A rotating screen is used to deposit the flock.

To summarize, flocked fabrics are:

• Made by attaching fibers to a fabric substrate; held by an adhesive or electronic bonding to make a pile figure or overall pile on fabric.

• Used in apparel, furnishing, and automotive fabrics.

Tufted-Pile Fabrics

Tufting is a process of making pile fabrics by stitching extra yarns into fabric. The ground fabric ranges from thin sheeting or fiberweb to heavy burlap or coarse warp knit and may be woven, knitted, or a fiberweb. Tufting developed as a hand craft. Early settlers used candle wicks and carefully worked them into bedspreads to create interesting textures and designs, and the making of candlewick bedspreads and hooked rugs grew into cottage industries. In the 1930s, machinery was developed to convert the hand technique to mass production (see Figure 15-26). Cotton rugs, bedspreads, and

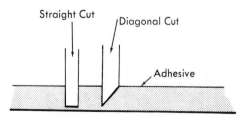

Fig. 15-23 *Flock with square-cut ends anchors more firmly.*

Table 15–6   Flocking Process

Mechanical Flocking	Electrostatic Flocking

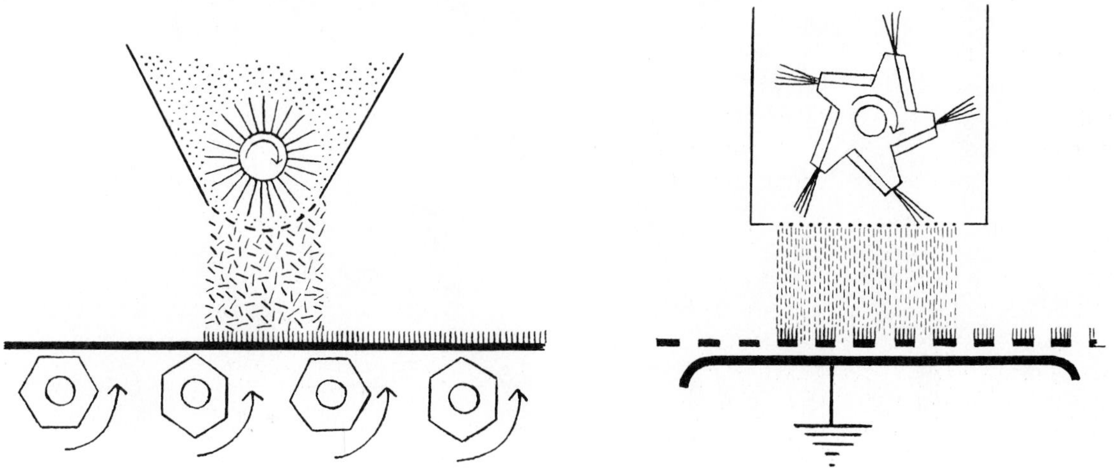

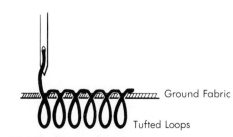

Fig. 15–25   (Courtesy of the Fibers Division of Monsanto Chemical Co., a unit of Monsanto Co.)

Mechanical Flocking	Electrostatic Flocking
1. Short fibers are sifted onto the adhesive-coated fabric. Vibration of beater bars causes fibers that do not fall flat against the adhesive to stand erect. Once erect, the fibers penetrate fully into the adhesive. The erect fibers help the free fibers to align themselves and to work down to the adhesive.	1. Flock passes through an electrostatic field that orients the fibers. In coating irregular surfaces, the lines of force are always perpendicular to the substrate, so this method is best for three-dimensional surfaces.
2. Most units consist of 6 to 20 beater bars and one or more sifting hoppers and run as high as 10 or more yards per minute.	2. Most units operate at speeds of 3–5 yards per minute.
3. Simpler in design, usually less expensive, and most widely used in the United States.	3. Can apply fiber to both sides of a fabric.
	4. Requires generators, proper insulation. Gives better end-on-end fiber orientation. Higher densities are possibilities.

(Courtesy of the Fibers Divison of Mosanto Chemical Co., a unit of Monsanto Co.)

robes were produced in many patterns and colors at low cost.

Tufting is done by a series of needles (see Figures 15-27 and 15-28), each carrying a yarn from a series of spools held in a creel. The backing fabric is held in a horizontal position and the needles all come down at once and go through the fabric at a predetermined distance, much as a sewing machine needle goes through fabric. For each needle, a hook moves forward to hold the loop as the needle is retracted. For cut-loop pile, a knife is attached to the hook and it moves forward as the needles are retracted to cut the loop. The fabric moves forward at a predetermined rate, and the needles move downward again to form another row of tufts.

The yarns must be opened and the fibers teased from the yarn. The tufts are held in place by bloom-ing or untwisting the yarn, by shrinkage of the ground fabric in finishing, and frequently by use of a coating on the back of the ground fabric.

Tuft density is the number of tufts per square inch and is related to the number of needles per inch and the number of stitches per inch. Computers

Fig. 15–26   How tufting stitches are made.

Fig. 15–27   *Tufting needles and yarn.*

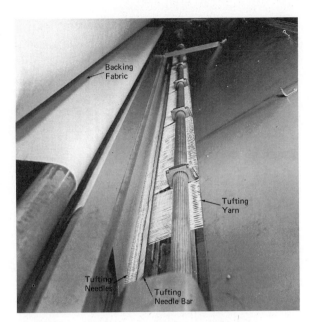

Fig. 15–28   *Needle area of tufting machine.*

control the tufting process. Patterns can be created quickly and easily by changing yarn color or type, tuft depth, and tuft type (cut or uncut). Thousands of patterns can be created quickly. The widespread use of carpets in homes, businesses, and industrial facilities is directly related to tufting, a low-cost method of producing carpeting.

Tufting is a less costly method of making pile fabrics because it is extremely fast and involves less labor and time to create new designs. Tufted apparel fabrics are made on 5/64-gauge machines. This gauge is the distance in inches between the tufting needles. Normal tufting specifications on this gauge call for 10–11 stitches per inch and a pile height of ⅛ inch. Tufted fabrics with a woven base are usually ½ inch or less in pile height.

Furlike tufted fabrics may be used for shells or linings of coats and jackets, but there are few other tufted apparel fabrics. Tufted bed-size blankets can be made in two minutes. Tufted blankets have not been successful in the United States but are being produced in Europe.

Tufted upholstery fabric is made in both cut and uncut pile. It is widely available. The back is coated to hold the yarns in place.

Carpeting of room-width size was first made by tufting in 1950; in 1990, approximately 90 percent of broadloom carpeting was made by tufting. A tufting machine can produce approximately 645 square yards of carpeting per hour compared to an Axminster loom, which can weave about 14 square

yards per hour. Variations in texture can be made by loops of different heights. Cut and uncut tufts can be combined. Tweed textures are made by the use of different-colored plies in the tufting yarns. Special dyeing and printing techniques have been developed to produce colored patterns or figures in which the color penetrates the tufts completely. A latex coating is put on the back of the carpet to help hold the tufts in place (Figure 15–29).

Tufted fabrics can be summarized as follows:

• Yarns carried by needles are forced through a fabric substrate and formed into cut or uncut loops.

• Tufted fabrics are cheaper than woven or knitted pile fabrics.

• Tufted fabrics are used in carpets and rugs, upholstery, coat linings, and bedspreads.

Tables 15-7 and 15-8 compare the different kinds of pile fabrics.

Laminates

Laminates include those fabrics in which two layers of fabric are adhered with an adhesive or foam. The term laminate refers to a fabric in which an adhesive was used; the term bonded refers to a fabric in which a foam was used. However, both terms are used interchangeably.

Introduced in 1958, bonding was originally a way to deplete inventories of tender or lightweight fabrics. Some converters were marginal operators who were not interested in quality. A bonder could buy

Table 15–7 **Look-Alike Pile Fabrics**

Furlike Fabrics—Used for Shells, Linings, Decubicare Pads, and Accent Rugs

	Woven-Warp Pile	*Sliver Knit*	*Tufted*
Fibers used	Cotton ground. Wool, acrylic, rayon, polyester pile	Cotton, olefin, or moda-crylic ground. Acrylic, modacrylic pile	Cheesecloth or soft, filled sheeting substrate. Acrylic, modacrylic pile
Cost	Most expensive	Variable	Least expensive
Characteristics	Pile firmly held in place. Tendency to "grin-through" in low-count fabrics	Most widely used. Dense underfibers and guard hairs possible, like real fur. Denser surface possible	Mostly used for sheepskin-type goods. Blooming of yarns and shrinkage of ground holds tufts in place

Carpets

	Woven-Warp Pile	*Filling Knit, Raschel Knit*	*Chenille Yarns*	*Tufted*	*Flocked*
Types and kinds	Wilton Axminster Velvet	Laid-in yarn	Usually woven to order	Most widely used. All kinds of textures Tufts held in by double back	Not very durable Limited pile height
Cost	Most expensive	Raschel knits expensive	Expensive	Inexpensive	Inexpensive

Velour

	Woven-Warp Pile	*Filling Knit—Jersey*	*Warp Knit*
Fiber content	Cotton	Cotton, polyester	Nylon, acetate
Characteristics	Heavy fabric, durable	Medium weight, soft, drapeable	Medium to heavyweight
End uses	Upholstery, draperies	Robes, shirts, jogging suits	Robes, nightwear

Velvet

	Woven-Warp Pile	*Tufted*	*Flocked*
Fibers	Rayon, nylon, cotton	Nylon	Nylon
Characteristics	Filament—dressy, pile flattens Cotton or nylon—durable Rich looking—heavyweight fabric	Pile not held in as firmly as woven, less expensive	Least expensive
End uses	Filament—apparel. Cotton, nylon—upholstery	Upholstery	Upholstery, draperies, bedspreads

Terrycloth

	Slack-Tension Weave	*Filling Knit—Jersey*
Characteristics	Usually cotton Holds its shape	All fibers. Soft, stretchy. Cotton does not hold its shape well. Very pliable
End uses	Towels, washcloths, robes	Baby towels and washcloths Baby sleepers, adult sportswear, socks

Table 15–8   Comparison of Pile Fabrics

Method	Types and Kinds	Fabrics—End Uses	Identification
Weaving	1. Filling floats cut and brushed up	1. Velveteen, corduroy	Filling pile
	2. Made as double cloth and cut apart	2. Velvet, velour	Warp pile
	3. Over wires	3. Friezé, Wilton and velvet carpets	Warp pile
	4. Slack tension	4. Terrycloth, friezé	Warp pile
Knitting	Filling knit: laid-in yarn Sliver knit Warp knit: laid-in yarn or pile loops	Velour, terry, fake fur, fleece	Stretchy—rows of knit stitches on wrong side More stable
Tufting	Yarns punched into substrate	Rugs and carpets Robes, bedspreads Upholstery Fake furs	Rows of stitches (like machine stitches) on wrong side
Flocking	Fibers anchored to substrate	Blankets, jackets Designs on fabric Upholstery	Fiber surface rather stiff
Chenille yarns	Pile-type yarns made by weaving Chenille yarns woven or knitted into fabric	Upholstery Outerwear fabric	Ravel adjacent yarns and examine novelty yarn

two hot rolls discarded by finishers and be in business. The fabric could be stretched as it went through the rollers. Consequently, many problems were associated with these bonded fabrics. The layers separated (delaminated) or shrank unevenly. There were problems with blotchy colors when the adhesive bled through to the technical face. Because of these problems, laminated fabrics have a poor reputation. However, the textile industry has worked to improve the quality of laminated fabrics and current laminates have greatly improved performance characteristics. Some advantages and limitations are given in Table 15–9. Figure 15–30 shows a laminate fabric with label.

Fig. 15–30   Bonded herringbone fabric and label.

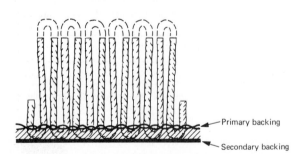

Fig. 15–29   Tufted carpet. Tufts are punched through primary backing. Secondary backing is bonded to primary backing to lock in pile.

Table 15–9   Laminated Fabrics

Advantages	Limitations
Less costly fabrics are upgraded.	Top-quality fabrics are not bonded.
Self-lining gives comfort.	Backing does not prevent bagging, so a lining may be beeded.
Stabilized if good quality.	Uneven shrinkage possible.*
Reduces time in sewing.	May be bonded "off-grain."
Interfacings may be eliminated.	May delaminate.*
Underlinings, stay-stitching, and seam finishing are not needed.	Hems, darts, and facings are stiff and boardy.
	Do not hold sharp creases.

*These are the two major problems.

LAMINATING PROCESS Knits are usually used as the *backing* fabric because they give with the stresses applied to the face fabric. Acetate and nylon tricot are most often used because of their low cost. The color of the backing can be a decorative feature in bonded laces.

Two methods of bonding are used (Figure 15–31):

1. Wet-adhesive method with aqueous acrylic adhesive or solvent urethane adhesive

2. Foam-flame method

In the *wet-adhesive method,* the adhesive is applied to the underside of the face fabric, and the liner fabric is joined by being passed through rollers. The fabric is heated twice, the first time to drive out solvents and to give a preliminary cure, and the second time to effect a permanent bond.

In the *foam-flame process,* polyurethane foam is the adhesive. Foam laminates consist of a layer of foam covered by another fabric or between two fabrics. The foam is made tacky first on one side and then on the other by passing under a gas flame. The final thickness of the foam is about 15/1,000 of an inch. This method gives more body but reduces the drapeability of the fabric. Another foam process generates the foam at the time it is to be applied, flowing it onto the cloth, and curing on the cloth.

Foam laminates were first visualized as thermal garments for outdoor workers because they are lightweight but warm. Foams were quilted to lining fabrics for a lining/interlining combination. Foam laminates today are made using all kinds and qualities of fabric with many different thicknesses of foam.

Laminated fabrics can be summarized as follows:

• Two or more fabrics are made to adhere together by an adhesive or flame-foam process.

• The laminating process is less expensive than the double woven or double knit processes.

• Laminating gives warmth without weight, when foam is one layer.

• Laminating makes possible the use of lightweight fabrics for outerwear.

• Laminated fabrics have body.

• Laminated fabrics do not hold sharp creases.

• Fabrics may be laminated off-grain, and may delaminate.

• Laminates are used in apparel, shoes, and industrial products.

Stitch-Bonded Fabrics

Stitch-bonded fabrics include those fabrics that combine textile structures by adhering fabric layers with fiber or yarn loops, chemical adhesives, or fusion of thermoplastic fibers. Stitch-bonded fabrics are divided into knit-through fabrics and quilted fabrics. Stitch-bonded fabrics can be produced from fiberwebs and any woven or knit fabric.

Knit-through fabrics are made in several ways. In the first process, a raschel warp-knitting machine knits yarns through a fiberweb structure. These fabrics can also be made by knitting fibers or knitting yarns around laid (not woven) warp and filling yarns. To make these knit-through fabrics, needles are used to create interconnected loops from yarns or fibers to stabilize the structure.

Araknit® is a knit-through fiberweb fabric used as a coating substrate. Arachne® and Maliwatt® are trade names for fabrics made by warp-knitting yarns through a fiberweb structure. These knit-through fabrics can be produced at high speeds and are used for

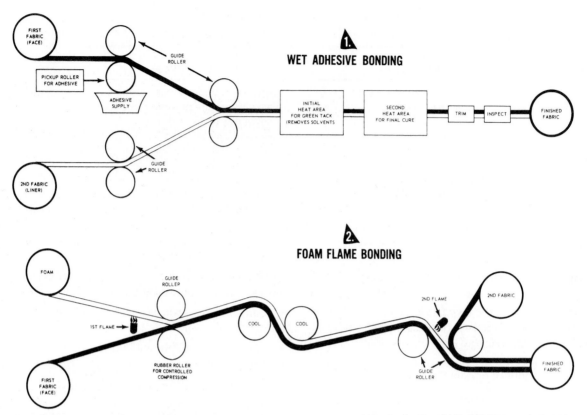

Fig. 15–31 *Two basic methods for producing bonded textiles. (Courtesy of* American Fabrics.*)*

furnishing items—such as upholstery, blankets, and window treatment fabrics—and industrial uses—such as insulation and interlining. Malimo® uses warp or filling or warp and filling laid-in yarns with warp-knitting yarns (see Figures 15-32 and 15-33). These fabrics can be produced at very high speeds and are used for tablecloths, window treatment fabrics, vegetable bags, dishcloths, and outerwear.

Fig. 15–32 *Malimo® fabrics: drapery and casement fabric.*

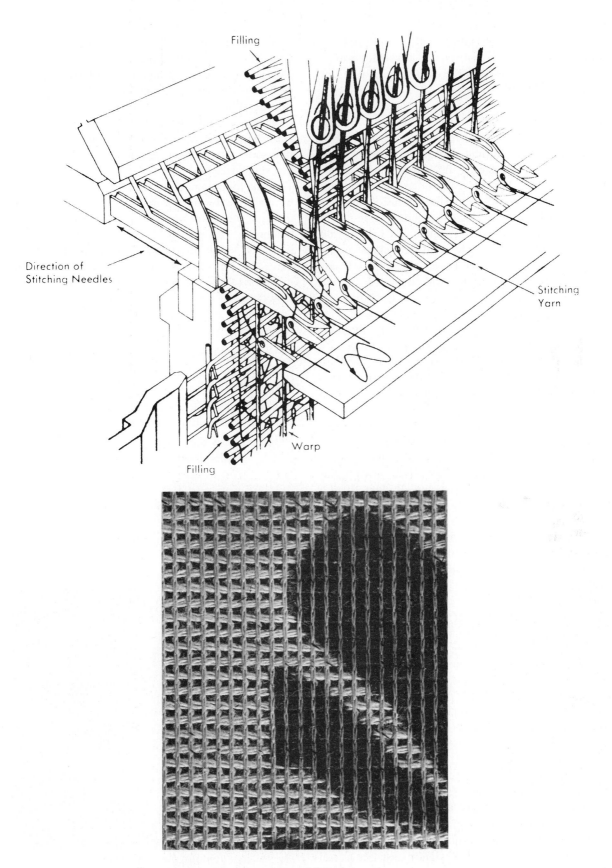

Fig. 15–33 *Malimo® textile machine* (top); *Malimo fabric* (bottom).

Some knit-through fabrics utilize split-polymer films from recycled carbonated-beverage bottles. These fabrics are used in the carpet, geotextile, and bale-wrap industries.

Quilted Fabrics

Quilted fabrics are multiplex fabrics consisting of three layers: face fabric, fiberfill or batting, and backing fabric. The three layers are stitch bonded with thread, chemical adhesive, or fusion by ultra-high-frequency sound. The bonding connects the layers in a pattern. The actual area physically bonded together is a very small percentage of the fabric's surface in order to get the high loft and bulky appearance desired in quilted fabrics.

Most quilted fabric is made by stitching with thread. The thread and type of stitch used in quilting are good indicators of the quality and durability of the finished fabric. A durable quilt will have a lock-type stitch with a durable thread. Twistless nylon-monofilament thread is often used because of its strength and abrasion resistance and because it is transparent and picks up the colors of the fabric.

Almost any thread can be used, but those designed for quilting are better than regular sewing thread. These threads are durable. The disadvantage of thread stitches in quilting is that the threads may break from abrasion or snagging. Broken threads are unsightly and the loose fiber is no longer held in place.

Any fabric can be used for the shell or covering. A fashion fabric is always used on one side. If the article is reversible or needs to be durable or beautiful on both sides, two fashion fabrics are used. If the fabric is to be lined or used as a chair covering or bedspread, the under layer is often an inexpensive fabric like cheesecloth, tricot, or a fiberweb fabric.

The wadding or batting may be foam, cotton, down, or fiberfill. Fiberfill is a modified-fiber type with crimp designed to help maintain loft and air space.

Quilting is usually done in straight or wavy lines. In upholstery and expensive quilts and comforters or bedspreads, the stitching may outline printed figures. This is a hand process. The machine quilting is guided by hand, and the fabric thus is more costly.

Beauty of fabric is important for all end uses. For ski jackets and snowsuits, a closely woven water- and wind-repellent fabric is desirable; for comforters, resistance to slipping off the bed is important; for upholstery, durability and resistance to soil are important.

Chemical adhesives seldom are used at present. Chemstitch is a trade name for a quilted fabric using chemical adhesives applied in a pattern. These fabrics are neither as appealing nor as durable as those produced by the other quilting methods.

Ultrasonic quilting requires thermoplastic fibers. Heat generated by ultra-high-frequency sound or ultrasonic vibrations melts thermoplastic fibers, fusing several layers. Figure 15–34 shows a Pinsonic Thermal Joining machine that heat seals thermoplastic materials by ultrasonic vibrations. The machine quilts seven times as fast as conventional quilting machines. This process is widely used on mattress pads and some lower priced bedspreads. It eliminates the problem of broken threads—a boon for institutional bedding in the hospitality industry. However, the outer layer may tear along the quilting lines. Figure 15–35 shows a *Pinsonic fabric*.

Quilted fabrics can be summarized as follows:

- One or two fabrics and wadding, batting, or foam are stitched together by machine or hand or welded by sonic vibrations.

- Quilted fabrics are bulky, warm, and decorative. However, stitches may break.

- Quilted fabrics are used in ski jackets, robes, comforters, quilts, and upholstery.

Supported-Scrim Structures

Supported-scrim structures include the foam- and fiber-type blankets currently on the market. These

Fig. 15–34 *Pinsonic Thermal Joining machine.*
(Courtesy of Branson Ultrasonics Corp.)

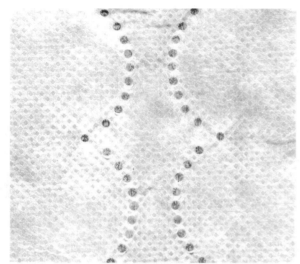

Fig. 15–35 *Mattress pad. Two layers of fiberweb fabric and fiberfill batt joined by Pinsonic Thermal Joining machine.*

fabrics use a lightweight nylon scrim, a loose warp-knit fabric, between two thin layers of polyurethane foam. A short nylon-flock fiber is adhered to the surface. These fabrics are attractive, durable, easy care, and inexpensive. Vellux and Vellux-Plus are two trade names.

Other types of supported-scrim fabrics include those that are needle punched with a scrim between the fiberweb layers. These fabrics are used industrially for roadbed-support fabrics and other applications requiring high stability.

ANIMAL PRODUCTS

The category of animal products includes leather and fur. These products are animals skins that are processed to maintain flexibility after being removed from the animal. In order to remove the skin, the animal must be killed. Animal rights activists object to this use of animals. Many people find products made of skins or hides attractive and functional regardless of the source of the product.

Leather

Leather is processed from the skins and hides of animals, reptiles, fish, and birds. It is an organic substance derived from living animals and therefore varies greatly in uniformity. Most leather in the U.S. is cow, pig, or lamb. These animals are raised primarily for meat or fiber, not for their hides or skins. Leather is a relatively unimportant by-product.

The hides from different animals differ in size, thickness, and grain. *Grain* is the marking that results from the skin formation and varies not only from animal to animal but also within one hide. Other factors influence the surface of hides: Animals scratch themselves, run into barbed-wire fences, and fight, causing scars that cannot be erased; brand marks or skin diseases mar the hides. Of 100 hides, it is estimated that less than 5 percent are suitable for conversion into smooth top-grain leather in aniline finish, 20 percent are suitable for smooth leathers with a pigment finish, and the remaining 75 percent must be embossed, buffed, snuffed, or corrected.

Dried skins and hides are stiff, boardy, nonpliable, and subject to decay. *Tanning* is the process in which skins and hides are treated with a chemical agent to make them pliable and water resistant. *Vegetable tanning,* the most expensive process, is done with an extract leeched from the bark of various trees. *Chrome tanning,* a solution of bichromate of soda, sulfuric acid, and glucose, makes soft, pliable leather. *Oil tanning* is used to make chamois. *Alum tanning* is used for white leather. Because of environmental concerns, vegetable tanning is becoming more common.

Skins go through many processes to become leather: salting; cleaning to remove the hair and epidermis; tanning; bleaching; stuffing; coloring or dyeing; staking; and finishing by glazing, boarding, buffing, snuffing, or embossing, depending on the desired end use. These many processes explain why leather is an expensive product.

The appearance of leather can be modified extensively in processing. Many finishes, including stuffing, snuffing, and buffing, are designed to camouflage flaws, scars, wrinkles, or irregularities in the skins. Fillers improve the appearance by covering these irregularities with a chemical, much like a cosmetic. Bleaching whitens the skin prior to dyeing. Staking is a drying process under tension to minimize skin shrinkage. Dyeing, printing, glazing, and embossing are finishing steps to add color, gloss, or texture to the skin. Many of these finishes add greatly to the appeal of the leather item. Unfortunately, many of these finishes are not fast to leather dry cleaning processes and are removed or altered during cleaning. In addition, fillers may be removed, allowing hide irregularities to appear. Dyes and prints may not be fast. Most leather cleaners are adept at finishing or reworking leather items so that the consumer is never aware that the original appearance has been replaced. However, the high cost of leather cleaning clearly reflects the additional efforts required of the dry cleaner.

Leather is a nonseparable-fiber product. As shown in Figure 15-36, the fibers are very dense on the skin side and less dense on the flesh side. Thick hides are often split or shaved into layers to make them more pliable and economical (Figure 15-37).

The first layer is called *top grain* and has the typical animal grain. It takes the best finish and wears well. It is also the highest quality and the most expensive layer. *Splits* have a looser, more porous structure and are cut across the fibers. They are not as smooth as top grain and tend to rough up during wear. Most split leathers are given an embossed finish or a suede finish. Although splits are not identified as such on product labels, top grain is usually mentioned. Splits are less expensive and lower in quality.

Leather is a durable product with a noticeable odor. It varies greatly in quality—not only from skin to skin but within one skin. Like wool fibers, leather from the backs and sides of the animal is better, whereas that from the belly and legs tends to be thin and stretchy or very coarse.

Leather picks up oils and grease readily. It requires special care in cleaning since it is stiffened by solvents. Most dry cleaners send leather and suede items to a specialist for cleaning. Leather cleaning removes soil, odor, and oil from the skin. Unfortunately, screen prints, dyes, and fillers may also be removed. Scars and other flaws like wrin-

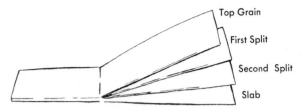

Fig. 15–37   *Split leather.*

kles, vein marks, and texture differences may appear. The oil can be replaced fairly easily. Dry cleaners can redye to bring the item closer to its original appearance. However, screen prints and wrinkles create problems that cannot be handled as easily (see Figure 15-38). Many consumers assume the dry cleaner is at fault when these problems occur. That may well be the case. Frequently, the problem lies with the manufacturer who selected the incorrect hide, process, chemical, or component to use in the item. For example, fusible interlinings in jackets may separate or shrink, causing bubbling or puckering of the leather. Screen prints may not be tested for fastness to dry cleaning before application to the leather.

Leathers are used for apparel, upholstery, wall coverings, athletic gear (balls, gloves, and saddles), luggage and bags, and accessories like wallets, lamps, and coasters.

Reconstituted leathers have been made by grinding up leather, mixing it with urethane, and forming

Fig. 15–36   *Cross-sectional drawing of a strip of leather, showing variations in density of fiber.*

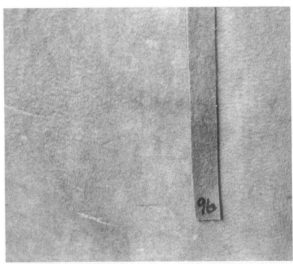

Fig. 15–38   *Pigskin suede after dry cleaning. The strip superimposed on the sample illustrates the original color and texture. Scars and other hide flaws are clearly visible.*

into sheets. This "leather" product is uniform in thickness and quality and is not limited in length and width.

SUEDE *Suede* is a popular leather for coats, jackets, dresses, trims, and furnishings like upholstery and wall coverings. The soft, dull surface is made by napping (running the skin under a coarse emery board) on the flesh side or on one side of a split to pull out the fibers. Suede is a very durable product, but it requires special care. Rain, wet snow, and other moisture damage suede. Cleaning of suede also should be done by specialists.

Furs

A *fur* is any animal skin or part of an animal skin to which the hair, fleece, or fur fibers are attached. Most fur is used in apparel, but fur is also used for throws and rugs, wall hangings, and animal toys. Fur garments are considered luxury items by the United States government. Consumers usually purchase furs because of their beautiful appearance rather than for their warmth, durability, or easy care. It is important to know about the kinds of fur, how fur garments are made, and how to care for them in order to make wise selections and to maintain the beauty of the garment.

Furs are natural products and therefore vary in quality. Good-quality fur has a very dense pile. If the fur has guard hairs they are long and very lustrous. The fur is usually soft and fluffy. The quality depends on the age and health of the animal and the season of the year in which it is killed.

Fur trapping has long been an important industry in all parts of the world. Fur farming, started in 1880, has been a boon to the fur industry because better pelts are produced as a result of scientific breeding, careful feeding and handling of the animals, and slaughtering them when the fur is in prime condition. Silver fox, chinchilla, mink, Persian lamb, and nutria are the common fur-bearing animals raised on ranches. By crossbreeding and inbreeding, new and different colored furs have been produced.

The cost of fur depends on fashion, the supply and demand for fashionable furs, and the work involved in producing the item. Chinchilla, mink, sable, platina fox, and ermine have always been very expensive.

Skins are gathered together from all over the world and sold at public auction. The four largest markets for fur are in St. Louis, New York, London, and Montreal.

Furs go through many processes before they are sold. Dressing of fur is comparable to tanning of leather and the purpose is the same—to keep the skins from putrefying and make them soft and pliable. Dressing must be more carefully done than with leather so that the surface hairs or fibers will not be damaged. After tanning, pelts are combed, brushed, and beaten. The final process is drumming in sawdust to clean and polish the hair and to absorb oil from the leather and fur. The sawdust is removed by brushing or vacuuming.

Many furs are dyed. Furs may be dyed to make less expensive furs look like the expensive ones. Muskrat may be dyed to resemble seal, rabbit may be stenciled to look spotted, and so forth. Furs are also dyed to improve their natural color as well as to give them unnatural colors—red or green, for example. Tip dyeing is brushing the tips of the fur and guard hairs with dye. Furs also are dip dyed, a process in which the entire skin is dipped in dye. Some furs are bleached and some are bleached and then dyed.

Furs require care to keep them beautiful. They should not be stored in damp places or in hot, humid places and never in plastic bags. Between seasons, if possible, garments should be sent to a furrier for cold storage; the furs are kept in special vaults in which the temperature and humidity are controlled. To restore luster and clean the garment, it is usually best to send it to a furrier once a year. Furs should never be dry cleaned, unless the furrier method is used. In this method, the fur is tumbled in an oil-saturated, coarsely grained powder. The powder absorbs soil, adds oil to the fibers and skin, and cleans the fibers without excessive abrasion and matting. The item must be carefully brushed and vacuumed to remove the excess powder. Often after furs have been cleaned, a small amount of the powder may be found in the pockets.

Furs should be protected from abrasion. Avoid sitting on fur garments. Hang them on a wide, well-constructed hanger and allow plenty of space between garments. Shake garments rather than brush them.

KEY TERMS

Film
Plain film
Nonreinforced film
Expanded film
Supported film
Foam
Fiberweb structure
Dry-laid fiberweb
Wet-laid fiberweb
Spun-bonded web
Spun laced web
Melt-blown fiberweb
Needle punching
Chemical adhesive
Batting
Wadding
Fiberfill
Resiliency
Resistance to shifting
Fusible fiberwebs
True felt
Netlike structure
Braid
Lace
Handmade lace
Leavers lace

Battenburg lace
Cordonnet lace
Reembroidered lace
Raschel lace
Multiplex fabric
Coated fabric
Lamination
Poromeric fabric
Suedelike fabric
Flock fibers
Tufting
Laminates
Wet-adhesive method
Foam-flame process
Stitch-bonded fabric
Quilted fabric
Knit-through fabric
Pinsonic fabric
Supported-scrim structure
Leather
Grain
Tanning
Top grain
Split leather
Suede
Fur

QUESTIONS

1. Why are fiberweb structures so important in the industrial products markets?
2. From the list of fabrication methods in this chapter (film, foam, fiberweb, lace, braid, coated, flocked, tufted, bonded, quilted, leather, and fur) identify which are made from these materials:
   solutions
   fibers
   yarns
   fabrics
3. Identify which fabrication methods combine two or more of the materials listed in question 2.
4. What performance can be expected from these products?
   a vinyl film (jersey supported) upholstered recliner chair
   a 100 percent polyester Leavers lace casement drapery for a master bedroom
   a quilted bedspread and matching draperies (50 percent polyester/50 percent cotton) for a hotel room
   a pair of leather slacks
   wall covering of a suedelike structure
   a poromeric raincoat of 65 percent polyester/35 percent cotton (outer fabric)

SUGGESTED READINGS

Batra, S. K., Hersh, S. P., Baker, R. L., Buchanan, D. R., Gupta, B. S., George, T. W., and Mohamed, M. H. (September, 1985). "Neither Woven nor Knit: A New System for Classifying Textiles." *Nonwovens Industry*, pp. 28, 30, 32, 34, 35.

Better Business Bureau of Milwaukee (1976). *Understanding Your Leather and Suede Garments.* Milwaukee, WI: Author.

Davies, Stan, and Owen, Phil (August, 1989). "Staying Dry and Keeping Your Cool." *Textile Month,* pp. 37–40.

Earnshaw, Pat (1982). *A Dictionary of Lace.* Aylesburg, Bucks, United Kingdom: Shires Publications.

Grayson, Martin, ed. (1984). *Encyclopedia of Textiles, Fibers, and Nonwoven Fabrics.* New York: John Wiley & Sons.

Schwartz, Peter, Rhodes, Trevor, and Mohamed, Mansour (1982). *Fabric Forming Systems.* Park Ridge, NJ: Noyes Publications.

Wagner, J. Robert (1982). *Nonwoven Fabrics.* Norristown, PA: Author.

SECTION 5

FINISHING

CHAPTER 16

Finishing: An Overview

OBJECTIVES

- To understand the general steps and sequence involved in fabric finishing.

- To recognize the ways fabrics can be modified in finishing.

- To relate finishing to fabric quality and end-use suitability.

*T*HE FOUR CHAPTERS IN THIS SECTION FOCUS ON converting a fabric from a raw form to the form consumers expect. In this process, the fabric is finished.

A *finish* is anything that is done to fiber, yarn, or fabric either before or after fabrication to change the *appearance* (what is seen), the *hand* (what is felt), or the *performance* (what the fabric does). All finishing adds to the cost of the end product and the time it takes to produce the item.

The sequence normally followed in textile processing is an involved one. Often several steps are repeated. A common sequence is fiber processing followed by yarn processing. Fabrication (producing a fabric) usually follows some preparation steps. In preparation, the yarn or fabric is made ready for additional steps in the sequence. Bleaching is almost always done before dyeing. Coloration is usually done before finishing and reworking (repairing). The following is a diagram of a normal pattern in finishing:

Fiber Processing → Yarn Processing →
Preparation → Fabrication → Bleaching →
Coloration → Finishing → Reworking

Finishing may be done in the mill where the fabric is constructed or it may be done in a separate establishment by a highly specialized group called *converters.* Converters operate in two ways: They perform a service for a mill by finishing goods to order, in which case they are paid for their services and never own the fabric; or they buy the fabric from a mill, finish it according to their own needs, and sell it under their own trade name.

A *permanent finish,* such as mercerization, lasts the life of the item. A *durable finish,* such as durable press, lasts longer than a temporary finish, but not for the life of the item. These finishes often require some manipulation, especially as the fabric ages. With durable-press finishes, older items may require some touch-up ironing. A *temporary finish,* such as simple calendering, lasts until the item is washed or dry cleaned. A *renewable finish,* such as some water-repellent finishes, can be applied with no special equipment, or it may be applied by the dry cleaner.

Some finishes—such as dyeing, printing, or embossing—are easy to recognize because they are visible. Other finishes—such as durable press—are not visible but have an important effect on fabric performance.

Consumers may have difficulty understanding the higher costs for fabrics with invisible finishes, like durable-press and soil-resistant finishes. Improved performance is expected, but the consumer needs to recognize the visible finishes and the need for nonvisible finishes, as well as the serviceability of the finish.

Many finishing processes are used on both woven and knitted fabrics. The processes are very similar for either type of fabric. The major differences that exist between finishing woven or knitted fabrics occur in the way the fabric is handled or transported. Woven fabrics have little give or stretch. Knits have a much greater potential for stretch; hence precautions need to be taken to minimize stretching during finishing of knits. Pile fabrics are handled so that pile matting is minimized.

Gray goods (grey, greige, or loom state) are fabrics (regardless of color) that have been produced but have received no wet- or dry-finishing operations. Some gray goods fabrics have names, such as print cloth and soft-filled sheeting, which are used only for the gray goods. Other gray goods names, such as lawn, broadcloth, and sateen, are also used as names for the finished cloth.

Converted, or *finished, goods* have received wet- or dry-finishing treatments such as bleaching, dyeing, or embossing. Some converted goods retain the gray goods name. Others, such as madras gingham, are named for the place of origin; still others, such as silence cloth, are named for the end use. Figure 16–1 shows a print-cloth gray goods and the various looks of the fabric with different finishing procedures.

Mill-finished fabrics can be sold and used without further finishing. Some may be sized before they are sold.

For years, *water-bath finishing* was standard. In water-bath finishing, the chemical was placed in a water solution and padded onto the fabric by immersing the fabric in the solution and squeezing out any excess. The fabric was heavy with water and required a lot of energy to move it and remove the excess water from it. A great deal of water was used to scour or clean the fabric. Recently, with water pollution and environmental concerns and energy costs, *foam finishing* has become an alternative means of adding a finish. Foam finishing uses foam rather than a liquid in applying the finishing chemical to the fab-

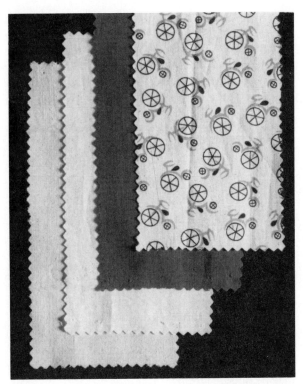

Fig. 16–1 *Print-cloth gray goods: as produced, bleached, piece dyed, printed* (from lower left to upper right).

ric. A foam is a mixture of air and liquid that is lighter weight than a solution of the liquid. Foam finishing is used because of the low-wet pickup (a much smaller amount of liquid is added to the fabric). In addition, energy is conserved in moving and drying the lighter fabric. The higher production speeds of foam finishing mean that the costs of finishing can be kept low. In foam finishing less water is used in scouring and cleaning. It is used to add both routine and special-purpose finishes to the fabric.

Another development in finishing is the use of *solvent finishing*. Solvent finishing was developed in response to a need to decrease water pollution and energy costs. In solvent finishing, a solvent other than water is used to mix the solution. Solvent finishing is not as popular as foam finishing because of the cost of solvents, expensive reclaiming processes, environmental concerns, regulatory issues, and health problems.

Computer control of finishing has also become extremely important. Computers provide automatic correction of processes, fabric tension, and finishing solutions and temperatures. Computerization allows for ease of planning and incorporates built-in menus to facilitate changing of recipes. Computer

systems also result in better control of environmental impact. For example, computer systems allow for efficient treatment of residue and recycling of recoverable chemicals from finishing.

The method of combining finishing steps is receiving attention from the industry. Combining steps minimizes space, chemicals, energy, water, and costs. In single stage preparation, desizing, bleaching, and scouring occur in one step rather than the three separate ones usually required.

This chapter discusses routine finishing. Routine finishing includes those steps in finishing that are done to most fabrics to prepare them for dyeing and special-purpose finishes. These routine finishes are often referred to as *preparation*. The normal order of production of a cotton/polyester, bottom-weight, plain-weave fabric is discussed. Because many steps of production are discussed in detail elsewhere, these steps are included in the discussion for continuity, but see other chapters for review. Routine-finishing steps for other fiber or fabric types are discussed at the end of this chapter.

ROUTINE-FINISHING STEPS

Fiber Processing

In *fiber processing*, the cotton fibers are processed separately from the polyester fibers because of the differences in the two fiber types. Synthetic fibers like polyester generally require little additional processing once the fiber has been produced if they are used in filament form. However, since this fabric is to be a cotton/polyester blend, the polyester fibers must be in staple form to be blended. Thus, the polyester fibers were produced as filament tow, crimped and cut or broken into staple fibers, baled, and shipped to the yarn spinning facility.

Since cotton is a natural fiber, considerably more processing is necessary. The fiber is grown, picked at the appropriate time, ginned, baled, and shipped to the yarn processing facility. The cotton's grade must be assessed because the suitability of the cotton fiber is matched to the end use based on its grade. Higher grades of cotton demand higher prices in the market. These prices fluctuate on a daily and seasonal basis, as do most agricultural commodities. Hence, the price of cotton is more likely to vary than that of the polyester fibers. The processing of these two fiber types is discussed in Chapters 4 and 8.

Yarn Processing

In *yarn processing* the fibers are aligned, blended, and twisted. Both fiber bales must be opened and dirt and soil removed. The compact fibers must be loosened and aligned in a parallel fashion before the yarns can be produced. However, since the properties of these two fibers differ significantly, the processing tends to be separate until well into the yarn production process; for blends, fibers are often combined at the roving stage. Once the fibers are blended, the appropriate amount of twist is added to the yarns. Generally, the warp yarns have slightly higher twist to facilitate the weaving process. After the yarns have been spun, they are wound on bobbins and shipped to the mill to be processed into fabric. Yarn processing is discussed in Chapter 10.

Yarn Preparation

Preparation involves several steps. The first steps involve the yarns and will be discussed before the fabrication step.

SLASHING In *slashing* the warp yarns are treated before being threaded into the loom for weaving. These yarns are coated with a mixture of natural starches or synthetic resins to enable the yarns to resist the abrasion and tension of weaving. Slashing adds a protective coating to the yarn to obtain optimum weaving efficiency. Slashing decreases yarn hairiness. This has become more important with faster, shuttleless looms. The sizing may contain a gum, starch, metal-to-fiber lubricant, preservative, defoamer, or a combination of these ingredients. For this cotton/polyester-blend fabric, the sizing is probably a mixture of a gum or starch and a lubricant or poly (vinyl alcohol). The filling yarns generally receive little if any treatment prior to weaving. The sizing must be removed after weaving in order for the finishes to bond with the fiber.

Fabrication

Fabrication normally follows the slashing step. In fabrication the fabric is woven, knitted, or created in some other manner. At the mill the cotton/polyester yarns are repackaged into the appropriate size unit for weaving. Warp yarns are threaded through the heddles in the harnesses and the spaces in the reed after slashing. Filling yarns are packaged for the specific type of loom to be used in weaving. Since shuttleless looms are so common in the U.S. textile industry, assume that this fabric will be made on such a loom. Filling yarn length is measured during weaving and the yarns are cut so that only the length needed for one insertion is available at any one time. The filling yarn is inserted in a shed that has every other warp yarn raised to create a plain weave. When the length of warp yarns has been woven, the fabric is removed from the loom and the cloth beam is transported to the finishing plant for appropriate finishing steps. For a more detailed discussion see Chapters 12 through 15.

Fabric Preparation

DESIZING In *desizing* the sizing added to the warp yarns in the slashing step is removed. Physical or chemical desizing may be done depending on the type of sizing and the fiber content of the fabric. Although sizing is present only on the warp yarns, all yarns in the fabric are treated since they will not be separated. In cotton-blend fabrics, physical desizing (agitation) with chemical desizing (an enzyme) may be done.

CLEANING All gray goods must be *cleaned* and made ready to accept the finish. Gray goods contain a warp sizing, which makes the fabric stiff and interferes with the absorption of liquids. The fabric must be desized before further finishing can be done. Also, fabrics are often soiled during fabrication and must be cleaned for that reason. Warp sizing, dirt, and oil spots have always been removed by a washing process—*degumming* of silk, *kier boiling* of cotton, and *scouring* of wool.

SINGEING *Singeing* burns free projecting fiber ends from the surface of the cloth. These protruding ends cause roughness, dullness, and pilling, and interfere with finishing. Singeing is the first finishing operation for all smooth-finished cotton or cotton-blend fabrics and for clear-finished wool fabrics. The fabric is passed between two gas flame bars or hot plates to singe it on both sides in one step. Fabrics containing heat-sensitive fibers such as cotton/polyester blends are often singed after dyeing because the melted ends of the fibers may cause unevenness in color. Singeing is one of the best solutions for pilling.

SCOURING *Scouring* is a general term referring to removal of foreign matter or soil from the fabric prior to finishing or dyeing. The procedure is related to the fiber content of the fabric. The foreign matter involved may be processing oils, starch, natural waxes, and tints or color added to aid in fiber identification during production. Common scouring chemicals are soaps or detergents. Scouring is generally done several times in finishing to wet out the fabric or to remove excess chemicals or soil. Wetted out fabrics are easier and more efficient to finish than dry fabrics.

Whitening

BLEACHING Most bleaches are oxidizing agents. The actual *bleaching* is done by active oxygen. A few bleaches are reducing agents and are used to strip color from dyed fabrics. Bleaches may be either acid or alkaline in nature. They are usually unstable, especially in the presence of moisture. Bleaches that are old or have been improperly stored lose their oxidizing power. In bleaching the goals are a uniform removal of hydrophobic impurities in the fabric and a high, uniform degree of whiteness of the fabric in order to get clear uniform colors when dyeing.

Any bleach will cause some damage and, because damage occurs more rapidly at higher temperatures and concentrations, temperature and concentration must be carefully controlled.

The same bleach is not suitable for all kinds of fibers. Because fibers vary in their chemical reaction, bleaches must be chosen with regard to fiber content.

The finisher uses bleaches to clean and whiten gray goods. The natural fibers are an off-white color because of the impurities they contain. Because these impurities are easily removed from cotton, most cotton gray goods are bleached without damage. The bleaching step is often omitted with wool because it has good affinity for dyes and other finishes even if not bleached.

Peroxide bleaches are common factory bleaches for cellulose and protein fibers and fabrics. *Hydrogen peroxide* is an oxidizing bleach. Peroxide bleaches best at a temperature of 180–200°F in an alkaline solution. These bleaching conditions make it possible to do peroxide bleaching of cellulose gray goods as the final step in the kier boil.

In the peroxide cold bleach procedure, the fabric is soaked overnight or for a period of 8 hours. This procedure is often used on cotton-knit goods and wool to preserve a soft hand.

OPTICAL BRIGHTENERS *Optical brighteners* are also used to whiten off-white fabrics. They are fluorescent-white compounds, not bleaches. The fluorescent-white compounds are absorbed by the fiber and emit a bluish fluorescence that masks yellow. At the mill, optical brighteners give best results when used in combination with the bleach rather than as a substitute for it. They are also added to the spinning solution of some manufactured fibers to optically brighten them, since bleach may not be effective on these fibers.

Further Preparations Steps

MERCERIZATION *Mercerization* is the action of an alkali (caustic soda) on a fabric. Mercerizing was a revolutionary development discovered in 1853 by John Mercer, a calico printer. He noticed that his cotton-filter cloth shrank and became stronger, more lustrous, and more absorbent after filtering the caustic soda used in the dye process. Little use was made of mercerization at that time because the shrinkage caused a 20–25 percent yardage loss, and the increased durability caused mill men to fear that less fabric would be used. In 1897, H. Lowe discovered that if the fabric were held under tension, it did not shrink but became lustrous and silklike.

Mercerization is used on cotton, linen, and some rayon fabrics for many different reasons. It increases the luster and softness, gives greater strength, and improves the fabric's affinity for dyes and waterborne finishes. Plissé effects can be achieved in cotton fabrics (see Chapter 17). Cotton is mercerized for luster in both yarn and fabric form.

Yarn mercerization is a continuous process in which the yarn under tension passes from a warp beam through a series of boxes with guide rolls and squeeze rolls, a boil-out wash, and a final wash (Figure 16–2).

Fabric mercerization is done on a frame that contains mangles for saturating the cloth; a tenter frame for tensioning the fabric both crosswise and lengthwise while wet; and boxes for washing, neutralizing the caustic soda with dilute sulfuric acid, scouring, and rinsing. In *tension mercerization* the fabric or yarn being mercerized is under tension. The concentration of the sodium hydroxide solution is high, generally around 20 percent. The sodium hydroxide causes the fiber to swell. Because of the tension during the swelling, the fibers become more

Fig. 16–2 *Mercerization of warp yarn. (Courtesy of Coats & Clark, Inc.)*

rodlike and rounder in cross section, and the number of convolutions decreases (Figure 16–3).

Tension mercerization results in:

• *Increased strength.* The molecular chains are less spiral in form and more oriented in length, making the fibers 30 percent stronger.

• *Increased absorbency* because the fiber swells. This opens up the molecular structure so that more moisture can be absorbed. The moisture regain is 11 percent. Mercerization is done primarily to improve the dyeability of cotton yarns and fabrics.

• *Increased luster* because the fibers become rounder with fewer convolutions and thus reflect more light. Mercerization for luster is done under tension and on long-staple cotton yarns and fabrics.

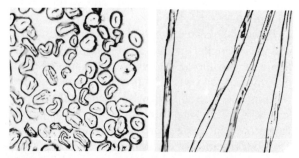

Fig. 16–3 *Photomicrographs of mercerized cotton: cross-sectional view 500 × (left); longitudinal view 250 × (right). (Courtesy of E. I. du Pont de Nemours & Company.)*

Greater absorbency results from mercerization because the caustic soda causes a rearrangement of the molecules, making more of the hydroxyl groups available to absorb more water and water-borne substances. Thus dyes can enter the fiber more readily. When they are fixed inside the fiber they have better colorfastness characteristics. Mercerized fabrics take resin finishes better for the same reason.

Increased strength is another important gain. Mercerized cotton fibers are stronger because, in the swollen fiber, the molecules are more nearly parallel to the fiber axis. When stress is applied, the end-to-end molecular attraction is harder to rupture than in the more spiral fibril arrangement.

Slack mercerization consists of dipping 100 percent cotton cloth in a 23 percent caustic soda solution, allowing it to react for 1½ minutes, and then washing and drying it. The cloth shrinks and the yarn crimp increases. The straightening of the crimp when stress is applied gives the stretch. One-way or two-way stretch can be obtained by variations in the mercerization conditions. Stretch is achieved in cotton by slack mercerization. Slack mercerization is done primarily to increase the absorbency and to improve the dyeability of cotton yarns and fabrics.

AMMONIATING FINISHES *Ammoniating finishes* are alternate finishes to mercerization used on cotton and rayon yarns and fabrics. Yarns or fabrics are treated with a weak ammonium solution at −33°C and are then passed through hot water, stretched, and dried in hot air. The finish is similar to mercerization but is less expensive and less polluting. The ammonia swells the fiber, but not to the degree that sodium hydroxide does. Fabrics that have had the ammonia treatment have good luster and dyeability. These fabrics do not dye to the same depth as mercerized fabrics, however. Because the amount of resin needed is less than with mercerized fabrics, ammonia-treated fabrics have better crease recovery and less loss of strength and abrasion resistance following wrinkle-resistant finishes than mercerized fabrics. Ammonia-treated fabrics are also less stiff and harsh than mercerized fabrics. Ammonia-treated fabrics have an increase in tensile strength of 40 percent and an increase in elongation of two to three times that of untreated cotton. These fabrics also are less sensitive to thermal degradation. Duralized and Sanforset are trade names that refer to means of improving the easy-care properties of heavy cotton fabrics like denim. Liquid ammonia treatments frequently are used as a substitute for mercerization on cotton sewing threads.

Coloration

Color is normally added to the fabric at this stage in the sequence. Properly prepared goods are critical to the quality of the dye or print. Dyeing and printing are discussed in detail in Chapter 19.

Finishing

SPECIAL-PURPOSE FINISHES *Special-purpose finishes* that would be appropriate for the cotton/polyester-blend fabric might include durable-press, soil-release, and a fabric-softening finish. These finishes usually follow dyeing to avoid interfering with the absorption of the dye by the fibers. These finishes are discussed in Chapter 18.

TENTERING *Tentering,* one of the final finishing operations, performs the double process of straightening and drying fabrics. In tentering, the fabric can be fed to the pins or clips at a speed slightly greater than that of the chains of the tentering frame. The result is that the amount of lengthwise shrinkage can be reduced to a degree.

Tentering is an important finishing step in terms of the fabric's quality. If the filling yarns are not perfectly perpendicular to the warp yarns, the fabric is off-grain. If the two ends of the filling yarn are not directly across from each other, the fabric will exhibit *skew.* If the center of the fabric moves at a slower speed than the two edges, the fabric will exhibit *bow* (see Chapter 12). Both of these off-grain problems can be eliminated by proper tentering. However, if a fabric was tentered off-grain, it will be printed off-grain as well. Some tentering frames have electronic sensors that help control the grain. The fabric may go through the tentering frame several times during finishing.

Tenter machines are of two types: the pin tenter and the clip tenter (Figure 16–4). The mechanism on the two sides moves around like a caterpillar tractor wheel, holding the fabric by a series of pins. More tension can be exerted by the clip tenter, but in cases where its use may damage the fabric, the pin tenter is used. The marks of the pins or the clips are often evident along the selvage.

Drying

Because of the frequent wetting of textiles in finishing, drying is also frequent, especially on cellulosics to minimize mildew and weight. The drying process usually uses hot air blowing past the textiles in an large convection oven at a temperature above the boiling point of water to remove the water quickly by evaporation. Fabrics in convection ovens are usually tentered as discussed in the previous section. Other means of drying fabrics, which are less efficient, include contact with hot metal rollers (conduction drying) and use of an infrared lamp, radio waves, or microwaves (irradiation).

LOOP DRYING Fabrics with a soft finish, towels, and stretchy fabrics such as knits are not dried on the tenter frame but on a *loop dryer,* where the drying can be done without tension. Many rayon fabrics are dried on loop dryers because of rayon's lower wet strength and soft hand.

HEAT SETTING In *heat setting* the fabric is usually placed on a tenter frame and passed through an oven where the time of exposure and the temperature

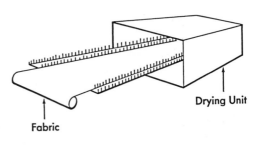

Fig. 16–4 *Tenter frames: clip tenter* (left); *drawing of pin tenter frame* (right).

are carefully controlled based on the fiber content and resins added to the fabric. The cotton/polyester fabric would require heat curing if it had been given a durable-press or soil-release finish or if the percentage of polyester was high enough, generally 50 percent or more, to give a degree of shrinkage control.

CALENDERING *Calendering* is a mechanical finishing operation performed by a series or stack of rollers through which the cloth passes. There are several types: the simple calender, the friction calender, the moiré calender, the Schreiner calender, and the embossing calender. Each produces a different finish (see Chapter 17).

Most calender machines have three rollers, but others may have two, five, or seven rollers. Hard-metal rollers alternate with softer rollers of foam, solid paper, or cloth-covered metal. Two metal rollers never run against each other.

The *simple calender* gives a smooth, flat, ironed finish to the fabric. The cloth is slightly damp before it enters the calender. The metal roll is heated. The cloth travels through the calender at the same speed the rollers rotate so they simply exert pressure to smooth out the wrinkles and give a slight sheen (Figure 16–5).

Reworking

INSPECTING Fabrics are *inspected* by pulling or running them over an inverted frame in good light. Fabric inspectors mark flaws in the fabric and record its quality at the same time. Fabric quality is a complex area related to the number of flaws, the severity of the flaws, and the length or size of the flaws. Mills and buyers must work together to define quality levels acceptable to both parties.

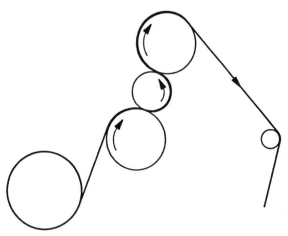

Fig. 16–5   Calender machine.

REPAIRING Flaws marked by the inspectors are repaired, if economically feasible or possible. Broken yarns are clipped, snagged yarns are worked back into the cloth, and defects are marked so that adjustments can be made when fabrics are sold. The fabric is then wound on bolts or cylinders ready for shipment.

ROUTINE-FINISHING STEPS FOR WOOL FABRICS

Carbonizing

Carbonizing, which is the treatment of wool yarns or fabrics with sulfuric acid, destroys vegetable matter in the fabric and allows for more level dyeing. Carbonizing is also done on recycled wool to remove any cellulose that may have been used in the original fabric. Carbonizing gives better texture to all-wool fabrics.

Crabbing

Crabbing is a wool-finishing process used to set wool fabrics. Fabrics are immersed in hot water, then in cold water, and passed between rollers.

Decating

Decating produces a smooth, wrinkle-free finish and lofty hand on woolen and worsted fabrics and on blends of wool and manufactured fibers. The process is comparable to steam ironing. A high degree of luster can be developed by the decating process because of the smoothness of the surface. The dry cloth is wound under tension on a perforated cylinder. Steam is forced through the fabric. Moisture and heat relax tensions and remove wrinkles. The yarns become set and are fixed in this position by cooling, which is done with cold air. For a more permanent set, dry decating is done in a pressure boiler. Wet decating often precedes napping or other face finishes to remove wrinkles that have been acquired in scouring. Wet decating as a final finish gives a more permanent set to the yarns than does dry decating.

Pressing

Pressing is the term used with wool or wool blends. In pressing the fabric is placed between heavy-metal plates that steam and press the fabric.

KEY TERMS

Finish
Converters
Permanent finish
Durable finish
Temporary finish
Renewable finish
Gray goods
Converted goods
Mill-finished fabrics
Water-bath finishing
Foam finishing
Solvent finish
Preparation
Slashing
Fabrication
Desizing
Cleaning
Singeing

Scouring
Bleaching
Optical brighteners
Mercerization
Slack mercerization
Ammoniating finish
Special-purpose finish
Tentering
Heat setting
Calendering
Reworking
Inspecting
Repairing
Carbonizing
Crabbing
Decating
Pressing

QUESTIONS

1. Differentiate among these terms: permanent finish, durable finish, temporary finish, renewable finish.
2. Why do yarns need to be finished before fabrication? What finishes are used?
3. At what stage is bleaching normally done? Why is it done at that time?
4. What problems can occur if tentering is improperly done? How does this affect fabric quality?
5. What terms are used in cleaning the following fibers?

   cotton
   silk
   wool

SUGGESTED READINGS

Needles, Howard (1986). *Textile Fibers, Dyes, Finishes, and Processes.* Park Ridge, NJ: Noyes Publications.

Powderly, Daniel (1987). *Fabric Inspection and Grading.* Columbia, SC: Bobbin International.

Trotman, E. R. (1984). *Dyeing and Chemical Technology of Textile Fibers.* New York: John Wiley & Sons.

CHAPTER

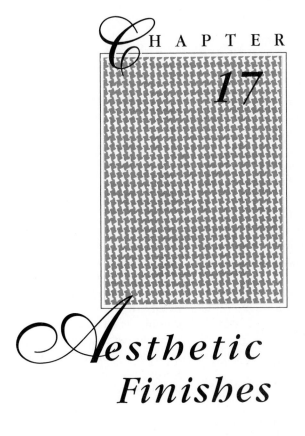

17

Aesthetic Finishes

OBJECTIVES

- To understand how finishes can alter aesthetic aspects of fabrics.

- To know the ways the aesthetic finishes can be applied to fabrics.

- To predict the performance of textiles with aesthetic finishes.

- To differentiate between applied designs and structural designs (recognize the quicker and less expensive imitation from the more expensive real thing).

Aesthetic finishes CHANGE THE APPEAR-ance and/or hand of fabrics. The finished fabric's name often reflects the change in appearance or the technique. For example, eyelet embroidery, ciré satin, and organdy are made by special finishes. Figure 17-1 shows several fabrics that were converted from print cloth. Percale is printed, chintz is waxed and friction calendered, plissé is printed with caustic soda, and embossed cotton is embossed. This fabric also could be flocked, embroidered, or surface coated.

Aesthetic finishes are also referred to as *applied design*. They are quicker and less expensive than incorporating the design as the fabric is produced (structural design). Table 17-1 compares applied and structural design.

Aesthetic finishes are grouped according to the change they produce in the fabrics:

1. Luster
2. Drape
3. Texture
4. Hand

The process, the effect, and the relationship of the finish to the fabric name will be explained for each group.

Many of these finishes are additive finishes that produce texture (body, stiffness, softness), luster, embossed designs, and abrasion resistance in the fabric. Some of these finishes mechanically distort or alter the fabric. Others use a chemical that changes the fabric. The permanence depends on the process, the fiber content, and the type of finish itself.

The *padding machine*, often called the "workhorse" of the textile industry, is used to apply dyes and finishing chemicals. These special chemicals are applied in either liquid or paste form, on one or both sides (Figure 17-2).

Padding is done by passing the fabric through the solution, under a guide roll, and between two padding rolls. The type of roll depends on the finish to be applied. The rolls exert tons of pressure on the fabric, forcing the finish into the fiber or yarn to assure good penetration. Excess liquid is squeezed off. The fabric is then steamed, cleaned, and dried.

The *backfilling machine* is a variation of the padding machine. It applies the finish to one side only, usually to the back of the fabric (Figure 17-3).

LUSTER

Luster finishes result in a change in the light reflectance of a fabric. Most finishes in this group increase light reflectance and improve the luster or shine of the fabric. The increase in luster may be over the entire fabric—as in the glazed, ciré, and Schreiner finishes—or it may be a localized increase in luster—as in the moiré and embossed finishes.

Glazed

Glazed chintz and polished cotton are two fabrics named because of the surface *glaze* that results from this finish. A *friction calender* is used to give a highly glazed surface to the cloth. If the fabric is first saturated with starch and waxes, the finish is temporary. If resin finishes are used, the glaze will be durable. The fabric is first passed through the finishing solution and partially dried. It is then threaded into the calender. The speed of the metal roller is greater than the speed of the fabric, and the roller polishes the surface.

Ciré

A *ciré finish* is similar to a glazed finish, except that the metal roll is hot, which results in more luster on the surface of the fabric. These fabrics often are made of thermoplastic fibers. Because thermoplastic fibers are heat sensitive, the surface of the fibers that comes in contact with the metal roll melts and flatten slightly and gives the highly polished appearance to the fabric. Ciré is a taffeta or satin fabric hot-friction calendered to give a high gloss, or "wet" look.

Moiré

These fabrics have a wood grain or watermarked appearance. To produce a *moiré pattern* on a fabric, two techniques can be used. In the first method, called *true moiré*, rib fabrics such as unbalanced taffeta or faille are used. True moiré is made by placing two layers of ribbed fabric face to face, so that the ribs of the top layer are slightly off-grain in relation to the under layer. The two layers are stitched or held together along the selvage and are then fed into the smooth, heated-metal roll calender. Pressure of 8 to 10 tons causes the rib pattern of the top layer

(a) (b) (c)

(d) (e)

Fig. 17–1 *Fabrics converted from print cloth: (a) gray goods; (b) roller printed; (c) waxed and friction calendered; (d) printed with caustic soda; (e) embossed calendered.*

to be pressed into the bottom layer and vice versa. Flattened areas in the ribs reflect more light and contrast with unflattened areas. This procedure can be modified to produce patterned moiré designs other than the traditional watermarked one.

In the second procedure an embossed-metal roll is used. The embossed roll has a moiré pattern engraved on it. When the roll passes over a ribbed fabric, the ribs are flattened in areas and a moiré pattern is created. If the fabric is thermoplastic and the roll is heated, the finish is permanent.

Schreiner

Fabrics with a Schreiner finish have a softer luster than most of the other luster finishes. The *Schreiner calender* (Figure 17-4) has a metal roller engraved

with 200–300 fine diagonal lines that are visible only under a magnifying glass. (The lines should not be confused with yarn twist.) Unless resins and thermoplastic fibers are used, this finish is temporary and removed by the first washing. The primary purpose of this finish is to produce a deep-seated

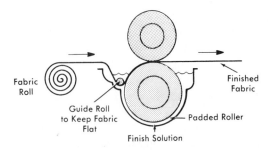

Fig. 17–2 *Padding machine.*

Table 17–1 Comparison of Structural and Applied Designs

Structural Designs	Applied Designs
Usually more expensive because decisions must be made farther in advance of market and process is more time consuming	Usually less expensive
Permanent design	Permanent, durable, or temporary
Woven figures are always on-grain (circular-knit jacquards may be skewed)	Figures may be off-grain
	May tender or weaken fabric
Kinds and Types	
Woven—jacquard, dobby, extra yarns, swivel dots, lappet designs, piqué, double cloth	Printed
	Flocked
	Embroidered
	Burned out
Knitted—jacquard single knits, jacquard double knits	Embossed
	Plissé
	Napped
Lace	Emerized
	Abrasive or chemical wash
Typical Fabrics	
Huck, damask, brocade, tapestry, shirting madras, piqué, dotted swiss, matelassé	Flock dotted swiss, embroidered linen, burned out, glazed chintz, moiré taffeta, embossed, frosted denim, sueded silk

luster, rather than a shine, by scattering the light rays. It also flattens the yarns to reduce the openness between them and give smoothness and cover. It can be used to upgrade a sleazy or lower quality

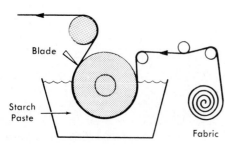

Fig. 17–3 *Backfilling machine.*

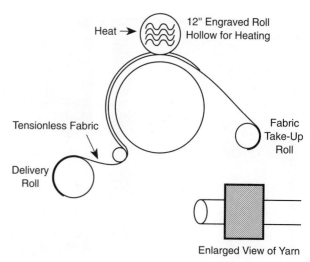

Fig. 17–4 *Schreiner calender machine for tricot.*

fabric. A Schreiner finish is used on cotton sateen and table damask to make them more lustrous and on nylon tricot to increase the cover.

Embossed

Embossed designs are created using an embossing calender that produces either flat or raised designs on the fabric. Embossing became a much more important finish after the heat-sensitive fibers were developed because it was possible to produce a durable, washable, embossed pattern. If the fabrics are made of solution-dyed fibers, they can be embossed directly off the loom and are then ready for sale.

The embossing calender consists of two rolls, one of which is a heated hollow, engraved-metal roll. The other is a solid-paper roll exactly twice the size of the engraved roll (Figure 17–5). The fabric is drawn between the two rollers and is embossed with the design. Embossing can be done to both flat and pile fabrics.

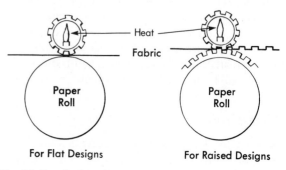

Fig. 17–5 *Embossing process.*

The process differs for the production of flat and raised designs. Raised-embossed designs will be discussed later in this chapter under the section on texture. Flat embossed designs are the simplest to produce. A metal, foam, or plastic roll engraved in deep-relief (Figure 17-6) revolves against a smooth-paper roll. The hot, engraved areas of the roll produce a glazed pattern on the fabric. Embossed brocades are an example of this type of design.

DRAPE

Drape finishes change the way a fabric falls or hangs over a three-dimensional shape. These finishes make the fabric stiffer or more flexible.

Crisp and Transparent

Transparent or parchment effects in cotton fabrics are produced by treatment with sulfuric acid. This fabric may be referred to as *parchmentized*. Since acid dissolves or damages cotton, the process must be very carefully controlled. Split-second (5–6 seconds) timing is necessary to prevent *tendering*, or weakening of the fabric. Several effects are possible: all-over, localized, or a plissé effect on either of the first two.

Because *all-over parchmentizing* produces a transparent effect, a sheer fabric of combed lawn is used. The goods are singed, desized, bleached, and mercerized. Mercerization is such an important part of the process that the fabric is mercerized again after the acid treatment to improve the transparency. The fabric is then dyed or printed with colors that will resist acid damage. The cloth is immersed in the acid solution and partial dissolution of the fiber surface takes place. On drying, this surface rehardens as a cellulosic film and gives permanent crispness and transparency. After the acid treatment, the cloth is neutralized in weak alkali, washed, and then calendered to give more gloss to the surface. This all-over treatment produces *organdy* fabric.

In *localized parchmentizing*, if the design is a small figure with a large transparent area, an acid-resist substance is printed on the figures and the fabric is run through the acid bath. The acid-resistant areas retain their original opacity and contrast sharply with the transparent background (Figure 17–7). If a small transparent design is desired, the acid is printed on in a paste form and then quickly washed off.

Burned Out

Burned-out effects are produced by printing a chemical on a fabric made of fibers from different fiber groups, such as rayon and polyester. One fiber, usually the less expensive or more easily dissolved fiber, is dissolved, leaving sheer areas. Figure 17–8 shows an *etched* rayon/polyester fabric. The rayon has been dissolved by acid. This finish is also known as etched or devoré.

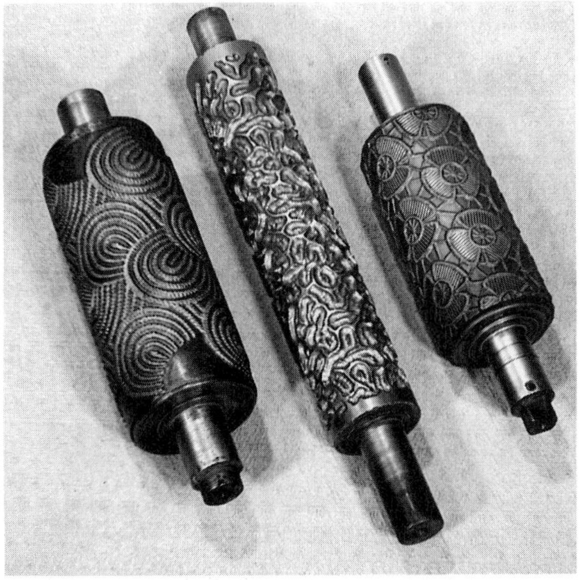

Fig. 17–6 *Embossing rolls. (Courtesy of Consolidated Engravers Corp.)*

Fig. 17–7 *Localized parchmentizing (acid finish) gives transparent background.*

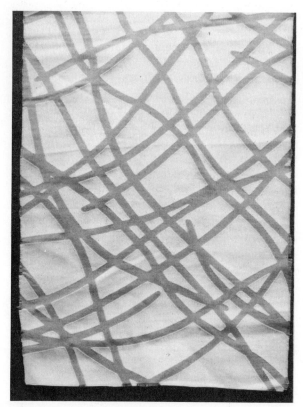

Fig. 17–8 *Burned-out design.*

Sizing

In *sizing*, or *starching*, the fabric is immersed in a mixture containing waxes, oils, glycerine, and softeners. For added weight, talc, clay, and chalk may be used. Gelatin is used on rayons because it is a clear substance that does not detract from the natural luster of the fibers but enhances it. Sizing adds stiffness, weight, and body to the fabric. The permanence of the sizing is related to the type of sizing and method of application. If the sizing is water soluble, it will be removed during washing. If the sizing is resin based and heat set, it will be permanent.

Weighting

Weighting is another technique used to add weight and body to a fabric. A metallic salt like stannic chloride is used. Salts that bond with the fiber are durable; others are a temporary surface coating. Silk may be weighted; however, weighted silks are not common today. Weighted silks are more sensitive to light damage and do not age well.

TEXTURE

Sheared

A *sheared fabric* is a pile or napped fabric in which the pile or nap has been cut to remove loose fiber or yarn ends, knots, and similar irregularities or surface flaws. Shearing is a finishing process done by a machine similar to a lawn mower. Shearing controls the length of the pile or nap and may create a patterned or a smooth surface. Sculptured effects are made by flattening portions of the pile with an engraved roller and then shearing off the areas that are still erect. Steaming the fabric raises the flattened portions.

Brushed

On a *brushed fabric* the surface of the fabric has been cleaned of fiber ends. Brushing follows shearing to clean the surface of clear-face fabrics. When combined with steaming, the nap or pile slants and is set in one direction, thus giving the up-and-down direction of pile and nap fabrics.

Embossed

Embossed fabrics also may have a raised design or pattern. The embossed design may be permanent if the fabric has a thermoplastic-fiber content or if a resin is used and heat set. Raised, or relief, designs require a more complicated routine than flat-embossed fabrics. The paper roll is soaked in water and then revolved against the engraved roll (without fabric) until the pattern of engraving is pressed into the paper roll. The temperature is adjusted to suit the fabric, which is then passed between the rolls.

Pleated

A *pleated fabric* is made by a special variation of embossing. Pleating methods are highly specialized operations done by either the paper-pattern technique or by the machine process.

The paper-pattern technique is a hand process and is therefore more costly, but it produces a wider variety of pleated designs. Garments in partly completed condition, such as hemmed skirt panels, are placed in a pleated-paper pattern mold by hand. Another pattern mold is placed on top so that the fabric is pleated between the two pleating papers. The whole thing is rolled into a cone shape, sealed, and then put in a large curing oven for heat setting.

The machine-pleating process is less expensive. The machine has two heated rolls. The fabric is inserted between the rolls as high-precision blades put the pleats in place. A paper backing is used under the pleated fabric and the pleats are held in place by paper tape. After leaving the heated roll machine, the pleats are set in an aging unit. The pleats may be stitched in place for permanent three-dimensional effects in apparel, upholstery, wall coverings, window treatments, and lampshades. Pleated fabric without stitching is used in similar products, but the pleats may soften with use.

Puckered Surface

Puckered surfaces are created by partial dissolution of the surface of a nylon or polyester fabric. Sculptured and "damasque" effects are made by printing a chemical, such as phenol, on the fabric to partially dissolve or swell it. Shrinkage occurs as it dries, thus creating a puckered surface.

Plissé

Plissé is converted from either lawn or print-cloth gray goods by printing sodium hydroxide (caustic soda) on the cloth in the form of stripes or designs. The alkali causes the fabric to shrink in the treated areas. As the treated stripe shrinks, the untreated stripes pucker. Shrinkage causes a slight difference in count between the two stripes. The treated or flat stripe increases in count as it shrinks. The upper portion of the cloth in Figure 17-9 shows how the cloth looks before finishing, and the lower portion shows the crinkle produced by the caustic-soda treatment. This piece of goods is defective because the roller failed to print the chemical in the unpuckered area.

The crinkle stripes can be narrow, as shown in Figure 17-9, or wide. In piece-dyed, wide-crinkle-stripe fabrics, the flat treated area may be a deeper color than the puckered area. The texture change is permanent, but can be flattened somewhat by steam and pressure.

Seersucker, plissé, and embossed fabrics can be very similar in appearance. These fabrics are frequently found in the same price range. Table 17-2 compares crepelike fabrics.

Flocked

Flocked fabrics are made to imitate pile fabrics. In a flocked fabric a surface fiber is applied to the fabric

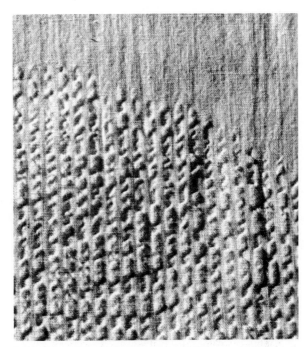

Fig. 17-9 *Plissé, showing treated* (bottom portion) *and untreated* (upper portion) *areas.*

after the base fabric has been produced. Flocking can be localized to imitate extra yarn weaves or all-over to imitate pile fabrics. See Chapter 15 for details of the process.

Tufted

Tufted fabrics are also made to imitate more expensive pile fabrics. In tufting, a surface yarn is stitched to the fabric to create a pile or three-dimensional effect. Tufting can be all over the fabric as in carpeting and upholstery, or in localized areas to create an imitation extra yarn weave or a fabric like that used in chenille bedspreads. See Chapter 15 for details of the process.

Embroidered

Embroidered fabrics can be produced either by hand or by machine. These fabrics are decorated with a surface-applied thread. The machine-embroidery operation uses zigzag stitches of various lengths very close together. There are two machines available for embroidery: the Schiffli and the multihead. The *Schiffli* embroidery machine is a frame 10 or 15 yards long (Figure 17-10) with 684 or 1,026 needles, respectively.

Table 17–2   Comparison of Crepelike Fabrics

High-Twist Natural or Manufactured Yarns (40–80 tpi)	High-Twist Thermoplastic Yarns	Bulky Yarn	Weave	Finish
Permanent crinkle. Flattens during use. Moisture will restore	Permanent crinkle. Retains appearance during use and care	Permanent crinkle. Does not flatten or need ironing	Crinkle does not flatten in use	Crinkle may flatten or be less prominent after washing
High potential shrinkage	Low potential shrinkage	Low potential shrinkage	Lower potential shrinkage	Lower potential shrinkage
Good drapeability	Good drapeability	Less drapeable	Less drapeable	Less drapeable
Stretches	Moderate stretch	Low stretch	Low stretch	Low stretch
Resilient, recovers from wrinkles	Resilient	Does not wrinkle	Wrinkles do not show because of rough surface	Wrinkles do not show because of rough surface
Dry cleaning preferable	Easy care	Easy care	Washable unless fiber content requires dry cleaning	Washable unless fiber content requires dry cleaning
Typical fabrics: Wool crepe Crepe de chine Matelassé Chiffon Georgette Silk crepe	Typical fabrics: Chiffon Georgette	Typical fabric: Silklike synthetics	Typical fabrics: Sand crepe Granite cloth Seersucker	Typical fabrics: Plissé Embossed

Fig. 17–10   *Schiffli embroidery machine.*

The designer makes a careful sketch of the embroidery pattern, which is enlarged several times and used as a guide for punching holes in a roll of thin, flexible cardboard. The perforated roll guides the placement of each stitch in the automated machine. An embroidered fabric is shown in Figure 17-11. Embroidering can be done on any kind of fabric.

Multihead embroidery machines can be used to create flat embroidery or pile embroidery. These machines are extremely versatile and can work with a variety of threads, ribbons, or bead/sequin strands. They can incorporate one or more colors of threads to create elaborate or simple designs in small or large scale. These machines are referred to as multihead because several machines are operated by the same computer system simultaneously (see Figure 17-12). Multihead machines are used to create designs and emblems that are sewn to other products like letter jackets, hats, and shirts. The machines are also used to stitch crests, logos, and other designs on finished items. (See Figure 17-13.)

Fig. 17–11 *Embroidered linen (right); printed to look like embroidery (left).*

Embroidered figures are very durable, often outlasting the ground fabric. The fabric is expensive compared to the same fabric unembroidered. Like other applied designs, the figure may or may not be on-grain.

Eyelet is an embroidery fabric with small, round holes cut in the fabric and stitching completely around the holes. The closeness and amount of stitching, as well as the quality of the background fabric, vary tremendously.

Expanded Foam

Another technique to create surface texture uses *expanded foam.* A colored compound is printed on the fabric. The compound expands during process-

ing to give a three-dimensional effect. Expanded foam patterns add three-dimensional texture to the fabric. These foams are durable, but create problems with pressing (see Figure 17–14).

Napped

Nap consists of a layer of fiber ends on the surface of the cloth, that are raised from the ground weave by a mechanical-brushing action. Thus napped fabrics are literally "made" by a finishing process. Figure 17–15 shows a fabric before and after napping .

Napping was originally a hand operation using several teasels (dried plant burrs shown in Figure 17–16) to gently brush up fiber ends. The raised fibers formed a nap that completely changed the appearance and texture of the fabric. Napping is less expensive than pile weave as a way of producing a three-dimensional fabric.

Napping is now done by rollers covered by a heavy fabric in which bent wires are embedded (Figure 17–17). Napping machines may be single action or double action. Fewer rollers are used in the single-action machine. Called pile rolls, they are all alike and travel at the same speed. The bent ends of the wires point in the direction in which the fabric travels, but the rollers are all mounted on a large drum or cylinder that rotates in the same direction as the cloth. The pile rolls must travel faster than the cloth to do any napping.

In the double-action napping machine, every other roll is a counterpile roll with wires that point

Fig. 17–12 *Multihead embroidery machine. (Courtesy of Baruden Co., Ltd. Distributed by Macpherson Incorporated)*

Fig. 17–13 *Multihead embroidered design showing two repeats of the pattern.*

in the direction opposite to those of the pile roll. The counterpile roll must travel slower than the cloth to produce a nap. When the speed of the rolls is reversed (pile rolls at slower speed and counterpile rolls at faster speed), a "tucking" action occurs. Tucking pushes the raised fibers back into the cloth and makes a smooth surface.

Napping results in a fabric with appealing characteristics. A napped surface and the soft twist of the filling yarns increase the dead-air space, providing good insulation. The fabric is soft and attractive. A dense mat of fiber ends on the surface imparts a degree of water repellency.

The amount of nap does not indicate the quality of the fabric. The amount may vary from the slight fuzz of flannel to the thick nap of imitation fur. Short compact nap on a fabric with firm yarns and a closely woven ground will give the best wear. Stick a pin in the nap and lift the fabric. A good, durable nap will hold the weight of the fabric. Hold the fabric up to the light and examine it. Press the nap aside and examine the ground weave. A napped surface may be used to cover defects or a sleazy construction. Rub the fabric between your fingers and then shake it to see if short fibers drop out. Thick nap may contain flock (very short wool fibers) . Rub the surface of the nap to see if it is loose and will rub up in little balls (pilling). Notice the pilling on the sweater in Figure 17-18.

Napped fabrics must be made from specially constructed gray goods in which the filling yarns are made of low-twist staple (not filament) fibers (see Chapter 11 for information about yarn twist). The difference in yarn structure makes it easy to identify the lengthwise and crosswise grain of the fabric. Figure 17-16 shows the warp and filling yarns from a camel-hair coat fabric before and after napping.

Fabrics can be napped on either or both sides. The nap may have an upright position or it may be "laid down" or "brushed." When a heavy nap is raised on the surface, however, the yarns are sometimes weakened.

Yarns of either long- or short-staple fibers may be used in napped fabrics. Worsted flannels, for example, are made of long-staple wool. The short-staple yarns used in woolen flannels have more fiber ends per inch and thus can have a heavier nap. In blankets, which may be heavily napped for maximum fluffiness, a fine-cotton (core) ply is sometimes used in the yarn to give strength.

Napped fabrics may be plain weave, twill weave, or knit. More filling yarn is exposed on the surface in a $\frac{2}{2}$ twill or a filling-faced twill; therefore a heavier nap can be raised on twill fabrics. The knit construction in napped fabrics is often used for extremely soft and flexible items.

Flannel is an all-wool napped fabric made in dress, suit, or coat weights. It may be made with

Fig. 17–14   *Fabric embellished with expanded foam.*

either worsted or woolen yarns, which may be yarn dyed. Worsted flannels are important in men's suits and coats and are used to a lesser extent in women's suits and coats . They are firmly woven and have a very short nap. They wear well, are easy to press, and hold a press well. Woolen flannels are fuzzier, less firmly woven fabrics. Because napping causes some weakening of the fabric, 15-20 percent nylon or polyester may be blended with the wool to improve the strength. *Fleece* is a coatweight fabric with a long brushed nap or a short clipped nap.

Cotton flannels flatten under pressure and give less insulating value than wool because cotton fibers are less resilient. The fibers are also shorter; thus there is more shedding of lint from cotton flannels. These fabrics are used in robes, nightwear, baby clothes, and sweatshirts. *Flannelette* is a plain-weave fabric that is converted from a gray goods fabric

called soft-filled sheeting. It is napped on one side only, has a short nap, and often has a printed design. The nap will form small pills and is subject to abrasion. *Suede* and *duvetyn* are also converted from

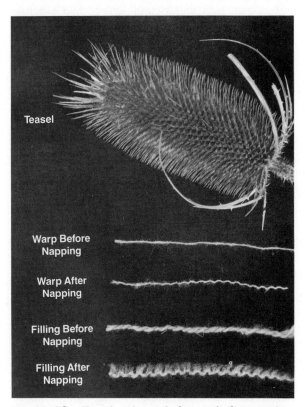

Fig. 17–16   *Teasel and yarn before and after napping.*

Before Napping   After Napping

Fig. 17–15   *Fabric before and after napping.*

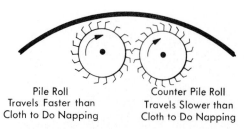

Pile Roll
Travels Faster than
Cloth to Do Napping

Counter Pile Roll
Travels Slower than
Cloth to Do Napping

Fig. 17–17   *Napping rolls.*

the same gray goods but are sheared close to the ground to make a smooth, flat surface. Of the two, duvetyn is lighter weight. *Outing flannel* is a yarn-dyed, white, or printed fabric that is similar in fabric weight and nap length to flannelette but is napped on both sides.

As the warp yarns in both flannelette and outing flannel are standard weaving yarns, it is easy to identify the grain of the fabric. Napped, knitted fabrics are often given pile-fabric names such as velvet or velour.

Fulled

Fulling is done on wool fabrics to improve the appearance, hand, body, and cover. Fabrics are fulled by moisture, heat, and friction—a very mild, carefully controlled felting process. A fabric that has been fulled is denser and more compact (see Figure 17-19).

Beetled

Beetling is a finish originally used on linen and fabrics resembling linen. As the cloth revolved slowly over a huge wooden drum, it was pounded with wooden-block hammers. This pounding continued

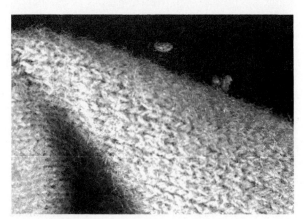

Fig. 17–18   *Pilling on a wool sweater.*

for hours. It flattened the yarns so they had an oval cross section, not a round one. The weave appeared tighter than it really was. The increased surface area gave more luster, greater absorbency, and smoothness to the fabric.

A contemporary method of producing a beetled fabric uses extreme pressure, resin, and thermoplastic fibers. In this case, the pressure flattens the yarns into the oval shape associated with beetled fabrics. The heat and resin result in a permanent flattening of the yarns. This finish is used on damask, crashes, and other linenlike fabrics.

Coronized

Coronizing is a process for heat setting, dyeing, and finishing glass fiber in one continuous operation. Since glass is low in flexibility, the yarns resist bending around one another in the woven fabric. Heat setting at a temperature of 1100°F softens the yarns so that they will bend and assume yarn crimp. Coronized fabrics have greater wrinkle resistance and softer draping qualities.

After heat setting, the glass fabric is treated with a lubricating oil; then color and a water-repellent finish are added. For this treatment, the Hycar-Quilon process is used. Hycar is an acrylic latex resin which, with the colored pigment, is padded on the fabric and then cured at a temperature of 320°F. This is followed by a treatment with Quilon, a water-repellent substance, and the fabric is again cured. The resin used in the color treatment increases the flexibility of the fiber.

Screen printing as well as roller printing can be done by the Hycar-Quilon process, since the color paste dries fast enough to allow one screen to follow another rapidly. The Hycar-Quilon process gives good resistance to rubbing off (crocking), which is one of the disadvantages of other coloring methods.

HAND

Emerizing

Emerizing, also known as peach skin, is a process used on fine silky fabrics of natural or manufactured fibers. It may be applied to polyester microfiber fabrics to improve their hand and comfort. The finish is usually applied to washed fabrics before they are heat set or dyed. The fabric moves at a speed of 15–20 meters per minute under two or more rollers. Each roller is coated with a different grade of emery

Fig. 17–19 *Wool cloth before* (left) *and after* (right) *fulling.*

or abrasive paper, from fine papers on the first roller to more abrasive paper on each additional roller. The process abrades the surface fibers and causes fibrils to split from the fibers. These fibrils give the fabric its soft hand and unusual appearance. The process damages the fabric and can decrease its tensile strength by as much as 60 percent. After emerizing, the fabrics are heat set and washed to remove the dust. Dyeing follows. Peach skin fabrics need to be handled carefully. Machine washing may abrade the fibrils and destroy the look of the fabric.

Abrasive or Chemical Washing

Abrasive or chemical washing are processes that were originally used on denim garments and have been popular in that application for several years under a variety of names, including acid wash, frosted, and pepper wash. These finishes are modified for application to other fabrications of cotton as well as a variety of fabrications of other fibers, like silk, polyester, and cotton/polyester blends. The washing process alters the surface of the fabric and damages it to some degree.

Many manufacturers are using these finishes on their products. The washing can be done by the sewing facility in an area of the plant referred to as the laundry. These processes require special equipment and knowledge and cannot be duplicated in the home. Some consumers have attempted stone washing at home with real stones. This usually results in an expensive repair or replacement of the washing machine.

CHEMICAL WASHES In this process a special chemical is added to the wash solution to alter the fiber's surface. Chemicals include alkalis, oxidizing agents, enzymes, and others that are specific to the fiber being treated. These chemicals may partially destroy the fiber and create irregularities, pits, pores, or other surface aberrations. Note that even though the term "acid wash" may be used , acid is not used in the process. This technique is used to produce fashion denims, comfort polyesters, and washed silks.

ABRASIVE WASHES With the abrasive washes, pumice or some other abrasive material is saturated with a chemical like potassium permanganate and tumbled with the fabric or garment for several hours. The abrasive material is removed and the chemical is neutralized in a bath. With fabrics like cotton, the abrasion is controlled by the length of time the fabric is treated and the style and type of pumice or stone used. With fabrics like silk that are lighter weight, the abrasion may result from tumbling against other fabrics in the chamber. Fabrics finished in this manner are referred to as stonewashed denim, sanded silk, and mudwashed silk.

Crepeing

Crepeing is a special compacting process to produce a fabric with a soft hand. Additional benefits include comfort stretch and soft drape. In crepeing the fabric is fed into the machine by a special blade at a faster rate than it is removed from the machine. Crepeing can create an all-over texture or a localized plisse effect.

Silk Boil-Off

In silk fabric sericin (gum) makes up about 30 percent of the weight. The boil-off finishing process removes the sericin and creates a looser, more mobile fabric structure. If the fabric is in a relaxed state while the sericin is being removed, the warp yarns take on a high degree of fabric crimp. This crimp and the looser fabric structure together create the liveliness and suppleness of silk, a suppleness that has been compared to the action of the coil-spring "Slinky" toy.

The properties are quite different when the boil-off is done under tension. The fabric crimp is much less, and the response of the fabric is more like that of a flat spring; thus the supple nature is lost. This helps to explain the difference between qualities of silk fabric.

Alkali Treatment

Manufactured fibers are normally processed under tension by a continuous method rather than by a batch method. Trilobal fabrics are processed in a completely relaxed condition. Finishing starts with a heat-setting treatment to stabilize the fabric to a controlled width, remove any wrinkles, and impart resistance to wrinkling. The next step is a very important caustic-soda (alkali) treatment, which dissolves away a controlled amount of the fiber. Similar to the degumming of silk, this step gives the fabric structure greater mobility. All remaining finishes are done with the fabric completely relaxed to get maximum fabric crimp. Figure 17–20 shows the effect of the alkali treatment on a fabric made of a circular-cross-sectional polyester.

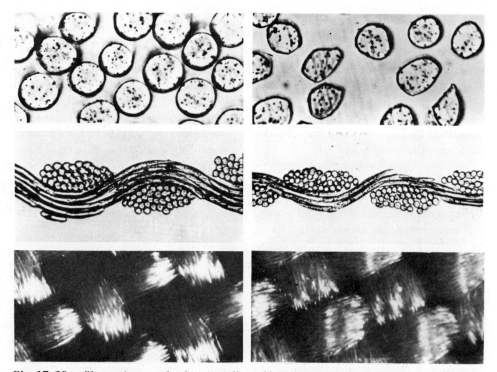

Fig. 17–20 *Photomicrographs showing effect of heat-caustic treatment. Original fabric on left; fabric after treatment on right. Dacron polyester fiber cross-section 1,000 × (top); fabric cross-section 200 × (center); fabric surface 50 × (bottom). (Courtesy of E. I. du Pont de Nemours & Company.)*

KEY TERMS

Aesthetic finishes
Applied design
Padding machine
Backfilling machine
Luster finish
Glazed
Friction calender
Ciré finish
Moiré pattern
Schreiner
Embossed design
Parchmentized
Tendering
Burned-out
Etched
Starching
Sizing
Sheared

Brushed
Pleated
Puckered surface
Plissé
Flocked
Tufted
Embroidered
Schiffli embroidery
Multihead embroidery
Eyelet embroidery
Expanded foam
Nap
Fulling
Beetling
Coronizing
Emerzing
Abrasive or chemical wash
Crepeing

QUESTIONS

1. What are the differences between embossed and plissé?
2. Explain the changes in serviceability of a fabric after it has been napped.
3. What kinds of fabrics are generally sheared? What is the purpose of shearing?
4. Describe the manner in which each fabric of these pairs was produced. Which are applied designs and which are structural?

    swivel dotted swiss and flocked dotted swiss
    extra yarn eyelash fabric and burned out
    plissé and seersucker
    tufted velvet and true velvet
    flocked corduroy and napped flannel

5. Predict the serviceability of each fabric listed in question 4.
6. Which of the finishes listed below would be permanent (last for the life of the fabric) and which would diminish with time or use? Why?

    heat-embossed nylon tricot
    pressure-embossed cotton
    burned-out rayon/polyester sheer drapery
    fulled wool gabardine
    water-soluble sizing on 100 percent cotton print cloth
    65 percent polyester/35 percent cotton glazed chintz upholstery (resin compound)
    100 percent polyester crepe de chine with caustic treatment

SUGGESTED READINGS

Jerg, Gunter, and Baumann, Josef (1990). "Polyester Microfibers: A New Generation of Fabrics." *Textile Chemist and Colorist, 22*(12), pp . 12–14.

Needles, Howard (1986). *Textile Fibers, Dyes, Finishes, and Processes.* Park Ridge, NJ: Noyes Publications.

Scott, Ken (April, 1990). "A Look at the Denim Processing Scene." *Laundry and Cleaning News International*, pp. 4–7.

Trotman, E. R. (1984). *Dyeing and Chemical Technology of Textile Fibers.* New York: John Wiley & Sons.

CHAPTER

18

Special-Purpose Finishes

OBJECTIVES

- To recognize the effects (both positive and negative) of special-purpose finishes.

- To relate special-purpose finishes to fabric, yarn, fiber, and end-use aspects.

- To understand the manner in which special-purpose finishes are applied.

- To recognize the problems special-purpose finishes are designed to eliminate or minimize.

SPECIAL-PURPOSE FINISHES ARE ALSO KNOWN as *functional finishes*. These are treatments that are applied to fabrics to make them better suited for a specific end use. Although they usually do not alter the appearance of fabrics, they improve performance. They help solve some consumer problems with textile products or make the fabric more suitable for a specific purpose. These finishes are organized by the performance aspect they address.

Special-purpose finishes add to the cost of the product, and their overall impact on performance may be difficult for consumers to recognize. This is especially true since the effect of the finish may be invisible or beyond consumer perception. For example, how does one measure the effectiveness of a soil-resistant finish since the fabric stays cleaner for a longer period of time? When finishes fail to perform at the expected or guaranteed level, consumers may complain. If the cost of the item is high or the yardage is great, civil lawsuits may be filed. For example, there may be lawsuits about carpeting in shopping malls if the carpet soils quickly or if the soil cannot be removed with appropriate treatment. This is especially common when guarantees have been made (see Chapter 21 for more information).

STABILIZATION: SHRINKAGE CONTROL

A fabric is *stabilized* when it retains its original size and shape during use and care. Unstable fabrics shrink or stretch, usually as a result of care. *Shrinkage*, the reduction in size of a product, is the more serious and more frequent problem.

The shrinkage problem begins in spinning, weaving, and finishing. Fabrics are under tension on the loom. In wet finishing, fabrics are pulled through machines in long continuous pieces and finally set under excessive warpwise tension that leaves the fabric with high residual shrinkage. Shrinkage occurs when these tensions are released by moisture and heat, as in laundering or steam pressing.

Shrinkage is used to advantage in the manufacture of some fabrics, as in fulling or shrinkage of crepe yarn in matelassé. Shrinkage is a disadvantage to the manufacturer and the consumer when it changes a product's dimensions.

There are two types of shrinkage: relaxation shrinkage and progressive shrinkage. *Relaxation shrinkage* occurs during washing or dry cleaning. Most relaxation shrinkage occurs during the first care cycle. However, many manufacturers and retailers test for shrinkage through three or more cleaning cycles because small amounts of relaxation shrinkage may continue to occur for several additional care cycles; this is *progressive shrinkage*. If the care is mild in the first cycle and more severe in later cycles, more shrinkage may occur during these later cycles than in the first cycle. For example, if the item was line dried in the first cycle and machine dried in later cycles, shrinkage will be more severe during machine drying. The following list groups fibers by the kind of shrinkage they normally exhibit:

1. *Cotton, linen, and high-wet-modulus rayon:* Exhibit relaxation shrinkage. No progressive shrinkage.
2. *Regular rayon:* Exhibits high relaxation shrinkage. Moderate progressive shrinkage.
3. *Wool:* Exhibits moderate relaxation shrinkage. High progressive shrinkage.
4. *Other properly heat-set manufactured fibers:* Exhibit relaxation shrinkage. No progressive shrinkage.

Mechanical-control methods or heat are used to eliminate relaxation shrinkage. Chemical-control methods are used to prevent progressive shrinkage.

Relaxation Shrinkage and Methods of Control

KNIT FABRICS Knit fabrics shrink because the loops may be elongated 10-35 percent lengthwise in knitting and wet finishing (Figure 18-1). During laundering, the stitches reorient themselves to their normal shape and the item becomes shorter and wider.

Fig. 18–1 *Knit stitches: (a) stretched; (b) relaxed.*

Minimal shrinkage of knits can be achieved by overfeeding the fabric between sets of rollers that result in lengthwise shrinkage. The increased use of polyester in blends with cotton knits permits the fabric to be heat set for stabilizing.

WOVEN FABRICS All woven fabrics shrink after the strains of yarn production, weaving, preparation finishes, and wet finishing are released, which occurs when the fabric gets wet. The warp yarns are under tension while they are on the loom, and the filling is inserted in a straight line. The filling takes on crimp as it is beaten back into the fabric, but the warp stays straight (Figure 18–2). When the fabric is thoroughly wet and allowed to relax, the yarns readjust themselves and the warp yarns also become crimped (Figure 18–2). This crimp shortens the fabric in the warp direction. With the exception of crepe fabrics, less change occurs in the filling direction.

Compressive shrinkage processes are used on woven fabrics of cotton, linen, and high-wet-modulus rayon. Regular rayons will not hold a compressive shrinkage treatment because of their high swelling and wet elongation.

In this process, a thick felt blanket is used since a thick blanket will shrink the fabric more than a thin one. The blanket, with the moist cloth adhering to its surface, is passed around a feed-in roll. In this curved position, the outer surface stretches and the inner surface contracts. The blanket then reverses its direction around a heated drum. The outer curve becomes the shorter, inner surface and the fabric adhering to it is compressed. The fabric, which is now against the drum, is dried and set with a smooth finish. The count will increase, and the fabric will actually be improved after compressing (Figures 18–3 and 18–4).

However, improper laundering may cause compressively shrunk fabrics to shrink as much as 6 percent. Tumble drying may also compress the yarns beyond their normal shrinkage.

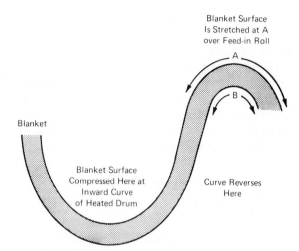

Fig. 18–3 *Reversal of curve causes change in size to compress fabric.*

London shrunk is a 200-year-old relaxation finish for wool fabrics that also removes production strains. A wet blanket—wool or cotton—is placed on a long platform, a layer of fabric is spread on it, and alternate layers of blankets and fabric are built up. Sufficient weight is placed on top to force the moisture from the blankets into the wool for about 12 hours. The fabric is hung to dry in natural room air. When dry, the fabric is subjected to hydraulic pressing by building up layers of fabric and specially made press boards with a preheated metal plate inserted at intervals and on the top and bottom of the stack. This setup of fabric, boards, and plates is

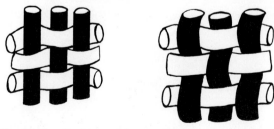

Fig. 18–2 *Position of the warp on the loom* (left); *after the fabric relaxes when it becomes wet* (right).

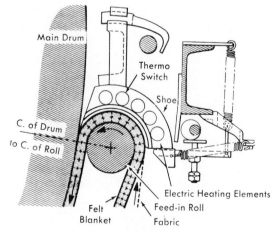

Fig. 18–4 *Closeup of compressive shrinkage process. The electrically heated shoe holds the fabric firmly on the outside of the blanket so that when the blanket collapses in straightening out, the fabric is shrunk accordingly. (Courtesy of the Sanforized Company.)*

kept under 3,000 pounds of pressure for 10–12 hours. London shrinkage is done for fine worsteds, not for woolens.

The label "Genuine London Process" or something similar is licensed by the Parrot Group of companies to garment makers all over the world. The permanent-set finish Si-Ro-Set, which produces washable, wrinkle-free wool fabrics, is now applied to some fabrics during London shrunk processing.

Progressive Shrinkage and Methods of Control

THERMOPLASTIC FIBERS Thermoplastic fibers are stabilized by *heat setting*, a process in which fabrics are heated at temperatures at or above the *glass transition temperature* (T_g) and then cooled. The T_g *temperature* is the point at which the amorphous regions of the fiber are easy to distort. It is lower than the melting point of the fiber and differs for various fibers. If properly heat set, fabrics will exhibit no progressive shrinkage and relaxation shrinkage will also be controlled (Figure 18–5).

WOOL FIBERS Washable wool is important in apparel and some furnishings and in blends with washable fibers. If wool fabrics are to improve their position in the competitive market with fabrics

made from wool-like fibers that have easy-care characteristics, they must be finished to keep their original size and surface texture during laundering. It might be assumed that people who can afford professional care will not be interested in washing wools. Another assumption might be that washable wools (those given a felting shrinkage-control treatment) are the poor- to medium-quality wools. Whether or not these assumptions are true, felting shrinkage is important today, as evidenced by the fact that patents for feltproofing wool continue to be issued. Figure 18–6 shows shrinkage of a wool sock after washing and drying.

To prevent felting shrinkage, the finish alters the scale structure by "smoothing off" the free edges and thus reduces the differential-friction effect that prevents wool fibers from returning to their original position in the fabric. The effectiveness of felting shrinkage treatments depends on the kind and amount of finish used and on the yarn and fabric construction. Worsteds need less finish than woolens. Low-count fabrics and low-twist yarns need more finish to give good washability. Treated-wool fabrics are usually considered machine washable, but care should be taken to use warm, not hot water and a short agitation period. Handwashing is preferable, because soil is easy to remove from the fiber and the handwashing process ensures lower temperature and less agitation. Machine washing may cause more loosening of fibers, which results in a fuzzy or slightly pilled surface.

Two methods are used to smooth off the free edges of the scales: surface coatings and halo-generation treatments. *Surface coatings* of a polyamide-

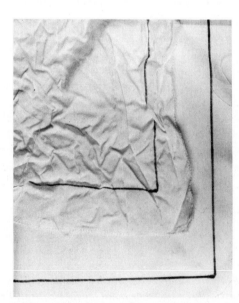

Fig. 18–5 *Comparison of thermoplastic fiber fabrics. Bottom fabric has been heat set. Note wrinkling and shrinkage of upper fabric (not heat set).*

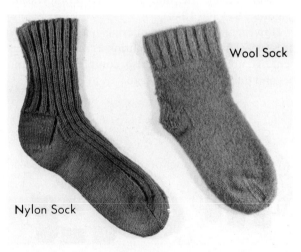

Fig. 18–6 *These socks were the same size when purchased. Nylon (left); wool (right).*

type solution are applied to mask the scales. This is a very thin, microscopic film on the fiber. In addition to controlling shrinkage, the coating tends to minimize pilling and fuzzing (one of the greatest problems in wash-and-wear wools), gives the fabrics better wash-and-wear properties, and increases resistance to abrasion. This process carries the trade name Wurlan.

Halogenation treatments, primarily with chlorine, are also used. They are low cost, can be applied to large batches of small items such as wool socks, do not require padding or curing equipment, and are fairly effective. Since the scales are partially dissolved, felting shrinkage is lessened. The processes damage the fibers and must be carefully done to keep the damage to a minimum. The scales are more resistant to damage than the interior of the fiber and should not be completely removed or there will be considerable reduction in wearing properties, weight, and hand. The fabric will feel harsh and rough. To maintain the strength of the fabric, 18 percent nylon fiber often is blended with the wool before weaving. The degradative process is especially good for handwashable items. A process combining chlorination and resin makes wool knits machine washable and dryer dryable. Shrinkage is less than 3 percent in length and 1 percent in width, and goods retain their loft and resiliency.

RAYON FIBERS The shrinkage of regular rayon varies with the handling of the fabric when wet. While it is wet the fabric can be stretched, and it is difficult to keep from overstretching it during processing. If it is dried in this stretched condition, the fabric will have high potential shrinkage; it will shrink when wet again and dried without tension because the moisture in the fabric adds enough weight to stretch it. It is almost impossible to determine this without laboratory or home testing.

Shrinkage-control treatments for rayon reduce the swelling property of the fiber and make it resistant to distortion. Resins are used to form cross-links that prevent swelling and keep the fiber from stretching. The resin also fills up spaces in the amorphous areas of the fiber, making it less absorbent. Aldehyde resins are superior to other resins because they do not weaken the fabric, are nonchlorine retentive, and have excellent washfastness. Treated rayons are machine washable, but the wash cycle should be short. High-wet-modulus rayon is also resin treated, mainly for durable-press purposes, because its shrinkage can be controlled by relaxation shrinkage-control methods.

SHAPE-RETENTION FINISHES

Even though care of contemporary textiles is a time-consuming task, it is hard to imagine the time and physical effort that it used to require! Imagine having to iron almost every item of apparel and bedding! With thermoplastic fibers, special shape-retention finishes, and modern washers and dryers, easy-care textiles are the norm. It is only the occasional object that requires the extra effort of ironing.

Theory of Wrinkle Recovery

Wrinkles occur when fabrics are crushed during use and care (creases and pleats made by pressing are desirable style features, however).Wrinkle recovery is dependent on *cross-links* that hold adjacent molecular chains together and pull them back into position after the fiber is bent, thus preventing the formation of a wrinkle. Fibers that have strong intermolecular bonds have good molecular memory. These fibers resist wrinkling and creasing, whereas fibers with weak bonds wrinkle and crease readily.

The cellulosic fibers do not have natural cross-links. Molecular chains are held together by weak hydrogen bonds. The hydrogen bonds of cellulose break with the stress of bending and new bonds form to hold the fiber in this bent position, thus forming a wrinkle. Resin cross-links give fibers a "memory" and good wrinkle recovery (Figure 18–7).

Urea formaldehyde was the first resin used to prevent wrinkles; other resins and improved resin combinations were developed later. Although fabrics treated with these resins were smooth, flat, and *wrinkle resistant*, they had poor abrasion resistance, lower tear strength, and a fishy odor.

Alternatives to the formaldehyde-based durable-press finishes have been identified. These include modified glyoxal-based reactants that decrease the formaldehyde release by 50 to 75 percent or reactants based on carboxylic acid derivatives. The carboxylic acid derivatives produce fabrics with better abrasion resistance, good durable press performance, and low shrinkage. However, color-fastness may be decreased. Unfortunately, both alternatives result in significantly higher costs of finished goods.

Resin finishes were first used in England in 1920 and in the United States in 1940 on rayon. The resin finishes were found to be equally good on cotton and linen fabrics.

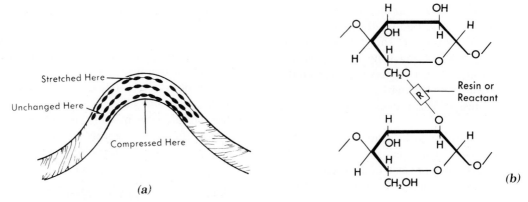

Fig. 18–7   *(a) Effect on internal structure when fiber is bent; (b) resin cross-link.*

Durable Press

Durable press is a descriptive term applied to items that retain their shape and their pressed appearance even after many uses, washings, and tumble dryings. The terms durable press and permanent press are used interchangeably, but durable is a more realistic description because the effectiveness of the finish decreases with age. Older items may require some touch-up ironing to meet appearance standards. Alternate terms for durable press are anticreasing and crease retention.

The two processes, *precured* and *postcured*, for durable-press items and fabrics are outlined here. The major difference in these two processes is the stage at which cutting, sewing, and pressing take place (Figures 18–8 and 18–9).

THE PRECURED PROCESS

1. Saturate the fabric with the resin cross-linking solution and dry.
2. Cure in a curing oven to form cross-links between molecular chains.
3. Cut and sew item. Press. (Yard goods for home sewing are made this way.)

THE POSTCURED PROCESS

1. Saturate the fabric with a resin cross-linking solution and dry.
2. Cut and sew the item and press shape with hot-head press.
3. *Cure* by putting pressed item into a curing oven at 300°–400°F.
4. Curing gives shape to the cellulosic fibers. The thermoplastic fibers were *set* by the hot-head pressing.

Problems associated with resin finishes—other than reduced tensile strength and abrasion resistance—are listed here:

1. Fabric stiffness and poor hand.
2. Chlorine absorption, which causes yellowing and loss of strength.
3. Offensive odors—fishy or formaldehydelike smell.
4. Color problems: "frosting," or loss of color on abraded edges; migration of color from the thermoplastic fibers to the cellulosic component as a result of the high curing temperature.

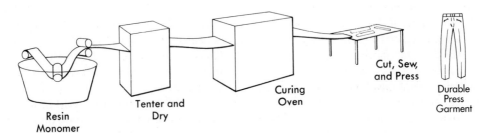

Fig. 18–8   *Precured process.*

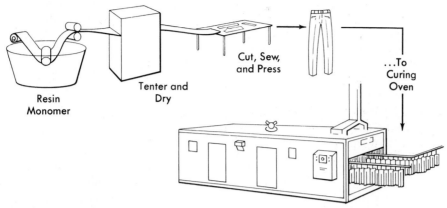

Fig. 18–9 *Postcured process.*

5. Soiling—especially the affinity of resins for oily soils. Soil-release finishes now help with this (see that section in this chapter).

6. Static pilling.

7. Construction problems—seam puckering, pressing-in or removing creases when altering items.

8. Health problems—sensitivity to formaldehyde (including breathing difficulty and sick building syndrome); a possible carcinogen.

Many of these problems have been solved or minimized, or alternative chemicals or processes have been developed.

By using blends of cotton/polyester instead of 100 percent cotton, less resin is needed. The high strength and abrasion resistance of polyester make these fabrics much more durable. Special pressing equipment has been developed for use on precured fabrics. Pretreating cotton with liquid ammonia or mercerizing cotton under tension adds strength to fabrics so they are not weakened as much from the finish. Polymer sizing added to the yarns before curing gives the fabric greater abrasion resistance.

Coneprest, by Cone Mills, is a process in which precured fabrics are made into garments. Where creases are desired the garment is sprayed with a substance that temporarily inactivates the wrinkle-resistant finish. The garments are then pressed under pressure to recur the finish.

Ameriset, developed by American Laundry Machinery Industries, is a finish process in which untreated fabrics are cut, sewn, and pressed. The garments are then placed in a gas chamber where formaldehyde and sulfur-dioxide vapor enters the fabric, causing cross-links in the cellulose fibers.

Creaset is a silicone-based finish by the company of the same name, Creaset, for all-wool and all-cotton fabrics.

DURABLE-PRESS WOOL Wool has good resiliency when it is dry, but it does not have durable-press characteristics when it is wet. *Durable-press wool* is achieved with resin treatments, but this must be accompanied by a treatment with shrink-resist resins in order to control wool's tendency to excessive shrinkage. Several procedures are used, but the one described here is typical. Si-Ro-Set is a trade name.

1. Flat fabric is treated with 1–2 percent of the durable-press resin and steamed (semidecated) for 3–5 minutes.

2. The item is made up, sprayed with more durable-press resin, and pressed. This gives the permanent-crease effect.

3. Shrink-resist resin is mixed with a dry cleaning solvent and the item is dry cleaned. The resin is then allowed to cure in the item for 3–7 days before it can be laundered.

Quality Standards and Care

Quality-control standards had not been developed during the wash-and-wear era and there was wide variation in fabrics, dependent on the economic objectives of the individual converter. To avoid problems, the industry developed standards for durable press and quality has been much more dependable. Registered trade names indicate to the consumer that the product has met certain performance tests. The consumer can also check the fabric for objectionable odor or excessive stiffness, which indicate poor processing. If the fabric is a blend, there should be an adequate amount of thermoplastic fiber to meet performance standards.

General care guidelines for durable-press items include the following:

- Wash these items frequently. Do not allow soil to build up. Resins have a special affinity for oil and grease, which should be removed quickly before they can penetrate.
- Pretreat stains, collars, and cuffs. Use a spot-removal agent on grease spots.
- Keep wash loads small. Crowding contributes to wrinkling.
- Heat sets wrinkles, so avoid heat as much as possible in the laundering process. Avoid wringing and squeezing. Use an automatic dryer if possible, but remove items promptly.

APPEARANCE-RETENTION FINISHES

Soil- and Stain-Release Finishes

Soil-release finishes function to reduce the degree of soiling of the fabric by repelling the soil or preventing a bond between the soil and the fabric. Thus these fabrics are easier to clean than those without soil-release finishes. Fluorochemicals are common, durable, and effective soil-resistant finishes.

Soil-release finishes definitely improve the fabric's performance in resisting soil, releasing soil, and retaining whiteness by resisting redeposition of soil from the wash water. Unfortunately, these finishes may not last the life of the item. Some are durable enough to last through 20–30 washings. Lack of permanence results from the surface application of the finish.

There are several companies that can be hired by design firms or consumers to add a chemically protective finish to fabrics on site, including products such as carpeting, upholstery, or wall coverings. These finishes impart soil and stain resistance. The firms provide a follow-up service as needed, a cleaning kit, and care instructions. There are also soil-resistant finishes the consumer can apply on site. However, research has shown that some of these finishes may actually increase soiling (Reagan, et al., 1990).

Soil-release finishes were developed because of the tendency of durable-press items to pick up and hold oily stains and spots. Oil affinity means that oil is absorbed into the resin or the fiber. Soil-release finishes either attract water and permit the soil to be lifted off the fabric or coat the fibers and prevent the soil from penetrating the coating.

Most durable-press items are blends of cotton/polyester. Untreated cotton is hydrophilic, and hydrophilic surfaces give the best oily soil-release performance, so cotton releases the oily soil when it is laundered. The resin finish, however, is hydrophobic and does not release the oily soil. Polyester is hydrophobic and oleophilic. It must be spot treated to remove oily soil from contact areas, such as the collar of a garment. When the polyester is coated with resin as it is in durable press, its oil affinity is increased. Finer fibers soil more readily than coarse fibers, and soil can penetrate low-twist yarns more easily than high-twist yarns.

Soil-release finishes make the surface less attractive to oil and more easily wetted—more hydrophilic. Many finishing materials fall into two general classes: They are mechanically or chemically bonded to the surface. Many soil-release finishes are organosilicon substances. Soil-release finishes include Scotchgard and Scotch Release by 3M, Visa by Milliken, and Teflon by Du Pont.

The soil-resistant process for carpets consists of a three-part program that combines a special carpet fiber (larger denier, modified cross section, and antistatic modification) with a stain-resistant finish and a treatment to block the dye sites on the fibers. When the dye sites are blocked, the fibers are no longer receptive to accepting color from stains. These blockers tend to concentrate near the surface of the fiber since that is the area most susceptible to staining. These finishes are most effective against the coloring agents found in food and beverages (acid dyes) and are not effective against coloring agents of other types like cationic or disperse dyes. The stain-resistant treatments are fluorochemicals or silicon based, which are not easily wetted by oil or water. These finishes may yellow with exposure to heat, ultraviolet light, or high relative humidity.

Abrasion-Resistant Finishes

Abrasion-resistant finishes are used on lining fabrics, especially for pockets. Thermoplastic resins fix fibers more firmly into the yarns so they do not break off as readily. In abrasion-resistant finishes an acrylic resin is often used. The resin may increase the wet soiling of the fabric. These resins are used in areas that receive high degrees of abrasion, such as pockets and waistbands. Blending nylon or polyester with cotton or rayon gives better resistance to abrasion than using finishes.

Antislip Finishes

Antislip finishes are used on low-count, smooth-surfaced fabrics. Fabrics are treated with resins, stretched, and dried under tension, causing the yarns to be bonded at their interlacing points. Antislip finishes are used to reduce seam slippage and fraying. Seam slippage occurs when the yarns in the seam slide toward the seam allowance. This results in an area next to the seam where only one set of yarns can be seen. Areas that have exhibited seam slippage have poor abrasion resistance and an unacceptable appearance. In some cases the seam can ravel completely. Antislip finishes are also called *slip-resistant*, or *nonslip, finishes*. The most effective and durable finishes are resins of urea or melamine formaldehyde.

Fume Fading–Resistant Finishes

Fume fading–resistant finishes are available for use on those fibers dyed with dyes susceptible to fading when exposed to atmospheric fumes or pollutants. The most common are acetate fibers dyed with disperse dyes. Of course, this problem was decreased significantly with the use of mass pigmentation. However, there are some cases where mass pigmentation is not economically practical. In these cases, fume fading-resistant finishes of tertiary amines and borax are used. These finishes are also known as antifume and atmospheric fading protective finishes.

Surface or Back Coatings

Metallic, plastic, or *foam coatings* are used on the back of fabrics to reduce heat transfer through the fabric, alter the appearance of the fabric, lock yarns in place, and minimize air and water permeability. Metallic coatings, which include aluminum, are used on apparel and window treatment fabrics. A very thin layer of aluminum is bonded to the back of a fabric for greater heat retention or to block heat transfer. In apparel, these coatings are found in winter coats for cold climates and specialized protective apparel for extreme temperature conditions such as fire fighting and space suits. In spacesuits the coating is on the exterior of the fabric to reflect heat from the sun when the wearer is in direct sunlight.

Plastic coatings reduce fabric soiling and give a smooth, leatherlike look to fabrics. (See Coated Fabrics, Chapter 15.) Problems of metallic and plastic coatings include cracking and peeling of the finish. In order to increase the life of these fabrics, care label instructions must be followed.

Acrylic-foam coatings are common on drapery fabrics. These back coatings are used to minimize air movement through the draperies, give a greater comfort factor by increasing the thickness of the fabric, and minimize the need to have a separate lining fabric. Draperies with the foam-back coating often are sold as self-lined draperies (Figure 18–10).

Latex back coatings are almost always used on tufted fabrics for furnishing uses. Tufted carpet and tufted upholstery use latex to lock the tufted yarns in place and to add dimensional stability to the fabric.

These coatings may have poor aging resistance. They may separate, peel, flake off, or experience a change in hand with age or exposure to degrading aspects in the environment, like heat or light. For example, acrylic-foam backings may become tacky or sticky. When used on draperies, these finishes may cause the drapery to stick together when it comes in contact with another portion of the fabric.

Light-Stabilizing Finishes

Light-stabilizing finishes incorporate light stabilizers or ultraviolet absorbers to minimize damage from light exposure. This is especially important in some furnishings, apparel, and many industrial products.

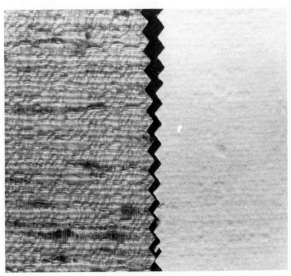

Fig. 18–10 Window treatment fabric with acrylic-foam coating: face (left) *and back* (right).

Products that are exposed to sunlight on a regular basis or to interior lighting that has a high percentage of ultraviolet light may require this finish. Artificial sources that may contribute to fading include regular fluorescent lights found in many office buildings and retail establishments. Products that require light stabilizers include tarpaulin and awning fabrics, tents, sewing thread for outdoor products, outdoor furniture, car interiors, and some carpeting.

COMFORT-RELATED FINISHES

Water-Repellent Finishes

A *water-repellent* fabric is resistant to wetting, but if the water comes with enough force, it will penetrate the fabric. A *waterproof* fabric is a fabric that will not wet regardless of the water exposure time or the force with which the water strikes the fabric. Waterproof fabrics are almost always films or coated fabrics. Waterproof fabrics are compared with water-repellent fabrics in Table 18–1. (The Federal Trade Commission has suggested the use of the terms durable and renewable in describing water-repellent fabrics.)

Water repellency is dependent on surface tension and fabric penetrability and is achieved by a combination of finish and fabric construction. Finishes that can be applied to fabric to make it repellent are wax emulsions, metallic soaps, and surface-active agents. They are applied to fabrics that have a very high warp count and are made with fine regular yarns.

Wax emulsions and *metallic soaps* coat the yarns but do not fill the interstices or spaces between the yarns. These finishes are not permanent and are removed in care. They can be renewed.

Surface-active agents have molecules with one end that is water repellent and one end that reacts with the hydroxyl (OH) groups of cellulose. After these agents are applied, heat is used to bond the finish to the fabric. This finish is permanent to washing and dry cleaning.

It is more difficult to select a water-repellent coat than a waterproof coat because the finish is not obvious and the label is the only source of information. However, the consumer can recognize some guides for buying. The fabric construction is far more important than the finish. The closer the weave, the greater the resistance to water penetration. The kind of finish used is important in selection because it influences the cost of care. The use of two layers of fabric gives increased protection, but the inner layer must also have a water-repellent finish or it will act as a blotter and cause more water to penetrate. Care is important in water-repellent fabrics. The greater the soil on the coat, the less water repellent it is.

Water-repellent finishes render fabrics stain resistant to water-borne stains, oil-borne stains, or both. Durable water-repellent finishes often hold greasy stains more tenaciously than untreated fabrics. Unisec, Scotchgard, and Teflon are trade names for finishes that give resistance to both oil- and water-borne stains. Hydro-Pruf and Syl-mer are silicone finishes that resist water-borne stains. Teflon, Scotchgard, and Fybrite are trade names for fluorocarbon finishes.

Table 18–1 Comparison of Waterproof and Water-Repellent Fabrics

Waterproof Fabrics	Water-Repellent Fabrics
Fabrics are films or low-count fabrics with a film coating.	High-count fabrics with a finish that coats the yarn but does not fill up the interstices of the fabric.
Characteristics	
No water can penetrate.	Heavy rain will penetrate.
Most plastic fabrics stiffen in cold weather.	Fabric is pliable and little different from untreated fabric.
Cheaper to produce.	Fabric can "breathe" and is comfortable for raincoats.
Permanent.	Durable or renewable finish.

Absorbent Finishes

Absorbent finishes are designed to increase the moisture absorbency of the fabric. These finishes increase the time needed to dry the fabric. They may aid in the dyeing of the fabric. Absorbent finishes are fair in durability. They are used on towels, diapers, underwear, and sportswear. They are applied as surface coatings for fibers and yarns. On nylon a solution of nylon 8 is used; on polyesters the finish changes the molecular structure of the fiber surface so that moisture is broken up into smaller particles that wick more readily; on cellulosics the finish makes them absorb more moisture. Fiber modifications and different fabric structures are more effective than finishes. Fantessa, Visa, and Zelcon are trade names.

Antistatic Finishes

Antistatic finishes are important in both the production and use of fabrics. Static charges that develop on fabrics cause them to cling to machinery in the factory and to people, attract dust and lint, and produce sparks and shocks.

Control of static buildup on natural-fiber fabrics is done by increasing humidity and using lubricants but these controls were not adequate with the thermoplastic fibers. Antistatic finishes were developed to (1) improve the surface conductivity so that excess electrons move to the atmosphere or ground; (2) attract water molecules, thus increasing the conductivity of the fiber; or (3) develop a charge opposite to that on the fiber, thus neutralizing the electrostatic charge. The most effective finishes combine all three effects. Most antistatic finishes are not durable and must be replaced during care. Most finishes use quaternary ammonium compounds. Washing aids such as fabric softeners also help to control static.

Incorporating antistatic substances into the fibers gives the best static control. Most manufactured fibers are produced in antistatic form especially for rugs, carpets, lingerie, and uniforms (see Chapter 6). Some trade names of antistatic fiber variants are Ultron nylon, Antron nylon, Staticgard nylon, and Anso nylon.

Fabric Softeners

Fabric softeners were developed to improve the hand of harsh textiles, which may develop as a result of resin finishes or heat setting of synthetics. Types of softeners include anionic softeners, cationic softeners, and nonionic softeners. *Anionic softeners* are usually sulfonated, negatively charged fatty acids and oils. These softeners are padded onto the fibers because of a lack of affinity for the fiber. Anionic softeners are often used commercially on cellulosic fibers and silk. *Cationic softeners* are most often used in domestic washing. These softeners have an affinity for the fiber. They tend to yellow with age and may build up on the fiber if used frequently, reducing the absorbency of the fabric. Cationic softeners may contain quaternary ammonium compounds, and these compounds may confer some incidental antibacterial properties. *Nonionic softeners* must be padded onto the fabric. These commercial softeners are usually a fatty acid.

Thermal Finishes

Polyethylene glycol (PEG) can be used as a *thermal finish* because of its ability to absorb or release heat in appropriate environmental conditions as it undergoes a phase change. The chemical can phase change from solid to liquid (absorb heat) or liquid to solid (release heat) several times. Thus, the wearer is warmed or cooled depending on the phase change that is occurring. The time span of these phase changes is generally in the range of 20 minutes. The finish is applied by Neutratherm as Polytherm. It is used on active sportswear. Besides the heat aspects, the finish also contributes antistatic characteristics, water absorbency, resiliency, soil release, and pilling resistance. Polytherm has also been investigated as an effective shrink-resist finish for machine-washable wools.

BIOLOGICAL CONTROL FINISHES

Moth Control Finishes

Moths and carpet beetles are likely to damage fibers containing protein, such as wool. In addition, insects are likely to cause damage to other fibers if soil is present. More than 100 species of insects have been known to damage textiles, including silverfish, crickets, cockroaches, and spiders. In most cases, a combination of soil as a food source and environmental conditions are necessary for a problem to develop. Manufactured fibers are not immune, but natural fibers are far more likely to fall victim to insect damage.

Moth control finishes are also known as fumigants, insecticides, insect repellent finishes, and other terms implying resistance to a specific insect pest, like silverfish or moths. Both moths and carpet beetles attack not only 100 percent wool but also blends of wool and other fibers. Although they can digest only the wool, the insects eat through the other fibers. The damage is done by the larvae, not the adult moth. Clothes moths are small, about ¼ inch long. Their larvae shun bright sunlight and live in the dark. For this reason, it is necessary to clean often under sofas, under furniture cushions, in the creases of chairs and garments, and in dark closets.

Most furnishing fabrics of wool are treated with a moth control or mothproofing agent. If information to that effect is not on the label, check into it.

Means of controlling insect damage include:

1. Cold storage, which decreases insect activity so damage is much less likely to occur. Museums use freezing to control insect problems in storage areas because the extreme conditions kill the insects. This technique is generally not practical for consumer use.

2. Odors that repel. Paradichlorobenzene and naphthalene (moth balls) can be used during storage, but use should be carefully monitored and only when absolutely necessary. Consumers should recognize that these insecticides are poisons and should be used with caution.

3. Stomach poisons. Fluorides and silicofluorides are finishes for dry cleanable wool.

4. Contact poisons. DDT is very effective but has been banned in the United States.

5. Chemicals added to the dye bath, which permanently change the fiber, making it unpalatable to the larvae. Surface and on-site applications may result in color loss or yellowing of carpet fibers.

Mold and Mildew Control Finishes

Molds and *mildew* will grow on and damage both cellulosic and protein textiles, although the problem is far more common on cellulosics. They will grow on, but not damage, thermoplastic fibers. These finishes are also known as fungicides or mildew-preventative finishes.

Prevention is the best solution to the problem because cures are often impossible. To prevent mold or mildew, keep textiles clean and dry. Soiled items should be kept dry and washed as soon as possible. Sunning and airing should be done frequently during periods of high humidity. An electric light can be used in dark, humid storage places. Dehumidifiers are very helpful.

If mildew occurs, wash the article immediately. Mild stains can be removed by bleaching. Mold and mildew growth is prevented by many compounds. Salicylanilide is often used on cellulosic fibers and wool under the trade names of Shirlan and Shirlan NA.

Antimicrobial Finishes

Antimicrobial finishes are used to inhibit the growth of bacteria and other odor-causing germs, prevent decay and damage from perspiration, control the spread of disease, and reduce the risk of infection following injury. Antimicrobial finishes are also known as *antibacterial, bacteriostatic, germicidal,* or *antiseptic finishes.*

These finishes are important in skin-contact clothing, shoe linings, hospital linens, and contract carpeting. The chemicals used are surface reactants, mostly quaternary ammonia compounds. Zirconium peroxides can be formed on the surface of cotton fabrics to give antimicrobial properties. Those substances can be added to the spinning solution of manufactured fibers for use in wall coverings and upholstery. Most diaper-service establishments add the finish during each laundering. Eversan and Sanitized are two trade names.

These finishes include chemical treatment, gas treatment, and irradiation treatment. Chemical antimicrobial finishes may cause yellowing and fading on nylon, which is especially important to prevent for carpet. The gas treatment involves exposure to ethylene oxide gas. Since the gas is a hazardous material, it is being replaced with irradiation sterilization, also known as electron beam sterilization. This treatment is cheaper, simpler, safer, and ideal for medical products like bandages, sutures, and surgical gloves. Since the beam can penetrate thermoplastic and foil packaging, items can be packaged and then treated. This process maintains the sterile environment until the package is opened.

SAFETY-RELATED FINISHES

Flame-Retardant Finishes

Each year a large number of fatalities and injuries result from fires associated with flammable fabrics. Financial loss from such fires is estimated in the millions of dollars. Five common causes of these fires are smoking in bed, starting fires with flammable liquids, children playing with matches and lighters, burning trash, and being caught in a burning structure.

Fabrics that burn quickly are sheer or lightweight fabrics and napped, pile, or tufted surfaces. Some items made from these constructions ignite quickly, burn with great intensity, and are difficult to extinguish. "Torch" sweaters, fringed cowboy chaps, and chenille berets are examples of some apparel items that caused tragic accidents. Some style features also present a fire hazard. Long, full sleeves, flared skirts, ruffles, frills, and flowing robes are examples in apparel.

Many terms are used when discussing the ability of a fabric to resist ignition, burn more slowly than normal, or self-extinguish once the source of ignition has been removed from the fabric. The following is a list of definitions from the American Society for Testing and Materials:

- *Fire retardance:* The resistance to combustion of a material when tested under specified conditions.

- *Flame resistance:* The property of a material whereby flaming combustion is prevented, terminated, or inhibited following application of a flaming or nonflaming source of ignition, with or without subsequent removal of the ignition source.

- *Flammability:* Those characteristics of a material that pertain to its relative ease of ignition and relative ability to sustain combustion.

Fabrics may be made flame resistant by using inherently flame-resistant fibers or fiber variants that have been made flame resistant by adding flame retardants to the spinning solution, or by applying flame-retardant finishes to the fabrics.

The burning characteristics of fibers are listed in Table 3–15. Fibers that are inherently flame resistant are aramid, modacrylic, novoloid, saran, PBI, sulfar, and vinal/vinyon matrix fibers. Fibers in which flame-retardant chemicals have been added to the spinning solution are some acetates, nylons, polyesters, and rayons.

Flame-retardant finishes function in a variety of ways. The finish may block the flame of fuel and hinder further flame propagation. A foam-containing, flame-extinguishing gas may be produced. The solid may be modified so that the products of combustion are not volatile or require excess heat to continue the fire.

Flame-retardant finishes are used on cotton, rayon, nylon, and polyester fabrics. Flame-retardant finishes must be durable (able to withstand 50 washings), nontoxic, and noncarcinogenic. Ideally, they should not change the hand and texture of fabrics or have unpleasant odors. Most of these finishes are not visible and they add significantly to the cost of the item, so the consumer is asked to pay for something that cannot be seen.

Flame-retardant finishes can be classified as durable and nondurable. These durable finishes are specific to fiber type and are usually phosphate compounds or salts, halogenated organic compounds, or inorganic salts. Examples of durable finishes for polyester and cellulosics include the trade names of Antiblaze and Pyroset. Many other flame-retardant finishes are sold by trade names in addition to these mentioned here but few consumer products are sold with the finish identified by trade name.

Flame-retardant finishes are less expensive than flame-resistant fibers or fiber variants. Knitting or weaving gray goods that can be given a topical flame-retardant finish when necessary is a more economical procedure for fabric producers.

Flame-retardant finishes generally require that a fairly high amount of finish be added to the fabric. Normal rates for cellulosics range from 5 to 30 percent of the weight of the fabric. For polyester, the normal rates are 1 to 10 percent of the weight of fabric. The range of add-on is related to the specific chemical used, the performance expectations for the product, and the cost of the finish. The finishes for cotton are of two general types. The first is referred to as the ammonium cure and provides excellent flame-retardant protection with minimal strength loss. However, it requires the use of special equipment so the investment in capital is great. The ammonium cure finish is more commonly used on apparel. The second type is the pyrovatex process by Ciba-Geigy, which uses conventional finishing equipment and a resin. The resin results in greater strength loss. This finish is more commonly used in furnishings.

CONCERNS AND LIMITATIONS Cost, durability, and care are the greatest problems for the consumer. The higher cost of research and development of fibers and finishes, testing of fabrics and products, and liability insurance result in a high cost of apparel and furnishing items. Because the items look no different, the consumer often thinks the item is overpriced. Because of government standards, the consumer has limited choice; for example, people who do not smoke in bed must pay a higher price for mattresses, because only those mattresses that pass flammability standards can be sold in interstate commerce. However, the safety component is present regardless of the consumer's preference.

Most of the topical finishes require special care in laundering to preserve the flame resistance. Labels should be followed carefully. Most labels indicate the following care procedures: Use phosphate detergents or do not use carbonate detergents, do not bleach, do not use soap, do not use hot water. In areas where phosphate detergents are banned, soft water and heavy-duty liquid detergents should be used.

Flame-retardant–treated fabrics may exhibit some problems for consumers. The hand may be harsh. The fabric may be less abrasion resistant than it would be without the finish. The finish may give the wearer a false sense of security. Remember, the fin- ish is designed to make the fabric flame retardant. It will not prevent the fabric from igniting or burning, although ignition and rate of burning will be slower with the finish.

Antipesticide Protective Finishes

Antipesticide protective finishes are designed to protect the wearer of protective clothing from pesti- cides. The finish is designed to prevent penetration of the chemical through the fabric and to aid in removal of the chemical during washing. It is expected that research in this area will continue.

KEY TERMS

Special-purpose finish
Functional finish
Stabilization
Shrinkage control
Relaxation shrinkage
Progressive shrinkage
Compressive shrinkage process
London shrunk
Heat setting
Glass transition temperature
T_g temperature
Surface coating
Halogenation
Shape-retention finish
Cross-links
Wrinkle-resistant finish
Durable press
Precured process
Postcured process
Quality-control standards
Soil-release finish

Stain-release finish
Abrasion-resistant finish
Antislip finish
Fume fading–resistant finish
Metallic coating
Plastic coating
Water-repellent finish
Waterproof
Water repellent
Absorbent finish
Antistatic finish
Fabric softener
Thermal finish
Moth control finish
Mold and mildew control finish
Antimicrobial finish
Flame-retardant finish
Fire retardance
Flame resistance
Flammability
Antipesticide protective finish

QUESTIONS

1. In what manner do the stabilization finishes work for the following products?
   100 percent wool sweater
   100 percent cotton upholstery of polished cotton
   100 percent acetate antique satin draperies
   65 percent cotton/35 percent polyester flannelette bedsheet
2. Differentiate between postcured and precured durable-press fabrics in both the process and product performance.
3. Compare and contrast water repellent and stain-repellent/soil-release finishes.
4. For what end uses are metallic, plastic, and foam coatings used? What purpose do these coatings serve?

5. For what fibers and products are moth control finishes likely to be used? How do they function?

6. How can flame retardancy be achieved with fabrics? For what products is flame retardancy mandatory or preferable?

SUGGESTED READINGS

Harris, Paul W., and Hangey, Dale A. (1989). "Stain Resist Chemistry for Nylon 6 Carpet." *Textile Chemist and Colorist, 21*(11), pp. 25-30.

Jackson, Doug, and Shinall, Keith (September, 1988). "Taking the Heat." *Industrial Fabric Products Review*, pp. 63-65.

Needles, Howard (1986). *Textile Fibers, Dyes, Finishes, and Processes*. Park Ridge, NJ: Noyes Publications.

North, Bernard F. (1991). "Reactants for Durable Press Textiles: The Formaldehyde Dilemma." *Textile Chemist and Colorist, 23*(10), pp. 21-22.

Reagan, Barbara M., Dusaj, Shailendra, Johnson, Diana G., and Hodges, Diane M. (1990). "Influence of Aftermarket Carpet Protectors on the Soiling, Flammability, and Electrical Resistivity of Nylon 6." *Textile Chemist and Colorist, 22*(4), pp. 16-20.

Trotman, E. R. (1984). *Dyeing and Chemical Technology of Textile Fibers*. New York: John Wiley & Sons.

Zeronian, S. Haig, and Collins, Martha J. (1988). "Improving the Comfort of Polyester Fabrics." *Textile Chemist and Colorist, 20*(4), pp. 25-28.

CHAPTER 19

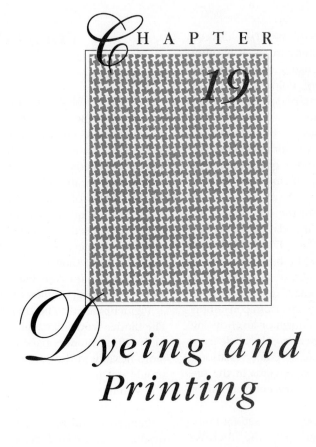

Dyeing and Printing

OBJECTIVES

- To understand the theory, techniques, and processes of dyeing or printing textiles.

- To relate quality and performance to the technique or process used in dyeing or printing.

- To differentiate among the stages of dyeing and types of printing.

- To relate dyeing or printing to the serviceability of textile products.

*C*OLOR IS ONE OF THE MOST IMPORTANT CHARAC-teristics of apparel and furnishing items. It is often the first feature for which consumers look. In this chapter the characteristics of color will be discussed from an identification perspective (when color was added to the product), a process perspective (how color was added to the product), a serviceability perspective (how color affects the serviceability of the product), and a problem-solving perspective (what kind of problems can develop because of color).

Consumers are not aware of the complex problems involved in achieving a particular color in a uniform manner on a textile product. They expect that the color will remain vivid and uniform throughout the life of the product, and that it will not create problems in use, care, or storage. It is remarkable that color creates as few complaints from consumers as it does, since achieving a uniform or level dyeing is a difficult process. Slight differences in fabric from different bolts can result in subtle color variations. These minor variations are very obvious in the finished product when seams join parts cut from different bolts.

To understand the complexities of adding color to a textile product, we begin with the fiber. As was discussed in Section 2, Chapters 3–9, fibers differ in their chemical composition. This difference can be seen in various properties and performance characteristics. In addition, any colored textile product may be exposed to a wide variety of potential color degradants, such as detergent, perspiration, dry cleaning solvents, sunlight, and makeup. To achieve a permanent or fast color, the dye must be permanently attached to or trapped within the fiber by using a combination of heat, pressure, and chemical assistants.

Color has always been important in textiles. Until 1856, natural dyes and pigments obtained from plants, insects, and minerals were used as coloring agents. Then William Henry Perkin discovered mauve, the first synthetic dye, and a whole new industry came into being. Europe became the foremost center for synthetic dyes, and it was not until World War I, when trade with Germany was interrupted, that a dye industry was developed in the United States. Since that time, many dyes and pigments have been developed, so that today there are hundreds of colorants or coloring agents from which to choose.

COLORANTS

Pigments

Color can be added to textile objects by either dyes or pigments. Because there are major differences between these coloring substances and the ways they are added to fabrics, the next few paragraphs differentiate between pigments and dyes.

Pigments are insoluble color particles that are held on the surface of a fabric by a binding agent. Their application is quick, simple, and economical. Any color can be used on any fiber, because the pigments are held on mechanically. Stiffening of the fabrics, crocking, and fading are some problems that may be encountered, however. Pigments also may be mixed with the spinning solution of manufactured fibers.

Pigments need to be bonded to the fiber surface. The binder works like a glue and binds the pigment to the fiber. Binders have become much softer and more flexible in the past few years. Ideally, binders should not interfere with the color of the pigment, nor with the hand and function of the fabric. Binders tend to be heat activated or catalyst activated.

Pigments tend to combine several ingredients to produce the desired appearance. Opacifiers help produce a pigment with good covering power. Some opacifiers produce a matte luster, others a full gloss luster, and still others a pearlescent or metallic luster. Thickeners produce a paste that does not migrate or spread from the area applied or where dark shades are needed. Thinners help with pastes that are too thick for one reason or another. Antibleeding agents eliminate the halo effect and keep the edges of a print sharp and clear. Softeners help maintain the fabric's soft hand after printing.

Pigments produce the color of the paste, although some other ingredients may alter the color. Pigment prints may be easier to match than dyes because the color is held on the surface. Dyes are more difficult to match because the chemical reactions that occur during dyeing may cause the dye to shift color. The hue shift is more difficult to control in dyeing compared to pigment printing.

Dyes

A *dye* is an organic compound composed of a chromophore, which is the color-producing portion of the dye molecule, and an auxochrome, which slightly augments or alters the color. The auxochrome also adds solubility to the dye and is a possible site for bonding to the fiber. Figure 19-1 shows examples of dye molecules.

Dye must be small particles that can be thoroughly dissolved in water or some other carrier in order to penetrate the fiber. Undissolved particles stay on the outside of the fiber and have poor fastness to crocking and bleeding. Dyes have great color strength; a small amount of dye is able to color large quantities of fabric. Pigments have much lower color strength; much more pigment is needed to color an equal amount of fabric. Most dyes bond chemically with the fiber and are found in the interior of the fiber, rather than on the surface where pigments are found.

A *fluorescent dye* absorbs light at one wavelength and re-emits that energy at another wavelength. Fluor-

escent dyes are used to make whites appear whiter and to mask yellowing of fibers. Fluorescent dyes are also used in safety clothing to increase the wearer's visibility at night and used in some items to give a bright, intense glow to the color. These dyes are used in costumes for the safety and glow-in-the-dark effects and in fashion apparel for bright, neonlike colors.

A *dye process* is the environment created for the introduction of dye by hot water, steam, or dry heat. Chemical additives like salt or acid are used to regulate penetration of the dye. A knowledge of fiber-dye affinity, methods of dyeing, and equipment results in a better understanding of color behavior.

The stage at which color is applied has little to do with fastness but has a great deal to do with dye penetration, and it is governed by fabric design. In order for a fabric to be colored, the dye must penetrate the fiber and either be combined chemically

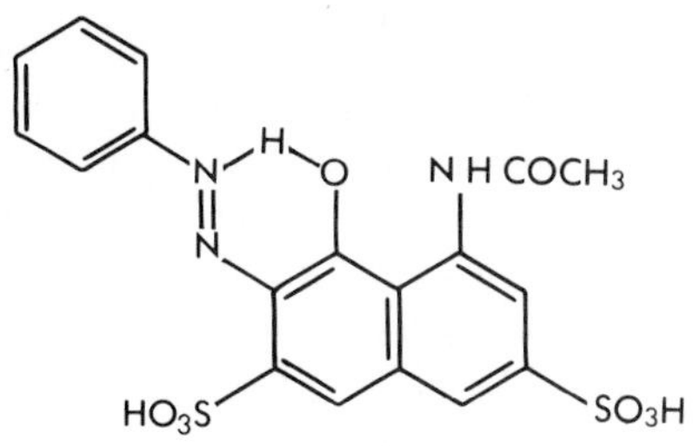

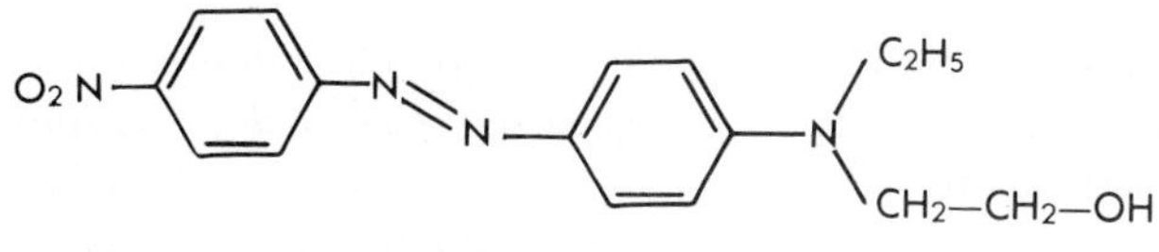

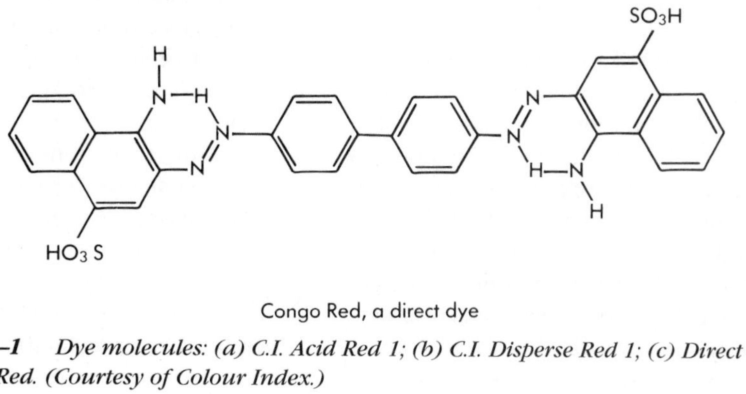

Fig. 19-1 *Dye molecules: (a) C.I. Acid Red 1; (b) C.I. Disperse Red 1; (c) Direct Dye Congo Red. (Courtesy of Colour Index.)*

with it or locked inside it. Fibers that dye easily are those that are absorbent and have dye sites within their molecules that react with the dye molecules. The dye reacts with the surface molecules first. Moisture and heat swell the fibers, causing the molecular chains to move farther apart so that reactive groups in the internal regions of the fiber are exposed to react with the dye. During drying the chains move back together, trapping the dye in the fiber. Wool dyed with an acid dye is a good example of a fiber that is absorbent and has many dye sites dyed with a dye that chemically reacts with the keratin of wool to color the fiber.

The thermoplastic fibers are difficult to dye because their absorbency is low. However, most of the manufactured fibers are modified to accept different classes of dyes. This makes it possible to achieve different color effects or a good solid color in blends of unlike fibers by piece dyeing.

No one dye is fast to everything, and the dyes within a class, a grouping of similar dyes, are not equally fast. A complete range of shades is not available in each of the dye classes; for example, some dye classes are weak in greens. The dyer chooses a dye suited to the color desired, the fiber content, the end use of the fabric, the performance expectations of the product, and the cost of the process. The dyer must apply the color so that it penetrates and is held in the fiber. Occasionally the manufacturer or the consumer selects fabrics for uses that are different from those that the fabric manufacturer intended. For example, an apparel fabric used for draperies may not be fast to sunlight. Suppliers or retailers should be notified when products or fabrics do not give satisfactory performance.

Dyes are classified by chemical composition or method of application. Table 19–1 lists the major dyes, along with some of their characteristics and end uses.

STAGES OF DYEING

Color may be added to textiles during the fiber, yarn, fabric, or product stage, depending on the color effects desired and perhaps on the quality or end use of the fabric. Better dye penetration is achieved with fiber dyeing than with yarn dyeing, with yarn dyeing than with piece dyeing, and with piece dyeing than with product dyeing. Good dye penetration is easier to achieve in products where the dyeing liquid or liquor is free to move between adjacent fibers. This freedom of movement is easiest to achieve in loose fibers. It is more difficult to achieve in products where yarn twist, yarn interlacing patterns, and seams or other product features minimize liquor movement.

As manufacturers and producers attempt to produce specific colors as needed, the trend is to add color to products as late in the processing as possible. However, this trend puts tremendous demands on dyeing. The earlier in processing color is added, the less critical is the uniformity or *levelness* of the dyeing. For example, in fiber dyeing, two adjacent fibers need not be exactly the same color since minor color differences in the yarn will be masked because of the small surface area of each fiber. However, the color must be level in products that are sewn before the color is added. Areas where the color is just slightly irregular will be apparent even to the casual observer and usually result in the item being labeled a second. Level commercial dyeing is not easy, as anyone who has attempted dyeing on a small scale can attest.

The stage at which the dye or pigment is added to the textile is discussed in this section. Dyeing can be done at any stage; printing is usually done at the fabric stage. However, some yarns are printed and some finished products are printed. Current product printing is usually in the form of a design applied to one area of the product, such as the designs on fronts or sleeves of active sportswear.

Fiber Stage

In the *fiber-dyeing process*, color is added before yarn spinning. Fiber-dyed items usually have a slightly irregular soft color like a heather or tone-on-tone gray.

1. *Mass pigmentation* is also known as *solution dyed*, *spun dyed*, *dope dyeing*, *mass coloration*, or *producer colored*. It consists of adding colored pigments or dyes to the spinning solution; thus each fiber is colored as it is spun. The color is an integral part of the fiber and fast to most color degradants. This method is preferred for fibers that are difficult to dye by other methods or where it is difficult to get a certain depth of shade. Colors are generally few because of inventory limitations. A common fiber that is mass pigmented is olefin. Black polyesters are often mass pigmented.

   Another type of dyeing similar to mass pigmentation is *gel dyeing*, in which the color is incorporated in the fiber while it is still in the soft gel stage. This occurs in the narrow time frame between fiber extrusion and fiber coagulation.

Table 19–1 Classification of Fiber Dyes

Dyes	End Uses	Characteristics
Acid (anionic). Complete color range.	Wool, silk, nylon, modified rayon. Modified acrylic and polyester.	Bright colors. Vary in fastness to light. May have poor fastness to washing.
Azoic (naphthol and rapidogens). Complete color range. Moderate cost.	Primarily cotton. May be used on manufactured fibers such as polyester.	Good to excellent lightfastness and washing. Bright shades. Poor resistance to crocking.
Cationic (basic). Used with mordant on fibers other than silk and wool and acrylic. Complete color range.	Used primarily on acrylics. Direct prints on acetate. Discharge prints on cotton. Used on modified polyester and nylon.	Fast colors on acrylics. On natural fibers, poor fastness to light, washing, perspiration. Tends to bleed and crock.
Developed. Dyes developed in the fiber. Complete color range. Duller colors than acid or basic.	Primarily cellulose fibers. Discharge prints.	Good to excellent lightfastness. Fair washfastness.
Direct (substantive). Largest and most commercially significant dye class. Complete color range.	Used on cellulosic fibers.	Good colorfastness to light. May have poor washfastness.
Disperse. Dye particles disperse in water and dissolve in fibers. Good color range.	Developed for acetate but used on most synthetic fibers.	Fair to excellent light and wash fastness. Blues and violets on acetate fume fade.
Fluorescent brighteners. Specific types for most common fibers.	Used on textiles and in detergents.	Mask yellowing and off-white aspects that occur naturally or develop with age and soil.
Mordant (chrome). Fair color range. Duller than acid dyes.	Used on same fibers as listed for acid dyes.	Good to excellent light and wash fastness. Dull colors.
Reactive or fiber-reactive. Combines chemically with fiber. Produces brightest shades.	Primarily used on cotton. Some are used on other cellulosics and wool, silk, or nylon.	Good light and wash fastness. Sensitive to chlorine bleach.
Sulfur. Insoluble in water. Complete color range except for red. Dull colors.	Primarily for cotton. Heavy work clothes. Most widely used black dye.	Poor to excellent light and wash fastness. Sensitive to chlorine bleach. Stored goods may become tender.
Vat. Insoluble in water. Incomplete color range.	Primarily for cotton work clothes, sportswear, prints, drapery fabrics.	Good to excellent light and wash fastness.

2. *Stock*, or *fiber*, *dyeing* is used when mottled or heather effects are desired. Dye is added to loose fibers before yarn spinning. Good dye penetration is obtained, but the process is fairly expensive (Figure 19-2).

3. *Top dyeing* gives results similar to stock dyeing and is more commonly used. Tops, the loose ropes of wool from the combing machine, are wound into balls, placed on perforated spindles, and enclosed in a tank. The dye is pumped back and forth through the wool. Continuous processes on loose fiber and wool tops are also done using a pad-steam technique.

Yarn Stage

Yarn dyeing can be done with the yarn in skeins, called *skein dyeing*; with the yarns wrapped on cones or packages, called *package dyeing*; or with the yarn wound on warp beams, called *beam dyeing*. Yarn dyeing is less costly than fiber dyeing but more costly than piece dyeing and printing. Yarn-

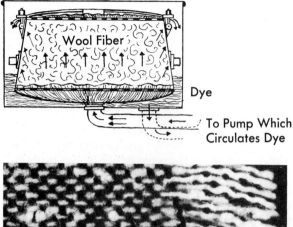

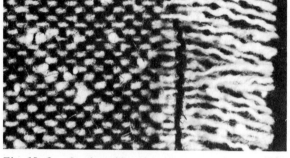

Fig. 19–2 *Stock or fiber dye: process and tweed fabric example.*

Fig. 19–3 *Yarn dyeing: process and fabric.*

dyed designs are more limited and larger inventories are involved (Figure 19–3).

Yarn dyeing is less expensive than fiber dyeing, but significantly more expensive than fabric or product types. Yarn-dyed fabrics are more expensive to produce because larger inventories of yarns in a variety of colors are required and more time is needed to thread the loom correctly. In addition, each time the pattern of color is changed, the loom needs to be rethreaded, which is another time-consuming and expensive task. Yarn-dyed fabrics are generally considered to be better quality fabrics, but it is rare to find solid-color yarn-dyed fabrics. It is much cheaper to produce solid-color fabrics by other processes. Yarn-dyed fabrics have stripes, plaids, checks, or other patterns due to the presence of yarns of different colors in different areas within the fabric. Examples of yarn-dyed fabrics include gingham, chambray, and many jacquard or dobby fabrics, both woven and knit.

Piece or Fabric Stage

When the bolt or roll of fabric is dyed, the process is referred to as *piece dyeing.* Piece dyeing usually produces solid-color fabrics. It generally costs less to dye fabric than to dye loose fiber or yarns. One other advantage is that decisions on color can be delayed so that fashion trends can be followed more closely.

CROSS DYEING *Cross dyeing* is piece dyeing of fabrics (Figure 19–4) made of fibers from different generic groups—such as protein and cellulose—or by combining acid-dyeable and basic-dyeable fibers of the same generic group. Each fiber type or different modification reacts with a different dye class. When different colors are used for each dye class, the dyed fabric has a yarn-dyed appearance. An example is a fabric made of wool yarns and cotton yarns dyed with a red acid dye and a blue direct dye, respectively. If the fabric was made with wool warp and cotton filling, the warp would be red and the filling blue.

UNION DYEING *Union dyeing* is piece dyeing of fabrics made of fibers from different groups, but unlike cross dyeing, the finished fabric is a solid color. Dyes of the same hue, but of composition suited to the fibers to be dyed, are mixed together in the same dye bath. Union dyeing is common; witness all the solid-color blend fabrics on the market. A frequent problem with these fabrics involves the different fastness characteristics of each dye class used. Aged, union-dyed fabrics may take on a heather

Fig. 19–4   Cross-dyed fabric.

look, due to the differences in colorfastness of the dyes. Piece dyeing is done with various kinds of equipment.

Product Stage

Before *product dyeing*, the fabric is cut and sewn into the finished product. Once the color need has been determined, the product is dyed. Properly prepared gray goods are critical to good product dyeing. Great care must be taken in the dyeing process to get a level, uniform color throughout the product. Careful selection of components also is required, or

buttons, thread, and trim may be a different color because of differences in dye absorption between the various product parts. Product dyeing is becoming more important in the apparel and furnishing industries with the emphasis on quick response to retail and consumer demands. Examples include towels, socks, T-shirts, slacks, and bed linens (see Figure 19–5).

METHODS OF DYEING

The method chosen for dyeing depends on fiber content, weight, dye, and degree of penetration required in the finished product. Time is money in mass production so that processes in which the goods travel quickly through a machine are used whenever possible. Dyeing and afterwashing require a great deal of water, and waste water causes stream pollution. Minimizing the environmental impact of dyeing and finishing is a major industry goal for the 1990s. (See Chapter 21.)

Many different methods and processes are used in dyeing. In this section, methods and products will be discussed. These methods tend to involve one of three procedures for combining the colorant with the textile: textile is circulated in a dyebath; dyebath is circulated around the textile; or both textile and dyebath are circulated together. The discussion presented here is general. Several references listed at the end of the chapter include greater details about dyeing.

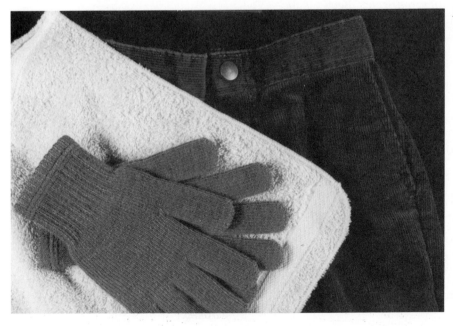

Fig. 19–5   Product-dyed items.

Batch Dyeing

Batch dyeing is also referred to as exhaust dyeing. In this process the textile is circulated through the dyebath. Batch dyeing can be used for textiles in any stage of production from fiber to product. The process has good flexibility in terms of color selection and cost is low, especially if done close to the product stage. Temperature can be controlled depending on the dye-fiber combination. Equipment used includes the beck, pad, and jig.

BECK, REEL, OR WINCH DYEING The oldest type of piece dyeing is *beck*, *reel*, or *winch dyeing* (Figure 19-6). The fabric, in a loose rope sewed together at the ends, is lifted in and out of the dye bath by a reel. The fabric is kept immersed in the dye bath except for the few yards around the reel. Penetration of dye is obtained by continued immersion in the slack condition rather than by pressure on the wet goods under tension. This method is used on lightweight fabrics that cannot withstand the tension of the other methods and on heavy goods, especially woolens. Reels are of various shapes—oval, round, octagonal.

In beck dyeing, a pressurized liquor ratio of 5:1 or 4:1 is used. Liquor ratio refers to the amount of solution compared to the amount of textile to be dyed. Thus, liquor ratios of 5:1 have five times as much liquid as textile in the process. This technique is generally used for fabric lengths ranging from 50 to 100 meters in rope or full width forms. It is simple, versatile, and low cost. Fabrics are subjected to low warp tension and bulking of yarns occurs. Beck dyeing uses large amounts of water, chemicals, and energy. It also causes abrasion, creasing, and distortion of some fabrics.

JIG DYEING *Jig dyeing* consists of a stationary dye bath with two rolls above the bath. The cloth is carried around the rolls in open width and rolled back and forth through the dye bath once every 20 minutes or so. It is on rollers for the remaining time.

This process has some problems with level dyeing. Acetate, rayon, and nylon are usually jig dyed (Figure 19-7).

In jig dyeing, much larger runs of fabric at open width are used; several thousand meters are common. Warp tension can be great because of the way the fabric is moved in the process. Fabrics that may crease in rope form are dyed in this manner, such as carpet, some twills, and some satins.

PAD DYEING *Pad dyeing* is a method in which the fabric is run through the dye bath in open width and then between squeeze rollers that force the dye into the fabric. Notice in Figure 19-8 that the pad box holds a very small amount of dye bath or dye liquor, making this an economical method of piece dyeing. The cloth runs through the machine at a rapid rate, 30-300 yards a minute. Pad-steam processes are widely used.

Package Dyeing

In package dyeing, the dyebath is forced through the textile. Normally, the textile is in the yarn stage and the yarn is wound on a perforated core of stainless steel, plastic, or paper and placed on a perforated spindle in a pressurized machine. This technique is also used for fiber and fabric dyeing. In beam dyeing, the yarn or fabric is wound on perforated beams. This technique is especially practical for fabrics whose warp is one color and filling another. In skein dyeing, the yarn skeins are hung in the machine and the dye circulates around the hanging skeins. This technique is used primarily for bulky yarns like acrylic and wool for knits and carpet. Liquor ratios for all types are high to ensure uniformity of the dyeing, usually ranging from 10:1 to 4:1 depending on the process, dye-fiber combination, and quality desired.

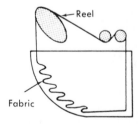

Fig. 19-6 *Winch dyeing.*

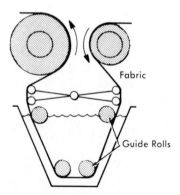

Fig. 19-7 *Jig dyeing.*

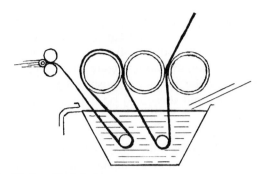

Fig. 19–8 *Pad dyeing.*

Combination Dyeing

In combination dyeing both the textile and the dye-bath are circulated. Several techniques are used here: jet dyeing, paddle machines, rotary drums, tumblers, and continuous dyeing.

JET DYEING In jet dyeing a technique similar to beck dyeing is used. Here the fabric is a continuous loop. The technique is especially useful for delicate fabrics of polyester. It involves vigorous agitation of the dyebath and the textile. Because of the rapid speed of the process (200–800 meters per minute), wrinkling of fabric is minimal. Low warp tension also assists in the development of bulk and fullness. High temperatures result in rapid dyeing, increased efficiency of dyes and chemicals, good fastness characteristics, and lower use of energy. However, equipment and maintenance costs are high, foaming can be a problem, and certain fabrics may be abraded in the process.

PADDLE MACHINES, ROTARY DRUMS, OR TUMBLERS Paddle machines and rotary drums are used primarily for product dyeing. Both the dyebath and the product are circulated by a paddle or rotation of the drum. Tumblers are similar to rotary drums except that they tilt forward for easier loading and unloading. Tumblers are used in product dyeing and in abrasive or chemical washes.

CONTINUOUS MACHINES *Continuous machines,* called *ranges,* are used for large lots of goods. They consist of compartments for wetting-out, dyeing, aftertreatment, washing, and rinsing.

In continuous dyeing, fabrics or yarns are used. The fabrics are usually cotton/polyester blends; the yarns are usually warp yarns for denim. Continuous dyeing is efficient for long runs, but color tolerances are generally relaxed for this method because of the variables involved. This technique is most com-

monly used in union dyeing of blends but it can be used in cross dyeing, too. In one-bath dyeing, both dyes are present in one bath. One-bath processes are used for disperse/direct dye combinations in many medium dark shades. The two-bath process is used for heavier weight goods, darker shades, or dyes that cannot be combined in one bath. In this process, the dye is added from two separate dye-baths.

The long-chain method is continuous dyeing of yarns. It usually involves indigo or a sulfur dye. Yarn is immersed in the dye, squeezed to remove excess dye, and skyed or exposed to air to oxidize and develop the color and fix the dye inside the fiber. Consecutive dips and skying progressively darken the shade until the desired color is reached. Indigo yarns may experience as many as sixteen separate dips to achieve a very dark navy blue.

PRINTING

Color designs are produced on fabrics by *printing* with dyes in paste form or by positioning dyes on the fabric with specially designed machines. Printing is used to add color in localized areas only. Wet prints use a thick liquid paste; dry prints are a powder print. Printed fabrics usually have clear-cut edges in the design portion on the right side and the color seldom penetrates completely to the wrong side of the fabric. Yarns raveled from printed fabrics show the color unevenly positioned on them.

Printing allows for great design flexibility. Patterns can be achieved with printing that are not possible from any other method.

The use of foams in printing is important. In *foam printing* the color is dispersed in the foam. The foam is applied to the fabric and the foam collapses. The small amount of liquid in the foam limits color migration.

Table 19-2 lists the various methods of creating printed designs.

Direct Printing

In *direct printing,* color is applied directly to the fabric in the pattern and location desired in the finished fabric. Direct printing is a common method of printing a design on a fabric because it is easy and economical.

BLOCK PRINTING *Block printing* is a hand process and probably the oldest technique for decorat-

Table 19–2   Printing Process

Direct	Discharge	Resist	Other
Block	Discharge	Batik	Jet
Direct		Tie-dye	Heat transfer
roller		Ikat	Electrostatic
Warp		Screen	Differential
		Flat	Foil printing
		Rotary	
		Stencil	

Fig. 19–9   *Carved wooden block and the print made using it.*

ing textiles. It is seldom done commercially because it is costly and slow. A design is carved on a block. The block is dipped in a shallow pan of dye paste and stamped on the fabric (Figure 19-9). Slight irregularities in color register or positioning are clues to block prints but these can be duplicated by other techniques.

DIRECT-ROLLER PRINTING *Direct-roller printing* was developed in 1783, about the time all textile operations were becoming mechanized. Figure 19-10 shows the essential parts of the printing machine. The fabric is drawn around a metal or high-density foam cylinder during printing (1 in Figure 19-10). A different printing roller applies each color. The printing roller (2 in Figure 19-10) is etched with the design. There are as many different rollers as there are colors in the fabric. In the diagram, three engraved rollers are used. Furnisher rollers are covered with hard rubber or brushes made of nylon or hard-rubber bristles. They revolve in a small color trough, pick up the dye paste, and deposit it on the rollers. A doctor blade scrapes off excess color so that only the engraved portions of the roller are filled with dye when it comes in contact with the fabric. The fabric to be printed, a rubberized blanket, and a back gray fabric pass between the cylinder and the engraved rollers. The blanket gives a good surface for sharp printing; the gray goods protects the blanket and absorbs excess dye.

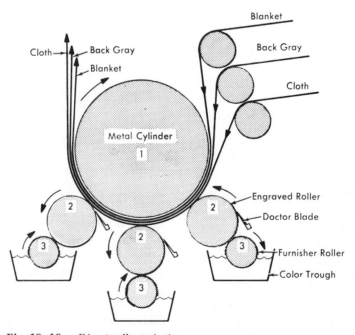

Fig. 19–10   *Direct-roller printing.*

Rayon and knitted fabrics are usually lightly coated with a gum sizing on the back to keep them from stretching or swelling as they go through the printing machine. After printing, the fabric is dried, steamed, or treated to set the dye. The sizing may cause water spotting during use or care.

Duplex printing is roller printing that prints on both sides of the fabric with the same or different patterns. In duplex prints, both sides of the fabric may be printed at the same time. However, the more common method prints the face and back in two steps.

WARP PRINTING *Warp printing* is a type of yarn printing done on the warp yarns prior to weaving. This technique gives an interesting, rather hazy pattern, softer than other prints. To identify it, ravel adjacent sides. Color in the form of the design is on the warp yarns. Filling yarns are white or solid color. Imitations have splotchy color on both warp and filling yarns. Warp printing is usually done on taffeta, satin ribbons, or cotton fabric, and on upholstery or drapery fabric (Figure 19–11). Since the practice is time consuming and expensive, it is not common.

Discharge Printing

Discharge prints are piece-dyed fabrics in which the design is made by removing color from selected areas of the fabric. Discharge printing is usually done on dark backgrounds. The fabric is first piece dyed in any of the usual methods. A discharge paste, which contains chemicals to remove the color, is then printed on the fabric using roller or screen techniques. Dyes that are not harmed by the discharging materials can be mixed with printing solution if color is desired in the discharge areas. The fabric is then steamed to develop the design, as either a white or a colored area. Better dye penetration is obtained with piece dyeing than with printing, and it is difficult to get good dark colors except by piece dyeing.

Discharge prints can be detected by looking at the back of the fabric. In the design area the color is often not completely removed and one can see evidences of the background colors, especially around the edges of the design. Background colors must be colors that can be removed by strong alkali. Discharge prints are usually satisfactory (Figure 19–12). However, the discharge chemical or bleach may cause tendering or weakening of the fabric in the areas where the color was discharged.

Resist Printing

Resist prints are fabrics in which color is prevented from entering the fabric during yarn or fabric dyeing.

BATIK *Batik* is generally a hand process in which hot wax is poured on a fabric in the form of a design. When the wax is set, the fabric is piece dyed. The wax prevents penetration of color into the wax-covered portions. Colors are built up by piece dyeing light colors first, waxing new portions, and redyeing until the design is complete. The wax is later removed by a solvent. Figure 19–13 shows a hand-produced batik from Indonesia. Figure 19–14 shows mass-produced yarn-dyed batiks from India.

Fig. 19–11 *Warp-printed fabric. Note the difference in yarn appearance and clarity of design between woven and raveled areas.*

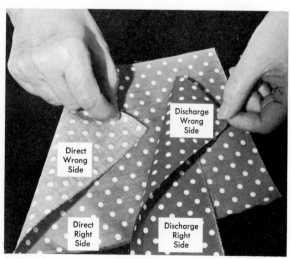

Fig. 19–12 *Discharge print versus direct print.*

Fig. 19–13   *Hand-produced batik.*

TIE-DYE   *Tie-dye* is a hand process in which yarn or fabric is wrapped in certain areas with fine thread or string. The yarn or fabric is then piece dyed and the string removed, leaving undyed areas (Figures 19-15 and 19-16). Manufacturing techniques using fabric in rope form have been developed to imitate tie-dyed fabric.

IKAT   *Ikat* is an ancient form of resist printing. In ikat, the yarn is tied for dyeing and weaving. The technique can be applied to only the warp yarns (warp ikat), only the filling yarns (filling ikat), or to both sets of yarns (double ikat). Ikat designs do not have precise edges. Ikat requires great skill in determining the placement of the design in the finished fabric (see Figure 19-17).

SCREEN PRINTING   *Flat-screen printing* is done commercially for small yardages, 50–5,000 yards, and often is used for designs larger than the circumference of the rolls used for roller printing.

The design is applied to the screen so that all but the figure is covered by a material that coats and permeates the pores in the screen, preventing the dye paste from moving through the screen. One screen is used for each color. The paste is forced through the open pores within the screen by a squeegee.

In the *hand process*, the fabric to be printed is placed on a long table. Two people position the screen on the fabric, apply the color, move the screen to a new position, and repeat the process until all the fabric is printed.

In the *automatic-screen process* the fabric to be printed is placed on a conveyer belt. A series of flat screens are positioned above and are lowered automatically. Positioning of the screen is carefully done to be sure print edges match. On screen-printed yardage, small areas along the selvage are used to align the print and may be used to identify a screen print. Color is applied automatically, and the fabric is moved automatically and fed continuously into ovens to be dried. For screen printing products, a similar process is used, but the equipment is specifically adapted to the type of product. Figure 19–18 shows a screen used in screen printing. Figure 19–19 shows a screen printer for T-shirts.

Rotary-screen printing is done with cylindrical metal screens that operate in much the same way as the flat screens, except that the operation is continuous rather than started and stopped as the

Fig. 19–14   *Mass-produced, yarn-dyed batiks.*

Fig. 19–15 *Tie-dye. This fabric was rolled on the bias, tied, and piece dyed. A second dyeing was done with the fabric rolled in the opposite direction.*

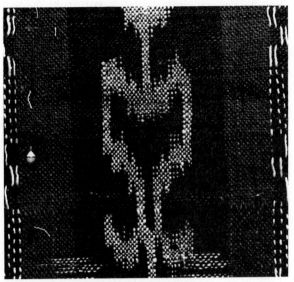

Fig. 19–17 *Ikat from Guatemala.*

screens are raised and lowered in the flat process (Figure 19-20). The rotary screens are cheaper than the copper rollers used in roller printing. Rotary screen printing is more common than flat-bed screen printing.

Screen printing is useful for printing large designs on fabrics. Screen printing has overtaken roller printing as the most common commercial printing method.

STENCIL PRINTING *Stencil printing* was the precursor of screen printing. The pattern is cut from a special wax paper or thin metal sheets. As in screen printing, a separate stencil is cut for each color. Color in a thick solution or paste is applied by hand with a brush or sprayed with an air gun. Stencilling is done on limited yardage.

Other Printing Methods

JET PRINTING *Jet printing* is a process that uses continuous streams of dye forced from jets. The ink-jet system is based on the method first introduced for use on carpets. In this system, small jets inject color into the fabric. The size of the nozzle, number of jets, and bleeding characteristics of the dye or pigment paste used determine the intricacy of the pattern, its size, and clarity. Ink-jet systems are available with 172 jets per inch. Textiles printed with this technique include carpeting, pile upholstery fabrics, toweling, and some apparel fabrics. Figure 19-21 shows a jet printing machine.

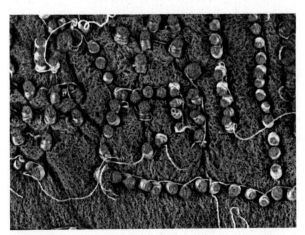

Fig. 19–16 *Tie-dye fabric showing thread used to make the design.*

Fig. 19–18 *Screen used in rotary screen printing. (Courtesy of Stork Screens B .V.)*

Fig. 19–19 *Printing machine used to print items after sewing. (Courtesy of Advance Process Supply)*

The ink-jet machine consists of a series of horizontal bars containing the dye, which is fed through small dye jets. The prepared cloth passes under the bars and by the use of an electronically controlled tape, dye is deposited in the proper place from the jets on the bars. Dye penetrates to the backing and patterns can be easily changed (see Figure 19–22).

Jet printing is an economical process for use with thick fabrics whose designs range from specific patterns to multicolored stripes, abstract splashes, or tie-dye effects. Several colors are applied in one operation from jets set in bars. The fabric moves over an inclined plane, dye is sprayed from jets onto the fabric, and the cloth then goes through heavy rollers that press the dye completely through the fabric.

HEAT-TRANSFER PRINTING *Heat-transfer printing* is a process in which designs are transferred to fabric from specially printed paper by heat and pressure (see Figure 19–23). The paper is printed by one of several paper-printing techniques: gravure, flexograph, offset, or converted rotary-screen. The fabric, yarn, or item is placed on a plastic frame and padded with a special solution. Paper is placed over the fabric and then covered with a silicone-rubber sheet.

This sandwich is subjected to high pressure at a temperature of 200°C for a few seconds during which the print sublimes and migrates from the paper to the fabric. In sublimation, a solid evaporates and recondenses as a solid in a new location.

The advantages of heat-transfer printing are better penetration and clarity of design, lower production costs, and elimination of pollution problems. Clear, photographic prints are possible with this technique. Transfer printing can be done on three-dimensional fabrics like circular knits without splitting them first and on three-dimensional products like garments.

Print papers using disperse dyes were developed for polyester-fiber fabrics and have been successful on high-polyester/cotton blends and on nylon. Cotton fabrics and 50/50 blends of cotton/polyester are treated with a resin that has an affinity for disperse dyes. Print papers with acid dyes for nylon, silk, and wool and with cationic dyes for acrylics are available.

ELECTROSTATIC PRINTING *Electrostatic printing* is similar to electrostatic flocking. A screen that has the design on it is covered with powdered dye mixed with a carrier that has dielectric properties. The screen is about ½ inch above the fabric. When

Fig. 19–20 *Rotary-screen printing. (Courtesy of Stork Brabant, B. V.)*

passed through an electric field, the dye-resin is pulled onto the material, where it is fixed by heat.

DIFFERENTIAL PRINTING *Differential printing* is a printing technique using screen printing on carpets tufted with yarns that have different dye affinities.

Foil Printing

In *foil printing*, a special adhesive is applied to the fabric by a flat-bed or rotary screen. The fabric is dyed and partially cured . The foil is a thin polyester film with a heat-sensitive release coating, covered with a very thin layer of aluminum and a clear or tinted lacquer. The metallic foil is transferred by a heat transfer press. The foil bonds only where the adhesive pattern exists on the fabric.

RECENT DEVELOPMENTS IN DYEING AND PRINTING

Recent advances in commercial coloration include dyes with environmental sensitivities and combinations of dyeing or printing processes. For example, Hypercolor casual wear by Generra uses a heat-sensitive dye combination that changes hue when exposed to heat, a metamorphic color system. The hue shifts are dramatic: from purple to bright blue, mauve to fluorescent pink, and green to hot pink. These cotton items are garment dyed in a process that combines an underlying pigment dye and another dye to achieve the special effect. When exposed to heat, the pigment dye shows through. A pair of Hypercolor socks is shown in Figure 19-24. These items are available in solids and graphics. For example, one graphic showing a man wearing a

Fig. 19–21 *Jet printing machine. (Courtesy of the Milliken Company)*

dark suit changes to a man wearing a sports jacket, shirt, and walking shorts.

Kanebo of Japan has introduced a system that incorporates tiny liquid crystals in a surface coating. The crystals change color depending on temperature. The coating is used on swimwear and trim; the high cost of the system limits its application to other products.

Fig. 19–22 *Jet-dyed carpets.*

Fig. 19–23 *Heat-transfer printing: design on paper* (left) *is transferred by heat to fabric* (center). *Design on paper is lighter after printing* (right).

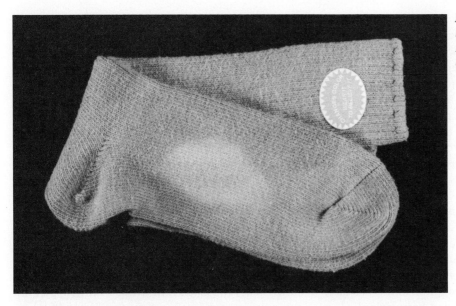

Fig. 19–24 *Socks with a heat-sensitive dye system. Note the lighter area that has been heated.*

Techniques that combine dyeing and printing, such as ginghams from India that have a batik top-dye, have become popular. Another example is yarn-dyed denim that is printed or overdyed. In overdyed denims, the yarn-dyed fabric is dyed another color. Often the overdyeing follows an abrasive or chemical wash. (See Chapter 17.)

Other developments in coloration relate to changes in the textiles industry, including technological advances and computer applications in dyeing and printing. The shift away from large runs of the same color or print continues. Speeds of 100 meters per minute do not contribute to extremely high quality or intricate prints. As quality increases in importance, production speeds and length of standard runs decrease. For example, in the 1950s and 1960s standard runs were 100,000 yards. By the 1980s, standard runs were less than 10,000 yards. In the 1990s, standard runs may be as short as 250 yards. Specialization of fabric or design type continues, especially in designer markets for apparel and furnishings. The industry is also strongly committed to minimal seconds, strict color control, and decreased dead time. Dead time refers to the time the equipment is not operating because of the need to change equipment components, like screens, or to change colors for different patterns. Dead time in screen printing has decreased to between 20 and 50 minutes, depending on the system and the complexity of the patterns involved.

Efficient use of dyes, chemicals, and water or other solvents is another concern of the industry. For example, with reactive dyes, standard utilization rates were 60–80 percent. Utilization rates are expected to increase to 85–93 percent in the next few years. Solvent dyeing systems, which are standard for some fibers like aramid, require high recovery rates, such as 98 percent, to be economically feasible. The growth of solvent dyeing has great potential, especially as water costs and water quality standards become greater. The use of solvent dyeing would allow expansion of dyeing into parts of the country where dyeing has not been done due to the limited availability of water.

The introduction of binders with greatly improved characteristics has done much to boost the popularity of pigment dyes and prints. Pigment-dyed products are on the market thanks to these new binders. In addition, in the near future there may be methods of spraying dispersions of pigments on fabrics and products to achieve solid shades with good fastness characteristics at a low price.

Computer applications relate to improved quality of dyed and printed goods, with the possibility of producing thousands of shades with minimal colors in overlap printing. Theoretically, it is possible to produce almost any color with the three primary colors and black, much as is the case in color xerography, depending on how much of each color is used. Computer use increases automation of the process and decreases costs associated with labor, raw materials, and inventory. Computer-aided design systems (CAD), computer-aided engraving systems (CAE), and computer-aided manufacturing systems (CAM) make it possible to create designs and convert them into fabrics in a matter of hours or days rather than months. CAD systems allow the textile designer to experiment with changes in scale and hue or saturation of the design. CAD systems also allow designers to quickly create coordinating prints for apparel and furnishing uses by selecting portions of the original design and copying it to another fabric. Computers also can automatically register the print so edges in the pattern match. Computer monitoring of dyeing and printing processes will decrease the environmental impact of these processes as manufacturers recognize the direct costs of inefficient use of materials and energy and incorporate closed-loop recycling of chemicals, solvents, water, and energy.

The progress in printing techniques has been so great that predictions for capabilities by the year 2000 include making direct imaging techniques available in retail stores. Consumers will be able to select the product in an acceptable ground or base color, select a pattern to be applied to the product, or design their own pattern and have it applied as they wait. Research on techniques currently used in color xerography on paper show that this technique can be modified for use on textiles. Fabric width, chemicals used in the process, and the relatively slow printing rate are some of the concerns limiting adaptation of this technique to textiles.

COLOR PROBLEMS

Good *colorfastness* is expected, but it is not always achieved. When one considers all the variables connected with dyeing and printing and the hostile environment in which fabrics are used, one can appreciate how good most colored fabrics are.

The factors that influence colorfastness are:

1. Chemical nature of fibers
2. Chemical nature of dyes and pigments
3. Penetration of dyes into the cloth
4. Fixation of dyes or pigments on or in the fabrics

The coloring agents must resist washing, dry cleaning, bleaching, and spot and stain removing with all of the variables of time, temperature, and substances used. They must be resistant to light, perspiration, abrasion, fumes, and other factors. Dyes for certain products, like car interiors and outdoor furniture, must use ultraviolet-light-stabilized dyes. Textiles used in furnishings may experience color problems from exposure to acne medication, bleaches, acids, and alkalis. These color-damaging agents are found in a host of materials with which furnishing textiles are likely to come in contact, such as vomit, drain and toilet cleaners, urine, plant food or fertilizers, insecticides, furniture polish, and disinfectants and germicides found in bathroom cleaners.

If the color is not fast in the fabric as purchased, it is not possible to make it fast. Salt and vinegar are used as exhausting agents for household dyes, but research does not support the theory that they will "set" color. If the dye could not be set using the knowledge of the dye chemist, the specialized equipment available in the dyehouse, and selected dyeing chemicals, the consumer will not be able to accomplish this task at home with salt, vinegar, or any other ingredient identified on some improper care labels.

Color loss occurs through bleeding, crocking, and migration or through chemical changes in the dye. *Bleeding* is color loss in water. In bleeding, other fibers present in the wash load may pick up the color. *Crocking* is color loss from rubbing or abrasion. In crocking, some color may be transferred to the abradant. For example, some tight-fitting denim jeans may color the front of the thighs during wear. *Migration* is shifting of color to the surrounding area or to an adjacent surface. An example of migration occurs with some red and white stripes when the white closest to the red takes on a pinkish cast. Atmospheric gases (fume fading), perspiration, and sunlight may cause fading as a result of a chemical change in the dye.

Certain vat and sulfur dyes *tender*, or destroy, cotton cloth. Green, red, blue, and yellow vat dyes and black, yellow, and orange sulfur dyes are the chief offenders. Manufacturers know which dyes cause the trouble and can correct it by thoroughly oxidizing the dye within the fiber. The damage is increased by moisture and sunlight, a problem that is sometimes critical in draperies. Damage may not be evident until the draperies are cleaned and then slits or holes occur (Figures 19-25 and 19-26). Sunlight, smog, and acidic atmospheric gases, as well as dyes, cause fabric damage.

Wear may remove the surface color of heavy fabrics (Figure 19-27). The movement of yarns during bending causes undyed fibers to work their way to the surface. Color streaks may result from uneven removal of sizing before the dye is applied because the portions of the fabric that did not come in contact with the dye were not even dyed. Some resin-treated fabrics show this sort of color change because either the dye was applied with the resin and did not penetrate sufficiently or the fabric was dyed after being resin treated, in which case there were not enough unused dye sites for the dye to be

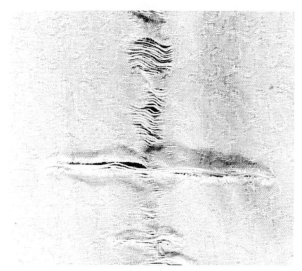

Fig. 19–25 *Cotton and rayon drapery fabric. After dry cleaning, yellowish streaks indicating fiber photo-degradation were obvious; after washing, splits had occurred in the fabric, resulting from fiber swelling in water and abrasion in the washer.*

Fig. 19–27 *Denim jeans; loss of surface color.*

anchored. The best way to check the dye penetration in heavy fabrics is to examine the fabric. In yard goods, ravel off a yarn to see if it is the same color throughout. In ready-to-wear, look at the edge of seams. In heavy prints, look at the reverse side. The more color on the back, the better the dye penetration.

A defect in printed fabrics occurs when two colors of a print overlap each other or where the edges are not clear. This defect is referred to as *out of register* (see Figure 19–28).

Printed fabrics may be printed off-grain. *Off-grain prints* create problems because the fabric cannot be both straight with the print and cut on-grain. If cut off-grain, the fabric tends to assume its normal position when washed, causing twisted seams and uneven hemlines. If cut on-grain, the print will not be straight. In an allover design this may not be important, but in large checks and plaids or designs with crosswise lines, matching at seam lines becomes impossible and slanting lines across the fabric are seldom desirable. Off-grain prints are created by incorrect finishing of the fabric. The gray goods are started into the tentering machine crooked or the

Fig. 19–26 *Tendering of cotton draperies caused by sulfur dye, atmospheric moisture, and heat.*

Fig. 19–28 *One color is printed on a fabric at a time. When colors are not properly aligned, they are out of register: (left) out of register; (right) in register.*

mechanism for moving the fabric does not work properly so that the two selvages move at slightly different speeds, or the fabric is not properly supported in the center of its width. The off-grain problem can easily be corrected at the mill.

Frosting often results from abrasion in cotton/polyester durable-press garments that have been dyed with two different but color-matched, dyes (union dyed). During wear, the surface is abraded and becomes lighter in color, while the unabraded or more durable area keeps its color.

Other problems related to dyeing and printing are concerns of the producer and manufacturer. These are problems related to the consistency of the color throughout the width and length of the fabric or from dye lot to dye lot. Manufacturers of apparel and furnishing items need to have a fabric that is consistent in color. The color needs to be the same from side to side (selvage to selvage); side to center (selvage to center), and end to end (from one end of the roll of fabric to the other). If the color is not consistent, the producer will have problems with product parts not *matching* in color. When several rolls of the same color fabric are required, it is important that all the rolls are consistent in color. Color matching equipment, like a colorimeter, is commonly used to assess color uniformity within or among fabric rolls.

The fastness of the dye often determines the method of care that should be used. The consumer must depend on the label, but some knowledge of color problems that occur in use and care will allow for more intelligent choices.

KEY TERMS

Pigment	Foam printing
Dye	Direct printing
Dye process	Block printing
Levelness	Direct-roller printing
Fiber dyeing	Duplex printing
Solution dyed	Warp printing
Producer colored	Discharge printing
Yarn dyeing	Resist printing
Piece dyeing	Batik
Cross dyeing	Tie-dye
Union dyeing	Ikat
Product dyeing	Flat-screen printing
Winch dyeing	Rotary-screen printing
Jig dyeing	Stencil printing
Pad dyeing	Jet printing
Cationic dyes	Heat transfer printing
Acid dyes	Electrostatic printing
Azioc dyes	Differential printing
Developed dyes	Foil printing
Direct dyes	Colorfastness
Disperse dyes	Bleeding
Fluorescent dyes	Crocking
Mordant dyes	Migration
Reactive dyes	Tendering
Sulfur dyes	Out of register
Vat dyes	Off-grain print
Solvent dyes	Frosting
Printing	Color matching

QUESTIONS

1. What are the visual clues to determine if a fabric has been dyed or printed? How can the product stage or the technique used in printing be determined?

2. Identify the coloration process (stage of dyeing or type of print) that was probably used for these products:
   solid blue cotton and nylon upholstery velvet
   patterned carpet of nylon for hotel lobby
   100 percent cotton chambray work shirt
   irregular or fuzzy plaid gingham
   floral pattern 100 percent rayon faille dress
   100 percent cotton T-shirt with local ski club name on front
   cartoon print on 100 percent polyester quilt for child's bed
   100 percent wool tweed upholstery
3. Describe the appearance and problems created by these color defects:
   poor leveling
   migration
   frosting
   bleeding
   side-to-side
4. What factors influence colorfastness? How can colorfastness be determined?
5. What dye class or classes are commonly used to color these fibers?
   cotton, rayon, flax, or ramie
   wool, nylon, or silk
   leather
   acetate, polyester
   olefin
   acrylic

SUGGESTED READINGS

Cook, Fred C. (December, 1990). "Q. R., Environmental Pressure Will Drive Dyeing, Printing." *Textile World*, pp. 83–85.

Crews, Patricia Cox (1989). "Effectiveness of Dye Setting Treatments on Cotton Fabrics Dyed with Direct, Reactive, and Vat Dyes." *Clothing and Textile Research Journal*, 7(4), pp. 1–7.

Kulkarni, S. V., Blackwell, C. D., Blackard, A. I., Stackhouse, C. W., and Alexander, M. W. (1986). *Textile Dyeing Operations.* Park Ridge, NJ: Noyes Publications.

Needles, Howard (1986). *Textile Fibers, Dyes, Finishes, and Processes.* Park Ridge, NJ: Noyes Publications.

Perkins, Warren, S. (1991). "A Review of Textile Dyeing Processes." *Textile Chemist and Colorist, 23*(8), pp. 23–27.

Trotman, E. R. (1984). *Dyeing and Chemical Technology of Textile Fibers.* New York: John Wiley & Sons.

Turner, G. Robert (1988). "Textile Printing in the 1990s." *Textile Chemist and Colorist, 20*(8), pp. 19–22.

SECTION 6

OTHER ISSUES RELATED TO TEXTILES

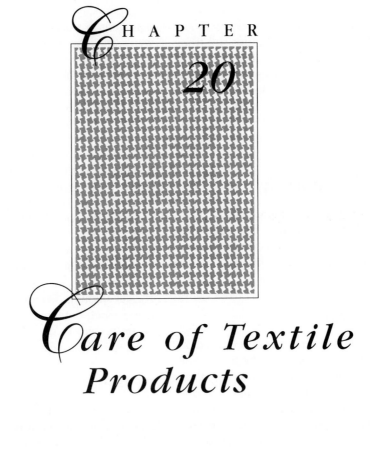

CHAPTER 20

Care of Textile Products

OBJECTIVES

- To understand the theory of detergency.

- To relate care requirements to fiber, yarn, fabrication, finish, dye, and construction of the textile product.

- To recognize the differences and similarities among the common cleaning procedures.

- To know the function of the various compounds used in cleaning textile products.

- To relate proper cleaning and storage to product serviceability.

*T*HE TERM *CARE* REFERS TO CLEANING PROCEdures or techniques necessary to remove soil from a textile product and return the product to its new or nearly new condition. Care can also refer to storage conditions. This chapter will deal primarily with commonly used cleaning procedures. However, a few brief comments will relate to storage. Table 20-1 summarizes standard care terminology.

LAUNDERING

In discussing *laundering*, it is important to understand the nature of soil and soiling, the manner in which a detergent and water work, and the additives that are used to improve the removal of soil or the appearance of the laundered item.

Soil and Soil Removal

Soil can be divided into several categories based on the soil type and how it is held on the fabric. Soil such as gum, mud, or wax can be held on the fabric mechanically. These soils can be removed mechanically by scraping or agitation. Soil such as lint and dust can be held on the fabric by electrostatic forces. If the electrostatic force is neutralized, the soil can be removed. Because water is such an excellent conductor of electricity, immersing the fabric in water neutralizes any static charge on the surface of the fabric. Water-soluble soils such as coffee, sodas, and sugar water are absorbed into the fiber. When the fabric is immersed in water, the water can dissolve the soil. Organic soils such as grease, oil, and gravy require the assistance of the chemical action of a detergent and heat to be removed. Of course, many soils are mixtures of these categories and are removed by a combination of thermal, mechanical, and chemical actions. If one aspect of removal is decreased, another aspect must be increased in order to maintain the degree of soil removal. For example, if the water temperature is decreased, either more detergent or more agitation will be required to be as effective.

Detergency

Detergency refers to the manner in which the soap or detergent removes soil. Adding soap or synthetic detergent to water lowers the surface tension of the water; thus the water wets things faster. Water does not bead up on surfaces, but spreads over the surface, wetting the surface. A *soap* or *detergent* molecule consists of an organic "tail" that has an affinity for organic soils and a polar "head" that has an affinity for water. Thus the two parts of the soap or detergent molecule literally dislodge the soil. Agitation breaks the soil into very tiny globules that are held in suspension until they are rinsed away (Figure 20-1). If hot water is used, the oily soils soften and are more likely to break into small globules. Because of the many functions of the ingredients in detergents, it is important to use the appropriate amount of detergent when doing the laundry. Instructions for the proper amount to use are included on the label. Much research has been done to determine these correct amounts. Do not guess; use a measuring cup. If too much detergent is used, detergent will build up on textiles in the wash. If too little detergent is used, soil will remain on the textiles.

Water

Water is used as the solvent because it is cheap, readily available, nontoxic, and does not require special equipment for use. Water has several aspects of importance in laundering: hardness, temperature, and volume. *Water hardness* refers to the kind and amount of mineral contaminants present. Water that contains mineral salts is referred to as *hard water*. The more mineral salts dissolved in the water, the harder it is. Hard water makes cleaning more difficult. In order to soften the water, the minerals must be removed, or *sequestered* (bonded to another molecule). The most common procedure for softening water is adding a water-softening agent, such as sodium hexametaphosphate, to the water or using an ion-exchange resin in a water softener.

Water temperature is important in determining the effectiveness of the laundry additives used. Some additives are more effective at certain temperatures. Water temperature is also important in removing certain soils. The following are water-temperature ranges as identified by the Federal Trade Commission in the Care Labeling Rule: cold water is 85°F, or the initial water temperature from a cold water tap; warm water is 90°F–110°F, or hand comfortable; and hot water is up to 150°F.

Water volume is important in order to allow for agitation, remove soil and keep soil suspended, and avoid wrinkling items in the load. Water volume is related to the amount of fabric present in the machine.

Soaps and Synthetic Detergents

Soaps and synthetic detergents are used to remove and suspend soils, minimize the effects of hard water, and alter the surface tension of the water.

SOAPS Soaps are salts of long, linear-chain fatty acids produced from naturally occurring animal or vegetable oils or fats. Soaps can react with hard water and produce insoluble curds that form a greasy, gray film on textiles and a ring on tubs. Soaps are effective in removing oily or greasy stains, but they are not vigorous soil-removal agents.

SYNTHETIC DETERGENTS Synthetic detergents are really mixtures of several ingredients: surfactant, builder, filler, antideposition agent, perfume, dye, and fluorescent-whitening agent (Figure 20–2 and Table 20–2). Detergent formulas are different in different parts of the country. The differences are related to the type of soil, water conditions, and laws. In this text the term detergent will be used to refer to the box or bottle of cleaning compound called a *detergent. Surfactants* are sulfonated organic compounds that are soluble in hard water and do not form an insoluble curd. Surfactants are vigorous soil-removal agents and are frequently sulfonated, long, linear-chain fatty acids. There are several types of surfactants: nonionic, anionic, and cationic. *Nonionic surfactants*, such as ethers of ethylene oxide, are used in liquids and recommended for use in cold or warm water because they become less soluble at high temperatures. *Anionic surfactants* are used in powders and are good for oily soils and clay-soil suspension. This category is the most common. These surfactants are usually linear alkyl sulfonates (LAS) and are biodegradable. Anionic surfactants are most effective in warm and hot water. *Cationic surfactants* are used primarily in disinfectants and fabric softeners.

Builders are used to soften the water, add alkalinity to the solution since a pH of 8–10 is best for maximum cleaning efficiency, emulsify oils and greases, and minimize soil redeposition. Builders include phosphates (usually sodium tripolyphosphate), carbonates (sodium carbonate), citrates (sodium citrate), and silicates (sodium silicate). Of these, phosphate builders offer the best performance over the widest range of laundering conditions. Phosphate builders have been banned or restricted in some parts of the United States, however, because of their role in water pollution. Carbonate builders do not contribute to water pollution. However, they combine with hard-water minerals to form water-insoluble precipitates that may harm the machine, fabric, and zippers. Citrate builders are much weaker at softening hard water and are used in heavy-duty liquid detergents. Sodium silicate functions as a builder when present in large concentrations. However, sodium silicate is often present in small concentrations because it also functions as a corrosion inhibitor.

Fillers, such as sodium sulfate in powder detergents and water and alcohol in liquid detergents, are used to add bulk to the detergent, allow for a uniform mix of the ingredients, increase the size of the micelle (the grouping of soap or detergent molecles that remove soil from fabric), protect washer parts, and minimize caking in powders. *Antiredeposition agents*, such as sodium carboxymethylcellulose, are used to minimize the soil redepositing from the wash water on the fabric. *Perfumes* are designed to mask the chemical smell of detergents and to add a "clean" smell to the wash. *Dyes* make the detergent look better and function as bluing.

Fluorescent-whitening agents are also known as *fluorescent-brightening agents, optical-whitening agents*, and *optical-brightening agents*. These compounds are low-grade or weak dyes that fluoresce, or absorb, light at one wavelength and reemit the energy at another wavelength. Thus it is possible to have whites that are "whiter than white." These ingredients do not contribute to soil removal; they mask soil and make yellow or dingy fabrics look white.

Other ingredients commonly found in detergents include fabric softeners and bleaches (which will be discussed later in this chapter), suds-control agents, and foam-control agents. Liquid detergents may contain alcohol to dissolve some ingredients of the detergent, assist in stain removal, and act as an antifreeze during shipping; hydrotopes to assist in keeping ingredients in solution; and opacifiers to give a rich, creamy appearance to the detergent.

Other Laundry Additives

Other *laundry additives* include bleaches, fabric softeners, water softeners, disinfectants, presoaks, pretreatments, starches or sizing, and bluing. Some of these additives are seldom used.

Table 20–1 Standard Care Terminology

1. Washing, Machine Methods

a. *Machine wash*—A process by which soil may be removed from products through the use of water, detergent or soap, agitation, and a machine designed for this purpose. When no temperature is given, e.g., "warm" or "cold," hot water up to 150°F (66°C) can be regularly used.

b. *Warm*—Initial water temperature setting 90°-110°F (32°-43°C) (hand comfortable).

c. *Cold*—Initial water temperature setting same as cold water tap up to 85°F (29°C).

d. *Do not have commercially laundered*—Do not employ a laundry that uses special formulations, sour rinses, extremely large loads, or extremely high temperatures or that otherwise is employed for commercial, industrial, or institutional use. Employ laundering methods designed for residential use or use in a self-service establishment.

e. *Small load*—Smaller than normal washing load.

f. *Delicate cycle or gentle cycle*—Slow agitation and reduced time.

g. *Durable press cycle* or *permanent press cycle*—Cool-down rinse or cold rinse before reduced spinning.

h. *Separately*—Alone.

i. *With like colors*—With colors of similar hue and intensity.

j. *Wash inside out*—Turn product inside out to protect face of fabric.

k. *Warm rinse*—Initial water temperature setting 90°-110°F (32°-43°C).

l. *Cold rinse*—Initial water temperature setting same as cold water tap up to 85°F (29°C).

m. *Rinse thoroughly*—Rinse several times to remove detergent, soap, and bleach.

n. *No spin* or *Do not spin*—Remove material at start of final spin cycle.

o. *No wring* or *Do not wring*—Do not use roller wringer, nor wring by hand.

2. Washing, Hand Methods

a. *Hand wash*—A process by which soil may be manually removed from products through the use of water, detergent or soap, and gentle squeezing action. When no temperature is given, e.g., "warm" or "cold," hot water up to 150°F (66°C) can be regularly used.

b. *Warm*—Initial water temperature 90°-110°F (32°-43°C) (hand comfortable).

c. *Cold*—Initial water temperature same as cold water tap up to 85°F (29°C).

d. *Separately*—Alone.

e. *With like colors*—With colors of similar hue and intensity.

f. *No wring or twist*—Handle to avoid wrinkles and distortion.

g. *Rinse thoroughly*—Rinse several times to remove detergent, soap, and bleach.

h. *Damp wipe only*—Surface clean with damp cloth or sponge.

3. Drying, All Methods

a. *Tumble dry*—Use machine dryer. When no temperature setting is given, machine drying at a hot setting may be regularly used.

b. *Medium*—Set dryer at medium heat.

c. *Low*—Set dryer at low heat.

d. *Durable press* or *permanent press*—Set dryer at permanent-press setting.

e. *No heat*—Set dryer to operate without heat.

f. *Remove promptly*—When items are dry, remove immediately to prevent wrinkling.

g. *Drip-dry*—Hang dripping wet with or without hand shaping and smoothing.

h. *Line dry*—Hang damp from line or bar in or out of doors.

i. *Line dry in shade*—Dry away from sun.

BLEACH Most *bleaches* are oxidizing agents. The actual bleaching is done by active oxygen. A few bleaches are reducing agents that are used to strip color from dyed fabrics. Bleaches may be either acid or alkaline in nature. They are usually unstable, especially in the presence of moisture. Bleaches that are old or have been improperly stored lose their oxidizing power.

Any bleach will cause damage, and because damage occurs more rapidly at higher temperatures and concentrations, these factors should be carefully controlled.

The same bleach is not suitable to all kinds of fibers. Because fibers vary in their chemical reaction, bleaches must be chosen with regard to fiber content. The sock in Figure 20-3 had been all white, but when bleached with a chlorine bleach, the wool-ribbed cuff section became discolored while the cotton foot remained white.

Liquid chlorine bleaches were, for many years, the common household bleaches. They are efficient bactericidal agents (disinfectants) and, as such, can be used for sterilizing fabrics. They are cheap and efficient bleaches for cellulosic fibers. The bleaching is done by hypochlorous acid liberated during the bleaching process. Because this tenders cellulosic fibers, the bleach must be thoroughly rinsed out. Chlorine bleaches are of no value on protein and thermoplastic fibers and, if used, will cause yellowing.

Table 20–1 (continued)

j. *Line dry away from heat*—Dry away from heat.

k. *Dry flat*—Lay out horizontally for drying.

l. *Block to dry*—Reshape to original dimensions while drying.

m. *Smooth by hand*—By hand, while wet, remove wrinkles, straighten seams and facings.

4. Ironing and Pressing

a. *Iron*—Ironing is needed. When no temperature is given, iron at the highest temperature setting may be regularly used.

b. *Warm iron*—Medium temperature setting.

c. *Cool iron*—Lowest temperature setting.

d. *Do not iron*—Item not to be smoothed or finished with an iron.

e. *Iron wrong side only*—Article turned inside out for ironing or pressing.

f. *No steam* or *Do not steam*—Steam in any form not to be used.

g. *Steam only*—Steaming without contact pressure.

h. *Steam press* or *Steam iron*—Use iron at steam setting.

i. *Iron damp*—Articles to be ironed should feel moist.

j. *Use press cloth*—Use a dry or a damp cloth between iron and fabric.

5. Bleaching

a. *Bleach when needed*—All bleaches may be used when necessary.

b. *No bleach* or *Do not bleach*—No bleaches may be used.

c. *Only nonchlorine bleach, when needed*—Only the bleach specified may be used when necessary. Chlorine bleach may not be used.

6. Washing or Dry Cleaning

a. *Wash or dry clean, any normal method*—Can be machine washed in hot water, can be machine dried at a high setting, can be ironed at a hot setting, can be bleached with all commercially available bleaches and can be dry cleaned with all commercially available solvents.

7. Dry cleaning, All Procedures

a. *Dry clean*—A process by which soil may be removed from products or specimens in a machine that uses any common organic solvent (for example, petroleum, perchlorethylene, fluorocarbon) located in any commercial establishment. The process may include moisture addition to solvent up to 75 percent relative humidity, hot tumble drying up to 160°F (71°C) and restoration by steam-press or steam-air finishing.

b. *Professionally dry clean*—Use the dry cleaning process, but modified to ensure optimum results either by a dry cleaning attendant or through the use of a dry cleaning machine that permits such modifications or both. Such modifications or special warnings must be included in the care instruction.

c. *Petroleum, fluorocarbon* or *perchlorethylene*—Employ solvent(s) specified to dry clean the item.

d. *Short cycle*—Reduced or minimum cleaning time, depending on solvent used.

e. *Minimum extraction*—Least possible extraction time.

f. *Reduced moisture* or *Low moisture*—Decreased relative humidity.

g. *No tumble* or *Do not tumble*—Do not tumble dry.

h. *Tumble warm*—Tumble dry up to 120°F (49°C).

i. *Tumble cool*—Tumble dry at room temperature.

j. *Cabinet dry warm*—Cabinet dry up to 120°F (49°C).

k. *Cabinet dry cool*—Cabinet dry at room temperature.

l. *Steam only*—Employ no contact pressure when steaming.

m. *No steam* or *Do not steam*—Do not use steam in pressing, finishing, steam cabinets, or wands.

8. Leather and Suede Cleaning

a. *Leather clean*—Have cleaned only by a professional cleaner who uses special leather- or suede-care methods.

Source: Federal Trade Commission (1984). *Writing a Care Label*. Washington, D.C.: U.S. Government Printing Office.

Powdered-oxygen bleaches, also called all-fabric bleaches, may be used safely on all fibers and colored fabrics. Their bleaching effect is much milder than chlorine bleaches.

Sodium perborate is a powder bleach that becomes hydrogen peroxide when it combines with water. It is a safe bleach for home use with all kinds of fibers. Powder bleaches are recommended for regular use in the wash water to maintain the original whiteness of the fabric rather than as a whitener for discolored fabrics.

Acid bleaches, such as oxalic acid and potassium permanganate, have limited use. Citric acid and lemon juice are also acid bleaches that are good rust-spot removers.

FABRIC SOFTENER *Fabric softeners* coat the fabric to increase the electrical conductivity of the fabric, minimize static charges, and decrease fabric stiffness. The types of fabric softeners include those added in the final rinse, those present in detergent, and those added in the dryer. The last two categories of fabric softeners have become much more convenient to use in the past several years. The instructions for use of the fabric softener need to be followed or problems may result. For example, dryer fabric softener sheets should be added to a cold dryer. If they are added to a warm or hot dryer, oil from the fabric softener may spot synthetic items. Fabric softeners have a tendency to build up on fabrics in a greasy layer, resulting in less absorbent

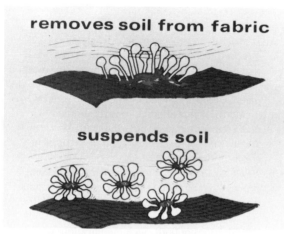

Fig. 20–1 *Mechanism of soil removal: detergent surrounds soil and lifts it off the fabric.*

fabrics. Hence it is not recommended that a fabric softener be used every time a product is laundered. Every other time or every third time is recommended, if necessary.

WATER SOFTENER *Water-softening agents* are found as builders in detergent or as separate

ingredients that can be added to increase the efficiency of the detergent if the water is especially hard. If a water-softening additive is used, a nonprecipitating type is recommended to avoid buildup of precipitates on washer parts and items in the wash.

DISINFECTANT *Disinfectants* include pine oil, phenolics, chlorine bleach, and coal-tar derivatives. These items are used occasionally to disinfect sickroom garments and bed and bath linens.

PRESOAK *Enzymatic presoaks* are used to remove tough stains. These additives contain enzymes—such as protease (for protein stains), lipase (for fat stains), and amylase (for carbohydrate stains)—that act as a catalyst and aid in removal of these soils. Enzymatic presoaks need more time to work than most other additives so a long presoak of one-half hour or more is recommended. Some people prefer to use the presoak overnight. Presoaks often include a builder and a surfactant to improve the efficiency of the presoak. These additives are not safe for use with protein fibers, such as silk and wool, and other specialty wool fibers.

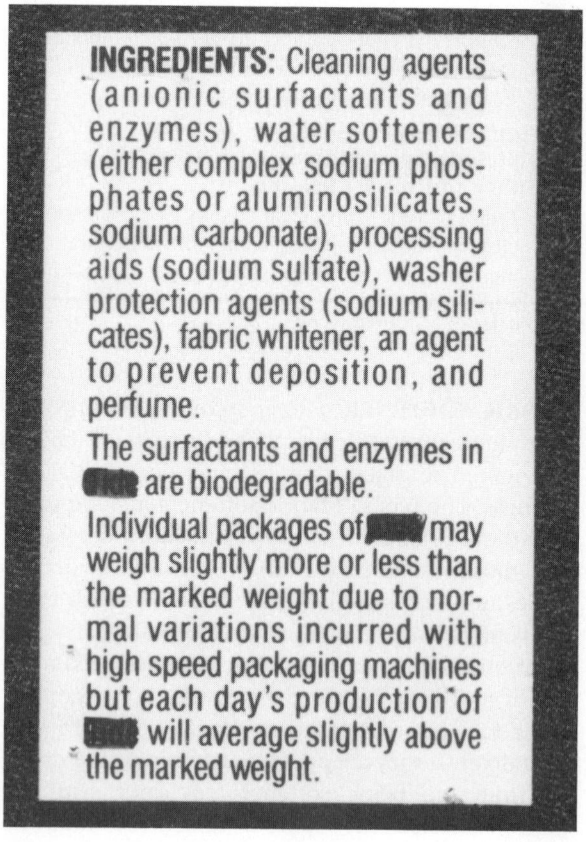

INGREDIENTS: Cleaning agents (anionic surfactants and enzymes), water softeners (either complex sodium phosphates or aluminosilicates, sodium carbonate), processing aids (sodium sulfate), washer protection agents (sodium silicates), fabric whitener, an agent to prevent deposition, and perfume.

The surfactants and enzymes in ▊▊ are biodegradable.

Individual packages of ▊▊ may weigh slightly more or less than the marked weight due to normal variations incurred with high speed packaging machines but each day's production of ▊▊ will average slightly above the marked weight.

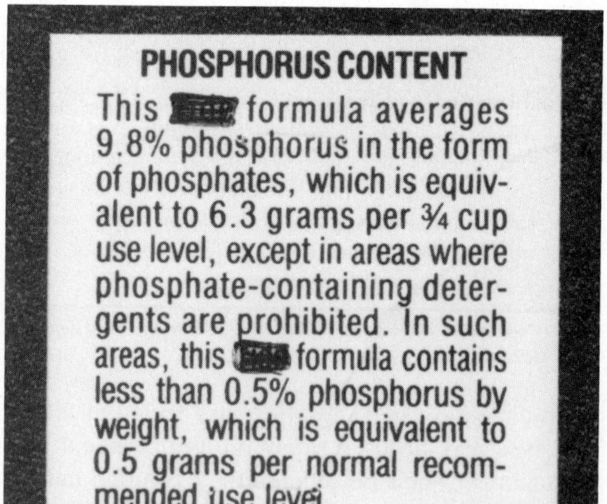

PHOSPHORUS CONTENT
This ▊▊ formula averages 9.8% phosphorus in the form of phosphates, which is equivalent to 6.3 grams per ¾ cup use level, except in areas where phosphate-containing detergents are prohibited. In such areas, this ▊▊ formula contains less than 0.5% phosphorus by weight, which is equivalent to 0.5 grams per normal recommended use level.

Fig. 20–2 *Detergent labels: ingredients* (left) *and phosphorus content* (right).

Table 20–2 Formulations of Detergents

	Heavy-Duty Powdered Detergents			Heavy-Duty Liquid Detergents	
Compound	With Builders	Without Builders	Compound	With Builders	Without Builders
Anionic surfactant	0–15%	0–20%	Anionic surfactant	5–17%	0–10%
Nonionic surfactant	0–17%	0–17%	Nonionic surfactant	5–11%	15–35%
Suds-controlling agent	0–1.0%	0–0.6%	Enzymes	0–1.6%	0–2.3%
Builders	23–55%	—	Builders	6–12%	—
Water softeners	—	0–45%	Formulation aids	7–14%	5–12%
Alkalis	3–22%	10–35%	Optical brighteners	0.1–0.25%	0.1–0.25%
Bleaching agents	0–5%	0–5%	Fabric softeners	0–2%	0%
Fabric softeners	0–5%	0–5%	Fragrances	a	a
Antiredeposition agents	0–0.5%	0–0.5%	Dyes	a	a
Enzymes	0–2.5%	0–2.5%	Water	Balance	Balance
Optical brighteners	0.05–0.25%	0.05–0.25%			
Anticorrosion agents	1–10%	0–25%			
Fragrances	a	a			
Dyes/bluing agents	a	a			
Formulation aids	0–1.0%	0–1.0%			
Fillers and water	Balance	Balance			

aComponent may be present in very small concentrations.

Source: *Chemical and Engineering News*, January 23, 1989, p. 35.

PRETREATMENT *Pretreatments* are another means of removing difficult stains. They are usually added directly to the stain shortly before the item is laundered. Pretreatment products often contain a solvent, surfactant, and builder.

STARCH OR SIZING *Starch* or *sizing* is used after washing to add body and stiffness to fabrics. Starch is seldom used today.

BLUING *Bluing* is a weak blue dye that masks yellowing in fabrics. Bluing is seldom used by itself today because it is incorporated in detergents as dyes. In addition, the use of fluorescent-whitening agents in detergents makes it unnecessary to add bluing.

Sorting

Before laundering, it is important to *sort* the items to be washed in order to minimize problems and remove soil as efficiently as possible. Sorting is often done by color, type of garment (for example, work garments separate from delicate items), type of soil, recommended care method, and propensity of fabrics to lint. During sorting, it is a good idea to close zippers and

buttons so they do not snag other items in the wash. It is also a good idea to check pockets for pens, tissues, and other items that may create problems during washing. In addition, this is the time to check items for stains, holes, or tears.

Table 20-3 summarizes the care required, based on fiber content. However, it is important to

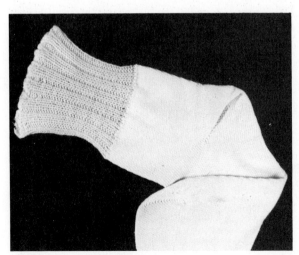

Fig. 20–3 *Cotton-and-wool sock after bleaching. Chlorine bleach caused wool in ribbed top to yellow and stiffen.*

remember that care is dependent not only on fiber content, but also on other things such as dye, fabrication, finish, product construction, type of soil, and extent of soiling.

DRYING

The *drying* procedure is usually specified on the care label. Machine drying is considered the most severe method because of the abrasion and agitation. Line drying may also be too severe for some items because wet fabrics are extremely heavy. Fibers that weaken when wet, such as wool and rayon, may be under too much stress if the item is hung to dry. Drying flat is the least severe method because the fabric is under little stress.

DRY CLEANING

In *dry cleaning*, the solvents include the following: perchloroethylene (perc), a petroleum solvent (Stoddard's solvent), or a fluorocarbon solvent (Valclene). Of these three, perc is most common. You may need to check with your dry cleaner as to which solvent is used in that system. Dry cleaning is referred to as dry because the solvent does not feel wet like water. Along with items labeled for dry cleaning, many machine-washable items may be dry cleaned.

A professional organization, the International Fabricare Institute (IFI), provides training and updates for dry cleaners, establishes a fair-claims adjustment guide for use in consumer complaints, and provides an evaluation service to members when problems develop. Members of IFI display an IFI plaque in their business.

Table 20–3   **Suggested Care of Textile Products by Fiber Group**

Fiber Group	Cleaning Method	Water Temperature	Safe to Use Chlorine Bleach	Dryer Temperature	Iron Temperature	Special Storage Considerations
Acetate	Dry clean*	Warm (100°–110°F)	Yes	Low	Very low	Avoid contact with nail polish remover
Acrylic	Launder	Warm	Yes	Warm	Medium	—
Cotton	Launder	Hot (120°–140°F)	Yes	Hot	High	Store dry to prevent mildew
Polyester/cotton DP	Launder	Hot	Yes	Warm	Medium	—
Flax	Launder	Hot	Yes	Hot	High For longest wear, do not press in sharp creases	—
Glass	Hand wash only	Hot	Yes	Line dry	Do not iron	Prevent fiber breakage by storing as flat as possible
Modacrylic	Launder	Warm	Yes	Low	Very low	—
Nylon	Launder	Hot	Yes	Warm	Low	—
Olefin	Launder	Warm	Yes	Warm	Very low	—
Polyester	Launder	Hot	Yes	Warm	Low	—
Rayon	Launder	Hot	Yes	Hot	High	Store dry to prevent mildew
Silk	Dry clean*	Warm	No	Warm	Medium	—
Spandex	Launder	Warm	No	Warm	Very low	—
Wool	Dry clean*	Warm	No	Warm	Medium, with steam	Protect from moths; do not store in plastic bags

*Or hand wash, avoiding excessive agitation and stretching.

In dry cleaning, the items are brought to the cleaners and identified with a tag that includes the special instructions, the owner's identification number, and the number of pieces in the group. Items are first inspected and treated at a spot board. Because a solvent is used, stains that are water soluble and other hard-to-remove spots must be treated at the spot board. Customers who identify stains for the dry cleaner make the cleaning task easier and ultimately improve their satisfaction with the cleaned product.

After treatment at the spotting board, items are placed in the dry cleaning unit to be tumbled with a charged solvent (solvent plus detergent plus a small percentage of water) (Figure 20–4). After tumbling, the solvent is reclaimed in the same unit or a separate unit called a *reclaimer*. The reclaimer serves the same function as a dryer in laundering, except that the solvent is condensed and filtered to be used again. Solvents must be reclaimed because of the cost. Filtering and distilling remove soil, color, odor, and other residue.

After the items are removed from the reclaimer, they go to the pressing area, where steam and special steam-air forms are used to give a finished appearance to the item. For example, pants are pressed with a topper that finishes the top part of the pants. Each leg is pressed separately with a press. Jackets, shirts, and blouses are finished with a suzie, a steam-body torso form (see Figure 20–5).

Additional treatments that many dry cleaners are equipped to do include replacing buttons; doing

Fig. 20–4   *Dry cleaning unit.*

minor repairs to items; replacing sizing, water repellency, and other finishes; adding permanent creases to pants; and cleaning fur and leather. Some dry cleaners can also clean and sanitize feather pillows and clean and press draperies.

Dry Cleaning of Leather and Fur

Because of the complex nature of leather and fur, products made of these materials or products that contain these materials should be cleaned by specialists. *Leather* and *fur* (furrier) *dry cleaning* involves removing soil without damaging the dye or finish and restoring oils that cleaning removes. This

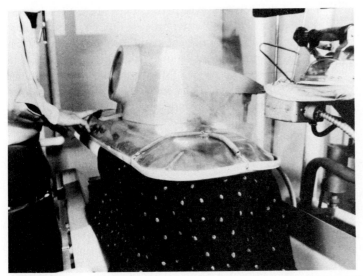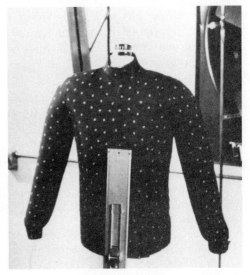

Fig. 20–5   *Pressing equipment: pants press* (left); *inflatable "suzie" for steaming blouses and shirts* (right).

is a complex and expensive process. Wide variations in hides or skins and processing create potential problems for the dry cleaner. Frequently, the leather/fur cleaner is required to redye or refinish the item to restore it to a form that will satisfy the customer. Because of the additional processing, leather and fur cleaning is expensive. Most dry cleaners do not clean these items themselves, but send them to a specialist.

Dry cleaners frequently see problems with leather dyes that are not fast to dry cleaning. This is especially common with high fashion items and items that combine leather trim with woven or knit fabrics. The problem is more common with apparel because apparel items are more likely to have leather trim. However, furnishing items made of leather or trimmed in leather may also present problems in dry cleaning.

OTHER CLEANING METHODS

This section discusses methods of cleaning carpets and upholstery. Table 20–4 lists upholstery cleaning codes.

Vacuuming

Vacuuming is the most common and most important method of cleaning carpets. Vacuuming removes soil that is not adhered to the fibers, especially particulate soil such as dust, lint, and dirt. Large particles such as small rocks, paper clips, and so on are generally not removed by vacuuming. Vacuuming is also used to remove soil from upholstered furniture and wall and window coverings. However, remember that vacuuming only removes particulate soil. Other types of soil must be removed by other means. For industrial and commercial carpets, it is critical that the vacuum cleaner be one with a heavy-duty rating that cleans deeply into the surface pile and that can withstand frequent, heavy use. Most vacuum cleaners used in the home are not of this type.

On any carpet, localized spots and stains should be treated as soon as possible after soiling. Carpet manufacturers provide a list of recommended cleaning compounds for specific stains. If carpets have an accumulation of oily soils or airborne dust and dirt that is not removed with regular vacuuming, corrective action should be taken. A variety of procedures are discussed in this chapter. However, before any of these other methods are attempted, a thorough vacuuming should be done first to remove surface soil and separate and loosen packed pile.

Wet Cleaning

Wet cleaning or *shampooing* of carpets is a method that uses water-based detergents and may require long periods of time to dry. A diluted water-detergent solution is worked into the pile with rotating brushes (thus this method is also referred to as the rotary brush method). A thorough wet vacuuming follows to remove the soil-laden solution. In some cases, several days may elapse before carpets are completely dry. It is generally recommended that the cleaning solution be tested on an inconspicuous area of the carpet before the entire surface is cleaned in this manner. Oversaturation of carpets can cause problems with fading and shrinkage. Solutions may not be completely removed, causing brown stains to appear on the surface of the pile yarns. The action of the brushes may permanently distort pile yarns. Select detergents that prevent dulling of the surface of the carpet, minimize rapid resoiling of the carpet, avoid creating problems with static electricity, and disinfect the carpet. After wet cleaning, problems with static electricity may develop if a water-based solution of an antistatic agent was originally applied to the carpet.

Dry Foam Cleaning

Dry foam cleaning or aerosol cleaning of carpet can be done by hand with a foam sprayed onto the carpet or by employing a machine that deposits a detergent solution as a foam on the carpet just ahead of an agitating brush. The brush works the solution into the carpet, loosens soil particles, suspends them in the foam, and the vacuum removes

Table 20–4 Upholstery Cleaning Codes

W	Use water-based upholstery cleaner only
S	Use solvent-based upholstery cleaner only
WS	Can use either water- or solvent-based upholstery cleaner
X	Do not clean with either water- or solvent-based upholstery cleaner; use vacuuming or light brushing only

the soil. The application of the foam, agitation, and vacuuming can be almost simultaneous. Hence, complete wetting of the carpet is avoided. Dry foam cleaning does not remove soil embedded in the carpet because the solution cannot work deeply in the pile. Dry foam processes allow the carpet to be used soon after finishing the cleaning, often within the hour. Dry foam cleaning may also be used to clean upholstery.

Hot Water Extraction

In the *hot water extraction* method a hot water-detergent solution is injected into the carpet. The solution is under pressure and wets the carpet quickly, but is almost immediately removed by a vacuum. As the water is removed by vacuuming, so too is the soil. Overwetting of the carpet can occur if an area is not treated quickly. To minimize rapid resoiling, the detergent must be completely removed. Since no brushes are used in this process, pile distortion is kept to a minimum. This method is sometimes referred to as steam cleaning, even though no steam is used in the process.

Powder Cleaners

Powder cleaners are absorbent powders combining detergents and solvents. The powder is applied in a dry form, sprinkled on the surface of the carpet or upholstery and brushed or otherwise worked into the pile. The powder combines with the soil and holds it in suspension until it is removed by vacuuming. It is recommended that the powder remain in contact with the fabric's surface for a short time before being removed by vacuuming. The method is fast, requires no time for drying, but removes surface soil only. Pile distortion is related to the vigor with which the powder is worked into the pile. This method may be referred to as dry extraction cleaning, absorbent powder cleaning, or absorbent compound cleaning.

Ultrasonic Cleaning

Ultrasonic cleaning requires that the carpet be removed from the use site and taken to a special cleaning facility. High-frequency sound waves attract the soil and remove it from the carpet fibers. At pre-

sent, this method cannot be used on carpets that cannot be removed from the location.

STORAGE

When products are not in use, they need to be stored. Many problems develop because the *storage* was not appropriate for the product. Short-term storage is not as likely to cause problems as long-term storage. All items should be stored clean and as free from wrinkles as possible. Care should be taken to protect items from insects, dust or dirt, excessive moisture, and light during storage. Most products should never be stored in direct contact with raw wood or wood finishes. Raw wood produces acid as it ages. Cellulosic fibers are degraded by acid, and brown or yellow stains may develop as a result of exposure to the wood (see Figure 20-6). Plastic bags from dry cleaners are provided as a service to avoid soiling freshly cleaned items during transport. These bags are not intended for storage and should be discarded immediately after the product is brought into the house. Items stored in dry cleaning bags may discolor because of the acids in the bag; build up static and attract dust; or trap moisture, creating an ideal environment for mildew. For more information regarding storage, see the appropriate fiber chapter.

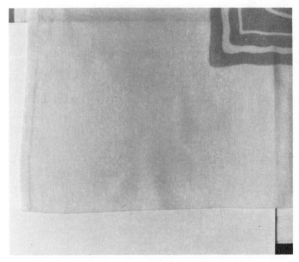

Fig. 20–6   *Yellowed cotton tablecloth stored next to wooden drawer bottom for several years.*

KEY TERMS

Care
Laundering
Soil
Detergency
Soap
Detergent
Water
Surfactants
Builders
Fillers
Antiredeposition agents
Perfumes
Fluorescent-whitening agents
Bleach
Fabric softeners
Water softeners
Disinfectants
Enzymatic presoaks

Pretreatments
Starch
Sizing
Bluing
Sorting
Drying
Dry cleaning
Leather cleaning
Fur cleaning
Vacuuming
Wet cleaning
Shampooing
Dry foam cleaning
Hot water extraction
Powder cleaners
Ultrasonic cleaning
Storage

QUESTIONS

1. Define detergency and explain what happens when a soiled textile product is cleaned.
2. Explain how the function of a soap can be adversely affected by hard water.
3. Why is water used in laundering and many other methods of cleaning?
4. How does dry cleaning differ from laundering?
5. Read the label on a box or bottle of detergent and explain the function of each ingredient listed.
6. What ingredients are present to minimize the effort of the person doing the laundry (i.e., what ingredients have been incorporated in one container to minimize the consumer having to keep track of additional other products)?
7. How does carpet or upholstery cleaning differ from laundering? How should selection of a specific method be made?

SUGGESTED READINGS

American Association of Textile Chemists and Colorists (1991). *Technical Manual, vol. 66*. Research Triangle Park, NC: AATCC.

Reznikoff, S. C. (1989). *Specifications for Commercial Interiors*. New York: Whitney Library of Design.

Soap and Detergent Association (1989). *Detergents: In Depth*. New York: Soap and Detergent Association. (Also consult previous editions of *Detergents: In Depth*.)

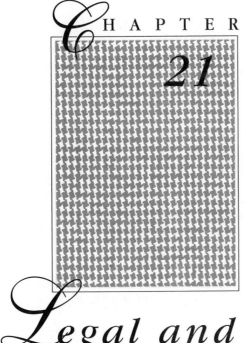

C H A P T E R

21

Legal and Environmental Issues

OBJECTIVES

- To understand labeling required by federal laws and regulations.

- To interpret labels on textile products correctly.

- To recognize the impact of textiles and of related activities on the environment.

- To know professional and consumer rights and responsibilities in terms of legal and environmental concerns.

*O*VER THE PAST SEVERAL DECADES, GOVERNMENT impact on the textile industry has evolved to affect fair trade practices, information labeling, safety regulations, environmental protection, and working conditions. It is clear that laws and regulations will continue to have an effect on the textile industry in terms of general operations, label requirements, environmental impact, design aspects, and health/safety concerns. This chapter focuses on those laws, regulations, and practices that are important to professionals in the industry. Some areas of discussion will relate more specifically to certain jobs or areas within the industry than others. However, it is beneficial to understand the importance of each of these issues to the industry. It is equally important to recognize where professional responsibilities imply legal responsibility.

LABELING

We begin this section on labeling of textile products with a discussion of laws and regulations. Each of these regulations or laws focuses primarily on providing the ultimate consumer with information. The justification for these *labeling requirements* is that with sufficient information, consumers should be able to make informed decisions regarding purchase of textile products, use of these items, and selection of appropriate care. Generally, these laws and regulations are the responsibility of the *Federal Trade Commission* (FTC) for interpretation and enforcement. The activities of the FTC are designed to protect not only the ultimate consumer, but also legitimate segments of the industry itself. It is the responsibility of the FTC to prevent unfair or deceptive trade practices. An example of such an unfair trade practice would include the marketing of a rayon/polyester blend crash in such a way as to suggest that it was made of flax, implied by the use of the term *linen*. Trade publications such as *Women's Wear Daily, Daily News Record*, and *Home Furnishings Daily* frequently carry articles describing current efforts of the FTC to prevent unfair or deceptive trade practices in the industry.

The first four laws and regulations deal with "truth-in-fabrics" aspects. For these to be fully beneficial, the consumer must have some knowledge about fibers and fabrics.

Silk Regulation, 1932

Silk may be weighted (treated with a solution of metallic salts) to increase the weight and hand of the fabric and improve its dyeability. However, weighted silk is not as durable as regular silk, and it wrinkles more easily. Because of these problems, the Federal Trade Commission ruled in 1932 that anything labeled pure silk or pure dye silk could contain no more than 15 percent weighting for black and no more than 10 percent for all other colors. Anything exceeding these levels is weighted silk. At present, very little silk on the market is weighted. However, museum collections have many weighted silk items that are disintegrating and shattering.

Wool Products Labeling Act, 1939 (Amended 1986)

Wool is often blended with less expensive fibers to reduce the cost of the fabric or to extend its use. The *Wool Products Labeling Act* of 1939 (amended in 1986) was passed to protect consumers as well as producers, manufacturers, and distributors from the unrevealed presence of substitutes and mixtures and to inform the consumer of the source of the wool fiber. This act applies to any textile product containing wool, unless otherwise exempt. Major exemptions include carpets, rugs, mats, and upholstery. The law requires that the label must give the fiber content in terms of percentage and the source of the fiber. The term *fur fiber* can be used for the fiber from any animal other than sheep, lamb, angora goat, cashmere goat, camel, alpaca, llama, and vicuña. Under the act, the fiber produced from those animals can be referred to as wool. The name of the manufacturer or the registered identification number of the manufacturer must also be on the label. The registered number is designated *WPL* or *RN*, where WPL refers to the wool product label, RN refers to the registered number, and the next several digits are the actual number. Finally, the act requires that the name of the country where the product was manufactured or processed be listed on the label. These labels must be sewn in the item; their location is designated in the act. The act does not state or imply anything regarding the quality of the fibers used in the product. Consumers must rely on their knowledge to determine the quality and suitability of the product.

The terms that appear on the labels of wool items are defined by the FTC as follows:

1. Wool—new wool or wool fibers reclaimed from knit scraps, broken thread, and noils. (Noils are short fibers combed out in the making of worsted wool.)

2. Recycled wool—scraps of new woven or felted fabrics that are garnetted or shredded back to the fibrous state and used again in the manufacture of woolens.

3. Virgin wool—wool that has never been processed in any way; thus knit clips and broken yarns cannot be labeled virgin wool.

Fur Products Labeling Act, 1952 (Amended 1980)

The *Fur Products Labeling Act* applies to furs, those items of animal origin with the hair/fiber attached. The act requires that the true English language name of the animal be used on labels for wearing apparel, and that dyed furs be so labeled. In addition, the country of origin must be identified. Finally, the use of used, damaged, or scrap fur must also be identified. The act has been amended to identify animals by name and has expanded the list of alterations to the natural fur to include tip dyeing, pointing (coloring the tips of the guard hairs), and other means of artificially altering the color or appearance of the fur. This law does not provide for a quality designation; poor quality fur is available on the market.

The law protects the consumer from buying furs sold under names resembling expensive furs. For example, prior to the enactment of this law, rabbit was sold under many names (some highly imaginative and some blatantly false), including lapin, chinchilette, ermaline, northern seal, coney, marmink, Australian seal, Belgian beaver, and Baltic leopard. "Hudson seal" was muskrat plucked and dyed to look like seal.

Textile Fiber Products Identification Act, 1960 (Amended 1986)

In 1958 Congress passed legislation to regulate labeling of textiles in order to protect the consumer through the enforcement of ethical practices and to protect the producer from unfair competition resulting from the unrevealed presence of substitute materials in textile products. *The Textile Fiber Products Identification Act* covers *all* fibers except those already covered by the Wool Products Labeling Act, with certain other exceptions.

Although the law was passed in 1958, it did not become effective until 1960. During this interval the Federal Trade Commission held hearings to discover inequalities or injustices that the law might cause. Then it established rules and regulations to be observed in enforcing the law. The list of manufactured fiber generic names in Table 21-1 was established by the Federal Trade Commission in cooperation with the fiber producers. A *generic name* is the name of a family of fibers all having similar chemical composition. (Definitions of these generic names are included with the discussions of each fiber.)

The following information, in English, is required on the label of most textile items, including apparel, outer coverings of furniture and mattresses/box springs, bedding, and toweling.

1. The percentage of each natural or manufactured fiber present must be listed in the order of predominance by weight. The percentage listed must be correct within a tolerance of 3 percent. This means that if the label states a fiber content of 50 percent cotton, the minimum can be no less than 47 percent and the maximum can be no more than 53 percent.

   If a fiber or fibers represent less than 5 percent by weight of the item, the fiber cannot be named unless it has a clearly established and definite functional significance. Where the fiber has a definite function, the generic name, percent-

Table 21–1 Manufactured Fibers' Generic Names

Cellulosic	Noncellulosic or Synthetic		Mineral
Acetate	Acrylic	Olefin	Glass
Triacetate*	Anidex*	PBI	Metallic
Rayon	Aramid	Polyester	
	Azlon*	Rubber	
	Lastrile*	Saran	
	Modacrylic	Spandex	
	Novoloid	Sulfar	
	Nylon	Vinal*	
	Nytril*	Vinyon*	

*Not produced in the United States.

age by weight, and functional significance must be listed. For example, a garment that has a small amount of spandex may have a label that reads "96% Nylon, 4% Spandex for elasticity."

2. The name of the manufacturer or the company's registered number such as WPL or RN must be stated. In many cases the company's registered number is listed with the letters and the number. (Trademarks may serve as identification, but they are not required information. Often a trademark is listed with the generic fiber name.)

3. The first time a trademark appears in the required information, it must appear in immediate conjunction with the generic name and in type or lettering of equal size and conspicuousness. When the trademark is used elsewhere on the label, the generic name must accompany it in legible and conspicuous type the first time it appears.

4. The name of the country where the product was processed or manufactured must be stated, such as "Made in USA." Country of origin is identified as the country where the item was assembled. For fabrics, it is the country where finishing occurred.

TRADE NAMES

A fiber may be given a *trade name* (*trademark*), which distinguishes the fiber from other fibers of the same generic family that are made and sold by other producers. A producer may adopt a single trade name, word, or symbol, which may be used to cover all (or a large group) of the fibers made by that company. For example, "Dacron" is no longer used to designate a single polyester fiber made by Du Pont, but is a broad descriptive name covering a family of related Du Pont polyester fibers, each of which is sold to the manufacturer by type number. Trade names are often protected by a quality-control program.

The fiber producer assumes the responsibility for promoting the fiber. The company must sell not only to its customers, the manufacturers and retailers, but to the customer's customer—the consumer.

Permanent Care Labeling Regulation, 1972 (Amended 1984)

In 1971 the Federal Trade Commission issued the *Care Labeling Regulation*. Because of some prob-

lems with the regulation, an amended version became effective in 1984. The rule requires manufacturers or importers of textile wearing apparel and certain piece goods to provide an accurate, permanent label or tag that contains regular-care information and instructions (relative to washing, drying, bleaching, warnings, and dry cleaning) and that is permanently attached and legible. The regulation specifies the location of the label by product type.

The regulation was developed because of consumer complaints regarding care instructions. The 1984 revision of the rule requires more specific, detailed information concerning only one care method for a product. The label should use common terms that have a standard meaning (see Table 20-1). The instructions must be in words, not just symbols, although symbols may also be used. When products are produced offshore and sold in the United States, they must meet U.S. care-labeling requirements. When a label identifies washing, it must also state the washing method, water temperature, drying method, drying temperature, and ironing temperature when ironing is necessary. Procedures to be avoided must be identified, such as "Only nonchlorine bleach, when necessary." If multiple care methods are appropriate for that product, the manufacturer is not required to list them on the label. If the care-label instructions are followed and some problem develops during care, the manufacturer is liable. However, if the care-label instructions are not followed, the manufacturer is not liable for any problems caused by improper care. Figure 21-1 shows several care labels for items of wearing apparel.

The rule applies to most items of wearing apparel. It does not apply to leather, suede, fur garments, ties, belts, and other apparel not used to cover or protect a part of the body. Certain other apparel items such as reversible garments are only required to have removable, not permanent, care labels. For piece goods, the information must be supplied on the end of the bolt, but neither the manufacturer nor the retailer are required to provide a label to be sewn to the finished product.

The Federal Trade Commission and the International Fabricare Institute are working together to identify problems with compliance with the labeling regulation and to minimize future problems with inadequate and incorrect care labels. Yearly reports by the IFI indicate that many problems encountered in cleaning are due to faulty or misleading care labels.

Fig. 21–1 Care labels for garments.

Laws and Regulations Related to Safety

Laws and regulations dealing with textile products and safety issues generally require that selected textile products meet a predetermined level of performance in terms of flammability. The procedure for flammability testing and a pass/fail scale identifying acceptable performance are included in these laws or regulations. Federal regulations are often referred to by the designation CFR (*Code of Federal Regulations*) with the identifying numbers indicating the product category into which they fall (see Table 21-2). Various governmental agencies are responsible for the enforcement of these safety standards, including the *Consumer Product Safety Commission* (a subdivision of the FTC) and the Department

Table 21–2 Flammability Categories of Product

Designation	Product Category
16 CFR 1610	Clothing textiles
16 CFR 1611	Vinyl plastic films used in apparel
16 CFR 1615	Children's sleepwear, sizes 0–6X
16 CFR 1616	Children's sleepwear, sizes 7-14
16 CFR 1630	Large carpets and rugs
16 CFR 1631	Small carpets and rugs
16 CFR 1632	Mattresses and mattress pads

of Transportation. Often these regulations are included as part of federal, state, or local building codes for interior furnishings for public-use areas.

Flammable Fabrics Act, 1953, and Its Amendment

Congress enacted the first national law dealing with flammable fabrics in 1953, following several apparel-fire deaths. The *Flammable Fabrics Act* prohibits the marketing of dangerously flammable material, including all wearing apparel, regardless of fiber content or construction. The act covers imported items or those in interstate commerce. One purpose of the law was to develop standards and tests to separate dangerously flammable fabrics from normally combustible ones.

The act was amended in 1967 to cover a broader range of apparel and interior furnishings with responsibilities for its implementation divided among the secretary of commerce, the secretary of health, education, and welfare, and the Federal Trade Commission. In 1972 the Consumer Product Safety Act was passed and the Consumer Product Safety Commission (CPSC), which has broad jurisdiction over consumer safety, was established. The responsibilities and functions, as stipulated in the Flammable Fabrics Act, were transferred to the CPSC. Federal standards were established under the direction of the Department of Commerce and later under the CPSC as shown in Table 21-3. These standards and/or test methods may be modified in the future depending on further research and evaluation.

It takes considerable time to develop a standard. First, facts must be collected to indicate a need. Then, a notice is published in the Federal Register that there is a need for a standard. Interested persons are requested to respond. Test methods are developed and published in a second notice. A final notice, which includes details of the standard and test method, is published with the effective date of compliance. One year is usually allowed so that merchandise that does not meet the standard can be sold or otherwise disposed of, and new merchandise can be altered (if necessary) to meet the standard.

Mandatory standards have been issued for children's sleepwear, sizes 0–6X and 7-14, large and small carpets and rugs, and mattresses and mattress pads. The *Upholstered Furniture Action Council* (UFAC) has issued voluntary standards for upholstered furniture. Figure 21-2 shows a photograph of a UFAC label.

Table 21–3   Federal Standards Implementing the Flammable Fabrics Act

Effective Date	Item	Requirements	Test Method
1954	Flammability of clothing Title 16 CRF 1610 (formerly CS 191-53)	Articles of wearing apparel except interlining fabrics, certain hats, gloves, footwear.	A 2 × 6 inch fabric placed in a holder at a 45⁰ angle exposed to flame for 1 second will not ignite and spread flame up the length of the sample in less than 3.5 seconds for smooth fabrics or 4.0 seconds for napped.
1954	Flammability of vinyl plastic film Title 16 CRF 1611 (formerly CS 192-53)	Vinyl-plastic film for wearing apparel	A piece of film placed in a holder at an angle of 45⁰ will not burn at a rate exceeding 1.2 inches per second.
1971	Large carpets and rugs Title CRF 1630 (formerly DOC FF1-70)	Carpets that have one dimension greater than 6 feet and a surface area greater than 24 square feet. Excludes vinyl tile, asphalt tile, and linoleum. All items must meet standards.	"Pill" test: 9 × 9 inch specimens exposed to methenamine tablet placed in center of each specimen does not char more than 3 inches in any direction.
1971	Small carpets and rugs Title 16 CFR 1631 (formerly DOC FF2-70)	Carpets that have no dimension greater than 6 feet and a surface area no greater than 24 square feet. May be sold if they do not meet standard if labeled: Flammable. (Fails U.S. Department of Commerce Standard FF 2-70.)	Same as for large carpets and rugs.
1972	Children's sleepwear, sizes 0-6X Title 16 CFR 1615 (DOC FF3-71)	Any product of wearing apparel up to and including size 6X, such as nightgowns, pajamas, or other items intended to be worn for sleeping. Excludes diapers and underwear. Items must meet requirements as produced and after 50 washings and dryings. All items must meet standard.	"Vertical Forced Ignition" test. Each of five 3.5 inch × 10 inch specimens is suspended vertically in holders in a cabinet and exposed to a gas flame along the bottom edge for 3 seconds. Specimens cannot have average char length of more than 7 inches.
1973	Mattresses (and mattress pads) Title 16 CFR 1632 (DOC FF4-72)	Ticking filled with a resilient material intended for sleeping upon, including mattress pads. Excludes pillows, box springs, sleeping bags, and upholstered furniture. All items must meet standard.	"Cigarette" test. A minimum of 9 cigarettes allowed to burn on smooth top, edge, and quilted locations of bare mattress. Char length must not be more than 2 inches in any direction from any cigarette. Tests are also conducted with 9 cigarettes placed between two sheets on the mattress surfaces.
1975	Children's sleepwear, sizes 7-14 Title 16 CFR 1632 (DOC FF5-74)	Same as preceding. All items must meet standard.	Same as preceding.

Fig. 21–2 *UFAC label. (Courtesy of Upholstered Furniture Action Council.)*

Some cities and states have established standards for additional textile items. Various sectors of industry have adopted voluntary standards for such items as tents, blankets, and career clothing for people who work near fire.

ASSESSMENT OF TEXTILE FLAMMABILITY Summaries of procedures and pass/fail scales are given here rather than full specifications due to space restrictions. The type of textile product category determines the procedure and pass/fail scale used to assess performance.

For large and small carpets and rugs, the methenamine pill test is required by CRF 1630. In this procedure, a piece of carpet 9 inches in diameter is placed in the bottom of an enclosed cube (open on the top) and held in place by a metal template with an 8-inch diameter hole. The methenamine pill is placed in the center of the carpet sample and ignited. Samples that burn to within one inch of the metal template fail. Eight samples are tested and seven must pass for the carpet or rug to pass the test. (Figure 21–3).

The Steiner tunnel test is another procedure used to assess carpet and rug flammability. It is required by many state codes and some federal agencies. This procedure requires a much larger sample (24 feet long, 20 inches wide) that is placed on the ceiling of a tunnel. A double gas jet burns for 10 minutes with an air draft designed to pull the flame into the carpet tunnel for a distance of approximately 4 feet. The distance the carpet sample burns is used to assess the flame-spread rating. Flame-spread ratings are based on a 100-point rating scale where 0 represents materials that will not burn and 100 represents the flammability of red oak flooring (classification A, flame spread 1–25; B, flame spread 26–75; C, flame spread 76–200).

The flooring radiant panel test is a third procedure used to assess carpet and rug flammability. This test is also used by many federal agencies. In this procedure, a sample 39 inches long by 8 inches wide is mounted horizontally, preheated, and ignited. The burn distance is measured and converted into a flame-spread index. Higher numbers indicate greater resistance to flame spread and greater safety.

Children's sleepwear testing requires that the fabric meet minimum flammability performance standards in order for products to be sold. The fabric must meet these performance requirements after 50 care cycles. The procedures are similar for 16 CFR 1615 and 16 CFR 1616. In both cases, the fabric is suspended vertically in a draft-free cabinet and exposed to an ignition flame for 3 seconds. Pass/fail ratings are based on burn time and burn length.

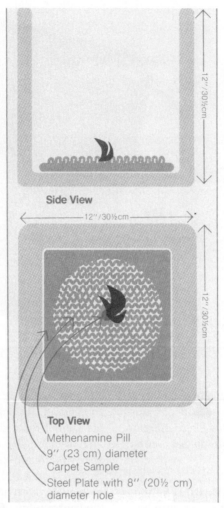

Side View

← 12″/30½cm →

Top View
Methenamine Pill
9″ (23 cm) diameter
Carpet Sample
Steel Plate with 8″ (20½ cm)
diameter hole

Fig. 21–3 *The methenamine pill test for carpets. (Courtesy of Center for Fire Research, Institute for Applied Technology, National Bureau of Standards)*

Regular apparel covered by 16 CFR 1610 is tested at a 45° angle (see Figure 21–4). Ignition is not necessarily guaranteed since the ignition time is 1 second. Based on burning behavior, fabrics are classified as Class 1 (fabrics suitable for apparel with a flame spread time greater than 7 seconds); Class 2 (fabrics suitable for apparel with intermediate flame spread); and Class 3 (fabrics unsuitable for apparel with flame spreads of less than 3.5 seconds). There are distinctions within the class ratings for brushed surface fabrics that are not included in this discussion.

Although the Consumer Product Safety Commission has indicated an interest in developing flammability standards for upholstered furniture and certain categories of adult apparel, no new standards covering these products have appeared. However, because of concern about the flammability of upholstered furniture used by consumers, the Upholstered Furniture Action Council has developed a voluntary flame retardant upholstery standard. Two categories of ignition propensity are identified. Class 1, the safer category, indicates no ignition occurred in the fabric classification test and char lengths were less than 1.75 inches. Class II identifies those fabrics that ignited in the fabric classification test. A hangtag is used to indicate the flammability rating.

In addition to the voluntary UFAC program, interior furnishings are regulated by several federal departments and agencies. The Department of Health, Education, and Welfare sets fire safety standards for health care facilities.

Mandatory and Voluntary Labeling Programs

Mandatory labeling rules specify acceptable and legal commercial practices for companies to follow.

Fig. 21–4 *The 45-degree angle test for apparel. (Courtesy of Atlas Electric Devices Co.)*

The law requires that the information be available and accurate, but requirements do not extend beyond that. Mandatory labeling includes fiber content requirements as specified in several laws and care labels.

Voluntary practices and labeling programs are often used in marketing textile products. Voluntary programs include certification and licensing programs, trademarks, trade names, and warranty programs. In many cases, the voluntary program also means an implied quality control program since products must meet company performance and quality specifications.

Warranties can be implied or written. Implied warranties indicate that the product is suitable for the purpose for which it was marketed. For example, an implied warranty for a raincoat says that it will not shrink significantly when wet. The written warranties offered for some apparel and furnishing items are legally binding and imply performance at a predetermined level.

Codes

Codes are systematic bodies of laws or regulations. Most codes are designed to guarantee a minimum level of safety and often follow a tragedy resulting in great loss of life, such as occurred in the 1986 hotel fire in Puerto Rico in which 96 people died. Federal, state, and local city or county codes for interiors often include in their purview textile products such as upholstery, wall and floor coverings, and window treatment fabrics. These codes enforce adequate standards of practice and uniformity of work. Codes generally provide minimum levels of performance and are designed to ensure safety for the people who live, work, shop, or otherwise use these buildings. Frequently codes deal with fire prevention and control the flammability of textiles used in interiors. Most fire prevention regulations are based on occupancy classification (business, apartment, industrial, mercantile, health care, educational, etc.); fuel load classification (museum, office building, retail shop, paint shop, warehouse, mobile home, underground structure, etc.); occupancy load (number of people); and type of occupancy (adults, children, elderly, or physically disabled). Unfortunately, building codes from the various agencies and government groups are not uniform. For example, federal agencies have adopted the Unified Building Code (UBC) and all standards and codes of the National Fire Protection Association (NFPA) and the American National Standards Institute (ANSI). However, county, city, and state codes often reflect situations unique to their geographic region, such as specific codes for high-rise apartment and office buildings.

The jurisdiction of codes depends on several factors, briefly discussed here. Federal codes are generally applicable to federal buildings or those built with federal funds, such as hospitals. State codes generally apply to state-owned buildings such as schools, state hospitals, and some public buildings where large crowds are common, such as exhibition halls. City and county codes are often incorporated in zoning ordinances. If two codes are applicable in a specific situation, the more stringent code generally prevails. Designers need to be sure that the textile products they select meet the specified code requirements. This may mean that products be tested following the standard procedure specified in the code and that adequate performance records be kept.

Besides knowing code requirements, designers should check with insurance company representatives early in the design process since their decisions may have a major impact on insurance rates for interiors. Designers should also be aware that finishes and fabrication methods may interfere with inherently flame-retardant fiber characteristics. All products, including those made from inherently flame-retardant fibers, should be tested to ensure that they meet code requirements. For example, the state of New York has a toxicity rule that requires companies to register their products with the state if they wish to sell in New York. In this rule two fire gas toxicity ratings exist: one for carpets and one for curtains, draperies, and wall coverings. The registration system removes the requirement of having each fabric individually tested at a cost per fabric of $2,000.

Codes applicable to upholstery fabrics include those listed for window treatment fabrics. The procedures identified in these codes assess flammability by a variety of methods. However, all regulate the length of time allowed for self-extinguishment of the flame and afterglow. The methods also identify the maximum allowable length or area of fabric burned or charred during the test. Samples tested include pieces of fabric, mock-ups of the upholstery and padding, and full-scale tests using an actual piece of upholstered furniture that is sacrificed in the procedure.

Wall coverings are rated for flammability, durability, and stain resistance and, depending on the applicable code, may need to meet any or all of these requirements. Window treatments usually are not regulated by codes, but those that cover a large surface area (more than 10 percent of the wall area) may be considered an interior finish. Codes most often cited for window treatment fabrics are those of the city of Boston, the city of New York, the state of California, and the commonwealth of Massachusetts.

The NFPA 701 Small Scale Test and the NFPA 702 Large Scale Test are used to assess the flammabilty of curtains, draperies, upholstery, and wall coverings. In these procedures, the sample is ignited and afterflame and length of char for both warp and filling directions are measured. The length of afterflame cannot exceed 2 seconds. In the large-scale test, dripping is also assessed. In the small-scale test, length of permissible char is dependent on the weight of the fabric; in the large-scale test, it cannot exceed 10 inches or 35 inches if the fabric is folded.

Interior textiles used in airplanes and motor vehicles are regulated by the Federal Aviation Administration and the Department of Transportation, respectively. Flame retardancy is mandated for all textiles used in the interiors of these vehicles including seat cushions and backs, seat belts, and interior roof, side, and wall panels. In addition, the standard extends to other items to augment the crashworthiness and emergency evacuation equipment of airplanes.

Tort

The category of *torts* includes behaviors that interfere with personal rights. Torts generally are categorized as either negligence or intentional torts. Negligence torts include substandard performance in regard to legal and regulatory requirements and contracts. Acceptable levels of performance are often referred to as professional standards of care and usually are identified in professional codes of ethics. For example, substandard performance could include a designer not checking to see that a fabric meets appropriate flame-retardant requirements for a product.

Intentional torts are wrongful acts performed in a deliberate fashion and may include deliberate misrepresentation and strict liability. For example, deliberate misrepresentation would include deliberately labeling a rayon/polyester crash as all-linen crash. Strict liability generally applies to the physical harm caused by a user or consumer of a product if it is defective and unreasonably dangerous. Strict liability, which holds people liable even in circumstances in which they were not negligent, applies to manufacturers, suppliers, retailers, and others.

Consumer Recourse

When consumers purchase products, they are entering into an implied contract. They expect the product to perform and to meet their needs. In most cases, textile products perform satisfactorily. In fact, it is amazing how well products perform given the care and wear they receive from consumers. However, at times products do not meet the consumer's expectations. Reasons for failure are varied, ranging from improper care labels to improper dyeing or finishing to improper use by consumers.

Problems with care labels are a great concern among consumers and within the industry. When care label instructions are followed and the result is disastrous, consumers expect to be compensated for their loss. Many stores take returns of this nature; however, some do not. In these cases, the consumer can complain to the manufacturer or the Federal Trade Commission, since incorrect care labels are prohibited by the Care Label Regulation. Other reasons for product failure include poor design, improper selection of dyes or finishes, improper processing of the fabric, or poor selection of the fabric for the end use. In all cases, manufacturers should be informed of the problem either by directly notifying them or by returning the item to the place where it was purchased. The address of the regional office of the Federal Trade Commission is in most telephone directories. Consumers should write to the Federal Trade Commission and include the manufacturer's name or RN/WPL number. The FTC can then identify the manufacturer and send the consumer the address for direct correspondence.

Industry professionals generally have a stronger position to take when products result in consumer complaints. Frequently, the professional is responsible for dealing directly with the unhappy consumer or for some process in the production. In either case, the professional's responsibility is to identify the source of the problem and suggest a solution that will satisfy both the consumer and the company.

ENVIRONMENTAL ISSUES

The condition of the environment has become a major concern worldwide and the textiles industry is no exception. *Environmental issues* affect production at all levels (fiber, yarn, fabric, finishes, dyes, and pigments), distribution of components (within facilities or to other facilities), and disposal of waste or otherwise discarded materials. These are areas of concern to producers, retailers, consumers, and service workers.

Two federal agencies work to protect the environment and create safe working conditions. The *Environmental Protection Agency* (EPA) enforces and regulates air, water, and noise pollution. The *Occupational Safety and Health Administration* (OSHA) develops and enforces standards for safety and educational training programs for workers. Many states also have environmental and worker safety departments. In addition, similar efforts are being made in other countries.

Environmental Impact

U.S. industries consume 142 billion gallons of water a day. The rate of water consumption has been steadily increasing over the past several years, especially in the textile industry. Aspects of production that have contributed to this increase in water consumption include dyeing and finishing of products (acid- and sandwashed fabrics) and a switch to soil-resistant carpets. However, regulations are restricting the use of fresh water and requiring that discharge water (water leaving the plant) meet more and more stringent guidelines.

The *Pollution Prevention Act* of 1990 is designed to reduce source pollution. This act focuses on preventing pollution rather than controlling it after it has been generated. One EPA project asks 600 companies to voluntarily limit the emission of 17 toxic chemicals to specific levels. By 1995, the emission goal would be 50 percent of the 1988 levels. Included in these 600 companies are many major fiber producers. In order to meet these goals, the 600 companies are focusing on these four categories, in this order: source reduction, environmentally sound recycling, treatment of toxic chemicals if necessary, and finally, disposal of waste materials in registered toxic dump landfills. Most companies have found that source reduction works best. Source reduction minimizes the generation of waste materials by substituting less hazardous or harmful materials when possible, and focuses efforts on product reformulation, process modification, improved cleaning standards and practices, and environmentally sound, closed-loop recycling. Companies have found that these new systems are extremely cost effective and pay for themselves in a few years.

The Pollution Prevention Act also requires a toxic release inventory. Many companies had never kept records of this nature. In many cases, the inventory has helped companies recognize practices that could be improved from both a profit and an environmental perspective. Additional practices that will become important in the next few years include new management and manufacturing practices, conservation of resources (especially nonrenewable resources), greater reliance on renewable energy sources, substitution of materials where possible, making more durable consumer goods, and rethinking industrial productivity so that product prices fully reflect environmental costs. Each of these potential practices will have a major impact on the industry and the consumer.

The *Clean Air Act* of 1970 focuses on the quality of the air. Concerns related to air quality include acid rain, toxic air emissions, and ozone. Acid rain is produced when water droplets in the air combine with air pollutants such as sulfur dioxide and nitrous oxides. Air emission guidelines are expensive for any industry, including the textile industry, to meet. It is clear that all industries will be required to meet guidelines and that the guidelines will steadily become more stringent as general attitudes and technology advance.

In the textile industry, stack emissions from steam-generating units or boilers have received quite a bit of attention. Efforts have been made by many segments of the industry to minimize smokestack emissions. Concerns include fly ash from coal-burning units, sulfur dioxide and nitrogen oxide (by-products of burning fuels that contribute to acid rain), and fume emissions from processes in the facility. Solutions to these problems are expensive to develop and time consuming to monitor. These added costs will be passed on to the consumer. As the cost of producing items in the U.S. increases, while meeting federal, state, and local environmental guidelines, many companies look to less regulated countries to produce their goods for lower costs. Although that solution is a cost-effective one in the short term, the U.S. continues to lose jobs and industries and developing countries find environmental pollution a major concern. There is no simple solution to this business and ethical problem.

The *Clean Water Act* of 1972 is concerned with toxic pollutants and the contamination of groundwater or surface water systems. Liquid waste disposal in the textile industry has changed significantly in recent years. Current regulations allow for disposal of many residual solids over adequate land area. Larger facilities have their own spray fields where smaller facilities pay for disposal. No federal regulations currently exist limiting the color of the discharge, but many companies are aware of public concern and currently remove color from effluents. Biological water treatment has been found to be effective for many chemicals found in textile mill discharge streams. However, dyes in the waste stream have received significant attention, not because of the amount of dye present, but because of the dyes' resistance to typical treatment systems. The problem will continue to exist because of the limited processes available to remove dyes and because of the expense involved in dealing with such a complex issue. Thousands of dyes are used by the textile industry and each dye presents a slightly different problem.

Several methods are used in the textile industry to minimize contamination of the water system. Reverse osmosis is one method currently under limited use in the U.S. to recover chemicals used in finishing textiles. Ultrafiltration is used to remove fabric impurities from waste water. By using ultrafiltration techniques, many textile companies have found that recovered and recycled materials have paid for the filtration systems in as little as 18 months.

In many states and areas in the U.S., phosphate builders in detergents are banned or restricted (see Table 21-4). Phosphates are one ingredient in the contamination of water systems that can be easily regulated. Phosphate builders in detergents are efficient chemicals in terms of soil removal from fabrics. With their restriction, more effort must be taken to achieve similar levels of cleaning.

Table 21–4 **States and Locations Banning or Restricting Phosphates in Laundry Detergents**

Akron, OH	Indiana	North Carolina
Chicago, IL	Maine**	Ohio*
Connecticut**	Maryland	Pennsylvania
Delaware	Michigan	Portland, OR
Florida**	Minnesota	Spokane, WA
Georgia	Montana*	Vermont
Idaho*	New Hampshire*	Virginia
Illinois*	New York	Wisconsin

*Some counties in these states.
**Phosphate content restricted to 8.7%

Heat emission from facilities is one concern of a public utility in the southeast. This utility is considering the possibility of heat recovery from the emissions via heat pumps.

Environmental Health and Safety

OSHA's formaldehyde standard became effective in February 1988. *Formaldehyde*, which has been identified as a carcinogen, is found in durable-press treatments, leather finishing, and some dyeing applications. Exposure limits were identified in the standard as 1.0 parts per million (ppm) over an 8-hour exposure time for a permissible exposure limit (PEL), 2.0 ppm within 15 minutes for a short-term exposure limit (STEL), and 0.5 ppm over 8 hours for an action level (AL).

OSHA has proposed modifying its formaldehyde standard. Included in this proposed modification would be a reduction in the permissible exposure limit from the current level of 1 ppm to 0.75 ppm, both averaged over 8 hours of exposure. OSHA would like to tighten the existing regulation so that workers who experience significant health impairment (based on a physician's professional judgment) would be transferred to an area with at least 25 percent less formaldehyde exposure. In addition, OSHA intends to amend the standard to require hazard warning labels for solid materials capable of off-gassing formaldehyde at levels from 0.1 ppm to 0.5 ppm and further clarify the warnings on materials capable of off-gassing above 0.5 ppm.

The EPA has issued permissible exposure levels for hundreds of chemicals that are known to be or are likely to be human carcinogens. One of the chemicals on the list is perchloroethylene (perc), one of the most common solvents used in dry cleaning. These regulations at federal and state levels restrict the use and disposal of perc. This could have a major impact on dry cleaning, dry cleaners, and consumers. The proposed standard has a compliance date of December 31, 1992. Permissible exposure limits are 25 ppm.

Indoor air quality has become a major concern. Indoor air pollution develops from many sources including textile products. Carpeting, carpet padding, fabrics used in furnishings and apparel, latex backcoatings, finishes, and dyes on textiles have all been identified as contributing to this problem. Buildings with poor ventilation and indoor air pollution are often referred to as having "sick building syndrome." Carpet has been specifically identified as a source of formaldehyde in these sick buildings. However, research into production of carpets shows that no formaldehyde is used to produce them. Carpets leaving production facilities have low levels of formaldehyde (1–25 μg/g). The source of the formaldehyde is unknown. In fact, one theory proposes that the carpet functions as a sink for formaldehyde (the carpet absorbs gaseous formaldehyde), thus lowering the levels in the environment by as much as 30 percent.

Multiple chemical sensitivity has been identified as a chronic problem for some people. Textiles that have been identified as contributors include carpet and installation materials (glues, pads, etc.) and formaldehyde-treated fabrics.

Disposal and Recycling

Concern for the environment also extends to disposal of textiles. Currently, very few textiles are *recycled*. Many recycling facilities refuse textiles because of the numbers of different fibers present, the small quantities of materials in each item, and the difficulties of shredding these items. Textiles tend to tangle contemporary shredders and cause them to malfunction or wear out quickly. Of course, one can consider the recycled wools and the used clothing/furnishing shops and donations to charitable institutions as recycling, but ultimately all textiles are disposed into the waste system. In 1987, a team of archaeologists from the University of Arizona began a study of seven landfills across the U.S. They

Fig. 21–5   *Floor mat made of recycled materials.*

carefully sorted, documented, and analyzed materials excavated from the landfills. What they found was that normally easily biodegradable items such as newsprint, textiles, and grass at least 10 years old remained intact. The content of landfills, by weight, was found to be 35.6 percent paper, 20.1 percent yard waste, 8.9 percent food waste, 8.7 percent metals, 8.4 percent glass, 7.3 percent plastics, 1.3 percent apparel, and 9.7 percent other materials.

Some groups concerned with waste disposal have been working to minimize the generation of waste at the point of production. These efforts include minimizing packaging and using quickly degradable packaging materials. Some companies have developed methods to convert some synthetic fibers and plastics into new products such as plastic bottles, carpet fibers, hazard fencing, and shoulder pads (see Figure 21-5). More efforts in this direction are needed.

KEY TERMS

Labeling requirements
Federal Trade Commission
Wool Products Labeling Act
WPL number
RN number
Fur Products Labeling Act
Textile Fiber Products Identification Act
Generic name
Trade name
Trademark
Care Labeling Regulation
Code of Federal Regulations
Consumer Product Safety Commission
Flammable Fabrics Act

Upholstered Furniture Action Council
Warranties
Codes
Torts
Environmental issues
Environmental Protection Agency
Occupational Safety and Health
   Administration
Pollution Prevention Act
Clean Air Act
Clean Water Act
Formaldehyde
Recycling

QUESTIONS

1. What information is required by law to be on sewn-in labels? What information is required to be present to consumers at point of purchase?
2. What rights do consumers have if they are dissatisfied with the performance or serviceability of a textile product?
3. What are the legal responsibilities of manufacturers, producers, and their employees regarding textile products?
4. What law or regulation deals with issues of safety?
5. What additional requirements might furnishings be required to meet depending on building codes?
6. What steps has the textile industry taken to minimize environmental impact in terms of production, distribution, and disposal of textiles or related materials?

SUGGESTED READINGS

Benning, Karen M. (May, 1988). "Formaldehyde." *Apparel Industry Magazine*, pp. 76–80.

Federal Trade Commission (March, 1984). *Writing a Care Label*. Washington, D.C.: Federal Trade Commission.

Fulmer, T. D. (May, 1990). "Toxic and Nontoxic Waste: What Is Ahead?" *America's Textiles International*, pp. 80–85.

Huer, Charles R. (1989). *Means Legal Reference for Design and Construction*. Kingston, MA: R. S. Means Company.

Reznikoff, S. C. (1989). *Specifications for Commercial Interiors*. New York: Watson-Guptill Publications.

CHAPTER 22

Career Exploration

OBJECTIVES

- To understand the importance of textile knowledge in professional roles.

- To recognize the need to communicate textiles information quickly and accurately to other professionals and consumers.

- To be aware of the diverse career options requiring some knowledge of textiles.

*N*OW THAT THE SCIENCE OF TEXTILES HAS been explored in some depth, it is helpful to know how this information relates to various careers. General terms and sample job titles are used here since each company, firm, or agency is organized differently. Also, the ability to apply knowledge and analyze products depends on both the textile product and the focus of the company, organization, or agency in the production pipeline. For example, the handling and marketing of a fabric being sold to a company that will sew it into a product differs from that of a fabric being sold directly to the individual customer.

DESIGN

Designers are responsible for creating the idea or design for a product, or selecting the components for a room setting. Designers work at all levels in the industry. They may design components such as yarns, fabrics, or patterns for prints, or apparel items, furnishing items, rooms, or other settings. Their creativity is of great importance, but they need to know what will sell, what will satisfy the consumer, what is within the capability of the company and its equipment, and what is within the price range of the target consumer. They also need to understand the performance of the textiles with which they work and must be able to select the appropriate materials to achieve the serviceability desired in the finished product. When working in manufacturing, designers need to understand the sewability of the materials and fabrics they select. For example, fabrics that are difficult to sew, heavy stiff fabrics like cotton denim and lightweight slippery fabrics like polyester ninon, demand higher piece rates because sewing machine operators cannot work as quickly with these fabrics. Designers need to know and be sure that their work meets the appropriate laws, regulations, and codes as established by the industry and government. Designers may need to be flexible enough to work at several quality levels and to work with knock-offs or less expensive copies of higher priced items. Most design work means problem solving and working within the company's niche, aiming to satisfy the company's target market while continuing to make a profit. Beginning positions in design include design assistant, assistant designer, or pattern maker. Design positions may be found in product development areas, especially in apparel production and retail businesses.

Design positions are also available in the entertainment field. Designers create the set or stage and dress the cast to convey the many visual aspects of the production. Positions in the entertainment area are more difficult to attain. A designer may have to spend several years as an assistant before achieving recognition as a set or costume designer.

The design area also includes the *artist* or craftsperson who creates one-of-a-kind items. Most artists specialize in one medium or type of object. For example, an artist may specialize in weaving large tapestries for public buildings or office spaces. Another artist may specialize in creating wearable art like kimonos, employing a variety of techniques including weaving, batiking, and quilting. Clearly, the artist needs to be able to select appropriate materials and have sufficient skill to execute the piece in an acceptable manner. Becoming a self-employed artist requires a great deal of effort, talent, and discipline.

MERCHANDISING

Working in the retail setting as a merchandise buyer or manager is an exciting career goal for many students. However, many positions in *merchandising* exist beyond the retail setting. There are buying positions in companies throughout the textile pipeline. For example, yarn companies buy fiber to use in their spinning facilities. Weaving and knitting facilities buy yarn to use in producing fabrics. Converters and dyeing/finishing plants buy dyes and chemicals to use in finishing fabrics. Sewing facilities buy fabric, wood and metal for furniture frames, padding, zippers, buttons, and a host of other materials and components to use in producing the finished item. Mail order has become big business; demand for merchandisers exists in that portion of the retail segment as well. Mail order positions include responsibilities directly related to buying or developing the merchandise presented in the catalog and those related to the production of the catalog, such as merchandising the product presentation, including organizing photo sessions. Another possi-

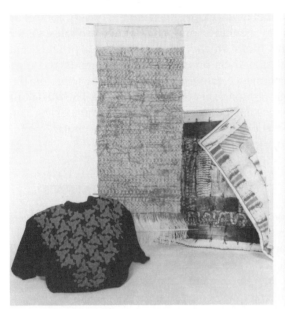 

Fig. 22–1 *Fiber artwork. (Courtesy of Patricia Kimle* (left) *and Teresa Heard* (right).*)*

ble option is in mall management, although many of these positions require some experience in the field. These professionals manage a mall facility, see that all retail space in the mall is rented, and publicize the mall via style shows, antique shows, and other events that bring the public to the mall. Mall management is also responsible for maintaining the right look of the mall and keeping the right mix of retailers in the mall for the target market.

Producers of textile products need someone to represent their product line to the retailer. Often this presentation takes place in a company showroom located at headquarers or in a merchandise center where similar merchandise lines are grouped together for buyers to see. Showroom managers and staff explain a company's line to retail buyers. Sales representative positions often require someone who is willing to travel and who is self-motivated. These positions may be quite demanding, but pay well and are exciting. Sales reps may represent several companies, product lines, or product types that complement each other. For example, a sales rep may carry the line of one company that produces women's dresses, a line of another company that produces coordinates aimed at the same target market, and jewelry that could be worn with either of these two lines. Fabric reps specialize in selling fabric to producers and consumer fabric stores.

Professionals in any of these positions need to be able to select products that will sell and that will satisfy the consumer. Often consumers assume that the employees of the retail establishment are knowl-edgeable about the products they carry. Consider the questions consumers ask about textiles: Will this item stain? How should it be laundered? Will it last? Will it be comfortable? These questions require textile knowledge to be answered correctly.

SOURCING

Sourcing is a relatively new career option that offers exciting and challenging positions in the industry. As a concept, sourcing is relatively simple: identifying the firm that can supply the item needed. In practice, sourcing is difficult. Sourcing agents need to understand textiles, textile products, production, marketing, quality assessment, and consistency of product or service quality. The ability to develop and understand specifications of products or services is critical. Sourcing agents also need to have good communication skills and a global perspective. For example, if a retailer wants to carry a specific item, a sourcing agent in that retail firm would investigate companies who produce items similar to what is needed, evaluate the products they produce, cost the products, and analyze the ability of each company to meet production deadlines. The sourcing agent usually recommends one or more companies to negotiate with for sample runs or contract terms.

Sourcing agents are often responsible for follow-up to ensure that the contract will be met, that items are shipped on time, and that shipping is handled in the agreed-on manner. When the source of production is offshore, sourcing agents need to be familiar with import/export requirements and regulations. For example, quotas refer to specific quantities of goods allowed to be imported from one country to another. Quotas are usually the result of agreements between the importing and the exporting countries. U.S. quotas are the most elaborate and detailed of any in the world. Imports are divided by product category. For apparel, they are further divided by fiber type and gender. Sourcing agents frequently work with customs officials to minimize problems or solve problems as they develop.

MARKETING

Marketing positions require people with imagination and creativity and an understanding of what motivates consumers to buy. Marketing positions may be in areas as diverse as advertising, journalism, and display. These professionals help the consumer become aware of the product, recognize its usefulness or desirability, and decide to purchase the product. Marketing and merchandising positions may be combined in some firms. A knowledge of the special features or design aspects of the product will assist in marketing it. Often textile knowledge gives a firm a boost in terms of its marketing because the firm can focus on the quality of the

product as developed through the quality control or quality assurance programs to increase sales. Other firms focus on the serviceability of a product and highlight their product testing programs and high performance ratings. Still other firms focus on the high fashion aspects of a product. A knowledge of textiles in all these areas provides an understanding of the product and an expanded vocabulary useful in marketing the product.

PRODUCT DEVELOPMENT

Product development specialists work in several areas in a company. Some individuals have a background in the social sciences, others in the physical sciences, and still others in business or design. In product development, target markets and consumer expectations for products are identified. *Prototypes* of products are developed, which may be an extremely time-consuming process with large numbers of people involved. For highly innovative products, product development works with research and development or the two may be combined in one department in a company. Prototypes (original product samples) are evaluated by combining performance testing with user, wear, or product testing. For example, in *performance testing* a new product may be tested for tensile strength, abrasion resistance, washability, and comfort using standard

Fig. 22–2 *Designer Susan McKeever displays boards depicting 1992 fashions created exclusively for J.C. Penney. (Courtesy of J.C. Penney Co., Inc.)*

Fig. 22–3 *Using the CAD system to develop designs for upcoming seasons. (Courtesy of J.C. Penney Co., Inc.)*

test methods and specialized testing equipment. At the same time, in *product testing* identical products may be used by consumers to see how the product performs for them and how they react to the product. This may occur several times as the prototype is modified based on results from the testing.

Product development does not cease once the product is on the market. Often, follow-up studies are conducted to see how the general public accepts the product. Later, further modifications may be necessary for the product to remain competitive. Note how often new detergents come on the market or how often detergents are labeled "new and improved." Development of a laundry detergent is just one area where textile knowledge is appropriate for a position in product development. The professional in this area needs basic textile knowledge to understand the components of the item being developed. Often the textile fiber used is the prime focus. For example, microfibers have created some unique design, production, and marketing problems.

Product development also involves developing the fashion design, selecting the most appropriate fabrication for the design, and sourcing accessories to go with the fashion item. For example, a firm may realize that one of its products is losing market share to a less expensive competitor. Thus, to remain competitive, the firm needs to produce the product for less. One way of remaining competitive is to use a less expensive, but equally serviceable

product. The firm may work with several mills to identify fabrics that meet their requirements and test these fabrics to determine their performance. Once performance has been determined, the firm may negotiate with a mill so that the most serviceable fabric is further modified to meet the firm's performance expectations at a price level appropriate for the final product. A similar kind of sequence may occur in-house as design modifications and product groupings are evaluated. Product development is an area in the textile industry that is increasing in importance.

QUALITY ASSURANCE

Quality assurance (QA), *quality control* (QC), and total quality management (TQM) are important areas in the textile industry. In general, quality engineers deal with producing an item at a specified level of quality in a manner that is as safe, cost-effective, and efficient as possible. Company standards and specifications identify requirements that products must meet in terms of fabric characteristics like weight and count or in terms of performance like colorfastness and dimensional stability. QA technicians, engineers, and managers develop these standards and specifications, work with suppliers to see that components and materials meet specifications, and test to be sure items purchased as well as items produced meet specifications and perform at the

Fig. 22–4 *Computer-aided design (CAD) used in the production of patterned textiles. (Courtesy of Stork Screens, B.V.)*

predetermined level. QA staff members may also develop the procedures or methods to make assessments quickly and accurately in order to solve problems in purchasing, product specifications, or production in a timely manner. QA professionals need to know textiles so that they can assess the quality of purchased items and identify possible sources of problems in production. For example, if an operator is having difficulty with seam puckering in a tightly woven fabric, the sewing thread may be too large, causing the yarns in the fabric to be distorted.

RESEARCH AND DEVELOPMENT

Many *research and development* (R&D) positions require the research and data processing skills, specialized understanding of the field, and statistical knowledge that are a major part of the courses for a degree at the master's or doctoral level. R&D positions can be found throughout the textile industry. For example, researchers study polymer science, fiber chemistry, yarn production, fabrication efficiency and flexibility, dyeing and finishing effects on the environment, development or modification of production machinery, and application of new technology to solve problems encountered in the textile industry, problems ranging from preventing carpal tunnel syndrome to managing clean air and water requirements to dealing with competition

from imports. Some researchers evaluate the appropriateness of textile products for specific end uses; others develop new end uses for existing textiles. Beginning positions in research and development may be as a technician, research scientist, or assistant engineer. R&D positions in the textile industry require a general knowledge of textiles and specific knowledge in a focus area.

PRODUCTION

Production careers deal with actually producing the textile or the textile product. There are positions at all levels of the industry from the raw material stage prior to fiber production, to the production of fiber, yarn, and fabric, to the dyeing and finishing of fabrics or products. Other positions are in sewn product facilities such as apparel, furnishing, and industrial production plants in the U.S. and most foreign countries. With the move of many production facilities offshore, there is a great demand for production management staff who are willing to work in the international arena. These positions are exciting and often very challenging. Beginning positions often are as assistant plant manager or assistant engineer. These positions require a combination of people skills and knowledge of the materials with which the facility works as well as the way the equipment works with or processes the materials. Obviously, essential knowledge includes some understanding of textiles such as ease of handling, melting point of thermoplastic fibers, elongation potential of knits, and so on.

GOVERNMENT

The U.S. government is one of the world's largest consumers of textile products. Hence, it should not be surprising that there are many positions in government agencies. Purchasing officers locate producers of specific textile products and verify that these items meet government requirements. The product or a prototype needs to be tested and evaluated to verify that its performance meets the government's stringent requirements. The performance of these items is evaluated by textile testing engineers using Federal Test Methods and Standards (FTMS). Since textile products purchased by the government must be domestically produced, *sourcing agents* are in demand. *Custom officials* and inspectors check to make sure that all imported goods meet the appropriate requirements in terms of quotas and labeling requirements, and are free of insects and disease organisms. For example, wool from certain countries is checked for anthrax, a highly contagious disease of sheep. Government employees may develop, enforce, or interpret standards, laws, and regulations. Government employees work with industry and business so that current guidelines and standards are met. Many positions are also available in the military, either as a member of the military or as a civilian employee. Research and development positions in government research facilities focus on textile products such as uniforms for adverse weather conditions, space suits, interiors for space vehicles and submarines, and suits that offer protection from biological and chemical warfare.

EDUCATION

Education positions can be formal, such as university/college or secondary school *educator*, or informal, such as home economist or consumer education specialist in extension, business, or industry. In the formal setting, an advanced degree or periodic additional coursework may be necessary. Many colleges and universities require a Ph.D. College/university faculty members teach specific classes related to their area of specialization and often do research or judge design competitions. A secondary teacher may be involved in several areas including family and child development, food and nutrition, and sex education. Secondary teachers may have additional responsibilities including making home visits and advising a student group or club.

In the informal setting, professionals have a wide variety of possible job descriptions. Some positions involve working with other employees of the com-

Fig. 22–5 *Developing color schemes for upcoming seasons. (Courtesy of J.C. Penney Co., Inc.)*

Fig. 22–6   Conducting a du-pro (during production) inspection of quality. (Courtesy of J.C. Penney Co., Inc.)

pany so that they better understand the consumer. For example, some *consumer education specialists* may help engineers understand problems consumers have with automatic washers and dryers. Many trade associations and businesses employ people with a background in education and textiles to write brochures describing the product, develop educational materials like the brochures handed out in class, write instructional books describing how to properly use the washer or serger, or produce audio-visual aids such as videotapes or slide sets. These people also may teach workshops to consumers or sales representatives and may be responsible for dealing with consumers who have questions related to the use of the product or who have a complaint with the product. It is not surprising, with this list of responsibilities, that an understanding of basic textiles is essential for these positions.

In extension positions, job titles include *extension specialist* or extension home economist. These professionals develop programs for state and regional use related to wide-ranging current concerns including cleaning clothing soiled with pesticides, disposing of leftover cleaning aids, recycling textiles in an environmentally safe manner, or storing textile heirlooms. They answer thousands of questions from consumers on an amazing array of topics, assess special needs in their geograhic areas, and develop programs and materials to meet these needs. Extension professionals develop and present educational materials to diverse and specific audiences including pesticide applicators, day care workers, or 4-H members.

MUSEUM OR COLLECTION WORK

Professionals in the museum field need an in-depth knowledge of textiles, production techniques, and evolution of design since dating an item and determining its cultural significance is often based on these specific details. *Curators* are responsible for the items in a museum's collection. This responsibility includes identifying the items for display. The

Fig. 22–7   Evaluating the wear resistance of upholstery fabrics. (Courtesy of J.C. Penney Co., Inc.)

curator is also responsible for selecting items to be added to the collection and maintaining the collection in good condition. In large museums with thousands of objects, this is a challenging position. The *conservator* performs hands-on cleaning and repair work and prepares objects for storage. Conservation requires an in-depth knowledge of the objects, how they were made, the materials and components in the objects, and how these materials age and react with environmental factors such as light, dust, and stains.

SUMMARY

Many exciting and challenging professional positions are possible with a background in textiles.

The variety and diversity of positions make it possible for anyone, regardless of interests, strengths, working habits, or geographic preferences to find a position in the textile industry or a closely related area.

All professional positions require a continual updating of information. The responsibility of finding information and keeping current is one that all professionals recognize. To keep current, make a habit of regularly reading professional journals and publications related to your area. Many professions have organizations so that members can meet others with similar interests on a regular basis and update their knowledge. In addition, workshops or short courses are offered through colleges/universities, professional organizations, or private concerns.

KEY TERMS

Designer	Quality control
Artist	Research and development
Merchandising	Production
Sourcing	Sourcing agent
Marketing	Customs official
Product development	Educator
Prototype	Consumer education specialist
Performance testing	Extension specialist
Product testing	Curator
Quality assurance	Conservator

QUESTIONS

1. Talk to a professional in your area of interest to determine the relationship of textiles knowledge to that career.
2. Based on your current career goal, how will you use your knowledge of textiles in performing the responsibilities of your job?
3. What efforts can you take to update your textiles knowledge on a regular basis as required in your future job or career?

SUGGESTED READINGS

Bureau of Labor Statistics. *Occupational Outlook Quarterly*, Washington, DC: U.S. Government Printing Office.

Hoeflin, Ruth, Pence, Karen, Miller, Mary G., and Weber, Joe (1984). *Career for Professionals: New Perspectives in Home Economics*, 2d ed. Dubuque, IA: Kendall/Hunt Publishing Co.

Krannick, Ronald L. (1983). *Re-Careering in Turbulent Times: Skills and Strategies for Success in Today's Job Market*. Manassas, VA: Impact Publications.

Smith, Devon Cottrell, ed. (1990). *The Fourth of July Guide to Careers, Internships, and Volunteer Opportunities in the Nonprofit Sector*. Garett Park, MD: Garett Park Press.

U.S. Department of Labor. *Occupation Outlook Handbook* (1990). Indianapolis, IN: JIST Works.

APPENDIX

FIBER NAMES
IN OTHER LANGUAGES

English	Chinese	French	German	Italian	Korean	Japanese*	Spanish
acetate	—	acetate	Acetat faser	acetato	—	—	acetato
acrylic	—	acrylique	Acryl nachgestellf	—	—	—	acrilico
cotton	mianhua	coton/cottonade	Baumwolle	cotone	myun	dahs-Shee-mehn	algodón
linen	mah bou	lin	Leinen	tela di lino	—	ah-Sah/Reen-neh-roo	lino
nylon	nilong	nylon	Nylon	nàilon	—	Nah-ee-rohn	nilón
olefin	—	—	—	—	—	—	olefina
polyester	huaxian	—	Polyester	poliestere	—	poh-Ree-eh-ste-roo	poliestero
ramie	—	—	—	—	mo shi	—	rame
rayon	—	rayonne	Reyon, Kunstseide	ràion	—	—	rayón
silk	sichou	soie	Seide	seta	beton	Kee-noo/Shee-roo-Koo	seda
wool	yangmao	laine	Wolle	lana	mo	OO-roo	lana

*based on pronunciation

GLOSSARY

Abrasion resistance is the ability of a fiber to withstand the rubbing or abrasion it gets in everyday use.

Abrasion-resistant finish is a process designed to improve the abrasion resistance of fabric. Commonly used in linings and pocket facings.

Abrasive wash is a finish designed to abrade a small portion of the fabric's surface to soften the hand and produce a slightly worn look in the finished product.

Absorbency is the percentage of moisture a bone-dry fiber will absorb from the air under standard conditions of temperature and moisture. Also known as moisture regain.

Absorbent finish improves the absorbency of the fabric; often used in apparel for better comfort.

Aluminum coating is a very thin layer of aluminum metal designed to minimize heat flow through the fabric or add a metallic sparkle to the product.

Ammoniating finish increases the absorbency of cotton and some other cellulosic fabrics. Often used in conjunction with durable-press finishes to minimize their negative effects.

Antifume-fading finish minimizes the effect of atmospheric fumes on sensitive dye-fiber combinations, such as disperse dyes on acetate.

Antimicrobial finish inhibits the growth of bacteria or destroys bacteria on textiles.

Antipesticide protective finish minimizes the wicking or absorption of pesticides by the fabric, thus protecting the user from exposure.

Antique satin is a reversible satin-weave fabric with satin floats on the technical face and surface slubs on the technical back created by using slub-filling yarns. It is usually used with the technical back as the fashion side for drapery fabrics and often made of a blend of fibers.

Antiredeposition agent is a compound used in detergents to keep soil suspended and prevent it from being deposited back on the fabric, causing a uniform grayish cast to the fabric.

Antiseptic finish (*See* Antimicrobial finish)

Antislip finish minimizes yarn slippage in fabrics; especially important in low-count, smooth filament-yarn fabrics in a satin weave.

Antistatic finish adds a compound to the surface of the fabric to absorb moisture, conduct electricity, or neutralize the buildup of static charges.

Appearance retention includes those aspects that influence the way a fabric looks during use, care, and storage.

Applied design includes those appearance aspects related to luster, drape, texture, hand, or design motif that are added to the fabric after it has been produced.

Bacteriostatic (*See* Antimicrobial finish)

Batik is a hand process in which wax is applied to the fabric in a design to prevent dye takeup, creating a pattern on the fabric. Batik may require several steps of wax application and dyeing.

Batiste is an opaque, lightweight, spun-yarn, plain-weave fabric with a smooth surface. When made of cotton or cotton/polyester, the yarns are usually combed. It can be made of all wool, silk, or rayon.

Battenberg lace is a hand-produced lace fabric made with narrow fabric tapes connected with thin yarn stitches called brides.

Bedford cord is a heavy, warp-faced, unbalanced pique-weave fabric with wide warp cords created by extra filling yarns floating across the back to give a raised effect.

Bengaline is a lustrous, durable, warp-faced fabric with heavy filling cords completely covered by the warp.

Beetling is a finish for linen or linenlike fabrics. The yarns are flattened to create a fabric that looks more regular and tighter.

Bleach is a compound that destroys the color compounds on fabrics. Bleach is generally used to destroy unwanted stains or yellowing on fabrics.

Bleeding is a problem with dyes. The dye leaves the fiber when the fiber gets wet, as in laundering. Dyes that bleed may be absorbed by other fibers, thus staining the originally uncolored fibers.

Blend is a fabric that consists of two or more generically different fiber types.

Block printing is a means of printing a fabric with a relief carved block so that only those areas protruding from the block transfer dye paste to the fabric.

Bonding produces a thick fabric from two thinner fabrics by use of an adhesive; also a means of producing a fabric from fibers with heat.

Bouclé is a woven or knit fabric with bouclé yarns. The loops of the novelty yarns create a mock-pile surface.

Bow is a type of off-grain fabric. The filling yarn sags in the center between the selvages.

Braid is a method of producing fabric by diagonal interlacing yarns; also a term describing any fabric made in such a fashion.

Breaking elongation describes the amount a fabric or fiber stretches at the breaking point.

Brightener (*See* Fluorescent brightening agent)

Bright fiber refers to a fiber in its original luster without the use of any delusterant.

Broadcloth is a close plain-weave fabric made of cotton, rayon, or a blend of either cotton or rayon with polyester. It has a fine rib in the filling direction caused by slightly larger filling yarns, filling yarns with a lower twist, or a higher warp-yarn count. High-quality broadcloth is made with plied warp and filling yarns. The fabric may be mercerized. It has a soft, firm hand. The term *broadcloth* is also used to refer to a plain- or twill-weave lustrous wool or wool-blend fabric that is highly napped and then pressed flat.

Brocade is a jacquard-woven fabric with a pattern that is created with different color yarns or with patterns in twill or satin weaves on a ground of plain, twill, or satin weave. It is available in a variety of fiber types and qualities.

Brocatelle is similar to brocade, but the pattern is raised and often padded with stuffer yarns. The pattern is warp faced and the ground is filling faced. Brocatelle is often a double cloth. It is mainly used in furnishings.

Brushing is a finishing step that removes fiber ends from the surface of fabric. Most common with pile fabrics.

Buckram is a heavy, very stiff, spun-yarn fabric converted from cheesecloth gray goods with adhesives and fillers. It is used as an interlining to stiffen pinch-pleated window treatment fabrics.

Builders are compounds used in detergents to augment the cleaning power of the surfactant. Builders sequester hardness minerals and adjust the pH of the solution to a more alkaline level.

Bunting (*See* Cheesecloth)

Burlap is a coarse, heavy, loosely woven plain-weave fabric often made of single irregular yarns of jute. It is used in its natural color for carpet backing, bagging, and furniture webbing. It is also dyed and printed for furnishing uses.

Burned-out is a fiber blend fabric. One fiber is dissolved in a selected area to create a pattern.

Butcher cloth is a coarse-rayon or rayon-blend fabric. It is made in a variety of weights. A Federal Trade Commission ruling prohibits the use of the word *linen* for this type of fabric.

Calendering is a common finishing technique in which fabric is passed between cylinders to achieve a specific effect. See the specific types of calendering: embossing, friction, moiré, Schreiner, simple.

Cambric is a fine, firm, plain-weave balanced fabric with starch, and has a slight luster on one side. It is difficult to distinguish from percale.

Canvas is a heavy, firm, strong fabric often made of cotton or acrylic and used for awnings, slipcovers, and covers for boats. It is produced in many grades and qualities. It may have a soft or firm hand. It is made in plain or basket weave.

Carbonizing is a treatment for wool in which acid removes cellulosic matter and prepares the fiber for dyeing.

Casement cloth is a general term for any open-weave fabric used for drapery or curtain fabrics. It is usually sheer.

Cavalry twill is a steep, pronounced, double-wale line, smooth-surfaced twill fabric.

Challis (shal'i) is a lightweight, spun-yarn, plain-weave balanced fabric with a soft finish. It can be made of any staple fiber or blend of fibers.

Chambray is a plain-weave fabric usually of cotton, rayon, or a blend of these with polyester. Usually chambray has white yarns in the filling direction and yarn-dyed yarns in the warp direction. Iridescent chambray is made with one color in the warp and a second color in the filling. It can also be made in striped patterns.

Cheesecloth is a lightweight, sheer, plain-woven fabric with a very soft texture. It may be natural colored, bleached, or dyed. It usually has a very low count. If dyed, it may be called *bunting* and could be used for flags or banners.

Chemical reactivity indicates the type of chemical reaction to which individual fibers are susceptible.

Chemical wash is a chemical finish in which the surface of the fiber is modified in some way by the chemical. Often used as a means of softening the fabric's hand, increasing the comfort, or modifying the appearance of the fabric.

Chiffon is a sheer, very lightweight, plain-weave fabric with fine crepe twist yarns of approximately the same size and twist used in warp and filling. The fabric is balanced.

China silk is a soft, lightweight, opaque, plain-weave fabric made from fine-filament yarns and used for apparel.

Chino is a steep-twill fabric with a slight sheen, often made in a bottom-weight fabric of cotton or cotton/polyester. Often it is made of combed two-ply yarns in both warp and filling and vat-dyed in khaki.

Chintz is a medium- to heavyweight, plain-weave, spun-yarn fabric finished with a glaze. Chintz may be piece dyed or printed. It is often referred to as glazed chintz.

Clip spot refers to a fabric in which design is created with an additional yarn that interlaces with the ground fabric in spots and floats along the technical back of the fabric. The floats are removed by shearing.

Cloque fabric is a general term used to refer to any fabric with a puckered or blistered effect.

Coated fabric is a multiplex fabric with a thin plastic film combined with a woven, knit, or fiberweb fabric.

Cohesiveness refers to the ability of fibers to cling together, especially important in yarn spinning.

Color problems refer to any aspect that creates difficulty for consumers, producers, or manufacturers due to dyes, pigments, or technique used in coloring the fabric. See specific types of color problems: bleeding, frosting, fume fading, migration.

Combination refers to a fabric of two or more generically different fiber types where ply yarns consist of strands of each generic type.

Corduroy is a filling-yarn pile fabric where the pile is created by long-filling floats that are cut and brushed in the finishing process. The ground weave may be either a plain or twill weave.

Coronizing is a finish specific to fiberglass to assist in yarn production and printing.

Count refers to yarns per inch in warp and filling direction in woven fabrics.

Course refers to the path of a yarn in a filling knit fabric as it moves across the fabric.

Cover is the ability to occupy space for concealment or protection.

Covert was first made in England, where there was a demand for a fabric that would not catch on brambles or branches during fox hunts. To make this tightly woven fabric, a two-ply yarn, one cotton and one wool, was used. Because the cotton and wool did not take the same dye, the fabric had a mottled appearance.

Cotton covert is always mottled. It may be made with ply yarns, one ply white and the other colored, or it may be fiber dyed white and a color. It is a $\frac{2}{1}$ twill, of the same weight as denim, and used primarily for work pants, overalls, and service coats.

Wool covert is made from woolen or worsted yarns. It may be mottled or solid color and may be suit or coat weight. It may be slightly napped or have a clear finish. The mottled effect is obtained by using two different-colored plies or by blending different-colored fibers.

Crash is a medium- to heavyweight, plain-weave fabric made from slub or irregular yarns to create an irregular surface.

Crease retention finish (*See* Durable-press)

Crepe refers to any fabric with a puckered, crinkled, or grainy surface. It can be made with crepe yarns, a crepe or momie weave, or a finish such as embossed or plissé. Examples of crepe fabrics include chiffon, crepe-back satin, georgette, and crepe de Chine. For more information, see these fabric names.

Crepe-back satin is a reversible satin-weave fabric in which the filling yarns have a crepe twist. The technical face has satin floats and the technical back looks like a crepe fabric. It is also known as *satin-back crepe*.

Crepe de Chine is a lightweight, opaque, plain-weave, filament-yarn fabric. It has a medium luster. Silk crepe de Chine usually is made with crepe yarns.

Crepe twist refers to a yarn with extremely high twist and great liveliness.

Cretonne is a plain-weave fabric similar to chintz, except that the finish is dull and the fabric is more likely to be printed with large-scale floral designs.

Crinoline is a stiff, spun-yarn, plain-weave fabric similar to cheesecloth, used in book bindings, hats, and stiffening for apparel.

Crocking describes a color problem in which abrasion causes color to transfer to the abradant.

Cross-dyeing describes a special type of dyeing fiber blends. Each fiber type present in the blend is dyed a different color.

Damask is a reversible, flat, jaquard-woven fabric with a satin weave in both the pattern and the ground. It can be one color or two. In two-color damasks, the color reverses on the opposite side. It is used in apparel and furnishings.

Delustered fiber describes a fiber with dull luster resulting from the incorporation of a white pigment within the fiber.

Denier describes yarn or fiber size and is defined as weight in grams for 9,000 meters of fiber or yarn.

Denim is a cotton or cotton/polyester blend, twill-weave, yarn dyed fabric. Usually the warp is colored and the filling is white. It is usually a left-hand twill that is commonly available with a blue (indigo) warp and white filling for use in apparel. It is available in a variety of weights.

Detergent is a chemical compound specially formulated to remove soil or other material from textiles.

Dimensional stability refers to a finish that minimizes fabric shrinkage or growth in use or during care.

Dimity is a sheer, lightweight fabric with warp cords created by using heavier-warp yarns at a regular distance, grouping warp yarns together, or using a basket variation where two or more warp yarns are woven as one. It may be printed or piece dyed. It may be made of combed-cotton yarns. *Barred dimity* has heavier or double yarns periodically in both the warp and filling.

Direct printing describes a process in which the color is applied to its final location as a paste or powder.

Discharge printing describes a process in which color is removed from piece-dyed fabric in specific locations.

Dotted swiss is a sheer, light- or medium-weight, plain-weave fabric with small dots created at regular intervals with extra yarns, either through a swivel weave or a clip-spot weave. Look-alike fabrics are made by flocking, printing, or using an expanded foam print.

Double cloth is a fabric made by weaving two fabrics with five sets of yarns: two sets of warp, two sets of filling, and one set that connects the two fabrics.

Double knit is a general term used to refer to any filling-knit fabric made on two needle beds.

Double weave is a fabric made by weaving two fabrics with four sets of yarns (two sets of warp and two sets of filling yarns) on the same loom. The two fabrics are connected by periodically reversing the positions of the two fabrics from top to bottom. Double weave is also known as *pocket cloth* or *pocket weave*.

Drape is the manner in which a fabric falls or hangs over a three-dimensional form.

Drawing describes a fiber finishing step in which a manufactured fiber is elongated after spinning to alter the molecular arrangement within the fiber, increasing crystallinity and orientation and resulting in a change in specific performance properties.

Drill is a strong, medium- to heavyweight, warp-faced, twill-weave fabric. It is usually a $\frac{2}{1}$ left-handed twill and piece dyed.

Dry cleaning describes a fabric cleaning process that uses an organic solvent rather than water.

Duck is a strong, heavy, plain- or basket-weave fabric. Duck comes in a variety of weights and qualities. It is similar to canvas.

Duplex printing describes a printing process in which both sides of the fabric are printed.

Durable finish lasts for the life of the product, but the performance diminishes with time.

Durable press describes a finish designed to maintain the fabric's smooth, flat, unwrinkled appearance during use, care, and storage.

Duvetyn is similar to suede, but is lighter weight and more drapeable. It has a soft, velvetlike surface made by napping, shearing, and brushing.

Dye is an organic compound with high color strength capable of forming a bond of some type with fibers.

Dyeing is the process of combining a fiber with a dye and achieving a bond of some type.

Elastic recovery is the ability of fibers to recover from strain.

Electrical conductivity is the ability to transfer electrical charges.

Electrostatic printing is a type of printing with a dye powder.

Elongation is the ability of a fiber to be stretched, extended, or lengthened.

Embossed refers to a finish in which a localized surface glazing of thermoplastic fibers is achieved or a three-dimensional effect is created to imitate a more elaborate fabric structure.

Embossed fabrics are created by applying a design with heated, engraved calenders. Often print cloths are embossed to imitate seersucker, crepe, or other structural-design fabrics.

Embroidered refers to stitching flat surface yarns to a fabric to create a pattern.

Emerized is a surface abrasion finish to alter the appearance, hand, and drape of the fabric.

Fabric is a planar substance constructed from solutions, fibers, yarns, fabrics, or any combination of these.

Faille (file) is a medium- to heavyweight, unbalanced, plain-weave fabric with filament yarns and warp-faced, flat ribs created by using heavier filling yarns. It has a light luster.

Fancy weave refers to any weaving method, other than plain, twill, or satin weave, used to create a fabric with a surface texture or pattern resulting from the interlacing pattern.

Fancy yarn describes a yarn with an irregular or unusual appearance compared to simple, basic yarns.

Felt is a fiberweb fabric of at least 70 percent wool made by interlocking the scales of the wool fibers through the use of heat, moisture, and agitation.

Felting refers to a method of producing a fabric directly from wool fibers by interlocking the fibers' scales.

Fiber is any substance, natural or manufactured, with a high length-to-width ratio and with suitable characteristics for being processed into a fabric.

Fiber blend refers to an intimate mixture of two or more generic fiber types in the yarns of a fabric. Usually used to refer to the presence of more than one generic fiber in a fabric.

Fiber dyeing is the addition of color, generally as dyes, to textiles while they are in fiber form. Also refers to adding pigment to fiber solutions before fibers are extruded.

Fiberfill is a lofty, weak structure of fibers designed to be incorporated as the center layer in a quilted fabric.

Fiber modifications are changes in the parent manufactured fiber to improve performance relative to a specific end use.

Fiberweb refers to a fabric made directly from fibers.

Filament refers to fibers that are extremely long (length measured in miles or kilometers); also refers to yarns made of these fibers.

Filament tow is an intermediate stage in the production of staple manufactured fibers; manufactured fibers produced in large bundles in filament length and crimped prior to cutting or breaking into staple fibers.

Filament yarn is a yarn made from filament fibers; smooth or bulky types are possible.

Filling refers to the yarns that interlace with warp yarns in a woven fabric; perpendicular to the selvage.

Finish is any process used to convert gray, unfinished goods into finished fabric.

Fire retardance is the resistance to combustion of a material when tested under specific conditions.

Flame-resistant finish is any finish that is designed to reduce the flammability of a textile.

Flannel is a light- to heavyweight, plain- or twill-weave fabric with a napped surface.

Flannelette is a light- to medium-weight, plain-weave cotton or cotton-blend fabric lightly napped on one side.

Flocking refers to the application of very short surface fibers to a fabric with an adhesive to produce an imitation pile appearance.

Fluorescent brightening agent is a compound used to mask the natural color of fibers or yellowing or other colors resulting from soil or aging.

Foam refers to a mixture of air and liquid used in the application of finishes, dyes, or pigments; also refers to a textile product in which a polymer is extruded with a high percentage of air mixed with the polymer to form a bulky, lofty sheet.

Foulard is a soft, lightweight, filament-yarn, twill-weave fabric. It is woven in a $\frac{2}{2}$ twill weave. It can be piece dyed or printed.

Friction calendering is a type of calendering in which one cylinder rotates more quickly than the other, result-ing in a shiny or polished appearance to the fabric; used to produce polished cotton with or without a resin.

Friezé is a strong, durable, heavy-warp-yearn pile fabric. The pile is made by the over-wire method to create a closed-loop pile.

Frosting is a problem with color retention due to the inability of the dye to penetrate deeply into the fiber. With abrasion, the surface components are removed, revealing the uncolored portion of the fiber. Also refers to a chemical or abrasive finish that deliberately produces this whitish cast on fabrics.

Full fashioning is the process of shaping knit garments during the knitting process by adding or decreasing stitches.

Fulling is a finish of woven or knitted wool fabrics that produces a tighter, more compact fabric by a carefully controlled felting process.

Fume fading is a color retention problem. Colors alter when exposed to gases, fumes, or other atmospheric pollutants.

Fume-fading-resistant finish refers to a finish designed to minimize the effect of atmospheric pollutants on dyes.

Functional finish (*See* Special-purpose finish)

Gabardine (gaberdine) is a tightly woven, medium- to heavyweight, steep- or regular-angle, twill-weave fabric with a pronounced wale. The fabric can be wool, a wool blend, or a synthetic-fiber content designed to look like wool. Gabardine can also be 100 percent texturized polyester or a cotton/polyester blend.

Gaiting describes the arrangement of needles in a double-knitting machine. (*See* Interlock and Rib Gaiting)

Garment dyeing (*See* Product dyeing)

Garnetted is a term for shredding wool yarns or fabrics to produce wool fibers for recycling.

Gauze is a sheer, lightweight, low-count, plain- or leno-weave balanced fabric made of spun yarns. It is often cotton, rayon, or a blend of these fibers. *Indian gauze* has a crinkled look and is available in a variety of fabric weights.

Georgette is a sheer, lightweight, plain–weave or momie-weave fabric made with fine-crepe yarns. It is crepier and less lustrous than chiffon.

Gingham is a yarn-dyed, plain-weave fabric that is available in a variety of weights and qualities. It may be balanced or unbalanced. It may be made of combed or carded yarns. If two colors of yarn are used, the fabric is called a *check* or a *checked gingham*. If three or more colors are used, the fabric is referred to as a *plaid gingham*.

Glazed chintz (*See* Chintz)

Gore-Tex is a poromeric multiplex fabric combining a thin film of PTFE with fabric to produce a water-impermeable but comfortable fabric.

Grain describes the relationship of warp to filling yarns in a woven fabric.

Gray goods (**grey goods** or **greige goods**) is a general term used to describe any unfinished woven or knitted fabric.

Grosgrain (grow′grain) is a tightly woven, firm, warp-faced fabric with heavy, round filling ribs created by a high-warp count and coarse filling yarns. Grosgrain can be woven as a narrow-ribbon or a full-width fabric.

Habutai is a soft, lightweight silk fabric. It is heavier than China silk.

Halogenation is a finish for wool that partially dissolves fiber scales in order to produce a washable fabric.

Hand is the way a fiber feels to the sense of touch.

Handkerchief linen is similar in luster and count to batiste, but it is linen or linen-look with slub yarns and a little more body.

Heat conductivity is the ability to conduct heat away from the body.

Heat sensitivity is the ability to soften, melt, or shrink when subjected to heat; see also thermoplastic.

Heat setting describes the process of producing fiber, yarn, or fabric stability through the use of heat.

Heat-transfer printing describes a process of adding color to fabric by using heat to cause a pattern printed on paper to transfer to the fabric.

Herringbone is a broken twill-weave fabric created by changing the direction of the twill wale from right to left and back again. This creates a chevron pattern of stripes that may or may not be equally prominent. Herringbone fabrics are made in a variety of weights, patterns, and fiber types.

Homespun is a coarse, plain-weave fabric with a hand-woven look.

Honan was originally of Chinese silk. Now it is made of any filament fiber. It is similar to pongee, but it has slub yarns in both warp and filling.

Hopsacking is a coarse, loosely woven suiting- or bottom-weight, basket-weave fabric often made of low-grade cotton.

Houndstooth check is a medium- to heavyweight, yarn-dyed, twill-weave fabric in which the interlacing and color pattern creates a unique pointed-check or houndstooth shape.

Huck or **huck-a-back toweling** is a medium- to heavy-weight fabric made on a dobby loom to create a honey-comb or bird's-eye pattern. Often the filling yarns are more loosely twisted to increase the absorbency of the fabric.

Inspection describes the finishing step in which fabric quality is assessed.

Intarsia is a type of filling-knit fabric in which yarns that appear on the surface of the fabric are discontinuous; a knit counterpart to a true tapestry weave.

Interlock is a firm, double-filling knit. The two needle beds knit two interlocked 1×1 rib fabrics. Both sides of the fabric look like the face side of jersey.

Interlock gaiting refers to the double needlebed arrangement. Needles in one bed are directly opposite needles in the other bed. Used to produce interlock and other double-knits.

Jean is a warp-faced twill of carded yarns. It is lighter weight than drill, and it has finer yarns but a higher warp-yarn count.

Jersey is a filling-knit fabric with no distinct rib. Jersey can be any fiber content and be knit flat or circular.

Jet printing is the application of color to fabric by spraying color through tiny nozzles to create the pattern.

Kersey is a very heavy, thick, boardy, wool-coating fabric that has been heavily fulled and felted. In kersey, it is difficult to see the twill weave because of the fulling and the short, lustrous nap. Kersey is heavier than melton. It may be either a single or a double cloth.

Knitting refers to the production of fabric by interlooping yarns.

Lace is an openwork fabric with yarns that are twisted around each other to form complex patterns or figures. Lace may be hand or machine made or made by a variety of fabrication methods including weaving, knitting, crocheting, and knotting.

La coste is a double-knit fabric made with a combination of knit and tuck stitches to create a meshlike appearance. It is often a cotton or cotton/polyester blend.

Lamé is any fabric containing metal or metallic yarns as a conspicuous feature.

Laminated fabric describes a multiplex fabric created by adhering two layers of fabrics with a thin foam.

Lawn is a fine, opaque, lightweight, plain-weave fabric usually made of combed-cotton or cotton-blend yarns. The fabric may be bleached, dyed, or printed.

Leno refers to any leno-weave fabric in which two warp yarns are crossed over each other and held in place by a filling yarn. Leno weaves require a doup attachment on the loom.

Lining twill is an opaque, lightweight, warp-faced twill of filament yarns. It may be printed.

Madras shirting is a light- to medium-weight, dobby-weave fabric in which the pattern is usually confined to vertical stripes.

Marquisette is a sheer, lightweight, leno-weave fabric usually made of filament yarns.

Mass pigmentation (*See* Solution dyeing)

Matelassé is a double-cloth fabric woven to create a three-dimensional texture with a puckered or almost quilted look. Matelassés are made on jacquard or dobby looms often with crepe yarns or very coarse cotton yarns. When finished, the shrinkage of the crepe yarn or the coarse cotton yarn creates the puckered appearance. It is used in apparel as well as in furnishings.

Melton is a heavyweight, plain- or twill-weave coating fabric made from wool. It is lighter than kersey and has a smooth surface that is napped, then closely sheared. It may be either a single or double cloth.

Mercerization is a finish in which cotton is exposed to sodium hydroxide to increase the fiber's absorbency, luster, and strength. See also slack mercerization and tension mercerization.

Metallic coating is a surface application of a thin layer of metal, usually aluminum, primarily to minimize heat transfer through the fabric or to add a metallic luster to the fabric.

Migration describes a color problem in which the dye shifts from the area where it was applied to adjacent areas of the same fabric or a fabric in close proximity.

Mildew control describes a finish that inhibits the growth of mold or mildew.

Mill-finished describes a fabric finished by the same company that produced the fabric; a type of vertical integration within the textile industry.

Milling (*See* Fulling)

Mixture is a fiber blend. Yarns of one generic type are present in one area in the fabric (i.e., the warp) and yarns of another generic type are present in another area of the fabric (i.e., the filling).

Moiré calendering describes a finish that produces a watermarked or wood-grain texture on the fabric; most common on rib or unbalanced plain-weave fabrics like taffeta.

Mold control (*See* Mildew control)

Moleskin is a napped, heavy, strong fabric often made in a satin weave. The nap is suedelike.

Monk's cloth is a heavyweight, coarse, loosely woven, basket-weave fabric usually in a 2×2 or 4×4 arrange-ment. Although it can be made in a 6×6 or 8×8 arrangement, it seldom is because of the low durability. It is often made of softly spun, two-ply yarns in oatmeal color.

Moth resistance describes a finish in which the wool fabric is treated to be unpalatable or harmful to insects.

Multiplex fabric describes a variety of fabrics that combine fibers, yarns, fabrics, or a combination of these into one fabric.

Muslin is a firm, medium- to heavyweight, plain-weave cotton fabric made in a variety of qualities. Muslin made with low-grade cotton fiber with small pieces from the cotton plant is often used in apparel design.

Napping is a finish in which fiber ends are brushed to the surface to produce a softer hand.

Neoprene describes a multiplex fabric combining a film of polychloroprene with a woven, knitted, or fiberweb fabric.

Net is a general term used to refer to any open-construction fabric whether it is created by weaving, knitting, knotting, or another method.

Ninon is a sheer, slightly crisp, lightweight, plain-weave fabric made of filament yarns. The warp yarns are grouped in pairs, but ninon is not a basket-weave fabric.

Organdy is a transparent, crisp, lightweight, plain-weave fabric made of cotton-spun yarns. The fabric has been parchmentized or treated with acid to create the crisp, wiry hand.

Organza is a transparent, crisp, lightweight, plain-weave fabric made of filament yarns.

Osnaburg (osnaberg) is a coarse, bottom-weight, low-count cotton fabric characterized by uneven yarns that have bits of cellulosic waste.

Ottoman is a firm, plain-weave, unbalanced fabric with large and small ribs made by adjacent filling yarns of different size that are completely covered by the warp.

Outing flannel is a medium-weight, napped, plain- or twill-weave, spun-yarn fabric. It may be napped on one or both sides. It is heavier and stiffer than flannelette.

Out-of-register is a problem with printed fabrics. The edges of a print do not match as the designer intended.

Oxford chambray is an oxford cloth made with yarn-dyed warp yarns, and white filling yarns. Sometimes a second color is used for the filling yarns.

Oxford cloth is a light- to medium-weight fabric with a 2×1 half-basket weave.

Parchmentizing is an acid finish to cotton fabrics that produces a thinner fabric with a crisper hand than the original fabric; used in the production of organdy.

Peau de soie is a very smooth, heavy, semidull, satin-weave fabric. It often has satin floats on both sides of the fabric. It can be made of silk, acetate, or other manufactured fibers.

Percale is a balanced plain-weave, medium-weight, piece-dyed or printed fabric finished from print cloths of better quality.

Permanent finish describes a finish whose effectiveness will not diminish with time or use.

Piece dyeing describes adding color to the textile when it is in fabric form. See also union dyeing and cross-dyeing.

Pigment is a colorant that is inorganic in nature; must be attached to the fiber with the use of a binding agent.

Pilling is the formation of the tiny balls of fiber ends and lint on the surface of the fabric.

Pinsonic quilting is the production of a multiplex fabric by heat-sealing face fabric, fiberfill, and backing fabric together in localized areas.

Piqué is a fabric made in a variety of patterns. It can be made on a dobby or jacquard loom with carded or combed yarns. Some piqués have filling cords. Most piqués have three or more sets of yarns.

Plastic coating is the surface application of a thin film to a fabric for increased luster and water repellency, or to minimize yarn slippage.

Pleating calender is a special type of embossing calendering that produces three-dimensional pleats in the fabric.

Plissé is a fabric usually finished from cotton-print cloth by printing with a caustic-soda (sodium hydroxide) paste. The paste causes the fabric to shrink, thus creating a three-dimensional effect. The stripe that was printed usually is darker in piece-dyed goods because the sodium hydroxide increases the dye absorbancy.

Polished cotton is a balanced medium-weight, plain-weave fabric that has been given a glazed-calender finish.

Pongee is a medium-weight, balanced, plain-weave fabric with a fine regular warp and an irregular filling. It was originally a tussah or wild-silk fabric, but now pongee is used to describe a fabric that has the general appearance of fine warp yarns and irregular filling yarns.

Poplin is a medium- to heavyweight, unbalanced, plain-weave, spun-yarn fabric that is usually piece dyed. The filling yarns are coarser than the warp yarns. Poplin has a more pronounced rib than broadcloth.

Power net is a raschel-warp knit in which an inlaid spandex fiber or yarn is used to give high elongation and elasticity.

Preparation refers to a series of steps to get yarns ready for weaving or dyeing or fabrics ready for dyeing, printing, or finishing.

Print cloth is a general term used to describe unfinished, medium-weight, balanced plain-weave, cotton or cotton-blend fabrics. These fabrics can be finished as percale, embossed, plissé, chintz, cretonne, or polished cotton.

Printing is the localized application of color to the surface of the fabric or yarn. See also resist printing, screen printing, direct printing, and roller printing.

Product dyeing refers to the process of adding color to the textile after it has been cut and sewn into the final product.

Quilted fabric is a multiplex fabric consisting of a face or fashion fabric, a layer of fiberfill or batting, and a backing fabric. The three layers may be connected with heat (pinsonic quilting) or thread (regular quilting).

Raschel knit is a general term for patterned, warp-knit fabric made with coarser yarns than other warp-knit fabrics.

Relaxation shrinkage refers to loss of dimensions resulting from tensions introduced during fabric production or finishing.

Renewable finish is a finish that, when its effectiveness has been decreased or destroyed, can be replaced by consumers, dry cleaners, or other firms.

Repairing is a finishing step in which minor flaws in fabrics are corrected.

Resiliency is the ability to return to original shape after bending, twisting, compressing, or a combination of these deformations.

Resist printing refers to a coloration process in which a portion of the yarn or fabric is treated so dyes will not be absorbed during dyeing; includes screen printing, ikat, and batik.

Reworking refers to repeating steps in finishing that were done incorrectly to achieve appropriate performance.

Rib gaiting refers to the double needle bed arrangement. Needles in one bed are directly opposite spaces in the other bed. Used to produce rib knits and other double knits.

Roller printing is the application of color in localized areas through the use of rollers.

Sailcloth is a bottom-weight, half-basket-weave (2×1), unbalanced fabric. It may be made of spun- or textured-filament yarns. It can be piece dyed or printed.

Sateen is a strong, lustrous, medium- to heavyweight, spun-yarn, satin-weave fabric that is either warp faced or filling faced. A warp faced, spun yarn fabric with a satin weave may be called cotton satin.

Satin is a strong, lustrous, medium- to heavyweight, filament-yarn, satin-weave fabric.

Schiffli embroidery is the application of decorative thread to the surface of a fabric to achieve a pattern, as in eyelet embroidery.

Schreiner calender etches hundred of fine lines on the surface of a fabric to increase cover, as in tricot, or add a subtle luster, as in sateen.

Scouring refers to a finishing step in which soil, excess chemicals, or fiber coatings such as natural waxes or oils are removed.

Screen printing is a process during which application of color to the surface of a fabric is controlled by a specially prepared screen so that dye or pigment paste penetrates the screen in selected areas only. Includes rotary and flat-bed screen printing.

Seersucker is a light- to heavyweight, slack-tension weave fabric. It can be made with a variety of interlacing patterns. Seersucker always has vertical crinkled or puckered stripes made by two sets of warp yarns. One set is under normal tension for weaving. The other set has a much looser, slack tension.

Serge is a general term used to refer to twill-weave fabrics with a flat, right-hand wale. The interlacing pattern is $\frac{2}{2}$. The fabric is often wool or wool-like.

Shagbark is usually a gingham with an occasional warp yarn under slack tension. During weaving, the slack-tension yarns create a loop at intervals giving the fabric a unique surface appearance.

Shantung is a rough-texture, plain-weave, filament-warp yarn and irregular-spun filling-yarn fabric. Shantung is heavier than pongee.

Shape-retention finish refers to any finish that controls wrinkling or creasing with heat or resin; includes crease-retention and durable-press finishes.

Sharkskin is a wool or wool-like $\frac{2}{2}$ twill made with alternating warp and filling yarns of two different colors and having a smooth, flat appearance. The twill line, unlike most of the wool-twill fabrics, is left-handed. Occasionally a plain-weave or basket-weave fabric is called sharkskin.

Shearing cuts away protruding fiber or yarn ends to achieve a level pile or surface nap; also can be done to achieve a sculptured effect.

Shrinkage control refers to finishes that minimize tension on fabrics during finishing to reduce shrinkage in consumers' hands.

Silence cloth is a white double-faced fabric used under table linens to minimize noise during dining.

Simple calendering is a mechanical finish. The fabric is passed between two rollers or calenders to remove wrinkles; the simplest calendering process, often precedes printing.

Sizing is a starch, resin, or gelatinous substance added to fabrics to increase body and abrasion resistance; especially important in preparing warp yarns for weaving.

Skew describes an off-grain problem. Filling yarns interlace with warp yarns at an angle less than or greater than 90°.

Slack mercerization is a treatment of cotton fabric with sodium hydroxide to increase absorbency; especially important as a preparation step in dyeing.

Slashing is the process of adding sizing to warp yarns prior to weaving.

Soap is a cleaning compound made from sodium or potassium salts of fatty acids.

Softener refers to a compound used to remove hardness ions from water (water softener); also a compound to improve the hand of fabric (fabric softener).

Soil describes contaminants on fabric.

Soil-release finish is a chemical surface coating on fabrics to improve the removal of soil during laundering or other cleaning procedure.

Solution dyeing describes the addition of colored pigments to polymer solutions prior to fiber extrusion.

Special-purpose finish includes all finishes designed to improve the performance of a fabric or minimize a problem with the fabric.

Specific gravity is the ratio of the mass of the fiber to an equal volume of water at 4°C.

Spinning refers to the process of producing a yarn from staple fibers; also refers to the production of a fiber by extruding a solution through tiny holes in a spinneret.

Spun-bonded describes a process of producing a fabric directly from fibers by adhering melt-spun fibers together before cooling.

Spun-laced describes a process of producing a fabric directly from fibers by entangling staple fibers with water to create a pattern in the fabric.

Stabilization refers to any finish that is designed to minimize shrinkage or expansion of fabric during care.

Stain-release finish (*See* Soil-release finish)

Stencil printing describes a process of adding color to a fabric by using a form to control where the color strikes the fabric; essentially a hand process.

Stiffness is the resistance to bending or creasing of a fabric.

Stitch-bonded fabric is a multiplex fabric in which fine lengthwise yarns in a warp knit are chain stitched to interlock the fiberweb base structure or inlaid yarns.

Stock dyeing refers to a fiber dyeing process in which loose fibers are colored.

Suede is a leather that has been brushed or napped to create a softer surface and more matte luster.

Suede cloth is a plain-weave, twill-weave, or knitted fabric that is napped and sheared to resemble suede leather. Suede cloth can be napped on both sides. Any suitable fiber can be used to refer to brushed leather.

Suiting is a general term for heavyweight fabrics. Suiting can be any fiber type or fabric construction.

Sunlight resistance is a finish or fiber modification to minimize the degradative effects of sunlight on fiber or dye.

Supported film is a multiplex fabric that combines a fiberweb, woven, or knitted fabric with a film for greater durability.

Supported-scrim structure is a multiplex fabric consisting of foam bonded to a yarn structure scrim; fibers may be flocked on the surface to simulate a pile or suede fabric.

Surah (*See* Foulard)

Surface coating is a finish, usually metallic or plastic in nature, applied to the face of the fabric.

Synthetic leather refers to a variety of fabrications or finishes that produce a surface that resembles leather in appearance or texture; some may be brushed to resemble suede.

Taffeta is a general term that refers to any plain-weave fabric with a fine, smooth, crisp hand made with filament yarns. The unbalanced taffetas have a fine rib made by heavier filling yarns and more warp yarns. Faille taffeta has a crosswise rib made by using many more warp yarns than filling yarns. Moiré taffetas have an embossed watermark design. Balanced taffetas have warp and filling yarns the same size.

Tanning is a finishing step in the production of leather to prevent rotting of the hide or skin.

Tapa cloth refers to a hand-produced fiberweb fabric made from the inner bark of selected trees.

Tapestry is a firm, heavy, stiff, jacquard-weave fabric made with several warp and filling yarn sets. Tapestry is also the term used for fabric made by hand in which the filling yarns are discontinuous. In handmade tapestries, the filling yarn is used only in those areas where that color is desired.

Temporary finish describes a finish that is removed during the first care cycle or that has a very short life span.

Tenacity describes the strength of a fiber; usually referred to as breaking tenacity, which describes the force at which the fiber ruptures or breaks.

Tendering describes the weakening of fibers due to exposure to degradants or due to a deleterious interaction between fiber, dye, or finish.

Tension mercerization is the process of treating cotton yarn, thread, or fabric with sodium hydroxide while under tension.

Tentering is a finishing step in which the fabric is stretched out to full width; often combined with other finishing steps like heat setting. If done incorrectly, contributes to bow and skew.

Terrycloth (terry) is a slack-tension, warp-yarn pile fabric. Terrycloth may have loops on one or both sides of the fabric. Terrycloth may have a jacquard pattern and may be made with plied yarns for durability. There are also weft- or filling-knit terrycloths.

Textile is a general term used to refer to fiber, yarn, fabric, or anything made from fibers, yarns, or fabrics.

Texturing refers to the process of adding bulk to yarns or modifying fabric surfaces.

Thermal finish describes a finish designed to minimize heat transfer through the fabric.

Thermoplastic describes a fiber's sensitivity to heat; fibers that melt or glaze at relatively low temperature.

Ticking is a general term used for fabrics of any weave used for mattress covers, slipcovers, and upholstery. It may also be used in apparel.

Tie-dye is a resist dyeing process. Portions of the fabric or yarn are tied to prevent dye absorption in the tied areas.

Tigaring is a surface napping of knit fabrics to produce a suedelike texture.

Tricot is a warp-knit fabric made with filament yarns with one or more bars. Tricot has fine, vertical wales on the technical face and horizontal ribs on the technical back.

Tufting is a method of producing an imitation pile surface by stitching yarns to the surface of an existing fabric; used to produce carpeting and upholstery.

Tweed is a general term used to refer to wool or wool-like fabrics made of flock or flake novelty yarns. Tweeds are most often made in plain, twill, or twill-variation weaves.

Union dyeing is dyeing a fabric made of two or more fibers to one solid color.

Velour is a general term used to describe pile fabrics. Velours tend to have dense, long, or deep pile. Velours can be woven or knitted.

Velvet is a warp-pile fabric most often made as a double cloth with five sets of yarns. One pair of ground warp and filling create one side of the fabric and a second pair of ground warp and filling create the other side. A fifth set of yarns (pile warp) interlace between the two sets of ground fabrics. The woven fabric is separated into two complete fabrics when the pile warp is cut. Velvet is usually a filament-yarn fabric.

Velveteen is a filling-pile fabric made with long gloats that are cut in the finishing process. The ground fabric can have a plain or twill weave. The pile in velveteen is short. Velveteen is usually a spun-yarn fabric.

Viyella™ is a medium-weight, twill-weave fabric made of an intimate blend of 55 percent wool and 45 percent cotton.

Voile is a sheer, lightweight, low-count, plain-weave, spun-yarn fabric in which the yarns have a high, hard, or voile twist to give the fabric a crisp hand. It has a lower count than lawn.

Waffle cloth is a dobby-weave fabric in which the interlacing pattern creates a three-dimensional honeycomb.

Wale refers to the diagonal line related to the interlacing pattern of twills; or the column of stitches made by one needle in a knit fabric.

Warp is the group of yarns threaded through the loom in a woven fabric; parallel to the selvage.

Waterproof refers to a coated or multiplex fabric that water will not penetrate regardless of the time water is in contact with the fabric or the force with which the water hits the fabric.

Water-repellent finish minimizes the wettability of a fabric; may result in stain resistance as well.

Weaving is the process of producing a fabric by interlacing two or more yarns at right angles.

Weighting is the treatment of silk with metallic salts to increase the weight, hand, and dye affinity of the fabric; may result in accelerated degradation of the silk.

Wicking is the ability of a fiber to transfer moisture along its surface.

Wrinkle resistance is the ability of a fiber to recover from deformations such as bending, twisting, or compressing.

Yarn is an assemblage of fibers, twisted or laid together so as to form a continuous strand that can be made into a textile fabric.

Yarn dyeing is a process of adding color, usually a dye, to yarns.

INDEX